The Psychology of Work and Human Performance

The Psychology of Work and Human Performance

Third Edition

Robert D. Smither
Rollins College

An imprint of Addison Wesley Longman, Inc.

New York • Reading, Massachusetts • Menlo Park, California • Harlow, England
Don Mills, Ontario • Sydney • Mexico City • Madrid • Amsterdam

Photo Credits
Page 8: © N.R. Rowan/Stock Boston; 13: © AT&T Archives; 47: © Jeff Greenberg/Photo Edit; 49: ©Bob Daemmrich Photo, Inc.; 68: © Mitchell Layton/Duomo; 119: © JB Boykin/The Picture Cube; 127: © ESS Corp., Maitland, FL. Used by permission; 152: © Eric Neurath/Stock Boston; 168: © Paul J. Sutton/Duomo; 283M: © R. Ellis/Sygma; 283L: © Les Stone/Sygma; 283R: © Pascal Le Segretain/Sygma; 285: © Stephen Jaffe/The Image Works; 444: Larry Lee/Mobil Corporation © 1996; 447: © NASA; 451T: © United States Postal Service; 451B: © United States Postal Service.

Executive Editor: *Rebecca J. Dudley*
Marketing Manager: *Jay O'Callaghan*
Project Editor: *Shuli Traub*
Text Designer: *Mary Archondes*
Cover Designer: *Wendy Ann Fredericks*
Cover Illustration: *© Diane Fenster/SIS*
Art Studio: *ElectraGraphics, Inc.*
Photo Researcher: *Julie Tesser*
Production Manager: *Alexandra Odulak*
Desktop Coordinator: *Joanne Del Ben*
Manufacturing Manager: *Hilda Koparanian*
Electronic Page Makeup: *York Graphic Services*
Printer and Binder: *Maple-Vail Book Manufacturing Group*
Cover Printer: *Coral Graphic Services, Inc.*

Library of Congress Cataloging-in-Publication Data

Smither, Robert D.
    The psychology of work and human performance/Robert D. Smither.
— 3rd ed.
      p. cm.
    Includes bibliographical references and index.
    ISBN 0-321-01256-9
    1. Psychology, Industrial.   2. Personnel management.   I. Title.
    HF5548.8.S563   1997
    158.7—dc21   97-27497
                                          CIP

ISBN 0-321-01256-9

Please visit our website at htp://longman.awl.com

12345678910—MA—00999897

To Henry Clay Lindgren

It is too often assumed that almost any young university graduate of sufficient intelligence can charge out of university and into industry and, armed with some rags and tatters of scientific method borrowed mainly from physics or chemistry, can proceed to make interesting findings. This belief ignores completely the mutual dependence and complexity of the facts of human association.

Elton Mayo

Contents in Brief

Contents in Detail   *ix*
To the Instructor   *xv*
To the Student   *xvii*

PART I An Introduction to Industrial and Organizational Psychology

Chapter 1   *The Field of Industrial and Organizational Psychology*   *1*
Chapter 2   *Research in the Organizational Setting*   *25*

PART II The Individual and the Organization

Chapter 3   *Recruiting and Selecting Personnel*   *57*
Chapter 4   *Assessing the Abilities of Personnel*   *93*
Chapter 5   *Training: Development, Methods, and Evaluation*   *131*
Chapter 6   *Appraising Performance*   *167*

PART III The Group in the Organization

Chapter 7   *Motivation: Understanding Differences in Performance*   *203*
Chapter 8   *Job Satisfaction*   *235*
Chapter 9   *Organizational Leadership*   *271*
Chapter 10 *Group Behavior in the Workplace*   *310*
Chapter 11 *Special Populations in the Workplace: Women, Minorities, and Older Workers*   *341*

PART IV Organizational Issues

Chapter 12 *The Nature of Organizations*   *371*
Chapter 13 *Organization Development*   *409*
Chapter 14 *Human Factors and Working Conditions*   *441*
Chapter 15 *I/O Psychology and Worker Health*   *470*

Glossary   *503*
References   *517*
Name Index   *563*
Subject Index   *579*

Contents in Detail

To the Instructor xv
To the Student xvii

PART I An Introduction to Industrial and Organizational Psychology

Chapter 1 *The Field of Industrial and Organizational Psychology* 1
Defining the Field of I/O Psychology 2
  Organizational Psychology and Organizational Behavior 4
  Areas of I/O Psychology 5
Theory and Its Application 8
Psychology in the Workplace: Three Historical Examples 10
  Scientific Management 10
  The Hawthorne Studies 13
  The Textile Mills of Ahmedabad 15
The Professional I/O Psychologist 16
  Work Environments 16
  Training 17
  Professional Life 18
I/O Psychology and the Workplace of the Future 18
Organization of This Book 20
Chapter Summary 22
Key Words and Concepts 23
Questions for Discussion 23

Chapter 2 *Research in the Organizational Setting* 25
Experimental Research 26
  Laboratory Experiments 27
  Field Experiments 30
  Natural Experiments and Ex Post Facto Studies 32
  Statistical Analysis of Experimental Data 33
  Evaluating the Experimental Method 35
Correlational Studies 36

  The Correlational Method 36
  Statistical Analysis of Correlational Data 39
  Evaluating the Correlational Method 40
Observational Studies 42
  The Observational Method 43
  Example of Observational Research 43
  Evaluating the Observational Method 44
Other Research Methods 46
  Survey Research 46
  Case Studies 48
  Focus Groups 49
Measurement Scales 49
Selecting a Research Method 50
Reliability and Validity in Research Studies 52
Evaluating Applied Research 53
Chapter Summary 53
Key Words and Concepts 55
Questions for Discussion 56

PART II The Individual and the Organization

Chapter 3 *Recruiting and Selecting Personnel* 57
The Importance of Effective Selection Procedures 57
The Predictor and Criterion in Personnel Selection 58
  Predicting Performance on the Job 59
  Fairness in Selection 60
  Affirmative Action Programs 66
Job Analysis 67
Personnel Recruitment 72
  The Recruitment Process 72
  Realistic Job Previews 74
Application Blanks and Biodata 76

Contents of the Application Blank   76
Using Biodata for Personnel Selection   77
The Employment Interview   80
Problems with the Employment Interview   80
The Interview Process   83
Improving Employment Interviews   87
*Applicant References and Letters of
Recommendation   88*
Preemployment Drug Testing   89
Chapter Summary   90
Key Words and Concepts   92
Questions for Discussion   92

**Chapter 4 *Assessing the Abilities
of Personnel 93***
A Brief History of Employment Testing   95
*Predicting Performance from Employment
Testing   96*
Establishing the Reliability of a Selection
Procedure   96
Establishing the Validity of a Selection
Procedure   97
Additional Approaches to Validity   104
Score Banding   106
*Determining the Usefulness of Improved Selection
Procedures   107*
Taylor-Russell Model   108
Other Utility Models   109
Types of Employment Testing   111
Measures of Aptitude and Ability   111
Personality Assessment   114
Integrity Testing   118
Individual Assessment   120
Interest Measures   121
Job Samples and Assessment Centers   122
New Approaches to Employment Testing   125
Genetic Screening   125
Computer-Adaptive Testing   126
Video-based Assessment   126
Chapter Summary   128
Key Words and Concepts   129
Questions for Discussion   130

**Chapter 5 *Training: Development, Methods,
and Evaluation 131***
A Brief History of Training   132
Designing a Training Program   133

Identify Training Needs   134
Establish Training Objectives   135
Develop Instructional Materials   136
Test and Refine Materials   137
Implement the Training Program   138
Evaluate the Program   138
Methods of Training   138
On-the-Job Training   139
Vestibule Training   139
Apprenticeship   141
Job Rotation   141
Lecture   142
Audiovisual Methods   143
Conferences   144
Sensitivity Training   144
Behavior Modeling   145
Programmed Instruction   146
Computer-assisted Instruction   147
Multimedia Training   148
Simulations   149
Games   150
Case Studies   150
Outdoor Experiential Training   151
Open Learning   152
Optimizing the Training Experience   153
Assessing Trainability   153
Training the Trainers   158
Evaluating Training Effectiveness   159
Case Study   161
Pretest-Posttest   162
Pretest-Posttest with a Control Group   162
After-Only with a Control Group   163
Solomon Four-Group Design   163
Other Considerations in Evaluation   163
Chapter Summary   164
Key Words and Concepts   165
Questions for Discussion   165

Chapter 6 *Appraising Performance 167*
*The Role of Performance Appraisal in the
Organization   169*
Uses of Performance Appraisal   169
The Importance of Performance
Appraisal   170
Criterion Development   171
Ultimate Criterion   171

Criterion Relevance   172
Criterion Deficiency   173
Criterion Contamination   173
Criterion Usefulness   174
Methods of Appraising Performance   174
Comparative Methods   175
Checklists   176
Rating Scales   177
Narrative Methods   179
Management by Objectives   180
The Appraisal Interview   181
Sources of Error in Performance Appraisal   182
Determining What to Measure   182
Errors in Rating   186
Biases of Raters   190
Peer Ratings and Self-assessments   194
Multirater Feedback   197
Upward Feedback   197
Designing a Performance Appraisal System   198
Evaluating Performance Appraisal   199
Chapter Summary   201
Key Words and Concepts   202
Questions for Discussion   202

PART III The Group in the Organization

**Chapter 7 Motivation: Understanding
                    Differences in Performance   203**
Defining Motivation   204
Need Theories of Motivation   205
Maslow's Hierarchy   205
Two-Factor Theory   207
Achievement Motivation Theory   209
Evaluating Need Theories   210
Equity Theory   211
Expectancy Theory   216
Behavioral Approaches to Motivation   219
Intrinsic Motivation   223
Goal-setting Theory   225
Evaluating Theories of Motivation   230
Chapter Summary   232
Key Words and Concepts   233
Questions for Discussion   234

Chapter 8 Job Satisfaction   235
Job Satisfaction and Life Satisfaction   236
Organizational Commitment   238

Measuring Job Satisfaction   240
Facets Versus the Global Approach   241
Measures of Job Satisfaction   242
Theories of Job Satisfaction   245
Need Fulfillment   246
Expectancy and Equity Approaches   247
Social Information Processing   247
Genetic Theory   248
Measuring Dissatisfaction   249
Absenteeism   249
Turnover   253
Tardiness   259
Deviant Behavior   259
Increasing Job Satisfaction   260
Compensation   261
Job Enlargement and Enrichment   264
Benefits   265
Chapter Summary   268
Key Words and Concepts   269
Questions for Discussion   269

Chapter 9 Organizational Leadership   271
The Leadership Position   273
Participative Versus Authoritarian Leadership   278
Leadership and Power   279
Personological Theories of Leadership   281
Trait Theories   281
Need for Power and Leadership   284
Evaluating Personological Theories
    of Leadership   284
Behavioral Theories of Leadership   286
Ohio State Studies   286
Contingency Model   287
Situational Leadership   289
Reinforcement Theory   289
Evaluating Behavioral Approaches
    to Leadership   291
Cognitive Theories of Leadership   291
Vroom-Yetton Decision-Making Model   292
Path-Goal Theory   293
Evaluating Cognitive Theories   296
Leadership as Social Interaction   296
Leader-Member Exchange   297
Charismatic Leadership   301
Transformational Leadership   302

Attributional Approaches to Leadership   304
Evaluating Social Interaction Theories   305
Chapter Summary   307
Key Words and Concepts   308
Questions for Discussion   308

Chapter 10 *Group Behavior in the Workplace 310*
Studying Group Behavior   311
Types of Groups   313
Primary and Secondary Groups   313
Reference and Designated Groups   315
Characteristics of Groups   316
Formation of the Group   316
Task Versus Process   318
Deindividuation   319
Norms and Deviance   319
Group Cohesion and Social Support   322
Resolving Conflict in the Workplace   323
Decision Making in Groups   325
Group Decisions   325
Group Polarization   327
Groupthink   328
Delphi Method   329
Interpersonal Skills Groups   329
Employee Involvement Programs   331
Teams in the Workplace   331
Autonomous Work Groups   333
Matrix Management   333
Quality Circles and Total Quality Management   335
Other Participative Decision-Making Models   336
Improving Team Performance   337
Chapter Summary   338
Key Words and Concepts   339
Questions for Discussion   340

Chapter 11 *Special Populations in the Workplace: Women, Minorities, and Older Workers 341*
Managing Diversity   342
Women in the Workplace   345
Women in Management   346
Salary Issues   349
Work–Family Conflicts   353
Sexual Harassment   355
Minority Employees   356

Hispanics in the Workplace   360
Older Workers   361
Social Stratification in the Workplace   365
Top Executives   365
Blue-Collar Workers   367
Chapter Summary   368
Key Words and Concepts   369
Questions for Discussion   369

PART IV Organizational Issues

Chapter 12 *The Nature of Organizations   371*
Studying Organizations   372
Qualities of Organizations   374
Classical Organizational Theory   375
Weber's Bureaucracy   375
Fayol's Functionalism   376
Qualities of Formal Organizations   377
Evaluating Classical Theory   378
Human Relations Movement   381
Theory X and Theory Y   381
Four-Function Typology   382
Evaluating Human Relations Theories   382
Contingency Theories of Organization   384
Industrial Organization Model   385
Differentiation and Integration   387
Mechanistic and Organic Systems   388
Sociotechnical Systems   389
Evaluating Contingency Theories   391
Organizational Culture   393
Organizational Socialization   395
Organizational Citizenship Behavior   397
Organizational Climate   398
Evaluating Organizational Culture   399
Postmodern Organizations   400
Japanese Organization   401
Lifetime Employment   402
Quality Circles   404
Seven S Theory and Theory Z   404
Chapter Summary   405
Key Words and Concepts   406
Questions for Discussion   407

Chapter 13 *Organization Development   409*
Origins of Organization Development   411
Diagnosis and Analysis   413

Resistance to Organizational Change 415
Barriers to Organizational Change 417
Overcoming Resistance to Change 418
Models of Planned Change 420
Lewin's Unfreezing-Moving-Freezing Model 420
Intervention Theory 421
Planned Change 422
Action Research 424
Organizational Transformation 425
Punctuated Equilibrium 426
Evaluating Models of Change 427
Organization Development Interventions 428
Individual Interventions: Interpersonal Interaction
  and Disclosure 429
Interpersonal Interventions: Third-Party
  Interventions 429
Team Development Interventions: Team
  Building 431
Organizationwide Interventions: The Leadership
  Grid® 433
Evaluating Organization Development 434
Ethical Issues in OD 434
Methodological Concerns 437
The Future of Organization Development 438
Chapter Summary 439
Key Terms and Concepts 440
Questions for Discussion 440

**Chapter 14 *Human Factors and Working
          Conditions 441***
Fatigue and Performance 443
Origins of Human Factors 445
The Human-Machine System 448
Designing the Work Environment 450
Illumination 450
Temperature 453
Noise and Vibration 455
Automatic Speech Recognition Systems 457
Space Arrangements 458
Human Factors and Automation 459

Computers in the Office 459
Telecommunications 460
Virtual Reality Simulations 462
Robotics 462
Accidents and Safety 463
Causes of Accidents 464
Reducing Accidents 466
Chapter Summary 467
Key Words and Concepts 468
Questions for Discussion 469

**Chapter 15 *I/O Psychology and Worker
          Health 470***
Issues in Worker Health 471
Historical Background 471
Employee Assistance Programs 472
Addictive Behavior in the Workplace 474
Alcoholism 474
Drug Use 477
Gambling 480
Stress 482
Characteristics of Stress 482
Environmental Stressors 484
Dispositional Stress 485
Stress and Type A Behavior 487
Stress Management Programs 488
Violence in the Workplace 489
AIDS in the Workplace 490
Health Promotion in the Workplace 493
Models of Employee Assistance Programs 496
Evaluating Employee Assistance Programs 497
Worker Health and the Future 499
Chapter Summary 500
Key Words and Concepts 501
Questions for Discussion 501

Glossary 503
References 517
Name Index 563
Subject Index 579

To the Instructor

Over the years, industrial and organizational (I/O) psychology has grown to become one of the most popular courses on many college campuses. This popularity is due, in part, to students increasingly recognizing that I/O psychology offers a framework for thinking about something most of us do most of our lives—work. In a larger sense, however, I/O psychology addresses issues—such as group dynamics, commitment to organizations, and leadership—that occur outside the workplace. So students are often able to see the relevance of I/O in ways that are perhaps not so obvious in other specialties of psychology.

On a more academic level, however, the widespread use of the "scientist-practitioner model" in industrial and organizational psychology has also affected the course's popularity. This model provides students and instructors with a framework for bringing together the theoretical aspects of the field with their applications in organizational settings. This immediate theory-to-practice aspect is one of the most appealing dimensions of modern industrial and organizational psychology. In addition, the subject matter of I/O allows students to take theoretical material from other psychology courses and apply it to real-life situations.

The *Psychology of Work and Human Performance* is designed to make optimal use of the scientist-practitioner approach. Whenever possible, theoretical points are illustrated by examples from the literature or from real life. Throughout the book, newsworthy topics—including the affirmative action debate, downsizing, violence in the workplace, virtual reality simulations, and others—are introduced to illustrate and expand more theoretical material.

Despite the particular attention I gave to making the book interesting to read, understanding psychological research remains the emphasis throughout the text. In some respects, this book has certain "hands-on" qualities, but the major focus throughout is still the rich body of I/O research. My overall goals in writing this book were to (1) provide a timely and research-based textbook that (2) capitalizes on the inherent interest of the subject matter of the field and (3) makes I/O psychology easily accessible to students.

A surprising amount of new knowledge has accumulated since the last edition of *The Psychology of Work*. This edition presents much of that new knowledge and adds materials not included in previous editions. For example, in addition to the topics covered in earlier editions, Chapter 2 (Research) has been expanded to include survey research, case studies, focus groups, and measurement scales; Chapter 3 (Selection) features the affirmative action debate, an expanded section on recruitment, and new research on making interviews more effective.

Chapter 4 (Assessment) now includes material on score banding and an expanded section on personality assessment; Chapter 5 (Training) has sections on multimedia training and open learning systems; and new material in Chapter 6 (Performance Appraisal) now includes downsizing, the appraisal interview, and multirater feedback. Chapter 7 (Motivation) contains expanded material on goal setting; Chapter 8 (Job Satisfaction) has larger sections on commitment and turnover, as well as sections on the relationship between job and life satisfaction; and Chapter 9 (Leadership) features new information on leader behavior.

Chapter 10 (Groups) includes new sections on resolving conflict and task versus process in groups; Chapter 11 (Special Populations) contains new research on women in management, work–family conflict, and expanded research on minorities in the workplace; and Chapter 12 (Organizations) now includes the psychological contract, organizational citizenship, and an expanded climate section.

Finally, Chapter 13 (Organization Development) has an expanded section on organizational diagnosis, third-party interactions, and the future of OD; Chapter 14 (Human Factors) now includes sections on fatigue and performance, automated speech recognition systems, and e-mail; and Chapter 15 (Worker Health) has a new section on violence in the workplace.

Throughout *The Psychology of Work,* I have kept the organizational focus in mind. As a result, the organizing model of *The Psychology of Work* moves from the individual to the group to the organization. Within the section of the book dealing with the individual, topics are presented in an order that reflects how a person experiences them on entering an organization. This model departs somewhat from other texts, but my experience has been that students understand I/O much better when it is presented in this order. Again, my goal was to write a readable, research-based survey text of industrial and organizational psychology. I hope that students and instructors enjoy using this book as much as I enjoyed writing it.

In preparing this book, I have been greatly assisted by many individuals. Some people who were particularly helpful include Paul Dyer, Marian Hasara, John Houston, Sandra McIntire, Leslie Miller, and Janan Smither. I would also like to recognize the contributions of my reviewers, whose helpful comments have made this book much stronger: T. L. Brink, Crafton Hills College; David Carkenard, Longwood College; George Diekhoff, Midwestern State University; Wanda Trahan, Southern Louisiana State University; Donald Truxillo, Portland State University; and Arthur Witkin, CUNY, Queens College.

Finally, I would like to express my thanks to Becky Dudley, Ellen MacElree, and Shuli Traub at Addison Wesley Longman, who were particularly helpful throughout this project.

To the Student

One reason I enjoy industrial and organizational (I/O) psychology so much is because its subject matter is so much a part of everyday life. For example, many things that happen in the classroom are similar to things that happen at work. Like workers on the job, students must fulfill tasks assigned to them by others, they must interact effectively with the leadership of the class and the "coworkers" around them, and, also like workers, students will eventually have their performances evaluated. So industrial and organizational psychology gives us a framework for understanding many events that happen both on the job and elsewhere.

A second interesting aspect of I/O is that it helps us understand the significance of real-life issues and events. For example, I/O researchers can help explain why, despite legal protection, women and minorities have failed to advance into management in large numbers; why organizations are currently so enthusiastic about employee participation in decision making even when research shows such programs are not necessarily effective; or even how e-mail is changing the workplace.

A third interesting aspect of industrial and organizational psychology is its emphasis on performance—on helping people to perform tasks at a high level of competence. Understanding performance requires I/O psychologists to draw on material from many different psychological specialties. For example, measurement, social psychology, perception and cognition, personality theory, experimental, and even abnormal psychology contribute to the subject matter of I/O psychology. At the same time, industrial and organizational psychologists also use knowledge from sociology, anthropology, physiology, and other fields in their work. Consequently, industrial and organizational psychology is one of the most interdisciplinary areas of psychology.

A final interesting aspect of industrial and organizational psychology is that it is both a theoretical and an applied science. That is, I/O psychologists work not only on theoretical issues, but on real-life problems as well. For example, some industrial and organizational psychologists study basic questions, such as how to do research in organizational settings, whereas others focus on applied problems, such as limiting employee absence or selecting individuals for high-risk occupations. The dual aspect of the field—its scientific and applied natures—has led many industrial and organizational psychologists to refer to themselves as scientist-practitioners. This term refers to individuals who are advancing our theoretical knowledge at the same time that they are solving practical problems.

In writing this book, I felt that understanding the linkage between theory and application was essential to understanding I/O psychology. Historically, managers used common sense to address issues that arose in the workplace, but today we have a tremendous body of research that can help managers make good decisions based on solid psychological principles. This is why it is important to understand the nature of I/O research before applying it to the workplace. I have tried to balance the "science" and the "practice" aspects of the field—in most cases, the findings from research reported here are illustrated by real-life examples.

One value that I kept in mind when writing this book is that I wanted students to see the linkage between the psychology of work and what happens—or will soon be happening—in their everyday lives. One of my reviewers flattered me by saying that he felt students could later keep this book at their work sites and refer to it when an organizational issue arose. The knowledge in this book is not purely abstract and theoretical; it has a relevance to what most people do most of their lives.

I hope you enjoy reading this book as much as I enjoyed writing it.

Robert D. Smither

CHAPTER 1

The Field of Industrial and Organizational Psychology

Defining the Field of I/O Psychology
Theory and Its Application
Psychology in the Workplace: Three Historical Examples
The Professional I/O Psychologist
I/O Psychology and the Workplace of the Future
Organization of This Book
Chapter Summary
Key Words and Concepts
Questions for Discussion

Since the dawn of human history, people have come together in groups to accomplish their goals. Although the first human goals focused on survival, today most of us are part of organizations that have a variety of goals. In many respects, the goals of the organization, whether it is a club, college, business, or government agency, have an important influence on our behavior. At the same time, however, our own goals, personalities, and behavior impact the organizations to which we belong.

When people work together in organizations, countless psychological processes come into play. Although they may not be aware of these processes, workers use psychology to persuade others, to make judgments about the capabilities of their coworkers, and to respond as effectively as possible to challenges that confront them. Since most people spend a good part of their lives interacting with others in the workplace, studying the psychology of work is obviously a useful undertaking.

In 1913 Hugo Munsterberg formalized the study of the psychology of work in his landmark textbook, *Psychology and Industrial Efficiency*. Munsterberg's book reflected the broadening of psychological research that had begun around the turn of the century. Psychologist Walter Dill Scott, for example, had published *The Psychology of Advertising* in 1908, and industrial engineer Frederick W. Taylor had published his book on worker productivity, *Principles of Scientific Management,* in 1911. (Taylor's work is discussed below.)

In the generations that followed Munsterberg, industrial and organizational (I/O) psychology became one of the most active research areas within psychology and related fields. During the 1920s, for example, many researchers worked on psychological measures to select employees, and in the 1930s, other researchers turned to studying the relationship between human behavior at work and productivity. During the 1960s, personnel selection again became a major interest for I/O psychologists as they focused on ways to ensure that personnel selection procedures are fair and accurate. By the 1990s, the diverse composition of the workforce, as well as the rapid rate of organizational change, became an area of focus for I/O psychologists.

Today, industrial and organizational psychologists constitute only about 7 percent of the almost 75,000 psychologists who belong to the American Psychological Association or the American Psychological Society, but virtually every complex organization has members dedicated to studying and modifying human behavior at work. Psychologists now study qualities of effective leaders, ways to create less stressful work environments, how to train people to use complex equipment safely, and virtually any topic related to human performance in the workplace.

Each chapter of *The Psychology of Work and Human Performance* begins with a brief history of the topic covered in that chapter. Table 1.1 is an overview of significant events in the history of I/O.

Defining the Field of I/O Psychology

Organizational Psychology
and Organizational
Behavior
Areas of I/O Psychology

Psychology is often defined as the scientific study of human behavior and cognition, or mental processes. **Industrial and organizational psychology** is the development and application of psychological principles to the workplace. Industrial and organizational psychologists are interested in such questions as:

- How do we create work environments where people can make the most effective decisions?
- Which is the best form of leadership: authoritarian, participative, or laissez-faire? How can we identify and nurture individuals who have leadership potential?
- Why do women and minorities typically have slower rates of promotion than White men?
- What motivates workers to be productive? What can we learn from the Japanese about productivity?
- What is the best way to deal with problems such as stress, alcoholism, and drug use in the workplace?

Table 1.1 IMPORTANT EVENTS IN INDUSTRIAL AND ORGANIZATIONAL PSYCHOLOGY

1881	Frederick W. Taylor's time-and-motion studies at the Midvale Steel Company
1892	Founding of the American Psychological Association
1908	Walter Dill Scott publishes *The Psychology of Advertising*
1911	Frank W. Gilbreth's study of bricklaying
1913	Hugo Munsterberg's classic text *Psychology and Industrial Efficiency* published
1917	U.S. Army begins administering Alpha and Beta intelligence tests
1918	Establishment of the *Journal of Applied Psychology*
1922	Max Weber introduces the concept of bureaucracy in *The Theory of Social and Economic Organization*
1924	Research begins at Western Electric's Hawthorne plant
1943	Office of Strategic Services (OSS) establishes a psychological screening process for selecting spies and saboteurs
1945	Establishment of the Society for Industrial and Organizational Psychology, Division 14 of the American Psychological Association
1947	Founding of National Training Laboratories in Bethel, Maine
1950	Beginning of Ohio State Leadership Studies
1951	Longwall coal-gathering method study
1952	Ahmedabad textile mill study
1956	Establishment of first AT&T assessment center
1961	Fitts and Jones' study of human error in aircraft accidents
1963	*Myart v. Motorola,* the first important unfair discrimination in employment case
1963	Equal Pay Act, requiring equal pay for the same or similar work
1964	Civil Rights Act
1970	Occupational Safety and Health Act
1978	*Bakke v. Regents of the University of California,* a case charging that setting quotas for minorities resulted in "reverse" discrimination against Whites
1978	*Uniform Guidelines on Employee Selection Procedures*
1983	Beginning of Project A, a review of the U.S. Army's system for selecting and classifying individuals applying for entry-level positions
1987	*Johnson v. Transportation Agency,* a case in which the U.S. Supreme Court ruled that women can receive preferential treatment in hiring, even in situations in which there is no proven history of discrimination
1988	*Price Waterhouse v. Hopkins,* the first U.S. Supreme Court case in which psychological research on sex stereotyping was used to prove unfair discrimination
1988	Founding of the American Psychological Society
1990	Americans with Disabilities Act, which extended protection of the Civil Rights Act to qualified disabled job applicants
1991	Civil Rights Act of 1991 reaffirmed provisions of the Civil Rights Act of 1964
1993	*Soroka v. Dayton Hudson,* a case in which an applicant challenged the job-relatedness of individual items on a personality inventory, settled out of court
1996	*Hopwood v. State of Texas,* in which the Fifth Circuit Court of Appeals ruled that race cannot be a criterion for admission to colleges in Texas, Lousiana, and Mississippi
1997	Federal Courts deliberate whether employers can limit caps on mental health insurance benefits.

As you might conclude from these questions, an important defining characteristic of industrial and organizational psychology is that it is an **applied science.** That is, the research generated by I/O psychologists is generally used in a real-life setting. Unlike **theoretical science,** which attempts to advance knowledge without attention to its practical or immediate value, I/O psychology largely focuses on areas or problems that are important or interesting to members of organizations. In fact, a major point of this book is that understanding both theory and its application is important for addressing I/O issues.

Another defining characteristic of industrial and organizational psychology is that it is a multidisciplinary activity. Not only do I/O psychologists use knowledge from areas of psychology, such as psychological assessment and learning theory, but they are also likely to draw on other fields, such as business administration, economics, communications, or sociology. When I/O psychologists approach a problem in the workplace, they frequently discover that understanding relevant material from related fields is essential for addressing the issue at hand.

Despite its already broad scope, however, industrial and organizational psychology has, in recent years, become even broader. Employers have been challenged to justify the usefulness and fairness of their selection procedures; companies have been challenged to develop flexible management structures that allow rapid response to change; and society has demanded that work become a psychologically rewarding and fulfilling experience as well as a means to make a living. When faced with these challenges, organizations often turn to the I/O psychologist for answers.

As we approach the beginning of the twenty-first century, we find that the demand for I/O psychologists is at an all-time high, and that within psychological specialities, the field is second only to clinical and counseling psychology in its popularity. At the same time, the related specialty of organizational behavior has become one of the most popular areas within the field of business administration.

Organizational Psychology and Organizational Behavior

At this point it is probably useful to clarify the distinction between organizational psychology and organizational behavior. Although the content within these two areas is often the same, they are differentiated by their conceptual approaches and historical backgrounds.

In psychology, topics are usually approached from the perspective of the *individual*. Even when psychologists study groups, they tend to focus on the cognitions or behaviors of the specific people who are members of the group. Consequently, **organizational psychology** looks at topics that relate the effects of individual behavior to organizational functioning such as the effects of employee absence on organizational productivity. The psychologists, of course, approach their topics from the perspective of psychology.

In contrast, **organizational behavior** has its roots in the field of management. Managers have always used psychological principles, but historically their knowledge in this area usually came from firsthand experience rather than from training. During the 1950s, however, an evaluation of the curricula of the nation's business schools recommended that business programs devote more time to studying psychology and other behavioral sciences. Today, all accredited MBA programs require courses in organizational behavior, and in many schools, organizational behavior is one of the first courses required of business students.

Organizational behavior specialists tend to deemphasize the individual approach and focus more on studying the *system* in which individual behavior occurs. Whereas industrial and organizational psychology generally moves from the study of individuals to the organization, organizational behavior moves from the organizational level to the study of individuals. In addition, I/O psychologists focus more on measurement than organizational behavior specialists do. Finally, organizational behavior developed as an amalgamation of several different fields, including I/O psychology, business administration, and sociology; I/O psychology, on the other hand, has always been rooted in psychology.

Not surprisingly, these conceptual distinctions became quite fuzzy when applied to a real work environment. Separating an individual's behavior from the organizational context in which it occurs is virtually impossible. Although their conceptual approaches may be different, the work of these two specialties in the real world is actually quite similar.

One final area of clarification concerns the differences between industrial psychology and organizational psychology. Historically, the first psychologists interested in behavior at work were industrial psychologists. These researchers studied issues concerning measurement and individual performance—how to select satisfactory workers, set standards for job performance, or train workers most effectively. Issues that focused on groups in the workplace—leadership and work group behavior, for example—were usually left to social and personality psychologists. Over time, however, the psychology of work expanded to include the study of these topics, and today the industrial and organizational psychologist is expected to know something about both individual performance and group behavior in the workplace.

Areas of I/O Psychology

Despite its long history, industrial and organizational psychology remains a dynamic and rapidly changing field. For example, I/O psychologists helped select spies in World War II, evaluated the effects of technology on British coal mines, and developed methods for training nuclear power plant operators.

For most industrial and organizational psychologists, productivity is a key value, and any aspect of the individual, group, or organization that affects productivity at work is likely to be an area of interest. For example, productivity can be affected by workers' abilities, their motivation, the environment in which they are expected to perform, or even their health. Consequently, researchers focus on a broad range of factors to determine how to evaluate and improve worker performance.

Although the traditional focuses of the field (e.g., personnel selection, performance appraisal, and worker motivation) remain important, in recent years industrial and organizational psychologists have become involved in other, less traditional areas. Developing effective work teams, determining the impact of work on family life and life satisfaction in general, and studying how management techniques from other countries might be applied to American work settings are some of the issues to which I/O psychologists have recently turned their attention. As suggested above, this broadening is testimony to the vigor and dynamism of the field. Some of the areas related to productivity in which I/O psychologists are presently involved, and can expect to be involved in the future, are listed below.

Job Analysis   Traditionally, **job analysis,** which is the study of the tasks necessary to accomplish a job, has been used to develop personnel selection procedures and set salary scales. Historically, many jobs have required standards such as a certain height, weight, age, or even gender. In recent years, however, job analysis has revealed that these requirements are often irrelevant to performance; that is, people who do not meet these standards are often capable of doing the tasks associated with the job. As the workforce becomes increasingly diverse, job analysts will be asked to determine whether such standards are fair—if, for example, a job really requires the physical strength of a man, or if the ability to speak English well is necessary to perform the job adequately.

Personnel Selection   **Personnel selection** is one of the most basic activities of any organization, and the study of methods for selecting the best employees is one of the oldest areas in industrial and organizational psychology. During the 1960s, however, the focus of personnel selection expanded from identifying applicants most likely to be successful to including methods for assuring the *fairness* of procedures. Groups that had often experienced exclusion from the hiring process complained that selection procedures discriminated against them on the basis of factors other than the ability to do the job. I/O psychologists have been in the forefront of evaluating procedures already in use and developing new procedures that select the best employees fairly. Two important recent developments in this area are the use of video selection procedures and a new interest in hiring older workers.

Training   Employee training is another area that has experienced rapid change in the past few years and is likely to change even more in the future. When people move into jobs for which their education and work experience have not prepared them, employers must provide training to assure a constant flow of qualified workers. At the same time, the rapid expansion of technology has made much previous knowledge obsolete, requiring the retraining of existing work groups. Finally, some equipment—such as airplane cockpits—has become so complex that special forms of training may be necessary for people to operate the equipment safely.

Organizational Commitment and Job Satisfaction In many respects, modern workers differ from workers of earlier periods. Better educated and less concerned about job security, many modern workers expect their jobs to be interesting, challenging, and personally satisfying. For these individuals, the sense of **job satisfaction** fulfillment that working brings is often more important than a paycheck or opportunities for promotion. During the 1990s, many employers became concerned about their workers' commitment to the organization. Today a large research effort is directed toward identifying the factors that affect levels of **organizational commitment.**

Improving the Organizational Structure Although the study of **organizational structure** goes back to the beginning of the twentieth century, this topic has recently become one of the most active research areas in industrial and organizational psychology. Whereas traditional theorists developed structures they believed would facilitate the smooth operation of a complex organization, more modern thinking suggests there is no one best way to run an organization. That is, each organization operates in a unique environment and has unique constraints on its actions. An important step away from traditional thinking in this area is the growth of participative management and self-directed work teams. In many cases the role of the manager in the workplace has changed as employees take on more responsibility for performance.

Human Factors and Working Conditions **Human factors**—the study of human–machine interactions—was formalized into an academic discipline in the 1940s, and is a field that is often independent of industrial and organizational psychology. Nevertheless, many I/O psychologists are involved in designing environments that allow workers to perform at the optimal levels of their abilities. Human factors psychologists design technologies that people are not afraid to use, air traffic control panels that minimize the chance of errors, and telecommunication systems that make face-to-face communication unnecessary. The photo on page 8 illustrates the complexity of a modern airplane cockpit.

Performance Appraisal In a sense, performance is the key to understanding many other areas of industrial and organizational psychology. Evaluating selection procedures, providing satisfying jobs, motivating workers, and selecting people for leadership positions are all tied to performance. Obviously, accurate appraisal of the performances of individuals is critical for efficient organizational functioning. Despite decades of research—the first performance appraisal instruments were de-

As this airplane control panel illustrates, technology can present challenges to workers' information processing abilities.

veloped in the 1920s—psychologists are still working to develop instruments that are accurate, meaningful, and easy to use, and training raters to use them.

Physical and Mental Health of Workers   When workers have physical or psychological problems, their performances are likely to suffer. For example, although psychologists have been interested in dealing with alcoholism in the workplace for decades, new issues— such as drug abuse, gambling, violence, and AIDS—have attracted the attention of many employers. Although industrial and organizational psychologists are not involved in treating individuals with these kinds of problems, they are often called on to assist management in developing programs that help minimize their occurrence.

Motivation and Leadership   **Motivation** and **leadership** are two traditional areas of industrial and organizational psychology that are highly interrelated. The job of the leader is to move workers toward goals. Without an understanding of what motivates workers, however, accomplishing those goals is often difficult. Conversely, not understanding what makes some leaders more successful than others also makes goals difficult to accomplish. Both motivation and leadership are among the most important, most studied, and least understood areas of I/O.

Theory and Its Application

The topics of motivation and leadership illustrate an issue that applies throughout most areas of psychology but is particularly relevant to the industrial and organizational psychologist. That is the question of theory and its application.

A **theory** is a set of related propositions used to explain a particular phenomenon. In contrast with theories based on common sense, **scientific**

theories are models or explanations that can be tested empirically; that is, researchers can use the scientific method to confirm or refute different aspects of the theory. The purpose of a theory is to explain facts and make predictions. For example, a researcher may develop a theory that hiring unskilled workers and training them in the company's procedures may be more efficient than hiring skilled workers and retraining them.

In general, psychologists prefer to develop knowledge through the use of theory rather than "common sense" approaches to knowledge. Unlike common sense, scientific theories are internally consistent, they do not ignore contradictory evidence, and they are broad in scope; that is, they are used to explain a variety of phenomena. Finally, theories are *parsimonious*—they try to explain phenomena with just a few principles. In other words, scientific theories move beyond common sense, which reflects the personal belief system of an individual, and provide a framework for testing more general principles.

In psychology in general, the most common method for testing a theory is experiments, but other methods, described in Chapter 2, are also used. The value of the experimental method lies chiefly in the fact that it can explain causality; that is, a well-designed experiment can determine if X causes Y. A researcher, for example, might use an experiment to determine if a new method of training employees leads to fewer errors in the workplace than the old training method.

For the experimental method to work, however, researchers need to control the environment in which the experiment takes place. Without control, researchers cannot be certain about the accuracy of their conclusions. They cannot be sure if the new training method caused the improvement, or if an extraneous factor—such as smarter employees or higher levels of motivation—brought about the change. Not surprisingly, research done in **applied settings,** such as offices or assembly lines, seldom has the kind of control found in a psychological laboratory. Consequently, research in applied settings is rarely as *elegant*—to use an experimental term—as that done in a controlled environment.

As suggested earlier, the purpose of theoretical research is to advance our knowledge in a particular area. We hope, for example, that a theory of what causes worker stress will further our understanding of worker performance. On the other hand, many times industrial and organizational psychologists are called on to solve problems first and worry about theory later. Typically, a company that has problems with worker stress is far more interested in handling that problem than in contributing to theoretical knowledge about the psychology of work.

Today, many industrial and organizational psychologists describe themselves as **scientist-practitioners.** This means that at the same time they are solving problems related to individual and organizational functioning, these psychologists are testing hypotheses and gathering data that advance science in general. In their daily activities, some I/O psychologists place a heavier emphasis on the "science" aspect of the field, whereas others emphasize the "practice" aspect. Probably more than any other area of psychology, I/O psychology is characterized by a constant interaction between theoretical and applied—or scientific and practical—approaches.

As suggested in Table 1.2, many industrial and organizational psychologists are involved in both developing and applying theories about behavior in the workplace. Both theory and its application are essential to the advancement of the field and of science in general.

In industrial and organizational psychology in particular, keeping the complementary nature of these two perspectives in mind is important. Whereas the academic researcher looks for knowledge derived from scientifically rigorous investigations, the sales manager is likely to look for knowledge that can be used immediately. The I/O psychologist needs to understand and appreciate the importance of both perspectives. Throughout the material presented here, this book tries to use real-life applications to illustrate theory.

Psychology in the Workplace: Three Historical Examples

Scientific Management
The Hawthorne Studies
The Textile Mills of
    Ahmedabad

As suggested above, psychology was being applied in organizational settings long before it existed as a formal field of study. For example, both Adam Smith and Karl Marx had strong opinions about human nature and its effect on behavior in the workplace. Smith believed that workers are influenced by appealing to their self-interest; Marx believed that self-interest by itself is an aberration, and that cooperative behavior is more natural to humans (Smither, 1984).

Although economists had been interested in the workplace for some time, psychologists began to study workplace behavior only around the beginning of the twentieth century. One way to understand the work of an industrial and organizational psychologist is to look at cases in which workplace behavior has been studied or explained in terms of psychological principles. Three "classic" approaches to understanding psychology in the workplace are described below.

Scientific Management

Scientific management is a school of thought about worker productivity developed by the industrial engineer Frederick W. Taylor. Taylor's work interests industrial and organizational psychologists because it was among the first to focus on the relationship between human behavior and productivity. At the same time, some of Taylor's ideas remain a part of management philosophy today.

Taylor, like Adam Smith, believed that workers' primary motivation is economic, and that individuals would work hard if they received appropriate financial rewards. Taylor also believed there is one best way to perform any particular job, and efficiency requires that procedures for performance be standardized. Once workers saw that standardized procedures make their jobs easier and increase productivity, Taylor believed they would work harder for the consequent benefits.

Table 1.2   THEORY AND ITS APPLICATION IN INDUSTRIAL AND ORGANIZATIONAL PSYCHOLOGY

	Theoretical Concern	Application
Job analysis	Precise measurement of tasks that constitute a specific job	Developing selection standards Setting salaries Developing training programs
Personnel selection	Development of procedures that lead to accurate predictions of employee performance Development of procedures that do not discriminate unfairly	Selecting employees who will be productive Avoiding problems with turnover, absenteeism, and low productivity Identifying leadership potential
Training	Development of methods that facilitate learning	Improving the skills of workers Ensuring a continuous supply of skilled workers
Job satisfaction	Identification and measurement of job aspects that are most rewarding to employees	Eliminating problems with turnover, absenteeism, and employee morale Developing policies and programs that encourage productivity
Organizational theory	Development of an organizational structure that facilitates functioning Development of plans for changing conditions	Improving communication Enhancing productivity Positioning organization for future environment
Human factors	Determination of how much information humans can process and act on at one time without diminishing performance	Designing work environments for productivity and performance Designing work environments for safety Improving design of consumer products
Performance appraisal	Development of psychometrically precise measurement techniques	Making accurate appraisals for personnel decisions Planning for training Identifying leadership potential
Motivation	Identification and understanding of the psychological processes involved in performance	Raising worker productivity Designing incentive programs
Leadership	Identification of psychological and environmental factors that affect leadership	Providing for the leadership of the organization Planning for the future

Taylor's initial work was in the area of determining the best procedures for performing jobs at the Midvale Steel Company in 1881. An obsessive researcher, he performed about 40,000 experiments to determine the best ways of cutting metal (Taylor, 1907). The method of these experiments was the **time-and-motion study,** in which a worker's movements were analyzed to determine the most efficient way of accomplishing a task.

In later years, however, Taylor became less interested in analyzing jobs and more interested in managing workers. He felt that if workers were paid on the basis of what they produced, rather than the time they spent working, productivity would increase. The **piecework** method of production introduced by Taylor required that workers receive a set amount of compensation for each piece of work they completed. According to Taylor, paying people for what they actually produce encourages high levels of production and is also the fairest method of establishing wage levels.

These two major elements of scientific management—the scientific study of jobs to determine the best way of doing them and compensation on the basis of piecework—were strongly resisted by many workers and managers. Many workers did not like being told how to accomplish their tasks, and often the introduction of the piecework system resulted in harder work for the same or lower wages.

Taylor's research had demonstrated that payment on the piecework system often led to amazing gains in productivity. But such gains also suggested something else: that employees had not been working as hard as they could have been before the introduction of piecework. When management realized that fact, often the production quotas were raised so that workers had to produce more to earn both the set wage and the bonus that was supposed to come from the piecework system. Although Taylor strongly objected to such practices, many workers considered "Taylorism" a form of exploitation. In 1912, in fact, Taylor's system of shop management was investigated by the U.S. House of Representatives.

Throughout his career, Taylor quarreled with both labor and management about these issues, but by the end of his life, he was recognized internationally as a major contributor to the study of human behavior in the workplace. Surprisingly, one of his admirers was Vladimir Lenin, who wrote in the April 28, 1918, edition of *Pravda:*

> The task that the Soviet government must set the people in all its scope is—learn to work. The Taylor system, the last word of capitalism in this respect, like all capitalist progress, is a combination of the refined brutality of bourgeois exploitation and a number of the greatest scientific achievements in the field of analysing mechanical motions during work, the elimination of superfluous and awkward motions, the elaboration of correct methods of work, the introduction of the best system of accounting and control, etc. . . . We must organise in Russia the study and teaching of the Taylor system and systematically try it out and adapt it to our own ends. (Lenin, 1965)

Although piecework can result in dramatic increases in productivity (Koretz, 1997c), its use is not as prevalent in the United States as it once was. Nonetheless, many other aspects of scientific management are still practiced. One review of Taylor's contributions (Locke, 1982) suggested that modern management continues to use Taylor's ideas about the standardization of work, the study of jobs, goal setting, and the scientific selection of workers.

The Hawthorne Studies

Probably no research has received as much attention from industrial and organizational psychologists as the **Hawthorne studies** conducted at the Hawthorne plant of the Western Electric Company (see below). This research, begun in the 1920s and lasting more than a decade, was a groundbreaking attempt to apply knowledge from the social sciences to an industrial setting. Of particular interest to Elton Mayo and F. J. Roethlisberger, the directors of the research, was identifying ways in which management and workers could cooperate to create a productive and satisfying work environment (Roethlisberger & Dickson, 1939).

Over the years, the researchers looked at a number of issues relevant to human behavior in the workplace. Two of the most famous parts of the study—the illumination experiments and the bank wiring observation room study—are described here.

The purpose of the illumination study was to determine how lighting affects productivity. Specifically, researchers wanted to see if workers would produce more when working under higher levels of illumination. In the first experiment in this series, illumination was raised for one group working under the experimental conditions and kept at the same level for another group working under control conditions. To the surprise of the researchers, the productivity of both groups increased.

In follow-up studies, productivity increased in all groups whether the researchers lowered or raised the levels of illumination. When lighting was finally

Hawthorne workers in the mica test room. (*Source:* AT&T Bell Laboratories. Reprinted with permission.)

lowered to a point about equal to the level of bright moonlight, productivity did not increase. The researchers had apparently stumbled onto a phenomenon that was not related to illumination.

Results of the illumination study are often used as an example of what has come to be known as the **Hawthorne effect,** a term that describes the phenomenon of individuals altering their behavior not because of specific changes in the environment, but because of the influence of the person making the changes. At the Hawthorne plant, attention from the researchers apparently motivated workers to raise their productivity. The illumination study demonstrated that interpersonal relations between workers and researchers, much more than levels of illumination, affected productivity. In the context of the 1920s, this was a significant finding.

A second important study from the Hawthorne research was not experimental, but simply an observation of workers assembling equipment in the bank wiring assembly room. These workers were organized along the lines of scientific management—they were paid based on the amount of their output. Although it was presumed to be in the best interest of the workers to produce as much as possible, managers had noticed that this was not what workers usually did. When a new employee joined the bank wiring assembly group, the new employee's productivity was typically high. Over time, however, this productivity dropped to a level no higher than the levels of more experienced workers.

Hawthorne employees were, in fact, practicing **work restriction**—putting limits on the amount of work that a worker accomplishes in a given period. In the bank wiring assembly room, experienced workers informally pressured high performers to lower their rates of productivity so that they were more in line with the group norm. As often occurs in piecework operations, the experienced workers were suspicious that higher productivity would lead to management's setting higher norms and expecting harder work for the same level of pay.

Although it would have been in the economic self-interest of the new employees to continue to produce at a high level, they did not do so. Even during the Great Depression, the time during which this particular study took place, the social norms established by the work group were more important than financial gain. This, too, was a surprise to the researchers. Starting from the perspective that self-interest is the major motivator in the workplace, the Hawthorne researchers did not expect social influences to be more important than money.

Today, neither of these findings seems particularly surprising, but to believers in scientific management, they were completely unexpected. In both cases, social relations—not illumination or financial reward—proved to be the critical factor in productivity. The Hawthorne studies indirectly gave rise to the human relations movement, a new approach to managing the industrial enterprise. This movement, which became particularly important in the period after World War II, encouraged the development of harmonious interpersonal relations at work as the most effective means to achieving higher productivity.

In the years since the Hawthorne research, a substantial body of literature critical of the effort has developed (Bramel & Friend, 1981; Parsons, 1974).

Critics typically fault the methodology, the narrow focus, or the assumptions underlying much of the research. Although such criticisms are important, the basic idea of the Hawthorne studies—that social relations play a critical role in the working environment—remains unchallengeable. The Hawthorne studies were an important step away from the mechanistic view of workers proposed by Taylor. The quote from Elton Mayo (cited in Roethlisberger & Dickson, 1939) at the beginning of this book is about the limitations of approaching behavioral phenomena ignorant of "the facts of human association."

The Textile Mills of Ahmedabad

The third study occurred in the textile mills of the Ahmedabad Manufacturing and Calico Printing Company in India (Rice, 1953). In June 1952, the company had installed automatic looms in one of its factories. In contrast with traditional methods of weaving, the new system introduced a number of changes, including the need for continuous attention to the loom by employees working in shifts. Individual jobs also became specialized, with each worker responsible for a small number of specific tasks. An additional change was the necessity of maintaining a humidity level between 80 and 85 percent in the loom shed so that yarn could stand the strain of the weaving process.

Despite management's high hopes, introducing the automatic equipment had resulted in lower productivity and a higher percentage of damaged goods. Although the possibility of increasing supervision was considered, this idea was rejected because the lines of management in the loom sheds were already too complicated. Under the mill's form of organization, some workers were responsible to as many as four supervisors.

After studying the problems of higher damage and lowered efficiency, A. K. Rice, a consultant from the Tavistock Institute of Human Relations, concluded that one problem was the way the mills were being managed. Drawing on the bureaucratic theory of management (discussed in Chapter 12), the textile company had developed a structure requiring the division of labor and specialization of tasks for each worker. Rather than performing several tasks at one loom, as workers had in the past, the new organization required workers to perform the same tasks at several looms. Similarly, rather than belonging to a specific work group, workers were reassigned to several groups. According to Rice, increasing the amount of supervision would probably have made the situation worse.

Eventually management recognized that applying traditional management theory was inappropriate for the loom operation. In an unusual step—particularly in the 1950s—management asked the workers what they thought would be a better system of organization. The workers, whose morale had remained high throughout the troubled period, eagerly responded. They formed small, internally led work groups, eliminated some lines of authority, moved to deemphasize job titles, and encouraged individuals to perform more than one task. Rather than having workers perform the same task in a variety of groups, the new organization encouraged workers to develop more cohesive teams. After these changes were instituted, performance improved and damage decreased.

The Ahmedabad study is a classic example of applying psychological principles in the service of efficiency. The workers knew better than management that developing stable work groups, rather than specializing tasks, would lead to greater efficiency. They also recognized that being partly responsible for a finished product was more efficient than being wholly responsible for only a small part of a finished product. In later years, the lessons of the Ahmedabad textile mills had an important influence on the formation of autonomous work groups at such companies as Volvo, Saab, and others.

The study of the textile mills at Ahmedabad is one of the most famous studies of a school of organizational theory known as **sociotechnical systems.** Sociotechnical systems, which is discussed in more detail in Chapter 12, focuses on two aspects of organizations—the social system, consisting of the network of interpersonal relationships among the organization's members, and the technical system, consisting of the tasks, equipment, and activities necessary to accomplish the goals of the organization. The basic principle of the sociotechnical approach is that technological change is likely to be disruptive if the social aspects of the workplace are not considered.

According to the sociotechnical approach, the best organization has an environment that facilitates the functioning of work groups in which employees have autonomy to decide how a task will be accomplished. These kinds of employee groups are more productive, and they also fulfill the social needs of workers. In recent years, the sociotechnical approach has become increasingly popular among some industrial and organizational psychologists.

The Professional I/O Psychologist

Work Environments
Training
Professional Life

Unlike some other psychological specialties, much industrial and organizational psychology takes place outside academic settings and in actual work situations. As previously suggested, there are advantages and disadvantages to the applied nature of the field.

Work Environments

Industrial and organizational psychologists who work primarily in academic settings typically teach and do research. They are often interested in the broader theoretical areas of the field, such as studying the general principles that govern learning, developing methods to measure performance as accurately as possible, or identifying factors that contribute to employee motivation. In addition, I/O psychologists who teach often provide consulting services outside the university. Organizations with problems sometimes call on these individuals for assistance. A survey of members of the Society for Industrial and Organizational Psychology (Borman & Cox, 1996) found that the areas in which I/O psychologists most frequently practiced included organization development, personnel selection, attitude surveys, and performance appraisal.

Another area in which industrial and organizational psychologists are active is management consulting. Consultants are specialists who work on specific problems for organizations. Management consultants may, for example, provide a company with a human relations training program, a fair and effective personnel selection procedure, or a strategic plan. Most consultants work on a contract basis for a variety of firms, addressing problems in different organizations, then moving on to work on other contracts. Because of the diversity of experience provided by their work, consultants use their knowledge of different situations to make recommendations to management. In the late 1980s, hundreds of management consulting firms were founded, and currently there are thousands of these firms in the United States and Canada.

In addition to those teaching and consulting, many industrial and organizational psychologists work full time for the government or for companies in the private sector. I/O psychologists have been instrumental in developing policies for both employees of the U.S. government—the nation's largest employer—and for private employers. Within the private sector, these individuals often work in personnel and human resources development departments, but they can also be found in production, marketing, and other areas.

Among all psychological specialties, industrial and organizational psychologists working in applied settings are among the highest paid. In 1995, the average starting salary for a nonacademic I/O psychologist holding a Ph.D. degree was $50,875 for jobs in consulting firms and $56,500 for jobs in business (American Psychological Association, 1996). Overall, however, the highest salaries for I/O psychologists are in the banking, financial, and insurance industries (Zickar & Taylor, 1996).

Training

As suggested above, the work of the industrial and organizational psychologist draws on knowledge from many different areas. Consequently, specialists from other fields often perform the same tasks as I/O psychologists. Human resources development specialists, trainers, and organization development consultants, for example, may become involved in areas pertinent to I/O. These allied fields have their own forms of certification, but practice as an I/O psychologist usually requires a doctorate or master's level degree.

Doctoral programs in industrial and organizational psychology generally focus on training students in the methods of research. An understanding of research is critical for a successful career in I/O, and individuals who work in either applied or academic settings are expected to be thoroughly trained in this aspect of the field. A typical doctoral program lasts four years and, in some cases, requires an internship in an organizational setting outside the university. Although some schools offer master's-only programs in I/O psychology, this practice is not widespread.

Professional Life

Many, if not most, industrial and organizational psychologists belong to the Society for Industrial and Organizational Psychology (SIOP), Division 14 of the American Psychological Association (APA). Other professional organizations to which I/O psychologists are likely to belong include the American Psychological Society, the International Personnel Management Association, the American Society for Training and Development, the Human Factors and Ergonomics Society, and the Academy of Management. In some cities, such as Los Angeles and Washington, D.C., smaller groups such as the Personnel Testing Council have a high proportion of industrial and organizational psychologists as members.

Although much of the applied work that industrial and organizational psychologists do is relevant only to a specific organization, much more is of interest to anyone working in related fields. Individuals doing research in I/O can publish their findings in journals such as the *Journal of Applied Psychology, Personnel Psychology, Academy of Management Journal,* and *Academy of Management Review*. These publications are all refereed; that is, submitted material is reviewed by more than one knowledgeable professional, each of whom evaluates the merits of the research and its usefulness to readers. Most of the studies cited throughout this book can be found in these journals, and students who are interested in learning about the most current topics of interest to I/O psychologists should look at recent issues.

Previously, the point was made that industrial and organizational psychology is a rapidly growing and dynamic field. The I/O psychologist has the unique opportunity of making substantial contributions to an area of life that concerns almost everyone—work. Although the course of preparation is long and challenging, the rewards—personal, financial, and those to society—make I/O psychology a very attractive career option. One goal of this book is to provide examples of both the attractiveness and the importance of the field.

I/O Psychology and the Workplace of the Future

One reason industrial and organizational psychology is becoming increasingly important concerns the ways in which the workplace is changing. During the 1980s, I/O psychologists, economists, managers, and many others began to recognize that the American workplace was undergoing a transformation that would change the psychology of work forever. Important developments in the composition of the workforce, the organization of the workplace, and the need to compete globally have introduced new areas of study for the I/O psychologist. As managers confront the rapidly accelerating pace of change, they are likely to turn to I/O psychologists to help them prepare for the workplace of the future.

One critical area of change concerns the composition of the workforce. According to a report issued by the U.S. Department of Labor (1991), the proportion of non-White workers will increase faster than the proportion of White workers. Hispanic workers, in particular, will constitute a greater share of the workforce. Almost certainly, this will require organizations to address questions of language requirements, special training programs, and differences in culture.

At the same time, the number of working women will also continue to increase, with Hispanic and Asian women entering the workforce at a faster rate than any other group. As a result, organizations will need to continue to pay close attention to issues of fairness in hiring, promotion, and other personnel decisions. Furthermore, the increased number of women in the workforce requires many employers to address other issues, such as child care arrangements, strength requirements for certain jobs, and the incidence of sexual harassment.

Jobs in service industries will expand as jobs in manufacturing become less available. Customer service is a key component in businesses that provide service, and many organizations will be required to develop special training programs and performance appraisal systems for dealing with customer service issues. According to the Department of Labor, businesses are going to place more emphasis on interpersonal and analytical skills—skills that traditional education sometimes fails to provide. During the next 25 years, exports are expected to increase, and manufacturers will be faced with the challenge of new technologies and with adapting their business practices to an international environment.

Finally, organizations are going to place a greater value on educated workers. Educated workers also place greater demands on organizations—they often expect greater benefits, participation in decision making, and a work environment that is personally rewarding. To attract these individuals, many companies will need to revise their structures, offer innovative compensation and benefit plans, and manage the interpersonal environment so that work provides more than just an income for the educated worker.

These are important challenges and, unfortunately, many companies are not well prepared to respond to them. Increasingly, experts in the psychology of work are going to be asked to help make the transition to the work environment of the future. Industrial and organizational psychologists have a critical role to play in making this transition successful.

Figure 1.1 illustrates some projected changes in the workforce, and Figure 1.2 illustrates the occupations expected to enjoy fast growth, high earnings, and large numbers of openings. Note that "Management analyst" and "Personnel, training, and labor relations specialist"—two careers related to I/O

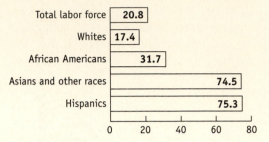

Total labor force	20.8
Whites	17.4
African Americans	31.7
Asians and other races	74.5
Hispanics	75.3

Source: U.S. Department of Labor. (Fall, 1991). Outlook: 1990–2005. *Occupational Outlook Quarterly.* Washington, DC: Bureau of Labor Statistics.

Figure 1.1 Workforce Growth by Race and Hispanic Origin (percent), 1990–2005

psychology—fall among these occupations. Other related occupations also predicted to have high growth rates between 1994 and 2005 include employment interviewers (35 percent), management consultants (35 percent), social scientists in general (23 percent), and psychologists (23 percent) (*Occupational Outlook Quarterly,* 1996).

Organization of This Book

As mentioned in the first part of this chapter, the areas of industrial and organizational psychology are varied and overlapping: Worker motivation is related to job satisfaction, leadership is related to group behavior, job analysis is related to personnel selection and training, and so forth. Consequently, it is almost impossible to define a precise boundary between industrial psychology and organizational psychology.

To facilitate understanding of the material, however, this book is divided into sections. Part I is a general introduction to the field and a discussion of the research methods that are used in applied settings. Part II focuses on the traditional areas of industrial psychology and, in general, addresses topics in the order that an individual entering a work environment experiences them—recruitment, assessment, selection, training, and performance appraisal.

Part III focuses less on the individual and covers areas more traditionally associated with organizational psychology and group functioning: worker motivation, job satisfaction, leadership, group behavior, and special populations in the workplace. Part IV covers topics more relevant to the organization as a whole: organizational theory, organization development, human factors and working conditions, and maintaining the mental and physical health of workers.

With regard to chapters, this book uses a system of **taxonomies,** or classifications. Each chapter begins with a listing of the broad areas related to

Occupations	Average weekly wages of full-time workers	Total job openings 1994–2005 (thousands)	Percent change 1994–2005
Lawyers	$1,131	268	28
Physicians	1,040	205	22
Systems analysts	845	481	92
Computer engineers	845	191	90
Management analysts	789	109	35
Residential counselors	694	158	76
Teachers, secondary school	690	782	29
Registered nurses	685	740	25
Teachers, special education	647	262	53
Writers and editors, including technical writers	633	111	22
Police patrol officers	632	271	28
Personnel, training, and labor relations specialists	611	129	22
Designers, except interior	590	113	32
Artists and commercial artists	575	117	23
Instructors and coaches, sports and physical training	530	119	35
Instructors, adult (nonvocational) education	530	107	29
Teachers and instructors, vocational education	530	104	27
Social workers	506	288	34
Heating, air conditioning, and refrigeration mechanics	497	125	29
Correctional officers	485	194	51
Licensed practical nurses	450	341	28

0   200   400   600   800   1,000 1,200

Usual training required
- ☐ Bachelor's degree or higher
- ☐ Postsecondary vocational training
- ☐ Associate's degree
- ☐ On-the-job training

Source: Bureau of Labor Statistics. (Projected job openings and percent change are from the BLS industry-occupation matrix; earnings, from the Current Population Survey; training, from research conducted for the *Occupational Outlook Handbook.*)

Figure 1.2 Fastest Growing Occupations, 1990–2005

the general topic, and within the chapter, a secondary taxonomy describes the materials covered in separate sections. These two systems of taxonomy introduce the concepts covered in the chapter. By familiarizing yourself with the concepts before beginning to read the chapter, you are likely to find the material more meaningful. Knowing the conceptual structure allows you to relate both material covered in the chapter and your own relevant experiences to the general topic. This method of taxonomies, used by educational psychologists to facilitate learning, should help you retain and recall chapter materials.

As with any field, industrial and organizational psychology has a specialized jargon. Each chapter has a list of key words and concepts discussed in that chapter, and the end of the book contains a glossary. Finally, each chapter ends with some questions for discussion.

Chapter Summary

Today, people work together in complex organizations that have a variety of goals. Organizational goals influence how people behave, but people also bring their own goals and patterns of behavior to organizations. This is why studying the psychology of work is important.

Industrial and organizational psychology is the development and application of psychological principles to the workplace. In general, industrial psychology focuses on issues related to measurement and individual performance. Organizational psychology focuses more on group behavior. These areas greatly overlap, however. I/O psychology is an applied science, and its approach is often multidisciplinary.

Although the topics studied by industrial and organizational psychologists have broadened in recent years, traditional areas of study include job analysis, personnel selection, training, organizational commitment and job satisfaction, organizational structure, performance appraisal, motivation, and leadership.

Industrial and organizational psychologists develop scientific theories and test them, but because their research is often done in the workplace rather than in a psychological laboratory, researchers do not always have the level of control over the research settings that they do in other areas of psychology. In addition, specialists in other areas may be interested solely in advancing theoretical knowledge, but the I/O psychologist is often called on to solve problems in real life. It is important to remember that both these approaches—the theoretical and the applied—are critical for the advancement of science.

Three classic approaches to studying psychology in the workplace are Frederick W. Taylor's scientific management, the studies done at the Hawthorne plant of the Western Electric Company, and the introduction of the automatic looms to the weaving sheds in Ahmedabad, India.

Many industrial and organizational psychologists teach and do research in academic settings, and they also provide consulting services outside the university. Others work as management consultants, providing contractual services to assist managers in solving organizational problems. Still other I/O psychologists work full time for the federal government or the private sector. Of all psychological specialties, I/O is among the highest paid.

Although individuals from other fields may work in the traditional areas of industrial and organizational psychology, most I/O positions require an advanced degree. Doctoral programs emphasize a solid background in research, and many require an internship in an organizational setting. There are a number of organizations to which I/O psychologists belong, and they publish their research in various scientific journals.

One of the most exciting challenges to industrial and organizational psychologists is the changing nature of the workplace. In the near future, the composition of the workforce will become more diverse, interpersonal and analytical skills in employees will become more important, and companies will need to develop more training programs for their employees. Industrial and organizational psychologists will undoubtedly play a key role in helping companies make the transition to the workplace of the future.

Key Words and Concepts

applied science (p. 4)
applied settings (p. 9)
Hawthorne effect (p. 14)
Hawthorne studies (p. 13)
human factors (p. 7)
industrial and organizational
   psychology (p. 2)
job analysis (p. 6)
job satisfaction (p. 7)
leadership (p. 8)
motivation (p. 8)
organizational behavior (p. 5)
organizational commitment (p. 7)
organizational psychology (p. 4)
organizational structure (p. 7)

performance appraisal (p. 7)
personnel selection (p. 6)
piecework (p. 12)
psychology (p. 2)
scientific management (p. 10)
scientific theory (p. 8)
scientist-practitioner (p. 9)
sociotechnical systems (p. 16)
taxonomy (p. 20)
theoretical science (p. 4)
theory (p. 8)
time-and-motion study (p. 12)
training (p. 6)
work restriction (p. 14)

Questions for Discussion

1. Although I/O psychologists constitute a small percentage of all psychologists, the field is growing rapidly. Why do you think this is so?
2. What is the difference between organizational psychology and organizational behavior? Which do you believe to be a better approach to understanding worker behavior?

3. What is the difference between common sense and a scientific theory? Which do you use more frequently in your daily life? Why?

4. What is the problem with piecework? Could you redesign your class so that students are paid on the basis of what they "produce"?

5. Do you believe you could learn more effectively if your class were organized on a sociotechnical model? Why or why not?

6. How do you envision the workforce and the workplace of the future?

CHAPTER 2

Research in the Organizational Setting

Experimental Research
Correlational Studies
Observational Studies
Other Research Methods
Measurement Scales
Selecting a Research Method
Reliability and Validity in Research Studies
Evaluating Applied Research
Chapter Summary
Key Words and Concepts
Questions for Discussion

Understanding research methods is important in all areas of psychology, but for the industrial and organizational psychologist, this understanding is critical. When organizations decide to invest time and resources in making changes recommended by an I/O psychologist, these recommendations must be based on well-designed studies conducted in a scientific manner. I/O psychologists must be able to justify their recommendations, design cost-effective research programs that answer the questions of management, and critique the research of others to determine its usefulness.

Typical research questions for an I/O psychologist might include the following:

■ After attending a human relations workshop, a manager wonders if communications training for employees will improve productivity.
■ A supervisor asks the personnel department if he can stop interviewing female applicants for a physically demanding position because the last two women he hired were unable to perform the job.

- Management is considering buying a computer-based training program to replace the traditional classroom lecture method, but wonders if such a change is worth the cost.
- The personnel department is not satisfied with the quality of candidates who apply through newspaper advertising and suggests the company hire a professional agency to do its recruitment.

In each of these cases, an industrial and organizational psychologist might be called on for advice. To back up this advice, the psychologist should be prepared to design a study or to provide examples of other studies that support specific views. Without supporting data, the psychologist's recommendations may not be cost effective—as in the case of purchasing computer-based training—or they may lead to legal challenge—as in the case of not interviewing women for physically demanding jobs.

As discussed in Chapter 1, doing good research in an organizational setting can be difficult. Whereas laboratory researchers have a large degree of control over their participants, a research study conducted in the workplace is much harder to control. Unlike human participants, rats cannot quit their jobs, intentionally sabotage research programs, or manipulate results to serve their own purposes. In other words, the complexities of dealing with animal behavior in the laboratory cannot be compared to the complexities of dealing with human behavior on the job.

In addition to controlling participants, the laboratory researcher usually has better control over the environment in which studies are conducted. Researchers in applied settings must often contend with a variety of factors that can affect results. Budget allocations, shifting priorities, or organizational politics are often beyond the control of the applied researcher. Additionally, the Hawthorne effect—discussed in Chapter 1—may make research findings misleading or uninterpretable. For all these reasons, researchers in organizational settings must be extremely cautious about the design of their studies.

Throughout the following chapters, many research studies about topics in industrial and organizational psychology are described. To understand and evaluate these studies, it is necessary to be familiar with the methods that the researchers used. This chapter looks at these methods, as well as the statistical techniques that researchers use to analyze their data.

Laboratory Experiments
Field Experiments
Natural Experiments and Ex
    Post Facto Studies
Statistical Analysis of
    Experimental Data
Evaluating the Experimen-
    tal Method

Experimental Research

One thing that can be said about all research methodology is this: The more rigorously scientific the method, the more difficult it is to do the research properly. In the social sciences, researchers must often compromise between methodological rigor and practical considerations in the design of their studies. For this reason, industrial and organizational psychologists typically use

experiments, in which researchers manipulate variables to study cause-and-effect relationships in control and treatment groups (Salkind, 1997), less frequently than correlational or observational studies.

Of the research methods discussed in this book, however, well-designed and well-conducted experiments are considered the most powerful. Because experimenters are obliged to keep control of the environments in which their studies take place, they are often able to infer **causality**—the particular reason that something occurs. The determination of causality, which is impossible in a correlational study and questionable in an observational approach, is the quality that gives the experiment its power. Table 2.1 illustrates the three experimental strategies that an industrial and organizational psychologist might use.

Laboratory Experiments

Although **laboratory experiments** are often designed to add to theoretical knowledge of a subject, sometimes their results can be used in applied settings. For example, laboratory studies of group behavior have had important implications for the practice of management in the workplace. Similarly, laboratory studies of the ways people make judgments have affected the development of systems for evaluating worker performance.

When conducting a laboratory experiment, the researcher creates a **controlled environment**—that is, an environment in which extraneous factors that may affect results are controlled. The purpose of the experiment is to test a **hypothesis,** which is a statement about the relationship between two or more variables. For example, a researcher may want to test the hypothesis that soothing music in the workplace will make employees drowsy and unproductive. Because testing this hypothesis in a real workplace may be too disruptive, the researcher may do the study in a psychological laboratory, with volunteers—or **participants**—taking the role of workers. In this example, the basic procedure would require some volunteers to perform a task while soothing music is being played, whereas others would perform the task with no music or with a different kind of music. The hypothesis would be tested by comparing the productivity of the participants in the "soothing" condition versus the productivity of those in the other conditions.

Another way to define the hypothesis is as a statement of the relationship between the independent and dependent variables. In this example, the soothing music would be the **independent variable,** which can be defined as the stimulus or aspect of the environment that the experimenter manipulates to determine its influences on behavior (Smith & Davis, 1997). The independent variable can be described as the input to the research—the different conditions to which the research participants are exposed, for example, or characteristics of the research participants themselves (Tabachnik & Fidell, 1989). Independent variables are sometimes referred to as **predictors** because they are hypothesized to predict performance on the dependent variable.

Table 2.1   THREE EXPERIMENTAL METHODS

	Rationale	Procedure
Laboratory experiment	Used when a researcher is able to control the environment in which the study takes place	1. Develop hypothesis 2. Select control group or use random assignment approach 3. Measure to assure comparability of groups 4. Administer treatment to experimental group 5. Measure both groups to determine changes 6. Determine if changes are due to chance factors 7. Make inference as to causality of changes
Field experiment	Used when a laboratory study is impossible or difficult to implement or when the researcher is concerned about the artificiality of the laboratory setting	As much as possible, researcher follows steps for laboratory experiment, although there may be problems with developing control groups or using random assignment. Additionally, extraneous factors in work environment may influence findings.
Natural experiments or ex post facto studies	Used when no control of environment is possible, control is not desired, or researcher wants to measure effect of changes that have already occurred.	1. Develop hypothesis 2. Identify groups to be studied 3. If possible, measure groups on independent variable 4. Allow change to occur 5. Measure groups on dependent variable 6. Perform statistical analysis if appropriate 7. Make inferences regarding causality if appropriate

The **dependent variable,** on the other hand, is the output variable—the response or behavior that is measured after the manipulation of the independent variable. In the example of the music research, productivity on the experimental task is the dependent variable.

In the simplest case—as in the music experiment—the researcher wants to determine whether a particular input is better than having no input. Testing this hypothesis would require two groups: the **experimental group**—those who listen to music while they perform the experimental task—and the **control group**—those who do not hear music while they are working. The purpose of the control group is to determine if no treatment results in the same performance as having a treatment. In this case, participants would be assigned to either the treatment group or the control group, exposed or not exposed to music while they are working, and then measured on their productivity.

In most experiments, the researcher works with a small number of participants and uses findings from the study to make **inferences** about a larger group. This is done with the use of inferential statistics, which allow the researcher to generalize from a smaller to a larger group. The small group that participates in the study is known as a **sample;** the larger group to which the findings will be applied constitutes a **population.** It is very important that the sample reflect the major characteristics of the population—that the sample be **representative** of the population. Otherwise, the researcher's conclusions may not be accurate.

In addition to making certain the sample is representative, assigning participants to the experimental or control groups is an important aspect of experimental research. To interpret results from a study with confidence, the researcher must be certain that members of the groups have similar characteristics. In most studies, researchers attempt to ensure that participants in these groups are comparable in age, level of education, work experience, and other factors. This is to guard against results from the study being influenced by factors outside the control of the experimenter. In general, researchers attempt to control these factors in two ways. A researcher may measure the average age or educational level of each group to ensure similarity, or the researcher may simply randomly assign participants to groups so that differences are spread equally.

In some cases, a researcher may not wish to use a control group. If, for example, the researcher has determined that soothing music does hinder performance, he or she may seek to determine whether the music has different effects depending on the task the workers are performing. In this study, type of task would be the independent variable. For example, the researcher would assign one group to a scheduling task and another to a sorting task, and then expose both to music while they are working. The final stage of the experiment would be to measure the performances of each group—performance would be the dependent variable—to determine if type of task affects reactions to music in the workplace.

Because of the need for control of the environment, conducting a laboratory experiment can become quite complex. In addition, sometimes conditions in a laboratory experiment are so different from conditions in the workplace that results from the experiment may not be applicable. Nonetheless, industrial and organizational researchers often use information from laboratory experiments as a starting point for further research in the work environment. Because a well-designed laboratory experiment can provide clear evidence of causality, I/O psychologists—particularly those in university settings—continue to consider the laboratory experiment a valuable research tool.

Example of a Laboratory Experiment Many people believe that employees can make more accurate appraisals of the quality of their work than their supervisors. Because employees actually do the work, the argument goes, they have a better understanding about what constitutes good performance. However, some researchers believe that self-assessments of performance are usually too lenient. (This question is explored more fully in Chapter 6.)

Two researchers (Jourden & Heath, 1996) were interested in testing the accuracy of individuals' perceptions of their performances. Business students who volunteered to participate in this study were assigned to one of three experimental conditions—working alone, working with one other person, or working in a group of four—and given 17 minutes to solve a group of word puzzles.

Afterward, all participants were asked to rate how they thought they did in solving the puzzles. Interestingly, people who worked in groups of four rated their individual performances higher than the participants working under other conditions. Participants working with one other person did not rate their performances particularly high or low, and those who worked alone rated themselves lower than other participants.

The researchers concluded that the belief that workers rate their own performances too highly may be incorrect. In this study, individuals gave themselves lower ratings when working alone than when they worked with others.

As illustrated by this example, the major value of the laboratory experiment is that it allows hypotheses to be tested with a high degree of control over the environment. The random assignment of participants to experimental conditions ensures comparability among groups, and experimenters can carefully isolate the variables they want to study. On the other hand, the laboratory experiment results in a certain amount of artificiality.

In the study described above, the obvious question that comes to mind is the similarity between the behavior of business students in a laboratory and that of employees in the workplace. As you will see in Chapter 6, the question of workers evaluating their own performances is more complicated than this one experiment can address.

Because of this concern about the comparability of environments, laboratory researchers can never be entirely certain their findings can be generalized from one setting to another. In the lab, attention is focused on relationships between just a few variables, but the real world consists of relationships among uncountable variables. Consequently, industrial and organizational psychologists must be cautious when asserting that findings from a laboratory study can be directly applied to the work environment.

Field Experiments

Field experiments attempt to circumvent the problem of the artificial nature of the laboratory method. Rather than assuming that findings from the lab will apply to a real-life setting, field researchers test their hypotheses in the workplace. Extending findings from the study described above, for example, researchers may wish to determine whether real workers rate their performances higher if they work together in a group.

The real-life setting offers several advantages over the laboratory. First, in contrast with student volunteers, participants in field studies will usually be affected by the results. Therefore, they may take their tasks more seriously. Second, employees participating in the study perform real work rather than an artificial task created by the experimenter. This, too, should add to the reality of the experiment. Finally, we may assume that people who are working to make mortgage and car payments are likely to behave differently from people who are participating in an experiment for class credit. Overall, we can expect the findings from the field experiment to be a more accurate representation of how people actually behave in the workplace.

The obvious disadvantage of the field experiment is the sacrifice of control. Without control, factors other than the independent variable may interfere in the course of the study and influence the results. Workers may go on strike or practice work restriction, supervisors may be reassigned, or the nature of the work may change. Another common problem in conducting a field experiment is management's reluctance to allow changes that might disrupt the work environment. Not surprisingly, managers whose own evaluations are based on the productivity of their subordinates usually resist jeopardizing that productivity.

Finally, field researchers rarely have control over the composition of their experimental and control groups. Workers who participate in a psychological study usually do not constitute a **random sample**—they are not representative of the population or are not randomly assigned to the experimental or control condition. The researcher may still conduct the study, but because the groups are not random, or because they may not be truly representative of a larger group, the study is referred to as a **quasi-experiment.** Quasi-experiments are not true experiments. Because of the field experimenter's frequent lack of control, most field experiments are actually quasi-experiments.

Because the field experimenter almost never has complete control over the environment, research design must be a compromise between scientific rigor and the demands of the situation. This can be a serious shortcoming in doing field research, but industrial and organizational researchers are often willing to sacrifice some control for the sake of realism.

Example of a Field Experiment   One question that concerns both researchers and managers is the relevance of management theories developed in the United States to workers in other countries. Welsh, Luthans, and Sommer (1993) conducted a field experiment to evaluate the effectiveness of three management techniques applied to workers in a Russian textile mill. The researchers first selected workers and randomly assigned them to groups that experienced three different motivational techniques. In this study, the motivational techniques were the independent variable.

The first group received extrinsic rewards—such as new blue jeans—for performance; the second group was taught how to diagnose functional and dysfunctional behaviors in the workplace, and members of the group were praised by their managers for good performance. The third group participated in meetings at which the workers could have input in decision making, a practice currently popular in the United States.

The researchers had previously measured the normal performances of the workers. They applied the three motivational techniques for two weeks, then withdrew the techniques to see if improvements in performance—which was the dependent variable—continued. Interestingly, the performances of the workers improved under the extrinsic reward and self-diagnosis systems, but actually declined under the participation model. From this study, the researchers concluded that management techniques developed in the United States should not be transferred to foreign settings without proper evaluation.

Natural Experiments and Ex Post Facto Studies

In cases in which experimenters do not exercise any control over the environment and simply observe and measure conditions and the effects of changes, the experimenter can be said to be performing a **natural experiment,** or an **ex post facto study** ("experiment after the fact"). This concept was introduced by Charles Darwin, who suggested that nature used survival of the fittest as a means of determining which species are best adapted to their environments. In many cases, organizations do ex post facto studies to evaluate the effects of changed conditions in the workplace, such as implementation of a new absence policy or the introduction of females into all-male work groups. Like the quasi-experiment, ex post facto studies are not true experiments.

Example of an Ex Post Facto Study Most people change jobs or occupations several times during their lives, but researchers are uncertain why. Do they change jobs for more money? more interesting duties? to relieve stress or boredom?

The "gravitational hypothesis" (McCormick, DeNisi, & Shaw, 1979) proposes that people gravitate toward occupations that fit with their ability level. That is, more intelligent people move toward more complex jobs and less intelligent people move toward less complex jobs. In a test of the gravitational hypothesis, two researchers (Wilk & Sackett, 1996) compared scores on measures of cognitive ability with job complexity and job changes over about 15 years. The researchers hypothesized that over time, people would move into jobs where requirements matched their mental abilities. Data about cognitive ability, job complexity, and job changes came from over 26,000 participants in a longitudinal study that had followed their careers since their graduation from high school in 1972.

Results from the study confirmed the hypothesis. Individuals who scored higher in cognitive complexity tended to move up in job complexity over their careers, and individuals who scored lower tended to move down. The researchers concluded that vocational counselors should gather as much information as possible about candidates' mental abilities and the complexity of the jobs they are interested in before making recommendations to their clients.

As this study illustrates, there are two defining characteristics of ex post facto studies. First, they concern real-life issues and settings, and second, they do not artificially manipulate the environment. The participants in this study made job changes over a 15-year period without any experimental manipulation of their work environments or decision-making processes.

However, the real-life quality of ex post facto studies illustrates both the strength and the weakness of such studies. Having no control of the environment precludes any Hawthorne-type effect, in which workers change their behaviors to meet experimenters' expectations. In this respect, implications from the results of an ex post facto study may be more accurate because they are derived from behavior in the workplace.

On the other hand, a lack of control allows the introduction of confounding variables that may influence the results. In this study, for example, the researchers had no information about any career counseling participants may have received and the impact the counseling might have had on their career decisions. Very likely, such counseling affected the career decisions of some of the participants.

Another problem with ex post facto research is the possibility that an unexpected change in the environment might negate the value of the study. If, for example, unemployment were high at the time of the research, participants might be willing to accept jobs that did not match their cognitive abilities. For these reasons, inferring causality from an ex post facto study is questionable.

Statistical Analysis of Experimental Data

After experimenters gather their data, they need to comfirm that their findings are not the result of chance—that is, that their treatment and not other factors caused a change. For this purpose, the researcher performs a statistical analysis—a **test of significance**—to see whether differences between groups or individuals are simply the result of probabilities or can be attributed to the researcher's experimental manipulation. Tests of significance help researchers avoid two types of errors. **Type I errors** occur when a researcher mistakenly believes there are significant differences when none exist; **Type II errors** occur when an experimenter overlooks significant differences that do exist (Mone, Mueller, & Mauland, 1996). Typical tests of significance used with experimental data include the *t* test and analysis of variance.

A *t* **test** is used when a researcher wants to determine that differences between two groups on one variable are not due to chance factors. In other words, results will apply to an entire population and not just the experimental sample. After calculating the formula for the *t* test—which can be found in any elementary statistics book or a statistical computer program—the researchers consult a t test table, which tells them the probability that their results are due to chance rather than to experimental manipulation.

Psychological researchers usually accept a finding as being the result of their experimental treatment only if the probability of it being a chance occurrence is less than 5 in 100. In scientific terms, this probability is expressed as $p < .05$. If the probability is less than .05—.01 or .001, for example—then the researchers are even more certain that their results were not due to chance. Although there is currently some debate about significance testing (APA, 1997), results in which there is a greater than 5 percent probability that they are due to chance are not usually considered sufficient to support a hypothesis.

If the researchers want to test differences in results between three or more groups, they may perform a more sophisticated analysis of variance. **Analysis of variance** (ANOVA) is a statistical method for combining several t tests into one operation. The purpose of the ANOVA procedure is to explain **variability,** or why some scores differ from the average score on a measure. The analysis of variance measures two kinds of variability: (1) the size of the differences between the mean scores of groups, and (2) the size of the differences between individual scorers within groups. An analysis of variance applied to the results of the performance rating study, for example, would consider both the difference between the average scores of the experimental conditions—working individually, with a partner, or in a group—as well as the variability of each subject from the average score for that subject's group.

Calculation of the analysis of variance formula—also found in statistics textbooks and computer programs—yields an **F ratio.** The F ratio is a numerical expression of the differences in the between-group and within-group scores and, like the t test, gives a measure of the likelihood that results from the study are due to chance. Similar to the t test procedure, the researcher uses the F ratio to look up a value in an F table to determine the level of significance of results from a study. Again, results in which the probability of their being due to chance is greater than .05 are not likely to be reported in the scientific literature. The analysis of variance is a statistical technique that can become quite complex. Some more sophisticated analyses of variance models that might be used to analyze data from an experiment include the **analysis of covariance** (ANCOVA) and the **multivariate analysis of variance** (MANOVA).

Finally, the **normal distribution** is another important concept in making inferences from a sample to a population. If a sample is representative of a population, then we can assume that the quality we are studying is normally distributed. That is, most people will score around the mean and only a few at the extremes. When this is the case, the distribution looks like a bell-shaped curve. When people score more frequently at either the high or the low end, then the distribution is said to be **skewed.** Examples of normal and skewed distributions appear in Figure 2.1.

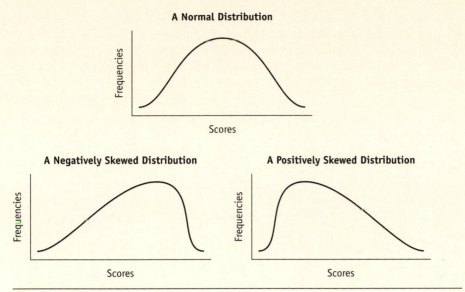

Figure 2.1 Distributions

Evaluating the Experimental Method

As stated above, the major advantage of the experiment is that the researcher can draw conclusions about causal relationships. In a properly controlled study with scientifically acceptable statistical results, the experimenter can safely say that X causes Y. Obviously, being clear about causality is important for the experimenter.

As powerful a research tool as the experiment may be, there are disadvantages connected with all three types of experimental methods. Researchers must consider these disadvantages when designing their experiments so as to minimize their undesirable effects. Some of these considerations are briefly described below.

1. Problems defining terms. If the researcher does not clearly define independent and dependent variables, results of the study will be difficult to interpret. Terms such as "higher productivity" or "improved performance," for example, are usually too vague to be useful. For example, would an experimenter be satisfied with higher productivity of 1 percent? 5 percent? 20 percent? For experimental results to be meaningful, it is critical that all variables be clearly defined.

2. Ensuring the similarity of groups being compared. The researcher must be certain that people who compose the groups being studied are similar, and that the study groups are similar to members of the group to which the results will be generalized. If participants are dissimilar, then results may be due to factors other than what the hypothesis suggests. For example, female workers may have attitudes different from those of male workers; employees from different ethnic backgrounds may approach their tasks differently. Comparing results of measures applied to dissimilar groups may be misleading and leaves open the possibility of alternative explanations of results.

3. The problem of confounding or extraneous variables. Experimental results may be affected by factors that interfere with establishing the relationship between the independent and dependent variables. These factors are beyond the control of the experimenter and are likely to obscure results. Even when researchers can control confounding variables, they may be creating an experimental situation that is unlike the environment in which business is normally conducted.

For example, a researcher may hypothesize that a new training course (the independent variable) will improve the sales performance of employees (the dependent variable). If the economy improves during the training, however, any increase in sales cannot be attributed to the training alone. In other words, conditions in the economy have confounded the relationship between the independent and dependent variables.

4. The expense of experiments. On a practical note, experiments can be costly and time-consuming. Planning and implementing a research program can be very expensive. If results from the experiment are unsatisfactory or flawed by error, then the experimenter must start again from the beginning. When important questions must be answered quickly, using an experimental approach may be inappropriate. Data collection, analysis, and interpretation are time consuming and require a level of skill the manager may not have.

Correlational Studies

The Correlational Method
Statistical Analysis of
   Correlational Data
Evaluating the Correlational Method

Sometimes researchers study the relationship between two factors without making inferences as to causality. Finding the cause is not necessary to demonstrate the relationship between the factors. For example, a researcher may wonder if there is a relationship between age and manual dexterity, or if the distance that workers live from the workplace is related to their attendance records.

The Correlational Method

To answer these kinds of questions, psychologists often use a statistical technique known as **correlation,** which is a measure of the extent to which two variables are related, not necessarily causally (Elmes, Kantowitz, & Roediger, 1992). As explained below, correlations are important because they allow a researcher to make predictions about values on one variable by knowing values on the second variable. In correlational studies, the term *predictor* is similar to the term *independent variable* in experimental research, and *criterion* is similar to *dependent variable*. Strictly speaking, researchers are performing an experiment whenever they have control over one or more of the independent variables. When researchers have no control over variables, a correlational research strategy may be appropriate.

The correlational approach differs from the experiment in several ways. First, as suggested above, the correlational method is aimed at determining the degree to which two variables are related, but it does not provide evidence for making judgments about causality. This method may show, for example, that workers who live far from the office are absent more frequently than those who live closer, but distance cannot be presumed to be the actual cause of absences.

Second, the correlational approach does not necessarily involve the manipulation of variables in a controlled environment. Rather, the researcher uses statistical analysis to determine whether a numerical score on one variable is related to a score on another. Since manipulation and control are not as important in the correlational study, correlational research is often easier to undertake than experiments. Many times correlational researchers do not have to take measures of variables, but can use data that already exist.

The relationship between the variables being considered in a correlational study is, in the simplest case, assumed to be linear. That is, data can be plotted on a graph, such as the examples depicted in Figure 2.2. Rather than plot such data, however, the researcher uses statistics to calculate a **correlation coefficient.** This coefficient is an expression of the degree of relationship between these two variables. As in the case of the experiment, the researcher then determines if the correlation coefficient is statistically significant—that is, that results are not due to chance factors.

Correlation coefficients are expressed as a number between -1.00 and $+1.00$, and the more two variables have in common, the greater the coefficient. **Positive correlations** mean that the more of one variable, the more of another (or the less of one, the less of another). We know, for example, that scores on measures of conscientiousness correlate positively with scores on job performance (Chapter 4).

Negative correlations mean the opposite of positive: the more of one variable, the less of another. An example of a negative correlation would be the relationship between time spent in a job and number of days absent. We know, for example, that the longer a person has worked for a company, the fewer days he or she is likely to be absent during a given period.

Finally, **zero correlation** means there is no relationship between variables. If a correlational analysis of the relationship between employee scores on a final exam in a sales training program to sales volume later yields a value near zero, this would be an example of a zero correlation that suggests the sales training program had no impact on sales volume.

Like the experiment, correlational research also starts with a hypothesis. In the example of commuting time and number of absences, the hypothesis may be that the longer the commuting time, the greater the frequency of absence. The correlational researcher collects data on the variables being considered—in this particular study, the commuting time and number of work days missed for each participant. Since there is no treatment or manipulation of the environment, there is no need to identify control or experimental groups.

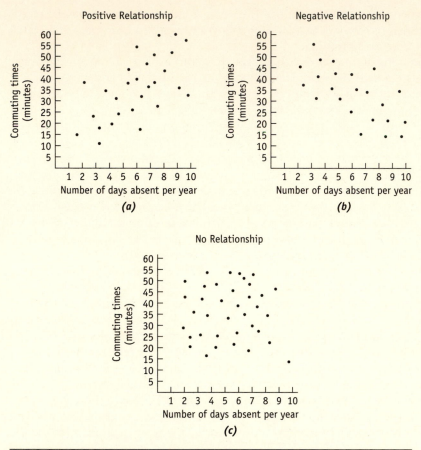

Figure 2.2 Correlations Between Commuting Time and Absenteeism
Figure *(a)* illustrates a positive relationship between two variables, in which the greater the commuting time, the greater the number of days absent. Figure *(b)* illustrates a negative relationship, in which the greater the commuting time, the fewer number of days absent. Figure *(c)* shows no relationship between the two variables.

Example of a Correlational Study In the 1990s, many companies adopted policies that emphasized customer service. **Customer service** refers to the practice of meeting customer expectations in order to generate customer satisfaction (Schneider & Bowen, 1995). Although it seems logical that an emphasis on customer service would lead to higher customer satisfaction, one researcher (Johnson, 1996) designed a study to test the hypothesis that creating an organizational environment that encouraged customer service resulted in higher customer satisfaction.

In that study, employees at 466 branches of a retail bank completed the Service Management Practices Inventory (Performance Research Associates & Questar Data Systems, 1988), a measure of employee perceptions about quality service. At the same time, almost 800 customers rated the quality of service of the bank. The researcher then correlated results from the employee survey with results from the customer survey.

Analysis of the results showed high correlations between sharing information about customer needs, training in customer service, and rewarding and recognizing excellent service and customer satisfaction with service at the bank. In other words, if a bank emphasized to employees the importance of customer service, customers were more likely to be satisfied with the bank.

Statistical Analysis of Correlational Data

The **Pearson product moment** is the formula most frequently used in calculating correlations. Calculation requires that scores on both variables be continuous; that is, they fall within a range and do not represent categories. Scores on a performance measure and number of months on the job are examples of continuous variables. (Categorical data, on the other hand, do not represent a range, but are "either-or" data, such as sex, race, skilled versus nonskilled, and so forth, that require a different form of correlational analysis.) For researchers who wish to look at more than one pair of variables, however, there are more complex methods of correlational analysis.

Multiple regression is a technique researchers use to determine which of several variables is the best predictor of a criterion. Multiple regression allows the researcher to determine how much each variable is responsible for predicting the criterion. Because it is usually more efficient to look at several predictors at one time rather than at each one separately, and because multiple regression gives a more accurate picture of the relationship between variables and the criterion, most industrial and organizational psychologists doing correlational research use multiple regression techniques. **Log-linear modeling** is a statistical technique related to multiple regression used when both the independent and dependent variables are categorical or nominal—that is, when the variables have no quantitative properties (White, Tansey, Smith, & Barnett, 1993).

Factor analysis is another statistical method related to correlation. Given a set of correlation coefficients, factor analysis determines whether there is an underlying structure within the data, or if there is some way in which large amounts of data can be rearranged. For example, suppose a researcher finds that praise from a supervisor, prestige associated with a job, salary level, and working conditions all correlate positively with a measure of job satisfaction. The researcher could use factor analysis to determine if these four variables relate to each other, or if they group together in a particular way. A factor analysis of the data might reveal that variables that have a psychological component—personal recognition and prestige—are related, whereas environmental factors—working conditions and salary level—relate to each other. In this case, the researcher has identified two factors—psychological and environmental—that relate to job satisfaction.

Box 2.1 describes a study in which factor analysis was used to predict the success of managers assigned to overseas jobs.

Many times industrial and organizational psychologists conduct research with small samples. As a general rule, the smaller the sample, the more difficult it is to achieve statistical significance. **Meta-analysis** (Glass, 1976; Hunter, Schmidt, & Jackson, 1982) is a statistical method related to correlation that allows the results of several studies to be combined and analyzed statistically in one study. In other words, researchers who use this approach can use the results from studies done in several different settings and, by controlling and adjusting the data, make conclusions that may be generalizable across a variety of situations.

Despite its widespread acceptance, meta-analysis is a sophisticated technique for analyzing data, and there are currently different techniques for performing the procedure (Johnson, Mullen, & Salas, 1995; Sagie & Koslowksy, 1993; Viswesvaran & Ones, 1995). In addition, meta-analytic procedures continue to be refined (Law, Schmidt, & Hunter, 1994).

Example of Meta-analysis In recent years, many employers have introduced "health promotion programs" (discussed in Chapter 15) into the workplace. These programs are designed to lower employee absence, turnover, and health insurance premiums. One typical health promotion program is smoking cessation, in which trained professionals offer workers different techniques to stop smoking cigarettes. In one study (Viswesvaran & Schmidt, 1992) meta-analysis was used to evaluate 633 smoking cessation studies that involved 71,806 participants.

Results from the studies were cumulated, then corrected statistically to give the best possible estimate of the average true effect of the different intervention methods. Some of the results of the meta-analysis showed that cardiac patients were most likely to quit smoking, and that hypnosis and acupuncture were among the most successful cessation techniques. Instructional methods in the workplace were also relatively effective, but simply receiving the advice of a physician was among the least effective ways to quit smoking. The researchers were surprised to learn that professional educators were more effective than health professionals in assisting people to stop smoking.

Evaluating the Correlational Method

Although the correlational researcher does not manipulate variables, several considerations relevant to the experiment are also important in correlational studies. If the researcher wants to make conclusions that can be generalized to a larger group, it is important that the characteristics of the individuals in the study be similar to those of the larger group.

As with the experiment, it is also very important that the researcher define terms precisely. For example, in the hypothetical study of commuting time and absence mentioned earlier, the researcher would need to distinguish between absences due to vacation and those due to illness or other reasons. Unclear definitions are likely to lead to unclear results.

Box 2.1   USING FACTOR ANALYSIS TO DESIGN A TRAINING PROGRAM FOR INTERNATIONAL EMPLOYEES

In recent years, many organizations have increased their international business, resulting in more of their employees being assigned to overseas positions. Interestingly, the rate of failure of managers assigned to foreign operations is surprisingly high. Although these managers often receive some form of cross-cultural training before being sent abroad, apparently the training is not usually sufficient to affect the failure rate.

Two researchers (Arthur & Bennett, 1995) hypothesized that cross-cultural training is ineffective because companies often don't know what they should be training for. That is, training programs could be more focused if trainers had more information about what makes an international assignee successful.

To identify the factors that affect performance overseas, the researchers surveyed 338 international assignees serving in 20 different countries. The average time spent abroad was 4.12 years, and the average age of the respondents was 43.19 years. Participants were asked to rate 54 factors believed to relate to success in an overseas assignment on a five-point scale. Some of the factors included are listed below:

Managerial ability	Creativity
Courtesy and tact	Tolerance
Confidence	Flexibility
Political sensitivity	Listening skills
Youthfulness	Knowledge of local language
Stable marriage	Intellectual curiosity

A factor analysis of the survey results revealed that the 54 items could be categorized into five factors The five factors related to success in an overseas assignment were, in descending order of importance:

1. *Family situation.* Successful international assignees had families that supported living abroad. The researchers concluded that including family members in cross-cultural training might be a good idea.

2. *Flexibility/Adaptability.* Successful employees had an openness and willingness to adapt to changing or unexpected situations.

3. *Job knowledge and motivation.* Skill in the areas of management, organization, and administration, as well as qualities such as perseverance, initiative, and alertness were also necessary for success as an overseas employee.

4. *Relational skills.* These included tact, empathy, patience, and tolerance.

5. *Extra-cultural openness.* Interestingly, openness to another culture was the least important of the five factors.

In the opinion of the researchers, cross-cultural training programs that address these five factors are more likely to result in employees who will be successful in their overseas assignments.

(*Source:* Arthur, W., Jr., & Bennett, W., Jr. (1995). The international assignee: The relative importance of factors perceived to contribute to success. *Personnel Psychology, 48,* 99–114.)

Nonetheless, the correlational approach offers several distinct advantages to researchers. First, calculating correlations is usually much faster and less expensive than performing experiments. Because of this, correlations are often done as a prelude to experimental studies.

Second, collecting data to use in correlational studies is often much easier than collecting data through experiments. Correlations are often calculated on data that already exist. For example, researchers can determine the relationship between variables in workers' personnel files and performance appraisal ratings. Many times there is no need to collect new data to determine relationships.

Third, because there is no manipulation of variables, correlational studies are less likely than field experiments or ex post facto studies to disrupt the workplace. Whereas managers may object to manipulating the working environment in order to measure changes, they may be more willing to allow questionnaires to be administered or data gathered from personnel files.

On the other hand, the most important disadvantage of the correlational method is its inability to determine causality. As suggested above, results demonstrating that the more of X, the more or less of Y, tell us nothing about X causing Y. Sometimes, not knowing the causal relationship between two variables makes findings unclear.

Related to the causality problem is the **third-variable problem.** Sometimes two unrelated variables are related to a third variable. For example, psychologists can demonstrate a negative correlation between waist size and IQ—people with higher IQs tend to have smaller waists. Does this mean that losing weight can raise a person's IQ? Although such a possibility would be convenient, the explanation for this relationship comes from the correlations of both these factors with socioeconomic level. In general, people from higher socioeconomic backgrounds have both smaller waists and higher levels of intelligence. Researchers must be careful not to draw inferences about variables because of their relationship to a third variable.

A third disadvantage of the correlational method concerns relying on data that have been collected by someone else. Industrial and organizational psychologists who use information from personnel files are well aware that such information can be misleading. When using existing data, the researcher must be careful to ascertain the accuracy of the information.

Observational Studies

The Observational Method
Example of Observational
   Research
Evaluating the Observa-
   tional Method

Sometimes a manager needs information immediately and there isn't sufficient time to design an experiment or to gather data for a correlational study. Similarly, a situation may be either too complex or too simple to warrant use of these methods. In other cases, managers may feel that they don't have the technical expertise or resources to do a proper experiment or correlational study.

Given these constraints, very likely the manager will use an observational research strategy. Overall, observation is the most common form of research done in applied settings.

The Observational Method

Observational studies are usually **qualitative** rather than **quantitative** in nature; that is, conclusions result from observing and describing, rather than from manipulating or measuring, behavior. For example, a supervisor may observe a bank teller to learn why the teller is making so many errors, or a management consultant may observe members of a department to find out why productivity is so low. As suggested in Chapter 1, findings from the bank wiring study at the Hawthorne plant resulted from observation.

Example of Observational Research

Over the years, some researchers have become interested in the idea of *emotional labor* (Morris & Feldman, 1996), which refers to managing feelings to create an impression that is part of a job. Emotional labor is an important part of many jobs. For example, waiters and waitresses, hotel desk clerks, and department store salespeople are usually expected to respond cheerfully to the requests of their customers, even when those requests are unrealistic. In jobs requiring emotional labor, simply knowing how to perform the tasks associated with the job is insufficient—the tasks must be performed with a particular emotion conveyed to the customer.

One researcher (Hochschild, 1983) was particularly interested in the emotional labor experiences of flight attendants and how they affected the attendants' attitudes about their jobs. To find out more about the emotional labor associated with being a flight attendant, Hochschild attended an airline attendant training school. At the school, the researcher learned that managers considered a smile one of the most important assets of an attendant. As one pilot explained to the group, smiling communicates confidence that the plane will not crash, that it will arrive and depart on time, and that the experience of flying is going to be enjoyable.

At the training center, obnoxious passengers were referred to as "irates," and much of the training was focused on maintaining a pleasant and smiling demeanor when dealing with irates. When students were asked to describe their own experiences with irates, some of the incidents reported included a passenger who threw coffee on an attendant, passengers who put their hands on the attendants as they passed with the drink cart, and passengers who complained about the food and cursed the attendants as if they had prepared the food themselves.

One important aspect of the training was teaching attendants to respond to these unpleasant situations while maintaining an appearance of cheerfulness. The instructor told the students that her method for dealing with irates was to pretend that something traumatic had just happened to the passenger and that was why the person was misbehaving. "If you think about the *other* person and why they're so upset, you've taken attention off yourself and your own frustration. And you won't feel so angry."

From the observation of the flight attendant training school, the researcher learned how important emotional labor is in the job performance of a flight attendant. Even if employees are completely proficient in the tasks associated with being an attendant, they will not succeed on the job if they cannot give the appearance of always being cheerful regardless of what the irates are doing to them.

Box 2.2 describes an observational approach to evaluating a salesperson's performance.

Evaluating the Observational Method

Properly designed, the observational study can be a rich source of data. More than the other methods discussed, the observational study attempts to understand the perspectives of the individuals involved in the research situation. Furthermore, the observational study allows for a wider variety of information to be gathered than either an experiment or a correlational study. In the Hawthorne research, for example, the more precise methodologies seemed to miss what was actually happening in the workplace. Along the same lines, it would be difficult to design an experimental or correlational study that provided the insights about the emotional labor of airline flight attendants.

Because observational studies are less structured than other methods, useful information relevant to other matters may emerge in the course of a study. For example, the supervisor observing the bank teller may incidentally note that very few customers come into the branch between 2 P.M. and 3 P.M., and that some tellers could be performing other duties during that period. Or the management consultant may discover that departmental morale is low because a favorite coworker is ill and not because of some company policy. Researchers relying on more structured methodologies may not be able to obtain these kinds of data.

Observational research is also useful as a prelude to more formal studies. By observing a situation or a phenomenon, researchers can develop hypotheses that can later be tested experimentally or statistically.

The major disadvantage of the observational study, however, relates to the problem of perception. People often have very different ideas about a situation, and this can affect their descriptions and conclusions. For example, one area where organizational members often differ is in their opinions of organizational communication. Very commonly, managers describe the quality of organizational communication as excellent at the same time that workers complain that management never tells them anything. It is unlikely that one of these groups is "right" and the other is "wrong"; rather, the quality of communication is a matter of perspective. In the bank wiring studies, for example, the researchers

---

Box 2.2   AN OBSERVATIONAL APPROACH TO THE ART
OF SELLING

One of the advantages of observational research is that it often provides information that is not necessarily obvious when experimental or correlational approaches are used. In particular, observations regarding the interactions between people such as managers and subordinates can be especially useful.

One area where interpersonal interactions can be critical is in sales. Although some people believe that telemarketing and sales via the Internet mark the end of the old-fashioned professional sales call, others believe that selling is an "art" that electronic media can never replace. From this perspective, establishing a customer's trust and responding to a customer's needs are skills that computers don't have.

One reporter decided to investigate how a sales professional interacted with his clients. Using an observational approach to study this question, the reporter spent a day visiting customers with a salesman for a sporting goods manufacturer. As the salesman drove his car into one retailer's parking lot, he commented that finding a space in the lot used to be much more difficult. The greater number of available spaces was the result of layoffs—a sign the company was having financial difficulties.

Sitting in the reception area, the salesman noticed other sales representatives who sold products of lesser quality—another sign of financial problems. Six weeks later, the company filed for bankruptcy.

In another meeting later the same day, another buyer told the salesman that he couldn't possibly buy any more merchandise because he had just discovered a substantial overstock. The buyer told the salesman that, in fact, he couldn't possibly pay for what he had already ordered. The salesman agreed to cancel the orders and then proceeded to persuade the customer to try some new items that might sell better. When the reporter later asked the salesman how he managed to turn a cancelled order into a different order, the salesman said he had been watching the reactions of the buyer. When the salesman agreed to cancel the order, buyer's hands had stopped shaking. The salesman took this to be a sign that the tension had passed and that the buyer might be receptive to new ideas.

After his experience with the salesman, the reporter concluded that electronic marketing can never substitute for the expertise of an experienced sales representative. The reporter's concluding comment, that salespeople "are the eyes and ears of a company; they make things work," reflected his view of what can be learned from an observational approach.

Source: Flavey, J. (1996, July 15). The art of selling. *Wall Street Journal,* p. A12.

---

explained worker behavior by concluding that workers did not understand the piecework system when, in fact, worker behavior was the product of patterns of social interaction (Bramel & Friend, 1981).

This problem of perception extends to researchers as well. Many times observations are done with several observers. If these observers are not clear about what they are looking for, or if they do not agree on how to define different phenomena, then their findings will be questionable.

Another problem with observation is that it often obscures base rates. **Base rate** refers to the frequency of an occurrence, and looking at situations without knowledge of the base rate can be misleading. The problem of a bank teller making errors of several dollars in balancing the drawer each day may seem more important to the supervisor than that of an employee making a larger mistake every few months. Without complete knowledge of the situation, the supervisor may misinterpret it. Because most observational studies do not rely on statistics, it is much more difficult to be certain about conclusions.

A final problem has to do with the overall acceptance of results derived from observational studies. Since good observational research is so difficult to do, many researchers—particularly those who work in academic settings—discount the method altogether. The possibility of error is so great that virtually any findings can be challenged by other researchers.

Other Research Methods

Survey Research
Case Studies
Focus Groups

Although experiments, correlations, and observations are the most traditional forms of research used in I/O psychology, there are several other important methods. Surveys, case studies, and focus groups are all described below.

Survey Research

Surveys—in which people are simply asked their opinions—are a common strategy for doing organizational research. For example, employers may survey workers about morale, about their feelings concerning a new absenteeism policy, or for suggestions to make the workplace safer and more productive. Surveys can be oral or written, but they are characterized by their use of a set of predetermined questions that are asked of all respondents. Researchers compile results from the survey and summarize their findings.

As in an experiment, the total group of employees is the population, but surveys often involve the use of a sample—a subgroup of the workforce that is assumed to be representative of the whole group. In other words, when the workforce is too large or too widely dispersed to be surveyed easily, researchers may survey a group of employees that reflects, for example, the experience, educational levels, gender, and racial composition of the population. Results from the sample are used to make inferences about the population. As suggested above, sampling is often used in experimental and correlational studies as well.

Surveys generally take one of three forms: mail survey, interview, or telephone survey. Because mail surveys are easy and relatively inexpensive to distribute, they are the most common form of survey. In addition, mail surveys usually offer confidentiality—an issue most employees consider important.

Telephone surveys get higher response rates and take less time than mail surveys, but sometimes workers are uncomfortable giving opinions to a faceless voice.

Disadvantages of mail surveys include the possibility of employees misunderstanding the questions, respondents answering only part of the questionnaire, or employees not returning the questionnaire. Since the average response rate for mail surveys is only 30 percent (Babbie, 1979), additional mailings may be necessary to reach the 50 percent response rate researchers consider adequate.

Interviews are oral surveys that offer some advantages over mail surveys. First, the interviewer can clarify the respondent's questions so that the responses will be more accurate and second, the interviewer can ask additional questions if unexpected information emerges from the interview. The major disadvantage of interviews, however, is that they are costly and time-consuming. Neither the interviewer nor the interviewee is "producing" during the interview, so a department's productivity may suffer during the interview period.

A second problem is bias. As with observations, the researcher must be very careful not to lead the respondent in certain directions and to report exactly what the respondent says. Given these constraints, it is not surprising that interviews work best when the group being studied is relatively small.

Telephone surveys are a compromise between mail surveys and interviews. They get higher response rates and take less time, but they also have limitations.

Not all workers have access to telephones, some workers are likely to be uncomfortable giving opinions to a faceless voice, and telephone interviews must be brief to be effective. Because of these constraints, industrial and organizational researchers use telephone surveys less frequently than mail surveys and interviews.

Statistical Analysis of Survey Data Although researchers sometimes use sophisticated methodologies to analyze survey data, the statistical analysis of survey data is not usually as complex as it is for experiments or correlational studies. Typically, survey researchers count **frequencies** (i.e., the number of times a response occurs) and calculate **means** or averages and **standard deviations** (i.e., the ranges within which most of the responses occur). Some survey data can be interpreted in terms of correlation coefficients, but experimental statistics are rarely applied to survey data. Consequently, survey techniques generally do not allow a researcher to infer causality.

One problem in analyzing survey data is nonresponses (Viswesvaran, Barrick, & Ones, 1993). Nonresponses can affect the external validity of survey conclusions because results are based on a subsample of the original sample and, as a result, may not be generalizable to the population. Researchers need to be careful that nonresponses do not distort their survey findings.

Case Studies

Case studies rely on in-depth information about an individual or a situation that is used to make decisions. The case method, widely used in business schools and in clinical psychology, relies on analogies for drawing conclusions. That is, researchers learn to recognize scenarios and various methods of problem solving, and they attempt to make the most appropriate match between the two. Although the case study resembles the observational approach described earlier, data for a case study may come from several sources, including—in addition to observation—telephone surveys, interviews, and other, more rigorous, research methods. Case studies also differ from observation in that they may focus on historical data, as opposed to observing an event or a behavior happening in the present.

There are several advantages to the case study approach. The major value lies in its ability to generate hypotheses that can be tested in more controlled studies. For example, employers may gather information about members of a productive work group, then test hypotheses about productivity in a field experiment using other groups. Along the same lines, case studies may generate several solutions to a problem without the use of more formal research methods. A discussion of absence problems in a work unit, for example, may identify several possible solutions that can be implemented without further research.

The case study is particularly useful in studying events that are unusual—such as the decision-making processes involved in the *Challenger* disaster. In these cases, researchers feel the in-depth information provided by a case study will lead to greater knowledge than controlled experiments or other kinds of studies. Finally, case studies can generate hypotheses to be tested in more formal studies, but they can also support hypotheses developed more formally. For example, a case study of a company that is laying off workers might provide support for psychological theories about the impact of stress on health and psychological well-being.

Drawbacks to the case study method include the inability to make inferences about causality. Because the events being studied did not take place in a controlled environment, there are likely to be many plausible hypotheses for explaining the situation. Second, case studies are particularly vulnerable to bias on the part of the researcher when collecting data and interpreting results—particularly when someone who has been involved in the case under study is participating in the research.

Finally, findings from case studies cannot automatically be generalized to larger populations. If the phenomenon under study is likely to occur in other settings—such as the stress resulting from layoffs—then perhaps findings from one case can be applied elsewhere. However, many case studies concern unique situations with many variables, so making inferences about other situations can be risky. It is important to remember that no two cases are ever exactly alike.

Focus Groups

Focus groups are a method for collecting qualitative data that involves a group of up to ten people discussing a topic of interest to the researcher. Members of the group do not know each other, but are selected on the basis of their relationship to the research topic. The researcher asks questions and steers the discussion, but the comments are unstructured and expressed in the words of the respondents.

The major advantage of the focus group is that participants provide a great deal of data that would probably not be revealed through surveys or questionnaires. In addition, the researcher can probe areas that are of particular interest. Like the case study, however, focus groups are limited by concerns about bias and questions about generalizability.

In a focus group, a small number of people who do not know each other discuss a topic of interest to a researcher.

Measurement Scales

In any study, one important question is the type of scale the researcher uses to measure variables. Not all variables can be measured on the same scale, however, and researchers have identified four different types of scales to be used with different variables.

Nominal scales refer not to scores, but to categories. Measures of sex, race, or occupation are examples of nominal scales. Nominal scales have no zero point, and the categories have no numerically based order. That is, one category is not numerically higher or lower than another. Identity is the only property of nominal scales.

Ordinal scales, on the other hand, have both identity and magnitude. That is, they reflect numerical differences between variables. A ranking system is a good example of an ordinal scale. When a supervisor ranks employees from best to worst, for example, the ranking reflects both category (the employee) and magnitude (the employee's rank).

Interval scales reflect identity and the magnitude of differences between variables, but they also use equal distance between units on the scale. However, interval scales have no true zero point. The most common example of an interval scale is the measurement of temperature. Although a thermometer has a zero point, zero does not mean the absence of temperature.

Finally, the most precise are **ratio scales,** which have identity, magnitude, equal intervals, and a true zero point. For this reason, ratio scales are considered the most precise form of measurement. Height, weight, and distance are examples of ratio scales.

Because different types of scales require different types of statistical analyses, researchers must be careful to use the correct form of measurement in their studies.

Selecting a Research Method

As suggested above, the industrial and organizational researcher is often constrained by a variety of factors. For example, managers may not appreciate the importance of research, they may be hostile to procedures that could interfere with worker productivity, or they may fear that research results will reveal shortcomings in their own performances. Because of these considerations, I/O researchers must select their research methods carefully.

Some typical questions an organizational researcher must address include the following:

- *Will my research design disrupt the productivity of the workforce?* If so, managers will be unlikely to cooperate unless the research question is sufficiently important to justify the disruption.

- *How soon will results from the study be available?* Managers have a preference for information that can be used immediately and are likely to be unenthusiastic about studies that will take months, or even years, to complete. In addition, the longer a study continues, the greater the likelihood that unforeseen factors—such as worker turnover—will interfere with the study.

- *Will results from the study be useful in a practical, as well as a scientific, sense?* Managers and researchers usually have different priorities. Although managers may recognize the potential merit of a research project, concerns about productivity—which, after all, is the basis for evaluating the performances of both workers and management—are likely to take precedence over scientific concerns.

- *How much will the study cost?* Although the cost of materials used in industrial research may not be great, the cost in time may be tremendous. I/O researchers must keep in mind that employees who are not fulfilling their job duties are costing their employers both their salaries and lost productivity. Managers are unlikely to participate in projects that prevent workers from accomplishing their assigned tasks.

- *What are the legal aspects of the research project?* Because many of the managerial practices that occur in the workplace are governed by law, most employers are unwilling to participate in research that jeopardizes employee confidentiality or gives the appearance of discriminating unfairly against certain groups. Organizational researchers need to keep legal considerations in mind when designing their studies.

As you can see from these questions, industrial and organizational research requires attention to many details that are not relevant to the typical laboratory experiment. I/O researchers must balance the rigor of their research design with the demands of accomplishing the research project in a work environment. For this reason, less rigorous approaches, such as observations and surveys, are the most common types of organizational research.

Nonetheless, the many studies cited in this book are testimony to the resourcefulness of industrial and organizational researchers. Applied research is usually much more difficult to do well than laboratory research, and it often has a critical and immediate impact on the lives of individuals. Researchers in I/O must always bear this in mind as they design and conduct their studies.

Reliability and Validity in Research Studies

By now it should be clear that performing good research is often a challenge, particularly when working in applied settings. In addition to the varieties of methods, there are two other important factors that must be considered: reliability and validity. Reliability and validity are such important issues in industrial and organizational psychology that they are addressed in more detail in Chapter 4 and are referred to throughout later chapters. In psychology, both research projects in general and the measures used in the research must have these two qualities, since even the most sophisticated research design is not useful if there is doubt about reliability or validity. This section briefly reviews these characteristics as they apply to research in general.

Reliability refers to consistency in measurement. A researcher must be certain that results obtained from one administration of a measure or treatment will not differ greatly from another administration. Reliability is determined by a correlational analysis. If, for example, employees scored high on a measure of job satisfaction at one time and scored low shortly thereafter, the measure would not be considered reliable if the situation had not changed. Given the difference between the first and second administration of the measure, the researcher could make no inference about the true level of job satisfaction.

There are several different ways of assessing reliability; these are discussed in more detail in Chapter 4.

Validity, a second necessary quality, refers to the accuracy of results from a study. Obviously research results must be accurate to be useful. Researchers (Schmitt & Klimoski, 1991) recognize four kinds of validity particularly relevant to studies done in organizations. **Construct validity** refers to the accuracy of hypotheses being addressed by the research. That is, studies with construct validity have hypotheses that are reasonable and that reflect organizational realities. A study that assessed managers' leadership ability on the basis of the number of memos they write to employees would probably have poor construct validity.

Statistical inference validity, on the other hand, refers to accuracy based on the size of statistical significance. An evaluation of the usefulness of an employee training program, for example, may find that participants increase their productivity 5 percent after completing the program. This increase may be statistically significant, but if the expense of the training program costs more than the 5 percent productivity gain, then the study probably does not accurately evaluate the training program. Because of concerns about the usefulness of statistical significance, some researchers have recently called for a reexamination of practices in this area.

Internal validity refers to the accuracy of a study in measuring what it is supposed to measure. A study of the qualities associated with absence from work that used only females as participants probably would not have internal validity because, in general, women are absent more frequently than men because of child care responsibilities.

External validity refers to generalizability, or whether findings from a study are relevant to situations outside the research setting. A laboratory study testing the relationship between high temperature and number of performance errors would have external validity if the findings could be shown to apply to tasks performed under high temperatures in a real-life work setting.

Because much of the research done by industrial and organizational psychologists affects the conditions under which people work—including salaries, promotions, and job tenure—it is critical that such research be properly designed and executed. Consequently, studies with questionable reliability or validity can cause tremendous damage. I/O psychologists must have a thorough understanding of these concepts. As suggested above, there are different strategies for demonstrating the validity and reliability of both studies and measures used in studies. These are discussed in greater detail in Chapter 4.

Evaluating Applied Research

One of the major points that was introduced in Chapter 1 is that industrial and organizational psychology is an applied field. That is, much of I/O research is designed for application to real-life settings rather than to advance theoretical knowledge. Even research done in academic settings usually has the purpose of adding to knowledge of issues relevant to organizational settings.

As also suggested earlier, however, many managers are more interested in "the bottom line" than they are in scientific precision. Consequently, the applied researcher often makes trade-offs and compromises between the conflicting demands of scientific practice and situational considerations.

Despite these constraints, psychological research has contributed immeasurably to the effective functioning of many organizations and to the lives of many workers. The following chapters contain many references to studies designed to have an impact on some organizational question. Students interested in a career in industrial and organizational psychology should review some of these original papers to see the elegance of a well-designed research project.

Chapter Summary

The successful study and practice of industrial and organizational psychology require an understanding of scientific research methods. A flawed research methodology may lead to inaccurate or misleading conclusions. Quality of research method is an issue that is particularly important when working in an applied setting. I/O psychologists typically use a variety of research methods, including experiments, correlational studies, observations, surveys, case studies, and focus groups.

There are three types of experiments. The laboratory experiment requires control over the environment in which the study takes place, and the researcher is able to manipulate variables and measure changes that occur. A field experiment uses the same methods, but the study takes place in real-life settings. In the field experiment, some compromise between control and realism is usually necessary. The natural experiment or ex post facto study occurs when the researcher does not manipulate the environment but simply measures changes that occur. Methods for analyzing data from experiments include the *t* test and the analysis of variance. The major value of the experimental method is that it allows the researcher to determine causality.

Correlational studies consider the relationship between two variables without regard for causality. Correlational research often uses existing data, and results indicate whether two or more variables are interrelated. Statistical methods for analyzing correlational data include the Pearson product moment, multiple regression, factor analysis, and a relatively new method, meta-analysis. Although correlational studies are often easier than experiments to accomplish, the inability to infer causality sometimes limits the usefulness of this approach.

In applied settings, observation is probably the research method most frequently used. Whereas experiments and correlations demonstrate causes and relationships between factors, the purpose of the observation is to describe a situation. Researchers observe behavior and make conclusions. Observation does not usually include statistical analysis, except when surveys are used.

Surveys can be oral or written, but they are characterized by their use of a set of predetermined questions to ask respondents. Surveys are typically done by mail, interview, or telephone, and results are usually analyzed in terms of frequencies, means, and standard deviations, although sometimes more complex statistical methods can be applied.

Case studies rely on analogies for reaching conclusions; that is, researchers learn to recognize scenarios and various methods of problem solving, then try to make the best match between the two. Case studies can be used to generate hypotheses, to try out several different solutions to a problem, and to study unusual cases in depth. However, problems connected with case studies include the inability to infer causality, bias on the part of the researcher, and difficulty in generalizing from one case to other situations.

Focus groups involve up to ten people discussing a topic of interest to the researcher. Their major advantage is that participants provide information that would probably not be revealed through surveys. Like case studies, however, focus groups are limited by concerns about bias and generalizability.

Some factors to consider when choosing a research method to use in the workplace include the likelihood of disrupting productivity, how soon results will be available, the usefulness of results in both a practical as well as a scientific sense, the costs involved in the study, and the potential legal impact on workers and employers.

Reliability and validity are two important factors in any research. Reliability refers to being certain that, in an unchanged setting, the results measured remain the same over time. Validity refers to accuracy. Four kinds of validity relevant to organizational research are construct validity, statistical inference validity, internal validity, and external validity. Because industrial and organizational research is likely to affect salaries, promotions, and other important factors in the lives of workers, studies with questionable reliability or validity can cause tremendous damage.

Key Words and Concepts

analysis of covariance (p. 34)
analysis of variance (p. 34)
base rate (p. 46)
case studies (p. 47)
causality (p. 27)
construct validity (p. 52)
control group (p. 28)
controlled environment (p. 27)
correlation (p. 36)
correlation coefficient (p. 37)
customer service (p. 38)
dependent variable (p. 28)
experimental group (p. 28)
experiments (p. 27)
ex post facto study (p. 32)
external validity (p. 53)
factor analysis (p. 39)
field experiment (p. 30)
focus groups (p. 49)
F ratio (p. 34)
frequencies (p. 47)
hypothesis (p. 27)
independent variable (p. 27)
inferences (p. 29)
internal validity (p. 52)
interval scales (p. 50)
laboratory experiments (p. 27)
log-linear modeling (p. 39)
mean (p. 47)
meta-analysis (p. 40)
multiple regression (p. 39)
multivariate analysis of variance
   (p. 34)

natural experiment (p. 32)
negative correlation (p. 37)
nominal scales (p. 50)
normal distribution (p. 34)
observational studies (p. 43)
ordinal scales (p. 50)
participants (p. 27)
Pearson product moment (p. 39)
population (p. 29)
positive correlation (p. 37)
predictors (p. 27)
qualitative (p. 43)
quantitative (p. 43)
quasi-experiment (p. 31)
random sample (p. 31)
ratio scales (p. 50)
reliability (p. 52)
representative (p. 29)
sample (p. 29)
skewed (p. 34)
standard deviation (p. 47)
statistical inference validity
   (p. 52)
surveys (p. 46)
t test (p. 33)
test of significance (p. 33)
third-variable problem (p. 42)
Type I error (p. 33)
Type II error (p. 33)
validity (p. 52)
variability (p. 34)
zero correlation (p. 37)

Questions for Discussion

1. What are the major differences among laboratory, field, and natural experiments or ex post facto studies? What is an example of each kind of study?
2. What is an example of a quasi-experiment?
3. What are the advantages of correlational studies over experiments? What are the disadvantages?
4. What makes good observational research so difficult? How might a researcher get around these problems?
5. In what situations is a survey methodology appropriate? a case study? a focus group?
6. In terms of measurement scales, what kind of a measure is a classification of race and ethnicity? an intelligence test? a list of employees in order of seniority?
7. In your view, what are the most important considerations in selecting a research method?
8. What is reliability? What is validity? Why are these so important?
9. If you wanted to evaluate the impact of offering free child care to employees, what would you use as your dependent variable? What research method would you use? Are there other methods for doing the evaluation?

CHAPTER | 3

Recruiting and Selecting Personnel

The Importance of Effective Selection Procedures
The Predictor and Criterion in Personnel Selection
Job Analysis
Personnel Recruitment
Application Blanks and Biodata
The Employment Interview
Applicant References and Letters of Recommendation
Preemployment Drug Testing
Chapter Summary
Key Words and Concepts
Questions for Discussion

How do you hire workers who will succeed on the job and avoid hiring those who won't? This basic question represents one of the most important challenges facing any organization. Before a qualified individual can be hired, however, employers need to understand which abilities and personal qualities will lead to success, and they need strategies for attracting and screening the best applicants. Chapters 3 and 4 look at the first steps in an employee's entry into an organization—personnel recruitment, assessment, and selection.

The Importance of Effective Selection Procedures

Every organization wants to hire the best employees. Individuals who work hard and add to productivity are valuable assets who must be selected carefully and rewarded appropriately. On the other hand, workers whose performances are poor or mediocre cost the organization in time spent recruiting, interviewing, training, supervising, and firing. Not only does the organization lose the money spent on the unacceptable employee, it also loses the productivity of a good employee who should have been hired in the first place.

Effective selection procedures clearly affect the bottom line. Working with survey data from 201 U.S. companies with more than 200 employees, two researchers (Terpestra & Rozell, 1993) compared the staffing practices of the organizations with their annual profit growth over a five-year period. In particular, the researchers wanted to know whether companies that used five specific staffing practices—follow-up studies of recruitment sources, studies of the validity of specific selection procedures, structured rather than unstructured interviews, cognitive ability and aptitude tests, and weighted application blanks—had greater profitability than companies that did not follow these procedures. Not surprisingly, results from the study found that companies that used any of the five procedures had higher profit growth than companies that did not.

In addition to profitability, the issue of fairness also affects the use of personnel selection procedures. Federal law requires that all individuals have equal opportunity with regard to employment. No employer is required to hire individuals who cannot do the work, but neither is an employer allowed arbitrarily to refuse to hire those who can. The enforcement of equal employment opportunity (EEO) legislation has significantly affected both the composition of the American workforce and the procedures by which employers select employees. Unfair discrimination can also have an impact on the bottom line. In November 1996, for example, Texaco, Inc., agreed to settle a racial discrimination lawsuit brought by its minority employees for more than $140 million, the largest EEO settlement ever.

This chapter first considers personnel selection from the perspective of how employment decisions are made, focusing on predicting performance, ensuring selection fairness, and using job analysis to set standards for hiring. The second part of the chapter reviews the elements of a typical selection process: employee recruitment, application blanks, interviews, references and letters of recommendation, and preemployment drug screening. Because employment testing is the most complicated selection procedure, it is discussed in detail in Chapter 4.

The Predictor and Criterion in Personnel Selection

Predicting Performance on the Job
Fairness in Selection
Affirmative Action Programs

Cheryl Ann Fischer was a junior at Case Western Reserve University when she lost her sight due to a degenerative disease. Despite her disability, Fischer graduated cum laude in 1987 with a degree in chemistry and applied for admission to the university's medical school that fall. When the medical school rejected her, Fischer complained to the Ohio Civil Rights Commission.

The commission agreed that Fischer had been discriminated against unfairly and filed suit against Case Western. In April 1996, however, the Ohio Supreme Court ruled in favor of the university. According to the court, sight is an important predictor of success in medical school and developing special educational programs for Fischer would have imposed an "undue burden" on the university.

Although most admission procedures are not as contentious as Fischer's case, admission to most American colleges or universities requires some evidence that the applicant can succeed in completing the curriculum. For example, most American students who plan to go to college are required to take a test to be admitted. Colleges and universities use scores from these tests—usually the Scholastic Aptitude Tests (SATs) or the American College Testing Program (ACTs)—to predict how well a student will perform in college, since people who score higher on these tests usually earn better grades than those who score lower. At many schools a cutoff score is set, and people who score below that point are not even considered for admission.

With regard to selecting applicants for admission to college, SAT or ACT scores can be thought of as a **predictor,** and the college grade point average (GPA) as a **criterion.** Recall from Chapter 2 that predictor and criterion are terms that describe two related phenomena. Most college officials believe that SAT or ACT scores and college GPA are related and that these scores can be used to predict success in college.

This process of predicting college performance on the basis of test scores is similar to the way employers make predictions about how individuals will perform on the job.

Predicting Performance on the Job

When selecting students for admission to their colleges, administrators need to be certain that the predictors they use are accurate—both valid and reliable. In other words, predictors must measure what they are supposed to measure, decisions based on predictor scores must be justifiable in terms of performance on the criterion, and different administrations of the predictor to the same person must have similar results.

Every day, thousands of personnel officers make decisions similar to those made by college admissions officials. They use some predictor—an employment interview, a reference check, a psychological test—to make judgments about the likelihood of an applicant's success on the job. If predictors do not lead to accurate judgments, employers will hire some people who cannot do the work adequately and reject some who can.

Although the usefulness of a procedure that leads to valid prediction of job performance seems obvious, not all companies have such procedures. A company in Oklahoma, for example, required applicants to read aloud from the works of Shakespeare as part of the selection process for the job of truck driver. Not surprisingly, a scientific evaluation of this requirement demonstrated that ability to read the works of Shakespeare was not a good predictor of truck-driving skill. Similarly, requiring an applicant to have a high school diploma has sometimes been found to be an invalid basis for predicting job performance, particularly for jobs requiring low levels of skill.

Many employers use grades as a predictor of job performance, but some people question their usefulness in employment decisions. One group of researchers (Roth, BeVier, Switzer, & Schippmann, 1996) performed a meta-analysis of studies that looked at the relationship between grade point average and supervisory ratings of job performance. Although the relationship was modest, grades did appear to have some predictive validity—higher grades correlated with higher performance ratings.

Having valid and reliable predictors is critical for effective selection. Poor predictors deny jobs to qualified individuals and lead to the hiring of unqualified workers. In addition, they waste company resources by ineffectively assessing employees' abilities. To develop the most useful employee selection procedures, psychologists must consider both the accuracy and the appropriateness of their predictors and their criteria. This chapter and the next discuss some commonly used predictors of job performance. Chapter 6 (Performance Appraisal) considers the criteria by which performance after hiring is judged.

Fairness in Selection

In addition to ensuring the validity of their predictors, employers must also make certain that their predictors are *fair*. Standards for fairness in selection have evolved over time through legal challenges and legislation. The first important employment discrimination case, *Myart v. Motorola* (1963), concerned the application of Leon Myart, an African American, for the position of television phaser and analyzer at Motorola, Inc. To become a phaser and analyzer, Motorola required applicants to score above a certain level on a five-minute intelligence test. Scores above this level were believed to be related to higher levels of job performance.

Although Myart had experience relevant to the job, he failed to score sufficiently high on the intelligence test to be hired. Myart filed a complaint with the Illinois Fair Employment Practices Commission alleging that he had passed the test but was being denied the job on the basis of racial discrimination. At the time of the testing, Motorola had hired 25 White applicants, but no African Americans.

The court awarded Myart damages of $1,000, but it did not require Motorola to give him a job. The court also ordered Motorola to stop using the intelligence test as a predictor, since employment decisions based on the comparison of scores from culturally "deprived" and culturally "advantaged" groups were considered unfair (Arvey, 1979a).

The Civil Rights Act of 1964 Although *Myart* was the first important challenge of selection procedures, the major impetus behind reviewing these procedures for fairness was passage of the **Civil Rights Act of 1964. Title VII** of the Civil Rights Act specifically states that employers are not allowed to make decisions about hiring, firing, segregating, or classifying employees on the basis of race, color, religion, sex, or national origin. Consequently, employment decisions based on any predictor that discriminates on these bases and disregards actual job performance are illegal.

The **Equal Employment Opportunity Commission (EEOC)** is the federal agency responsible for enforcing Title VII. Box 3.1 summarizes some of the major court cases that have challenged the fairness of selection procedures, and Box 3.2 (p. 64) lists legislation that has extended equal employment opportunity legislation to other groups, including disabled workers.

Since passage of the Civil Rights Act, many employers have revised their employee selection practices to avoid **adverse impact,** a situation in which the selection rate for groups protected under Title VII falls below 80 percent of the group that has the highest selection rate. If, for example, 50 majority individuals apply for jobs and 25 are hired, the **selection ratio**—the number of applicants divided by the number hired—for the majority is 50 percent. To avoid adverse impact, the hiring rate for minorities must be at least 80 percent of the 50 percent rate—in this case, 40 percent.

Federal standards for demonstrating the validity of a selection procedure are described in the *Uniform Guidelines on Employee Selection Procedures* (EEOC, 1978), which are discussed in Chapter 4. There are at least two important benefits from the federal requirements governing employee selection.

First, establishing the validity of selection procedures is essential to the efficient operation of any organization. Valid predictors of employee performance identify both the unacceptable applicants before they are hired, as well as those people who are going to perform at the highest levels. The use of scientifically developed selection guidelines results in a much better "fit" between applicant and job responsibilities, higher levels of productivity, and lower turnover rates. In fact, even a slight improvement in selection procedures can save thousands of dollars.

Second, use of the EEOC guidelines has been essential in guaranteeing equal opportunity for all job applicants. Historically, certain selection procedures unfairly kept some groups out of different jobs. By making sure that selection procedures are fair, more employment opportunities are available for women, minorities, and disabled applicants. Largely due to the efforts of industrial and organizational psychologists, selection procedures today are much fairer than they were in the past.

Despite this progress, challenges to fairness in employee selection remain. For example, some evidence suggests that discrimination on the basis of race and sex is still common in agencies that provide temporary employees. Using an agency does not exempt an employer from fairness requirements, however, and it seems likely that fairness in using contingent employees will be an area of greater scrutiny in the future (Ryan & Schmit, 1996).

The Civil Rights Act of 1991 During the 1980s, many legislators began to believe that certain court decisions had eroded some of the provisions of the Civil Rights Act of 1964. The **Civil Rights Act of 1991** was designed to restore these provisions and to protect the ways in which individuals can challenge employment practices they consider unfair. For example, legal precedent

Box 3.1 PERSONNEL SELECTION AND THE COURTS

Over the years, the practice of personnel selection has been affected by a number of important legal decisions. Some of the most important cases are summarized here.

Myart v. Motorola (1963)

The first major employment discrimination case and the precedent for government regulation of fairness in hiring.

Griggs v. Duke Power Company (1971)

One of the most far-reaching decisions in EEO law. Individuals hired or promoted at Duke Power were required to have a high school diploma or pass an equivalency exam. Since this requirement resulted in the hiring of fewer African-American employees, and Duke Power had not demonstrated that the diploma requirement was related to job performance, the U.S. Supreme Court unanimously held that Duke Power had discriminated unfairly. The court also held that although the employer had not intended to discriminate, it is the consequence of an employment practice that is significant. Additionally, the court held that the individual need only demonstrate discrepancies in hiring practices; the burden of proof that procedures are either nondiscriminatory or a business necessity then shifts to the employer.

Bakke v. Regents of the University of California (1978)

After failing to be accepted to medical school because certain slots were reserved for minority candidates, Bakke, a White male, filed suit against the University of California under the Equal Protection Clause of the Fourteenth Amendment. In a divided decision, the U.S. Supreme Court ruled that the doctrine of equal protection under the law must hold for all groups, and not only those protected under Title VII. The court held that race can be considered in making admissions to universities, but that quota systems are clearly illegal.

Johnson v. Transportation Agency (1987)

A male employee filed suit after a female employee who scored lower on a qualifying examination was chosen for a supervisory position. The U.S. Supreme Court ruled that the employer could give the job to the woman despite the fact that the employer had no history of unfair discrimination against women. The court held that such favorable treatment for women can be justified because of existing inequities in our society.

Wards Cove Packing Company v. Antonio (1987)

A group of Filipino and Alaskan natives filed suit against a salmon cannery, alleging that skilled jobs were reserved for White employees. In a split vote, the court ruled that statistical evidence of a disparity between a group's representation in a job category and in the population at large was insufficient to shift the burden of proof to the employer. The *Wards Cove* ruling was an important impetus for passage of the Civil Rights Act of 1991, which shifted the burden of proof back to the employer.

Price Waterhouse v. Hopkins (1988)

Hopkins was a top performer in her accounting firm, but her promotion to partner was delayed because of alleged problems with interpersonal skills. One colleague advised her to "walk more femininely, talk more femininely, dress more femininely, wear make-up, have her hair styled, and wear jewelry." Hopkins filed a sex discrimination suit, alleging that sexual stereotyping on the part of her employer had prevented her promotion. In a 6–3 decision, the U.S. Supreme Court found Price Waterhouse guilty of sex stereotyping, which is forbidden by Title VII of the Civil Rights Act of 1964.

Soroka v. Dayton Hudson (1991)

Soroka applied for a job as a security guard at a department store. As part of the screening process, the store required applicants to complete a personality measure designed to identify people with mental health problems. Soroka filed suit against the department store, alleging that individual questions about his religious beliefs and sexual practices violated his civil rights. This case was significant because current legislation requires that overall test scores be predictive of performance, but does not require validity evidence for individual items on a measure. Soroka won the first round; Dayton Hudson appealed, but settled out of court in 1993.

Adarand Constructors, Inc. v. Peña (1995)

A nonminority subcontractor lost a bid to a minority subcontractor on a Department of Transportation project even though the nonminority bid was lower. The nonminority company challenged the DOT process, but the Tenth Circuit Court of Appeals affirmed the award to the minority company. The Supreme Court justices reversed this decision, however, and asked for a strict judicial review to see whether the DOT's affirmative action program represented a "compelling government interest." The decision in this case notified employers that henceforth the courts would scrutinize affirmative action programs more closely to determine whether they were actually fulfilling their purposes.

Hopwood v. State of Texas (1996)

Race has long been a criterion in college and university selection policies, so administrators were surprised when the Fifth Circuit Court of Appeals ruled that the University of Texas Law School could not consider race in its admission process. Although the case was appealed to the Supreme Court, justices declined to review the decision. Because the ruling came from the Fifth Circuit, only Texas, Louisiana, and Mississippi were barred from considering race, but officials in other states wondered if similar rulings would occur in their areas. This decision appeared to negate the *Bakke* decision of 20 years earlier.

Box 3.2   FAIRNESS TOWARD OTHER GROUPS

After the passage of the Civil Rights Act in 1964, the federal government extended equal employment opportunity to groups such as older workers, the disabled, Vietnam veterans, and pregnant employees. Some of this legislation is described briefly below.

Age Discrimination Act of 1967

This act prohibits discrimination against workers between ages 40 and 65 and eliminates mandatory retirement for federal workers. It was amended to raise the upper limit to age 70 in 1978.

Rehabilitation Act of 1973

This act requires federal contractors to develop affirmative action plans for hiring disabled individuals and prohibits discrimination against the disabled.

Vietnam Era Veterans Readjustment Assistance Act of 1974

Government contractors are required to develop affirmative action plans to attract and promote qualified disabled veterans and veterans of the Vietnam era. Contractors must also list with local employment services all suitable openings, and employment services are required to give Vietnam veterans preference in referrals.

Pregnancy Discrimination Act of 1978

Discrimination against an employee because she is pregnant is illegal. In general, medical coverage and leaves of absence must be provided for pregnant women if they are provided for nonpregnant employees. If coverage and leaves of absence are not available to any employee, then it is not necessary to provide them for pregnant employees.

Americans with Disabilities Act (1990)

This far-reaching act forbids discrimination against qualified individuals with disabilities. In only three cases can employers refuse to hire an applicant with a disability: (1) if hiring such a person causes undue hardship in terms of the company's making accommodations for the disabled worker; (2) out of a business necessity; or (3) because the presence of a disabled person would pose a direct threat to the health or safety of either the disabled person or another worker.

---

had established that after an unfair discrimination complaint is filed, the burden of proof lies with the employer. The landmark case *Griggs v. Duke Power Company* (1971) established the principle that when hiring practices negatively affect protected groups, employers must justify their actions even if they had no intention of discriminating unfairly.

In *Wards Cove Packing Company v. Añtonio* (1987), however, the U.S. Supreme Court shifted this burden to the plaintiff. In this case, two salmon canneries in Alaska defended their practice of dividing their jobs into the categories of skilled and unskilled, then housing and feeding the predominantly White skilled employees separately from the predominantly non-White unskilled workers. In this case, the court ruled that plaintiffs had to demonstrate how the hiring practices in question were *not* related to business necessity, rather than companies demonstrating that such practices were related. Given the financial resources of most individuals, this burden greatly limited their ability to pursue employment discrimination complaints.

To a large degree, the Civil Rights Act of 1991 reversed the *Wards Cove* ruling, shifting the burden of proof back to the employer. In addition, the act required that hiring practices be focused on improving job performance and not merely on the unspecified goals of the employer. Requiring a high school diploma, for example, can be justified only if the employer can demonstrate that having a diploma is related to job performance. Under the 1991 Civil Rights Act, employers cannot require a high school diploma solely because they want to improve the overall educational level of their workforce.

Although the Civil Rights Act of 1991 addressed several other issues, its basic purpose was to protect or reaffirm provisions of the Civil Rights Act of 1964. The original form of the 1991 act provoked a sharp political division between the president and Congress, but in its final form, it represented a compromise between the legislative and executive branches of government.

One important compromise was the outlawing of **subgroup norming,** which refers to the practice of using different norms on a predictor for making decisions about members of different groups. Recognizing that different groups score at different levels on tests, some employers had begun to keep separate norms for different racial groups. The United States Employment Service, for example, kept different norms on African-American, Hispanic, and White groups so that the score necessary to be at the 90th percentile in terms of performances differed among the groups.

There are three basic arguments for subgroup norming or adjusting scores depending on one's racial group (Sackett & Wilk, 1994). First, score adjustment helps disadvantaged individuals overcome obstacles that members of the majority may not have faced. Second, score adjustment helps compensate for tests that are inherently biased against minorities (test bias is discussed more fully in the next chapter). Third, because no selection system is completely fair, score adjustment makes the overall selection process less harmful to minorities.

Although all of these arguments are debatable, the overall rationale for subgroup norming is to avoid using the same standards to compare people from different cultural or ethnic backgrounds. Nonetheless, subgroup norming does often make race a criterion of employment. With the passage of the Civil Rights Act of 1991, this practice was forbidden. As then-Senator Bob Dole stated, the act "means exactly what it says: race-norming or any . . . adjustment of scores or cutoff points of any employment test is illegal"(*137 Congressional Record,* 1991, S15472).

Affirmative Action Programs

One approach to ensuring fairness in the workplace has been through the use of affirmative action programs. According to a 1995 Presidential Review Commission, **affirmative action** refers to "any effort to expand opportunity for women or racial, ethnic, and national origin minorities by using membership in those groups that have been subject to discrimination as a consideration." The basis for affirmative action is Executive Order 11246, which requires federal government contractors or subcontractors with more than 50 employees and contracts worth more than $50,000, as well as banks and certain other employers, to have written affirmative action plans to eliminate employment discrimination based on race, color, sex, religion, or national origin.

Such plans, which usually necessitate hiring on the basis of race or gender, often appear to contradict the provisions of either Civil Rights Act. A number of court rulings, however, have specified the circumstances under which employers may give preferential treatment to certain groups. Affirmative action plans can be used, first, if the employer can demonstrate that the goal of the plan is to compensate for past inequities in hiring. Second, the plan must not unnecessarily damage the interests of other unprotected groups. Third, the plan must include provisions for nonprotected groups, and fourth, the plan must be reasonable (Kleiman & Faley, 1988).

Reverse discrimination refers to a situation in which a nonminority individual feels his or her rights have been violated in favor of a protected group. In *Terry v. EEOC* (1996), for example, a White male attorney who worked for the Equal Employment Opportunity Commission was awarded $150,000 plus additional damages because he had been passed over for promotion at least ten times between 1984 and 1992 in favor of women and minority employees. In addition, the EEOC was found guilty of retaliating against the attorney after he filed a complaint alleging unfair discrimination.

During the mid-1990s, affirmative action came under attack from a variety of sources. One argument against affirmative action and EEO legislation is that its primary impact has been to create bureaucratic agencies. Another argument is that companies create affirmative action and EEO departments whose mission is to justify existing organizational practices when the organization is challenged (Edelman, 1992). Finally, federal courts are increasingly scrutinizing the statistics and surveys—known as **disparity studies**—that are used to justify municipal set-aside programs for minorities. In a number of cases, such studies have been found to be so flawed that the judges demanded the programs be discontinued (Barrett, 1996). Perhaps reflecting these concerns, voters in California voted in 1996 to disallow preferences based on race or sex in public hiring, contracting, and college admissions.

Some evidence also suggests that affirmative action can have negative effects on an individual basis. For example, one study (Heilman, Rivero, & Brett, 1991) found that people who believe they have been selected on the basis of a racial or gender preference have less positive views of themselves, and others in the organization stigmatize them as incompetent (Heilman, Block, & Stathatos, 1997). In addition, some evidence (Heilman, McCullough, & Gilbert, 1996; Kravitz & Platania, 1993; Saal & Moore, 1993) suggests that preferential selection, rather than selection based on merit, produces negative reactions in people who do not benefit from the selection.

Another problem with affirmative action is that its goal may be to reapportion jobs so the economic status of minorities or women improves, but using race or gender as a criterion does not necessarily address this problem (Malos, 1996). That is, an affirmative action policy can benefit minorities of higher economic status at the same time that it excludes Whites of low economic status, which is clearly not the intent of affirmative action. Critics argue that policies that focus on an applicant's socioeconomic status, rather than on race or gender, are more in keeping with the goal of raising the status of disadvantaged individuals.

Despite these concerns, most major employers still recognize affirmative action considerations when making hiring decisions.

Box 3.3 considers some fairness issues regarding hiring in professional sports.

Job Analysis

In addition to fairness, one of the most important considerations when making an employment decision is the requirements for successful job performance. An accurate selection decision requires a thorough understanding of job tasks, which is usually acquired through job analysis.

Job analysis is the procedure for identifying the duties or behaviors that define a job and is the foundation of virtually every other area of industrial psychology, including performance appraisal, training, and human factors.

Job analysis is also the basis for **job evaluation,** the procedure for setting salary scales. According to the Equal Pay Act of 1963, the worth of a job must be evaluated in terms of four aspects: the skill, responsibility, and effort required for the job and the working conditions associated with the job. Two instruments for evaluating jobs are the Midwestern Industrial Management Association job evaluation system and the Factor Evaluation System developed by the U.S. Civil Service (Collins & Muchinsky, 1993).

Job analysis information can be collected in a number of ways including observation, individual interview, group interview, technical conference, questionnaire, diary, critical incidents (described in Box 3.4, p. 70), equipment design information, recordings of job activities, or employee records. Possible "agents" to do the collecting are professional job analysts, supervisors, job incumbents, or even a camera in the workplace. Figure 3.1 (p. 69)shows the steps in a typical job analysis.

In one study (Love, Bishop, Heinisch, & Montei, 1994), for example, a modified job analysis was used to develop selection procedures for American manufacturing employees who were applying for jobs in an automobile plant 80 percent owned by Japanese. Because of the preponderance of the Japanese ownership, the

Box 3.3   UNFAIR DISCRIMINATION IN PROFESSIONAL SPORTS

Although minorities sometimes experience unfair discrimination in certain jobs, most people believe that professional sports offer exceptional opportunities for minorities. For example, African Americans make up about 11 percent of the general labor force, but they constitute more than 75 percent of professional basketball players, more than 50 percent of professional football players, and more than 25 percent of major league baseball players. These occupations pay extremely well, with many players earning over $1 million annually.

Nonetheless, some people argue that even in sports, minorities are not treated as well as their White counterparts. For example, African Americans may be well represented among players, but they hold a small percentage of managerial or executive positions. Further, they are not well represented in key positions, such as pitcher in baseball and quarterback in football. Along the same lines, prize money for professional female tennis players is often lower than prize money for male players, even in the same tournaments.

One researcher (Kahn, 1991) reviewed the literature to determine whether there were recognizable patterns of unfair discrimination in professional sports. In general, he found major league baseball to be the fairest in terms of salary, and that segregation in playing positions was slowly fading. In contrast, however, professional basketball showed consistent evidence of salary discrimination—White players were often paid more than African-American players with equal performance records. Finally, professional football also showed a pattern of unfair discrimination, with African-American players more often excluded from quarterback, linebacker, and kicker positions. Position discrimination was also likely to lead to salary discrimination, since salaries for these key positions were higher.

Research into racial or gender discrimination in professional sports illustrates an important psychological principle known as the *availability heuristic,* which holds that

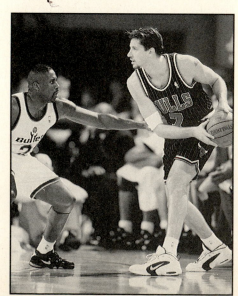

when people are asked to make judgments, they are likely to rely on information they have readily at their disposal. Unfortunately, this may lead to incorrect conclusions. When thinking about professional sports, for example, most people are likely to think of the high number of African Americans they see on sports teams, and the high salaries of African-American players such as Penny Hardaway. A more thoughtful analysis, however, suggests that appearances of equal—or greater—opportunity for minorities may mask important differences in the ways players are treated.

Source: Kahn, L. M. (1991). Discrimination in professional sports: A survey of the literature. *Industrial and Labor Relations Review, 44,* 395–418.

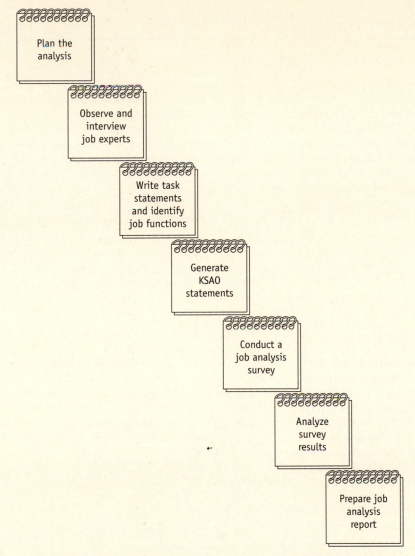

Source: Reproduced by special permission of the Publisher, Psychological Assessment Resources, Inc., 16204 North Florida Avenue, Lutz, Florida 33549. From the *Job Analysis Kit* by Sandra McIntire, Ph.D, Mary Ann Bucklan, and Deonda R. Scott. Copyright © 1995 by PAR, Inc. Further reproduction is prohibited without permission of PAR, INC.

Figure 3.1 Job Analysis Steps

management of the company stressed qualities often associated with Japanese management such as interpersonal skill, team orientation, and high-quality production.

The job analysis identified 140 behaviors critical to success, and a work simulation was developed to help screen applicants. The work simulation included three phases: introduction to the task and goal setting; motor production; and group discussion about the production process. Based on the company's success

Box 3.4 METHODS OF JOB ANALYSIS

Functional Job Analysis

Functional job analysis (FJA) focuses on the interaction among the task, the individuals responsible for accomplishing the task, and the environment in which the task is to be performed (Fine, Holt, & Hutchinson, 1974). When assessing the abilities necessary to perform the job, analysts look at such factors as how *data* (the worker's involvement with information and ideas), *people* (communication and interaction), and *things* (the use of machines and tools) affect performance. In addition, jobs are analyzed in terms of the *amount of autonomy* the worker has, the *complexity of reasoning* required, and the *use of mathematics and language.*

Critical Incidents Technique

In contrast with functional job analysis, where experts make judgments about the content of a job, the *critical incidents technique (CIT;* Flanagan, 1954) uses actual episodes of on-the-job behavior. In other words, CIT asks employees for specific examples of on-the-job behaviors that demonstrate both high and low levels of performance. In the language of job analysis, these employees are known as "subject matter experts," or SMEs, and their reports are analyzed to determine the most important aspects of a job.

Job Elements Approach

The *job elements approach* to job analysis focuses on the *elements* that a worker uses in performing a specific job. Job elements include knowledge, skills, and abilities, or KSAs, as well as willingness, interest, and personal characteristics, sometimes referred to as Os, for other factors (Primoff, 1975).

In the first step of a job elements approach to job analysis, SMEs participate in a brainstorming session in which they identify as many of the elements of a particular job as possible, then rate them on their importance. Using a statistical procedure developed by Primoff, analysts next develop a "crediting plan," which describes the KSAs necessary for successful job performance.

Position Analysis Questionnaire

The *Position Analysis Questionnaire (PAQ)* was developed by McCormick, Jeanneret, and Mecham (1972) on the assumption that there is an underlying taxonomy to all

at selecting employees, the authors concluded that job analysis can be an important tool in dealing with cultural differences that may affect selection.

In recent years some researchers have criticized traditional techniques of job analysis because of the changing nature of the workplace. That is, the pace of change has increased so much that some researchers feel traditional job analysis methods take too long to be helpful to employers. In addition, reorganization of the workplace into teams has led to a decline in the number of jobs performed by one person only (Sanchez, 1994). Nonetheless, the Department of Labor has begun an initiative to analyze virtually all jobs in the U.S. economy to help match people with jobs (Peterson, Mumford, Borman, Jeanneret, & Fleishmann, 1995).

jobs. In other words, in contrast with the other methods, the *PAQ* approach focuses on broad categories common to all jobs rather than on individual elements of specific jobs.

Given the thousands of tasks for one job that the other methods may identify, *PAQ* attempts to put these data into a more manageable form. *PAQ* reduces all jobs to 194 elements, which are classified in terms of six broader dimensions: information input; mental processes; work output; interpersonal activities; work situation and job context; and miscellaneous aspects.

Abilities Requirements Approach

One limitation of all the methods discussed above is that, with the exception of the *PAQ,* they are not very useful in determining physical requirements for job performance. Lack of knowledge about physical requirements can lead to problems in many areas, particularly in personnel selection and employee turnover. Employers who assume that women are unable to accomplish tasks requiring physical strength and consequently avoid hiring them may be discriminating unfairly.

Fleishman (1975; Fleishman & Quaintance, 1984) developed a taxonomy of physical and cognitive abilities to describe the performance standards of any job called the *abilities requirements approach.* According to Fleishman, *abilities* are the foundation on which skills are built. Whereas operating heavy equipment is a *skill,* some of the *abilities* required include static strength, choice reaction time, multilimb coordination, and rate control.

Generic Work Behavior

Although the abilities requirements approach identifies mental and physical abilities necessary for job performance, one researcher (Hunt, 1996) noted that there is no taxonomy of nonjob-specific, nonability-dependent performance dimensions. Working with data from the Employee Rating Form of the PDI Employment Inventory (Paajanen, Hansen, & McLellan, 1993), Hunt analyzed supervisor ratings of 18,146 entry-level employees to identify generic work behaviors. Findings from the study revealed eight generic behaviors common to entry-level jobs: industriousness, thoroughness, schedule flexibility, attendance, off-task behavior, unruliness, theft, and drug misuse.

Some suggestions for making job analysis more responsive to changing environments include gathering information about jobs from customers and technical experts rather than job incumbents and their supervisors only; analyzing jobs in terms of the work that will be done in the future; and shifting the focus of analysis from specific tasks to work functions or larger units of analysis (May, 1996). In addition, some research (Borman, Dorsey, & Ackerman, 1992) suggests that, along with information about tasks, a more complete job analysis focuses on the amount of time allocated to specific tasks. Successful and unsuccessful stockbrokers, for example, have the same tasks, but they vary considerably in which tasks require more of their time.

Box 3.4 describes some formal models of job analysis.

Information gathered from a job analysis is often used to write a job description. The **job description** contains information about the tasks to be performed, equipment to be operated, working conditions, nature of supervision, and factors such as the hours of work, salary, and opportunities for promotion.

Although job descriptions often provide useful information about lower-level jobs, they tend to be less useful when describing managerial or executive positions, where duties, hours, and working conditions are less structured. Consequently, job descriptions of such positions usually do not provide an accurate picture of the job in question.

Job specifications define the knowledge, skills, abilities, and other factors necessary to accomplish a job. These are derived from the job description and are useful in evaluating an employee's performance. Their greatest utility, however, is usually in determining the predictors to use when making a hiring decision.

The rest of this chapter looks at the standard employee selection process: recruitment, application, interview, reference check, letters of recommendation, and preemployment drug screening. As each aspect is discussed, remember that every step of the employment process must meet the federal requirements for validity and fairness. If the employer has based the selection procedure on a thorough job analysis, however, the likelihood of choosing valid predictors is usually greatly increased.

Personnel Recruitment

The Recruitment Process
Realistic Job Previews

The purpose of **recruitment** is to persuade individuals to consider or to apply for a position with a particular employer. As every college student knows, some organizations plan elaborate strategies for attracting applicants, whereas others make little or no effort to recruit employees. In recent years, the movement in American industry toward downsizing has caused most companies to reconsider their recruitment strategies.

The Recruitment Process

Some of the methods of recruitment that organizations use include rehiring former employees, hiring people referred by current employees, using employment agencies, advertising, and accepting referrals from schools. Most research suggests that informal methods of recruiting—referrals by other employees and people who simply walk in and apply, for example—lead to longer job tenure than more formal methods (Rynes, 1991). Some research (Latham & Leddy, 1987) found that newspaper or employment agency recruits were likely to be less involved and satisfied with their jobs than self-referred employees. In addition, one study (Kirnan, Farley, & Geisinger, 1989) found that the best life insurance agents were informally referred by other agents, sales managers, or district managers.

There are at least two possible explanations for why informally recruited employees perform better. One is that these employees have greater knowledge about the job and are less likely to quit because they have more realistic expectations (the impact of realistic expectations on job turnover is discussed below). A second explanation relates to personality factors, such as confidence and self-esteem, that may affect job performance. In one study, people who had higher levels of self-esteem were more likely to use informal methods of job search, whereas those with lower self-esteem relied more on formal methods, such as newspaper advertising and employment agencies (Ellis & Taylor, 1983).

One of the most important aspects of the recruitment process is the person doing the recruiting. In a survey of college recruitment practices of Fortune 1000 companies, Rynes and Boudreau (1986) found that the average recruiter had been with the company almost five years, and that half the college recruiters were human resource professionals and half were line managers. Interestingly, almost none of these individuals had received training in recruitment, nor was the success of their recruitment evaluated. Recruiters were likely to be evaluated on how they conducted themselves during the recruitment period, but not on the quality of the individuals they recruited.

Although it may be reasonable to assume that recruiters look for the most qualified applicants, some research suggests that, at least in the college setting, other factors are more important than qualifications. In a study of how recruiters made their job offers, Graves and Powell (1988) found that subjective qualifications—communication skills, enthusiasm, initiative, and knowledge about the position—were the best predictors of an employment offer. In this study, objective qualifications such as knowledge, experience, and GPA were not related to interview outcomes. In another study by the same researchers (Graves & Powell, 1995), female recruiters rated male applicants more qualified than female applicants, but male recruiters did not distinguish between genders in rating applicant qualifications.

Just as recruiters may be influenced by factors other than objective qualifications, some evidence suggests that applicants also try to influence the recruitment process by managing the impressions they are making on interviewers. In one study (Stevens & Kristof, 1995), for example, students participating in campus recruitment typically emphasized personal qualities and described themselves as hardworking, competent, confident, socially adept, goal-oriented, flexible, and effective leaders.

Another study (Gatewood, Gowan, & Lautenschlager, 1993) found that organizational image was an important factor in attracting recruits. When applicants were familiar with a company's advertising, used its products, or had studied the organization in school, they tended to have a higher opinion of the company. This suggests that simply having more information about a company creates a positive attitude in the minds of applicants. In addition, students respond more favorably to recruiters they believe to be an accurate representative of the employer (Rynes, Bretz, & Gerhart, 1991).

Applicants' knowledge about a job also affects the recruitment process. For example, when jobs are posted, salary and location seem to be important in deciding whether to apply (Barber & Roehling, 1993). However, when applicants have little knowledge about the job in question, the knowledgeability of the recruiter and a good presentation about the company are likely to affect individual acceptance of a job offer (Rynes, Heneman, & Schwab, 1980). Research also suggests that applicants prefer their recruiters to be young, but not too young. One study of engineering recruitment found that students were more satisfied with recruitment if the recruiter was the same gender as the job applicant and had a similar educational background (Maurer, Howe, & Lee, 1992). There is little evidence, however, that the race of a job recruiter affects an applicant's acceptance of an offer.

Another factor that can affect recruitment is the job search strategy of applicants. For example, individuals who are assertive in seeking a position are likely to be more successful than those who are not (Schmit, Amel, & Ryan, 1993). As the job search begins, people typically consider a variety of opportunities, then narrow their focus to fewer companies as the search continues. Although they tend to rely on formal sources for information about jobs initially, as time passes, job seekers rely more on informal sources such as friends and contacts (Barber, Daly, Giannantonio, & Phillips, 1994).

Apparently the efficiency with which applications are processed also affects the recruitment process. Delays create a particularly bad impression if the applicant has received other job offers (Rynes, Bretz, & Gerhart, 1991). Also, students are more inclined toward organizational recruitment if they have little job experience or begin their job search later than their peers. In contrast, they are less favorable toward recruitment if they dislike the job characteristics or the recruiter who interviews them.

Realistic Job Previews

Under traditional recruitment plans, only the positive characteristics of a job are communicated to applicants. A number of studies have suggested, however, that employers could lower turnover rates considerably if they would be more honest in describing jobs to candidates. Results from several studies (McEvoy & Cascio, 1985; Vandenberg & Scarpello, 1990; Wanous, 1992) indicate that providing a **realistic job preview (RJP)** of a job to applicants results in higher job satisfaction, organizational commitment, and retention.

Unrealistic job previews are likely to attract applicants who have unrealistic expectations about a job that may affect their satisfaction and commitment to the organization. In contrast, **realistic recruitment**—the presentation of "*all pertinent* information *without distortion*" (Wanous, 1980)—increases the job survival rate. There are several explanations for this, including fostering the perception that the organization is honest, helping applicants understand exactly what is expected of them, strengthening a commitment to join an organization, and reducing overly positive expectations about a job (Meglino, DeNisi, & Ravlin, 1993).

In a study of the effects of realistic recruitment, Dean and Wanous (1984) provided three groups of bank tellers with either a booklet giving a realistic preview of the teller job, a booklet providing general information, or no preview of the job. Individuals who received either booklet were more likely to quit a training course during the first weeks, whereas those who had received no preview were more likely to leave after 20 weeks. The realistic preview and early—rather than late—withdrawal of some employees resulted in considerable savings to the organization.

In a study of realistic job previews with U.S. Army trainees (Meglino, DeNisi, Youngblood, & Williams, 1988), researchers provided subjects with two kinds of previews: a "reduction" preview, designed to curtail trainees' overly optimistic expectations, and an "enhancement" preview, designed to allay trainees' overly pessimistic expectations. Soldiers who heard both kinds of job previews had lower turnover than those who heard only one type of preview or no preview, but soldiers who heard only the preview designed to reduce their expectations had higher turnover.

Another group of researchers (Meglino, DeNisi, & Ravlin, 1993) looked at the effect of previous job experience on reactions to realistic job previews. Participants in the study were 1,117 individuals who had applied for a job as a correctional officer. During the interview process, half the applicants had been randomly assigned to view a video that emphasized the excessive amount of paperwork, difficulties in dealing with inmates, high levels of stress, and possibility of being injured on the job. Interestingly, applicants who had previous correctional experience were less likely to accept an offer of employment after viewing the video, whereas those without experience were more likely to accept.

Although there seems to be agreement that RJPs are useful in screening out people who will later be dissatisfied with the job and consequently increase the job tenures of those who stay, no one is exactly certain why RJPs work. Some is researchers have related the success of informal recruiting methods to RJPs. When friends have recommended someone for a job, they have almost certainly given the job seeker some preview of what the job is like (Swaroff, Barclay, & Bass, 1985).

It is important to note, however, that although RJPs may increase job tenure, they do not appear to be related to performance. That is, there is no evidence that individuals who are told about the aspects of a job make better employees than those who are not told. In a meta-analysis of experiments with RJPs, Premack and Wanous (1985) summarized the results of research as follows:

> Specifically, RJPs appear to lower initial expectations about a job and the organization, to increase the number of candidates who drop out from further consideration for a job, to increase initial levels of organizational commitment and job satisfaction slightly . . . and to increase job survival.

According to Wanous (1989), RJPs can be more effective if certain procedures are followed. Content of the RJP should focus on aspects most important to the job, aspects most related to turnover, and aspects most misperceived by employees. In general, information presented should not be too negative, and applicants tend to believe job descriptions given by real employees rather than by actors. Finally, the RJP should come early in the recruitment process so that the employer will expend time and effort only on recruits who are seriously interested in the position being previewed.

Contents of the Application Blank
Using Biodata for Personnel Selection

Application Blanks and Biodata

In most cases, applicants must complete an application blank or furnish a resume to be considered for a position. From information such as educational background and work experience, employers make judgments about the probable success of a candidate. In terms of cost, applications and resumes are two of the most efficient ways to make personnel decisions. In addition to efficiency, application blanks have face validity; that is, they ask for information that appears to be relevant to job performance. They are also easy to administer, and information from the application can be verified.

The use of an application is subject to the considerations of validity and fairness discussed above. As with all personnel selection procedures, using application blanks to discriminate unfairly is illegal, and applicants are required to furnish only information that is job-related. For this reason, employers typically avoid asking any questions that could give the appearance of an employment decision being made on grounds unrelated to job performance. When questions about race or sex, for example, appear on an application blank, they are usually for statistical purposes and are not used in the selection process.

Contents of the Application Blank

As a general rule, questions about age, sex, race, arrest (but not conviction) records, marital status, height, weight, and other areas are omitted from the application blank unless they can be shown to be related to job performance. In such cases, these questions are allowable because they provide information about a **bona fide occupational qualification (BFOQ).** BFOQs are standards necessary to perform a job successfully. For example, although hiring on the basis of race is prohibited, being Chinese may be a BFOQ for a job in a film about China. Unless appearance is a BFOQ, requiring submission of a photograph before being hired is a questionable practice. As in all aspects of personnel selection, the employer must be able to demonstrate that any information gathered on the application blank relates to performance on the job.

In some cases, certain items on the application blank are better predictors of job success than others. Experience operating a drill press, for example, is probably more strongly related to job success than merely having attended a class about drill presses. Consequently, an employer may use a **weighted application blank,** in which responses that are most predictive of actual job performance have more "weight" in the employment decision.

Although there are advantages to the application blank, an obvious concern for the employer is the accuracy of the information supplied. Not surprisingly, applicants often interpret or inflate information to make themselves look more appealing. In an interesting study of the relationship between claims of abilities and actual job performance, Anderson, Warner, and Spencer (1984) asked applicants for clerical positions to rate their abilities on a variety of job tasks. To determine how much applicants were inflating their qualifications, a number of bogus abilities—that is, meaningless phrases—were included in the rating sheet. The researchers found that applicants who rated themselves highest on bogus factors such as "matrixing solvency files" and "planning basic entropy programs" were actually the poorest typists.

Using Biodata for Personnel Selection

Another approach to applications is the use of **biographical inventory,** or **biodata,** which is basically an expanded application blank. In addition to the usual questions, the biographical inventory asks about areas such as recreational activities, early childhood experience, and health.

The rationale behind the use of biodata is as follows. People are born with certain hereditary influences, and as they grow, they learn to adapt to their environments. Over time, they put themselves in situations that are reinforcing to them, and eventually their life histories can be studied for an identifiable pattern of choices. The biodata model holds that future behavior can be predicted from the choices a person has made in the past (Mumford & Stokes, 1992).

When employers screen biodata in the form of resumes or application blanks, they look for evidence of both ability to perform the job and personal characteristics that the employer feels are important to the job. For example, grades and work experience are sometimes used to infer math ability, whereas holding an elected office in a club can suggest leadership and interersonal skills (Brown & Campion, 1994).

Biodata items often resemble items on personality inventories, but they differ from personality measures in their focus on concrete aspects of a person's life history rather than on reported feelings, values, or questions about the future (Smither, 1989). Typical biodata items include the following:

- How old were you when you got your first job?
- What was your favorite subject in high school?
- What was your greatest accomplishment in your last job?

Overall, biodata have been shown to be a useful predictor of job performance (Stokes, Mumford, & Owens, 1994). In one test of the biodata approach, for example, researchers asked cadets at the U.S. Naval Academy to write autobiographical essays that were used to generate biodata items. These items were later asked of different cadets to predict success at the academy.

Scores on the biodata inventory predicted military and academic performances, as well as peer ratings of leadership ability (Russell, Mattson, Devlin, & Atwater, 1990).

Another study (Mael & Ashforth, 1995) looked at biodata items and turnover among newcomers to an organization. Over 2,500 male Army recruits completed biodata forms three days after their induction. In addition, 1,082 active duty soldiers participated in the study. Biodata factors most related to attrition were a preference for rugged outdoor activities; respect for authority, property, and institutions; membership in groups or sports teams; and intellectual or achievement orientation. Soldiers who scored high on these factors were more likely to reenlist.

Finally, one group of researchers (Snell, Stokes, Sands, & McBride, 1994) looked at the relationship between results from biodata forms filled out by college freshmen and their occupational attainment almost 20 years later. Results from the study indicated that adults who had chosen careers in science, medicine, and technology had reported similar social and academic experiences as freshmen. Table 3.1 lists some of the biodata factors used in this study.

Despite these interesting results, there are some considerations regarding the use of biodata. First, biodata may predict job performance, but they are often criticized for lacking content and construct validity (Katzell, 1994; Schmidt, Ones, & Hunter, 1992). In other words, researchers are not certain how biodata work. Some research (Mumford, Costanza, Connelly, & Johnson, 1996), however, suggests that the careful selection of items can generate scales that demonstrate both content and construct validity.

Second, applicants may object to the personal nature of some of the questions on the biographical inventory. For example, Mael, Connerley, and Morath (1996) found that people objected to biodata items that asked them to recall traumatic events or inquired about religion or intimate matters. Items that were verifiable, more transparent in purpose, and more impersonal were more acceptable to participants in the study.

Third, biodata are subject to faking, and applicants may be able to guess the response the employer favors. Consequently, employers need to take precautions against faking when developing a biodata instrument (Becker & Colquitt, 1992; Kluger & Collela, 1993; Stokes, Hogan, & Snell, 1993). Interestingly, however, some research suggests that people generally give honest answers when completing biodata forms (Shaffer, Saunders, & Owens, 1986). Finally, some evidence (Whitney & Schmitt, 1997) suggests biodata responses are affected by race.

Regardless of the specific approach, the rationale behind using the application blank to select employees is that previous experience and behavior are believed to predict future success. Proponents of biodata believe that biographical items have greater validity in predicting job performance because (1) they are factual rather than abstract (as in employment testing) or impressionistic (as in an interview); (2) applications contain only relevant information and do not allow for irrelevancies that may distract from judgment; and (3) applications are direct—they do not rely on interviewers' opinions about such traits as

Table 3.1 TYPICAL BIODATA FACTORS

Factor	Description
Academic achievement	Had high grades and very high standing in high school class; were very competitive and successful in academic situations
Athletic participation	Were very active in athletic activities; rated past performance in physical activities very high; often engaged in team sports; enjoyed physical education courses
Popularity	Dated regularly; had many close friends; were well liked by both male and female classmates
Parental freedom versus control	Had parents who allowed more freedom and independence and were less punitive and critical
Socioeconomic status	Had parents who attained high educational degrees and held high-occupational-level jobs; enjoyed high family income and social class
Parental interest and support	Had close, warm relationships with both parents; had parents who were interested in their activities and frequently gave attention and praise
Scientific interests	Had high grades and enjoyed science and laboratory courses
Verbal aggressiveness	Enjoyed discussion courses and tried to make others see their point of view; questioned teachers on subject matter
Social adjustment	Rarely felt depressed; were satisfied with social status with peers; seldom "took things out" on parents or friends
Positive academic attitude	Had teachers who were more successful in arousing academic interests and allowed more class participation and discussion; liked high school teachers to a greater degree; felt high school education was adequate
Mechanical interests	Enjoyed building things and repairing devices on their own initiative; belonged to school-subject-matter clubs, such as for science and math, as well as to hobby clubs, such as for hot rods and crafts; read business and sports magazines
Religious involvement	Were very active in church, religious, or charitable organizations; went more often to church and had stronger religious beliefs in comparison with their peers
Sibling friction	Had more siblings close to their own age; argued or fought more often with siblings; experienced more friction and feelings of competition with siblings

Source: Snell, A. F., Stokes, G. S., Sands, M. M., & McBride, J. R. (1994). Adolescent life experiences as predictors of occupational attainment. *Journal of Applied Psychology, 79,* 131–141.

ambition, sociability, and dependability (Asher, 1972). Overall, research suggests that when the information supplied is truthful, both traditional applications and biodata are effective in predicting job performance.

In summary, application blanks and biodata are useful in selecting the best employees when (1) they do not ask questions that discriminate unfairly; (2) the information obtained can be shown to be job-related (see Box 3.5 for examples of illegal questions); and (3) the truthfulness of the information supplied is certain. Finally, application blanks are far less expensive to administer than other forms of personnel selection, especially employment interviews.

Problems with the Employment Interview
The Interview Process
Improving Employment Interviews

The Employment Interview

For virtually every job opening, employers require an interview at some point. The employment interview and the application blank are two of the most common personnel practices and a critical part of the selection process. Despite the almost universal use of interviews, however, applicant performance in the typical unstructured employment interview is one of the worst predictors of job performance and probably the part of the selection process most likely to lead to questions about fairness.

Problems with the Employment Interview

Decades of research confirm a number of discouraging aspects of employment interviews, including the following:

1. In most cases, unstructured interviews are neither reliable nor valid for identifying good candidates (Mayfield, Brown, & Hamstra, 1980; Zedeck, Tziner, & Middlestadt, 1983). Although the *intrarater* reliability of interviews is great, *interrater* reliability is moderate to low. That is, interviewers may be personally consistent in their ratings of applicants, but they often disagree with the ratings of other interviewers (Heneman, Schwab, Fossum, & Dyer, 1986).

2. Rather than approaching each candidate with an open mind, interviewers develop stereotypes of the ideal job candidate and compare candidates to this model (Rowe, 1989; Webster, 1982).

3. Interviewers pay more attention to negative than to positive information (Binning, Goldstein, Garcia, & Scattaregia, 1988; Webster, 1982).

4. For lower-level employees, interviewers typically make up their minds in about the first four minutes of the interview (Springbett, 1958). Once an interviewer makes a decision, further information is useless (Farr, 1973; Webster, 1982).

Box 3.5   QUESTIONS TO AVOID; QUESTIONS TO ASK

Experts from the Society of Human Resource Management (SHRM) have identified a number of questions to ask applicants, as well as questions to avoid.

Age

Don't ask "How old are you?" or "Date of birth?"

Ask "If you are under 18, will you be able to furnish a work permit after employment?"

Medical

Don't ask "Do you have any health-related problems that may affect your ability to do this job?" or "How many days were you absent from work last year?"

Ask "Can you perform the essential job functions listed in the job description?" and "Will you be able to comply with our company's policy of 10 sick days per year?"

National Origin

Don't ask "Are you a U.S. citizen?" or "What language do you speak at home?"

Ask "Are you legally eligible to work in the U.S.?" and "The job requires fluent English; can you meet this requirement?"

Religion

Don't ask "What clubs and organizations do you belong to?"

Ask "List memberships in any professional organizations that you feel would enhance your application, excluding any whose name would indicate the race, religion, creed, color, national origin, or ancestry of its members."

Education

Don't ask "Dates of attendance," which could reveal the applicant's age and create an appearance of age discrimination.

Ask "How many years of school did you attend?"

Source: Bahnsen, E. (1996, November). Questions to ask, and not ask, job applicants. *HR News.* Alexandria, VA: Society for Human Resource Management.

---

5. Interviewers often form opinions about candidates based on personal qualities such as attractiveness, likeability, initiative, and intelligence rather than on objective qualifications such as education or job experience (Hitt & Barr, 1989; Liden, Martin, & Parson, 1993; Raza & Carpenter, 1987). These impressions are likely to be unrelated to job performance (Kinicki, Lockwood,

Hom, & Griffeth, 1990). In addition, attractive candidates of either sex are preferred over unattractive candidates, although this bias is less common in more experienced managers (Marlowe, Schneider, & Nelson, 1996).

6. Both male and female applicants are rated lower when they apply for jobs outside traditional sex roles (Cash, Gillen, & Burns, 1977; Cohen & Bunker, 1975; Heilman & Saruwatari, 1979). The more masculine a female applicant dresses, the more favorably her performance in the interview is judged (Forsythe, Drake, & Cox, 1985). Applicants whose dress resembles typical dress within the organization are regarded more favorably (Rafaeli & Pratt, 1993). Applicants who are overweight, and females in particular, are judged less favorably (Pingitore, Dugoni, Tindale, & Spring, 1994).

7. Although gender seems to have little effect on interviewer rating of applicants, interviewers do seem to be influenced by race. On some occasions, minorities are rated more favorably than Whites, and on others less favorably, irrespective of actual qualifications (Campion & Arvey, 1989). Interviewers also tend to rate candidates of their own race more favorably (Prewett-Livingston, Feild, Veres, & Lewis, 1996). Researchers presently recognize that race affects interview outcomes, but they are not yet certain how (Harris, 1989).

8. Training only occasionally improves interviewer performance (Dougherty, Ebert, & Callender, 1986; Maurer & Fay, 1988). Since the interview is a form of social interaction, it is unrealistic to think that three or four days of training will change behaviors that have developed over a lifetime (Webster, 1982).

9. A valid employment screening test easily outperforms unstructured interviews in identifying good candidates (Fear, 1984; Webster, 1982).

10. The interviewer's opinions about a candidate's performance in the interview are likely to be influenced by information on the application blank. That is, interviewers who regard an application favorably are more likely to have a favorable view of the candidate after the interview, whereas negative opinions about an application often lead to negative ratings of a candidate's interview performance (Dougherty, Turban, & Callender, 1994; Macan & Dipboye, 1990).

Despite these problems, interviews remain one of the most common personnel practices. Regardless of the scientific value and success rate of almost any other validated personnel selection device, virtually every employer will want an individual to be interviewed before hiring. One researcher, in fact, referred to the selection interview as an art form—since the typical interview has so little scientific validity, good results can only be the result of the skill of the interviewer (Webster, 1982).

The idea that the skill of the interviewer is more important than the structure of the interview is an important point. One reason research on the employment interview has been so negative is that most studies have focused on the success of interviews in general and have not considered the success of individual interviewers. In fact, however, interviewers vary widely in their competence, and only in recent years have researchers addressed the question of what makes an interviewer effective (Dreher, Ash, & Hancock, 1988; Eder & Buckley, 1988; Pulakos, Schmitt, Whitney, & Smith, 1996). In addition, some research (Dalessio & Silverhart, 1994) suggests that interviewers pay more attention to interviews when results from testing are poor; when test results are good, interviewers give less weight to the interview in making decisions.

Another point about interviews is that they have generally been studied from the perspective of selection only. That is, researchers have largely focused on the interviewer's reaction to the applicant, but not the applicant's reaction to the interview process. When qualified applicants are scarce, the recruitment aspect of the employment interview may be as important as the selection aspect (Barber, Hollenbeck, Tower, & Phillips, 1994).

Interestingly, recent reviews of interview research have been much more positive than earlier research. For example, one meta-analysis (Conway, Jako, & Goodman, 1995) found that interviews were more reliable when interviewers were trained, questions were standardized, a procedure for evaluating responses was used, and ratings were based on multiple measures. Another study (Huffcutt & Arthur, 1994) found that results from structured interviews can predict job performance as well as mental ability tests for entry-level jobs. Some evidence (Huffcutt, Roth, & McDaniel, 1996) also indicates that interview ratings correlate with cognitive ability, particularly when interviews are less structured.

In an influential meta-analysis of studies of the validity of employment interviews, one group of researchers (McDaniel, Whetzel, Schmidt, & Maurer, 1994) concluded that interview validity is affected by different aspects of the interview process. For example, structured interviews are more valid for predicting job performance than unstructured; individual interviews are more valid than board interviews; interviews are equally valid for predicting job performance and performance in training; and situational interviews are more predictive than job-related interviews, which, in turn, are more predictive than psychological interviews.

The Interview Process

Most research considers the interview as a unitary process, but in fact, the interview has three distinct phases: the initial period, when the interviewer forms an impression of the candidate from the resume, references, and test scores; the face-to-face interview itself; and the final period, in which the interviewer makes judgments about the suitability of the candidate for the position. As suggested above, some evidence suggests—not surprisingly—that postinterview impressions about a candidate are strongly influenced by preinterview impressions, and less by the content of the interview itself (Macan & Dipboye, 1990; Phillips & Dipboye, 1989).

Many times interviewers look at the fit between the applicant and the needs of the organization. *Fit* refers to firm-specific qualifications—the applicant's personal values, political orientation, hobbies, style of dress, and so forth, compared to those of other members of the organization. Another way of thinking about fit is in terms of the compatibility between an individual and an organization (Kristof, 1996).

Once an employer is convinced of an applicant's general qualifications, the employer is likely to look at the issue of fit before making a job offer. Research suggests that the employer makes the fitness decision using criteria different from those associated with general employability. In addition, the judgment about fit tends to be stricter and often focuses on a candidate's values or other qualities (Adkins, Russell, & Werbel, 1994; Finney, 1996; Rynes & Gerhart, 1990).

Most research supports the importance of assessing fit in the selection process. In one series of studies (Caldwell & O'Reilly, 1990), for example, managers who developed specific criteria for assessing a candidate's fit with the organization hired more successful employees. In another study (Guthrie & Olian, 1991), executives whose previous experiences fit well with the company that hired them were likely to stay in their positions longer, irrespective of their objective qualifications. Finally, two researchers (Rajagopalan & Datta, 1996) found that high-performing CEOs were more often chosen on the basis of their fit with the hiring firm rather than their knowledge of industry conditions.

For most entry-level jobs, both qualifications and fit are assessed in one interview. For higher-level jobs, however, the interview process typically has additional stages during which candidates must meet more than one interviewer. Regardless of who does the interviewing, however, every individual who meets with the candidate needs to be carefully trained so that unfair or nonjob-related questions are avoided. In no case should interviewing be left to individuals who are unfamiliar with EEO considerations.

As a general rule, interviews take one of four forms:

1. Traditional interview. In this wide-ranging discussion of an applicant's background, the interviewer moves about from topic to topic, focusing on anything that may be of interest or may provide information relevant to job performance. This form of interview is the most common, least reliable, and most likely to result in charges of unfair discrimination.

2. Structured interview. This procedure resembles an oral questionnaire, in which all applicants are asked the same questions. The interviewer is not permitted to go into areas that are not structured into the interview. Although this format limits the information the employer can obtain, it is the least likely to result in EEO complaints (Mayfield, Brown, & Hamstra, 1980). In addition, the structured interview, which is usually developed from a job analysis, yields the greatest amount of job-related information.

Comparisons of interviews using structured and unstructured approaches suggested that structured interviews are superior in identifying better candidates (Weisner & Cronshaw, 1988; Wright, Lichtenfels, & Pursell,

| **Box 3.6** | STRUCTURED INTERVIEW QUESTIONS |

Examples of Structured Interview Questions

Future-oriented question: Suppose you had an idea for a change in work procedure to enhance quality, but there was a problem in that some members of your work team were against any type of change. What would you do in this situation?

(5) Excellent answer (top third of candidates)—Explain the change and try to show the benefits. Discuss it openly in a meeting.

(3) Good answer (middle third)—Ask them why they are against change. Try to convince them.

(1) Marginal answer (bottom third)—Tell the supervisor.

Past-oriented question: What is the biggest difference of opinion you ever had with a coworker? How did it get resolved?

(5) Excellent answer (top third of candidates)—We looked into the situation, found the problem, and resolved the difference. Had an honest conversation with the person.

(3) Good answer (middle third)—Compromised. Resolved the problem by taking turns, or I explained the problem (my side) carefully.

(1) Marginal answer (bottom third)—I got mad and told the coworker off, or we got the supervisor to resolve the problem, or I never have differences with anyone.

Note: Both questions are intended to assess conflict resolution and collaborative problem-solving knowledge, skills, and other requirements.

Source: Campion, M. A., Campion, J. E., & Hudson, J. P., Jr. (1994). Structured interviewing: A note on incremental validity and alternative question types. *Journal of Applied Psychology, 79,* 998–1002. Used by permission.

1989). In a two-year study involving more than a thousand applicants for sales clerk positions, for example, researchers (Arvey, Miller, Gould, & Burch, 1987) found a structured interview to be a valid predictor of job performance.

In another study of structured interviews, Pulakos and Schmitt (1995) tested the predictive validity of two forms of interview questions. *Experience-based questions* ask applicants to explain what they did in past jobs or life situations; *situational questions,* on the other hand, ask how a candidate would respond to a hypothetical situation. In this study, the experience-based interview questions yielded higher validities than the situational questions.

Box 3.6 contains some typical structured interview questions.

3. Semistructured interview. In this format the interviewer uses broad areas and categories as a basis for questions. When something of particular interest is mentioned by the candidate, the interviewer probes this area in more depth. In general, the semistructured interview provides the most information with the least risk of charges of unfair discrimination and is preferred by most professionals (Webster, 1982).

4. Stress interview. Developed as a selection device for spies during World War II, the stress interview attempts to determine how a candidate holds up in unpleasant or difficult situations. Typically, an employer using the stress technique will denigrate or minimize any accomplishments a candidate mentions, then watch to see if the applicant becomes angry, defensive, or anxious. Other typical stress techniques include seating candidates so light shines directly in their eyes, continuous telephone interruptions so candidates can never finish a sentence or a thought, offering messy food without a plate or napkins, or seating a candidate in an unbalanced chair.

In contrast with the other approaches, stress interviews aim to make the candidate uncomfortable. Since most experts agree that the most effective interviews are those with a high degree of rapport between the candidate and the interviewer, most professional interviewers avoid stress techniques.

When candidates meet the interviewer they are likely to be nervous, which, given the tendency of some interviewers to make up their minds in just a few minutes, is particularly unfortunate. A good interviewer is aware that candidates may be nervous, avoids jumping to conclusions, and tries to help the applicant relax. One technique to help the applicant feel at ease is to ask a friendly but complex question about an area that the candidate feels comfortable discussing (e.g., "I see from your resume that you enjoy skiing. Have you had much opportunity to ski this winter?").

One approach the interviewer may use is to keep in mind two questions: (1) *Can* the applicant do the work? and (2) *Will* the applicant do the work? (Goodale, 1989). The first question has to do with qualifications, whereas the second addresses such issues as motivation, personality, and fit with the organization. As the interview progresses, the interviewer probes for information concerning both the ability and the willingness of the applicant to do the job.

After the preliminaries, the interviewer typically moves into the body of the interview. During this part, the candidate is asked in detail about achievements, failures, interests, and goals. The interviewer makes no verbal judgments, but simply encourages the candidate to speak at length. When certain topics are omitted or the candidate strays from the subject at hand, the interviewer carefully guides the applicant back. At no time does the interviewer provide information the candidate can use to slant his or her background to fit the position.

Most professional interviewers recommend taking detailed notes during the interview. The interviewer records what the candidate is saying and how it is being said (e.g., confidently or with hesitation). If the applicant makes negative comments or admits to career failures, the interviewer should *not* record these as they are being said; the candidate is likely to notice that negatives are being noted and subsequently speak more cautiously. When the applicant moves on to other areas, however, then the negative comments should be noted.

In general, the effective interviewer does nothing that may make the candidate feel defensive. Since the purpose of the interview is to get as much relevant information as possible, the interviewer does not want to make the applicant nervous. Difficult questions should be withheld until the candidate feels sufficient rapport to be candid with the interviewer. Although it is legitimate to ask disabled persons if they feel their disabilities will affect job performance, for example, such a question should not be asked in the opening phase of the interview.

After all the necessary information has been obtained, the interviewer should ask the candidate if there is any information about the company the interviewer can supply. As the interview ends, the professional interviewer will be listening closely for any offhand comments the candidate may make. Assuming the interview is over, applicants often make unguarded statements that may reveal something the interviewer has missed. For the interviewer, the interview is not finished until the applicant has left the room.

Improving Employment Interviews

Many people have asked the obvious question why, if interviews are neither reliable nor valid and fraught with EEO dangers, employers still use them. There are several answers to this question.

First, interviews can be quite useful if the interviewer is highly skilled. Second, using interviews for personnel selection is sometimes more practical than developing job-related tests and measures. Third, regardless of the negative research, employers continue to believe they have the skills and insight necessary to select the best candidates.

On a more positive note, recent research has indicated that there are a number of steps employers can take to make interviews more effective. Evidence mentioned earlier in this chapter clearly shows that structured interviews can be useful in predicting job performance. Developing a rating system for evaluating responses also improves predictions based on interview results. Finally, employers can determine which of their interviewers are most effective in hiring good applicants and learn from them how they reach their recommendations.

Two other promising approaches to employment interviews are behavioral description interviewing and computerized interviews.

Behavior Descriptions in Interviews In the **behavior description** or situational approach to interviews (Janz, 1989; Janz, Hellervik, & Gilmore, 1986; Latham, 1989), selection standards are based on critical incidents examples of both good and bad performance. Information from these incidents is used to formulate questions about hypothetical situations. Applicants describe how they would handle the situations based on their experiences or judgment. Afterward, responses are evaluated in terms of the level of performance indicated, and the highest scorer gets the job.

Orpen (1985) compared the behavior description approach to unstructured interviews in predicting the job performances of life insurance salespeople. Interviewers using either approach were asked to predict the future job performance of applicants. The behavior description method predicted performance significantly more accurately than an unstructured interview. Along the same lines, Latham and Saari (1984) found that the performance levels of workers in a newsprint mill were accurately predicted by scores on situational interviews conducted three years earlier.

Computerized Interviews   One common complaint about the selection interview is that it is so easily manipulated—candidates with strong social skills and weak credentials are often able to influence the interviewer into making them a job offer. In one study, researchers tried to control the effect of social influence by having applicants respond to a **computerized interview,** in which candidates answer questions presented to them on a computer (Martin & Nagao, 1989).

Interestingly, candidates offered fewer socially desirable responses and were more honest about reporting GPA and test scores. On the other hand, higher-status applicants resented the computer approach. This suggests that the computerized interview may not be appropriate in all situations, particularly when job duties are largely unstructured.

Applicant References and Letters of Recommendation

In an often-cited study of the usefulness of references as a predictor of job performance, Browning (1968) correlated preemployment ratings of teachers with their performance ratings one year after being hired. Overall, the relationship between quality of references and job performance was quite weak. Browning found that the best predictor of job performance was information from the application blank—the greater the number of years an applicant had taught, the higher the level of job performance.

In general, the value of references or letters of recommendation in making an employment decision has not been well researched. It seems logical to assume, however, that both references and letters of recommendation are likely to be of limited value in assessing the suitability of a candidate, since few applicants are going to supply the names of individuals who will give bad recommendations (Knouse, 1989). In a review of letters of recommendation, Muchinsky (1979) found their usefulness in predicting job performance was almost negligible. Along the same lines, other researchers (Hunter & Hunter, 1984; Reilly & Chao, 1982) have found low correlations between references and job performance.

A second problem related to references and letters of recommendation is the reluctance of many employers to give information that might be considered harmful to an applicant. **Defamation** occurs when an employer makes a false statement that is injurious to the former employee. In one case, when an employer who was asked for a reference described a former employee as irrational and ruthless, a jury awarded the employee more than $2.5 million in damages (Martin & Bartol, 1987).

Not surprisingly, some employers fear their references or letters could lead to legal challenge, so they decline to give any opinion on employee performance. In recent years, however, many states have passed laws that grant employers immunity from lawsuits when they provide performance information to prospective employers. However, employers may not disclose information that violates the civil rights of the employee (Meindertsma, 1996).

One important use of references and letters of recommendation is to avoid charges of negligent hiring. **Negligent hiring** refers to a situation in which an employer knowingly puts an employee into a situation where that employee may harm a third person (Ryan & Lasek, 1991). In *Maloney v. B&L Motor Freight, Inc.* (1986), for example, a company was sued when one of its truck drivers picked up a hitchhiker and then raped her. Although the employer did not know that the driver had a history of raping hitchhikers, the court found B&L Motor Freight guilty of negligent hiring because of the company's superficial investigation of the applicant's background.

For references or letters of recommendation to be useful, the evaluator needs to determine how well and for how long the reference has known the applicant, the nature of their relationship (e.g., friend, boss, relative), and the work that was performed in the previous position. In one study of letters of recommendation, Knouse (1983) found that personnel directors tended to rate letters that mention specific examples of performance more favorably than those containing more general comments. "Increased sales volume 30 percent," for example, is more favorably regarded than "hardworking, persevering, and efficient."

If references are candid and knowledgeable, they can be a valuable source of information about an individual. Still, decisions made on the basis of references must also meet the standards for validity and fairness, and there has been some litigation regarding reference checks.

Overall, given the constraints of making decisions on the basis of references, this approach does not seem to be a particularly useful method for selecting employees. On the other hand, the threat of being charged with negligent hiring probably necessitates continued use of references and letters of recommendation for making hiring decisions.

Preemployment Drug Testing

As the use of illicit drugs became more prevalent during the 1980s, many employers instituted a drug test as the last step before hiring. Employee drug use is an important issue because drug usage can diminish performance and lead to accidents and theft. In one study (Parish, 1989), for example, employees who had tested positive for drug use at the time of hiring had a 28 percent higher turnover rate and a 64 percent higher rate of disciplinary warnings compared to employees who had not tested positive at hiring. In another study (Winkler & Sheridan, 1989), employees who tested positive for drugs used more medical benefits, were absent more often, and had more automobile accidents than employees who had tested negative.

One group of researchers (Stein, Smith, Guy, & Bentler, 1993) looked at the relationship between adolescent drug use and job performance and satisfaction later in life. In this study, high school students in the Boston area completed questionnaires about drug use. Ten years later, the former students were contacted and asked to complete questionnaires about their current situation. Several interesting findings emerged from this study. First, adolescent drug use did not predict adult drug use, nor did it predict later job behaviors or satisfaction. However, participants who had continued drug use into adulthood had more problems and less satisfaction with their jobs. Adults who used several drugs—alcohol, marijuana, cocaine, and hard drugs such as LSD, heroin, and PCP—had more problems at work and more terminations.

Drug testing of job incumbents is a controversial area that has had many legal challenges, but few cases have challenged the right of an employer to test for drugs before making a job offer. Today most Fortune 500 companies test applicants for drugs before making an employment offer. Although the need for such programs may be obvious to employers, they can have a negative impact on applicant attitudes toward recruitment. One study (Crant & Bateman, 1990), for example, found that college students were more likely to have a negative attitude toward companies with preemployment drug screening programs.

Another laboratory study (Rosse, Ringer, & Miller, 1996) found that job applicants who were required to take an integrity test or a urinalysis were significantly less satisfied than those who had no drug screening. Interestingly, participants in the study objected more to completing personality measures than to a urinalysis. Finally, another study (Rosse, Miller, & Ringer, 1996) found that drug users had more negative reactions than nonusers to either paper-and-pencil measures of drug use or urinalysis.

Given the dangers created by the use of illicit drugs in the workplace, however, it is unlikely that applicant reactions will cause employers to scale back their drug-testing programs any time soon. Because the use of illicit drugs affects many aspects of the psychology of work, this topic is covered in more detail in Chapter 15.

Chapter Summary

Personnel recruitment and selection are two of the most important functions within any organization, particularly because of the high costs associated with poor hiring procedures.

Employers must be certain that the procedures they use to select employees lead to accurate predictions about job performance. Otherwise, they may hire applicants whose performances will be disappointing and reject applicants who can do the work successfully. Additionally, employers must be certain that the predictors they use are fair. Fairness is a concept that has been defined through legislation and by the courts. Proper use of valid and fair selection procedures has improved the efficiency of many organizations and also has increased job opportunities for groups that have traditionally been excluded from certain occupations.

Before the recruitment and selection process begins, employers should have a clear understanding of the requirements of the job under consideration. Industrial and organizational psychologists have developed a number of methods for analyzing jobs, and courts have set standards for proper job analysis.

The basic steps in the employee selection process include recruitment, application, interview, testing, and reference check. Recruitment sources vary in their effectiveness, particularly with regard to employee tenure. An important aspect of recruitment, however, is the performance of the recruiter. Giving applicants realistic information about jobs seems to reduce turnover. Application blanks can be a good source of information for making hiring decisions. Employers must be careful about the questions they ask, however.

Biodata are used in some applications; they ask questions about aspects of the personal life of the applicant that are related to performance on the job.

Interviews, the area of greatest research, are often unreliable and invalid in selecting the best employees. Interviewers are likely to use stereotypes in making decisions; focus on negative, rather than positive, information; make quick decisions; and allow the race of applicants to influence decisions. Evidence suggests that a valid employment screening test easily outperforms interviewers in identifying good candidates.

Generally speaking, interviews can be classified as one of four types: traditional, structured, semistructured, and stress. Professional interviewers tend to avoid the stress technique, preferring to develop rapport to gather information about applicants. Although researchers have been critical of the validity of employment interviews in predicting job performance, newer studies suggest that structured interviews can be as useful as employment testing.

Recent research has suggested some ways in which interviews might be improved. Some newer approaches include behavior descriptions in interviews and computerized interviews.

Overall, relying on information provided by references or letters of recommendation seems to be a poor method for selecting employees. Employers will probably continue to use these methods of screening, however, in an effort to avoid negligent hiring.

The final step in employment screening is often a drug test, since research suggests that employees who use drugs are less productive than those who do not.

Key Words and Concepts

adverse impact (p. 61)

affirmative action (p. 66)

behavior description (p. 87)

biodata (p. 77)

biographical inventory (p. 77)

bona fide occupational
   qualification (BFOQ) (p. 76)

Civil Rights Act of 1964 (p. 60)

Civil Rights Act of 1991 (p. 61)

computerized interview (p. 88)

criterion (p. 59)

defamation (p. 88)

disparity studies (p. 66)

Equal Employment Opportunity
   Commission (EEOC) (p. 61)

job analysis (p. 67)

job description (p. 72)

job evaluation (p. 67)

job specifications (p. 72)

negligent hiring (p. 89)

predictor (p. 59)

realistic job preview (RJP) (p. 74)

realistic recruitment (p. 74)

recruitment (p. 72)

reverse discrimination (p. 66)

selection ratio (p. 61)

semistructured interview (p. 85)

stress interview (p. 86)

structured interview (p. 84)

subgroup norming (p. 65)

Title VII (p. 60)

traditional interview (p. 84)

weighted application blank
   (p. 76)

Questions for Discussion

1. What are the predictors and the criterion in your industrial/organizational psychology class? Do you feel the predictors are valid? Do you feel they are fair?

2. What are the major differences between the Civil Rights Acts of 1964 and 1991?

3. What are the arguments for and against affirmative action? What is your opinion on this issue?

4. How would you design a recruitment program that would appeal to college students and also result in hiring the best employees?

5. In your opinion, what kind of biodata items might predict success as a lawyer? a college professor? an automobile salesperson?

6. What are some of the problems with employment interviews? How can interviews be improved?

7. What is your opinion of preemployment drug testing?

CHAPTER 4

Assessing the Abilities of Personnel

A Brief History of Employment Testing

Predicting Performance from Employment Testing

Determining the Usefulness of Improved Selection Procedures

Types of Employment Testing

New Approaches to Employment Testing

Chapter Summary

Key Words and Concepts

Questions for Discussion

At some point during the recruitment, application, interview, and reference check process, applicants are often asked to take an employment test. Of all methods of personnel selection, employment testing has historically been the most controversial. Applicants may object to personality measures as being an invasion of privacy, minority candidates may believe that tests of cognitive ability are biased against them, and employers may be uncertain that test results actually predict job performance. Despite these misgivings, measures of ambition, intelligence, manual dexterity, and other factors have been routinely administered to applicants for all types of jobs for decades. Some people have even written books and articles about "outsmarting" employment tests.

The establishment of federal standards for employee selection, discussed in Chapter 3, affected all selection procedures, but they had a particularly profound impact on employment testing. In 1972, the Equal Employment Opportunity Commission (EEOC) was given power to prosecute employers who did not comply with the federal standards. In one of its most famous actions, the EEOC filed suit against AT&T, alleging that unfair selection procedures were resulting in underrepresentation of women in outdoor craft jobs, and of men in clerical and operator positions. The suit was settled out of court, with AT&T agreeing to pay $15 million to 15,000 women and minority male employees for past discrimination in hiring and promotion practices. The company also agreed to pay

Box 4.1 THE BUSINESS OF EXECUTIVE SELECTION

During the 1990s, more and more firms developed special test procedures—or hired a firm that specialized in developing such procedures—for selecting executives. One reason behind this renewed interest in testing is the poor track record of traditional methods of selection. In many industries, a failure rate of 35 percent of senior executives is considered normal. Considering the cost of hiring a senior manager can easily go over $100,000, failure rates this large are unacceptable.

Another factor in testing's new popularity is problems with the employment interview mentioned in Chapter 3. Many candidates now read books and study videotapes to improve interview performance, and many interviewers make the common mistake of choosing someone they like over someone more competent. Although structured interviews can be useful in predicting performance, duties at the executive level are often unclear, making structured interviews less useful.

Typical areas covered by executive testing include communication, analysis and organization, attention to detail, management style, motivation, and personality. Testing can be entirely paper-and-pencil (or computer), or it can include interviews and activities such as assessment centers (described below). Costs for testing range from about $300 at the most basic level up to $4,000 or more. Although executive testing is not inexpensive, many employers now feel that the results of testing justify its cost.

Source: Dobrzynski, J. H. (1996, September 2). Executive tests now plumb new depths of the job seeker. *The New York Times,* p. A1.

$23 million per year in salary increases to women and minority workers who had been moved to higher paying jobs without being credited for seniority.

The AT&T case demonstrated to employers the high costs of using poor predictors. After 1972, some employers abandoned their testing programs out of fear of prosecution. In such cases, employers were willing to sacrifice the effectiveness of their selection procedures to avoid lawsuits. On the other hand, other employers that had been using carefully developed and validated selection tests, such as Sears, Exxon, and DuPont, rarely abandoned them.

Today, after countless studies of the effectiveness of personnel selection procedures, meta-analyses of existing research, and reexaminations of results from testing, it is clear that valid and reliable employment tests can be used to predict employee performance. Employment decisions based on test results are often more accurate than those based on applications, interviews, references, or letters of recommendation. Despite the earlier controversies, personnel testing became popular again in the 1980s and is enjoying something of a boom in the 1990s. Box 4.1 describes the current interest in testing applicants for managerial positions.

Of course, accepted scientific procedures for development and administration must be followed for an employment test to be useful. This chapter continues the discussion begun in Chapter 3 and looks at some of the issues surrounding psychological testing for employee selection and the types of tests employers use to screen applicants.

A Brief History of Employment Testing

Although psychological testing had been used for many years, the personnel selection program developed by the Office of Strategic Services (OSS) during
World War II was probably the major source of its popularity. In 1942, the
president and Congress had authorized the establishment of the OSS for the
purpose of recruiting secret agents to gather information about the enemy and
engage in destructive activities behind enemy lines.

During its first year of operation, the OSS—the forerunner of the Central
Intelligence Agency (CIA)—selected agents without the benefit of any professional screening process. As it became apparent that many of these recruits
could not handle the pressure of clandestine activity, the OSS responded by instituting a three-day psychological screening program for potential agents.

Some of the methods and instruments used by the OSS to predict an individual's performance as a spy and saboteur included the Personal History Form
(a detailed application blank); a measure of mental ability; a sentence-comple-
tion test; a health questionnaire; a vocabulary test (as a measure of intelligence);
a map-reading test; leaderless problem-solving activities; and tests of propa-
ganda skills, observation and memory, mechanical comprehension, and teaching skills. During the screening, the psychologists and psychiatrists carefully observed the recruits in a variety of settings, making judgments about such
qualities as emotional stability, anxiety level, and sociability.

The OSS screening program was one of the first scientific efforts to develop
measures for selecting individuals for jobs, and its success was a major factor in
the widespread adoption of employment testing in industry after World War II.
AT&T, for example, developed a selection procedure to identify executives
based on the "realistic" approach of the OSS program. AT&T's assessment
center screening technique, described in more detail below, became one of the
most widely emulated personnel selection procedures.

Interestingly, the original impetus for establishing the OSS personnel selection procedures was the British program introduced during World War I,
which, in turn, had been developed from the work of German military psychologists. In 1917, the U.S. Army had instituted the Army Alpha and Beta intelligence tests to screen recruits, and in 1921, James McKeen Cattell had organized the Psychological Corporation, which became a major publisher of
psychological tests. During the 1930s and 1940s, tests such as the Thurstone
Personality Scale and the Allport Ascendance-Submission Test were used to
identify "cooperative" employees (Hogan, Carpenter, Briggs, & Hansson,
1984). Despite their decline in popularity during the 1960s and 1970s, employment tests, and particularly measures of cognitive abilities and skills, became increasingly popular in the 1980s. During the 1990s, employers also
showed a renewed interest in personality assessment—particularly in measuring
how such qualities as honesty and conscientiousness relate to job performance.

As suggested above, valid and reliable employment tests are, in most cases, better predictors of performance than applications, interviews, references, or letters of recommendation. Research now suggests that these alternative procedures usually do not predict performance as well, are no less vulnerable to charges of unfair discrimination, and can result in other problems for employers. When General Electric dropped its aptitude testing program in the 1960s, for example, many individuals were subsequently hired who simply were not promotable. As a result, GE soon experienced a shortage of individuals qualified for management positions (Schmidt & Hunter, 1981).

Predicting Performance from Employment Testing

Establishing the Reliability
    of a Selection Procedure
Establishing the Validity of
    a Selection Procedure
Additional Approaches to
    Validity
Score Banding

Effective personnel decisions are usually based on accurate predictors, and accuracy is determined by demonstrating both the reliability and the validity of a predictor. Recall from Chapter 2 that reliability is a measure of how consistent scores on a predictor are, and validity concerns the relationship between the predictor and the criterion. The different approaches to establishing the reliability and validity of a selection procedure are discussed below.

Establishing the Reliability of a Selection Procedure

A predictor such as an employment test is said to be reliable if it is consistent in measurement. That is, applicants who take the test at one time are likely to achieve similar results in future administrations of the test. In addition, measures must be reliable in order to be valid.

Tests that are not reliable are obviously of little use to an employer. If, for example, a candidate for an accounting position scored well on the first administration of an accounting aptitude test, but poorly on the second, the employer would have difficulty predicting future job performance. A judgment about future performance based on either test result might be incorrect.

There are several ways to determine the **reliability** of a measure. The most direct method is **test-retest.** In this approach, a test is administered to a group of individuals twice, usually not within less than a two-week period. Scores from the first administration are correlated with scores from the second administration. The resulting coefficient is considered an estimate of reliability, and the higher the correlation between the two sets of scores, the more reliable the test.

There are some problems associated with establishing reliability through the test-retest method, however. First, results on the second administration are likely to be affected by material the employee has learned or remembered between administrations. Additionally, if the period between administrations is too long, the size of the group at the second administration is likely to be smaller. As is the case with all statistical procedures, it is harder to achieve significant results with small samples. Finally, on a purely practical note, an employer may regard assembling a group for the second administration of a measure too costly or time-consuming.

Another approach to measuring the reliability of an employment test is the **equivalent forms** method. Equivalent forms of a test are developed by assembling a large pool of questions, then randomly dividing the questions into two tests. Both tests are assumed to measure the same skills or qualities, and applicants are required to take both forms. Candidates for pharmacist's assistant positions, for example, would be required first to take Form A of a Knowledge of Pharmacology Test, then to take Form B sometime later. If scores on the two tests have a significant positive correlation, the employer can then assume that the tests are comparable, and that each test is reliable. Although the equivalent forms method is highly regarded by psychologists, sometimes the burden of creating and administering two forms precludes use of this method.

A third approach to estimating reliability is **internal consistency.** Internal consistency assumes that for each applicant, performance on each test item will be consistent with performance on every other item. Responses to items are correlated with each other, and an average intercorrelation is determined. This average is then adjusted according to the total number of items on the test. The resulting coefficient is an estimate of the test's reliability. For a perfectly reliable test, performance on one item would allow the employer to predict performance on every other item. Internal consistency is based on the assumption that test items are homogeneous—that is, all items measure the same concept.

Split-half reliability is another form of internal consistency. In this approach, test results for each individual are divided into two equal parts. Each part is then scored as if it were a separate test, and a correlation is calculated for the two sets of scores for each individual. If the correlation coefficient is significant, then it can be assumed that the test is reliable. Both forms of internal consistency are affected by the number of items on the measure, with more items increasing the likelihood of establishing reliability.

The methods for establishing reliability are summarized in Table 4.1.

Establishing the Validity of a Selection Procedure

As suggested previously, validity relates to the appropriateness of a predictor. In general, **validity** refers to the accuracy of a test in measuring what it is supposed to measure. A test designed to measure ambition, for example, would be considered valid if items on the test were related to the psychological characteristic of ambition. A question about an applicant's level of aspiration, for example, is more likely to be related to ambition than a question about the applicant's age.

For many years researchers accepted the premise that the validity of a measure was one of three types: criterion-related, which consists of the subtypes predictive and concurrent; content; or construct. Demonstrating these four basic

Table 4.1   METHODS FOR ESTABLISHING THE RELIABILITY OF A MEASURE

	Procedure	Considerations
Test-Retest	Results from one administration of a measure are correlated with results from a second administration some time later	Results may be affected by practice or by memory
Equivalent forms	Two versions of a measure are developed and administered to the same persons; results from the two measures are then correlated	Results may be affected by practice or by memory; comparability of measures may be difficult to determine
Internal consistency	Performance on each item of a measure is examined to determine consistency in response between items	Reliability coefficient will be lowered if items are not homogeneous; measure length will also affect reliability
Split-Half	A measure is split into two parts and results from each part are correlated to obtain a reliability coefficient	Reliability coefficients will be affected by the length of the measure

kinds of validity required different research strategies, and employers were required to use the strategy most appropriate for their work setting. When the federal government established its guidelines on employee selection, it recognized only these four ways of demonstrating the accuracy and fairness of a predictor.

Increasingly, however, psychologists have questioned the traditional approaches to establishing the validity of a predictor. This questioning has focused on two areas. First, in the federal guidelines for selection, and in many textbooks and journal articles, validity is discussed in terms of which "type" it is. In fact, focusing on the type of validity may be misleading. Criterion-related, content, and construct actually are not *types* of validity, but merely *strategies* for determining validity. Validity itself is a unitary concept.

Second, although federal guidelines for establishing the validity of a predictor consider these three approaches equally useful, more recent thinking suggests that each of these kinds of validation strategies demonstrates something different (Landy, 1986). Characteristics of the individual strategies are discussed below.

Criterion-Related Validity **Criterion-related validity** compares applicant scores on a predictive measure with some other criterion score of job performance. For example, to determine the validity of using an accounting test to make hiring decisions, an employer would correlate scores on the test with supervisory ratings of accountants' job performances. As pointed out earlier, there are two approaches to determining criterion-related validity: concurrent and predictive.

An employer using the **concurrent validity** approach administers some measures or tests to employees already working for the company. From these results, the employer identifies the qualities or abilities found in the best employees and uses these as a basis for designing a selection procedure for job applicants. A software firm, for example, may find that the best programmers score high on a measure of deductive reasoning. Using this information, employers might require job applicants to take a test of deductive reasoning and then base their hiring decisions, at least in part, on deductive reasoning score.

In most cases, the concurrent validity approach is relatively easy to accomplish—employers simply correlate scores on a predictor with some criterion measure of job performance. However, there are some problems associated with this method. One problem, for example, is that using job incumbents to set standards for applicants may result in hiring standards that are too high. Incumbents probably developed skills on the job that applicants will not have. For example, some research (Duesbury & O'Neil, 1996) suggests that scores on spatial ability measures can be improved by training on computer-aided design software. Because of this, comparing scores on spatial ability between job incumbents and applicants may result in the rejection of candidates with good potential.

A second problem with concurrent validity is that individuals who are superior employees are likely to have moved on to better jobs, and those who are inferior may have been terminated. The workers who are left do not constitute a random sample, and setting hiring standards based on their skill levels may lead to poor decisions. Shrinkage in the pool of job incumbents would result in a **restriction in range,** which refers to the loss of subjects at the extreme high and low levels of performance. Although there are procedures for correcting for restriction in range, these procedures are rarely applied, or sometimes are applied improperly (Hoffman, 1995; Sackett & Ostgaard, 1994). Additionally, employees previously hired may have been selected under biased conditions, and therefore may not be representative of the applicant pool as a whole.

Finally, people who already hold jobs may not respond to employment testing in the same way as those who are trying to be hired. Job incumbents may be less concerned with making a favorable impression, they may know what answers the company is looking for, or they may not be motivated to try their best, since they have already been hired. In a study of highway maintenance workers (Arvey, Strickland, Drauden, & Martin, 1990), for example, applicants for the job scored significantly higher than incumbents on a measure of motivation.

Overall, the problem with the concurrent validity approach is that job applicants and job incumbents are not necessarily comparable groups. From a scientific viewpoint, this greatly limits the usefulness of a concurrent validation strategy. Consequently, many researchers prefer to use a predictive validity strategy that avoids comparison between applicants and incumbents.

Under the **predictive validity** strategy, an employer requires applicants to complete a measure whose scores the employer feels will be predictive of job performance. However, actual hiring decisions are not based on this measure, but rather on whatever selection procedures the employer already has in place.

Some time later—6 months or a year, perhaps—some rating of employee performance is correlated with test results to determine what qualities identify the best and worst performers. This information is then used to set the standards for hiring future employees.

Although the predictive validity approach avoids unfair comparisons, it also has some limitations. For example, a predictive strategy takes considerably longer to implement than a concurrent strategy. Particularly as the pace of organizational change accelerates, it would not be unusual if job content changed during the period between administration and validation of test procedures. If this occurs, then results of the study would be open to question.

Another problem with predictive validity is that many employers are unwilling to pay someone to administer employment tests that cannot immediately be used in hiring decisions.

Finally, despite the shortcomings of the concurrent validity approach, some researchers have argued that this much easier method works as well as predictive validity (Barrett, Phillips, & Alexander, 1981; Schmitt, Gooding, Noe, & Kirsch, 1984). On the other hand, other researchers have suggested that selecting a validation strategy on the basis of what "works" is not scientifically appropriate. They argue that selection of a validation strategy should be based on proper understanding of the question to be answered or the hypothesis to be tested (Guion & Cranny, 1982; Landy, 1986).

Content Validity   The **content validity** method of validating a selection procedure relies on a measure that contains representative elements of the job in question; that is, applicants are tested on their abilities to perform tasks that are actually part of the job. For example, measuring knowledge of plants is probably a valid approach for predicting the performance of a botanist. Similarly, a test of driving skills—rather than ability to read aloud from the works of Shakespeare—is probably content valid for assessing performance as a truck driver.

Content validity has the advantage of focusing directly on skills necessary to perform a job. This approach does not require a waiting period, and the relationship between the predictor and job performance is usually easier to demonstrate than in other validation methods.

A content validity strategy requires a job analysis to be certain that the skills being tested for the predictor are actually relevant to successful job performance. A standard of scoring 50 words per minute on a word processing test, for example, may not be valid for predicting performance if the job consists mostly of producing graphs or charts. In an important case centered around content validity for a selection procedure (*Kirkland v. New York Department of Correctional Service,* 1974) the court ruled that a proper job analysis is critical to developing content valid selection procedures.

Despite the fact that content validity often appears to be the most direct approach to demonstrating the job-relatedness of employment testing, designing measures based on content validity is not always practical. Developing a selection device that sampled all the elements of the job of general practice physician, for example, would probably be impossible.

Other standards for developing a selection procedure based on content validity established in *Kirkland* include the following: (1) material on the selection examination must be directly related to the job; (2) material must be weighted to reflect its importance in job performance; and (3) the difficulty of the examination must match the difficulty of the job in question.

In addition to these requirements, tests based on content validity will probably lead to better decisions if they are administered in an atmosphere similar to that in which the work is performed, and individuals taking the tests have a high degree of response freedom. In other words, applicants should have more than the three or four possible responses typically found on a multiple-choice test. In this way, test content will more accurately reflect the actual job conditions (Dreher & Sackett, 1981).

Content validity may also be less valid as a predictor of *future* performance, since it measures performance at the time of testing. Because most employment tests are designed to *predict* which applicants will do well, a content validity approach is not appropriate in situations in which new employees will undergo a training program.

Construct Validity **Construct validity** refers to the identification of a hypothetical concept—as opposed to an observable behavior—considered relevant to job success. In *Myart v. Motorola* (1963), for example, the employer considered intelligence relevant to performance as a television phaser. In the example of the computer programmers cited above, deductive reasoning was a construct believed to be related to job performance. Some other typical constructs employment tests measure include honesty, leadership, mechanical ability, mathematical skills, and visual acuity.

Suppose an employer wants to determine the validity of a newly developed Inventory of Managerial Potential. To do this, the employer needs to know the correlation between scores on the inventory and scores on other measures relevant to successful performance as a manager. These other measures may include communication skill, ability to organize and delegate, budgeting skill, and so forth. If test scores significantly correlate with scores on these other measures, then the employer has validity evidence for the existence of the construct "managerial potential." If the managerial potential inventory measures the necessary standards for predicting performance, then it could be a useful selection device.

Construct validity is the most theoretical of the approaches to validating selection procedures, and it is sometimes considered the most difficult to use because the selection procedure measures a hypothetical construct rather than an actual job-related behavior. Researchers need to be particularly careful with regard to the scientific properties of the other instruments they use to establish the construct validity of a measure.

Nevertheless, most researchers have now adopted the position that all strategies for demonstrating validity are actually demonstrating construct validity (Messick, 1995). For example, although content validation relies on observation of test performance relevant to job performance, test performance is really only a strategy for inferring the existence of some construct. A word processing test may be considered content valid for the job of secretary, but in actuality, the test is simply a means of making a judgment about the construct of "secretarial ability." Similarly, criterion-related validation requires observation or measurement of a construct previously observed or measured in a criterion group.

Theoretically, results from a study based on construct validity should be similar to results based on other validity strategies. Although few researchers have compared the approaches to validity, Carrier, D'Alessio, and Brown (1990) obtained criterion-related values on 300 items in a structured interview guide used to select life insurance agents, then asked supervisors to rate the items in terms of their content validity. The researchers found no significant differences between the criterion-related and content approaches to establishing validity.

Validity and Construct Equivalence. Once an employment test has been validated, employers are likely to use the test as long as they believe it identifies good employees. Over time, however, the validity of a test may decline. Changes in the workforce and increased knowledge about test contents may make measures less useful for predicting performance. Some researchers have proposed a strategy for dealing with these problems based on construct equivalence.

Construct equivalence (Turban, Sanders, Francis, & Osburn, 1989) refers to administering experimental tests at the same time that applicants are taking tests that have already been validated. Results from the experimental tests are not used for hiring decisions, but are compared to the other results to develop newer tests. The basic idea of construct equivalence is that the experimental tests measure the same construct as the previously validated tests. In this way, employers can update their selection inventories regularly so that validity of their measures is maintained over longer periods of time.

Table 4.2 summarizes some of the considerations about the different types of validation strategies.

Validity Generalization and Situational Specificity

Sometimes researchers evaluate their selection procedures using **validity generalization,** a form of meta-analysis (see Chapter 2) that analyzes results from studies that used the same or very similar predictors (James, Demaree, Mulaik, & Ladd, 1992). When the correlation coefficient between employment test scores and job performance ratings is not significant, for example, validity generalization may be used to see if the coefficient is being affected by a small sample size.

For many years, some people argued that employment tests were not useful in predicting job performance because the size of the correlation between test score and performance was often low. After reviewing the validity coefficients of hundreds of selection procedures, Ghiselli (1966) concluded that the validity of selection procedures in predicting performance was largely situational. In other words, due to factors unique to each testing situation—number of tests administered, small samples, unreliable tests or criteria, and so forth—scores on a measure such as the Inventory of Managerial Potential mentioned above might lead to valid prediction of performance in one setting but not in another.

Table 4.2 ADVANTAGES AND LIMITATIONS OF STRATEGIES USED TO DETERMINE THE VALIDITY OF A MEASURE

	Procedure	Advantages/Limitations
Criterion-related	Scores on a measure are compared with some criterion of job performance	
	Concurrent validity requires comparing the scores of one group to those of individuals for whom criterion data already exist	Easy to accomplish but relies on comparisons of dissimilar groups; may not meet scientific standards for establishing validity
	Predictive validity requires comparing the scores of one group with criterion data collected at a later date	Avoids unfair comparisons and meets scientific and legal standards; longer period for establishing validity may result in misleading findings
Content	The measure contains elements that will actually be performed on the job; validity is established by correlating test scores with some measure of job performance	Avoids a lengthy waiting period for validation of a psychological construct; job-relatedness is usually obvious; may require a job analysis; some jobs are too complex to be sampled adequately
Construct	Scores on a measure of a hypothetical construct are correlated with scores on other measures whose validity has already been established	Development of measure may be easy; requires solid understanding of psychometrics and test construction in order to meet scientific standards

According to this view, measures have **situational specificity,** and each employer who wishes to use such a test needs to do his or her own validity study, rather than rely on those done in other settings.

In 1977, Schmidt and Hunter proposed that the low validity coefficients reviewed by Ghiselli in different employment settings were actually due to statistical rather than situational factors. Specifically, in most of the studies reviewed by Ghiselli, the sample size was so small that it was improbable that the correlation between test performance and job performance would reach statistical significance. Consequently, validity of the predictor could not be demonstrated. If, on the other hand, sample size could be increased by combining test results from different settings, then the significance of the validity coefficient for an employment test could more easily be demonstrated.

Consider, for example, the Inventory of Managerial Potential. Suppose five employers who are using it to predict performance find validity coefficients in the .20 to .30 range. Although such values are likely to be insignificant if sample sizes are small, the coefficient is more likely to be significant if the five samples are combined. Significant results would suggest that the test is a valid predictor of performance.

Validity generalization has been defined as the degree to which inferences from test scores can be transported across different situations (Burke, 1984). Considerable evidence has now accumulated supporting the idea that the validity of employment testing in predicting job performance can be generalized across situations (Schmidt, Hunter, Outerbridge, & Trattner, 1986; Schmidt, Law, Hunter, Rothstein, Pearlman, & McDaniel, 1993; Schmidt, Pearlman, Hunter, & Hirsch, 1985). In a review of different studies of cognitive aptitude tests, for example, Schmidt and Hunter (1981) concluded that "the situational specificity hypothesis is false and that validity generalization is always possible."

Despite the promise of validity generalization, however, there are still some concerns about the method. An obvious concern when using results from several studies is the quality of the research being combined. Researchers using studies done by others are unlikely to be able to correct for mistakes in data coding or biased reporting of results by the original authors. When the data used for the validity generalization study are flawed, the results are questionable. Also, procedures for performing validity generalization analyses require a number of judgment calls by researchers that may affect findings (Russell, Settoon, McGrath, Blanton, Kidwell, Lohrke, Scifres, & Danforth, 1994).

Despite these concerns, many psychologists and employers now rely on validity generalization to demonstrate the usefulness of employment testing.

Additional Approaches to Validity

In addition to those discussed above, two other forms of validity often considered relevant to the personnel selection process are face validity and synthetic validity.

Face Validity   **Face validity** refers to the apparent validity of a measure. For example, response to a question about the difference between a gallon and a liter may appear to be validly related to performance as a gas station attendant, but in fact, it may or may not be. Similarly, some questions on the U.S. State Department's examination for foreign service officer candidates ask about architecture and ballet. Although these items do not have face validity—that is, they do not appear to relate to performance as a visa officer, for example—they are believed to relate to overall performance in the diplomatic corps. Face validity alone is obviously an unacceptable basis for establishing the relationship between an employment test and job performance.

Interestingly, a lack of face validity in an employment test can sometimes lead to problems for employers. When job candidates feel they are being asked questions that are irrelevant to the job for which they are applying, they may challenge the testing procedure. Although the employer may demonstrate the validity of the seemingly irrelevant questions, the employer will nevertheless have the burden of responding to legal challenge. In *Soroka v. Dayton Hudson* (1991), for example, job applicants who had applied for positions as security guards claimed that questions about their religious beliefs and sexual preferences on a preemployment psychological test were an invasion of their privacy. Although such questions are an accepted part of many similar tests, the court found in favor of the applicants.

Although face validity has not been widely studied, some research suggests it can affect an applicant's perceptions of an organization. One study (Macan, Avedon, Paese, & Smith, 1994), for example, compared applicants' reactions to two selection procedures—tests of cognitive ability and an assessment center (discussed below). Although applicants reacted favorably to both methods, they felt the assessment center was more face valid than the cognitive tests. Applicants who had more favorable views of the selection procedures were more satisfied with the selection process, the job, and the organization as a whole.

Another study (Steiner & Gilliland, 1996) found that college students—potential job applicants—in France and the United States expressed favorable reactions to selection decisions based on interviews, work-sample tests, and resumes rather than ability tests or personality measures. Finally, one group of researchers (Smither, Reilly, Millsap, Pearlman, & Stoffey, 1993) found newly hired managers felt that simulations, interviews, and measures of vocabulary and math were more job-related than personality, biodata, or cognitive ability tests that contained abstract items. Results from both of these studies suggest that, irrespective of validity, the type of selection procedures companies use can affect the attractiveness of an organization and may indirectly impact recruitment.

Synthetic Validity **Synthetic validity** is a technique developed to deal with the problem of small sample sizes (Lawshe, 1952; McCormick, 1959; Primoff, 1955). Because statistical significance is less likely to be found in small groups, a researcher may have difficulty demonstrating the validity of a selection procedure for a job with relatively few applicants. The synthetic validity approach aggregates valid predictors into one larger instrument.

Using this approach, researchers first look at a number of jobs that contain elements of the job they are studying. Each component relevant to predicting performance of the job under review is validated. The researcher then assembles the results to determine what constitutes the best predictor for each part of the job being studied. The two most common approaches to synthetic validity are the J-coefficient and the Job Components Model (Mossholder & Arvey, 1984). In essence, both of these methods compare aspects of the job in question to aspects of similar jobs found in other settings.

Suppose, for example, a personnel psychologist wanted to develop a valid procedure for selecting retail clerks. With only a small group of clerks to study, developing a specific selection procedure and performing a validity study would not be cost effective. The psychologist therefore selects the elements of the retail clerk job that are the most important—sociability, mathematical aptitude, and honesty, for example—and looks at procedures used for selecting other employees in different positions that require the same skills or characteristics. Since those procedures are known to be valid, the psychologist adapts them into a package used to select retail clerks.

Although synthetic validity may be useful to an employer, it is important to note that federal law does not recognize this approach as sufficient to demonstrate the fairness or effectiveness of a selection procedure.

Score Banding

Sometimes selection test scores will be shown to be valid predictors of performance, but the mean scores differ between groups of applicants. For example, a welding test may be useful in predicting job performance, but the mean test score of White males may be consistently higher than the mean scores of females and minorities. If the employer selected only applicants who scored highest on the test and rejected those who scored lower, then females and minorities would probably be underrepresented in the workforce. In this case, if the employer rejects females and minorities who probably can do the job successfully, the employer may be accused of discriminating unfairly because of **test bias.**

In many cases, differences in test scores between two groups may be much larger than differences in job performance. If test score is used as the ultimate criterion for selection—as illustrated in Figure 4.1—majority candidates will be selected at a greater rate than minority candidates, resulting in adverse impact. Over the years, some alternative strategies for handling this kind of situation have been developed (Cascio, Outtz, Zedeck, & Goldstein, 1991; Murphy, 1994). Although subgroup norming (Chapter 3) is one method for dealing with this problem, the Civil Rights Act of 1991 forbade that practice.

Currently, many researchers are interested in a procedure known as score banding. **Score banding** refers to considering all scores that fall within a certain range equal. That is, because differences between scores within a range are insignificant, performance differences are also likely to be insignificant. For example, a measure with a possible 100 points might be divided into bands of eight points. Individuals who score from 93 to 100 would be treated equally, and employers would select employees from this band until it is depleted. In this way, sex or race differences would be ignored.

Banding is not without critics. In the example above, differences between 93 and 100 are considered insignificant, whereas the difference between 92 and 93, a much smaller range, is significant (Schmidt, 1991). Other criticisms are that the appeal of banding is based in politics rather than science, and that banding creates substantial restriction in range between candidates within a band (Kriska, 1995; Schmidt & Hunter, 1995). Nonetheless, some researchers feel banding is a viable method for avoiding adverse impact, and in *Officers for Justice v. Civil Rights Commission* (1992), the Ninth Circuit Court of Appeals upheld banding as an acceptable method for selecting police officers in San Francisco.

As suggested earlier, researchers have now accumulated considerable evidence that scientifically developed employment tests are not differentially valid. In other words, workers who score high on a valid test usually perform at a

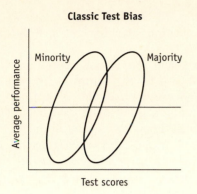

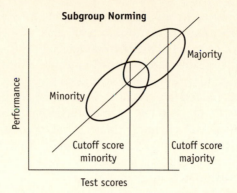

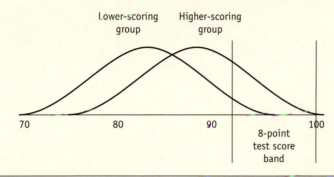

Figure 4.1 Test Bias and Score Banding
Classic test bias occurs when groups perform equally well on the job but one group scores higher than the other on an employment test. Subgroup norming occurs when one group scores higher than another on an employment test and different cutoff scores for hiring are set. In score banding, all scores are combined and segmented into bands. Scores within a band are considered equal.

higher level than individuals who score lower—regardless of race, sex, or ethnic group (Maxwell & Arvey, 1993). Given the substantial body of supportive research, the usefulness of scientifically developed employment tests now seems incontrovertible.

Determining the Usefulness of Improved Selection Procedures

Taylor-Russell Model
Other Utility Models

From the foregoing discussion of reliability and validity, it should be apparent that personnel selection can be a very expensive operation. If the people making a selection decision make a mistake that results in hiring an unsuccessful employee or the employee's leaving after training, the organization suffers a tremendous cost. Additionally, unless an organization keeps careful records, such costs are likely to go undetected.

Research shows that even a modest improvement in selection procedures can result in surprising savings to an organization. In a study comparing selection procedures for hiring school principals (Hogan, Zenke, & Thompson, 1985), for example, researchers found that using a more valid assessment center-type approach rather than the traditional interview saved $58,672. Other researchers (Schmidt, Hunter, McKenzie, & Muldrow, 1979) estimated that if the validity coefficient for the federal government's selection procedure for computer programmers were .30, and 20 percent of the applicants were hired, the government could save about $64,725 per applicant.

Utility analysis is a technique used to determine the institutional gain or loss anticipated from various courses of action (Cascio, 1982). Blum and Naylor (1968) defined the utility of a selection device as "the degree to which its use improves the quality of individuals selected beyond what would have occurred had that device not been used." Three utility models frequently used in personnel selection are Taylor and Russell (1939), Naylor and Shine (1965), and Brogden-Cronbach-Gleser (Cascio, 1982).

Taylor-Russell Model

The Taylor-Russell model estimates the utility of a selection device from the validity coefficient, the selection ratio—the percentage of the total number of applicants actually hired—and the percentage of employees who perform successfully on the job and who were hired without the benefit of a specific selection procedure. If these three pieces of information are known, then an employer can consult the **Taylor-Russell tables** to determine how many employees must be hired to reach a certain level of satisfactory performance.

For example, if a plumbing firm uses a measure of mechanical ability that has a validity coefficient of .30, selects 50 percent of job applicants, and considers 60 percent of present employees to be satisfactory, then consulting the Taylor-Russell tables (see Table 4.3, p. 110) shows that continued use of the same procedures will result in 69 percent of the newly hired employees performing at a satisfactory level. If the employer improves the validity coefficient of the selection procedures to .70 and maintains the same selection ratio, then 84 percent of those hired will be satisfactory. If the plumbing firm keeps the percentage of satisfactory employees at 80 percent, the validity coefficient at .70, and the selection ratio at 50 percent, then 96 percent of all new hires will be satisfactory.

Although the idea behind the Taylor-Russell tables is appealing, sometimes employers have trouble distinguishing between satisfactory and unsatisfactory performance. Since the method divides employees into these two categories only, there is no way to determine the ranges of successful or unsuccessful performances. Certain employees may be good at some job tasks and poor at others, or satisfactory employees may be either excellent or barely successful. Consequently, relying solely on the Taylor-Russell model to make hiring decisions may equally result in selecting excellent or barely successful employees.

Other Utility Models

Two other utility models are the Naylor-Shine model and Brogden-Cronbach-Gleser model.

Naylor-Shine Model In contrast with the Taylor-Russell model, the **Naylor-Shine model** (Naylor & Shine, 1965), assumes a linear relationship between validity and utility. In other words, rather than simply dichotomizing performance into successful and unsuccessful, the Naylor-Shine model assumes that higher validity coefficients result in higher utilities (i.e., better performance). As a result, this model does not require the setting of a cutoff (satisfactory/unsatisfactory) score.

Brogden-Cronbach-Gleser Model One limitation of both methods of estimating utility discussed above is that they do not consider the dollar cost of selection procedures. Employers using the Taylor-Russell tables or the Naylor-Shine model may be able to determine that they are getting better performances from their employees, but they cannot estimate the dollar value of the performances. Given the expense of developing and validating selection procedures, such information would obviously be useful to an employer.

The **Brogden-Cronbach-Gleser model** (Brogden, 1949; Cronbach & Gleser, 1965) uses the Naylor-Shine tables to determine the dollar value of performance. If an employer knows the validity coefficient for current selection procedures, the selection ratio, and the standard deviation of the criterion expressed in dollars—that is, an estimate of the dollar value of the average worker's performance—then the dollar value of improved selection procedures can be determined.

The Brogden-Cronbach-Gleser model has been used to estimate the value of the performance of computer programmers, budget analysts, insurance counselors, district sales managers, and others. In a study of food and beverage sales managers, for example, Cascio and Silbey (1979) found that the estimated value of the performance of superior managers—those whose performance levels were one standard deviation above average performance—was $39,500. In terms of dollars, superior managers were therefore almost 30 percent more valuable to the organization than average managers.

Although there are some methodological concerns about estimating the value of performance in dollars (Becker, 1989; Hazer & Highhouse, 1997; Orr, Sackett, & Mercer, 1989; Raju, Burke, & Normand, 1990), the potential usefulness of utility analysis should be apparent. Employers can determine the rela-

Table 4.3 TAYLOR-RUSSELL TABLES

Employees Considered Satisfactory	r	.05	.10	.20	.30	.40	.50	.60	.70	.80	.90	.95
60 Percent	.00	.60	.60	.60	.60	.60	.60	.60	.60	.60	.60	.60
	.10	.68	.67	.65	.64	.64	.63	.63	.62	.61	.61	.60
	.20	.75	.73	.71	.69	.67	.66	.65	.64	.63	.62	.61
	.30	.82	.79	.76	.73	.71	.69	.68	.66	.64	.62	.61
	.40	.88	.85	.81	.78	.75	.73	.70	.68	.66	.63	.62
	.50	.93	.90	.86	.82	.79	.76	.73	.70	.67	.64	.62
	.60	.96	.94	.90	.87	.83	.80	.76	.73	.69	.65	.63
	.70	.99	.97	.94	.91	.87	.84	.80	.75	.71	.66	.63
	.80	1.00	.99	.98	.95	.92	.88	.83	.78	.72	.66	.63
	.90	1.00	1.00	1.00	.99	.97	.94	.88	.82	.74	.67	.63
70 Percent	.00	.70	.70	.70	.70	.70	.70	.70	.70	.70	.70	.70
	.10	.77	.76	.75	.74	.73	.73	.72	.72	.71	.71	.70
	.20	.83	.81	.79	.78	.77	.76	.75	.74	.73	.71	.71
	.30	.88	.86	.84	.82	.80	.78	.77	.75	.74	.72	.71
	.40	.93	.91	.88	.85	.83	.81	.79	.77	.75	.73	.72
	.50	.96	.94	.91	.89	.87	.84	.82	.80	.77	.74	.72
	.60	.98	.97	.95	.92	.90	.87	.85	.82	.79	.75	.73
	.70	1.00	.99	.97	.96	.93	.91	.88	.84	.80	.76	.73
	.80	1.00	1.00	.99	.98	.97	.94	.91	.87	.82	.77	.73
	.90	1.00	1.00	1.00	1.00	.99	.98	.95	.91	.85	.78	.74
80 Percent	.00	.80	.80	.80	.80	.80	.80	.80	.80	.80	.80	.80
	.10	.85	.85	.84	.83	.83	.82	.82	.81	.81	.81	.80
	.20	.90	.89	.87	.86	.85	.84	.84	.83	.82	.81	.81
	.30	.94	.92	.90	.89	.88	.87	.86	.84	.83	.82	.81
	.40	.96	.95	.93	.92	.90	.89	.88	.86	.85	.83	.82
	.50	.98	.97	.96	.94	.93	.91	.90	.88	.86	.84	.82
	.60	.99	.99	.98	.96	.95	.94	.92	.90	.87	.84	.83
	.70	1.00	1.00	.99	.98	.97	.96	.94	.92	.89	.85	.83
	.80	1.00	1.00	1.00	1.00	.99	.98	.96	.94	.91	.87	.84
	.90	1.00	1.00	1.00	1.00	1.00	1.00	.99	.97	.94	.88	.84
90 Percent	.00	.90	.90	.90	.90	.90	.90	.90	.90	.90	.90	.90
	.10	.93	.93	.92	.92	.92	.91	.91	.91	.91	.90	.90
	.20	.96	.95	.94	.94	.93	.93	.92	.92	.91	.91	.90
	.30	.98	.97	.96	.95	.95	.94	.94	.93	.92	.91	.91
	.40	.99	.98	.98	.97	.96	.95	.95	.94	.93	.92	.91
	.50	1.00	.99	.99	.98	.97	.97	.96	.95	.94	.92	.92
	.60	1.00	1.00	.99	.99	.99	.98	.97	.96	.95	.93	.92
	.70	1.00	1.00	1.00	1.00	.99	.99	.98	.97	.96	.94	.93
	.80	1.00	1.00	1.00	1.00	1.00	1.00	.99	.99	.97	.95	.93
	.90	1.00	1.00	1.00	1.00	1.00	1.00	1.00	1.00	.99	.97	.94
	r	.05	.10	.20	.30	.40	.50	.60	.70	.80	.90	.95

An example from the Taylor-Russell tables. If a plumbing firm considers 60% of its current employees satisfactory (the top quarter of the table), has a selection ratio of .50 (hires 50% of those who apply), and uses a predictor with a validity coefficient of .30 (column r in the table), then 69% of the newly hired employees will be satisfactory. If the employer raises the validity coefficient of the selection procedure to .70, maintains a selection ratio of .50 and still considers 60% of current employees satisfactory, then 84% of the newly hired will be satisfactory employees.

(*Source:* Taylor, H. C., & Russell, J. T. (1939). The relationship of validity coefficients to the practical effectiveness of tests in selection: Discussion and tables. *Journal of Applied Psychology, 23,* 565–578.)

tionship between the cost of developing new selection procedures and performance benefits from the new procedures. Utility analysis shows the employer the dollar value of the higher validity coefficients resulting from improved selection.

Some people believe, however, that the complexity of the utility analysis procedure limits its attractiveness to employers. In one study, for example, applying utility analysis reduced managerial support for implementing a valid selection procedure. In this study, researchers (Latham & Whyte, 1994) provided a group of managers with four selection scenarios and asked them to choose the one they preferred. In the control condition, a standard description of validation procedures was provided. The second scenario included the information in the control condition as well as a section that contained a description of work previously done for another client and an expectancy table that could be used to predict performance.

The third condition included the control information and a utility analysis that estimated the financial gain from using the selection procedure. Finally, the last scenario included the information, the expectancy table, and the utility analysis. Participants were then asked to rate their preferences. Interestingly, the managers preferred the straightforward approach of the control method over use of both the expectancy table and the utility analysis. Apparently the managers were more receptive to methods they could understand than to the more technical procedures.

Types of Employment Testing

Measures of Aptitude and
   Ability
Personality Assessment
Integrity Testing
Individual Assessment
Interest Measures
Job Samples and Assess-
   ment Centers

As should be apparent from the foregoing discussion, not all personnel selection procedures are equally useful, valid, or fair. The following section describes some of the most commonly used instruments and methods of predicting performance. These fall into four broad categories: tests of aptitude and ability, personality measures, interest measures, and job samples.

Measures of Aptitude and Ability

Aptitude and ability tests measure the potential of an individual to perform a particular job. **Aptitudes**—as in mechanical aptitude—refer to an ability to learn. **Abilities** are the foundation for learning skills. These tests can be categorized into those that measure cognitive abilities and those that measure physical skills.

Measures of Cognitive Ability **Cognitive ability** tests measure different aspects of intelligence such as inductive and deductive reasoning, memory, spatial ability, verbal and quantitative skills, and mechanical comprehension. Many researchers (e.g., Barrett & Depinet, 1991; Schmidt & Ones, 1992) believe that cognitive ability, sometimes referred to as *general mental ability,* is the best predictor of job performance. In fact, a review of recent research in the area of cognitive ability and personnel selection (Borman, Hanson, & Hedge, 1997) concluded that the majority of researchers in this area now believe that general mental ability is more important for predicting job performance than specific abilities. As discussed in Chapter 1, some evidence (Wilk & Sackett, 1996) also suggests that people gravitate toward jobs that are commensurate with their cognitive abilities.

An example of a cognitive measure widely used for employment screening is the Wonderlic Personnel Test, which consists of 50 questions covering verbal and numerical skills, logic, direction following, and spatial relations. The test is designed to determine the applicant's ability to learn a job, to understand instructions, and to adapt and solve problems that occur on the job. Additionally, the Wonderlic attempts to provide information an employer can use to control employee turnover by matching employee abilities with levels of job demands. That is, applicants with high scores are recommended for jobs that are more demanding rather than for routine clerical or production jobs. Although the validity of the Wonderlic has been challenged in several court cases, its usefulness as a predictor of clerical performance has largely been upheld.

Mechanical abilities can be measured by such tests as the Purdue Mechanical Adaptability Test, the Bennett Mechanical Comprehension Test, or the D.A.T. Space Relations Test. These kinds of tests measure ability to understand the relationships between parts of mechanical objects. Similarly, trade tests may ask about specific knowledge necessary to perform a job successfully. Some questions from trade tests appear in Box 4.2.

One study (Hanisch & Hulin, 1994) looked at the effectiveness of a selection procedure that combined aptitude and ability testing followed by participation in a training course prior to selection. Results from the study suggested that adding a training component to the aptitude and ability tests improved the validity of the selection procedure.

Measures of Physical Ability   Physical tests measure abilities such as reaction time, finger dexterity, rate control, strength, flexibility, and stamina (Fleishman & Hogan, 1978; Hogan, 1991). These skills are obviously important for occupations such as construction worker, deep sea diver, professional athlete, combat soldier, or quality control inspector.

Despite the large number of jobs that depend on physical abilities, research linking physical abilities and selection is still rather scarce (Borman, Hanson, & Hedge, 1997). Nonetheless, one researcher (Hogan, 1991) proposed that physical abilities used on the job can be categorized in three ways. *Muscular strength* refers to both muscular power and endurance; *cardiovascular endurance* refers to capacity for sustaining physical activity; and *movement quality* involves skilled performance such as balance and coordination and is particularly important in athletic performance. In a meta-analysis of the role of physical ability in job performance (Blakely, Quiñones, Crawford, & Jago, 1994),

Box 4.2   TRADE TEST QUESTIONS

Trade tests assess the knowledge of job applicants in particular skill areas. The following are questions relevant to positions as painter, cook, and auto mechanic.

Painter

1. What do you do to knots and sappy places before painting?
2. When is puttying done on new woodwork?
3. What is the brightest yellow used?
4. What do you use to bleach an exposed oak door before refinishing?
5. What device is used for working just outside a single window on a high building?

General Cook

1. What do you use to clear boiled coffee?
2. How would you cook lamb chops or steaks for children?
3. How hot an oven should you have for biscuits?
4. Do you start soup in hot or cold water?
5. What do you put on fried sweet potatoes to make them brown?

Auto Mechanic

1. What joint is there between the differential and the transmission?
2. What regulates the height of gasoline in the carburetor?
3. What are the marks on the flywheel used for?
4. If a cylinder is scored from overheating, what repairs are necessary to put it in good condition?
5. What tool would you use in trueing up bearings?

Answers

Painter: **1.** shellac **2.** after priming **3.** chrome **4.** oxalic acid **5.** jack   *General cook:* **1.** egg shell **2.** broil **3.** 450 degrees **4.** cold **5.** sugar   *Auto mechanic:* **1.** universal **2.** float valve **3.** timing **4.** rebore and regrind **5.** scraper

Source: Adapted from H. E. Burtt (1970), *Principles of employment testing,* rev. ed. Westport, Conn.: Greenwood Press. Used by permission.

researchers found that strength is an important component in physically demanding jobs and that the most effective method for measuring strength is simulations.

A continuing problem with physical tests is that some male groups generally score higher than females and certain ethnic minorities (Arvey, Landon, Nutting, & Maxwell, 1992; Hogan & Quigley, 1986). Height, weight, and strength requirements may also eliminate disabled applicants. This is not a problem if test scores are predictive of performance, but physical standards, as all other selection procedures, require a thorough validation against the criterion of job performance. Until a fully automated workplace eliminates a need for physical standards, employees and applicants are likely to continue to challenge these kinds of requirements (Hogan & Quigley, 1986).

Personality Assessment

Although there are a variety of definitions for personality, in terms of personnel selection, **personality** can be defined as "a person's distinctive interpersonal characteristics, especially as described by those who have seen that person in a variety of situations" (Hogan, Hogan, & Roberts, 1996). As suggested earlier in this chapter, personality measures were initially used to determine the "cooperativeness" of employees. Today personality assessment is used to measure a wide range of characteristics, including persistence in salespeople, responsibility in bank employees, and service orientation in waiters.

Personality Measures During the 1960s and 1970s, the use of personality inventories for personnel selection fell into disfavor with many employers. This was largely due to two factors. First, the EEO requirement that such tests be shown to be related to job performance led some employers to feel that relying on tests that were based on content—rather than construct—validity would lessen the chance of unfair discrimination. Some employers, for example, believed validating word processing skill as a predictor of performance as a secretary was easier and "safer" than validating personality constructs relevant to the same job, such as sociability and responsibility. Additionally, personality measures were particularly vulnerable to the charges of cultural bias that were prevalent during that period.

A second reason for the decline in favor of personality measures was research suggesting that scores on these measures were not particularly useful in making predictions about performance. Reviews by Guion and Gottier (1965), Ghiselli (1966, 1973), and others concluded that validity coefficients derived from correlating scores on personality measures with ratings of job performance were too low to recommend use of such tests. Other authors objected to personality measures as an invasion of privacy or suggested they could easily be faked.

These criticisms of personality measurement for personnel selection provoked a series of research that continues today. In a meta-analysis of 97 studies comparing results from personality measures with job performance, for example, Tett, Jackson, and Rothstein (1991) found that personality factors are significantly related to job performance, and that many studies underestimate the importance of personality in job performance. According to these researchers, personality scales are particularly useful if the employer selects the qualities to measure on the basis of a job analysis. In a study of personality factors affecting performance as an accountant, for example, Day and Silverman (1989) found that personal qualities such as the willingness to take on difficult tasks, to work long hours, and to be serious about work were predictive of supervisor ratings.

Today, most industrial and organizational psychologists recognize the importance of personality characteristics in predicting performance. During the 1990s, in fact, interest in the relationship between personality and behavior on the job became stronger than ever. Although some researchers still believe assessment should focus on observable behaviors, most now accept the relevance of personality to job performance.

Personality inventories do not sample specific behaviors necessary for job performance. Rather, they attempt to identify personal qualities that are related to successful performance or to screen out individuals who may not be successful in a position. **Objective personality measures** require individuals to give a structured response—such as "True" or "False"—to questions such as "I am considered outgoing by my friends," "Someone has been following me," or "Most people would be better off if they would talk less and work more."

Projective personality measures, on the other hand, require unstructured responses. For example, a candidate may be asked to finish the sentence "My father. . . ." Responses to projective measures reflect an individual's view of the world and because of this, there are no right or wrong answers. The subjective nature of projective measures makes them virtually impossible to validate and as a result, they are rarely used for selection.

In addition to being objective or projective, personality measures can focus on either a candidate's psychological profile in general or on a specific quality related to job success. One of the most well-known measures of personality in general is the Minnesota Multiphasic Personality Inventory (MMPI; Hathaway & McKinley, 1940), a personality inventory designed to measure psychopathology. Its 10 clinical scales are often used to screen applicants for high security jobs, such as police officer or nuclear power plant operator. Assessing the mental health of applicants can be tricky, however, and although the MMPI is widely used for screening in high-risk occupations, its validity for predicting job performance even in these jobs is questionable (Butcher, 1979; Cortina, Doherty, Schmitt, Kaufman, & Smith, 1992).

In most cases, the personality measures used for personnel selection are based on the assumption that the applicant is normal, and that the need to screen for psychopathology is minimal. Typically, employers look at a candidate's levels of sociability, intelligence, responsibility, and ambition. The California Psychological Inventory (CPI; Gough, 1975), for example, measures "normal" characteristics, such as self-control, social presence, intellectual efficiency, and dominance. Dominance, in fact, has been found to be one of the best predictors of managerial potential (Megargee & Carbonell, 1988). Other commonly used measures of normal personality include the 16PF (Cattell, Eber, & Tatsuoka, 1970) and the Hogan Personality Inventory (HPI; Hogan, 1985). In addition to a personality profile, the HPI has subscales for predicting the performances of managers, service employees, and salespeople (Hogan, 1992).

Like most general measures of personality, these instruments all contain items to identify **motivated distortion,** or faking. Motivated distortion occurs when a person wants to project a particular image and answers questions in ways that promote that image. Most instruments offer formulas to correct for distortion, although some evidence suggests these corrections can affect the validity of the instrument (Christiansen, Goffin, Johnston, & Rothstein, 1994). Also, some research (Schmit, Ryan, Stierwalt, & Powell, 1995) suggests that applicants tend to give more positive responses to items on personality inventories when they are applying for a job than they do in other settings. Overall, however, motivated distortion does not appear to have a major impact on personality inventory validity (Barrick & Mount, 1996).

Another frequently used personality measure is the Myers-Briggs Type Indicator (MBTI; Briggs, Myers, & McCaulley, 1985), which is based on C. G. Jung's theory of psychological types (Jung, 1921). The MBTI classifies people into one of 16 personality types based on the way they take in and interpret information. Employees are identified as being introverted or extraverted, sensing or intuiting, thinking or feeling, and judging or perceiving. In general, the MBTI is not used in hiring; rather, it is more commonly used by employers to select special project teams or improve communication in the workplace. The MBTI is incredibly popular with both employees and employers—almost 2 million individuals take the MBTI each year—but evidence for its reliability and validity remains questionable (Zemke, 1992). As a personality measure, the MBTI is probably best used in the context of organization development (Chapter 13), and not for personnel selection.

One of the most influential models in current personality research is the **five-factor theory** (Digman, 1990; Salgado, 1997). Five-factor researchers believe that the basic dimensions of personality are extraversion, emotional stability, agreeableness, conscientiousness, and culture or intelligence, and that all human behavior is related to these qualities. In a review of the relationship between five-factor dimensions and (1) performance and productivity ratings; (2) ratings of performance in training; and (3) promotions, salary, and turnover, Barrick and Mount (1991) analyzed five-factor inventory results from almost 24,000 individuals in five occupational groups.

These researchers found conscientiousness to be the one factor related to all of the criteria concerning job performance. In other words, being conscientious was necessary for success in all five occupations. In addition, the extraversion score was a valid predictor for performance as a manager or a salesperson, and both culture and extraversion were related to success in a training program. Interestingly, these researchers found that agreeableness was not related to any of the performance measures, suggesting that being pleasant is not necessarily related to job success.

In another study that used five-factor theory, the same authors (Barrick & Mount, 1993) found that conscientiousness and extraversion were related to job performance when managers had a high degree of autonomy in their positions. The researchers concluded that autonomy may moderate the validity of certain predictors of performance. Along the same lines, one researcher (Stewart, 1996) found the relationship between extraversion and sales performance was affected by organizational reward structure.

In summary, just as some researchers have concluded that cognitive ability is the best predictor of job performance, others (Barrick & Mount, 1991; Hough, Eaton, Dunnette, Kamp, & McCloy, 1990) have concluded that conscientiousness is the best predictor of job performance.

> The preponderance of evidence shows that individuals who are dependable, reliable, careful, thorough, able to plan, organized, hardworking, persistent, and achievement oriented tend to have higher job performance in most if not all occupations. Conscientiousness has emerged as perhaps the most important trait motivation variable in personnel psychology. (Mount, Barrick, & Strauss, 1994)

Some evidence suggests that supervisor observations of conscientiousness and extraversion can be better predictors of job performance than self-assessments through personality inventories. In fact, one study (Dunn, Mount, Barrick, & Ones, 1996) found that the qualities managers most often looked for in applicants were general mental ability and conscientiousness. When managers were concerned about the possibility of counterproductive behavior, however—such as theft or drug use—they looked for conscientiousness, agreeableness, and emotional stability. The researchers concluded:

> After choosing among applicants and following their success at work, it seems reasonable that managers eventually gain an accurate perception about what characteristics are and are not related to performance. In other words, even though managers may know nothing about validities of predictors in a scientific sense, they may well intuit them in a practical way, which is based on their own observations of workers over time.

Not all researchers accept the five-factor model of personality as the best predictor of employee performance. For example, Schmit and Ryan (1993) found that the five-factor model fit a group of college students, but it did not fit a group of job applicants as well, suggesting the possibility that the model may not be equally appropriate for assessing personality in all groups. Other researchers have suggested that a model of personality that uses more than five factors is more appropriate for personnel selection (Cellar, Miller, Doverspike, & Klawsky, 1996; Hough & Schneider, 1996).

Along the same lines, Crant (1995) challenged the five factor model by proposing that *proactive personality* might better predict performance than extraversion and conscientiousness. Proactive behavior occurs when people take action to influence their environments and proactive individuals show initiative, take action when presented with opportunities, and persevere. One hundred forty-six real estate agents completed measures of proactive personality, conscientiousness, extraversion, and general mental ability. The criteria for the study were number of houses sold, number of listings generated, and commission income. In this study, proactive personality was a better predictor of performance than the other variables, including the five-factor dimensions of extraversion and conscientiousness.

Finally, one group of researchers (Rosse, Miller, & Stecher, 1994) wondered whether applicants might object to the use of personality measures in employment screening. All applicants for jobs at a Colorado resort completed an application, an interview, and a reference check, but only some were required to take a personality inventory, and a third group completed both a personality inventory and a measure of cognitive ability.

When asked to report their attitudes afterward, applicants who completed the usual selection procedure and a personality measure were the least satisfied, and satisfaction was significantly greater when applicants completed both personality and cognitive ability measures. The researchers concluded that applicant reactions to selection procedures are likely to be more positive if employers use interviews alone or interviews, personality measures, and ability tests together rather than interviews and personality measures only. Interestingly, applicant reactions to selection procedures appear to be unrelated to how well they do in the process (Macan, Avedon, Paese, & Smith, 1994; Smither, Reilly, Millsap, Pearlman, & Stoffey, 1993).

Integrity Testing

As suggested above, some employers are interested in specific personality dimensions rather than in an employee's general psychological profile. One of the most common concerns of employers today is employee honesty. Theft and fraud are serious matters, and researchers have developed several methods for identifying applicants who may steal from an employer. Historically, many employers used a polygraph, or lie detector test, for screening applicants, but problems associated with the validity of results led Congress to curtail its use (see Box 4.3). As a result, employers have increasingly turned to paper-and-pencil measures of honesty, usually referred to as **integrity tests.**

Integrity tests originally focused solely on identifying applicants who would steal from an employer. Research suggests that job applicants most likely to steal typically believe themselves to be honest people in a dishonest world. As a result, they rationalize that dishonest behavior is the norm (London House Press, 1987). Attitudes that predict theft generally fall into five areas: (1) frequent thoughts about stealing; (2) greater tolerance toward those who steal; (3) a belief that most people steal; (4) a belief that thieves won't inform on each other; and (5) finding justifications for theft (Murphy, 1993).

Typical integrity tests include the London House Personnel Selection Inventory, Reid Report, and Stanton Survey. Items on these measures ask about attitudes toward dishonesty and instances when an applicant may have done something dishonest.

Box 4.3 LIE DETECTORS

In response to continuing problems with information leaks, President Ronald Reagan signed National Security Decision Directive 84 in January 1984. This directive would have expanded mandatory use of polygraph ("lie detector") tests for federal employees, but congressional opposition caused the president to suspend the directive.

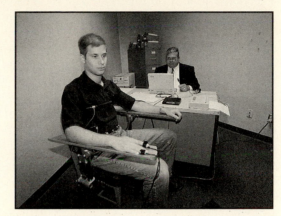

Polygraphs operate on the principle that increased perspiration, respiration, or blood pressure are indications of anxiety caused by dishonesty. In a standard polygraph procedure, an inflated cuff is attached to a person's arm, a rubber tube is placed around his or her chest, and small electrodes on his or her hand. After establishing a physiological base rate for the person, the examiner then asks questions. Any fluctuation in the physiological base rate is seen as a possible indication of discomfort, anxiety, or lying.

According to professionals, the proper use of polygraphs requires: (1) a well-trained examiner; (2) carefully prepared objective questions; (3) a calm atmosphere; and (4) a willing, cooperative subject. In many situations, these are difficult conditions to fulfill.

Overall, polygraphs have been shown to be of limited usefulness in personnel selection. Although they are sometimes used in companies where employees have direct access to cash or commodities, such as jewelers, department stores, banks, drug stores, or electronic equipment dealers, many researchers question their validity. For example, some research (Honts, Raskin, & Kircher, 1994) shows that polygraph results can be affected by biting the tongue, pressing the toes to the floor, or using mental countermeasures such as counting backwards when being interviewed. Along the same lines, validity seems to differ between administrations of polygraphs in the laboratory and in the field (Bradley, McLaren, & Carle, 1996).

Although polygraphs are designed to determine whether an individual is lying, job candidates are typically rejected on the basis of confessions they make, not on the results of the test. Finally, many of the questions asked during a polygraph test are probably illegal. For these reasons, most employers avoid using polygraphs in personnel selection.

Sources: Bradley, M. T., MacLaren, V. V., & Carle, S. B. (1996). Deception and nondeception in guilty knowledge and guilty action polygraph tests. *Journal of Applied Psychology, 81,* 153–160; and Honts, C. R., Raskin, D. C., & Kircher, J. C. (1994). Mental and physical countermeasures reduce the accuracy of polygraph tests. *Journal of Applied Psychology, 79,* 252–259.

An alternative approach to integrity testing is measuring an applicant's tendencies toward counterproductive behavior in general, which includes not only a tendency to steal, but also a range of antisocial behaviors, including absenteeism, carelessness, or intentionally destructive behaviors (Hogan & Hogan, 1989). These measures look at broader personality factors and generally do not contain direct references to theft. Typical personality measures of integrity include the PDI Employment Inventory (Paajanen, 1986), the Reliability Scale of the Hogan Personnel Selection Series (Hogan & Hogan, 1989), and the London House Employment Productivity Index (Terris, 1986).

Although there are numerous methodological problems in determining the validity of integrity tests, one review (Sackett & Wanek, 1996) concluded that, in general, both approaches to integrity testing—identifying applicants who may steal versus measuring applicant responsibility in general—were beneficial to employers. Other evidence suggests that combining an integrity test with a measure of conscientiousness improves predictions about performance.

One study (Collins & Schmidt, 1993), for example, used integrity tests to identify differences between white-collar criminals and people in positions of authority who had not committed criminal acts. Overall, the noncriminals scored significantly higher on dimensions related to conscientiousness, whereas the criminals scored significantly higher on social extraversion and extracurricular activities.

Another study (Bernardin & Cooke, 1993) looked at honesty in 111 employees who worked in a major retail convenience store chain. The researchers followed the employees over a three-year period and compared scores on integrity measures with rates of termination for theft. Results from the study indicated that scores on the integrity measures did significantly predict which employees would steal. In a laboratory study in which participants attempted to manipulate the results of integrity testing, results also supported the validity of integrity testing (Cunningham, Wong, & Barbee, 1994). Finally, a meta-analysis of 665 validity coefficients from integrity tests (Ones, Viswesvaran, & Schmidt, 1993) concluded that "integrity test validities are substantial for predicting job performance and counterproductive behaviors on the job, such as theft, disciplinary problems, and absenteeism."

Individual Assessment

Sometimes employers need in-depth information about an individual to make an employment decision. Most frequently this occurs when the employee is being considered for a position with a high level of responsibility. **Individual assessment** refers to the practice of one psychologist evaluating an individual (Ryan & Sackett, 1987). In most cases, this evaluation is based on a variety of assessment techniques, and it typically requires two hours to one full day of testing.

In the typical individual assessment, assessees complete an ability test, such as the Watson-Glaser Critical Thinking Appraisal, and an objective personality inventory, such as the 16PF. In some cases, assessors use projective personality measures, such as sentence-completions or the Rorschach Inkblot Test. In addition, assessors usually require an in-depth interview and completion of a personal history questionnaire. Less frequently, assessors use simulations, check references, survey other workers about the individual, or ask for a health evaluation.

Ryan and Sackett (1992) surveyed psychologists who practice individual assessment to determine the measures they most commonly used. Most frequently mentioned were the Wechsler Adult Intelligence Scale Revised, the Watson-Glaser Critical Thinking Appraisal, the MMPI, 16PF, CPI, and Myers-Briggs. Other information most frequently requested included educational background, previous work history, current job, career goals, hobbies, self-assessed needs and strengths, as well as questions about the person's parents, spouse, and children.

Individual assessment can be quite valuable in providing an in-depth evaluation of an employee or job applicant, but there are some drawbacks to this approach to personnel selection. An obvious problem is cost. A second problem is the personal nature of the information gathered; employees may not wish to provide such detailed information about their backgrounds or personalities. In addition, from a scientific standpoint, individual assessment is particularly open to bias on the part of the assessor. In a study comparing individual assessments of the same people, Ryan and Sackett (1989) found differences in assessors' opinions about the suitability of job candidates. Companies that use individual assessment need to be certain about the competence of the individuals they use to do the assessments.

Interest Measures

Interest measures are an inventory of the degree to which a person's interests correspond to the interests of individuals in specific occupations. Applicants are asked how much they feel they would enjoy certain careers or activities, and their responses are then compared to the responses of individuals in different occupations. In other words, these inventories determine whether an individual has the same interests as a lawyer, a forest ranger, a gas station attendant, and so forth.

Three commonly used interest inventories are the Kuder Occupational Interest Inventory (Kuder, 1964), the Strong-Campbell Interest Inventory (Strong & Campbell, 1966), and the Self-Directed Search (Holland, 1979). All three use a theory of vocational choice developed by Holland (1966). According to Holland, all occupations can be classified into one of six types: realistic, investigative, artistic, social, enterprising, or conventional. Based on personality factors, individuals typically prefer occupations that fall within a particular group.

Although interest inventories are often used at the college and high school levels to help students identify potential career directions and by the military to determine job placement, they are less often used by employers. Since no evidence indicates that interest inventories predict performance, some employers consider them of limited value, at least in personnel selection.

Table 4.4   DIMENSIONS MEASURED IN AN ASSESSMENT CENTER

General mental ability
Oral communication skills
Written communication skills
Human relations skills
Forcefulness (what kind of an impression does this person make on others?)
Likeability
Awareness of social environment (how skilled is this person at interpreting the behaviors of others?)
Self-objectivity (does this person recognize his or her own assets and liabilities?)
Behavior flexibility
Need approval of peers
Inner work standards (desire to do a good job)
Resistance to stress
Tolerance of uncertainty
Range of interests
Energy
Organizing and planning
Decision making
Creativity

Source: Campbell, R. J., & Bray, D. W. (1993). Use of an assessment center as an aid in management selection. *Personnel Psychology, 46,* 691–699.

Job Samples and Assessment Centers

The **job sample** approach to selecting employees relies on content validity. Applicants provide samples of their work, which the employer then uses to make an employment decision. Examples of job samples include an artist's portfolio, a journalist's magazine or newspaper articles, or a biologist's research findings. The employer uses work already done to make decisions about future performance. From the job sample, the employer may also determine whether an applicant will need additional training.

One well-known job sample technique used to predict the managerial potential of candidates is the **assessment center.** As discussed in the opening of this chapter, this approach was developed by the OSS to select spies during World War II. Because of enthusiasm about its effectiveness, the assessment center was refined at AT&T and applied to selecting individuals for other, less exotic occupations. Since the 1950s, the assessment center approach has spread to many other companies. Table 4.4 lists the variables studied in the first assessments at AT&T.

In the typical assessment center, candidates for promotion are evaluated on a combination of performance factors and personality factors relevant to handling situations likely to occur in management. Typical performance factors include creativity, communication skill, ability to prioritize, and thoroughness;

typical personality factors include persuasiveness, interpersonal perceptiveness, and self-acceptance (Shore, Thornton, & Shore, 1990). Individuals are nominated to participate by their supervisors or, in cases in which it is important to avoid bias in nominations, they can nominate themselves. The candidates participate in management games, leaderless group discussions, and other simulations typical of a manager's work.

One of the most common assessment center exercises is the **in-basket activity,** a simulation that requires a candidate to organize and respond to materials typically found in a manager's in-basket—memos, letters, phone messages, and so forth. Although in-basket activities are, at least theoretically, both face and content valid, some researchers have questioned their usefulness for making predictions about managerial performance. Brannick, Michaels, and Baker (1989), for example, found little evidence for the validity of predictions based on in-basket scores, and Russell (1987) found little relationship between in-basket scores and effective interpersonal behavior, a quality that most researchers consider essential for effective performance as a manager. Along the same lines, Houston and Smither (1992) found that results from in-basket exercises were unrelated to scores on personality-based managerial potential inventories.

Despite these findings, in-baskets remain popular with employers. One suggestion for improving the validity of an in-basket activity, however, is to develop an exercise for a specific job, rather than use a generic product bought from a test supplier (Schippmann, Prien, & Katz, 1990).

In the assessment center, rating is usually done by managers who are two or three levels above the candidates and who are unfamiliar with the participants. These observers are first trained in assessment procedures; they then spend two or three days observing candidates perform. At the end of the assessment center, the observers write evaluations about each candidate. From these evaluations, the future management of a company will often be drawn.

In an interesting evaluation of the assessment center method, McEvoy and Beatty (1989) compared assessment center ratings of law enforcement agency managers with subordinates' ratings of the managers. Although the researchers found evidence supporting the validity of the assessment center for predicting managerial success, subordinate ratings of performance were often more accurate than the assessment center ratings. According to the researchers, subordinate ratings were as good at predicting managerial success as cognitive ability tests, biodata, peer evaluations, or traditional assessment centers. In another study of assessment centers (Shore, Shore, & Thornton, 1990), peer ratings of performance in an assessment center were more likely than self-ratings of performance to agree with the ratings of professional assessors, a finding that has important implications for performance appraisal (Chapter 6).

In a study of the validity of predictions based on assessment center results (Gaugler, Rosenthal, Thornton, & Bentson, 1987), the researchers concluded that (1) assessment centers are useful for predicting managerial success; (2) they are more valid when the group being assessed contains a larger proportion of females; (3) using a greater variety of assessment exercises increases validity; and (4) peer ratings improve assessment center validity.

Although most evaluations of assessment center selection have focused on male candidates, Ritchie and Moses (1983) followed the career paths of 1,633 females who had been evaluated in assessment centers. Seven years later, scores from the assessment center correlated positively with measures of career success. Aside from being validity evidence for the assessment center method, results also suggested that the abilities and personal characteristics of male and female executives are similar.

One feature of the assessment center that appeals to many employers is its reliance on a content validity approach to predicting job performance. That is, the exercises that participants do during the assessment are usually similar to the actual job duties of executives.

Nonetheless, findings from several studies suggest researchers still are unclear on what makes assessment centers effective. In one study (Schneider & Schmitt, 1992), for example, the form of assessment center exercises—group discussion versus individual decision making, for example—was a better predictor of results than the content of the exercises. Another study (Harris, Becker, & Smith, 1993) found that rating assessees on overall performance in the assessment center led to different results from rating assessees after each exercise. Along the same lines, Kleinmann (1993) found that participants who are able to recognize the dimension an assessment center exercise is measuring do better in that exercise. Another study (Groffin, Rothstein, & Johnston, 1996) found that assessment centers and personality measures appear to assess different domains of managerial performance. Finally, some research (Spychalski, Quiñones, Gaugler, & Pohley, 1997) suggests that organizations vary greatly in the training provided to assessors. Findings such as these suggest that assessment centers may be measuring performance on the exercises rather than personal qualities that lead to effective managerial performance. Nonetheless, the general consensus among personnel selection researchers is that assessment centers can provide valid predictions about job performance (Borman, Hanson, & Hedge, 1997).

A final interesting aspect of the assessment center approach is that although the method does seem to predict promotability, its usefulness for predicting performance is much less clear (Turnage & Muchinsky, 1984). This research suggests that employees who attend assessment centers are likely to be promoted, but their future job performances may not be outstanding.

On the other hand, some research suggests that employees who attend assessment centers change their behaviors after the experience (Gaugler et al., 1987). This suggests that assessment centers may be useful as developmental interventions rather than measures of performance. One study (Jones & Whitmore, 1995) that followed assessees over a ten-year period after the assessment found that although results from the assessment did not predict promotions, participants who followed developmental suggestions from the assessment were more likely to be promoted later.

Finally, employers need to be careful when setting standards for judging assessment center results because assessment centers can perpetuate the status quo (Segal, 1996). That is, managers who are doing the assessing may look for qualities similar to their own and inadvertently create a situation of adverse impact, which can lead to legal challenge.

New Approaches to Employment Testing

Genetic Screening

Genetic Screening
Computer-Adaptive Testing
Video-based Assessment

Genetic screening refers to testing applicants for constitutional factors that may affect job performance. One type of genetic screening, **cytogenetic monitoring,** refers to testing to determine whether an employee's chromosomes are being affected by exposure to harmful chemicals or radiation on the job. In general, there are few legal issues involved in cytogenetic monitoring (Bible, 1990). Genetic screening for the purpose of making an employment or promotion decision, on the other hand, is more controversial.

Testing for genetic deficiencies and the impact of such testing on employment decisions is a recent development that has been not been widely studied by industrial and organizational psychologists. Today, scientists can identify genes that are linked to hemophilia, cystic fibrosis, sickle-cell anemia, and other diseases. If evidence of a genetic disposition toward disease appears during a routine preemployment health screening, an employer may want to use this information when making a hiring decision. The employer may be concerned that the genetic defect will hinder job performance, or that illness associated with the disorder will result in higher insurance premiums.

Results from genetic screening can be used to disqualify applicants if the employer can demonstrate a bona fide occupational qualification (BFOQ); that is, a legitimate business reason for rejecting the individual. For example, an employer may reject applicants with a tendency toward hypercholesterolemia—a type of heart disease that occurs more frequently in African Americans—if the employer can demonstrate that job duties require working under high levels of stress. In addition, employers can reject applicants if they can demonstrate the applicants would pose a direct threat to the health and safety of others in the workplace.

For decisions based on genetic screening to comply with either Civil Rights Act, however, the employer must test *all* applicants, and not only those more highly at risk for genetic disorders. In the example cited above, for instance, the employer who wishes to use genetic information when making an employment decision must test *all* applicants for hypercholesterolemia, not just African Americans (Zeitz, 1991). In addition to the Civil Rights Act, other legislation that may affect the use of genetic screening for employment decisions include the Rehabilitation Act of 1973 and the Americans with Disabilities Act of 1990.

Computer-Adaptive Testing

Historically, all applicants have been required to take the same employment tests. With the advent of new theories of testing, as well as the proliferation of computers in the workplace, employers are now able to tailor employment tests to the ability of the test taker (Guion, 1991). Applicants with a high level of ability, for example, no longer need to spend time answering questions that are below their ability.

At the computer terminal, the applicant is first presented with a question of average difficulty. If the applicant misses the question, the computer is programmed to offer an easier question; if the applicant answers correctly, the computer presents a more difficult question. By varying the level of difficulty, the computer program obtains a precise estimate of the applicant's ability.

In addition to providing a precise estimate of ability, **computer-adaptive testing (CAT)** uses fewer items and takes less time than paper-and-pencil measures. In addition, computer-adaptive tests appear to be as reliable and valid as other forms of testing (Anastasi, 1988; Overton, Harms, Taylor, & Zicker, 1997). The major disadvantage of computer-adaptive tests, however, is their cost. The test program must have a large pool of easy, average, and difficult questions in its memory, and developing such a program can be expensive. Because of this, CAT is probably most effective when large numbers of applicants or employees are being screened. Otherwise, although computer-adaptive testing is appealing from a scientific standpoint, it may simply be too impractical for most employers.

In another approach to using computers for selection, however, one group of researchers (Schmitt, Gilliland, Landis, & Devine, 1993) developed a computerized testing procedure for selecting secretaries. The procedure first trained, then tested, the applicants on a variety of tasks. One advantage of the system was that it minimized the role of the administrator in the selection process. The researchers concluded that computers can play a role in adding innovations to the entire selection process.

Video-based Assessment

Several researchers (Hunter & Hunter, 1984; Schmitt et al., 1984) have pointed out that scores from simulations are among the best predictors of job performance. By replicating job situations, simulations allow applicants to

Scene from a video assessment. This photograph shows the filming of a video selection system for measuring customer service in the supermarket industry. Applicants will be presented with a number of situations likely to occur in the supermarket, then asked how they would handle such situations. Video assessment provides a realistic job preview at the same time it measure applicant suitability. (*Source:* ESS Corp., Maitland, FL. Used by permission.)

behave as if they were on the job. A problem with simulations, however, is their cost—development and administration of job simulations can cost hundreds of thousands of dollars. **Video-based assessment** is a relatively new selection technique that uses video to simulate job situations (see photo).

In the typical video assessment, actors portray workers in situations that require a decision. Applicants see a brief scenario, then are asked how they would respond to the situation. In most cases, the applicant responds to a multiple-choice question that is flashed on the screen. Answers are tallied electronically and results are available at the end of the testing session.

One advantage of video assessment is that it provides applicants with a realistic job preview. They see the kinds of duties the employee will be expected to fulfill, problems likely to occur in the workplace, and the setting in which the job is performed. In this way, video assessment provides a great deal of information about the company and the job at the same time the applicant is being tested.

In terms of validity, predictions made on the basis of video assessment results are quite high—comparable to those made from assessment center results (McIntire & Thomas, 1990). Although video assessment is expensive to develop, administration is relatively inexpensive. Results are scored automatically at the end of the test session, and applicants receive a realistic job preview at the same time they are being tested. Some research (Chan & Schmitt, 1997) also found fewer race differences in performance on video assessment vs. paper-and-pencil situational tests.

Scott, McIntire, and Burroughs (1992) compared the performances of groups of bank tellers who had been selected by either video assessment or traditional procedures. The first group of tellers was selected using the traditional application, telephone screening interview, unstructured interview, and reference check. The second group was selected using the same procedure, but members of the group were also administered the video test before, or following, the employment interview.

In terms of objective performance, tellers hired after passing the video test were better workers than tellers selected using the traditional process. Applicants who experienced the video assessment made fewer and less costly mistakes, took fewer sick days, and had less turnover.

Although there is not yet much scientific evaluation of video assessment, this technique offers a promising new direction for selection research. Some major concerns about video assessment, however, are its cost, which can be prohibitive for small and medium-sized companies; the importance of making the assessment an accurate reflection of the job and the situations the employee will face; and some evidence (Weekley & Jones, 1997) that video assessments may primarily be measuring cognitive ability. Although personnel departments fulfill a variety of functions for the organization, few have the expertise to write, film, and produce high-quality video assessments. Nonetheless, video assessment seems likely to become an important assessment tool in the future.

Chapter Summary

During the personnel selection process, applicants are likely to be asked to take some form of an employment test. Employment testing has historically been one of the most controversial areas in industrial and organizational psychology. Nevertheless, considerable scientific evidence has now accumulated demonstrating that testing is one of the best ways of predicting job performance.

Although employers had been using psychological tests since World War I, widespread application began after the success of the OSS screening program during World War II. During the 1960s and 1970s there was a decline in test usage, but employment testing has once again become popular among employers. In the 1990s, employers became increasingly interested in personality assessment.

For predictors to be useful, they must have the qualities of reliability and validity. Reliability can be demonstrated by several methods, including test-retest, equivalent forms, and internal consistency.

Historically, validity has been seen as being one of three kinds: criterion-referenced, content, and construct. Recent thinking has suggested, however, that there are not three kinds of validity, but three strategies or methods for demonstrating validity. Validity itself is a unitary construct. Many psychologists also believe that all validity is construct validity. Current research suggests that, in some cases, validity can be generalized across situations; that is, the validity of a predictor need not be demonstrated in each setting where it is used.

Synthetic validity refers to a method of combining parts of tests that have been shown to lead to valid predictions about job performance. Face validity refers to the apparent validity of a measure.

Test bias occurs when average scores on some measure differ between groups but the groups are both able to perform the job in question. Although subgroup norming is a strategy for dealing with this problem, the Civil Rights Act of 1991 prohibits use of this method. Score bonding is a recent approach to avoiding test bias that has interested many researchers and practitioners.

In recent years, employers have become interested in evaluating the usefulness of their selection procedures. Such evaluations are referred to as utility analysis, and three approaches are the Taylor-Russell model, the Naylor-Shine model, and the Brogden-Cronbach-Gleser model.

Employment tests can be broadly categorized into four types: aptitude and ability, personality, interest, and job samples. Aptitude and ability tests measure the potential of an individual to perform a specific job. Typical cognitive ability tests measure different aspects of intelligence, whereas physical ability tests measure such qualities as visual acuity, reaction time, and finger dexterity.

Personality measures identify personal qualities of applicants that are considered necessary for job success. Typical personality measures used for employment screening assess qualities such as assertiveness, ambition, and conscientiousness. Integrity testing is a form of personality assessment that focuses on an applicant's honesty, and individual assessment is an in-depth look at one person. Interest measures assess the degree to which a person's interest correspond to the interests of individuals in specific occupations.

Job samples are examples of applicant performance that the employer uses as a basis for making a decision about performance. Such samples include an artist's portfolio, a professor's publications, or letters typed by a clerical assistant. The assessment center is one of the most popular job sample methods of employment testing. Participants in assessment centers are evaluated on creativity, communication skill, and ability to prioritize; personality factors assessed include persuasiveness, interpersonal perceptiveness, and self-acceptance. Most researchers agree that assessment centers can be valuable in identifying managerial potential.

Three of the newest approaches to personnel testing are genetic screening, computer-adaptive testing, and video-based assessment.

Key Words and Concepts

abilities (p. 111)

aptitudes (p. 111)

assessment center (p. 122)

Brogden-Cronbach-Gleser
   model (p. 109)

cognitive ability (p. 111)

computer-adaptive testing (CAT)
   (p. 126)

concurrent validity (p. 99)

construct equivalence (p. 102)

construct validity (p. 101)

content validity (p. 100)

criterion-related validity (p. 98)

cytogenetic monitoring (p. 125)

equivalent forms (p. 97)

face validity (p. 104)

five-factor theory (p. 116)

genetic screening (p. 125)

in-basket activity (p. 123)
individual assessment (p. 120)
integrity tests (p. 118)
interest measures (p. 121)
internal consistency (p. 97)
job sample (p. 122)
motivated distortion (p. 116)
Naylor-Shine model (p. 109)
objective personality measures
   (p. 115)
personality (p. 114)
predictive validity (p. 99)
projective personality measures
   (p. 115)

reliability (p. 96)
restriction in range (p. 99)
score banding (p. 106)
situational specificity (p. 103)
synthetic validity (p. 105)
Taylor-Russell tables (p. 108)
test bias (p. ??)
test-retest (p. 96)
utility analysis (p. 108)
validity (p. 97)
validity generalization (p. 102)
video-based assessment
   (p. 127)

Questions for Discussion

1. Why do you think some people resist the idea that employment tests can be used to predict performance successfully?
2. What are the methods for establishing reliability? In your opinion, which would be most useful to an employer?
3. What are the methods for establishing validity? In your opinion, which would be the most useful to an employer?
4. What is situational specificity? Can you think of an instance in which it would be a problem?
5. What are the arguments in favor of score banding? Do you agree with the score banding approach?
6. If you were putting together a group of assessment intruments for selecting construction workers, what would you use? What would you use to select department store managers? psychology professors?
7. What advantages do assessment centers offer over paper-and-pencil measures? What are the disadvantages? Which approach do you prefer? Why?
8. Of all the selection methods discussed in Chapters 3 and 4, which do you consider the least useful? Why? Which do you consider the most useful? Why?

CHAPTER | 5

Training: Development, Methods, and Evaluation

A Brief History of Training

Designing a Training Program

Methods of Training

Optimizing the Training Experience

Evaluating Training Effectiveness

Chapter Summary

Key Words and Concepts

Questions For Discussion

After recruitment, testing, and hiring, many workers next experience training. Training is one of the largest personnel functions, with American companies budgeting just under $60 billion in 1996 to provide training for almost 59.6 million workers (Industry Report, 1996). As sizable as this figure may be, it does not include the additional $13 billion associated with hardware, services, and in-house staff. Of all the human resource functions discussed in this book, training is probably the most expensive.

Although learning is a traditional area of interest for psychologists, translating educational theory and research into training programs is not always a straightforward process. Adult learners have unique motivations, values, and constraints that affect their abilities to learn. Additionally, most training programs have constraints placed on them by the organizations in which they operate. Unlike public school classes, training programs that do not receive positive reviews may be cancelled.

Allocation of resources is another important factor that affects the development of training programs. Some companies, for example, may find that improved personnel selection procedures can minimize or eliminate the need for training programs. Although some corporate officers may consider training essential for organizational effectiveness, others may feel that training classes are a luxury or an unimportant part of operations.

Given the projected changes in the workforce discussed in Chapter 1, however, as well as the recent emphasis on providing low-income individuals with job training as part of welfare reform, training is likely to continue to be one of the most active areas in industrial and organizational psychology in the future.

This chapter looks at the process of developing an effective training program, the methods available to trainers, and the methods by which training programs can be evaluated. Like the employment interview, training is one of the areas of I/O psychology in which theory and practice converge only occasionally. For example, despite the thousands of programs and the billions of dollars spent on training, the effectiveness of these programs is only occasionally evaluated scientifically. Along the same lines, many individuals are chosen to be trainers because of their expertise in particular areas—and despite the fact that they have no knowledge of educational theory or practice. These kinds of contradictions are important to remember as we discuss training.

A Brief History of Training

Historically, the first training of workers occurred on the job. Soldiers, merchants, artisans, and others learned to accomplish their assigned tasks by actually attempting to do them at the worksite. The typical form of this worksite training was apprenticeship, the practice of learning a trade from the teaching of a skilled craftsman.

Although still widely practiced today, apprenticeship has a long history: The first rules governing its practice appeared in 2100 B.C. in the Code of Hammurabi. Usually associated with the craft industries, apprenticeship was once the method of training doctors and lawyers. Even in the 1920s in the United States, for example, people could become attorneys by apprenticing themselves to a practicing lawyer for several years, then passing a bar examination.

One of the first schools in the United States devoted specifically to industrial training was the Ohio Mechanics Institute, established in Cincinnati in 1828. By the end of the nineteenth century, many American industries had recognized the need for training programs and had established factory schools, particularly for mechanics. Today the most popular topics for employee training are computer skills, technical material, management, and communication (Industry Report, 1996).

Almost every large company offers its employees some kind of in-house education and, as suggested above, training has become a multibillion-dollar industry. In addition to its traditional role in raising productivity, training has recently become an important area in I/O psychology because of the rapid advances in technology that require new knowledge from employees.

Because of breakthroughs in electronics, data processing, and communications, many industries are acquiring sophisticated equipment that did not exist five—or even three—years ago. Consequently, those who are expected to operate the equipment are unlikely to have the necessary skills. Since technological expansion typically leads to rapid obsolescence of equipment, even these operators are likely to require constant retraining to keep current. Some research suggests that modern workers can expect to experience some kind of training on the job or elsewhere five to eight times during their careers. As long as the pace of technological change remains rapid, training is likely to continue to be a growth area in I/O psychology.

Designing a Training Program

Identify Training Needs
Establish Training Objectives
Develop Instructional Materials
Test and Refine Materials
Implement the Training Program
Evaluate the Program

How do organizations decide what kinds of training they need? Although simple observation of performance may give some indication, proper planning for future needs requires a much more detailed and controlled approach. As illustrated in Figure 5.1, establishing a training program is basically a six-step process. The six steps are explained as follows.

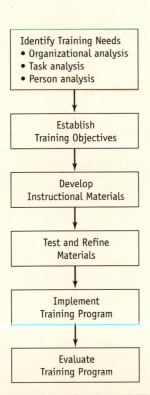

Figure 5.1 Establishing a Training Program

Identify Training Needs

Although most companies recognize the need for training, assessing the specific needs of employees is not usually a priority for organizations. Given the cost of the training effort, it is surprising more organizations don't attempt to find out what training their employees lack. For a training program to be optimally effective, organizations must analyze training needs at the levels of the organization, the task, and the person expected to do the task.

Organizational analysis requires taking a broad overview of areas such as the role of training in the organization, the current state of organizational effectiveness, and organizational plans for the future. For example, the usefulness of a training program for accounting clerks will obviously be affected by an organization's plans to upgrade its accounting software.

In addition to assisting in planning, the organizational analysis may identify ways in which the training should be structured to be most effective. An organizational analysis might indicate, for example, that the need for training would be greatly lessened if the selection process were improved. Similarly, the analysis may suggest that decentralized training is more effective than sending trainees to the home office for a two-week training course.

Another important aspect of the organizational analysis is the specification of goals. When the organization's goals are not clear, trainers may not know which programs to develop or who will decide how the program will be implemented. In addition, training programs cannot be evaluated if goals are unclear.

Other factors in the organization may also affect training development. Specifically, the needs assessment must determine whether the organization will support the transfer of skills learned in training to the workplace. If trainees learn new methods of communicating or doing their jobs, then are not encouraged by their supervisors to use their new knowledge, the training effort will be wasted.

Finally, the organization needs assessment should focus on the resources available for the training effort. The organization must provide the space and equipment for the training, but more importantly, it must have personnel qualified to do the training. Given the rapid changes in both equipment and personnel in many companies, the needs assessment may reveal that the organization must make some adjustments before it can undertake an effective training program.

Task analysis is a form of job analysis, but the task analysis focuses more specifically on what a trainee needs to learn to do the job properly. By studying the actual work performed through observation and interview, training developers can identify areas that need the most attention. Obviously, areas of satisfactory performance need not be addressed during the training program. Data from the task analysis may also suggest that jobs be restructured, with certain tasks being deleted from one job and more logically assigned to another, or that more efficient procedures be developed.

After developing a list of job tasks, the assessor then identifies the knowledge, skills, and abilities (KSAs) necessary to perform the job successfully. Through further analysis, the assessor determines which KSAs are the most important and makes these the foundation for the training course.

Making training relevant to specific job-related tasks is important to ensure that employees support the training program. For example, one group of researchers (Ford, Smith, Sego, & Quiñones, 1993) asked ground equipment mechanics in the U.S. Air Force their opinions of a training program 8 and 12 months after its completion. Mechanics who had experienced a wider variety of tasks covered by the training were more supportive of the program than mechanics who had experienced a narrower range of tasks. In addition, mechanics who scored higher on a measure of self-efficacy (discussed below) were also more supportive of formal training programs.

Finally, the training developer needs to do a **person analysis.** This consists of looking at qualities of the individuals who will be doing the work described in the task analysis. Do the workers targeted for training have the background and skills to make optimal use of the training? Which tasks give the workers the most problems? Using interviews, observations, reviews of production, and performance appraisal records, the training developer can tailor the materials to the specific needs of those who will be expected to accomplish the job tasks.

One element of person analysis that is sometimes overlooked is simply asking employees if they feel they need training. Interpreting employee responses may not be a straightforward process, however, since employees sometimes believe a request for training is an admission of incompetence. Nonetheless, an employee survey may highlight aspects of the job in which training is needed that the training needs analyst may overlook. In a survey of training needs among managers (Ford & Noe, 1987), for example, lower-level managers expressed a need for training in administrative matters, and both lower- and higher-level managers expressed a need for training in interpersonal skills.

Establish Training Objectives

Unfortunately, training programs are often developed with vague or unspecified goals. For example, trainees are expected to learn to "improve communication skills" or "raise productivity." Without concrete and specific goals to be accomplished, training is likely to be unfocused and limited in its success.

As much as possible, training goals should be measurable. For example, "increase sales volume 20 percent over last year" is better than the vague goal of "increase productivity." Similarly, rather than "improve communication," a training goal might specify "decrease employee grievances 40 percent over last year." If a goal is not measurable, then it will be difficult to determine whether the training has been successful. Considerable research (discussed in Chapter 7) has demonstrated that having specific goals facilitates both job performance and academic learning.

Another consideration related to training objectives is the manner in which goal accomplishment will be evaluated. Goals can be stated in terms of behavior (e.g., "at the end of the course, participants will be able to solve 75 percent of equipment maintenance problems without requiring special assistance"); productivity ("participants will increase their production volume 50 percent over the next six months"); trainee opinion ("90 percent of the trainees will rate the program as 'excellent.'"); or other ways. Some attention should be directed toward the type of objective established.

Develop Instructional Materials

Different training situations require different kinds of materials. Although on-the-job is probably the training method used most often, it is not usually the most effective. Effective training requires selecting materials that will accomplish the goals of the program and that are appropriate to the group to be trained.

Regrettably, training seems to be an area that is particularly susceptible to fads. As new materials and methods are developed, some trainers are anxious to use this "state-of-the-art" material. Although such material can be effective, the trainer first needs to make an objective evaluation of its usefulness. Some relevant considerations include the following:

- Is this material appropriate to the skill and educational levels of the targeted training group?
- Does it focus on the areas most important to successful performance of the job?
- Which method—lecture, audiovisual, behavior modeling, and so forth—will provide the optimal cost–benefit trade-off?
- To what method will the trainees be most receptive?
- What method am I most successful in using?
- How long will these materials and methods be useful? Will they be outdated in a short time?

Transfer of Training During the design of the training program, training developers need to consider how course participants will use what they have learned in training to do their jobs. **Transfer of training** refers to transferring knowledge from a training course to performance in the workplace by (1) using course material, and (2) being able to generalize that learning to similar situations (Baldwin & Ford, 1988). Transfer of training is hindered by poorly designed materials that are not relevant to the tasks required for successful job performance, ineffective communication of good materials, or terminating training before the workers have learned the material.

Two key concepts that affect transfer of training are physical fidelity and psychological fidelity (Goldstein, 1992). **Physical fidelity** refers to the similarity between equipment or materials used in a training situation and those actually used on the job; **psychological fidelity** refers to employees attaching similar meanings to their experiences in training and in the workplace. In many cases, physical fidelity is easier to achieve than psychological fidelity. Employers can create a control panel similar to those used in commercial airlines, for example, but creating the stress associated with flying through turbulence is more difficult.

Obviously, lessons from a training experience are more likely to be transferred to job performance if the equipment or materials used in training resemble actual work equipment as closely as possible, and the training requires performance of behaviors used on the job. Since it is usually impossible to include all the equipment and every job behavior in a training environment, courses must be designed so that the most important elements of the job are included.

One approach that seems to allow for a more effective transfer of training is through worker self-management, by which workers learn to evaluate their own performances and set goals for improvement (Gist, Bavetta, & Stevens, 1990). In a sense, self-management focuses on the process, as well as the goal, of a learning situation. If workers learn self-management of the skill development process, the training is more likely to transfer to the workplace.

One other consideration with regard to transfer of training: Most transfer of training studies assume that trainees automatically have the opportunity to use their training in the workplace. In fact, this isn't always the case. One study of a group of pilots (Ford, Quiñones, Sego, & Sorra, 1992), for example, found that transfer of training was affected by the supervisor's perception of a pilot's capabilities, skills, and likeability. That is, the supervisor did not automatically give employees who had experienced training the opportunity to use that training. Along the same lines, a study of supermarket managers (Tracey, Tannenbaum, & Kavanagh, 1995) found that stores that supported continuous learning were more likely to support using what was learned in training.

Test and Refine Materials

In the fourth stage of the process, the trainer tests the materials with a group of employees. This can be done formally or informally. Formal evaluation of materials would follow the steps discussed below in the section on evaluating training programs—pretest and posttest with a control group, for example. Although formal evaluation is the optimal procedure from a scientific vantage point, it may not be optimal from the perspective of time and costs.

More likely, the trainer will undertake an informal evaluation of the program. The trainer will determine the reactions of the group to the training, as well as the reactions of those who supervise the trained employees. Anecdotal or informal evidence of changes in productivity, error rates, morale, or other variables may also be noted.

With this information, the trainer can make changes so that goals are clearer, training content is more focused, or more pertinent material is included.

Implement the Training Program

When the trainer is reasonably certain that the training program meets the requirements, the program can be implemented. During the implementation phase, the trainer uses sound educational practices to facilitate learning. Course participants should have opportunities to practice what they have learned, and the instructor should provide feedback on their performances.

In an interesting study of social context and training performance, Martocchio (1992) told one group of computer trainees that they were receiving an "opportunity," whereas another group received no special instructions. Trainees in the opportunity condition learned more and experienced less computer anxiety than trainees in the neutral condition. In a similar study (Martocchio & Webster, 1992), trainees experienced higher performances and more positive attitudes when they received positive rather than negative feedback on their performances in the course. Finally, another related study (Martocchio, 1994) found that trainees who were told computer ability was an acquirable skill experienced less anxiety and greater feelings of confidence than trainees who were told that computer ability is a fixed entity.

Evaluate the Program

In the final stage of program development, the training experience is evaluated. As suggested above, this seems to be the weakest link in the training enterprise, since few training programs are scientifically evaluated. Probably the most obvious consideration with regard to evaluating a training program is that it should be done by someone other than the person who designed and delivered the program. In this way, impartiality of the results will be enhanced.

Since proper evaluation is such an important part of developing a training program, it will be considered in some detail later in this chapter.

On-the-Job Training
Vestibule Training
Apprenticeship
Job Rotation
Lecture
Audiovisual Methods
Conferences
Sensitivity Training
Behavior Modeling
Programmed Instruction
Computer-assisted
  Instruction
Multimedia Training
Simulations
Games
Case Studies
Outdoor Experiential
  Training
Open Learning

Methods of Training

Training programs take many forms. Although on-the-job training remains perhaps the most common format, modern trainers have used research from psychology and education to develop a variety of techniques. The following section discusses some of the methods of training. Methods that occur at the actual job site are on-the-job training, apprenticeship, vestibule training, and job rotation. Off-site methods include lecture, audiovisual methods, conferences and sensitivity training, behavior modeling, programmed instruction, computer-assisted instruction, multimedia instruction, simulations, games, case studies, and outdoor experiential training. Recently, some managers have become interested in open learning as a training method.

Most training programs use a variety of these techniques. Advantages and disadvantages of the different methods are compared in Table 5.1, which appears on page 154.

On-the-Job Training

For most employees, training consists of learning on the job. In a survey of managers at Honeywell Corporation, for example, employees estimated that they learned only about 20 percent of their job duties in formal training sessions and 80 percent on the job. Not surprisingly, most companies rely heavily on **on-the-job training (OJT).**

In a typical on-the-job program, new employees are placed with more experienced workers, who give them directions about what to do. The practicality and reasonableness of this approach are appealing. New employees get hands-on experience of the job, some productivity occurs during the training period, and the only major cost to the company is the productivity of the experienced worker. Additionally, there is no concern about transfer of training, since the situation has a high degree of physical and psychological fidelity.

Despite both its widespread use and face validity, however, OJT is not an especially effective training method, particularly because it is rarely approached systematically. The critical variable in OJT is the teaching skills of the employee assigned to do the training. If the trainer communicates ineffectively or provides incorrect information, then successful training is unlikely. At the same time, the trainer may have duties that must also be accomplished. Although the trainee may make some contribution to productivity, it is unlikely that this contribution will equal the lost productivity of the experienced worker.

Another consideration with OJT is that the actual work setting may not be the best environment for learning new skills. Job pressures, such as machine-paced production or demands from customers, may hamper the new employee's ability to learn.

Despite these problems, OJT can be successful with the proper planning, a good instructor, and a supportive environment (Malcolm, 1992). Box 5.1, for example, describes a successful OJT program for homeless people.

Vestibule Training

Vestibule training is a type of on-site program that avoids some of the problems associated with OJT. Rather than disrupt the flow of work, trainees are provided with an area outside the main production site where they can practice the skills necessary for successful job performance. In many respects, this approach is similar to simulation, which is discussed below.

Box 5.1   MARRIOTT'S WELFARE-TO-WORK PROGRAM

When Congress passed the Welfare Reform Act in 1996, few people realized that welfare reform would add two million very difficult to place individuals to the workforce over the next five years.

One company that has already responded to providing jobs for people on welfare is the hotel chain Marriott International, Inc. In the past few years, Marriott has hired more than 600 welfare recipients to full-time jobs.

Marriott's welfare-to-work program has faced a number of challenges. Presently, its employees drive the welfare trainees to work, arrange day care, help with housing, provide them with suitable clothing, and provide coaching on appropriate behavior in the workplace.

Although Marriott recognizes the benefits to society of providing work for people on welfare, there are other considerations behind the program. First, providing training for welfare recipients is another method for dealing with the chronic need for hotel workers. Second, the federal government helps pay part of the training cost. Finally, if Marriott can decrease turnover among its employees, the training will pay for itself.

Not everyone on welfare qualifies for the Marriott program. Applicants need a sixth grade reading ability, and they must pass a drug test and demonstrate a desire to work. Only about 25 percent of those who apply are accepted into the program.

According to Marriott trainers, one of the greatest challenges of the program is instilling corporate values into people who may not have worked in many years. One applicant, for example, turned down the training because it would conflict with her bowling schedule; another missed training because she needed to clean her house for out-of-town guests.

Nonetheless, 80 percent of the people accepted into the welfare-to-work program finish the training and accept jobs at Marriott. Some have progressed from the kitchen to higher level jobs and have even been named "employee of the month" in their hotels. In Marriott's view, the welfare-to-work program makes for both good social policy and good business.

Source: Milbank, D. (1996, October 31). Hiring welfare people, hotel chain finds, is tough but rewarding. *Wall Street Journal,* p. A1.

In the vestibule training program, professional trainers, rather than experienced workers, provide guidance about the proper procedures for task accomplishment. These trainers are more aware of the educational considerations relevant to training and are free of the pressures of accomplishing duties other than training the new employees.

An important consideration when comparing vestibule and on-the-job training is cost. Although the productivity of an experienced worker is not lost in vestibule training, the trainee is unlikely to make any contribution to productivity. Additionally, the company has the expense of maintaining equipment and space not directly engaged in production, as well as the salaries of the trainers and the materials used in the training program.

To prevent problems with transfer of training, the company also needs to be certain the vestibule experience closely approximates the actual work experience. Sometimes companies use older or outmoded equipment for vestibule training, which obviously may create problems when the new employee assumes regular responsibilities.

Apprenticeship

As mentioned above, **apprenticeship** is probably the oldest form of training. In addition to learning on the job, apprentices are required to spend at least 144 hours in classroom or shop training. On the average, apprenticeship programs last four years; during this period, trainees usually earn less than journeymen—the skilled craftspeople who have completed the program.

For many occupations, completing an apprenticeship program is necessary for acceptance into a union, and union membership is a prerequisite to getting a job. The basic idea behind apprenticeship is that labor and management cooperate so that there is always an adequate supply of skilled workers.

Although the combination of on-the-job, classroom, and shop training characteristic of apprenticeship programs can be quite effective, there are also some problems associated with this approach. One major problem is the length of the apprenticeship experience. Over the four-year training period, the tasks that constitute a job may change, and the person who has completed the course may still be unprepared to perform successfully on the job.

A second problem related to the length of the training is the availability of jobs when the apprentice finishes the program. In cyclical industries such as homebuilding, where apprenticeship is common, the availability of jobs depends on the economy. In these kinds of industries, a trainee may emerge from a program to find there are few jobs available.

Job Rotation

Job rotation is a training strategy often used with management trainees, but it can be used with blue-collar workers as well. Under this system, employees spend designated periods of time in different kinds of positions. For example, an employee may spend one month in accounting, one month in marketing, and a third month in personnel before settling into a regular assignment.

A unique advantage of job rotation is that it allows trainees to develop an appreciation for the specific role of their jobs in the organizational structure. At IBM, for example, engineering, manufacturing, and financial employees are frequently sent out with salespeople to learn about customer attitudes toward the company. Through such exposure, the company hopes that employees will realize the importance of their own jobs.

Job rotation is particularly useful for trainees—such as MBAs—who are uncertain about their career plans. Through exposure to a variety of jobs, they may be able to determine the best fit between job tasks and their abilities. At Land's End, a mail order clothing company, for example, employees often work one day a month in another department to learn about other parts of the business. In Land's End's "job enrollment" program, employees can train for a job elsewhere in the company before a job is available, then move into the job when a vacancy occurs (Stamps, 1996).

One group of researchers (Campion, Cheraskin, & Stevens, 1994) looked at the antecedents and outcomes of job rotation among employees of the finance department of a large pharmaceutical company. In this study, workers who were younger or who had a high level of education or performance were more likely to be chosen to participate in a rotation program. Job rotation was also related to being promoted or getting a raise, and employees who experienced rotation reported improved knowledge and skills.

Drawbacks to job rotation, however, include those that affect OJT training: Productivity is likely to be lost, the quality of training depends on the abilities of the employee assigned to do the training, and the worksite environment may not facilitate learning new skills. An additional problem occurs when employees are assigned to areas in which they have no interest but nevertheless must "serve out their time."

Lecture

Certainly every student is familiar with the **lecture** method of training. The major advantage of classroom lectures is their efficiency—large amounts of information can be transmitted in short periods of time to large numbers of people.

The skill of the presenter is a key consideration in the effectiveness of the lecture method. When the lecturer is a noted expert or an entertaining speaker, such experiences can be informative and personally rewarding. On the other hand, when a lecturer is ill-prepared, boring, or does not allow for questions from the audience, then the training experience is not likely to be successful. Since communication in a lecture is typically one-way, and learning is passive rather than active, trainees have no way of determining if they understand the material. The lecture method also lacks hands-on experience for the trainees. This kind of experience can be essential for job success.

At Dunkin' Donuts, for example, store managers were originally trained by listening to 12 weeks of lectures about what they could expect once they were assigned to their stores. During the training period, turnover was 50 percent, and the average shop tenure for managers was only 9.2 months. The training program was eventually revamped so that trainees could have more experience with the actual work done on the job.

Although lectures still constitute an important part of the training, Dunkin' Donuts trainees presently spend four weeks learning how to make donuts and maintain the equipment and two weeks learning management skills.

One of the elements of the final exam is to produce 140 twelve- to thirteen-ounce donuts in eight hours. The improvement in training procedures was undoubtedly a factor in the drop of trainee turnover to .05 percent and the increase in average store manager tenure to 26 months.

Lectures have also been shown to be less effective than other methods when training managers. In a meta-analysis of management training studies, Burke and Day (1986) found that lecture and lecture/discussion were not as effective as either modeling or lecture/discussion with role play. Similarly, Gist (1989) found that managers trained to generate innovative ideas through a modeling approach significantly outperformed managers who had been trained through a lecture approach.

Some suggestions for making lectures more interesting include allowing questions and answers, putting participants in small groups to discuss the material, and requiring students to debate different sides of the material being presented (Broadwell & Dietrich, 1996).

Audiovisual Methods

Traditional **audiovisual methods** of training include films, slide presentations, videotapes, and closed circuit television; newer methods include interactive video discs, digitized text projectors, and interactive audiocassettes.

Because presentation costs are minimal, audiovisual methods are particularly good when material has to be presented many times. Additionally, audiovisual materials can often be made more interesting than a lecture. For example, at a well-known chain of pizza restaurants, new employees see a film of how *not* to be a good waitress. The waitress in the film writes down the wrong order, spills drinks on the customers, and argues with the customers about the bill.

Videotapes have emerged as an important training method that is considerably less expensive than training using films. Particularly in occupations in which self-presentation is important, seeing a videotape of one's performance can be quite useful. In the life insurance industry, for example, where clients often reject proposals from salespeople, learning to counter customer objections is an important part of training. At Life of Virginia, agents are allowed to borrow videotape equipment and practice handling objections with friends or coworkers, who play the part of the customer. When agents feel their performances are satisfactory, they send a videotape for evaluation by their superiors. Management reviews the tapes and makes suggestions as to how the agents can improve performance and increase sales.

In another innovative use of video, the American Hotel and Motel Association developed a video without narration or dialogue to use in training housekeepers. Using music, animation, computer graphics, and sound effects, the video allows housekeepers to see the jobs they are expected to perform. The advantage of the video was that it used no language, since many housekeepers have limited skill in English (Hequet, 1996).

One of the newest audiovisual methods is teleconferencing, in which training is provided by satellite from a central location to audiences in different places. Although teleconferencing was once an expensive form of training, prices today are lower, and a number of companies use the teleconference method. Cray Research, a maker of high-speed computers, for example, broadcasts its training classes to other sites, and employees can also receive graduate training in audio engineering by teleconference from the University of Minnesota (D. Sheridan, 1992).

Some drawbacks to audiovisual methods can include the cost of film preparation, which is typically $90,000 for a half-hour film (Hequet, 1996). Another disadvantage is the one-way communication and the inability of trainees to determine whether they understand the material, as well as difficulties in adding or deleting material. The effectiveness of some training films is also limited by problems with aesthetics. Artificial or contrived settings, poor acting, and dated costumes can distract the trainee from the lesson the film is designed to present.

Conferences

Conferences bring together several people who have specialized knowledge about particular areas that they share with each other. The conference may be used to solve problems, inform others about new information or developments, or improve communication among individuals. This method requires little more than a discussion leader, a meeting place, and the participants' time. In contrast with lectures, the conference method encourages individual participation and feedback, and the trainer can determine whether participants understand the material.

The Leadership Institute is a conference program set up by Marquette University for employees of Harley-Davidson in which one of the courses focuses on values. In this course, employees compare their personal values with the values of Harley-Davidson, then discuss ways of integrating both sets of values into the way they do their work. The five key Harley-Davidson values appear in Box 5.2.

Although the effectiveness of conferences is influenced by the quality of the material and the presenter, group dynamics also play an important part in making the program a success. The person leading the conferences needs to be skilled in group facilitation skills. Group dynamics are covered in more detail in Chapter 10.

Sensitivity Training

Sensitivity training, which is also covered more fully in Chapter 10, is a conference technique that focuses on improving interpersonal communication skills between training participants. Through a series of group meetings, partic-

Box 5.2 VALUES AT HARLEY-DAVIDSON

At Harley-Davidson, all employees are expected to learn and abide by five key values that were developed as part of a reorganization in the late 1980s. Employees can take a course and become certified to teach others about the values.

The values are printed on a laminated card given to each employee:

1. Tell the truth.
2. Be fair.
3. Keep your promises.
4. Respect the individual.
5. Encourage intellectual curiosity.

Source: Filipczak, B. (1996, February). Values keep Harley-Davidson on the road to success. *Training,* pp. 38–42.

ipants learn to communicate more effectively, listen to their coworkers more carefully, and appreciate the viewpoints of others. Although this approach was highly regarded in the 1950s and 1960s, its popularity has lessened considerably. Improved communication can have important effects on productivity and morale, but these effects are not always easy to identify—nor are they always positive. Sensitivity training is still widely practiced, however, among clinical and counseling psychologists, educators, and others in the helping professions.

Behavior Modeling

Behavior modeling is a method of training that draws on Bandura's (1969) work on learning and behavior. Specifically, modeling theory holds that individuals often learn best by observing, then practicing, a behavior. Employees simply watch someone who is effective at performing the desired behavior, then practice until they can perform the behavior themselves. For example, authoritarian bosses may use behavior modeling to practice being more considerate toward employees, car salespeople may use the technique to practice closing a deal, or service personnel may use the method to practice handling difficult customers.

Behavior modeling as a training method relies chiefly on role playing as its instructional method, but techniques such as lecture and videotape can be used as well. Basically, the elements of this approach consist of five steps:

1. Viewing the desired behavior;
2. Using written materials or other study aids to assist in performing the desired behavior;
3. Rehearsing the behavior;
4. Receiving social reinforcement for successful performance of the behavior; and

5. Transferring the behavior from the training setting to the workplace (Decker, 1983).

In a study of the behavior modeling approach, Meyer and Raich (1983) evaluated the effects of a training program on the productivity of individuals selling large appliances, televisions, and radios. In this study, sales associates were first presented with "learning points" (i.e., written materials about selling), then watched videotapes of an effective salesperson. Finally, the trainees practiced the same situation while receiving feedback from their instructors.

In the six-month period following the training, hourly commissions of the sales associates who had participated in the behavior modeling program increased 7 percent, whereas the commissions of those who had participated in the more traditional training—the control group—declined 3 percent. An additional finding from this study was that those who had received the experimental treatment were less likely to leave the company than those who had not received the behavior modeling training.

In another test of the behavior modeling approach, managers participated in computer software training using either a computer-assisted tutorial (see the section on CAI below) or behavior modeling. Managers who received the behavior modeling approach were more successful at learning the software than those who had received the tutorial (Gist, Schwoerer, & Rosen, 1989). In a similar study (Simon & Werner, 1996), computer trainees learned more effectively using behavior modeling rather than self-paced instruction or lecture.

The obvious consideration with regard to behavior modeling is the quality of the model. As is the case with the lecture, successful application of the method depends on the skill of the presenter. Additionally, it is important that the modeling situation resemble closely the actual job situation. Otherwise, transfer of training problems are likely to occur.

Programmed Instruction

As suggested above, a consideration common to several training techniques is the quality of the instructor or leader. If this individual does not do the job well, then the quality of the training experience will be diminished.

Programmed instruction (PI) is a method for coping with this problem. The major feature of PI is that it is self-paced and does not require interaction with an instructor. Trainees are provided with material, divided into units of increasing difficulty, that they are expected to learn. When they feel they have learned the material within a unit, they then answer a series of questions. If their answers are correct, they are instructed to advance to the next unit. Incorrect answers are explained, and if too many are missed, the learner is instructed to go over the unit again before proceeding to the next section. Material in the PI program is hierarchical. That is, it is necessary to understand the preceding unit in order to learn the next unit.

Programmed instruction is effective in shortening the time necessary to learn. Trainees set their own pace, they receive immediate feedback on their performances, and successful completion of the program indicates they have learned all the necessary material.

There are many attractive features to programmed instruction, but a key consideration is the quality and timeliness of the material being presented. Developing a training program that is segmented into comprehensive units is typically a lengthy process. Additionally, PI is not usually very flexible. When changes in job procedures and tasks occur, the program must be updated or revised so that the trainees receive all the necessary information. When workbooks or other printed material are used for PI, constant changes may become unwieldy. For this reason, many proponents of PI now recommend the use of computers.

Computer-assisted Instruction

Computer-assisted instruction (CAI) is an extension of the programmed instruction method. A computer program assesses the knowledge of the individual trainee, then delivers training material appropriate to that trainee's level. As with programmed instruction, trainees receive constant feedback about their performances, and they cannot advance to more difficult material until they have mastered the more basic.

In computer-adaptive training, which resembles computer-adaptive testing (CAT) used in personnel selection, the level of difficulty of the material is adapted to the knowledge and abilities of the computer user. This is a particular advantage of this method, since teaching does not have to occur at the level of the "lowest common denominator," as in lectures or conferences. At Hewlett Packard, for example, systems operators and managers are trained on a multimedia program that includes full-stereo audio, text, graphics, music, and animation on a mixed-mode CD-ROM that allows participants to proceed at their own pace (Spitz, 1992).

Like programmed instruction, CAI requires that considerable time and care be spent in developing useful and effective materials. Additionally, there may be some concern about certain groups of employees who are not used to working with computers. Evaluations of CAI suggest, however, that trainees generally react positively, and that training time is usually shortened (Wexley & Latham, 1981). In addition, as CD-ROMs become more available, this form of training is likely to become more widely used.

Two researchers (Dossett & Hulvershorn, 1983) evaluated a CAI program designed to teach electronics to U.S. Air Force personnel. Individuals experiencing regular classroom training were compared to individuals working both alone and in pairs on a CAI electronics program. Although achievement scores for all three groups were similar, both groups of CAI-trained personnel completed their training faster than the classroom group, and individuals working in pairs were faster than either group. The researchers concluded that CAI can be effective when used by pairs of employees, and that this can offset costs associated with CAI training.

One company that has made extensive use of CAI is Motorola, a maker of portable cellular telephones, microprocessors, and other high-technology items. Since rapid change seems to be a defining characteristic of high-tech industries, constant enhancement of employee skills through training is critical. To facilitate training for employees responsible for maintaining Motorola's complex manufacturing equipment, a computer-based training program was developed. Working alone on terminals in cubicles, employees learned about the procedures for keeping the equipment functional and repairing breakdowns. Employees were allowed to take their terminals home for additional practice.

An unexpected benefit of the Motorola program was the identification of several high performers who had previously received poor ratings from their supervisors. Most of these individuals were not native speakers of English, and consequently had been unable to communicate well. Since many of the jobs they had been assigned required more verbal than technical skills, they were able to be reassigned to more difficult and challenging work.

Another company that has adopted computer-assisted training is Shell Oil, which has almost 200 interactive video training programs. Employees sit at terminals and work through the programs at their own pace. Shell estimates that, despite their development costs, the interactive videos resulted in considerable savings to the company. Development and presentation of a traditional course on statistical quality control, for example, was estimated to cost $3 million, but the same course on interactive video cost only $100,000 (Zemke, 1991). Finally, Federal Express uses an interactive video system that is updated every six weeks. Employees take a job knowledge test every six months, and results from the test are part of an employee's performance review (Galagan, 1991).

Multimedia Training

Multimedia training uses a variety of methods, usually focused around computers and using CD-ROMS and the World Wide Web. In many respects, multimedia training is the "cutting edge" of training systems (Multimedia Training in the *Fortune* 1,000, 1996). Although multimedia methods presently constitute only 16 percent of all training, this figure is expected to double in the very near future.

In most companies multimedia training is most frequently used to teach computer skills, but recent applications include safety, interpersonal skills, and customer service. Not surprisingly, employees in information systems departments are usually the heaviest users of multimedia training.

Advantages of multimedia include its availability at all times and accessibility over wide geographic areas. In addition, employees can move through the material at their own pace. A major disadvantage is cost, since not all employees have computers with a CD-ROM drive, color monitor, sound card, and graphics card. Another obvious disadvantage is updating data, hardware, and software. Nonetheless, this method of training is likely to become increasingly widespread.

Simulations

Simulations are typically used when the training situation calls for a high degree of realism. For example, because of the importance of minimizing errors in flight, airline pilots and astronauts spend many hours using equipment that simulates flight conditions.

Transfer of training is an important issue in simulations. Because simulation equipment is often expensive to build, trainers need to be certain that what the trainee learns is applicable and useful in the workplace. For this reason, simulation equipment in particular must have both physical and psychological fidelity. In other words, the simulation experience must use equipment that resembles the actual work equipment as closely as possible and must require performance of the behaviors that are used on the job.

One area in which simulation is widely used is the nuclear power plant industry. Babcock and Wilcox, the company that built most of the nuclear power plants in the United States, maintains a large simulation facility in Lynchburg, Virginia. Utility companies can arrange to rent the facility for their employees to receive hands-on experience in both operating a power plant and handling emergencies.

At Three Mile Island (TMI), site of the worst nuclear accident in the United States, classroom training was originally emphasized over simulation. For example, as part of their training, operators were required to memorize 50 different procedures to use in case of an emergency (Feuer, 1985). Unfortunately, the emergency that occurred in March 1979 was not covered in the procedures, and employees were uncertain how to respond. After the accident, training at TMI was revised to emphasize simulations over classroom learning. At a cost of $15 million, the parent company of TMI installed a control room simulator that is an exact replica of the one used in the workplace.

Flight simulation is based on an exact replica of the cockpit and aerodynamic characteristics of a particular aircraft. In addition to practical considerations, flight simulation is important from a theoretical perspective because results from these simulations are often used in studies of transfer of training (Adams, 1989). Interestingly, several studies (Diehl & Ryan, 1977; Orlansky & String, 1977; Semple, Hennessy, Sanders, Cross, Beith, & McCauley, 1981) have shown that transfer of training from flight simulators can be surprisingly low. Nonetheless, flight simulators are used for training because they are much less expensive than training in an aircraft, they operate independent of weather, and they allow trainees to repeat a task several times in one training session.

Although simulations can be quite effective in training employees, they can also be expensive to develop and maintain. Many companies do not have the resources to develop an effective simulation program. Along the same lines, establishing physical fidelity by using state-of-the-art equipment in the training facility may be impractical.

Games

One training technique often used in business schools and the military is **games.** Games allow participants to practice making decisions and to see the outcomes of those decisions. Most games have three elements: roles, scenarios, and an accounting system. Roles are assigned to players and describe the behaviors inherent in the roles; scenarios are situations described by maps, statistical reports, company histories, and so forth. The accounting system is the method by which the performances of an individual or a team are evaluated.

Games are particularly useful when situations are ill-defined or several possible solutions to a problem are available. By experiencing the process of decision making, many times players can decide on actions that would not necessarily have occurred to them otherwise. When players participate as teams, there is also the opportunity to observe, and perhaps discuss, the way players interact with each other.

Limitations of games include high development costs, the possibility of low psychological fidelity, and the likelihood that participants will not take the exercise seriously. Also, for some partipicants, winning becomes more important than learning. In these situations, the usefulness of this approach becomes questionable.

Case Studies

Case studies are written descriptions of an organizational problem that has no correct solution. Trainees are asked to study the problem and develop recommendations, then meet in groups to discuss their answers. Case studies are designed to teach critical thinking, creativity, communication, and feedback. At Corning, Inc., a major manufacturer of glass products, for example, employees learn about gender issues and sexual harrassment through case studies and feedback sessions.

Although case studies are one of the most popular training techniques, critics suggest that they generally fail to accomplish longer-range goals. Specifically, case studies often help trainees learn ways to fix a problem, but they are rarely useful in understanding why the problem occurred in the first place. In this way, case studies promote problem solving, but they do not address deeper issues, such as organizational policies or goals. In addition, the case study approach often does not allow for the effective transfer of training back to the organization, and trainees receive no hands-on experience. Finally, many trainers regard case studies as one of the dullest ways to do training (Owenby, 1992).

Outdoor Experiential Training

One of the newest forms of training requires trainees to perform tasks such as climbing trees or whitewater rafting. **Outdoor experiential training (OET)** is a unique form of training in that it has virtually no content. In other words, the method itself—rather than the information presented—is designed to encourage employee creativity and communication so that problems in the workplace can be addressed more effectively (Tarullo, 1992). OET programs typically last from one to five days.

The rationale behind holding training outdoors is that workers can step outside behaviors typical of the workplace. Social norms, such as titles, modes of dress, and formal communication, are discarded as workers attempt to cross a log suspended 60 feet above the ground or scale a 10-foot wall. When such norms are discarded, people become more honest and open to change. The activities in OET are designed to heighten participants' sense of arousal so that feelings of trust, support, and cooperation can develop. Theoretically, OET works best with individuals who work together as a team.

Despite its popularity, no studies have yet demonstrated clearly the effectiveness of OET as a training technique. Nonetheless, some research (Wagner & Roland, 1992) suggests that although individual behavior does not seem to change after OET, group behavior does. Specifically, groups that participated in OET were rated by supervisors as more cohesive, clearer about goals, and more effective 15 months after an outdoor training program. When groups were balanced in numbers of male and female participants, improvements in problem solving and effectiveness were particularly significant.

In general, employees react favorably to OET, even when they initially objected to participating. Still, there are some considerations about implementing this form of training. First, OET is, in a sense, a kind of sensitivity training, and changes related to productivity and behavior, rather than attitude, may be difficult to detect. Second, most OET programs require a certain level of physical ability; trainers using OET need to be careful not to discriminate unfairly against employees who are unable to perform outdoor tasks.

Third, OET exposes employees to dangers that are not found in most work sites, so employers need to be certain that they have the resources to deal with injuries that might occur during OET. In one case (Sample & Hylton, 1996), for example, a 59-year-old woman participating in an outdoor experience fell off a log and broke her leg. Ten months after the accident, the woman sued; the jury, finding her employer negligent, awarded the woman $875,000.

Finally, changes that emerge from OET may not be due to the experience itself. Rather, OET may create a Hawthorne effect, where employees change their behavior because of the attention focused on them, rather than because of the method or content of the training program. In addition, sending an entire

Outdoor experiential training is designed to build trust and improve communication among participants.

work group away for several days is extremely expensive. If results from OET are from a Hawthorne effect, employers can almost certainly find less costly and dangerous ways to provide training in creativity and openness.

Open Learning

Some researchers have recently proposed that because of the rapid pace of change in the workplace, much training is likely to be informal and outside standardized programs. **Open learning** refers to workers learning on their own material that is presented in writing or through a computer, audio- or videotapes, or an interactive video system. In an open learning program, workers have more autonomy to decide what to study, as well as the manner in which they will proceed.

The open learning system has several desirable characteristics. First, it is flexible—workers can choose the time and place they will participate. Second, open learning does not depend on a trainer. Third, open learning gives responsibility for learning to individuals, so only people who are motivated will participate in the training.

Warr and Bunce (1995) followed the progress of junior managers who undertook a four-month open learning training program. Topics covered in the program were communication, problem solving, budgeting, hiring people, and health and safety. At the end of four months, managers who had expressed a positive attitude toward training in general and used an analytic (i.e., cognitive) rather than a behavioral learning strategy had learned the most. In addition, supervisor ratings of performance improved between the beginning of the program and four months later, suggesting that the participants were successfully learning the material.

Another important consideration in open learning is the motivation of trainees to learn the material. Maurer and Tarulli (1994) looked at the role of individual characteristics, the work environment, and possible outcomes in predicting which employees would participate in development activities. In terms of the work environment, results showed that when an employer encouraged employee development activities and when social support at the job site was not great, employees were more likely to participate. The best predictors of development activity, however, were qualities of the individual. Specifically, career insight, perceived need for skill enhancement, job involvement, and self-efficacy motivated employees toward development programs.

As should be clear to you by now, designing and implementing a training program can be complicated and expensive. Table 5.1 summarizes the various methods of training in terms of the rationale, advantages, and disadvantages of each, and Figure 5.2 illustrates the most commonly used methods of training.

Optimizing the Training Experience

Assessing Trainability
Training the Trainers

Even the best designed training programs can fail if attention is not paid to two other areas: the readiness of the employees for the training and the abilities of the trainers. If employees are apathetic and unmotivated, then training materials of even the highest caliber are unlikely to be successful. If the presenters know little or nothing about teaching, or are themselves apathetic and unmotivated, then the program is equally likely to fail. The following sections consider some issues relevant to assessing the trainability of workers and the abilities of training staff.

Assessing Trainability

Interestingly, the trainability of employees is often not addressed in the training literature. Yet it stands to reason that certain employees are more suitable for training, and that training will enhance their value to the company more than the value of others. These facts should be kept in mind when managers identify candidates for a training program.

Two necessary preconditions for learning are trainee readiness and trainee motivation (Goldstein, 1986). Readiness refers to both the maturational and the experiential backgrounds of the employees. Programs that do not consider the skills necessary to accomplish the training are likely to be limited in their effectiveness. For example, word processing classes for employees who do not type well or investment management seminars for individuals who do not have some understanding of accounting may not be particularly useful.

Recall from Chapter 4 that general cognitive ability has been shown to be an important predictor of job performance. Cognitive ability is also an important component of success in training (Ree, Carretta, & Teachout, 1995). However, a common problem with training programs is the presumption of a certain level of literacy among course participants. This is an important consideration, since some research (Mumford, Weeks, Harding, & Fleishman, 1988)

Table 5.1 METHODS OF TRAINING

Method	Advantage	Limitation
On-the-job training	Hands-on-experience; some productivity; low costs; few transfer of training problems	Effectiveness depends on skill of instructor; lost productivity of instructor; job pressures may interfere with training
Vestibule training	Does not disrupt workplace; professional trainers are aware of educational practices; few transfer of training problems	Can be expensive to provide equipment and space; worker contributes no productivity; companies sometimes use outdated equipment for training
Apprenticeship	Combines classroom learning with job experience; allows companies to plan supply of workers	Length of training may make training content outdated; job availability may be cyclical
Job rotation	Trainees learn how their jobs fit with organizational structure; helps trainees identify careers that appeal to them	Lost productivity; quality of training depends on instructor; job pressures may interfere with learning; trainees waste time in areas not relevant to their actual job assignments
Lecture	Efficient in presenting large amounts of material to large groups of people	Success depends on skills of presenter; passive learning; no hands-on experience for trainees
Audiovisual methods	Allows material to be presented many times; often more interesting than lecture; low presentation costs	Can be expensive to develop; does not allow trainees to get feedback; difficulty adding or deleting material
Conferences/ sensitivity training	Requires only discussion leader and participants; encourages participation and feedback	Linkage between training and performance is unclear
Behavior modeling	Appears to be a very effective training method; workers practice behavior and receive immediate feedback	Learning depends on skill of model; important to consider transfer of training issues
Programmed instruction (PI)	Shortens training time; trainees get immediate feedback; they proceed at their own pace; program cannot be finished unless trainee knows the material	High development costs; concerns about timeliness of material; method is not very flexible
Computer assisted instruction (CAI)	Training is tailored to the level of trainee; seems to work well in high-tech industries	High development costs; trainees must know how to operate computers
Multimedia training	Always available; available in different sites; self-paced	Expensive to create and maintain; requires special equipment
Simulations	High degree of physical fidelity in training; transfer of training assumed to be high	Simulators can be quite expensive to develop and maintain; psychological fidelity may be hard to establish
Games	Allows participants to practice making decisions and see outcomes of decisions	Often has problems with transfer of training; trainees may not take the game seriously
Case studies	Designed to teach critical thinking; creativity, communication, and feedback	Do not teach analytical skills or deeper issues; problems with transfer of training
Outdoor experiential training (OET)	Allows trainees to interact outside traditional roles; focuses on interpersonal relations between employees	Little evidence of linkage to performance; possibility of injury or unfair discrimination
Open learning	Flexibility; does not require trainers; participants are self-motivated	No guarantee participants will finish the program; no check to see if they are learning materials correctly

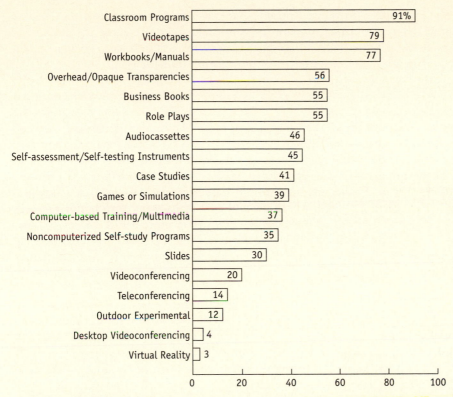

Figure 5.2 Percentage of Companies Using Different Instructional Methods

suggests that educational background is more predictive of success in a training program than course content, experience of the instructor, hands-on practice, or other situational variables.

When employees are deficient in reading and study skills, remedial instruction may be necessary before participants can be expected to learn the new material. However, some experimental research (Quiñones, 1995) suggests that being assigned to a "remedial" training program has a negative impact on trainee attitudes.

The manner in which material is presented also affects performance in training. Substantial evidence suggests that less able learners do better when instruction is highly structured, and that more able learners do better with less structured instruction (Snow & Lohman, 1984). Additionally, high levels of anxiety are known to lower educational achievement.

One approach to improving the effectiveness of a training program is to use a test or exercise to assess training readiness. These measures, like personnel selection procedures in general, must be valid and reliable predictors of performance. In one study (Dunbar & Novick, 1988), for example, scores from the

Armed Services Vocational Aptitude Battery (ASVAB) overpredicted the success of men in a clerical training program and underpredicted the success of women. This undesirable situation illustrates the importance of being certain about the validity of measures used for assessing trainability.

Another approach to predicting success in training is to use a work sample. In a typical trainability test, workers are taught how to perform a task, and then a supervisor observes as the workers attempt the task. The supervisor notes the number of errors the workers make, then makes a judgment about the workers' likelihood of success in a training program. When such tests have a high degree of physical and psychological fidelity, they can be quite useful.

One other factor that appears to affect training readiness is **self-efficacy.** Self-efficacy is a belief in one's ability to perform a specific task (Bandura, 1986). In general, people who have high self-efficacy perform better on tasks than those who have low self-efficacy (Eden & Aviram, 1993; Mathieu, Martineau, & Tannenbaum, 1993). In the study of computer software training mentioned above, managers with high self-efficacy scores performed significantly better on a software performance task than managers who had low self-efficacy.

One study (Saks, 1995) looked at the relationship between self-efficacy and training among newly hired entry-level accountants. When the accountants had low self-efficacy initially, training increased feelings of self-efficacy, ability to cope, job performance, and job commitment. In this study, training also proved to be an important source of socialization for new employees (socialization is covered more fully in Chapter 12).

The second precondition for learning is motivated employees. Worker motivation, which is discussed in Chapter 7, is a complicated topic that offers a variety of explanations for job performance. Researchers are presently uncertain whether the factors that motivate workers' job performances are the same as those that motivate their performance in training. Nevertheless, it is reasonable to assume that workers who are motivated to perform well in a training course are likely to do better than those who are unmotivated, apathetic, or hostile to training.

One study (Stewart, Carson, & Cardy, 1996) looked at the relationship between personality factors and training among 130 employees at a hotel/resort in the Southwest. The hypotheses of this study were that employees who had received training in self-leadership (i.e., self-observation, goal setting, self-reinforcement, and so forth) would improve their customer service behavior, and that employees who scored high on a measure of conscientiousness would be more customer-service oriented than those who scored low. In this study, training in self-leadership did not improve customer service behavior, but the personal quality of conscientiousness was a significant predictor of job behavior. Self-leadership training did, however, improve conscientiousness scores.

In another study (Martocchio & Dulebohn, 1994), researchers looked at providing feedback that attributes performance success to causes outside the trainees' control. Employees participating in a software training program received one of two messages regarding their performances. All employees were first told they had performed at an average level, but then half received a message that attributed their performances to the difficulty of the program they were learning, whereas others received a message that they needed to work harder. Employees who received the second message, which implied that training performance was under their own control, expressed more confidence about their ability to learn the material and did, in fact, learn more.

In one study (Baldwin, Magjuka, & Lohrer, 1991), two groups of workers were given an opportunity to choose the type of training they would experience, whereas a third group was given no choice. In fact, however, all groups received the same training program. Members of the group assigned to the training method they "selected" had higher motivation to succeed in the training program than the other two groups. More importantly, members of the group that had no choice had higher motivation to succeed than the group whose members specified a choice that they did not get. Apparently being offered a choice of training and having it denied is more harmful to motivation than having no choice. In a similar study (Hicks & Klimoski, 1987), trainees who received a realistic preview of a training program were more motivated to attend the training sessions. Finally, Mathieu, Tannenbaum, and Salas (1992) found that proofreaders reacted more positively to a training program if they chose, rather than were assigned, to participate.

For the most part, researchers have not addressed the personal characteristics associated with success in training. Some studies have suggested, however, that trainees are more likely to be successful if they have higher levels of need for achievement (Baumgartel, Reynolds, & Pathan, 1984), locus of control (Noe & Schmitt, 1986), and general intelligence (Ree & Earles, 1991; Robertson & Down, 1989). Also, some evidence (Smith-Jentsch, Jentsch, Payne, & Salas, 1996) suggests that when training addresses problems workers have already experienced on the job, participants perform better.

Despite our limited knowledge about trainability, most researchers agree on certain general principles regarding motivation and training. First, participants in training are likely to experience higher levels of motivation when they understand the relevance of what they are expected to learn. If the material to be covered will help them perform their jobs more easily or will lead to rewards such as higher skill levels and salaries, then trainees may be more positively oriented toward the training program.

Second, the instructor should make the goals of the training program clear from the outset. Setting goals focuses the attention of the participants and establishes an incentive to achieve. Additionally, some evidence suggests that participants do better if they help set their own goals.

Third, the teaching method should be appropriate for the kind of skill to be taught. Trainers need to be certain that their teaching methods fit the task to be learned. Additionally, the difficulty level of the materials must be appropriate to the aptitudes of the workers.

Finally, the instructor needs to provide feedback and other reinforcers to course participants. In addition to informing the participants about their performances, the instructor should use social reinforcement, such as demonstrating confidence in trainees' abilities and using trainees' knowledge and experiences in the training program. Probably the most basic reinforcement for learning is simply making the material interesting.

Training the Trainers

Being a successful trainer is much more complicated than merely being a good teacher. In addition to teaching skills, the effective trainer must be able to diagnose problem areas, develop a program to address those problems, administer a training program, and evaluate the training programs of others.

Several qualities are important in becoming a successful trainer. First, trainers must have knowledge of the organizational environment in which they operate to assess properly the appropriateness of training methods. Computer-assisted instruction (CAI), for example, might be highly regarded at IBM, but not be acceptable as a method for training social workers. Trainers need to appreciate the values of the environments in which they work.

Second, trainers obviously need professional knowledge of the area in which they teach. Although some training packages—particularly programmed instruction—are designed so they can be administered by anyone, it is usually not good practice to have an individual unfamiliar with an area be responsible for teaching it. Trainers should have knowledge of the relevant field, or at least knowledge of a related area and time to become sufficiently familiar with the area to be taught. At the same time, the trainer's background should rest on solid credentials and not merely reflect some faddish ideas currently popular in training circles.

Third, trainers must be in their positions because they want to be trainers, and not for other reasons. Unfortunately, the axiom "Those who can't, teach" often applies to individuals who do training. Trainers should be selected because they enjoy the work and can provide high levels of performance and not because they are unsuccessful doing other work, are motivated by a desire to work with people rather than numbers or objects, or are nearing retirement. Historically, the majority of professional trainers have had backgrounds in either psychology or education.

Finally, the trainer must have some understanding of the general principles of education. Most formal training in organizations uses one of two approaches: mastery or learning time. Mastery (Bloom, 1976) requires that an instructor constantly monitor the progress an individual makes in learning new material and that corrective instruction be provided until the employee has mastered the required skill.

Learning time (Fisher, Berliner, Filby, Marliave, Cahen, & Dishaw, 1980), on the other hand, focuses on mastering the new skills within a specific time period. Even though an employee may achieve mastery, time is allocated so that skills can be practiced or more advanced skills developed. Learning time draws on the considerable body of research with academic students showing that the more time students have to practice materials, the better they learn them. In a meta-analysis of studies that considered the effect of overlearning, for example, Driskell, Willis, and Copper (1992) found that **overlearning,** which refers to the continuous practice of a behavior after it is acquired, did significantly affect retention of material.

In addition to training methods, trainers must know something about the successful communication of instruction. These include explaining the purpose of the training course; providing clear directions to participants; providing for participant questions, feedback, and practice; and adapting teaching strategies to fit the abilities of the participants. Although considerable research indicates that such methods facilitate learning, regrettably, not all trainers or teachers (or professors) seem to be able to put them into practice.

In summary, successful training is the product of success on three levels: the readiness of the trainees, the appropriateness of the method, and the abilities of the trainer. Although a good trainer may compensate for poor materials, or good materials for a poor trainer, all three factors must be considered to optimize training time and budgets.

Evaluating Training Effectiveness

Case Study
Pretest-Posttest
Pretest-Posttest with a
  Control Group
After-Only with a Control
  Group
Solomon Four-Group
  Design
Other Considerations in
  Evaluation

As suggested above, properly researched, developed, and administered training programs can contribute greatly to an employee's productivity. Inferior programs, on the other hand, contribute little or nothing to productivity, waste organizational resources, and, in some cases, even lower productivity. The effectiveness of a training program can only be determined through evaluation.

In addition to productivity concerns, training programs should be evaluated for at least two other reasons: cost and fairness. Research has shown that the greatest cost of a training program is not its development, but the productivity lost while people attend the training sessions. Since some training methods, such as computer-assisted instruction, can be quite expensive, companies need to know which methods are the most effective for their employees.

Another consideration relevant to evaluating training programs is fairness. As mentioned in Chapter 3, training falls under the same legal guidelines as personnel selection, and companies must be careful to maintain proper standards of admission when selecting workers to attend training programs. Furthermore, if future promotions are based on job performance, then employers must see that training content is relevant to performance. Although it seems logical that what is taught in training would be used on the job, this can be determined only by job analysis.

Table 5.2   KIRKPATRICK'S CRITERIA

Reaction: This refers to participants' feelings or attitudes toward the training intervention, usually collected by means of a questionnaire that assesses participants' opinions on various aspects of the training intervention using structured rating scales. How participants reacted to behavior modeling, for instance, would be an example of an outcome at this level.

Learning: The assessment of learning involves determining how much of the training material participants have absorbed. This includes the principles, theories, facts, techniques, and attitudes that the training is designed to convey. A variety of techniques, including paper and pencil tests, simulations, and peer evaluations, can be used to test learning. Although favorable reactions may create a positive atmosphere, they do not always lead to learning.

Behavior: This level focuses on the use of learned material in the workplace. Since learning demonstrated in a training environment may not be applied on the job, participants' performance following the training intervention indicates to what extent behavior has actually changed. The evaluation of job performance should target aspects of the job related to the training objectives. Behavior rating scales are frequently used in this type of evaluation.

Results: This category deals with the relationship between the results of the training intervention and organizational goals. Results include outcome measures such as productivity, turnover, job satisfaction, accident rates, and grievances. The selection of results measures should be based on the intended outcome of the intervention.

It is ironic that companies interested in improving the productivity of their employees through training often do not evaluate the effectiveness of the programs they adopt. Even when they do evaluate, often their research plans or the instruments they use to make an evaluation are faulty or look at only one or two dimensions (Kraiger, Ford, & Salas, 1993; Ostroff, 1991). In a survey of over 100 firms that claimed to evaluate their training programs, Kirkpatrick (1978) found that 75 percent used the reaction of the trainees as a basis for evaluation, less than 20 percent measured behavioral changes, and about 15 percent looked at on-the-job results as measured by supervisor ratings. For a variety of reasons, these evaluation strategies are all likely to provide unclear results.

One influential model for considering the effectiveness of training looks at four levels of criteria (Kirkpatrick, 1959a, 1959b, 1960a, 1960b). *Reactions* refer to participants' feelings about a training program and are not necessarily linked with job performance. *Learning* is the absorption of material covered in the training program. *Behavior* refers to use of learning on the job; and *results* are goals of the training program. Table 5.2 describes Kirkpatrick's criteria.

When evaluators consider a training outcome, they need to be conscious of the level at which they focus their analysis. For example, Campion and Campion (1987) used Kirkpatrick's levels of analysis to evaluate the outcome of an interview training program. They found that participants had positive reactions to the training and learned about interviewing during the training course

(Levels 1 and 2), but their performances in interviews and the number of job offers received were not significantly greater than those of individuals who had not participated in the interview training (Levels 3 and 4).

Another important consideration is whether determining the effectiveness of a training program is worth the cost of the evaluation design (Yang, Sackett, & Arvey, 1996). Although researchers can design rigorous evaluations, sometimes these evaluations are not cost effective.

Nonetheless, there are several research strategies of varying scientific rigor for evaluating a training program. These approaches are explained below and illustrated in Figure 5.3.

Case Study

In the **case study** approach, the evaluator looks at performance after training. The evaluator may interview those who participated, observe their work methods, or even collect quantitative data about productivity after the training. After the data are collected, the evaluator assembles the results into a report that is circulated among management.

For obvious reasons, the case study approach is unlikely to be either valid or reliable. Because the evaluator did not take a measure of how well the employees were doing before the training—that is, establish a base rate—the evaluator cannot conclude that the training caused or affected productivity after the training program. Although the evaluator may suspect there are improvements, if the evaluator did not collect data before the training program, then the conclusions are open to question.

Second, if the evaluator did not compare the employees with another group that did not experience the training, he or she cannot reasonably attribute changes in productivity to the training program. Other variables may have intervened to affect employee behavior.

Finally, case studies often use observation as the major methodological tool, and though observation can be valuable, it also has some shortcomings. If the evaluator is biased either for or against a training program or a particular instructor, for example, this bias might be reflected in the evaluation. Taking an objective view of the situation is not necessarily easy.

Pretest-Posttest

The **pretest-posttest** method is somewhat more rigorous than the case study, but there may still be problems interpreting the results. In this case, the evaluator measures the training group on some variable before the training program, then measures the group afterward to see if performance has improved. For example, an evaluator may record the number of errors made by bank tellers before a training program, then determine if the number has decreased—or increased—after the training. If a test of significance reveals that the difference could not be due to chance, the evaluator might then conclude that the training was effective.

Although the evaluator has taken care of the base rate problem, another problem was not considered. Without comparing the training group to a group that did not experience training, the evaluator cannot be certain that something else did not cause the change in the error rate. Intervening variables—such as a change of branch managers, a new salary system, or new furnishings (remember the Hawthorne effect!)—may have led to changes in behavior that lowered the number of errors. In the absence of a control group, the evaluator cannot be certain that the training is responsible for the changes. Unfortunately, the case study and the pretest-posttest methods are the most common approaches used by evaluators in assessing the effectiveness of a training program.

Pretest-Posttest with a Control Group

In combining the above procedure with a control group (**pretest-posttest with a control group**), the evaluator looks at base rates for both a training group and a group that does not experience the training program. If a test of significance indicates the differences in scores on a posttest are probably not due to chance, then the evaluator is much safer in concluding that the training had an effect. This is clearly a much better evaluation design than either the case study or pretest-posttest methods.

After-Only with a Control Group

In another method, **after-only with a control group,** a pretest is not necessary if the evaluator randomly assigns employees to training. For example, the evaluator starts with a group of tellers and randomly assigns some to a training program and some to the control group. Random assignment presumably spreads differences in the two groups evenly, and differences that emerge from a posttest can be attributed to the training program. Some evidence suggests that after-only tests are more desirable than pretest-posttest designs when costs for administration of the evaluation are high (Arvey, Maxwell, & Salas, 1992).

Solomon Four-Group Design

Although the **Solomon four-group design** is not widely used because of its complexity, it does provide a means of determining the effect of pretesting on training outcomes. An evaluator may be concerned that participating in a pretest affects training. That is, workers are learning job-relevant information from the pretest as well as from the formal training. Simply evaluating training outcomes without considering the effects of the pretest would therefore give a distorted picture of training effectiveness.

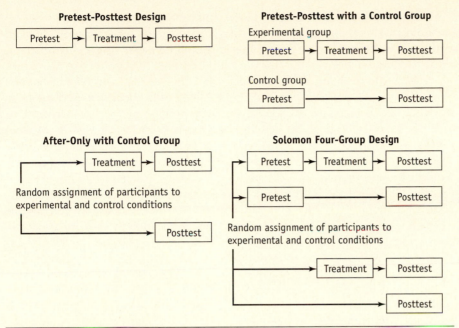

Figure 5.3 Evaluation Designs
Organizations cannot be certain about the effectiveness of their training without an evaluation. This figure illustrates four methods of evaluation. The pretest-posttest is the easiest to perform, but its usefulness is questionable. Evaluators who use a pretest-posttest with a control group or after-only design can be more certain of their results. The Solomon four-group design, which controls for the effects of a pretest, is the most sophisticated and most difficult to implement.

The Solomon four-group design addresses this problem. In this evaluation procedure, the trainees are divided into four groups. The first group experiences pretesting, the treatment, and posttesting; the second experiences only pre- and posttesting. The third group receives no pretest, but only the treatment and a posttest; whereas the fourth group receives only the posttest.

Other Considerations in Evaluation

Three other points about the evaluation of training programs should be mentioned. First, evaluating the usefulness of a training program, like evaluating the usefulness of a personnel selection procedure, is very much influenced by the number of trainees in the evaluation. The greater the number of trainees, the more confidence the evaluator can have in the findings. All of the methods described above require at least 20 cases—still a rather small number—to perform a proper evaluation.

Second, evaluating a training program solely from a behavioral perspective may be shortsighted. Presently, many training programs are being revised to focus on the cognitive factors that affect performance. As illustrated by the simulation examples cited earlier, understanding the ways in which trainees use reasoning and memory may be more useful than simply teaching individuals to perform specific behaviors. The evaluator should be aware of the differences in these two approaches.

Finally, the training evaluator needs to consider cost and benefit factors. The experimental designs described above will identify changes in performance, but they are inadequate for identifying how much change has occurred or whether a target level of performance has been reached (Sackett & Mullen, 1993). For example, accounting clerks may benefit from attending university accounting classes, but sending the clerks to off-site classes may not be cost effective. Proper evaluation of training procedures needs to consider both changes in performance and the relationship between these changes and the associated costs.

Internal referencing is a training evaluation strategy that may be less costly because it uses only one group of participants (Haccoun & Hamtiaux, 1994). In this pre-post single group design, the evaluator includes both relevant and irrelevant items in the pre- and postmeasures. Participants are measured on differences on both sets of items both before the training and after. Training effectiveness is inferred when changes on the relevant items are greater than changes on the irrelevant items.

One other approach to evaluating training is utility analysis, which was discussed in Chapter 4. Mathieu and Leonard (1987), for example, evaluated the effectiveness of a training program for supervisors in a bank. According to their analysis, the bank increased the value of employee performance $34,000 in the year following a supervisory skills training program. Utility analysis has also been used to compare the effectiveness of different kinds of training (Morrow, Jarrett, & Rupinski, 1997).

Chapter Summary

Training is one of the most expensive personnel functions. Although considerable research on the learning process is available, not all of it is immediately applicable to training adults to improve their job performances.

Probably the earliest form of training was apprenticeship, but formal training programs began to be established by companies in the United States around the turn of the century. Current interest in training has been heightened because of employers' need to train unskilled individuals and rapid changes in the technological industries.

The design of a training program requires six steps: (1) identification of needs, which requires organizational, task, and individual analyses; (2) establishment of objectives; (3) development of materials; (4) testing of materials; (5) implementation; and (6) evaluation. Transfer of training is an important consideration during the development of materials.

Trainees must have the requisite skills and be motivated for training to be maximally effective. Similarly, trainers must have some knowledge of sound educational practices.

Some methods of training that occur at the worksite include on-the-job, vestibule, apprenticeship, and job rotation. Off-site methods include lecture, audiovisual methods, conferences, sensitivity training, behavior modeling, programmed and computer-assisted instruction, multimedia training, simulations, games, case studies, outdoor experiential training, and open learning. There are advantages and disadvantages to each of these methods.

When planning a training program, two other important considerations are the trainability of the participants and the abilities of the trainers.

Despite the high costs and pervasiveness of training programs, very few programs are evaluated in a scientific fashion. There are several methods of doing an evaluation, but better methods include the pretest-posttest with a control group, after-only with a control group, and the Solomon four-group design. Two additional factors that should be considered in doing an evaluation include making certain that the sample size is sufficiently large and defining the relationship between changes in performance and the costs of the training program.

Key Words and Concepts

after-only with a control group
(p. 163)
apprenticeship (p. 141)
audiovisual methods (p. 143)
behavior modeling (p. 145)
case studies (p. 150)
computer-assisted instruction
(CAI) (p. 147)
conferences (p. 144)
games (p. 150)
internal referencing (p. 164)
job rotation (p. 141)
lecture (p. 142)
multimedia training (p. 148)
on-the-job training (OJT)
(p. 139)
open learning (p. 152)
organizational analysis (p. 134)

outdoor experiential training
(OET) (p. 151)
overlearning (p. 159)
person analysis (p. 135)
physical fidelity (p. 136)
pretest-posttest (p. 162)
pretest-posttest with a control
group (p. 162)
programmed instruction (PI)
(p. 146)
psychological fidelity (p. 137)
self-efficacy (p. 156)
sensitivity training (p. 144)
simulations (p. 149)
Solomon four-group design (p. 163)
task analysis (p. 134)
transfer of training (p. 136)
vestibule training (p. 139)

Questions for Discussion

1. Why has training become such an important area of industrial and organizational psychology?

2. What are the primary considerations in developing instructional materials?
3. What is transfer of training? What aspects of your industrial/organizational psychology class will transfer outside the classroom?
4. How do you feel about the lecture method of training? How can it be improved?
5. What kinds of training have you experienced in jobs you have held in the past?
6. Why do you think outdoor experiential training became popular? Do you think it is effective?
7. How would you select workers for training? What qualities or experiences would you look for? How would you select trainers?
8. Why do you think training is rarely evaluated?

CHAPTER 6

Appraising Performance

The Role of Performance Appraisal in the Organization
Criterion Development
Methods of Appraising Performance
Sources of Error in Performance Appraisal
Designing a Performance Appraisal System
Evaluating Performance Appraisal
Chapter Summary
Key Words and Concepts
Questions for Discussion

During the 1990s, many major American companies began **downsizing,** a process by which companies try to become more efficient by becoming smaller. By the middle of the decade, for example, General Motors had announced plans to eliminate 69,650 jobs; Sears, Roebuck, 50,000 jobs; and IBM, 38,500 jobs.

This restructuring has had a significant impact on businesses and workers. When companies decide to eliminate thousands of jobs, they need to plan carefully which employees they will keep and which will be let go. Although there are many considerations in a downsizing program, a key element is assessing the performances of workers. Organizations obviously want to keep productive employees and terminate the unproductive.

Evaluating the productivity of employees after they are hired is one of the most important functions of any organization. Regardless of the strengths identified during the personnel assessment, selection, and training process, most employees will eventually be evaluated on the quality of the work they do. Performance appraisal allows a company to identify the strengths and weaknesses of its personnel, and it allows workers opportunities to receive salary increases and promotions. Ideally, the people doing the rating should be experts at judging performance. They should be completely familiar with the job, have experience as a rater, rate performance immediately after observation, and be publicly accountable for the ratings they give.

In reality, however, all of the conditions for accurate performance appraisal are rarely met. Judges make errors in their ratings, rating instruments don't capture all aspects of performance, and the pressures of meeting production demands interfere with performance appraisal accuracy.

Nonetheless, two researchers (Weekley & Gier, 1989) hypothesized that ratings done at Olympic sporting events fulfill the criteria for expert raters in ideal conditions. Becoming an Olympic judge requires attending a judges' school and as many as 20 years of practice at rating sports performances. These researchers reviewed records from Olympic figure skating events to determine if expert ratings in ideal conditions resulted in reliable and valid performance ratings. Not surprisingly, the researchers concluded that using expert raters in ideal conditions results in performance appraisals far more reliable and valid than those made in most organizations.

Despite the importance of performance evaluation, virtually no organization has either expert raters or ideal conditions for supervisors to rate their subordinates. It is interesting to note that most of the research in performance appraisal has been done in laboratory settings that often bear little resemblance to the real world. This is an important distinction since real-life performance appraisals are likely to be influenced by social factors and, as a result, tend to be more lenient than laboratory studies of performance (Harris, Smith, & Champagne, 1995).

Performance ratings equal to those made by Olympic judges are a kind of ultimate criterion (described below) that many employers and researchers strive to achieve. In fact, the practice of performance appraisal has become one of the most important specialities in industrial and organizational psychology. Developing an accurate appraisal system is a complex task that affects the lives and careers of virtually all workers. This chapter looks at the methods by which standards for performance are determined, methods for evaluating employee performance, and ways of ensuring the fairness of an appraisal system.

Judges at the Olympics must meet the highest standards for accuracy.

The Role of Performance Appraisal in the Organization

Uses of Performance
  Appraisal
The Importance of
  Performance Appraisal

Performance appraisal is the evaluation of employee performance in light of predetermined standards. Such standards can be *behavioral* ("Produces reports of consistently high quality"; "Answers telephone promptly"), *trait-based* ("assertive," "ambitious," or "dependable"), or *criterion-referenced* (sales volume; number of errors; for police, number of arrests; and for professors, number of publications). It is important to note that these three types of performance criteria differ in the emphasis they give to the *process* by which a job is done versus the *outcome* of performance. Performance appraisal systems that take a behavioral or trait-based approach focus on the way an employee does a job. Criterion-referenced systems, on the other hand, focus on the outcome of performance. Both aspects are important, however. If, for example, employees are having trouble meeting their sales quotas (a criterion), they need feedback on the process by which they are attempting to meet their goals.

In most cases, employers regularly assess performance and use the assessment to make recommendations about a worker's future status. These recommendations can result in salary adjustments, new assignments, or changes in job structure . Although performance appraisal may seem to be the last stage of the hiring and entry process, it actually relates to the very first part. Employers cannot know what to expect of applicants without determining what constitutes satisfactory and unsatisfactory performances. For this reason, some industrial and organizational psychologists consider performance appraisal the most fundamental personnel issue.

Appraisal can take many forms, and it can be formal or entirely informal. Although most employers now use quantitative appraisal methods such as checklists, scales, or rating sheets, some simply tell their employees informally how they are doing. In some cases, employers do not rely on formal performance appraisal procedures. For example, salespeople paid by commissions are typically well aware of their sales volumes and how they are doing before they receive performance reviews, and bank tellers who must balance their drawers every afternoon are similarly well informed about their performances. In fact, some research (Fedor, Rensvold, & Adams, 1992; Larson, 1989) suggests that employees who suspect they are doing poorly on the job informally seek feedback about their performances so they can improve before the more formal appraisal meeting.

Uses of Performance Appraisal

In a survey of how companies use performance appraisal, one group of researchers (Cleveland, Murphy, & Williams, 1989) found companies most often used appraisals for salary decisions and performance feedback, and least often for evaluating their personnel systems. Other uses of performance appraisal include counseling, training, making retention/discharge decisions, setting goals for the employee, performing job analysis, or developing employment standards. Also, performance appraisal can identify areas in which employees need additional training.

In most large organizations, appraisal requires a supervisor to rate an employee on several job dimensions, then to meet with the employee to discuss the employee's performance. Typically, companies have guidelines on how frequently a performance review must occur. Many companies review performance at the end of a training period and thereafter on a yearly or a more frequent basis. Revenue officers at the Internal Revenue Service, for example, are evaluated several times during a three-month training period, then not again until one year from being hired.

At the time of the performance appraisal, the supervisor reviews the elements of the job that the employee is expected to perform and assigns a rating as to how well the employee has done during the period under consideration. In some appraisal systems, the supervisor and the employee agree on goals the employee is expected to accomplish before the next review. These goals provide the employee with concrete standards by which performance can be assessed, and they can be an important part of the performance evaluation. In one case in which the employer left goals undefined (*Weahkee v. Perry,* 1978), a Native American employee of the Equal Employment Opportunity Commission sued the chairman, claiming that he had not been given specific instructions on how to improve before being fired from his job as complaint investigator.

Interestingly, many managers have a negative attitude toward performance appraisal—they dislike telling an employee about areas that need improvement, so they give an employee only high ratings or avoid giving feedback altogether. Most large organizations, however, have rules and procedures to make certain the performance appraisal occurs at regular intervals. Performance appraisal training, in which managers learn how to give both positive and negative feedback to the employee, is one of the training programs most frequently presented in organizations (Lee, 1991).

The Importance of Performance Appraisal

As suggested in Chapter 3, performance is the criterion by which most employees are evaluated. From such evaluations, employers can determine the effectiveness of a personnel selection system, identify employees with leadership potential, and make decisions about future staffing needs. Because of this, performance assessment systems must meet scientific standards for reliability and validity.

Title VII of the Civil Rights Act of 1964 prohibits the classification of an employee in a way that limits the employee's promotional opportunities because of race, color, religion, sex, or national origin. Because performance appraisal is used to make decisions about an employee's future, the appraisal system is legally required to be fair. (In practice, however, the courts have been less concerned about the validity of the performance appraisal system than about selection system validity [Werner & Bolino, 1997].)

Performance appraisal is also important from a theoretical or scientific perspective. The accurate measure of behavior is a critical part of the science of psychology. Not surprisingly, many industrial psychologists are interested in developing and refining methods to provide as accurate a picture of employee performance as possible. Identifying criteria to determine job success and appraising employee performance in light of those criteria are interesting questions from both theoretical and applied perspectives.

Criterion Development

Ultimate Criterion
Criterion Relevance
Criterion Deficiency
Criterion Contamination
Criterion Usefulness

One of the most critical issues in developing an appraisal instrument is identifying the criteria—or standards—of acceptable and unacceptable performance. For example, supervisors must be able to determine how many pairs of shoes a salesperson must sell, or how few errors an airline ticketing agent can make, for their performances to be classified as "excellent," "good," or "poor." Additionally, employers need criteria to determine when performance warrants dismissal. For these reasons, identifying an appropriate criterion is an essential part of developing a fair and useful performance appraisal system. The proper setting of a criterion begins with a job analysis.

Ultimate Criterion

A **criterion** is "a dependent or predicted measure for judging the effectiveness of persons, organizations, treatments, or predictors of behavior, results, and organizational effectiveness" (Smith, 1976). In other words, the criterion is the standard by which performance is judged. As suggested above, sales volume and lack of errors are possible criteria for judging performance in certain occupations.

The **ultimate criterion,** a hypothetical concept introduced by Thorndike (1949), refers to a standard that contains all possible determinants of job success. According to psychometric theory, meeting the ultimate criterion would result in perfect job performance. Of course, setting standards for perfect performance is usually not practical because some individuals may exceed even the standard of perfection that has been set.

Because of the difficulties inherent in setting a standard of perfect performance, the ultimate criterion is used only as a concept by which real-life criteria are judged. In the case of performance appraisal, most criteria are developed by

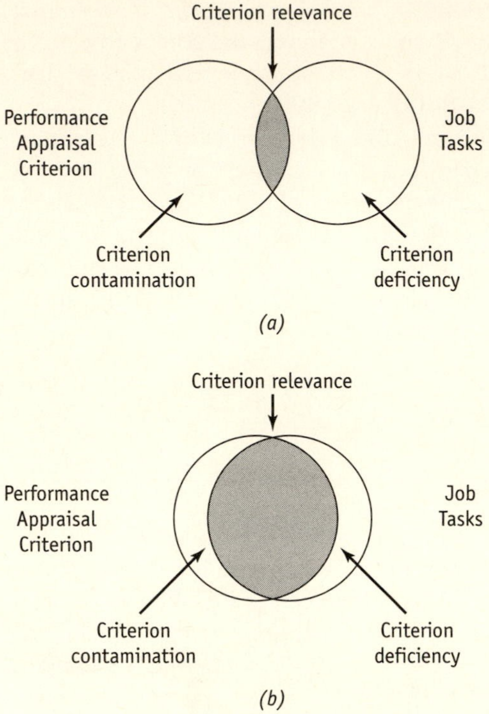

Criterion relevance

Performance Appraisal Criterion   Job Tasks

Criterion contamination   Criterion deficiency

(a)

Criterion relevance

Performance Appraisal Criterion   Job Tasks

Criterion contamination   Criterion deficiency

(b)

Figure 6.1 Criterion Relevance, Contamination, and Deficiency
When the performance appraisal criterion is *contaminated,* workers are judged on behaviors that are not necessary to perform the job successfully. When the criterion is *deficient,* workers are not being judged on all the behaviors necessary for successful job performance. Where the criterion overlaps, the actual job tasks represent *relevance.* Figure (*a*) illustrates a poor appraisal system, in which the criterion does not adequately reflect job tasks. Figure (*b*) is a much better system because the criterion and job tasks overlap.

first setting a minimally acceptable level of performance. Three dimensions on which criteria are judged are relevance, deficiency, and contamination. These dimensions are discussed below and illustrated in Figure 6.1.

Criterion Relevance

A standard for appraisal is considered relevant if it is an important part of job success. Ideally, employers judge employee performance only on the knowledge, skills, and abilities pertinent to doing a job successfully. For example, appearance may be a useful criterion in evaluating the performances of sales representatives, but it is probably irrelevant for evaluating diesel mechanics. **Criterion relevance,** therefore, refers to using only criteria that are relevant to successful job performance.

Evaluating the relevance of performance criteria can be tricky. What some supervisors consider essential for successful performance may be considered irrelevant by others. As is the case with selection procedures, employers need to be able to demonstrate that both the method and the criteria they use to judge employee performance are relevant and accurate. This is probably best demonstrated through job analysis.

Criterion Deficiency

If the standard used to judge performance does not contain all the elements necessary for success, the criterion is said to be deficient (Goldstein, 1992). In other words, **criterion deficiency** occurs if successful job performance requires an ability that is not judged during the performance appraisal. For example, success as a manager almost certainly requires some skill in communication; if a performance appraisal form does not require an evaluation on this dimension, then the criterion is deficient.

Criterion deficiency in performance appraisal can be a serious problem for an organization. Since employees expect promotions and raises to be based on fulfilling specified goals, evaluation on the basis of a factor that does not appear on the appraisal form can be unfair. For example, a salesperson may achieve a high sales volume but receive low performance ratings because the salesperson's superiors consider the methods used to achieve that volume unorthodox. Unless the appraisal procedure has a provision for "Use of established company procedures for making sales," downgrading the salesperson's performance is not justifiable.

Criterion Contamination

When extraneous factors appear in the performance evaluation, the criterion is said to be contaminated. In other words, **criterion contamination** occurs when employees are evaluated on criteria that are not relevant to their job performances. A rating on appearance, for example, may be a contamination if appearance is not relevant to success on the job. Three common types of criterion contamination are listed below (Goldstein, 1992).

1. Opportunity bias occurs when workers have different opportunities for success. A salesperson who is assigned to an area of high economic growth, for example, is likely to be more successful than one who is assigned to an economically depressed area. In this case, performance is affected by factors other than individual effort or ability.

2. Group characteristic bias occurs when factors about the work group, such as interpersonal relations, obscure the accuracy of a performance appraisal. In the case of the bank wiring room (Chapter 1), for example, performance was affected by the dynamics of the work group: Workers lowered their productivity in order to maintain positive social relations. Evaluation on the basis of production alone gave an inaccurate picture of worker abilities.

3. Knowledge of predictor bias occurs when a supervisor allows the evaluation to be biased by some knowledge about the employee. Factors such as quality of the college attended, performance in an assessment center, or personal relationships with other employees may affect a supervisor's ratings of a new worker. A supervisor who has some reason to expect job success or failure from an employee may inadvertently contaminate the appraisal process. As is the case with criterion deficiency, contamination can be a serious problem in achieving fair and accurate performance appraisals.

Interestingly, some researchers (McManus & Brown, 1995) have developed a biodata instrument for selecting salespersons that avoids criterion contamination by adusting sales results for differences in economic conditions. For the most part, however, this approach has not been applied to performance appraisal.

Criterion Usefulness

Although criteria for judging performance may be developed scientifically, these criteria must be useful within the organizational setting. In general, performance standards in real-life settings represent a compromise between the scientific and the judgmental. Blum and Naylor (1968) identified 14 qualities necessary for a useful criterion. According to these authors, a criterion must be reliable, realistic, representative, related to other criteria, acceptable to the job analyst, acceptable to management, consistent from one situation to the next, predictable, inexpensive, understandable, measurable, relevant, uncontaminated and free of bias, and discriminating.

As should be obvious from the foregoing discussion, performance appraisal is an area in which there is likely to be conflict between theory and its application. Whereas the researcher may be looking for the best system from the perspective of psychological measurement, the manager needs something that is practical and easy to use.

Methods of Appraising Performance

Comparative Methods
Checklists
Rating Scales
Narrative Methods
Management by Objectives
The Appraisal Interview

Once a criterion for performance has been identified, an instrument for rating individual performance needs to be developed. Through the years, organizations have used a variety of techniques for recording the rater's view of employee performance. Choice of appraisal method is important because it affects both appraisal accuracy and employee satisfaction with the appraisal process (Giles & Mossholder, 1990). In addition, newer research (e.g., Hartel, 1993) suggests that characteristics of the rater also affect performance ratings.

Despite these obstacles, psychologists have put great effort in trying to identify a rating format that most accurately reflects employee performance. The following section describes the major approaches, and Table 6.1, which appears at the end of this section, summarizes the advantages and limitations of the different performance appraisal methods.

Comparative Methods

Comparative methods consider the performance of a worker relative to the performances of others. Overall, these procedures, which include ranking, paired comparisons, and forced distributions, are usually easier to implement than other approaches to appraisal.

A **ranking system** requires supervisors to place employees in order from best to worst, usually along a dimension such as productivity or overall performance. Supervisors can then clearly identify their best and worst employees. Additionally, ranking usually provides a high degree of interrater reliability and is straightforward and easy to implement.

The major problem with ranking, however, is that it does not really give an indication of performance. For example, the best telephone order clerk may process 20 orders per hour, whereas the second handles 10 and the third, 5. Ranking would not indicate the large variance in order processing skill. Similarly, 20 orders per hour may be the slowest speed of a group of order clerks in another department.

An additional problem with ranking is that it becomes cumbersome with large numbers of employees. If a supervisor has to rank 30 employees, the top 5 and the bottom 5 may be easy to identify, but there may not be much difference among the remaining 20. Finally, ranking gives no information about criteria. The best order clerk may be well above or well below the criterion. Ranking tells the supervisor only that certain employees are better than others.

Paired comparisons is a method in which the supervisor lists all possible pairs of employees, then identifies the better employee of the pair. The billing clerk is compared with the new accounts clerk, for example, the new accounts clerk with the file clerk, the billing clerk with the file clerk, and so on. After the supervisor has rated all possible comparisons of employees, the individual who has been the better employee the greatest number of times receives the highest ranking.

Forced distribution requires the supervisor to set up categories ranging from poor to outstanding, then to assign employees to the different categories. To avoid errors of either leniency/severity or central tendency, the supervisor rates the employees across a normal distribution. For example, a supervisor may be required to assign 10 percent of her employees to the "poor" category, 20 percent to "below average," 40 percent to "average," 20 percent to "above average," and 10 percent to "outstanding."

Although paired comparisons and forced distribution, like ranking, have the advantage of being easy to use, they also have the same problem with criteria. In a comparative framework, there is no direct indication whether an employee's performance is superior or unacceptable. All employees may be superior or unsatisfactory, but the only information available is whether they are better or worse than other employees. Comparing their standing to other employees gives no indication of quality of their own performances. Because of this criteria problem, many raters do not like these approaches so, overall, use of comparative methods is not widespread.

Checklists

Checklists are lists of traits or behaviors the supervisor marks as relevant to the performance of the employee. As with comparisons, checklists are easy to develop and use, but they have some of the same problems as comparisons. A disadvantage of the simplest checklist is its being "all or none." For example, employees are rated as "cooperative" either all of the time or none of the time.

An additional disadvantage with the simple checklist is that all behaviors or traits relevant to a job are considered equally important. In most jobs, duties vary in importance. A salesperson may receive high ratings for punctuality, but low ratings for sales volume. On a checklist, these two aspects of the job may be considered equally important, although they are not.

The **weighted checklist** avoids this problem by discriminating among the importance of various job duties. Since some aspects of job performance are more important than others, different numbers of points are assigned for individual job tasks. For example, the maximum number of points a salesperson can earn for punctuality may be 5, whereas volume of sales may be worth 80 points. Ideally, both the rater and the employee are aware of the values of different tasks, so employees direct their efforts appropriately.

A problem that can occur with the checklist is a tendency toward leniency or severity on the part of a rater. Since supervisors are aware they are rating an employee positively or negatively, such knowledge may interfere with rating accuracy; that is, a supervisor may realize that some employees are doing a poor job but may not wish to give them lower ratings.

The **forced-choice checklist** format was developed because of leniency problems in rating U.S. Army officers during World War II. In this checklist format, supervisors are presented with groups of four statements about different aspects of job performance. Two of the statements appear to be negative; the other two appear positive. Of the latter two, only one is relevant to appropriate job performance. Of the two negative statements, only one is relevant to unacceptable job performance.

Because the rater cannot determine the positive nature of a statement simply by looking, biases are reduced. In addition, raters are not allowed to score the evaluation instrument, but must send it elsewhere for scoring.

Although the forced-choice checklist seems to control leniency, two disadvantages are obvious. First, developing such a scale requires the assistance of skilled professionals, and creating four adequate and plausible performance descriptors is costly and time-consuming. Second, supervisors are generally not receptive to using rating forms when they do not know what the outcome will be. For these reasons, the forced-choice checklist is not widely used.

Rating Scales

Rating scales allow employee performance to be assessed along a continuum that typically ranges from "all the time" to "never." This approach provides a more accurate view of individual performance than ranking or checklist formats.

Graphic rating scales, introduced in 1922, are the oldest quantitative performance appraisal technique (Eichel & Bender, 1984). These scales typically use a trait description with a continuum on which a worker is rated. Employees, for example, may be rated as "highly responsible," "very responsible," "responsible," "occasionally responsible," or "not responsible." The manager marks where the employee falls on a particular dimension on a continuum.

Graphic rating scales are easy to develop and use, but proper application requires a precise understanding of what constitutes the behavior being described. For example, supervisors may have problems distinguishing between "responsible" and "highly responsible" performance if such terms are not well defined.

Mixed-standard scales (MSS) were developed by Blanz and Ghiselli (1972) to minimize halo and leniency errors (described below) in performance appraisal. The rationale behind MSS is that ratings will be more accurate if the rater is provided with descriptions of behavior at different levels (Barnes-Farrell & Weiss, 1984).

In this format, three critical incidents descriptive of "good," "average," and "poor" performance are collected and summarized into statements on a rating form. These statements appear randomly, so it is impossible for the rater to determine the value of a statement. Raters mark a "+" when employee performance exceeds the standard, "−" when it is below the standard, and "0" when it is equal to the standard. Figure 6.2 is an example of a mixed-standard rating scale.

Although the mixed-standard scale seems to control bias, questions about its reliability have been raised. Additionally, the scale has the disadvantage of being time-consuming to develop and difficult to use, and some research (Hughes & Prien, 1986) suggests that results can be scored in several different ways. Overall, evaluations of the MSS approach have been mixed.

Another evaluation instrument that has become popular in recent years is the **behaviorally anchored rating scale (BARS),** introduced by Smith and Kendall (1963). The BARS appraisal instrument has specific paragraphs describing actual work behavior considered "excellent," "good," "poor," and so

---

Listed below are a number of descriptions of behavior relevant to the job of patrol officer. Your task is to carefully examine each example, and then to determine in your own mind the answer to the following questions: Is the patrol officer to be rated "better than this statement," "worse than this statement," or "does this statement fit this patrol officer?"

If you believe that the person you are rating is "better than the statement," put a "+" in the space to the right of the statement. If you believe that the person is "worse than the statement," put a "−" in that space. If you believe that the statement "fits" the patrol officer, put a "0" in that space.

Be sure that you write either a "+", a "−", or a "0" after each of the statements listed below.

	Rating
(II) 1. The officer could be expected to misinform the public on legal matters through lack of knowledge. (P)	+
(III) 2. The officer could be expected to take the time to carefully answer a rookie's question. (G)	0
(II) 3. This patrol officer never has to ask others about points of law. (G)	−
(I) 4. The officer could be expected to refrain from writing tickets for traffic violations which occur at a particular intersection which is unusually confusing to motorists. (G)	+
(I) 5. The patrol officer could be expected to call for assistance and clear the area of bystanders before confronting a barricaded, heavily armed suspect. (A)	+
(III) 6. The officer could be expected to use racially toned language in front of minority-group members. (P)	+
(II) 7. This officer follows correct procedures for evidence preservation at the scene of a crime. (A)	0
(I) 8. The patrol officer could be expected to continue to write a traffic violation in spite of hearing a report of a nearby robbery in progress. (P)	+
(III) 9. This officer is considered friendly by the other officers on the shift. (A)	+

Note: (I), (II), and (III) to the left of the items indicate the performance dimension; (G), (A), and (P) following the items refer to Good, Average, and Poor performance levels, respectively.

Source: Adapted from Landy, F. J. (1985). *Psychology of work behavior,* 3rd ed. Chicago, IL: Dorsey Press, pp. 182, 183. Used by permission.

Figure 6.2 Mixed-Standard Rating Scale

forth. Consequently, the supervisor has concrete examples of how behaviors should be categorized on the rating form. On an evaluation form for secretaries, for example, a rating of "excellent" along the dimension of "telephone skills" may be described as "answers the telephone promptly and politely; takes thorough messages." The descriptor "lets telephone ring for long periods; is rude or abrupt to callers" would be an example of "poor" telephone skills.

The BARS approach improves appraisal accuracy by providing the rater with concrete examples of performance. For example, one group of researchers (Fogli, Hulin, & Blood, 1971) developed a BARS instrument by first interviewing 43 grocery personnel to obtain critical incidents of behavior. The researchers categorized the incidents into eight categories, then, as a check on reliability, they asked 15 grocery store employees to place the incidents into the eight categories to see if their ratings agreed with those of the researchers. In the final step, 97 grocery employees created the appraisal instrument by rating each incident on a continuum from good to bad. The authors concluded that involving grocery employees in every step of the research, as well as expressing the final criteria in language specific to the grocery industry, made the final instrument more acceptable to employees.

Although the BARS approach appears straightforward, most research has shown BARS to be only slightly better than other methods. Because of this, some researchers believe the BARS instrument may not be as useful as other types of scales, particularly in light of the effort and expense of its development (Jacobs, Kafry, & Zedeck, 1980; Kingstrom & Bass, 1981).

Latham and Wexley (1977) introduced an innovation on the BARS technique called the **behavioral observation scale (BOS).** In this approach, evaluators collect information about critical incidents and use these data to develop categories of job tasks. Unlike BARS, however, BOS uses a continuum to measure how often (e.g., "almost never" versus "almost always") an employee performs a specific task. In a comparison of BOS with other evaluation methods, Fay and Latham (1982) found BOS to be both more accurate and more practical.

Nonetheless, other research on BARS, BOS, and mixed standard scales has not demonstrated the superiority of any particular approach (Landy & Farr, 1980). One criticism of all three is that although they allow a rater to determine whether a worker is performing a task successfully overall, none considers variability in performance. For example, some researchers (Steiner, Rain, & Smalley, 1993) have argued that looking at whether employees regularly perform at maximum levels, for example, would improve accuracy of ratings. In that particular study, participants were asked to rate the excerpts of an instructor delivering a lecture at four different times rather than only once. By rating several times, the raters obtained more precise information about the instructor's overall performance. The researchers concluded that the "distributional" approach to performance appraisal was more accurate than the BOS approach.

Finally, an obvious disadvantage of BOS is that, like the BARS technique, BOS requires a considerable investment in time and effort to develop.

Narrative Methods

Although the present trend is in the direction of using quantitative performance appraisal formats, **narrative methods** are still widely used, particularly for evaluating executives. Narrative methods work best when duties are complex or unstructured, or when development of a quantitative measure does not seem to be justified.

One of the oldest narrative methods of performance appraisal is the **evaluation essay,** where a supervisor describes a worker's strengths and weaknesses, areas where improvement is necessary, potential goals for the employee, and other personal qualities. A particular advantage of the essay is that it can iden- tify aspects of performance that may not be obvious through the use of the other formats.

There are several considerations about the essay approach to performance appraisal. First, essays require a considerable investment in time, and a manager who supervises 30 employees may have trouble finding the time to write 30 or more pages of evaluation. Additionally, the supervisor's memory about perfor- mance may not be as good when writing the twentieth essay as it was when writing the first.

Second, supervisors may have no guidelines as to what should be included in the essay or the depth of the analysis. Should a supervisor, for example, men- tion a management trainee's poor appearance in an evaluation essay when the supervisor is uncertain if the employee's dress affects current performance?

Finally, the quality of the essay as a performance appraisal instrument also depends on the writing skills of the rater. A supervisor who is a skilled writer may have the reputation of doing high-quality performance appraisals, when in fact these appraisals may be inferior to those of someone less eloquent. Judging the quality of rating skill by the writing skill of the rater is a good example of a halo error (described later).

Critical incidents, discussed in Chapter 3, is another narrative approach to performance appraisal. Supervisors keep records of positive and negative behav- iors on each employee. Critical incidents appraisal has the advantage of being based on actual, rather than inferred, behavior. Like the essay, however, the critical incidents approach is costly, time-consuming, and possibly inaccurate. Also, employees may react negatively to the fact that a supervisor is keeping an ongoing record of their behavior.

Management by Objectives

A final approach to performance appraisal particularly popular among managers is **management by objectives (MBO).** MBO was developed in the 1950s by Peter Drucker (1954) and is widely applied in organizations today.

Under an MBO system, a manager identifies seven or eight specific results that an employee is expected to achieve by a certain date. The manager may help the employee plan "action steps" necessary to achieve the objectives, or the steps to achieve the goals may be left entirely to the employee. Generally, objectives are set in consultation with the employee, since MBO seems to be more successful in organizations with a participative management style. Auto- cratic management and MBO do not seem to work well together.

An advantage of the MBO approach is that employees are clear about what is expected of them before the next review period. With this information, man- agers can also plan for the future and evaluate other aspects of the operation. Another advantage of the MBO system is that it is flexible. Although most of the other systems discussed take time to develop and implement, MBO ap- proaches can be developed, modified, or adapted in a matter of days.

Table 6.1   SUMMARY OF PERFORMANCE APPRAISAL METHODS

Method	Types	Considerations
Comparative methods	Ranking Paired comparisons Forced distribution	Easy to develop and use; provides comparisons of employees but not a true indication of performance
Checklists	Simple Weighted Forced-choice	Simple form is easy to develop and use but considers all behaviors equally important; some problems with leniency with weighted form; forced choice controls leniency but is difficult to develop
Rating scales	Graphic Mixed-standard Behaviorally anchored rating scale (BARS) Behavioral observation scale (BOS)	Graphic is easy to develop and use but requires clear understanding of ratings; mixed standard controls bias but is difficult to develop and use; BARS heightens rating accuracy but is expensive to develop; BOS may be particularly useful for feedback but also expensive to develop
Narrative methods	Evaluation essay Critical incidents	Works best when duties are unstructured; allows appraiser to cover many areas; time-consuming to complete; subject to halo
Management by objectives (MBO)		Employees are clear on what is expected; employees may be involved in determining objectives; MBO can have a narrow focus; does not consider environmental factors that may affect performance

A disadvantage of MBO is that its narrow focus may exclude other areas of the job that are important for performance. An employee may become preoccupied with the goals that are outlined for accomplishment to the exclusion of other, less important job duties. Also, MBO obviously is more useful for higher-level employees. Individuals who have routine and repetitive jobs will not get much out of the MBO system.

Finally, some people consider MBO an "all-or-none" approach. An employee either reaches a goal or does not. Intervening variables, such as poor economic conditions, cannot be accounted for in an MBO system.

Table 6.1 summarizes the advantages and disadvantages of the different performance appraisal methods.

The Appraisal Interview

Regardless of the rating form used, most performance appraisals require an interview between the rater and ratee at some point. This can be part of the appraisal process itself, or it can come at the end of the evaluation. In most cases, employees are asked to comment on what they perceive to be their strengths and areas where they feel they need development.

The supervisor discusses these opinions with the employee and adds any areas of strength or weakness that the supervisor has observed. At the end of the interview employees are often asked to come up with goals or plans for improvement.

Like the selection interview, the **appraisal interview** will be more effective if the supervisor works from a structured format. Additionally, the supervisor needs to be aware of the EEO considerations relevant to performance appraisal and not behave in any way that could imply unfairness during the appraisal process or the interview.

Determining What to Measure
Errors in Rating
Biases of Raters
Peer Ratings and Self-assessments
Multirater Feedback
Upward Feedback

Sources of Error in Performance Appraisal

As previously mentioned, two major problems in performance appraisal are determining a criterion and being certain that the measurement of performance related to that criterion is accurate. Three sources of error related to measurement—determining what to measure, errors in rating, and biases of raters—are discussed below.

Determining What to Measure

One of the most difficult problems in performance appraisal is determining what to appraise. For example, many factors affect job performance, including job complexity, task difficulty, number of tasks to be performed, or number or quality of product produced (Quiñones, Ford, & Teachout, 1995). Nonetheless, most performance appraisals focus on an employee's personal qualities, the employee's behavior, or objective criteria used to measure the employee's productivity.

Traits are qualities, such as ambition, flexibility, or laziness, that are ascribed to an individual's personality. In the early days of performance appraisal, almost all companies used the trait approach to evaluate workers on personality dimensions believed related to job performance. Typical trait measures in early appraisal systems included initiative, innovation, loyalty, cooperation, and potential for advancement. Although the trait approach is less popular today, it is still used to evaluate performance in many settings. Figure 6.3 is an example of a trait rating form.

The trait approach is simple to use, easy and inexpensive to develop, and seems to represent the way most people think. Employers identify the qualities they feel are most relevant to performing a specific job and use those qualities as criteria for employee evaluation. In some cases, the critical incident method of job analysis is used to develop trait rating forms for performance appraisal.

The trait approach to performance appraisal relies on construct validity. That is, the employer assumes that measures of a psychological construct can predict job performance. As with all performance predictors, however, proper

Employee _____

Position _____

Supervisor _____

Date _____

Rate the employee on the following:

Job Know-How	1 Low	2	3 Average	4	5 High
Productivity	1 Low	2	3 Average	4	5 High
Communication Skills	1 Low	2	3 Average	4	5 High
Cooperation	1 Low	2	3 Average	4	5 High
Initiative	1 Low	2	3 Average	4	5 High
Dependability	1 Low	2	3 Average	4	5 High
Attendance	1 Low	2	3 Average	4	5 High

Figure 6.3 Trait Rating Form
As you can see from this example, trait rating forms are very easy to use. However, employers who use this approach must be able to demonstrate that each trait is relevant to job performance.

use of the trait approach requires scientific evidence that these qualities relate to job performance—evidence of which is based on criterion-related validity. So traits themselves may be constructs, but their validity in predicting job performance is usually demonstrated through a criterion-related strategy.

Despite the advantages of this approach, there are other considerations relevant to using a measure of traits to evaluate performance. Specifically, the job of the supervisor is to evaluate performance, not the *causes* of the performance. Whereas a supervisor may be quite skilled in assessing the quality of an employee's welding, the supervisor may be less skilled in determining that employee's level of "initiative" or "leadership potential." As long as the employee produces satisfactory work and gets along with the other workers, personality characteristics are probably irrelevant to performance.

Another problem with the trait approach is that it assumes the trait elements on the appraisal form are necessary for successful job performance when, in fact, successful performance may depend on other factors. Individual workers of different temperaments may use different approaches to a task, and all approaches may be successful. Requiring that automobile salespeople receive high ratings on assertiveness, for example, assumes that a less direct, "soft-sell" approach is not effective—which may simply be untrue for some salespeople.

Because virtually all individuals think in trait terms, however, some researchers (e.g., Hogan, 1985) have argued that ignoring personality traits limits the usefulness of the appraisal. When workers are equal in skill levels, factors such as motivation and values measured in trait terms may be important in determining who is promoted. Some research (Krzystofiak, Cardy, & Newman, 1988) suggests that raters actually rely more on their ideas about personality than on behavior when making performance judgments. One study (Heneman, Greenberger, & Anonyuo, 1989), for example, found that if supervisors liked an employee, they were more likely to attribute effective performance to the employee's personal characteristics. For employees they did not particularly like, effectiveness was more likely attributed to conditions in the environment than to personal qualities.

One personal quality that has often been linked with job performance is intelligence. Although Binet originally measured intelligence as a unitary construct, widely used employment tests such as the Differential Aptitude Test (DAT) and Armed Services Vocational Aptitude Battery (ASVAB) focus on specific components of intelligence. One group of researchers (Ree, Earles, & Teachout, 1994) tested whether measures of specific abilities would predict performance better than a general intelligence score in a study of 1,036 U.S. Air Force enlistees.

The researchers compared test scores on dimensions such as numerical operations and coding speed with performance in jobs such as jet engine mechanic, information systems radio operator, and personnel specialist. Although scores on specific subtests were significantly related to performance, most of the variance in performance was attributable to general intelligence. In a similar study involving 1,400 navigator and pilot training students in the Air Force, Olea and Ree (1994) also found that general intelligence is a better predictor of performance than scores on measures of specific abilities. These findings suggest that a global estimate of intelligence may be a better predictor of performance than looking at specific factors.

On the other hand, some researchers believe that performance appraisal should be based on employee behaviors. The major argument in favor of using **behavioral performance appraisal** over a trait system is that behaviors can be observed, whereas traits must be inferred by the person doing the rating. Some employers prefer behavioral appraisals because they fear that traits cannot be directly linked to performance, and that legal issues about performance appraisal may arise.

Although this line of reasoning seems logical, some evidence suggests that, in real life, the trait approach may be as useful as a behavioral approach (Borman, 1979; Borman & Dunnette, 1975). In addition, some researchers (Landy & Farr, 1980) have argued that the development of accurate and useful behavior-based performance appraisal systems can be confounded by the fact that even raters who have been trained to be objective often revert to using their own ideas about personality over time. Whereas a behavior-based appraisal system may be more psychometrically sound and logically defensible, evidence from applied settings suggests that the issue of traits versus behaviors is not that straightforward.

In addition, the use of behavioral criteria may not always reflect exactly what a supervisor uses when rating an employee. In one study (Werner, 1994), for example, 116 supervisors of secretaries in a large state university completed questionnaires about the behaviors they would use in judging subordinate performance. Not surprisingly, the supervisors considered dimensions associated with the role of secretary—job knowledge, productivity, and attendance—most important. However, supervisors also considered behaviors not specifically related to secretarial duties, such as cooperation and teamwork and putting forth extra effort.

A third approach to appraising performance is **objective criteria,** in which a supervisor evaluates employee performance in light of some concrete criterion. There are two major categories of objective criteria used for performance appraisal: production data and personnel data (Guion, 1965).

Production data focus on output, such as amount of goods produced, sales volume, number of letters typed, and so forth. Although output seems to be a straightforward measure of performance, this is not always the case. Sometimes output can be affected by variables beyond the individual worker's control, and the supervisor needs to be aware of this.

Another way of looking at production is in terms of quality—for example, the absence of errors or the amount of materials accepted by quality control inspectors. A final form of production data is trainability; in this case the supervisor bases ratings on the amount of time it takes an employee to reach a certain level of competence.

A second category of objective criteria is personnel data. This category includes number of absences, length of job tenure, rate of promotion, and number of accidents. Although personnel data may be related to performance, the supervisor using these criteria should be aware that they are not as direct an indication as production data.

Although objective criteria would appear to be a straightforward method for evaluating employees, studies that compare objective measures of performance with other forms of performance appraisal generally show only a modest correlation (Bommer, Johnson, Rich, Podsakoff, & MacKenzie, 1995). This suggests that supervisors make their judgments about employees based on factors other than objective criteria alone.

Some researchers (Austin, Humphreys, & Hulin, 1989; Barrett, Caldwell, & Alexander, 1985) have questioned whether criteria should be fixed or dynamic—that is, should appraisals reflect fluctuations in worker performance? Historically, industrial and organizational psychologists have argued that performance increases as a worker learns the job, then plateaus as the worker becomes familiar with the job requirements (Avolio, Waldman, & McDaniel, 1990; Jacobs, Hofmann, & Kriska, 1990).

The argument for dynamic criteria, however, is that workers perform at differing levels over time, and that more accurate appraisals take this factor into consideration. Another approach to dynamic criteria is to make a distinction between performance that is typical (i.e., what the employee usually does) and maximum (i.e., what the employee does when, for example, he or she is being observed). Few performance appraisal systems make a distinction between typical and maximum performances (DuBois, Sackett, Zedeck, & Fogli, 1993).

In one study (Deadrick & Madigan, 1990), for example, the performance levels of 509 sewing machine operators continually shifted over a six-month period, suggesting that more accurate appraisals would reflect these kinds of changes.

Along the same lines, Hofmann, Jacobs, and Gerras (1992) looked at performance data for two groups of major league baseball players—batters and pitchers. Among the batters, performance increased steadily during the first five years of their careers, then began a steady descent. For the pitchers, on the other hand, performance was more varied, with the best performances coming in the seventh year and declining steadily in the next three years. The researchers concluded that this evidence of one group improving its performance while the performance of the other group diminished argues against the plateau theory of job performance. To be accurate, performance appraisal in this case would need to take a dynamic approach. Figure 6.4 illustrates the changing performances of the baseball players.

Errors in Rating

Regardless of the validity of the criterion and the scientific nature of the appraisal instrument, errors in rating can occur when raters misjudge performance. This is an important point, and one to which industrial and organizational psychologists have devoted increasing attention. For example, some evidence suggests that the accuracy of performance ratings taken in an employee's first year are often questionable. In a study of performance appraisal ratings of almost 10,000 employees in 79 different organizations, Hirsch (1990) found that ratings made by a single supervisor in the first year were not reliable. In her view, reliability of rating early in an employee's career could be improved by using several different raters for each employee.

As in the employment interview, the cognitive processes of the person doing the appraisal are likely to be a critical factor in accuracy. Typical errors in rating include halo, leniency/severity, central tendency, similar-to-me, proximity, logical error, social influence, and context errors.

The **halo effect** (Guilford, 1954) has been written about extensively in the performance appraisal literature (Murphy & Reynolds, 1988; Pulakos, Schmitt, & Ostroff, 1986). Supervisors who make halo errors identify one positive or negative element about an employee and base their ratings on their perceptions of this one aspect. Employees who have excellent attendance, for example,

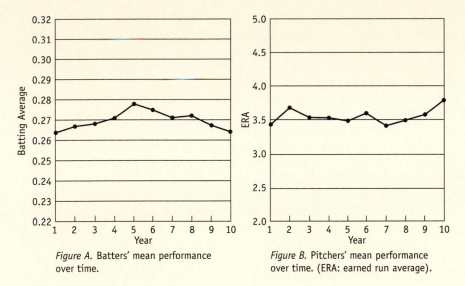

Figure A. Batters' mean performance over time.

Figure B. Pitchers' mean performance over time. (ERA: earned run average).

Source: Hofmann, D., Jacobs, R., & Gerras, S. (1992). Mapping individual performance over time. *Journal of Applied Psychology, 77*(2), p. 189. Copyright © 1992 by the American Psychological Association. Adapted by permission.

Figure 6.4 Performance Appraisal and Baseball Players
In a study of how performance changes over time, researchers found that players improved their batting averages during the first five years, but the averages declined over the next five years. The performance of pitchers, on the other hand, started out strong, reached a plateau, then declined in the ninth and tenth years. The researchers considered this evidence against the plateau theory of job performance.

might be rated higher on other aspects of job performance even though attendance may be irrelevant to performance. (The attendance halo can be relevant to professors' ratings of students as well.)

Another common example of halo is the assumption that individuals who have been invited to assessment centers are superior employees simply because they were invited to the center. They receive higher performance ratings because they attended the center rather than because of their actual job performance.

Some researchers have interpreted halo as being performance appraisal based on general merit rather than on a specific performance dimension. That is, halo reflects a manager's general impression about a worker. Interestingly, some research (Nathan & Tippins, 1990) suggests that interpreting halo in this light may increase the validity of performance ratings overall. When this occurs, halo is no longer an error, but makes a meaningful contribution to performance appraisal. Although intriguing, this interpretation of halo has not yet been accepted by most researchers in this area. Despite the number of studies that have considered the role of halo in performance appraisal, there seems to be increasing disagreement about both what the concept means and its usefulness (Balzer & Sulsky, 1992; Murphy, Jako, & Anhalt, 1993).

Some of the approaches used to control halo effects include special training for raters, giving individual attention to supervisors during the rating task, practicing simulations before ratings, keeping a diary of information relevant to appraisal, and having raters listen to a short lecture on halo before beginning the rating task.

Leniency/severity errors occur when supervisors do not make meaningful distinctions between workers but rate everyone at the extremes of rating scales. Leniency is an overly positive evaluation of an employee's performance and may occur if the supervisor has a personal relationship with the employee or if the supervisor does not feel comfortable telling the employee that his or her performance has been less than satisfactory. Leniency may also be a product of supervisors wanting their employees to reflect favorably on supervisory management style or of the attractiveness of the employee. Severity, on the other hand, refers to the practice of finding all performance inadequate.

Is leniency a product of environmental factors or the personal qualities of the rater? One group of researchers (Kane, Bernardin, Villanova, & Peyrefitte, 1995) hypothesized that certain individuals tended always to give lenient ratings, then looked at police sergeants' ratings of patrol officers, head nurses' ratings of nurses, and supervisors' ratings of social workers. Results from the study supported the hypothesis—even when the appraisal system changed and new formats were used, certain individuals continued to give lenient ratings to subordinates.

When raters do not distinguish among the performances of employees, or when they find no excellent or poor performances, they are making **central tendency errors** (Guion, 1965). This refers to the practice of giving everyone mediocre ratings—no one is rated exceptionally good or bad. One means of controlling central tendency is by requiring supervisors to rate employees in terms of a normal curve or forced distribution, with a predetermined percentage of employees to be rated "excellent" and "unsatisfactory." Some research (Ganzach, 1995) suggests, however, that raters tend to give more weight to negative than to positive attributes, so this approach should be used with caution.

Similar-to-me errors (Wexley & Yukl, 1977) occur when supervisors use themselves as a criterion for job performance. Errors of this kind include evaluating employees in terms of how similar their methods of doing the work are to those of the supervisor, or how personally similar employees are to the supervisor (Wayne & Liden, 1995).

Comparing employee and supervisor performances is particularly unfair, since most supervisors achieve their positions because of their superior performances. In one study (Dobbins & Russell, 1986), managers who had rated employees' performances as poor were more likely to punish an employee if they disliked him or her, but less likely to take any action if they liked the employee.

Zedeck and Blood (1974) identified two other sources of error: **proximity errors and logical errors.** Proximity errors occur when employees are rated similarly on dimensions that occur together on the rating form. Employees receive favorable ratings on punctuality and attitude, for example, because these two dimensions are in the same section of the rating sheet. Logical errors are the result of the rater linking two dimensions that are actually unrelated, such as absenteeism and tardiness. Some evidence (Sanchez & De La Torre, 1996) also suggests that raters make more errors when they have high demands on their memories.

Social influence errors occur when interpersonal factors in the workplace affect performance ratings. That is, ratings are influenced by social relationships between the rater and the ratees. In a study of performance rating among teachers, for example, Zalesny (1990) found that raters' confidence about their ratings were influenced by interacting with other raters, and that experience in rating also affected judgments about performance. In this study, novice raters were less certain about their own ratings of a teacher's performance when other raters appeared confident about their ratings. Experienced raters, on the other hand, were less certain when other raters presented persuasive justifications for their own ratings.

Borman, White, and Dorsey (1995) looked at interpersonal factors and performance ratings among a group of first-tour U.S. Army soldiers. In that study, soldiers were measured on cognitive ability, job knowledge, and task proficiency, and rated by supervisors on personal factors such as sense of humor, friendliness, and dependability. Results from this study confirmed previous findings that ability, job knowledge, and technical proficiency were the most influential factors in performance rating. In terms of personal characteristics, dependability had the greatest influence on ratings; friendliness did not have a significant impact. In another study (Duarte, Goodson, & Klich, 1994), employees who had good relationships with their bosses were rated higher, even when objective measures of performance were not high. In other words, if the boss likes the employee, their social relationship can influence performance appraisal more than performance of job duties.

Context errors refers to rating an employee in the context of other employees or on the employee's previous performance (Kravitz & Balzer, 1992; Sumer & Knight, 1996; Woehr & Feldman, 1993). In this case, the supervisor fails to consider actual performance during the period covered by the ratings, but relies instead on comparisons with other employees or on how the employee has performed in the past. For example, some research (Martell, Guzzo, & Willis, 1995) suggests that when raters form favorable evaluations of ratees, subsequent evaluations will ascribe more favorable and fewer ineffective behaviors to the employee.

Particularly when performance is inconsistent, raters are likely to rely on factors other than objective performance to make assessments (Steiner & Rain, 1989). Ratings are also influenced by stereotypes of qualities associated with different occupations (Kinicki, Hom, Trost, & Wade, 1995). One approach to controlling context errors is the use of a diary, in which raters make notes about job performance that they can use when they complete the rating form. Unfortunately, however, one experimental study of the effect of using diaries to eliminate context errors actually appeared to increase the number of these errors

(Maurer, Palmer, & Ashe, 1993). In this particular study, checklists were better at controlling contextual errors than were diaries. On the other hand, a field study (DeNisi & Peters, 1996) found the use of diaries improved appraisal accuracy among managers in a transportation company.

Finally, one might expect a negative relationship between rating error and appraisal accuracy; that is, the more errors the rater makes, the less accurate the rating. Some research (Murphy & Balzer, 1989; Sulsky & Balzer, 1988), however, suggests the relationship between error and accuracy is not particularly strong. For example, a meta-analysis of studies of error in performance appraisal (Murphy & Balzer, 1989) found a small negative correlation between error and accuracy of ratings. The researchers suggested that the measures of error used in these studies may not be valid, which means that the knowledge about measuring errors made in performance appraisal may be less certain than once believed.

In an interesting approach to controlling error, two researchers (Kulik & Ambrose, 1993) proposed that ratings of performance done by a computerized monitoring system might differ from ratings based on visually monitoring performance. In theory, computerized performance monitoring (CPM) has the advantage of being free of social influences and might result in more accurate ratings. CPM has been widely used in the insurance, communication, and banking industries, but in most cases it is complemented by a visual observation of performance. In a laboratory study of a computerized versus a visual appraisal of secretarial performance, the researchers found that raters relied more on what they observed than on information provided by the computerized system. In another study (Stanton & Barnes-Farrell, 1996), some participants expressed dissatisfaction with an electronic performance monitoring system.

Finally, two researchers (Van Scotter & Motowidlo, 1996) proposed that the context in which performance occurs can be broken down into two components: job behaviors and the interpersonal behaviors that support the work environment. That is, in addition to rating workers strictly on performance, supervisors might also appraise helpful and cooperative behavior, as well as effort, persistence, and self-discipline. In a study of performance among U.S. Air Force mechanics, the researchers found these two dimensions to be distinct parts of the performance context.

Biases of Raters

Sometimes performance appraisal accuracy is contaminated by characteristics of both the raters and the ratees. The sexes of the rater and the ratee may affect the performance appraisal, although the direction of the effect is unclear. Deaux and Taynor (1973), for example, found that female employees generally receive lower performance ratings than males, even when the rater is female. On the other hand, other researchers (Peters, O'Connor, Weekley, Pooyan, Frank, & Erenkrantz, 1984) found that female retail store managers were likely to be rated higher than males, regardless of performance.

Along the same lines, female raters may be more lenient than male raters. In a laboratory study of performance appraisal, for example, Benedict and Levine (1988) found that female raters were more likely to delay appraisals, to delay scheduling feedback sessions, and to distort performance ratings in a positive direction.

Interestingly, Schmitt and Hill (1977) found that males who work in traditionally masculine occupations, such as management, tend to get higher ratings than females in the same occupations; females who work in traditionally low or nonskilled occupations, however, receive higher ratings than males (Bigoness, 1976; Hamner, Kim, Baird, & Bigoness, 1974). Along the same lines, some researchers (Sackett, DuBois, & Noe, 1991) found that women receive lower performance ratings—irrespective of objective factors—when they constitute a small percentage of a work group.

Race also seems to have some effect on appraisal. In a study of the organizational experiences of African-American managers, for example, researchers found that supervisors rated African Americans lower than Whites on performance (Greenhaus, Parasuraman, & Wormley, 1990). In a meta-analysis of studies that focused on race effects in performance appraisal, Kraiger and Ford (1985) found that the race of both the rater and the ratee did affect performance evaluation, but that these effects became less important as the percentage of minorities in a work group became greater. This contrasts with the finding that sexual composition of a work group may affect performance appraisal (i.e., women receive lower ratings when they constitute a small percentage of the work group), but the *number* of minorities in a work group appears unrelated to performance ratings (Sackett, DuBois, & Noe, 1991).

One study (Sackett & DuBois, 1991) looked at race differences in almost 14,000 performance appraisals. In a sample of both military and civilian workers, White employees received higher ratings from both African-American and White raters, and there were no significant differences between African-American and White ratings of White employee performance. However, African-American raters tended to rate African-American employee performances higher than White raters. Another study that involved over 100,000 participants (Mount, Sytsma, Hazucha, & Holt, 1997) found that African-American raters rated both White and African-American managers higher than White raters.

These results suggest that the earlier finding that people rate members of their own race higher is more complicated than first believed. In addition, some researchers have argued that racial effects on performance appraisal become quite small when such factors as education and experience are controlled (Pulakos, White, Oppler, & Borman, 1989; Waldman & Avolio, 1991).

Considerable evidence suggests a negative relationship between age and performance appraisal. In other words, older employees are judged to be less productive than younger (Ferris, Yates, Gilmore, & Rowland, 1985; Waldman & Avolio, 1986). Such a bias appears to be unfounded, however. In a review of studies linking performance and age, Waldman and Avolio found little support for the belief that performance declines with age except when the job requires strength or speed. (The performances of older workers are considered in more detail in Chapter 11.)

In another study linking performance appraisal with age, Lawrence (1988) looked at the relationship between performance ratings and an employee's age compared with ratings of the employee's peers. Lawrence hypothesized that employees who were younger than other employees at the same level in the organization would be perceived as more effective and receive higher performance ratings. Similarly, employees older than their organizational peers would receive lower ratings. For the most part, Lawrence's hypothesis was supported, suggesting that organizations have informal norms about the kinds of performances expected of different age groups.

Some research suggests that supervisors with appraisal experience are better at rating than those who are inexperienced, and employees who are high performers also produce better ratings (Landy & Farr, 1980). However, one laboratory study (Richman & Quiñones, 1996) found that inexperienced raters were better than experienced raters at estimating the frequency with which a task was performed.

Attitudes toward the worker being rated can also affect appraisals. One study (Klaas & DeNisi, 1989), for example, found that supervisors were more likely to give negative performance ratings to unionized employees who had filed a grievance against them, and they were especially negative if the grievance had been decided in favor of the employee. Another study (Robbins & DeNisi, 1994) found that a supervisor's positive or negative affect toward a ratee influenced performance evaluation.

On the other hand, a third study (Fried & Tiegs, 1995) found that supervisors who were experiencing stress on the job were more likely to give higher ratings. Presumably the supervisors who were experiencing stress avoided low ratings to minimize conflict with their subordinates.

Another interesting aspect of rating accuracy is accountability. Mero and Motowidlo (1995) tested the effects of holding raters accountable for their ratings. In an experimental study involving undergraduate students, participants who were required to write an explanation for their ratings of the performances of other students were more accurate in their ratings than raters who did not have to justify the ratings they gave.

Many people believe that training raters about the different types of errors and biases and ways to avoid them improves performance appraisal accuracy. Research suggests, however, that the benefits of training tend to dissipate with time (Davis & Mount, 1984; Kraiger & Ford, 1985). Methods supervisors have developed over the years for evaluating performance are probably not easily changed, just as the patterns of interaction used in the employment interview are also difficult to modify. Nonetheless, supervisors with substantial performance appraisal experience provide more accurate appraisals than those with less experience (Smither, Barry, & Reilly, 1989).

In an effort to improve rating accuracy, Hedge and Kavanaugh (1988) evaluated three approaches to training raters: *training to reduce effects (RET)*, in which supervisors heard a lecture about common errors in performance appraisal; *training to improve observational skills*, in which supervisors saw a videotape that illustrated appraisal errors; and *decision training*, which used a videotaped lecture focusing on strategies for making decisions. Interestingly, RET was useful in reducing halo and leniency errors, but had no effect on improving rating accuracy. In fact, the two other strategies were more useful in improving the accuracy of performance appraisals.

In recent years, some researchers have become interested in **frame-of-reference training** (FOR; Bernardin & Buckley, 1981) for performance appraisal. FOR starts with the identification of raters who possess their own ideas about performance standards. These raters then read a job description and discuss the qualifications they think necessary for successful performance. Raters next read descriptions of critical incidents of outstanding, average, and poor performance and make judgments about each case. Finally, the raters are informed about the correct rating for each incident and they discuss how to reconcile their personal ratings with the correct ratings.

The main idea of FOR is to present raters with a context for making judgments about performance. FOR typically involves emphasizing the different dimensions of performance, defining these dimensions, providing examples of each dimension, and practice using the dimensions. Several studies of FOR (Day & Sulsky, 1995; Stamoulis & Hauenstein, 1993; Sulsky & Day, 1994; Woehr, 1994) suggest that raters who receive this form of training are more accurate in their ratings and have better recall of actual performance.

Another approach to controlling error in performance appraisal is having employees rated by both their immediate supervisor and other supervisors who know their work. Although the immediate supervisor makes the ultimate appraisal, input from the other supervisors may make the overall rating more objective. The drawback is finding several supervisors who are familiar with the work of a particular employee, which may not always be possible.

As suggested earlier, more recent research has considered other aspects of the job, the rater, or the ratee that may affect performance appraisal. In one influential study, for example, Hunter (1983) argued that cognitive ability, job knowledge, and task proficiency were the major determinants of ratings. More recently, some researchers (Borman, White, Pulakos, & Oppler, 1991) evaluated the role of four additional factors they considered potentially relevant to performance rating: achievement orientation, dependability, disciplinary actions taken against the employee, and commendations received. The researchers found that the expanded model offered a more complete explanation of performance ratings, and that task proficiency and disciplinary actions had the most direct effect on ratings.

Along the same lines, one study (Sutton & Woodman, 1989) considered the **Pygmalion effect** and its relationship to job performance. As you may recall from other psychology classes, the Pygmalion effect occurs when a person communicates expectations about the behavior of another, which consequently brings about a change in the second person's behavior. The most well-known example of the Pygmalion effect occurs in the classroom, where students who are believed by their teachers to be superior in fact turn out to be superior at the end of the school year (Rosenthal & Rubin, 1978).

In the study of the Pygmalion effect and its relation to job performance, sales managers in two department stores were told that certain subordinates had exceptional sales potential when, in fact, the subordinates had been chosen randomly. Two and a half months after the study began, supervisors were asked to rate the performances of their employees. Although they could recall the names of the employees who had been rated as potentially high performers, those employees did not receive particularly high ratings. According to the researchers, these findings suggest that although the Pygmalion effect might impact student performance, it is less important in judging performance in the workplace.

Finally, two researchers (Judge & Ferris, 1993) hypothesized that typical appraisal error research that focused on one or two variables alone failed to reveal the importance of social factors in performance appraisal. Results from this study of nurses and their supervisors identified a number of social factors that seemed to affect ratings. Some of these factors included how the supervisor felt nurses would rate their own performances; the personal feelings of a supervisor toward a nurse; the work relationship between the supervisor and the nurse; and the similarity of the supervisor and the nurse in terms of demographic factors. Less important in rating were the supervisor's experience or the supervisor's opportunity to observe the nurse's performance. Figure 6.5 illustrates the social factors the researchers found to be affecting performance ratings.

Peer Ratings and Self-assessments

Do peers do a better job of rating than supervisors? Following the line of argument that the person who does the job knows it better than anyone else, some researchers have argued that **peer ratings** and **self-assessments** may be more accurate than supervisory ratings (Kraut, 1975; Mumford, 1983). Unfortunately, research findings on this question are unclear.

In general, peers give more lenient ratings than supervisors (London & Wohlers, 1991). When supervisors and subordinates are asked to list critical incidents of a job, the resulting lists are likely to be quite different. This suggests that supervisors and subordinates view the same job differently, and that they have different opinions about what constitute exemplary and unacceptable performances (Murphy & Cleveland, 1991).

In a study of performance appraisal in a multinational firm, for example, Mount (1983) found that managers tended to base their appraisals on the specific tasks within a job, whereas workers based their evaluations on overall performance. In another study, Mount (1984) compared the self-assessments of

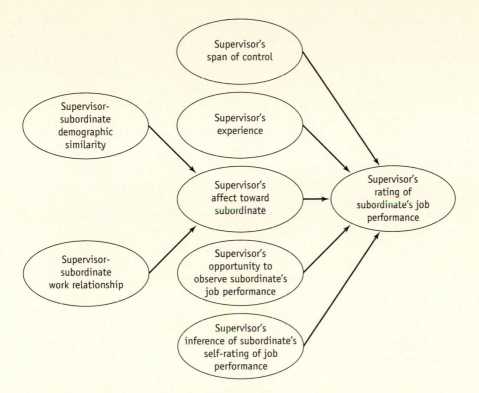

Source: Judge, T. A., & Ferris, G. R. (1993). Social context of performance evaluation decisions. *Academy of Management Journal, 36*(1), p. 95. Used by permission.

Figure 6.5 Social Factors in Performance Appraisal
In a study of the social factors that influenced performance appraisal, researchers found that what the supervisor inferred about how the nurse viewed his or her own performance was the best predictor of overall rating. Other important factors were the similarity between the supervisor and the nurse, their work relationship, and the supervisor's personal reaction—irrespective of performance—to the nurse.

middle managers with assessments from their superiors and their subordinates. Interestingly, the evaluations of the superiors and subordinates were similar, but both were different from the managers' self-assessments. In a review of studies of self-assessment and peer assessment, Harris and Schaubroeck (1988) found a modest correlation between self-rating and supervisor ratings of performance, but a much stronger relationship between supervisor ratings and peer ratings.

Another study (Hauenstein & Foti, 1989) found that law enforcement supervisors evaluated negative performance more negatively than patrol officers, suggesting that the supervisors viewed such incidents more seriously. Two laboratory studies of performance appraisal (Saavedra & Kwun, 1993) found that the highest performers in work groups were the most precise evaluators.

In another study of peer assessments, McEvoy and Buller (1988) found that employees favored peer assessment when results were used for feedback and developmental purposes; they were less enthusiastic when peer ratings were used for performance evaluation and wage determination. Another study (Yammarino & Waldman, 1993) found that supervisors and job incumbents could agree on which aspects of a job were important, but agreement about performance of those aspects was much lower.

Two researchers (Martell & Borg, 1993) hypothesized that groups might be more accurate in rating performance than individuals. Almost two hundred students were asked to view a film of the behavior of a police officer and then rate the officer's performance both individually and in a four-person group. Behaviors were rated immediately or after a five-day delay. Interestingly, individual and group ratings did not differ in the immediate rating situation, but groups remembered behaviors more accurately than individuals in the delayed condition. Groups were also more lenient in their ratings.

Overall, the literature on peer assessment suggests that supervisors and their subordinates typically evaluate different aspects of performance. In other words, supervisors and workers have different ideas about what constitute the important aspects of a job. For example, when workers in a broadcast company were asked to evaluate their jobs, they rated certain aspects as more important than did supervisors rating the same jobs. When the employees and supervisors were asked to resolve any differences in their ratings, employees were more likely to lower their ratings than supervisors were to raise theirs (Huber, 1991). In a related study among bank employees (Williams & Levy, 1992), researchers found that employees who had greater knowledge of the performance appraisal system were more likely to give ratings that were similar to those given by supervisors. Overall, however, supervisor ratings of performance have higher interrater reliability than peer ratings (Viswesvaran, Ones, & Schmidt, 1996).

One area that has not been widely studied is subordinate rating of supervisor performance. In a study of workers in a Fortune 100 firm, however, London and Wohlers (1991) asked managers to rate their own performances at the same time they asked subordinates to rate their managers' performances. The relationship between self-ratings and subordinate ratings was only somewhat significant, but improved over time. Interestingly, female supervisors were more accurate than male supervisors in their self-ratings, but all ratings showed—not surprisingly—a leniency bias.

This tendency for supervisors and employees to see the same job differently makes it difficult to determine whose evaluation is more accurate. At present, peer assessments and self-assessments may be useful in helping employees identify areas in which they feel they need further development, but their accuracy in assessing performance is much less certain. For example, some research (Farh, Dobbins, & Cheng, 1991) suggests that self-ratings may be influenced by culture. In a study of 982 leader-subordinate dyads in Taiwan, for example, workers tended to rate their own performances less favorably than did their supervisors. The researchers referred to this phenomenon as a *modesty bias* and pointed out that this is the opposite of the leniency bias that typifies most

American workers' self-ratings. However, a study of self-ratings of workers in China (Yu & Murphy, 1993) found Chinese workers as likely as their American counterparts to overrate their own performances.

Multirater Feedback

In recent years, managers have become interested in **multirater feedback,** in which individuals receive appraisal information from a combination of subordinates, peers, supervisors, or customers. The idea behind multirater feedback is that jobs have many dimensions and different constituencies can offer unique perspectives about job performance. In addition, multirater feedback is often used for developmental purposes to identify areas in which an individual might improve his or her performance (London & Smither, 1995). Finally, evaluations from several sources are less likely to contain errors than ratings from one source only.

One popular form of multirater feedback is **360° feedback,** which represents a full circle of feedback. In the typical 360° assessment, performance information is collected from an employee's supervisor, peers, direct reports, and, possibly, customers. Supervisors and customers tend to judge performance in terms of accomplishments; peers generally have more information about an individual's work style; and direct reports are the best source of information about leadership and managerial behavior (Howard, Byham, & Hauenstein, 1994). In most 360° systems, these evaluations are compared with a self-evaluation done by the employee.

Some research (Nowack, 1993) suggests that multirater feedback is a cost-effective alternative to the assessment center. There are some important differences in these methods, however. Figure 6.6 compares multirater assessment and assessment centers.

Upward Feedback

Another alternative to traditional forms of performance appraisal is **upward feedback,** in which subordinates rate the performance of their immediate supervisor. Information from upward feedback is typically used to help managers make developmental plans, although it can also be used as part of a more traditional performance appraisal. Although upward feedback has become a popular management practice in recent years, not many managers or researchers have evaluated its effectiveness.

One group of researchers (Smither, London, Vasilopoulos, Reilly, Millsap, & Salvemini, 1995), however, collected upward feedback information on 238 managers in large corporations. Managers were rated by their subordinates on qualities such as communication, support, fairness, and commitment to quality. Results from the study showed that managers whose initial levels of performance were moderate or low improved their performances six months after receiving the upward feedback. This suggests that upward feedback can have an important effect on improving performance. In another study (Atwater, Roush,

Multirater Assessment	Assessment Center Method
Behaviors	
On-the job	Elicited by stimulations
Performance	Proficiency
Typical	Optimal
Current assignment	Future assignment
Observers	
Untrained	Trained
Different standards	Common standards
Low interrater agreement	High interrated agreement
Familiar with target	Unfamiliar with target
Observations	
Much information irrelevant	Most information relevant
Competing demands	Focused on appraisal task
Diffuse	Concentrated
Extended time	Single time
From memory	Immediate
More halo	Less halo

Source: Howard, A., Byham, W. C., & Hauenstein, P. (1994). *Multirater assessment and feedback.* Pittsburgh: Development Dimensions International.

Figure 6.6 Multirater Assessment Versus Assessment Center

& Fischthal, 1995), student leaders improved their performances after receiving feedback from their followers.

Some research (Antonioni, 1994) suggests that the results of upward feedback are affected by the accountability of people doing the ratings. In a study of the performances of 38 managers in an insurance company, Antonioni asked some raters to sign their names to the feedback, whereas another group provided feedback to the managers anonymously. Managers who received the feedback felt information provided from specific individuals was more valuable than information provided anonymously—perhaps because raters who were identifiable tended to inflate their ratings of the managers. Overall, raters expressed a preference for providing anonymous feedback.

Designing a Performance Appraisal System

Given all these considerations, designing a performance appraisal system may seem a formidable task. Formidable or not, employers need performance appraisal systems to evaluate the effectiveness of their employees, selection systems, training programs, and supervisory practices. In addition, performance appraisal is governed by Title VII of the Civil Rights Act, so employers need to be able to justify personnel decisions based on employee performance.

Some guidelines for developing a performance appraisal system are:

1. To be effective, performance appraisal must be based on job analysis. Without an understanding of the tasks involved in successful performance, appraisals may seem arbitrary and may not lead to improvements in employee performance.

2. From the job analysis, criteria for judging performance can be set. Criteria must be free of contamination and not deficient. At the same time, standards must be sufficiently high to ensure organizational goals are accomplished. Interestingly, criteria are the cornerstone of the performance appraisal process, but few researchers have considered how such standards are set (Bobko & Colella, 1994).

3. The instrument used to rate performance must be appropriate for the appraisal situation. No method is without drawbacks, so employers should consider the tasks to be evaluated, the persons who will do the evaluation, and the costs involved when designing a performance appraisal form.

4. People who do the rating must be trained in how to use the procedure. Employers often assume their systems are straightforward, but in light of the variety of errors raters make, this is rarely the case. Also, raters need to understand the importance of fairness and the legal considerations of performance evaluation.

5. Performance appraisal should occur at regular intervals—typically every six months or annually. Given the reluctance of some supervisors to do appraisals, management must make certain that the appraisals are occurring and that employees are getting accurate feedback about their ratings.

6. Finally, performance appraisal systems, like training programs, require occasional evaluation. The ultimate goal of a performance appraisal system is to improve performance. Employers need to know whether the system is fulfilling its goal, and if problems are occurring in terms of the criteria, the rater, or the format, adjustments will need to be made.

Evaluating Performance Appraisal

Like personnel selection, performance appraisal has generated a lot of interest among industrial and organizational psychologists in recent years. Particularly in an era of downsizing, employers need to be clear about which of their employees are the best performers.

Box 6.1 PERFORMANCE APPRAISAL AND POLITICS

Although developing a fair and accurate appraisal system has always been a challenge, performance appraisal has become even more difficult in recent years. Managers are now often required to evaluate teams rather than individuals, downsizing has increased the number of workers reporting to a single manager, and changing organizational structures sometimes makes consistent observation of an employee's performance difficult for managers.

According to a recent story in the *Wall Street Journal,* 90 percent of a group of employees surveyed felt their appraisal systems were ineffective. Typical complaints included managers treating appraisals like a ritual to be endured, not taking the appraisal process seriously, and saving all negatives and dumping a year's worth of complaints on an employee at the annual appraisal session.

Sometimes the appraisal process can result in negative behavior. According to the *Wall Street Journal:*

> 98% of 151 Philadelphia-area managers encountered some type of aggression after giving employees negative appraisals. More than two-thirds of the bad reaction was verbal rather than physical. But a Los Angeles city technician killed four of his bosses last year shortly after getting a poor review. (Schellhardt, 1996)

Because of incidents like these, some people feel that researchers have underestimated the importance of social factors in performance appraisal. That is, systems for evaluating performance usually do not address either the antecedents—the manager's workload, the organizational structure, and so forth—or the consequences of the appraisal interview. This is an important issue that may change the direction of performance appraisal research.

As suggested earlier, however, the issue of theory versus practice is particularly relevant for performance appraisals. Researchers want to develop methods that are psychometrically precise, whereas employers need something that is practical and easy to use.

An additional issue is the politics of performance appraisal. Many employees do not believe performance—regardless of how it is measured—is the basis for salary and promotion decisions. In their view, performance appraisal is largely a political process. This suggests that the interpersonal aspects of the appraisal process may be more complicated than researchers have considered. Perhaps in the future, researchers will pay more attention to this largely unexplored aspect of performance appraisal. Box 6.1. discusses some of the political aspects of performance appraisal.

Performance appraisal is obviously an area in which practitioners must make trade-offs between psychometric precision and usefulness. For some employers, many of the methods described above are simply too difficult to develop and implement. In these cases, the method of performance appraisal used becomes a compromise between its costs and its benefits. Two aspects of performance appraisal cannot be compromised. As is the case with selection procedures, all performance appraisal standards and methods must be related to job performance, and they must be fair.

Chapter Summary

Performance appraisal is the evaluation of employee performance in light of predetermined standards. As such, it is governed by federal regulations about fairness in employee selection.

Setting criteria for satisfactory and unsatisfactory performances may be difficult. Although considerable effort may be expended in attempting to develop objective standards for judging performance, such standards nonetheless remain somewhat arbitrary.

Performance appraisal can take several forms. Comparative methods include ranking, paired comparisons, and forced distribution. Checklist methods include the weighted and the forced-choice checklists. Graphic rating scales, mixed-standard scales, behaviorally anchored scales, and behavioral observation scales are examples of scalar approaches.

The appraisal essay and critical incidents are two narrative methods of performance appraisal. An approach that is popular with management is MBO, or management by objectives, in which employees are simply appraised on whether they accomplished specific goals. Finally, performance can also be appraised in terms of such objective criteria as sales volume or production levels.

Results from performance appraisal are usually shared between a supervisor and an employee in an appraisal interview.

Some sources of error in performance appraisal include deciding whether to measure traits, behaviors, or objective criteria. Other rating errors include the halo effect, leniency/severity, similar-to-me, central tendency, logical and proximity errors, social influence, and context errors.

Raters may also have biases. Some evidence suggests that women rate more leniently than men and that race has an impact on performance appraisal. Other factors that affect appraisal include age, experience with rating, attitude toward the employee, and accountability. In some cases, these biases may be overcome with training.

Peer ratings and self-assessments are new forms of performance appraisal, but their usefulness is limited because peers and managers rate aspects of performance differently from those rated by individual employees. Multirater feedback refers to gathering performance data from a variety of sources and is particularly useful in employee development. Some research also suggests that upward feedback can help improve performance.

When an employer chooses an appraisal system, several considerations must be kept in mind. The most accurate systems are based on job analysis, the system must be appropriate to the job setting, raters need training, appraisals should occur at regular intervals, and the performance appraisal system should be evaluated regularly. Nonetheless, politics seem to be part of any appraisal system.

Key Words and Concepts

appraisal interview (p. 182)

behavioral observation scale (BOS) (p. 179)

behavioral performance appraisal (p. 184)

behaviorally anchored rating scales (BARS) (p. 177)

central tendency errors (p. 188)

checklists (p. 176)

context errors (p. 189)

criterion (p. 171)

criterion contamination (p. 173)

criterion deficiency (p. 173)

criterion relevance (p. 172)

critical incidents (p. 180)

downsizing (p. 167)

evaluation essay (p. 179)

forced-choice checklist (p. 176)

forced distribution (p. 175)

frame-of-reference training (p. 193)

graphic rating scales (p. 177)

group characteristic bias (p. 173)

halo effect (p. 186)

knowledge of predictor bias (p. 174)

leniency/severity errors (p. 188)

management by objectives (MBO) (p. 180)

mixed-standard scales (MSS) (p. 177)

multirater feedback (p. 197)

narrative methods (p. 179)

objective criteria (p. 185)

opportunity bias (p. 173)

paired comparisons (p. 175)

peer ratings (p. 194)

performance appraisal (p. 169)

proximity errors and logical errors (p. 188)

Pygmalion effect (p. 193)

ranking system (p. 175)

rating scales (p. 177)

self-assessments (p. 194)

similar-to-me errors (p. 188)

social influence errors (p. 189)

360° feedback (p. 197)

traits (p. 182)

ultimate criterion (p. 171)

upward feedback (p. 197)

weighted checklist (p. 176)

Questions for Discussion

1. Why is it so difficult to rate performance accurately?
2. What are the criteria on which your performance in this class will be judged? Will there be any problems with relevance, deficiency, or contamination?
3. Of the three approaches to rating—traits, behaviors, and objective criteria—which do you think will yield the most accurate ratings? Could different approaches be more accurate in different types of settings?
4. What are some common errors raters make? How might these errors be avoided?
5. What is your opinion of peer assessment? self-assessment? Why aren't the two more widely used?
6. Do you think 360° feedback is a promising method of appraisal? What might be some problems with this approach?
7. If you were designing a performance appraisal form, which of the many formats (pp. 175–181) would you choose? Why?

CHAPTER 7

Motivation: Understanding Differences in Performance

Defining Motivation

Need Theories of Motivation

Equity Theory

Expectancy Theory

Behavioral Approaches to Motivation

Intrinsic Motivation

Goal-setting Theory

Evaluating Theories of Motivation

Chapter Summary

Key Words and Concepts

Questions for Discussion

I had 150 employees; well, that was just like a little town of 150 people. We had some good people, we had some excellent people, we had some people who were just average, then we had some that we were not too proud of. Those that we were not too proud of, we would try and get rid of.

E. E. FARRELL, CARNIVAL OWNER

In most work settings, there are some employees whose performances are excellent, some employees who are average, and some that management is "not too proud of." Just as individual workers differ in knowledge, skills, and abilities, they also vary in their levels of motivation. In fact, motivation within an individual worker can vary from day to day, or even from hour to hour. This is why motivation is one of the most complex—and important—topics in industrial and organizational psychology.

In this section of *The Psychology of Work*, we begin to focus on issues that affect the way people work together. When people come together in groups, their behavior is likely to differ from when they are alone. Within the work group, behavior is affected by the policies companies use to motivate their workers toward higher performance levels. At the same time, these policies are likely to affect workers' satisfaction with their jobs, another group-related topic.

The last chapters of this section, which discuss leadership, group behavior, and different groups within the workplace, look directly at psychological phenomena related to relationships within work groups and between management and workers. Motivation is a critical aspect that affects the relationship between the leader and the group.

Defining Motivation

From the perspective of industrial and organizational psychology, **motivation** is the force that moves people to perform their jobs. Workers with high levels of motivation want to achieve and perform to the best of their abilities, whereas low levels of motivation lead to poor performance, apathy, and turnover. Motivation is a topic of vital interest to employers, and probably more time, money, and management training courses have been expended in this area of the psychology of work than any other.

The psychological study of motivation attempts to understand why people do what they do. This study is not straightforward, however, since motivation is not observable, and motives can only be inferred from behaviors or self-reports. Another complication is the fact that motivation is both psychological and physiological.

For example, our understanding of physiological motivations, such as the need to fulfill hunger, thirst, and sex drives, is much more advanced than our understanding of psychological motivations such as the need to achieve, be praised, or be loved. The examples of Taylor's piecework system and the bank wiring room study at Hawthorne, discussed in Chapter 1, illustrate the complexities of worker motivation.

In addition to complexity, motivation is another area where theory and application sometimes conflict. Whereas most academic researchers focus on identifying the sources of motivation, employers are usually interested in what improves performance. Rather than being concerned about advancing our knowledge of human nature, employers are more interested in raising levels of production. The point raised in Chapter 3 with regard to interviews—that there is often little linkage between individuals studying the process and people doing the interviewing—seems to be equally true for the topic of motivation. Although the amount of research concerning the motivation of workers is substantial, successful application of that research has been limited.

Another complicating aspect of motivation concerns the unit of study. Most theories of psychological motivation focus on processes occurring within the worker, but it is also possible to approach motivation from the perspective of job design (e.g., Wong & Campion, 1991). That is, it may be possible to raise worker motivation by making tasks more appealing, irrespective of the initial level of motivation. This "job design" approach to motivation is considered more fully in Chapter 8.

In recent years, some researchers (Kidwell & Bennett, 1993) have looked at what might be called the opposite of motivation—the tendency to avoid work. According to these theorists, there are three ways of withholding effort. **Shirking** (Jones, 1984) refers to withholding effort because of self-interest or opportunism, and **social loafing** (Williams & Karau, 1991) refers to reducing one's effort when working with others on the same task. Finally, **free riding** (Albanese & Van Fleet, 1985) refers to obtaining the benefits of a group effort without expending a proportional amount of individual effort. The propensity to withhold work is influenced by factors such as group size, turnover rates, and the altruism of other group members and is an area that has not been widely researched.

Motivation is a wide-ranging subject that touches on many of the other areas covered in this book, including job satisfaction, leadership, and group behavior. This chapter looks at eight theories of worker motivation that have been popular among industrial and organizational psychologists.

Need Theories of Motivation

Maslow's Hierarchy
Two-Factor Theory
Achievement Motivation
  Theory
Evaluating Need Theories

Probably the most popular theories about worker motivation focus on drives within the worker. The notion that individuals are motivated or not motivated to do well on the job is usually explained in terms of psychological needs that differ according to individual experience. These theories hold that motivation has a psychodynamic base—that individual motives originate in childhood and are usually unconscious.

This approach to explaining motivation is referred to as **need theory.** Need theories include Maslow's need hierarchy, Herzberg's two-factor theory, and McClelland's achievement motivation theory.

Maslow's Hierarchy

Abraham Maslow is considered one of the fathers of humanistic psychology. Originally trained as a behaviorist, Maslow said that he became disenchanted with the behaviorist model (discussed below) because it could not explain the psychological development of his baby daughter. From his research, Maslow concluded that all the humans have an innate drive toward wholeness and growth, as well as a need to fulfill their highest potentials.

According to Maslow (1954), individual motivation is hierarchical, and accomplishing goals on higher levels cannot occur until goals at lower levels are met. In all humans, the first level of needs concerns phenomena necessary for survival, such as food, shelter, and warmth. When those needs are met, individuals require that their environments be consistent, orderly, and secure.

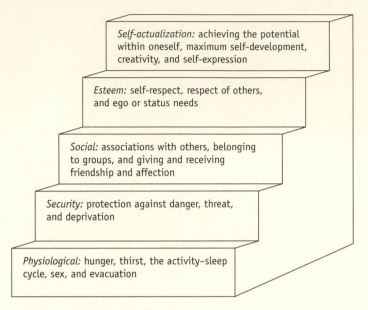

Source: Data based on Hierarchy of Needs from "A Theory of Human Motivation" in *Motivation and personality,* 3rd edition, by Abraham H. Maslow, revised by Robert Frager et al. Copyright 1954, 1987 by Harper & Row, Publishers, Inc. Copyright © 1970 by Abraham H. Maslow. Reprinted by permission of Harper & Row, Publishers, Inc.

Figure 7.1 Maslow's Hierarchy of Needs

At the third level of the hierarchy, individuals need intimate relationships. The fourth level of needs focuses on esteem, and the final and highest level of the hierarchy relates to self-actualization needs. **Self-actualization** is a process in which the individual moves toward a state of self-improvement, happiness, and satisfaction. Some of the historical figures Maslow considered to have been self-actualized include Abraham Lincoln, Ludwig van Beethoven, Thomas Jefferson, and Eleanor Roosevelt. Maslow's **hierarchy of needs** is illustrated in Figure 7.1.

Although Maslow was initially describing a theory of personality, in later years he turned his attention to the operation of the need hierarchy in the work environment. How might his model apply to claims workers in an insurance company, for example? First, the workers would be concerned with first-level needs such as earning enough money to provide the essentials for survival. Once survival needs are met, security needs such as an orderly and predictable work environment become important, the second level.

In the third stage of development, workers need respect and positive social relations with their coworkers. They need to be liked and have pleasant interactions with others in the workplace. When the workers are satisfied with the social environment, they next want to fulfill their esteem needs—to achieve, be competent, and gain approval and recognition. Finally, in the highest state of Maslow's hierarchy, the claims workers want to fulfill their unique potentials and abilities.

According to Maslow, motivation is affected by the level at which an individual is performing. Providing salary raises (level one) will not be very useful if a worker desires social contact (level three) or praise (level four). In Maslow's framework, managers first need to determine the level at which an individual worker is functioning, then help the worker meet the needs appropriate to that level. If such a determination is not made, the motivators offered are likely to be ineffective.

Alderfer (1972) used Maslow's hierarchy to develop a theory based on the needs of **existence, relatedness, and growth (ERG),** which is also the Greek word for *work*). In essence, ERG theory collapses Maslow's five levels into three. Instead of being hierarchical, however, Alderfer saw motivation as continuous. That is, individuals can move back and forth along the continuum rather than upward through the hierarchy.

Evaluating Maslow's Hierarchy Although Maslow has been influential in many areas of psychology, his hierarchy of needs has been of limited value in the psychology of work. Psychological theories based on biological movement, growth, and expansion appeal to many people, but scientific evidence supporting such theories is scarce. Some of the problems related to Maslow's theory of motivation include the difficulty in determining the level of need at which workers are functioning; the difficulty determining what may be an appropriate reward once a worker's level has been identified; a lack of scientific evidence that the levels of Maslow's hierarchy exist; and the assumption, common to all psychological need theories, that the hypothesized needs are universal across cultures. Despite these shortcomings, Maslow's theory remains popular among managers.

Two-Factor Theory

According to Herzberg's **two-factor theory** (Herzberg, 1966; Herzberg, Mausner, & Snyderman, 1959), people are motivated by two aspects of the work environment: hygiene factors and motivators. **Hygiene factors** are conditions that occur in the working environment such as salary, management, and working conditions.

Motivators, on the other hand, are opportunities for professional advancement, growth, and satisfaction. Although individuals may complain about a lack of hygiene factors, the supply of motivators is the critical issue affecting performance. If motivators are in sufficient supply, workers will continue to perform at high levels. If motivators are scarce, even high-quality hygiene factors are likely to be insufficient to keep employees motivated. Typical motivators and hygiene factors are illustrated in Figure 7.2.

According to Herzberg, employees are likely to complain if hygiene factors are lacking, but hygiene factors alone will not lead to high levels of performance. Over the long run, performance depends on the motivators associated

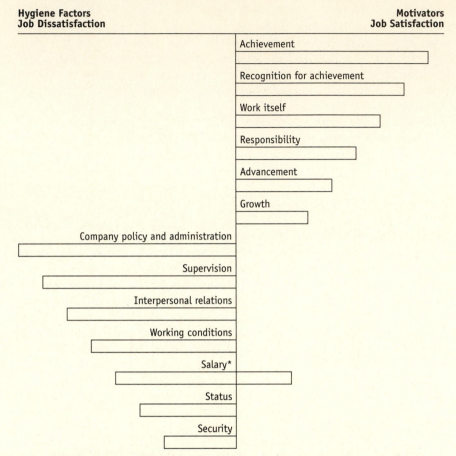

* Because of its ubiquitous nature, salary commonly shows up as a motivator as well as a hygiene factor. Although primarily a hygiene factor, it also often takes on some of the properties of a motivator, with dynamics similar to those of recognition for achievement.

Source: Herzberg, F. (1982). *The managerial choice: To be efficient and to be human,* 2nd ed. (rev.). Salt Lake City: Olympus Publishing. Reprinted by permission of the author.

Figure 7.2 Hygiene Factors and Motivators

with the job. The employer who wishes to motivate must make certain that the job itself—and not the conditions surrounding it—is satisfying and provides opportunities for professional growth.

Although two-factor theory is appealing on an intuitive level, empirical tests of the theory do not provide much support. Typical problems related to the two-factor approach are that employers are likely to have difficulty determining what is a hygiene factor and what is a motivator for each individual worker, in addition to difficulties developing strategies for using that information.

Achievement Motivation Theory

Achievement motivation theory, introduced by David McClelland (1961), has been extremely popular with managers and, unlike other need theories, continues to generate interest among researchers. McClelland originally used his theory to explain the rise and fall of civilizations, but he later applied his approach to explaining worker performance. McClelland says that although individuals have many needs, need for achievement is critical in determining individual levels of performance.

Need for achievement is an acquired, rather than an innate, need. According to McClelland, children interact with a variety of stimuli in their environment as they grow, and when they become bored with the familiar, they look for something more complex and interesting. If parents encourage this search for the more complex, then children will develop a psychological need to master more complex stimuli. In terms of motivation, McClelland defines need for achievement as "competition with a standard of excellence."

Individuals with a high need for achievement generally try to do a good job at whatever they attempt. Achieving individuals focus on personal improvement, generally prefer to work alone, and like feedback on their performance. From a managerial perspective, an appealing aspect of need for achievement is that it can be increased with training. Participants in achievement motivation training learn to diagnose their own levels of achievement need, identify higher levels, and take the steps necessary to reach higher levels. Typical materials used in the training include games, paper-and-pencil exercises, outside readings, and tests.

Achievement is generally not the only need operating in the work environment, however. According to McClelland, many workers have a stronger **need for affiliation** than they do for achievement. For these individuals, the social relations of working are more important than fulfilling job duties. People with a high need for affiliation prefer to work in groups, and they are as concerned with the process by which work is accomplished as they are with the final product.

Interestingly, high achievers are not necessarily the most successful performers in the work environment. In some cases, maintaining positive social relations becomes more important than work accomplishment. In a study of bank employees, for example, Smither and Lindgren (1978) found that managers had lower levels of need for achievement than lower-level workers. At that stage in their careers, the managers apparently relied on social relations, rather than achievement, to further their advancement.

High need for achievement does appear to be related to success as an entrepreneur, however. In a study that followed high-performing start-up firms over a five-year period, for example, researchers (Miner, Smith, & Bracker, 1994) found that a desire for personal achievement, as well as a desire to plan and set goals, were related to the success of the firms.

McClelland (1975) later introduced the notion of a **need for power** as an additional influence on motivation. In a study of individual managers from different large U.S. corporations, McClelland and Burnham (1976) concluded that a high level of need for power, which refers to a need to influence others, is a critical factor for success.

People who are high in need for achievement and low in need for power may be good workers, but McClelland suggests that they are not management material. On the other hand, workers who are motivated primarily by affiliation needs will also have problems managing, since they are likely to make exceptions to rules to satisfy other employees. McClelland argues that this kind of person actually creates poor morale because the workers who do not ask for exceptions perceive the treatment of others as unfair to themselves.

According to achievement motivation theory, the best managers have a greater need for power than a need to be liked, but their need for power is directed toward organizational goals rather than personal aggrandizement. In a study of 1,649 individuals across seven organizational settings, for example, Stahl (1983) found that individuals high in both need for achievement and need for power were also high in managerial motivation. Similarly, individuals who were low on both of these qualities also had low managerial motivation.

In McClelland's original research, individual need for achievement was measured by responses to the Thematic Apperception Test (TAT; Murray, et al. 1938). The TAT is a projective measure consisting of cards with vague pictures in black and white and one blank card. People make up stories about the cards and an administrator analyzes the stories for themes such as achievement, affiliation, and power needs (Veroff, Atkinson, Feld, & Guinn, 1974). Needs for achievement, affiliation, and power can also be assessed by objective measures.

In one study that looked at task motivation theory—which resembles need for achievement theory—and entrepreneurship (Miner, Smith, & Bracker, 1989), researchers found that individuals who scored high on a measure of task motivation were more likely to be the founders of firms that grew quickly in both number of employees and annual sales. A comparison group of manager/scientists who had not founded their own firms showed lower scores on the task motivation inventory. Results from this study suggest that need for achievement may be a significant factor in the success of new businesses.

Evaluating Need Theories

Need theories are like many theories in psychology: some are appealing intuitively and appear to offer some insight into motivations, but they do not hold up very well under empirical testing. This does not make the theories useless, but it does limit their applicability. As several researchers (Tuzzolino & Armandi, 1981; Wahba & Bridwell, 1976; Wanous & Zwany, 1977) have pointed out, need theories are not particularly helpful in developing practical techniques for motivating workers.

A major problem in using need theories to explain worker motivation is determining levels of need. As was suggested with Maslow's hierarchy, an individual supervisor may be incapable of identifying the level of achievement of a worker or the motivators within the work environment. Even if one accepts the evidence for most of these approaches, assessing need levels requires psychological sophistication usually beyond that of the normal supervisor.

Another problem with need approaches is their psychodynamic base. If, as some theorists argue, childhood experience determines adult levels of motivation, then changing such levels will be difficult. Need theories suggest that patterns of cognition and behavior developed over a lifetime can be modified by consultants or skilled managers. Psychologists who believe in a psychodynamic viewpoint would argue that changing longstanding behavior patterns is both difficult to accomplish and difficult to maintain. Aside from the practical problems, expecting a supervisor or manager to bring about personality changes may also raise ethical questions.

Finally, need theories generally ignore or minimize the importance of factors in the environment that affect motivation. Some researchers consider the environment the major factor in worker motivation. This line of argument, sometimes referred to as **social information processing** (Salancik & Pfeffer, 1977, 1978), suggests a worker's motivational levels are more the product of factors in the worker's immediate environment than of instinctual needs or needs acquired in early childhood.

One quality common to need theories of worker motivation is that needs are often unconscious, irrational, and not easily manipulated. As such, it may be difficult or impossible for managers to influence the motivations of their subordinates, or perhaps even for workers to change their own levels of motivation.

Equity Theory

In contrast with need theory, equity theory (Adams, 1965) takes a more rational perspective toward motivation. According to **equity theory,** the level of effort a person expends reflects the person's perceptions of fairness. That is, a worker's performance is directly related to the perceived payoff, particularly as compared to the payoffs of other workers. Employees work hard if they believe the payoffs are substantial, and they avoid work if they believe the payoffs are not worth the effort.

Equity theory is based on the notion of **exchanges.** A worker exchanges a certain amount of effort and expects to get certain things in return. According to the theory, any time there is an exchange there is the possibility of inequity, and when there is inequity, people change either their beliefs or their behaviors to bring the situation into equilibrium. Equity theory is related to Festinger's (1957) theory of cognitive dissonance. **Dissonance theory** holds that tension occurs when a person has two beliefs with psychologically opposite implications. When dissonance occurs, people are motivated to change their beliefs. For example, a worker may hold the beliefs that "I worked really hard on that job" and "I was poorly rewarded for all that work." According to dissonance theory, the worker will change either his or her beliefs or his or her behavior to deal with the opposite implications of those beliefs.

Equity theory was originally used to explain how individuals responded to money as a motivator, but since its introduction, the theory has been modified, expanded, and applied throughout social psychology and other areas. Like dissonance theory, the basic idea behind equity theory is that inequities cause tension and that individuals who experience either favorable or unfavorable inequities will be motivated to reduce that tension. Any exchange that results in equity or inequity involves four factors (Adams, 1965):

1. **Inputs**—what is brought to the exchange
2. **Outcomes**—the results of the exchange
3. **Person**—any individual for whom equity or inequity exists
4. **Other**—any individual with whom Person is in an exchange relationship, or with whom Person compares him- or herself

Simply stated, equity theory holds that workers adjust their performances by comparing the rewards they receive with those received by others. Consider, for example, two salesclerks in a department store. Although one salesclerk works much harder than the other, they are paid at the same rate. The clerk who works harder (Person) feels tension that results from inequity. The ratio between that clerk's salary (Outcome) and performance (Input) is not as great as that of the clerk who receives the same salary for less work (Other). According to equity theory, this situation can be represented as follows:

$$\frac{O_p}{I_p} < \frac{O_a}{I_a}$$

Equity theory holds that the behavior of any of the people—in this case, the worker or her coworker—who perceive inequity in a situation is likely to change. If, for example, Person feels the situation is unjust, then Person—the hardworking salesclerk—will feel tension and will try to relieve this tension in one of the following ways.

First, she may **alter inputs** by working less hard. Second, she may try to **alter outcomes** (defined as an attempt to change Person's status) by trying to get a raise. A third strategy is to **leave the field** altogether by transferring to another department or resigning. Fourth, the clerk may **act on Other** by sabotaging the coworker's work as a means of getting even for the inequity. Finally, Person may reduce tension by **altering the object of comparison;** that is, she may decide the difference in effort is not really that great.

Equity theory is a cognitive theory holding that motivation is based on the perceptions of the individuals involved. If the salesclerk does not realize or mind that her coworker is working less hard, then no state of inequity would exist. Equity and inequity are not "real"—they exist only in the mind of the

Person and nowhere else. If, however, the other clerk in this example recognized the inequity of receiving privileges while Person received none, the theory suggests that she also would seek to bring about a situation of equity.

In its original formulation, equity theory argued that all workers attempt to bring a situation into equity. Some researchers (Huseman, Hatfield, & Miles, 1987) have argued, however, that not everyone reacts to inequity in the same way and that there are at least two other approaches to an inequitable situation. *Equity sensitives*—the type described in the original theory—work to bring a situation into equity, but *benevolents* prefer situations in which they put forth more effort and experience lesser outcomes than their peers. *Entitleds,* on the other hand, feel that whatever benefits they receive are due them.

Equity theory has often been used in studies of the motivational effects of salary. In one study (Greenberg, 1989), for example, white-collar workers were asked about the importance of various features of the workplace such as desk space, privacy, windows, and office decor just after experiencing a 6 percent pay cut because of slow sales, then asked again a few months later, when full pay was reinstated.

According to equity theory, workers would adjust their thinking about what they valued at work in order to achieve the perception of equity. Results from the study confirmed this prediction. After workers experienced the pay cut, they emphasized the importance of features of the workplace other than salary. When normal pay was reinstated, however, other features again became significantly less important than salary.

In two other applied studies, Lord and Hohenfeld (1979) and Duchon and Jago (1981) used equity theory to test predictions about the performances of major league baseball players. In 1976, free agency—a situation in which a player lets his contract expire, plays one additional year with his team, and then is able to negotiate with other teams for a new contract—was introduced. Players who elected to become free agents often experienced pay cuts of as much as 20 percent during the year after their contracts had expired and before they had joined a new team.

Lord and Hohenfeld used equity theory to predict that lower pay relative to the pay of other players (outcomes of Others) would result in a decline in performance (inputs of Person) during the year prior to signing a new contract. In terms of number of home runs, runs batted in, and runs scored, the performances of the players were, in fact, lower than they had been in the previous three years. This situation is represented in Box 7.1.

In an extension of this study, however, Duchon and Jago found that Lord and Hohenfeld's predictions did not hold up in the years after free agency was instituted. These researchers found that outputs (performance) actually *increased* during the year prior to signing a new contract, and that performance declined during the first year after joining a new team. According to Duchon and Jago, the fact that the original study had been based on the first year of free agency, when players and owners were uncertain about outcomes, influenced results.

BOX 7.1   INPUTS AND OUTCOMES OF MAJOR LEAGUE BASEBALL PLAYERS

Free agency (first year)

Perceived Inequity:

	Free Agent	Other Players
Outcome:	Salary cut	Same salary
Input:	Regular level of performance	Regular level of performance

$$\frac{\text{Salary cut}}{\text{Regular level of performance}} < \frac{\text{Same salary}}{\text{Regular level of performance}}$$

Result: Lowered level of input to reduce inequity

Free agency (following three years)

Perceived Inequity:

	Free Agent	Other Free Agents
Outcome:	Poor contract offers	Good contract offers
Input:	Lower level of input	Regular level of performance

$$\frac{\text{Poor contract offers}}{\text{Lower level of input}} < \frac{\text{Good contract offers}}{\text{Regular level of performance}}$$

Result: Higher level of input to reduce inequity

As you can see from this illustration, free agents who experienced a salary cut and continued at the regular level of performance felt inequity when they compared their salaries to those of other players. This was likely to result in a lowered level of input. Over time, however, players observed that free agents who maintained their performance levels got better contract offers. In this case, performance was raised to reduce feelings of inequity.

After 1976, when ballplayers saw that poor performances during the year before signing a new contract jeopardized earnings, performances actually improved. Since both studies demonstrated the importance of ballplayer perceptions about fairness in influencing performance, both sets of researchers considered their study supportive of equity theory.

Finally, Howard and Miller (1993) extended the study of equity and professional baseball and developed a model to predict underpaid, equitably paid, and overpaid players. Using measures of performance such as stolen bases, hits, runs batted in, errors, home runs, and other variables, the researchers found that outfielders were most likely to be underpaid and shortstops were most likely to be overpaid. Table 7.1 summarizes the results of their study.

In another example of how equity theory might be applied to a work setting, Adams and Freedman (1976) suggested that one of its best uses is in creating "obligations"—situations in which employers use praise and rewards so employees feel they must perform at high levels in order to reduce inequities in the situation. For example, employees in an insurance company were assigned to work in other departments because their own offices were being refurbished. One group was temporarily assigned to work in the offices of coworkers with higher status; one group was assigned to the offices of coworkers with lower status; and the

TABLE 7.1   UNDERPAID, EQUITABLY PAID, AND OVERPAID BASEBALL PLAYERS

Position	*n*	Underpaid	Equitably Paid	Overpaid
Catcher	76	36	33	7
First base	51	18	24	9
Second base	50	21	22	7
Third base	52	19	24	9
Shortstop	47	14	21	12
Outfield	157	101	42	14
Total	433	209	166	58

Source: Howard, L. W., & Miller, J. L. (1993). Fair pay for fair play: Estimating pay equity in professional baseball with data envelopment analysis. *Academy of Management Journal, 36,* 882–894. Copyright © 1993.z

third group was assigned to offices of equally ranked coworkers. In terms of equity theory, the first group was being "overpaid" in work environment, the second group was "underpaid," and the third group was treated equitably.

Performances of all three groups were compared. The performance of the group in the equitable condition did not differ from the performance of a control group of equal status that had not been moved from its office. The overpaid group, however, performed significantly better than the group in the equitable condition, and the underpaid group performed significantly worse (Greenberg, 1988). (In addition to providing confirming evidence for equity theory, this research suggests that the quality of office environments—a hygiene factor—can affect performance.) Finally, one other test of equity theory (Griffeth, Vecchio, & Logan, 1989) found that people were more tolerant of inequity when they were working with a person they liked.

Evaluating Equity Theory   As suggested above, considerable research supports equity theory. Because much of this research has taken place in the laboratory and not in applied settings, however, it is sometimes difficult to evaluate the usefulness of equity theory in explaining employee motivation. In an experimental study of equity theory using high-status job titles as compensation for underpayment, for example, Greenberg and Ornstein (1983) found that people who felt they earned their high titles were better performers, whereas the performances of people who received an unearned title declined over time. Although equity theory would predict such an outcome, would this be the case in a real-life work setting? Given the state of present knowledge about equity theory, it is difficult to be certain.

There are a few other considerations with regard to equity theory. As with all cognitive approaches, behavior is the result of *perceptions*—how an individual views a situation. As any psychologist or employer knows, diagnosing or predicting individual perceptions of events is not always a straightforward undertaking. For example, certain individuals may be bothered by *any* perception of inequity, but others will have a large tolerance for inequities. It is unlikely that a manager can be consistently accurate in judging how employees perceive a situation. One of the major criticisms of equity theory, in fact, is that it is not very useful unless an employer knows how an employee determines if a situation is equitable or inequitable (Cropanzano & Folger, 1989; Locke & Henne, 1986).

A second problem with equity theory relates to the tension that supposedly occurs when inequities exist. According to Adams and other researchers, both disadvantageous and advantageous inequity will result in tension. Although support for disadvantageous inequity (Person feeling outcomes do not match inputs) leading to behavioral or cognitive change has been demonstrated—that is, workers change their behaviors if they feel the situation is disadvantageous to them—support for the opposite proposition is much less clear. More recent research suggests that advantageous inequity, in which employees recognize they are receiving more for their inputs than others, does not necessarily lead to a change in performance.

Finally, equity theory does not contain the elements of either time or history (Vecchio, 1982). In other words, considering instances of behavior without considering the background leading up to the perception of inequity may result in an unrealistic view of the situation. For example, workers who feel they have been slighted in the past may continue to feel disadvantageous inequity regardless of what outcomes occur.

Overall, equity theory can be recognized as an approach that has had wide implications in industrial and organizational, as well as social, psychology. Like most of the theories discussed thus far, however, empirical evidence from applied settings is more difficult to obtain than evidence from laboratory research. Again, relying on managers to determine the perceptions of employees and then to use this information to improve performance makes equity theory difficult to apply in the workplace.

Expectancy Theory

Expectancy theories of motivation focus on three elements: the effort an individual expends, the individual's beliefs about probable outcomes, and the value the individual places on those outcomes. **Expectancy theory** recognizes that efforts, values, and outcomes affect each other and influence performance. Probably because expectancy is the most quantifiable and the most theoretically precise theory of motivation, it has until recently been the most popular approach among psychologists doing work in this area (Schneider, 1985).

Although there are several precursors to expectancy theory, Vroom (1964) is generally credited with its formal introduction. Like equity theory, expectancy is a cognitive and rational model of motivation, in which workers estimate probabilities and make choices among alternatives. Unlike need theories, which focus on influences in a person's past, expectancy theory centers on *outcomes*—that which is likely to happen in the future. The basic idea behind expectancy theory is that *force*—the motivation to act—is the result of the worker's expected results and how much perceived value those results hold.

According to Vroom, worker motivation is the product of several factors. First, a worker has choices among several outcomes. People who sell on commission, for example, can work hard in hopes of higher income, or they can take a more relaxed approach, probably resulting in lower income. The perceived desirability of these outcomes is referred to as the **valence.** It is important to recognize that valences are based on perceptions that individuals have toward predicted outcomes. They differ from *values* because they are only projections of what something is worth. For example, the occupation of stockbroker may have a high positive *valence* for some individuals who are not stockbrokers. If they become stockbrokers and dislike the job, however, then actual experience will hold a negative *value* for them.

Expectancy relates to the probability of an outcome occurring. Hard work may result in a strong expectancy that a promotion will result, but it may result in a weak expectancy if the boss's son is competing for the same position. Expectancies take values ranging from +1.00, meaning absolute certainty of an outcome, to −1.00, meaning absolute uncertainty. **Force** is that which compels a person to act. Typically, force will be the strongest positive, or the weakest negative, outcome.

Although Vroom's original formulation of expectancy theory implied that all behavior could be explained by understanding a worker's perceptions of outcomes, more recent research suggests that the theory may not be as generalizable as once believed. For example, Miller and Grush (1988) looked at the expectancies of two groups of individuals—one group of people who paid more attention to their own personal norms than to social influences, and another group of people who were more attentive to social norms than to their own beliefs. Although expectancies did affect the behavior of the individuals attentive to their personal norms, expectancies had little effect on the behavior of people influenced by social norms. Apparently expectancy theory works less well for people whose main reference point is the expectations of the people around them.

Extending the research on free agents in major league baseball described above, one researcher (Harder, 1991) proposed a synthesis of expectancy theory with equity theory to explain free agent performance. Research regarding salaries in major league baseball suggest a free agent's "slugging percentage" (i.e., the total number of bases attained by the player with base hits divided by the total times at bat) is more predictive of salary than batting average alone. Using this measure, number of home runs is more predictive of salary than batting average.

According to expectancy theory, free agents probably had the expectancy that more home runs hit would lead to higher salaries, so they put more effort into hitting home runs. According to equity theory, however, free agents also perceived that their inputs for high batting averages were not being equitably rewarded, and consequently put less effort into raising batting averages. This, in fact, was what happened. In the year before salary would be determined, players put significant effort into their home runs and less effort into their batting averages.

Self-efficacy (Bandura, 1977), a concept mentioned in Chapter 5, has also been linked with expectancy theory and motivation. In terms of job performance, self-efficacy refers to workers' beliefs in their abilities to accomplish a job in a satisfactory manner. Although the linkage between expectancy and self-efficacy is obvious, expectancy theory focuses chiefly on a worker's perception of the amount of effort necessary to accomplish a task. Self-efficacy is more encompassing, however, because it focuses on the way workers decide about the amount of effort necessary. In this sense, self-efficacy actually influences expectancy (Gist & Mitchell, 1992).

Self-efficacy is an important psychological construct that has been used to predict life insurance sales (Barling & Beattie, 1983), research productivity (Taylor, Locke, Lee, & Gist, 1984), success in training (Frayne & Latham, 1987), and student exam scores (Thomas & Mathieu, 1994). Another interesting study (Eden & Zuk, 1996) found that experimentally improving the self-efficacy of naval cadets lowered their tendency to seasickness. Other researchers (Lindsley, Brass, & Thomas, 1995) proposed that widespread feelings of efficacy within an organization can lead to "efficacy-performance" spirals that lead to ever higher levels of performance. Another study (Gellatly, 1996) found that expectancy was also influenced by a person's level of conscientiousness.

Although the concept has not yet been fully explored as a motivational theory of work and researchers are not yet clear on the best way to measure it (Lee & Bobko, 1994), self-efficacy appears to hold some promise for understanding job performance.

Evaluating Expectancy Theory   Several advantages of the expectancy approach to understanding worker motivation are apparent. First, expectancy theory is a model that can be applied in many different situations, not only at work. Marketing managers, for example, could use expectancy theory to determine which product consumers are likely to purchase.

Second, the expectancy model can reflect changing conditions or even be used to bring about changes in performance. Performance can be improved by (1) instituting new outcomes; (2) changing the expectancies of existing outcomes so that the more desirable are more likely to occur; or (3) changing the valences of existing outcomes.

On the other hand, expectancy theory is not something of immediate use to most supervisors. Most managers prefer approaches such as those of Maslow or Herzberg over mathematically precise models. Determining expectancies and valences requires considerable research and calculation. Also, although the model is designed to reflect dynamic situations, rapidly changing work environments may undermine the accuracy of its predictions.

Another questionable aspect of expectancy theory is its assumptions that workers have enough information to make rational decisions and that, regardless of information availability, workers make rational decisions. It is easy to see that information about job situations is not always available and that many people make decisions based on emotions.

As suggested above, the expectancy model was, until recently, the most popular theory of motivation used by academic psychologists, and it has been refined or expanded by several researchers (Naylor, Pritchard, & Ilgen, 1980; Staw, 1982). Ironically, the mathematical precision and theoretical elegance of the expectancy model are the qualities that limit its applicability. Nonetheless, in recent years there has been a revived interest in equity theory (Klein & Wright, 1994; Mento, Locke, & Klein, 1992; Shepperd, 1993; Summers & Hendrix, 1991). However, results from a recent meta-analysis (Van Eerde & Thierry, 1996) were not supportive of expectancy theory as a predictor of work-related criteria.

Behavioral Approaches to Motivation

Approaches to motivation that use a behavioral framework—such as **operant conditioning**—are not usually considered theories of motivation in and of themselves. Rather, these approaches apply the principles and methods of learning theory to behavior that occurs in the work environment. Individuals who use behavioral approaches to explain worker performance rely on the theories of John B. Watson, B. F. Skinner, and other learning theorists. In recent years, the behavioral approach to worker motivation has been more fully developed by Luthans and Kreitner (1985) and given the title of **organizational behavior modification (OBM).**

From a behaviorist perspective, because motivation is a hypothetical construct that cannot be observed, it is not a particularly useful concept. Therefore, researchers or managers should focus on observable behavior and events that influence behavior, rather than on mediating variables—such as achievement motivation—that cannot be observed.

What can be observed in the workplace are instances of desirable and undesirable behavior. Desirable workplace behaviors include working on the weekend to meet deadlines, taking special classes to improve skills, or being helpful toward other workers. Undesirable workplace behaviors include being tardy, producing inferior goods, or ignoring customers. In these cases, the behavioral theorist would like to increase desirable behaviors and eliminate the undesirable.

One way to increase desirable behaviors is to control the stimuli that affect employees. For example, a manager who wants employees to work weekends could communicate the importance of this behavior to the employees. Along the same lines, the manager could arrange a particularly appealing work environment for those who work on weekends. Given these stimuli, the hoped-for response is weekend work.

TABLE 7.2   MODELS FOR INFLUENCING BEHAVIOR

Goal   A manager wants employees to get their work done on time.

Procedure	Operationalization	Behavioral Effect
Positive reinforcement	The manager compliments employees when work is done on time.	Increases the desired behavior (meeting deadlines)
Negative reinforcement	The manager removes disliked job duties if employees consistently hand in assignments on time.	Increases the desired behavior (meeting deadlines)
Punishment	Each time an assignment is handed in late, the manager increases the employee's workload by adding one extra assignment the following day.	Decreases the undesirable behavior (handing in assignments late)
Extinction	The manager ignores the employee when a work assignment is handed in late.	Decreases the undesirable behavior (handing in assignments late)

Another way to influence behavior is to rely on reinforcement theory, the behavioral approach most often used by managers. According to reinforcement theory, what people do is determined by the consequences of their actions. A manager influences behavior by manipulating these consequences. Procedures for influencing behavior are summarized in Table 7.2.

The final steps of an organizational behavior modification program are evaluation and maintenance; that is, the manager evaluates employee behavior after the reinforcement is applied to see if the behavior is in line with what the manager desires. If the behavior is desirable, the manager should plan a program of occasional reinforcement to ensure that the behavior is maintained over time.

For example, a U.S. factory in Mexico had serious problems with tardiness, with almost 15 percent of the workforce being late on a regular basis. Management decided to reinforce promptness by paying workers a few extra pesos per day (amounting to about 16 cents at the time) for starting work early. At minimal cost to the employer, tardiness dipped from 15 percent to 2 percent (Carlson & Sperduto, 1982). Recall from Chapter 2 that providing the Russian textile workers with rewards for performance raised their productivity, but allowing them to participate in workplace discussions did not (Welsh, Luthans, & Sommer, 1993).

Successful implementation of a behavioral approach to motivating workers requires several steps. First, supervisors need to identify the goal they want workers to accomplish. Take, for example, a clerical employee who is constantly behind in his work. After careful observation, the supervisor decides that limiting the amount of time the worker spends on the telephone talking to friends will result in more time for fulfilling job duties. The goal of the intervention in this example is to limit the amount of time spent on nonwork-related telephone calls.

In the second part of the program, the supervisor determines a baseline to assess progress. The supervisor needs to know how much time the employee spends on the telephone in contrast with the amount of time the supervisor considers acceptable. When the supervisor has determined an acceptable amount of time spent on personal calls, this becomes the goal of the behavioral management program.

In the third part of the program, the supervisor attempts to change the employee's behavior using a strategy of positive reinforcement, negative reinforcement, punishment, extinction, or a combination of these approaches. Using a **positive reinforcement** approach, the supervisor may offer the worker incentives, such as being able to leave early for spending less time on the telephone, praising the worker for good performance, or promising a raise if work is finished on time.

If a strategy of **negative reinforcement** is chosen, the supervisor may remove some of the duties the clerical worker dislikes if the worker spends less time on the telephone and more time working.

If the supervisor selects **punishment** as a reinforcement strategy, she may criticize the employee's work, warn about dismissal, or make the employee stay late to make up for time spent on the telephone.

Finally, with regard to the strategy of extinguishing the employee's behavior by ignoring it, this approach, if not used in combination with the other strategies, is unlikely to be successful, since talking to friends is obviously a rewarding experience that the employee would like to continue.

This example illustrates how implementing a behavioral approach to worker motivation requires careful planning. Managers need to identify the goals they want to accomplish, and they need to develop a system for influencing behaviors that will lead to those goals. Although raises, criticism, praise, advancements, and special privileges can be thought of as reinforcements and punishments, managers must be able to determine which of these the employee values. For the worker in the example above, social contact is obviously an important reinforcer. In the case of the Mexican workers, on the other hand, money was the reinforcer. Box 7.2 illustrates some of the approaches that may be taken to implement a schedule of reinforcement.

One group of researchers (Banker, Lee, Potter, & Srinivasan, 1996) looked at a behavioral incentive plan in a large retail firm. In this company, management instituted a bonus system for employees who exhibited high levels of customer service, which would translate into greater sales. As the researchers had predicted, the positive reinforcement of a bonus led to greater sales and greater customer satisfaction. However, when supervisors monitored the performances of workers more closely—a form of punishment—the levels of sales and customer satisfaction decreased.

BOX 7.2   RATIO AND PERFORMANCE

Regardless of the strategy selected, an employer can increase effectiveness by choosing a schedule for reinforcement. Types of reinforcement schedules are summarized below.

Continuous Reinforcement

In this case, a supervisor rewards a desired performance every time it occurs, such as giving workers compliments each time they reach a certain goal. Over longer periods of time, however, this strategy is difficult to implement and is not very practical in the work environment.

Partial Reinforcement

One problem with continuous reinforcement is that workers eventually stop performing the desired behavior if they are not reinforced every time it occurs. Partial reinforcement, in which workers are reinforced only occasionally, will sustain behavior over a longer period of time. The schedules described next are varieties of partial reinforcement.

Fixed Ratio

This is a type of partial reinforcement in which a worker is rewarded after a specific number of performances. For example, a life insurance salesperson may earn bonuses for every $100,000 worth of insurance sold. An advantage to this approach is that the faster workers perform, the more reward they receive.

Fixed Interval

This is the schedule of reinforcement in operation at most work settings and, unfortunately, one of the worst ways to influence behavior. Rewards are certain to come at a designated time, regardless of performance. For example, paychecks arrive every two weeks and raises come at yearly performance appraisal meetings. Employees who do little work are paid as regularly as those who excel.

Variable Ratio

In this case, reinforcement comes after an average number of responses. For example, an employee may make ten customer calls, but the reward does not necessarily come after the tenth call. The salesperson cannot know when the reinforcement will arrive; it may come after the second call or after the fifteenth call. Since the worker perceives that there is always the possibility of a reward, there will be continuous motivation to work.

Variable Interval

In this case, reinforcement comes after an average period of time. Rewards may come weekly for a while, then come monthly or semiannually. As in the case of variable ratio, because the worker always feels the possibility of a reward, performance levels are likely to be higher.

Evaluating Reinforcement Theory Although the reinforcement approach has been shown to work in a variety of settings, there are some considerations before implementing such an approach. First, managers must be clear about which rewards and punishments they have available. Sometimes resources are not adequate to provide the reinforcements that motivate workers. Additionally, jobs may be so boring or so demanding that a manager may have difficulty identifying reinforcers to raise levels of motivation.

Second, the manager must be able to specify the behavioral change being sought and design a program for accomplishing the goal. Certainly not all workers respond to the same reinforcers, so the supervisor must determine what reinforcement works with whom. This aspect of planning a reinforcement program can be tricky. Some studies, for example, show that male employees tend to set a high value on rewards such as increased salary and potential for advancement, whereas females often put greater value on job security and flexible working hours. Similarly, individuals from other cultures may hold values that are not common in the American workplace. The manager who wishes to act as behavior analyst must be able to ascertain these differences.

Third, once a reinforcement system has been implemented, managers need to make special efforts to see that desirable behaviors are sustained. This is one of the most dangerous aspects of using cash as a reward system. Unless a manager is willing to provide ever higher amounts, money is likely to lose its effectiveness as a reinforcer over time.

Fourth, in contrast with other theories, individual motivation in the reinforcement framework is entirely extrinsic. That is, its success depends on factors in the environment, and not on the internal state of the employee. Because of this, managers need to monitor the situation to make certain there are sufficient rewards and punishments to keep performance levels high.

A final problem with reinforcement theory is that some managers or workers may see it as manipulative. Not everyone is comfortable with shaping behavior through a system of rewards and punishments. Although the idea of improving performance by giving people what they enjoy seems logical, some workers may object to having their behavior "shaped."

Intrinsic Motivation

Another approach to worker motivation that challenges the behavioral approach is Deci's model of intrinsic and extrinsic motivators (Deci, 1975a, 1975b, Deci & Ryan, 1985). **Intrinsic motivation** is a cognitive theory that argues that the internal state of a worker determines level of effort. This view contrasts not only with behavioral theories, where individual performance is the product of rewards and punishments, but also with traditional need theory, where individual performance is affected by childhood experience. The intrinsic motivation model suggests that motives, emotions, and cognitions cause behavior, rather than vice versa.

According to Deci, individuals are motivated by drives for competence and self-determination or autonomy. Consequently, individuals engage in two kinds of behaviors: seeking challenging situations, and conquering those challenges (Deci, 1975a). Consequently, people like stimuli that offer the potential satisfactions of demonstrating competence and autonomy.

Intrinsic motivation offers a challenge to the behavioral model in particular, since, according to this theory, some "reinforcers" could actually lead to lower performance. When workers are motivated by outcomes chosen by others such as higher pay, promotions, or threats from a supervisor, their autonomy is being denied. Working for these kinds of extrinsic motivators actually disconfirms workers' feelings of self-determination. As a result, workers are not motivated to perform as well as they would if they were given opportunities to demonstrate their competence and self-determination. In addition, extrinsic motivators can distract workers' attention from their goals (Shalley, 1995).

Extrinsic rewards may improve performance in the short run, but the best way to motivate workers is to provide opportunities that confirm their feelings of competence and self-determination. Conversely, motivation suffers if workers experience situations in which their feelings of competence and self-determination are disconfirmed. Good supervisors recognize this fact and structure the workplace so there are opportunities for demonstrating competence and self-determination.

In a test of the role of self-determination in the performances of technicians and field managers of an office machine company, for example, Deci, Connell, and Ryan (1989) trained managers to encourage self-determination in their employees. Over time, as managers became more supportive of employees' self-determination, employee satisfaction with the organization increased. When business conditions were bad, however, employees worried more about pay and job security than about self-determination, an outcome that supports Maslow's views on motivation.

Empowerment, which refers to giving workers the capacity to act to solve organizational problems (Smither, Houston, & McIntire, 1996; Spreitzer, 1995), is a concept sometimes used in conjunction with intrinsic motivation. Employees who are empowered are motivated to do their jobs because they want to do them, and not because management is manipulating the environment in which the task is performed. Empowered employees take responsibility for accomplishing their tasks and are less inclined to rely on bureaucratic procedures and managerial direction.

According to some researchers (Thomas & Velthouse, 1990), empowerment occurs when employees experience the following:

1. *Meaning,* which involves a fit between requirements of a work role and a person's beliefs and values;
2. *Competence,* which refers to self-efficacy regarding work;
3. *Self-determination,* or a sense of choice in choosing a course of action; and

4. *Impact,* or the degree to which a person can influence outcomes at work.

Working with survey data from 393 middle managers from a *Fortune* 50 organization, Spreitzer (1996) found that managers felt empowered when goals were clear, when spans of control were large and managers had more latitude in decision making, and when the organization had a climate that encouraged participation.

Evaluating Intrinsic Motivation Intrinsic motivation is a cognitive theory that has provoked considerable controversy. Radical behaviorists—those who rely chiefly on reinforcement to explain behavior—are particularly hostile to the intrinsic approach. They argue that the methodology of Deci's original research was faulty, that hypothesizing the existence of internalized states is not necessary, and that all that Deci argues can be explained by a reinforcement model. These arguments appear to have some merit, especially since some researchers have been unable to replicate Deci's original findings (Farr, 1976; Scott & Erskine, 1980). In addition, some research suggests that reward is detrimental only in unusual circumstances (Eisenberger & Cameron, 1996).

Another problem with intrinsic motivation is definitions. Identifying a dependable method of determining what is intrinsically motivating to individual workers has long been elusive. An additional problem is determining the relationship between motivation and the qualities of competence and self-determination. If boss tells subordinates that future promotions depend on taking classes to improve their skills outside of working hours, the workers may or may not feel that their self-determination has been violated. Some workers might resent the night class requirement, but others might be grateful for the suggestion.

Although Deci's theory is intriguing, it appears to suffer from a problem common to most cognitive theories. In our present state of knowledge, it is virtually impossible to make any certain connections between cognition and behavior. What people think and what they do are, in many cases, unrelated or even contradictory. Intrinsic motivation may yet provide useful insights into worker performance, but thus far, both clear scientific evidence of support and a means of operationalizing the model in the workplace are lacking.

Goal-setting Theory

One fact that researchers have demonstrated repeatedly over the years is that goal setting improves performance (Mento, Steel, & Karren, 1987). Goals act as motivators, and research in both applied and experimental settings shows that difficult goals produce higher levels of performance than either no goals or simply instructions to "do your best" (Locke & Latham, 1990; Tubbs, 1986). When workers know a particular level of performance is expected of them, they are motivated to try to reach that level, even though it may be difficult. In addition, when group members are committed to a goal, performance of the group improves (O'Leary-Kelly, Martocchio, & Frink, 1994).

In an often-cited study, Latham and Saari (1982) used a goal-setting approach to improve the job performances of logging truck drivers. At this particular company, drivers were responsible for delivering loads of logs to the mill. When the drivers did not work fast enough, however, logs would pile up at the loading dock and the work of other employees would be disrupted. A review of company operations found that some drivers were taking longer lunch hours, stopping along the road to visit their friends, or were simply apathetic about their job performance.

In the first part of the study, loggers were divided into experimental and control groups. The control group was given no instructions, but the supervisor of the experimental group introduced a weekly goal of trips per day to the mill. This goal was intentionally difficult but attainable. Drivers were told that there would be no negative consequences for not meeting their individual goals. However, the supervisor posted the target number of trips next to the name of each driver on a bulletin board and, at the end of the day, recorded the number of trips actually accomplished.

Although there were no significant differences between the number of trips by the experimental and control groups before initiation of the goal-setting program, important differences emerged later. Specifically, over an 18-week period, the experimental group made 1,800 additional trips to the mill. Based on the value of a load of logs, the annual increase in deliveries amounted to $2.7 million.

Goal setting focuses on the task to be accomplished. As discussed in Chapter 6, management by objectives (MBO) is a goal-setting procedure that requires managers to put on paper which goals are to be accomplished and by whom. Although the MBO approach has been shown to be very successful with management, at least in the short run, Latham and Locke (1979) suggest that it can be just as successful for all levels of workers. Box 7.3 is a sample MBO plan.

Goal setting also appears to be an effective motivational technique in other cultures. In a study of 92 Caribbean women who sewed children's clothing, Punnett (1986) found that women who were given specific difficult goals outperformed those who were told "do your best" or given no goals.

One of the most interesting aspects of goal setting is that it works so well in the absence of visible reinforcement. In the original Locke-Latham (1990) model of goal setting, goals themselves are not seen as motivating. What actually motivates is the self-dissatisfaction caused by discrepancies between what people do and what they hope to achieve. These discrepancies motivate people to try harder to produce a positive self-image (Earley, Northcraft, Lee, & Litchy, 1990; Wood & Bandura, 1989).

Since the fact that having goals improves performance is well established, more recent research has focused on the situations in which goal setting works best. For goals to be successful motivators, they must meet the following criteria:

BOX 7.3   MBO PLAN

As suggested below, goals that are specific, time-limited, and challenging but achievable are most likely to be accomplished. Management by objectives (MBO) requires managers and employees to put onto paper which goals are to be accomplished and by whom. Many times, managers develop these goals in consultation with the employee. Part of an MBO plan for a sales representative might include the following:

Employee: _____

Position: _____

FIRST-QUARTER OBJECTIVES

Objectives	Action Steps	To Be Accomplished By:
1. Attend new product training sessions at Seattle plant	1. Clear calendar during week of training 2. Arrange travel	March 15
2. Visit five new prospects each month	1. Identify prospects from trade show responses 2. Telephone to arrange appointment 3. Arrange travel	By the 20th of each month By the 25th By the 30th
3. Train junior salesperson	1. Consult with trainee to determine best time to meet 2. Plan materials to be covered in training session 3. Hold session 4. Hold follow-up session	February 28 March 10 March 20 September 20

1. Goals must be specific. "Do your best" seems to be as ineffective a motivator as having no goal.

2. Goals must have time limits. Knowing that a goal must be reached by the end of the year will not affect performance as much as having a lesser goal to accomplish in one month.

3. Goals must be challenging but achievable. Interestingly, research shows that people are more motivated to work for goals that seem difficult than they are to work for easy goals. Higher goals elicit higher levels of performance.

The method by which a goal is determined to be difficult, however, can affect performance (Wright, 1990), and workers who have experienced a clear and well-documented review of their performances are more committed to their goals than those whose progress toward goals is not reviewed (Tziner & Kopelman, 1988). In addition, factors such as public knowledge of a goal and the worker's having an internal locus of control and a high need for achievement also affect commitment to a difficult goal (Hollenbeck, Williams, & Klein, 1989).

Finally, having goals can affect the ways in which workers perform their tasks (Audia, Kristof-Brown, Brown, & Locke, 1996), and some research (DeShon, Brown, & Greenis, 1996) suggests that the success of goal setting may be affected by the complexity of the task.

Latham and Locke (1979) identified two other conditions necessary for successful performance: the worker must be committed to the goal and resources must be available for its accomplishment. If workers do not see the value in what they are asked to do, if they object to the end product, or if they fail several times at achieving a goal, then their performances are likely to suffer (Vance & Colella, 1990). Although earlier research suggested that employee participation in setting goals improved performance, more recent research suggests that employees do as well when goals are assigned (Tubbs, 1986; Tubbs, Boehne, & Dahl, 1993). Although the concept of commitment is not yet entirely understood (Tubbs, 1993), some factors that affect commitment to goals are peer influence, an employee's personal values, rewards for goal accomplishment, feelings of self-efficacy, and expectancy of success (Locke, Latham, & Erez, 1988).

Some research suggests that workers' stating they are committed to a goal does not mean they actually accept the goal (Hollenbeck, Klein, O'Leary, & Wright, 1989; Tubbs & Dahl, 1991). One of the newer areas of research in motivation theory focuses on intention, defined as "a cognitive representation of both the objective (or goal) one is striving for and the action plan one intends to use to reach that objective" (Tubbs & Ekeberg, 1991). Applying the intention model to goal setting suggests that workers may accept a goal, but they may not be fully committed to the steps necessary to achieve the goal. In other words, just being favorably disposed to a goal does not indicate commitment to its accomplishment. Furthermore, some research (Wright, O'Leary-Kelly, Cortina, Klein, & Hollenbeck, 1994) suggests that commitment is affected by workers' feelings of self-efficacy.

Can commitment to a goal be harmful to an organization? Wright, George, Farnsworth, and McMahan (1993) hypothesized that people who are committed to achieving a difficult goal would be less likely to help others attain their goals. In this experimental study, student volunteers were assigned easy, moderate, or difficult goals and asked to perform an order-processing task. During the 20 minutes participants were given to accomplish the task, a confederate of the experimenters repeatedly asked volunteers for help during the experimental period. Results from the experiment indicated that people who commited themselves to difficult goals were less likely to help people around them. The researchers concluded that having goals may affect other areas of organizational functioning and that researchers need to pay attention to those areas as well.

In one study that looked at goal setting and incentives and success as a hockey player (Anderson, Crowell, Doman, & Howard, 1988), members of a hockey team with three years of losing seasons were assigned to one of three interventions: feedback, goal setting, or praise. Feedback, in the form of posting individual performance records in the locker room, improved performance significantly, and the setting of individual goals improved performance even more. Praise also improved performance, but in a less consistent fashion.

Results from the study confirmed the researchers' belief that sports performance can be improved if coaches take a careful, analytical approach to studying the individual performances of athletes and that goal setting in combination with reinforcement can make a significant difference in team performance. In addition, some research (Weingart, 1992) suggests that group performance is more likely to be successful if members plan how to accomplish the group goal.

In an interesting study of how goals can affect job design, one group of researchers (Doerr, Mitchell, Klastorin, & Brown, 1996) looked at production procedures in various fish processing plants. In the "push" production setting, workers performed their assigned task, then moved the fish to the next worker, whether or not that worker was ready. In the "pull" setting, fish were passed to the next worker only when he or she was ready for them. Workers in both production settings were assigned to conditions of having no goals, individual goals, or group goals. The greatest increase in productivity occurred in the pull setting when workers had group goals. These results suggest that goal setting can also be affected by job design.

Finally, some researchers (Barrick, Mount, & Strauss, 1993) considered the relationship between personality factors and goal setting among appliance sales representatives. Results showed that sales representatives high in conscientiousness were more likely to set goals and be committed to their accomplishment. This led to both greater sales volume and higher supervisory ratings.

Evaluating Goal Setting Of all the theories of motivation discussed in this book, goal setting is presently generating the most research. Although many of these studies were done in the laboratory with student subjects, more and more researchers are applying findings from this research to the workplace.

Also, goal setting now appears to be a more complicated theory of motivation than when it was first proposed. The initial work in goal setting stated that goals need only be specific, difficult, and time-limited to be effective. More recent research, however, has shown goal acceptance is a critical element in goal setting. At present, researchers are focusing on both the ways in which goal commitment is measured (Tubbs, 1994; Wright et al., 1994) and the conditions that make workers more willing to accept goals.

Evaluating Theories of Motivation

As stated in Chapter 1, one of the goals of this book is to bridge some of the gaps between industrial and organizational theory and its application. For example, the elegance of theoretical models is often lost on the manager who must respond to job pressures. Similarly, ad hoc applications of motivational techniques without any theory behind them tell us little that is useful over a longer period. Nowhere is the gap between theoretical knowledge and application greater than in the area of motivation. Table 7.3 compares some different aspects of the theories of motivation.

Although each of the theories discussed in this chapter has been the target of substantial research, widespread practical application of any particular theory remains elusive. Whereas we may use expectancy theory to explain the performances of sales representatives, for example, it is much more difficult to use this model to develop a strategy for managing a department.

Along the same lines, we may believe one employee's poor sales performance is due to an inherent lack of achievement motivation, whereas another's excellent sales record is due to a combination of both high need for achievement and high need for affiliation. Basing job changes or reassignment of workers on our suspicions about psychological needs, however, may not be an effective management strategy.

Four of the psychological approaches to motivation discussed in this chapter—need, equity, expectancy, and intrinsic motivation—require some understanding of how an employee perceives the work environment. For these theories to be effective, managers must to be able to identify employee needs, perceptions of equity, or valences. If managers misperceive how their employees view the work situation, then applying any of these theories of motivation is unlikely to be successful. Obviously, this is not a task that a busy manager without advanced training in the behavioral sciences can easily fulfill.

Behavioral theories and goal setting differ from the other theories in one important way. Whereas psychological needs or perceptions are the basis for the other theories, reinforcement and goal setting focus on the extrinsic world of the employee. Understanding of the internal state of the worker is not necessary to apply either of these theories. Reinforcement requires only a knowledge of what a worker finds desirable.

Goal-setting theory requires even less information—the act of setting a goal seems to motivate workers regardless of need levels, valences, or reinforcement. Because these two theories are simpler to operationalize than the others, reinforcement and goal setting are probably the most widely applied theories of motivation in the work environment.

One important factor that has not been addressed by most theories of motivation is the effect of gender or culture on performance. Cognitive theories work only when the cognitions of the target group are understood, and tradi-

TABLE 7.3   MOTIVATIONAL THEORIES COMPARED

Theory	Rationale	Considerations
Need Theories		
Hierarchy of Needs	Workers are motivated by a drive toward psychological growth but must fulfill needs at four other levels first	The Maslow hierarchy has great intuitive appeal to some managers but little empirical support
Two-Factor Theory	Workers are motivated by conditions in the work environment, known as hygiene factors, and opportunities for growth and satisfaction, known as motivators	Determining what is a hygiene factor and what is a motivator is not straightforward; little research supports the theory
Achievement Motivation Theory	Workers are motivated by needs for achievement, affiliation, and power	Motivations are established in childhood, but training courses can modify needs; managers may have difficulty manipulating drives that originated in childhood
Equity Theory	Worker motivation is based on employee perceptions about fairness in the workplace	Managers need to understand how workers perceive their situations, which may be difficult to do; aspects of the theory are not supported by research
Expectancy Theory	Motivation is based on the amount of effort needed to accomplish a task, the possibility of success, and the value the worker places on the outcome	Expectancy theory is well researched and supported, but application to the workplace may be too complex for most managers
Behavioral Approaches	Managers motivate workers by manipulating the environment and by providing reinforcements	Behavioral theories focus on observable behavior rather on what a manager assumes an employee thinks about the work environment; to be effective, the system needs careful planning and maintenance over time
Intrinsic Motivation	Workers are more motivated toward tasks that increase feelings of competence and autonomy	The manager must provide tasks that fulfill the conditions of competence and autonomy, which is likely to be difficult in some cases; also, some researchers dispute the idea that extrinsic rewards may be demotivating
Goal-Setting Theory	Workers perform best when they have specific, time-limited, and difficult goals	Goal setting is presently the motivational theory of greatest interest to researchers; although it appears to be promising, recent research suggests goal setting is more complex than once believed

tional managers may not be equipped to deal with the values of other cultures. Particularly with regard to foreign operations, such practices as serving tea in the afternoon may be more motivating than the promise of increases in wages over long periods of time. When evaluating theories of motivation, it is important to remember that most concepts about motivation have been developed with White male, sex-segregated, or college student groups that do not represent the diverse workforce of the future.

Nonetheless, these theories have made important contributions to our understanding of what motivates individuals to act in any environment. They are useful as frameworks for expansion of a theory or for developing new theories. Most importantly, the theories of motivation may eventually provide an understanding of worker behavior that can lead to more humane and productive work environments.

Chapter Summary

Motivation is the force that moves people to perform their jobs. As such, it is not observable, but must be inferred. It is an important but difficult area to study.

Need theories of motivation focus on psychological deficiencies in workers. Maslow's need hierarchy, Herzberg's two-factor theory, and McClelland's achievement motivation theory all argue that personality characteristics are responsible for individual levels of performance. Although need theory is appealing on an intuitive level, not much empirical research supports that approach.

Equity theory is based on the individual worker's view of the fairness in the work situation. Individuals compare the outcomes of their performances with the outcomes of the performances of others. If either advantageous or disadvantageous inequity exists, the employee then feels tension. Responses to tension include altering inputs, altering outcomes, leaving the field, or acting on the other employee. Successful application of equity theory to the work environment depends on a manager's understanding of employee perceptions. Developing this understanding may be difficult.

Expectancy theory has historically been the most popular theory of motivation among academic psychologists. Like equity theory, expectancy is a cognitive and rational model, in which the worker estimates probabilities and makes choices among alternatives. The basic idea behind the model is that the motivation to act results from a worker's expected results, the effort needed to achieve those results, and the value the worker places on that particular outcome. Self-efficacy is often related to expectancy theory.

Behavioral models of motivation come from the perspective of learning theory. Simply put, worker performance is influenced by manipulating stimuli—such as work environments—and by applying positive or negative consequences for performance. Proper application of the reinforcement model requires developing a program for accomplishing a precise goal, evaluating the program, and providing reinforcement so the behavior is maintained over time.

An alternative to the reinforcement model is intrinsic motivation theory. This approach suggests that the application of extrinsic motivators, such as raises and promotions, may actually lower motivation and performance over time. Rewards such as these are chosen by others, and they diminish a worker's feelings of self-determination and competence. On the other hand, rewards that reinforce feelings of competence and self-determination—intrinsic motivations—are more effective than those that are imposed from outside. This theory has not been widely tested outside the laboratory, however.

The number of studies supporting goal setting as a means of motivating has led to considerable interest in this area. Goals seem to act as motivators, and difficult goals are more motivating than easy goals or having no goals. For the goal-setting approach to work, however, goals must be specific, have time limits, and be challenging but achievable. Additionally, the workers must be willing to accept the goals, and management must be able to provide the necessary tools and environment to accomplish the goals. Management by objectives is a kind of goal-setting approach.

Overall, there is a considerable gap between theories of motivation and their application in the work environment. Although some supporting research exists for each theory, each has its limitations. Reinforcement theory and goal setting have probably had the widest application in the work setting simply because they are easier than the other theories to understand and implement. Because of the changing nature of the American workforce, it is possible that the theories of motivation discussed here may have limited relevance in the future. Nevertheless, they will form the basis for new theories.

Key Words and Concepts

achievement motivation theory
  (p. 209)
act on Other (p. 212)
altering the object of comparison
  (p. 212)
alter inputs (p. 212)
alter outcomes (p. 212)
dissonance theory (p. 211)
empowerment (p. 224)
equity theory (p. 211)
exchanges (p. 211)
existence, relatedness, and
  growth (ERG) (p. 207)
expectancy (p. 217)

expectancy theory (p. 216)
extinction (p. 220)
force (p. 217)
free riding (p. 205)
goal setting (p. 225)
hierarchy of needs (p. 206)
hygiene factors (p. 207)
inputs (p. 212)
intrinsic motivation (p. 223)
leave the field (p. 212)
motivation (p. 204)
motivators (p. 207)
need for achievement (p. 209)
need for affiliation (p. 209)

need for power (p. 210)

need theory (p. 205)

negative reinforcement (p. 221)

operant conditioning (p. 219)

organizational behavior
  modification (OBM) (p. 219)

other (p. 212)

outcomes (p. 212)

Person (p. 211)

positive reinforcement (p. 221)

punishment (p. 221)

self-actualization (p. 206)

self-efficacy (p. 218)

shirking (p. 205)

social information processing
  (p. 211)

social loafing (p. 205)

two-factor theory (p. 207)

valence (p. 217)

Questions for Discussion

1. What motivates you? Why? Are you motivated for different things at different times? What determines your motivational level?

2. What are examples of shirking, social loafing, or free riding? Do they ever occur in class?

3. Why do you think need theories are so appealing to most people? Do you think these theories are credible?

4. Do perceptions of advantageous or disadvantageous equity theory ever affect your behavior? How so?

5. What is the basic idea behind expectancy theory? How would expectancy theory explain the performance of students in a psychology class?

6. If you were designing a program to improve your grades, how would you use positive reinforcement, punishment, negative reinforcement, or extinction to achieve your goal?

7. In intrinsic motivation theory, reinforcers can lead to lower performance. How could this be possible? Do you agree with this viewpoint?

8. What is empowerment? Do you, as a student, feel empowered? If not, what would it take for you to be empowered?

9. What are the conditions under which goals lead to successful performance? Why is it so difficult for many people to achieve their goals?

10. Of all the theories of motivation, which best explains your performance? Why?

CHAPTER | 8

Job Satisfaction

Job Satisfaction and Life Satisfaction
Organizational Commitment
Measuring Job Satisfaction
Theories of Job Satisfaction
Measuring Dissatisfaction
Increasing Job Satisfaction
Chapter Summary
Key Words and Concepts
Questions for Discussion

Why do people like their jobs? In opinion surveys of workers over many decades, almost 80 percent of respondents have consistently stated that they are satisfied with the work they do. Certainly not all jobs have prestige, high salaries, or pleasant working conditions, however. Long hours, dangerous environments, and high stress are just a few of the negative factors that are typical of some jobs. Nonetheless, some people are willing to endure these negatives—and more—for the sake of their positions.

Since the turn of the century, employment conditions for most American workers have steadily improved. In most cases, salaries have increased, hours have shortened, and many workers now participate in decision making. Despite these changes, however, some modern workers continue to press for further modifications to the traditional employment model. Flexible hours, company-sponsored child care, and workplace democracy are just a few of the demands that modern workers are making and, in many cases, achieving. Table 8.1 shows how workers rank the importance of the different aspects of their jobs.

This chapter looks at job satisfaction, one of the most intriguing areas of industrial and organizational psychology. Job satisfaction specialists want to know what makes a job enjoyable to workers and what kinds of changes in the work environment make workers more satisfied. Since changes workers were demanding at the turn of the century are now taken for granted, learning about job satisfaction may provide clues as to what work will be like in the future.

Table 8.1   WHAT WORKERS VALUE

The following table indicates what percentage of workers considered different facets of jobs as very important and what percentage were satisfied with the level they currently had.

	Very Important	Completely Satisfied
Good health insurance and other benefits	81%	27%
Interesting work	78	41
Job security	78	35
Opportunity to learn new skills	68	31
Annual vacations of a week or more	66	35
Being able to work independently	64	42
Recognition from coworkers	62	24
Having a job in which you can help others	58	34
Limited job stress	58	18
Regular hours, no nights or weekends	58	40
High income	56	13
Working close to home	55	46
Work that is important to society	53	34
Chances for promotion	53	20
Contact with a lot of people	52	45

Source: Braus, P. (1992). What workers want. *American Demographics, 14,* 30–37.

Job Satisfaction and Life Satisfaction

Another reason job satisfaction is important is because it seems to be related to satisfaction with life in general. Since work is a major component of most people's lives, it stands to reason that satisfaction in one area affects satisfaction in others. To test this hypothesis, two researchers (Judge & Watanabe, 1993) evaluated the relationship between life satisfaction and job satisfaction using survey data from a group that represented the U.S. workforce in demographic and occupational characteristics. Figure 8.1 illustrates the factors group members felt were important for both job and life satisfaction.

Researchers collected data on satisfaction twice, the second time five years after the first. Results showed that life satisfaction and job satisfaction are clearly related, that each influences the other, and that both forms of satisfaction continue to be related over time. Furthermore, life satisfaction has a greater influence on job satisfaction than vice versa. In terms of the researchers' model, only race was not significantly related to life satisfaction, whereas education, wages, hours worked, and job tenure were unrelated to job satisfaction.

In a similar study, Judge and Locke (1993) looked at the relationship between "dysfunctional thought processes" and job satisfaction. Basing their

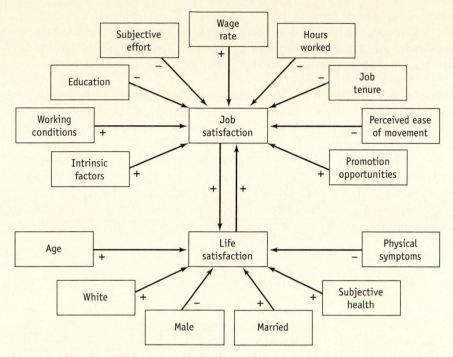

Source: Judge, T. A., & Watanabe, A. (1993). Another look at the job satisfaction-life satisfaction relationship. *Journal of Applied Psychology, 78,* 939–948.

Figure 8.1 Job and Life Satisfaction
As the figure illustrates, the researchers found that job satisfaction and life satisfaction were related to each other, with several factors affecting both forms of satisfaction. A "+" indicates a positive correlation between a factor and satisfaction; a "−" indicates a negative correlation.

hypotheses in cognitive theories of depression, the researchers asked 217 university employees to complete surveys on dysfunctional thought processes, personal estimates of well-being, and job satisfaction. Results from the study supported the idea that dysfunctional thoughts affect both life and job satisfaction:

> To the degree that people believe that they must be dependent on others for self-worth, believe that they must be perfect in terms of task mastery and not making mistakes, and overgeneralize from a single event to a grand conclusion, they decrease the chances that they will enjoy their jobs and their lives in general. . . . Those who are depressed more than average are more likely to believe that they are no good, that life is no good, and that things will never change for the better. Such a triad . . . of self-defeating conclusions virtually guarantee negative affect with respect to one's life in general and one's job in particular.

Along the same lines, a meta-analysis of studies reporting relationships between life and job satisfaction (Tait, Padgett, & Baldwin, 1989) found a strong relationship between these areas—people who were satisfied with their jobs were more likely to be satisfied with life in general, and vice versa. According to these researchers, job satisfaction and life satisfaction are so intertwined that they should not be studied separately. Another study (Johnson, Ryan, & Schmit, 1994), for example, found that attitudes toward job satisfaction were also related to customer satisfaction.

Finally, job satisfaction can also affect academic performance. In a study of satisfaction and performance in schools (Ostroff, 1992), 13,808 teachers were surveyed about their job satisfaction. The researcher also collected 24,874 surveys of student satisfaction with their teachers, as well as objective measures of academic achievement, student behavior, teacher turnover, and administrative performance. Results of the research showed that schools at which the teachers were more satisfied with their jobs had greater student satisfaction, higher academic achievement, fewer problems with student behavior, lower turnover, and higher ratings of administrative performance.

Organizational Commitment

During the 1990s, employers became increasingly concerned about employee loyalty. After an era of downsizing, many employers began to worry that their best employees were not feeling committed to their organizations and might leave. As a result, companies such as Ford, Boeing, and Xerox implemented programs to "retain, retrain, and reassure nonunion and white-collar workers" (White & Lublin, 1996). In talks with the United Auto Workers, for example, Ford agreed in 1996 to retain at least 95 percent of its current blue-collar jobs for three years.

The concern at these companies was that employees no longer felt strong levels of organizational commitment. Organizational commitment is related to job satisfaction, job involvement, and a concept known as work centrality. Although all these concepts are related, each describes something different. **Job involvement** refers to a person's psychological identification with the job (Kanungo, 1982). **Work centrality** refers to the degree of importance that work in general plays in a person's life (Paullay, Alliger, & Stone-Romero, 1994). **Organizational commitment,** on the other hand, refers to a belief in the organization's goals and values, a willingness to expend effort on behalf of the organization, and a desire to remain in the organization (Williams & Hazer, 1986).

When organizational commitment is high, employees are likely to stay at their jobs longer and possibly expend more effort than if their commitment is low (Tett & Meyer, 1993). Low organizational commitment has been related to lower job satisfaction (Mathieu, 1991; Mathieu & Zajac, 1990), turnover (Blau & Boal, 1989; Farkas & Tetrick, 1989), and absenteeism (Mathieu & Kohler, l990a). One study (Romzek, 1989) found that people who were more committed to their jobs were more satisfied with both their work and nonwork lives, whereas uncommitted people expressed less satisfaction in both areas.

Interestingly, commitment does not seem to be strongly related to performance (Hackett, Bycio, & Hausdorf, 1994; Mathieu & Zajac, 1990). That is, employees can be psychologically attached to an organization but not be particularly good workers. Some researchers (Becker, Billings, Eveleth, & Gilbert, 1996) decided to see if commitment to the organization differs from commitment to a particular supervisor. The researchers obtained completed questionnaires about work situations from 469 graduates of a large northwestern university and permission from the graduates to ask their supervisors about the graduates' performances. Results from this study showed that workers distinguish between commitment to their supervisors and commmitment to the organization, and that commitment to a supervisor was the better predictor of performance.

To be committed to the organization, employees must be "engaged," or psychologically involved with activities occurring in the organization. One researcher (Kahn, 1990) looked at the factors that drew employees of two organizations—a camp for wealthy adolescents and a prestigious architecture firm—into situations that might affect their levels of organizational commitment. Using observation and in-depth interviews, Kahn concluded that people are more likely to become engaged in organizational events when they (1) perceive tasks as being personally meaningful; (2) feel a lack of fear about negative consequences to self-image, status, or career; and (3) have the physical and emotional resources to commit to an organizational event.

Commitment is not a unitary construct, however, and some researchers (Becker, 1992; Dunham, Grube, & Castañeda, 1994; Hunt & Morgan, 1994) have argued that commitment can be to the organization as a whole or to constituent parts, much as satisfaction can be considered either global or in terms of different aspects of a job. Furthermore, employees can be committed to an organization because of emotional ties, or because they have no alternatives (Meyer, Allen, & Gellatly, 1990). Other reasons for commitment include "investments"—time, effort, friendships, titles, and so forth—an employee makes in a job, as well as a moral commitment to the organization's goals and values (Jaros, Jermier, Koehler, & Sincich, 1993).

Some research (Meyer, Allen, & Smith, 1993) suggests that commitment can be conceptualized as having three components. According to those researchers, "Employees with a strong **affective commitment** remain with the organization because they want to, those with a strong **continuance commitment** remain because they need to, and those with a strong **normative commitment** remain because they feel they ought to." In other words, some employees are committed because they have an emotional tie to the organization, some have investments in the organization that make leaving too costly, and others simply feel obligated to stay.

Apparently the perceived level of organizational commitment can affect a person's career. In one study (Shore, Barksdale, & Shore, 1995), researchers asked managers to rate their employees on affective commitment and continuance commitment at the same time that the researchers collected data on other aspects of employee performance and potential. Results from the study showed that when a manager believed an employee was high in affective commitment, the manager tended to rank that employee higher on both job performance and promotability. In contrast, when commitment was seen as a result mostly of investments in the organization, the employee was ranked lower on these dimensions. In this study, managers valued affective commitment more than continuance commitment.

In another study that compared continuance commitment with affective commitment, Shore & Wayne (1993) found that employees with high affective commitment were better "organizational citizens" than those with high continuance commitment. That is, when workers had emotional ties to an organization, they were more likely to engage in positive behaviors that were not part of the job description.

Emotional commitment to the organization is stronger when employees feel the organization cares about their well-being (Eisenberger, Fasolo, & Davis-LaMastro, 1990). When employees are worried about the future of their jobs, however, they express lower commitment, less trust in the organization, and lower job satisfaction (Ashford, Lee, & Bobko, 1989).

Can commitment lower stress during organizational turmoil? Begley and Czajka (1993) looked at the relationship between stress and commitment among the staff of a psychiatric division in a hospital that was experiencing downsizing. Workers were asked about job satisfaction, intention to quit, and stress measures such as work-related depression, work-related irritation, and somatic complaints. Interestingly, workers who were high in organizational commitment were less likely to feel stress after the downsizing.

Finally, commitment varies over time, and one researcher (Cohen, 1993) found that level of commitment was a better predictor of turnover in newer employees than in employees in later career stages. One researcher (Randall, 1987) has argued that commitment can have both positive and negative effects on individual workers and on the organization. For example, low-commitment employees may create an atmosphere of tension and conflict that, at the same time, fosters creativity. Similarly, high commitment often leads to low turnover and higher productivity, but it can also encourage conformity or even a willingness to commit illegal acts for the "good" of the company.

Measuring Job Satisfaction

Facets Versus the Global
Approach
Measures of Job
Satisfaction

For a number of reasons, defining job satisfaction is not a clear-cut process. As suggested above, satisfaction at work is a complex phenomenon involving factors such as salary, working conditions, supervision, individual motivation, and the work itself. Since job satisfaction appears to be related to satisfaction off the job, employers could conceivably have no control over the satisfaction of their workers. Additionally, there is confusion about the consequences of job satisfaction: Does satisfaction mean productivity will be higher or turnover will be lower?

Despite the fact that the vast majority of employees express satisfaction with their jobs, measuring satisfaction is not always a direct process. In addition to simply asking employees if they are satisfied, many researchers have focused on factors such as turnover and absenteeism that would seem to indicate a lack of job satisfaction. This approach regards these factors as behavioral indicators of dissatisfaction, although even this is subject to interpretation. An employee may enjoy work, for example, but on certain days he or she may enjoy staying at home more. Absence on those occasions would not seem to indicate job dissatisfaction.

Facets Versus the Global Approach

For our purposes, we can use Locke's (1976) definition of job satisfaction: "a pleasurable or positive emotional state resulting from the appraisal of one's job or job experiences." Theoretically, there are two approaches to job satisfaction. The **facet approach** focuses on factors related to the job that contribute to overall satisfaction. These include salary, supervision, relations with coworkers, the work itself, working conditions, and promotional opportunities. This approach holds that workers may feel different levels of satisfaction toward the various facets, but the aggregate of these feelings constitutes job satisfaction.

An alternative to the facet approach is global job satisfaction. Rather than asking a worker about facets of the job, the **global approach** simply asks if the worker is satisfied overall. The global approach suggests that satisfaction is more than the sum of its parts, and that workers can express dissatisfaction with facets of the job and still be satisfied generally.

A recurring question for researchers is which approach—global or facet—more accurately measures job satisfaction. Although it would seem logical that overall job satisfaction would result from levels of satisfaction with job facets, some researchers have suggested that a global approach might be more useful. In a study of employees in a scientific engineering firm, for example, Scarpello and Campbell (1983) found that a simple 1 to 5 rating of how satisfied workers were with the job in general predicted turnover better than the sum of facet scores.

Nevertheless, most research takes a facet approach to job satisfaction. Rice, McFarlin, and Bennett (1989), for example, used a discrepancy approach that looked at the contrast between real and ideal working conditions to measure job satisfaction on a number of facets. Workers were asked how much they *have* of facets (e.g., hourly pay, health insurance, and contact with the supervisor) versus how much they *want*. This approach to measuring satisfaction with facets yielded more information about overall satisfaction than simply asking workers if they were satisfied with a particular facet of a job.

Another recurring question for researchers is the relationship between job satisfaction and productivity. During the human relations movement of the 1950s (discussed in Chapter 11), the belief that satisfied workers would perform better was widespread. But after hundreds of studies of job satisfaction, it appears that the relationship between satisfaction and productivity is not as straightforward as once assumed. For example, dissatisfied employees can be highly productive, just as satisfied employees can be highly unproductive.

Some researchers have focused on the question of job satisfaction among women and minorities. Since these two groups have traditionally held jobs with lower levels of responsibility and compensation, perhaps their satisfaction is lower. In fact, the evidence on this point is unclear. Although White employees report greater satisfaction than minorities, the difference in reported satisfaction is not significant. Even though greater dissatisfaction among women and minorities seems plausible, evidence is not yet supportive of this position.

Finally, Kacmar and Ferris (1989) considered the relationship between age and job satisfaction on a number of facets. That study is particularly interesting becuse older workers tend to have higher-status jobs or have been in the organization longer, and both status and tenure affect satisfaction. Even after controlling for these two variables, however, these researchers found that age did seem to affect job satisfaction. Specifically, satisfaction on several facets tends to dip between the ages of 20 and 30, and 30 and 40, but to increase after 40. Some of the results of this study are presented in Figure 8.2.

Measures of Job Satisfaction

As mentioned above, there are two ways to measure job satisfaction. Indirect methods consider "withdrawal" behaviors—turnover, absenteeism, and tardiness—as evidence of a lack of job satisfaction. Absenteeism and turnover are discussed more fully below. Direct measures of job satisfaction, on the other hand, include the Job Descriptive Index (Smith, Kendall, & Hulin, 1969), the Kunin (1955) faces scale, and the Minnesota Satisfaction Questionnaire (Weiss, Dawis, England, & Lofquist, 1967).

The Job Descriptive Index (JDI) measures satisfaction in five categories: the work itself, supervision, pay, promotions, and coworkers. Each category has a series of adjectives that respondents are asked to mark as "Yes," "No," or "?" depending on how they relate to the job in question. Scores within the categories can be summed to give some indication of facet satisfaction, or all five scores can be summed as a measure of global satisfaction. The JDI is the most popular direct method of measuring job satisfaction. Figure 8.3 (p. 244) illustrates examples from the JDI.

The Kunin faces scale is a one-item global measure of job satisfaction. Respondents are presented with a series of faces showing expressions ranging from smiling to frowning and are asked to indicate the face that best expresses their feelings about their job. Because the scale uses virtually no words, it is particularly useful in measuring job satisfaction among illiterate and non-English-speaking employees. Dunham and Herman (1975) developed a version that uses female faces. Figure 8.4 (p. 245) illustrates the faces scale.

The Minnesota Satisfaction Questionnaire (MSQ) asks questions about worker satisfaction and dissatisfaction regarding facets such as the competence of the supervisor, doing things that do not violate a worker's personal princi-

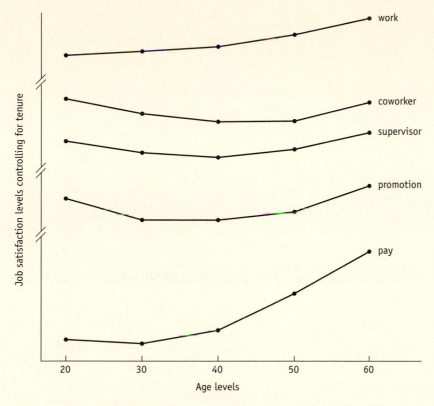

Source: Kacmar, K. M., & Ferris, G. R. (1989). Theoretical and methodological considerations in the age-job satisfaction relationship. *Journal of Applied Psychology, 74* (2), 205. Copyright© 1989 by the American Psychological Association. Adapted by permission.

Figure 8.2 Job Satisfaction over the Life Span
As you can see from the graph, satisfaction with most facets of a job declines between ages 20 and 30. Between ages 30 and 40, satisfaction with supervisors and promotion opportunities stays at roughly the same level, satisfaction with coworkers declines, and satisfaction with the work and salary increases. After age 50, satisfaction with all facets—and pay in particular—increases.

ples, and the chance to be "somebody" in the community. The scale can be scored in total or it can be scored in subsets that indicate extrinsic and intrinsic satisfaction. Normative data for occupations have been collected so that employers can compare levels of satisfaction and dissatisfaction for their employees with similar groups. Figure 8.5 (p. 246) illustrates the short form of the MSQ.

Finally, some researchers (Villanova, Bernardin, Johnson, & Dahmus, 1994) have looked at job satisfaction in terms of organizational fit. As you may recall from Chapter 3, fit refers to the relationship between job duties and individual characteristics. The Job Compatibility Questionnaire (Bernardin, 1989) measures how workers feel about specific aspects of a job. In a test of worker preferences and turnover among people working as concessionists, box office

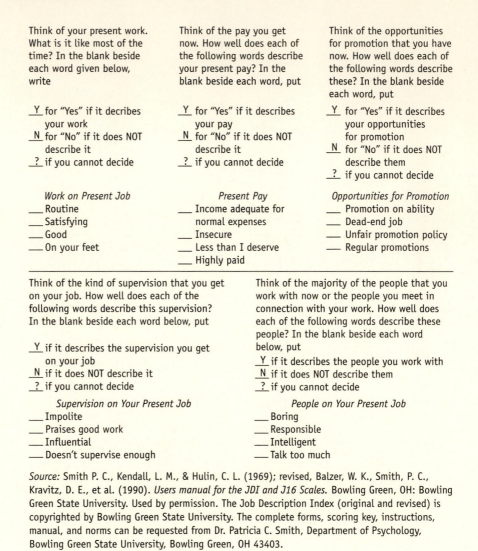

Think of your present work. What is it like most of the time? In the blank beside each word given below, write

_Y_ for "Yes" if it decribes your work
_N_ for "No" if it does NOT describe it
_?_ if you cannot decide

Work on Present Job
___ Routine
___ Satisfying
___ Good
___ On your feet

Think of the pay you get now. How well does each of the following words describe your present pay? In the blank beside each word, put

_Y_ for "Yes" if it describes your pay
_N_ for "No" if it does NOT describe it
_?_ if you cannot decide

Present Pay
___ Income adequate for normal expenses
___ Insecure
___ Less than I deserve
___ Highly paid

Think of the opportunities for promotion that you have now. How well does each of the following words describe these? In the blank beside each word, put

_Y_ for "Yes" if it describes your opportunities for promotion
_N_ for "No" if it does NOT describe them
_?_ if you cannot decide

Opportunities for Promotion
___ Promotion on ability
___ Dead-end job
___ Unfair promotion policy
___ Regular promotions

Think of the kind of supervision that you get on your job. How well does each of the following words describe this supervision? In the blank beside each word below, put

_Y_ if it describes the supervision you get on your job
_N_ if it does NOT describe it
_?_ if you cannot decide

Supervision on Your Present Job
___ Impolite
___ Praises good work
___ Influential
___ Doesn't supervise enough

Think of the majority of the people that you work with now or the people you meet in connection with your work. How well does each of the following words describe these people? In the blank beside each word below, put

_Y_ if it describes the people you work with
_N_ if it does NOT describe them
_?_ if you cannot decide

People on Your Present Job
___ Boring
___ Responsible
___ Intelligent
___ Talk too much

Source: Smith P. C., Kendall, L. M., & Hulin, C. L. (1969); revised, Balzer, W. K., Smith, P. C., Kravitz, D. E., et al. (1990). *Users manual for the JDI and J16 Scales.* Bowling Green, OH: Bowling Green State University. Used by permission. The Job Description Index (original and revised) is copyrighted by Bowling Green State University. The complete forms, scoring key, instructions, manual, and norms can be requested from Dr. Patricia C. Smith, Department of Psychology, Bowling Green State University, Bowling Green, OH 43403.

Figure 8.3 Sample Items from the Job Descriptive Index

employees, and ushers in movie theaters, researchers (Villanova et al., 1994) found that low compatibility between preferences and job characteristics predicted turnover. That is, workers who expressed dislike for typical theater employee duties such as cleaning bathrooms several times a day and interacting with senior citizens frequently were more likely to quit or be fired.

The job compatibility approach offers an interesting alternative to traditional measures of both job satisfaction and selection. Instead of focusing on the match between a worker's knowledge, skills, and abilities and the requirements of a job, this approach matches worker preferences with job requirements. Although job compatibility is not yet well researched, it offers a promising approach to furthering our understanding of the concept of fit.

Expectancy and Equity Approaches

Both the expectancy and the equity approaches to job satisfaction are based in motivational theory. Expectancy theory holds that satisfaction is the result of what workers expect for their efforts compared to what they actually receive. Equity theory, on the other hand, argues that satisfaction results from perceptions of fairness about inputs and outcomes.

Value discrepancy theory (Locke, 1976) emphasizes the importance of a worker's values rather than needs in determining job satisfaction. In contrast with needs, values are acquired over time, and workers make judgments about their jobs in terms of how much they value different aspects. They then compare how much they have of that aspect to how much they want. The difference between what they have and what they want influences their job satisfaction.

For example, a worker may want opportunities for promotion, but the company may not have many promotional opportunities available. In that case, satisfaction will depend on how much the worker values promotions. If the value is strong, job satisfaction will be low. If, on the other hand, the worker would like a promotion but doesn't feel strongly about the matter, job satisfaction will be impacted less negatively.

Similarly, **facet satisfaction theory** (Lawler, 1973) emphasizes the application of equity theory to determining job satisfaction. In this model, workers make judgments about their satisfaction with different facets of a job compared to what they think they should have based on their input. To a large degree, what workers feel they deserve will be influenced by the amount of effort they see others putting forth and the rewards they receive.

According to the theory, satisfaction occurs when workers get what they believe they should get. Interestingly, in keeping with equity theory, the model holds that workers who receive more than they feel they should are likely to feel guilty.

Although there are attractive aspects of both of these theories, overall empirical support has not been strong for either one. Not surprisingly, both suffer from the same shortcomings as the expectancy and equity theories mentioned in the last chapter.

Social Information Processing

The **social information processing** approach to job satisfaction holds that satisfaction or dissatisfaction results from comparing oneself with other workers. This position, argued by Salancik and Pfeffer (1977, 1978), suggests that facets of a job are not as important as perceptions about how a worker is doing compared with other workers. For example, a worker who takes a new job cannot accurately gauge his or her satisfaction without observing similar individuals who are satisfied or dissatisfied.

Proponents of the social information processing approach argue that job characteristics are not inherently pleasing or displeasing. Rather, pleasing or displeasing are attributions that are socially constructed. Only through a process of comparisons with others can an individual worker know how he or she is doing.

Social information processing provides an interesting contrast with the need fulfillment theories of both job satisfaction and motivation. Rather than coming from within, worker attitudes and behavior are socially derived. Social information processing emphasizes the importance of the social environment in shaping individual behavior, a topic that perhaps has not been as widely explored as it ought to be in industrial and organizational psychology.

Genetic Theory

The **genetic theory** of job satisfaction considers dispositional factors to be the major determinant of satisfaction. Work in this area is based on the observation that some people appear to be satisfied or dissatisfied with their jobs regardless of their situations. For example, people who score high on measures of **negative affectivity**—a term referring to anxiety, irritability, and neuroticism—usually have less favorable attitudes toward their jobs (Levin & Stokes, 1989). Because personality factors such as intelligence, information processing styles, and interests have been shown to be genetically based, some researchers proposed that satisfaction with work might be related to genetics as well.

One group of researchers (Arvey, Bouchard, Segal, & Abraham, 1989) asked 34 identical twins who had been separated at about six months of age to complete the Minnesota Satisfaction Questionnaire. Because the twins had been separated so early, researchers were confident that environmental influences would have had little effect on any similarities in their attitudes toward job satisfaction. Results from the study showed a significant correlation between the twins' attitudes toward their jobs. Further analysis revealed that the separated twin pairs had also chosen jobs that were similar in terms of complexity, motor skill requirements, and physical demands.

The researchers concluded that organizations may have less control over job satisfaction than previously believed. In addition, satisfaction with past jobs may predict satisfaction with future jobs. Although environmental factors still affected satisfaction, a significant part of satisfaction could be traced to the worker's genetic background.

In a discussion of this study, two other researchers raised a number of concerns (Cropanzano & James, 1990). In particular, they were concerned about influences in the environments into which the twins had been adopted as well as factors such as attractiveness and interaction upon reunification that may have influenced the twins' reported attitudes toward their jobs. These researchers concluded that insufficient evidence exists to support the genetic theory of job satisfaction—a conclusion the original researchers rejected (Bouchard, Arvey, Keller, & Segal, 1992).

In another study that looked at the genetic component of work values (Keller, Bouchard, Arvey, Segal, & Dawis, 1992), researchers compared the attitudes of identical and fraternal twins who were reared apart. Pairs of identical twins held similar attitudes toward five work values: achievement, comfort, status, safety, and autonomy. The fraternal twins, on the other hand, had similar attitudes only on achievement. The researchers concluded that genetic factors also play a part in what people value in work.

The genetic approach to job satisfaction offers an interesting alternative to other environmental or cognitive explanations. Although too new to be strongly supported by research findings, initial studies suggest that genetics do play a part in attitudes toward work. Researchers in this area are quick to point out, however, that genetics are only part of job satisfaction, and that environmental factors cannot be ignored.

Measuring Dissatisfaction

Absenteeism
Turnover
Tardiness
Deviant Behavior

For many years researchers have used turnover, absenteeism, and tardiness rates as indirect measures of job satisfaction. Although more recent research suggests that the relationship between satisfaction and these withdrawal behaviors is not as clear as once assumed, they are still widely studied. In other words, despite the intuitive appeal of the idea that satisfied workers are less likely to be absent or tardy or to quit, numerous studies have failed to demonstrate a strong relationship between these factors and job satisfaction. Some research on withdrawal behaviors is discussed below.

Absenteeism

Every day, about one million American employees are absent from their jobs (Dalton & Enz, 1988). Whether voluntary or involuntary, absenteeism costs employers $40 billion per year. In addition to its costs, absenteeism can be dangerous. For example, coal miners who filled in for absent workers and who were less familiar with procedures, environments, and coworkers had more accidents than miners who were not absent (Goodman & Garber, 1988). Not surprisingly, both researchers and employers have spent considerable effort learning about and attempting to deal with this problem, and hundreds of studies have considered the effects of absenteeism on performance.

Although absenteeism is a problem found in almost any workplace, there are several issues that make studying absenteeism somewhat tricky. For example, absenteeism can be measured in terms of *frequency* and *duration*. Is frequent absence more harmful to productivity than infrequent absence that is longer in duration?

Another problem is the way absence is reported. In many studies of absence, researchers have relied on archival records. Since archival records are kept for organizational purposes and not for research, there is usually no way of determining their accuracy. In other cases, researchers have relied on self-reports of absenteeism, which are sometimes inaccurate. For example, one study (Johns, 1994b) found that employees of a large utility company underestimated their own absence rates, and that managers of the same company estimated that their work groups had absence rates lower than the company average. In another study that looked at accuracy in reporting absenteeism, two researchers (Harrison & Shaffer, 1994) found that employees estimated their own absences to be significantly lower than company norms, and they estimated that company norms for absence were higher than they actually were. Workers also tended to overestimate the absences of their peers.

Despite these considerations, researchers have collected a substantial body of knowledge about absenteeism. For example, Rhodes and Steers (1978, 1990) formulated a popular model of absenteeism. According to this model, illustrated in Figure 8.6, attendance is the combination of attendance motivation and ability to attend. **Attendance motivation** is the product of job satisfaction plus pressures to attend (e.g., economic conditions, incentives, and personal standards). **Ability to attend** relates to factors such as health and transportation. In an evaluation of the Steers and Rhodes model, Brooke (1986) suggested that three other areas that affect attendance are levels of job involvement, perceptions of fairness about the pay system, and the worker's involvement with alcohol.

When employees do not have the *ability* to attend, there is little an employer can do. When an employee is *unmotivated* to attend, on the other hand, managerial intervention may lower absence rates. In a study of avoidable absence among public utility employees, for example, Dalton and Mesch (1991) found that 60 percent of all absences were avoidable (i.e., were not due to illness or a transportation problem) and that 25 percent of the employees accounted for almost all of the absences during one year.

In addition to monitoring absence policies, teaching self-management may be an effective approach to increasing attendance. Latham and Frayne (1989) followed the attendance records of state government employees who had been trained to set goals for attendance, develop a schedule of reinforcement, monitor their own attendance behavior, and brainstorm about problems and solutions for avoiding job absence. In comparison with a control group that had not experienced the training, the experimental group was absent significantly less frequently in the months following the self-management training.

Another model of absenteeism (Baba & Harris, 1989) suggests that absence is a function of (1) individual differences, including age, tenure, number of children, and mental health; (2) work-group factors, including the rate of absenteeism in the group and the individual's rate compared to other work-group members; and (3) situational factors, such as the worker's attitude toward absence, the consequences of being absent, and job involvement. In a test

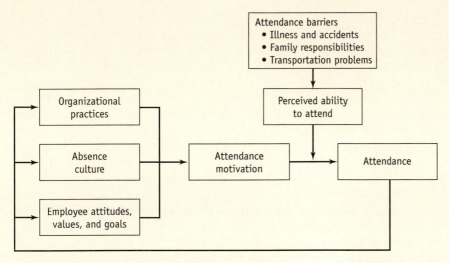

Figure 8.6 A Diagnostic Model of Employee Attendance
In this model, organizational practices such as absence policies and management expectations affect an employee's perceived ability to attend. Ability to attend is also affected by attendance barriers that are largely outside the control of the employee. Organizational practices interact with the absence culture—the shared understanding about absence acceptability—and the personal values and goals of the employee to affect attendance motivation. Attendance motivation and the perceived ability to attend together affect actual attendance.

of this model based on the absence records of administrative employees of an aerospace company, Baba (1990) found comparative absence, job involvement, and age related to both frequency of absence and time lost. Interestingly, number of children was negatively related to both frequency and time lost. That is, workers with fewer children were more likely to be absent than were those with more children.

Two researchers (Steel & Rentsch, 1995) looked at absenteeism and its relationship to job satisfaction, job involvement, demographic variables, and stress in 419 federal employees. This study was unusual because of the length of the period covered—almost six years. Results showed absenteeism can be successfully predicted over the long term. Gender and education were particularly useful in predicting absenteeism, with women and the less educated having more absences. Job satisfaction and job involvement scores were also negatively related to absenteeism, but stress was not related.

One study (George, 1989) looked at the relationship between mood and absence. Among department store employees, workers who scored high on **positive affectivity**—defined as having more positive mood states and an overall sense of well-being (Tellegen, 1982)—were absent less frequently. This study also confirmed the relationship between job tenure and absence, with newer employees more likely to be absent than those with longer tenure. In another study that looked at employee perceptions of how much an organization cares about employee well-being (Eisenberger, Fasolo, & Davis-LaMastro, 1990), researchers found absence to be lower when employees felt support from their employers.

Another way of looking at absenteeism is in terms of an "absence culture" (Nicholson & Johns, 1985), in which different groups within an organization develop their own norms regarding acceptable absence levels. For example, in a study of transit employees (Mathieu & Kohler, 1990a), researchers found that different groups of employees had different rates of absence. From these results, researchers concluded that managers might deal with absenteeism more effectively by addressing the problem at a group rather than an individual level. Possible interventions might include absence feedback delivered to groups, group goal setting regarding absence, and incentives based on attendance of the group as a whole.

In another study of absence culture (Markham & McKee, 1995), researchers looked at attendance among employees of five sewing factories in which perfect attendance was the official company goal. Analysis of the data suggested that although the company had one absence policy, individual supervisors had their own standards regarding absenteeism. In addition, various workgroups had their own ideas about the level of absence that was acceptable. The researchers concluded that, irrespective of individual variables, worker absenteeism is affected by standards set by supervisors and their coworkers. In a related study of bank tellers and hospital employees, Blau (1995) found that organizational culture affected the occurrence of tardiness—another withdrawal behavior often linked with absenteeism.

Apparently working conditions can also affect attendance. Some researchers (Melamed, Ben-Avi, Luz, & Green, 1995) looked at the effects of work monotony on job satisfaction and absenteeism in hospital workers. In this study, monotonous tasks required vigilance and attention but offered little stimulation. Not surprisingly, workers who performed the most monotonous tasks had the lowest levels of job satisfaction and experienced higher levels of psychological distress.

In terms of absence, however, monotony had little impact on men, but women who had monotonous jobs were absent significantly more often than women who did not have monotonous jobs. The researchers concluded that redesigning jobs to make them less monotonous can affect satisfaction and absenteeism.

Another interesting finding regarding absence and organizational culture is that economic conditions affect absence rates. Markham and McKee (1991) analyzed absence data for a large textile manufacturer that was experiencing downsizing. The researchers found that as the size of the workforce shrank, employees were absent less frequently. In addition, workers were less likely to be absent when unemployment rates were high.

Several studies have suggested that because of child care demands, female employees are more likely than male employees to be absent. In an interesting study of absence rates, however, one group of researchers found that absence rates of women were significantly higher than those of men only during the winter, and were similar throughout the other seasons (Markham, Dansereau, & Alutto, 1982). These authors suggested that children are more likely to be ill during the winter, and consequently mothers are more likely to stay home during that time.

Another consideration with regard to the higher absence rates of women is the kinds of jobs they occupy. Many women hold jobs that are lower in the occupational hierarchy and pay less than those held by men. Consequently, absence in those positions may be seen as less serious than when it occurs among higher-level employees, and the employees may feel less compelled to come to work.

Does absenteeism indicate a lack of job satisfaction? Three meta-analyses of the job satisfaction, absenteeism, and turnover literature (Hackett & Guion, 1985; Mitra, Jenkins, & Gupta, 1992; Scott & Taylor, 1985) found that these two variables are related. In other words, people who are less satisfied with their work do seem to be absent more frequently. In addition, people who are absent more frequently have higher turnover rates.

As you can see from the studies cited above, the relationship between absence and turnover is not completely straightforward. Nonetheless, we know that absence is affected by both ability and motivation to attend, that women and employees with lower educational levels are absent more frequently, and that people with higher job satisfaction are absent less frequently. Absence also seems to be affected by norms set by workgroups, as well as by economic conditions and the work environment.

One final point: In most studies, absenteeism is considered a reaction to aversive work conditions, but one researcher (Youngblood, 1984) has raised the interesting idea that workers may like their jobs but, on certain occasions, find nonwork activities more appealing. (This is undoubtedly the case with students who fail to attend classes as the weather gets warmer.) In these cases, absence is probably not related to dissatisfaction.

Turnover

Turnover is a serious problem for employers because of the related expenses. Most employers know there are costs associated with turnover, but they are usually unaware just how high those costs can be. For example, the turnover rate among salespeople is typically 27 percent annually, with the cost of replacing a salesperson who leaves after six months approaching $100,000 (Bertrand, 1989).

Because of the high turnover costs, industrial and organizational psychologists have spent more than 30 years trying to understand why people leave their jobs. Although the study of turnover would seem to be straightforward, we still are not very skilled at predicting who is likely to quit. For this reason, researchers have developed a number of approaches to try to explain turnover.

One meta-analysis (Williams & Livingstone, 1994) reviewed 55 studies that had considered the relationship between measures of performance and turnover. The meta-analysis revealed that performance was most strongly related to turnover when rewards were contingent. That is, when good performance resulted in rewards not received by others, good employees were more likely to stay and poor employees to leave. In addition, this study found that poor performers were more likely to leave regardless of economic conditions and the availability of other jobs. These results support the idea that poor performers are more likely than good performers to quit.

In a laboratory study of job satisfaction and performance, Olson-Buchanan (1996) also found that when people filed a grievance against a supervisor or working conditions, performance was likely to decline and turnover became more likely.

Some researchers (Barrick, Mount, & Strauss, 1994) have looked at the qualities of individuals who leave their jobs because of downsizing or reductions in force. Although most people assume that involuntary turnover is the result of a poor match between worker characteristics and job requirements, Barrick and his associates hypothesized that personality factors might play a role in involuntary turnover. In a group of 227 appliance salespersons, poor supervisory ratings and low sales volume were found to be the factors most related to involuntary turnover.

However, the personality characteristics of conscientiousness and general mental ability (GMA) were also positively related to supervisory ratings and sales volume. The researchers concluded that level of conscientiousness and GMA are possible predictors of who is going to be fired. In a related study (Barrick & Mount, 1996), levels of conscientiousness and emotional stability were negatively related to turnover among truck drivers.

In another interesting study of involuntary turnover, researchers (Spera, Buhrfeind, & Pennebaker, 1994) asked professional workers who had been terminated to write about the experience of being fired. Compared with a control group that did not write about being fired, the experimental group found new jobs signficantly more quickly. Interestingly, the experimental and control groups did not differ in amount of job-seeking activity, but the researchers proposed that those who wrote about the experience of job loss used the expressive writing to move beyond their negative feelings and search for work more effectively.

In recent years researchers have looked at turnover from both its "push" and "pull" aspects. Push theories focus on individual peceptions and attitudes about jobs that affect the likelihood to quit. Pull theories, on the other hand, consider qualities of the marketplace, such as the supply and demand of labor, and their impact on turnover (Lee & Mitchell, 1994). In general, I/O psychologists have focused more on push theories that consider turnover form the perspective of the individual worker.

For example, one "push" model of turnover describes the process as follows:

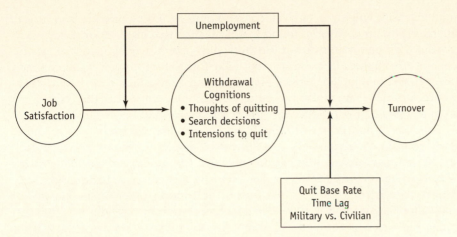

Source: Hom, P. W., Caranikas-Walker, F., Prussia, G. E., & Griffeth, R. W. (1992). A meta-analytical structural equations analysis of a model of employee turnover. *Journal of Applied Psychology, 77,* 890–909. Copyright © 1992 by the American Psychological Association. Adapted by permission.

Figure 8.7 Factors That Affect the Turnover Process
In this model, job satisfaction affects a worker's thoughts of quitting, decisions about a job search, and intentions to quit. However, these thoughts are also affected by the general availability of employment. Other factors that affect turnover are the general rate of turnover within the occupation (quit base rate), the duration of time between quit decisions and quitting (time lag), and whether one were in the military (military quit decisions were less affected by unemployment rates and more likely to be acted on).

1. An evaluation of the current job and assessment of current levels of dissatisfaction;
2. An evaluation of the attractiveness and attainability of other jobs;
3. Some expression of the intention to leave; and
4. Turnover (Youngblood, Mobley, & Meglino, 1983).

Figure 8.7 presents a similar model of the turnover process (Hom, Caranikas-Walker, Prussia, & Griffeth, 1992).

Other research (Gerhart, 1990b; Steel, 1996), however, suggests the linkage between turnover and labor market conditions is not yet fully understood. For example, some researchers (Hulin, Roznowski, & Hachiya, 1985) have argued that economic conditions ("pull" factors) are more relevant for marginal and temporary employees, whereas job satisfaction (a "push" factor) is more relevant for professional workers. Other studies (Carsten & Spector, 1987; Gerhart, 1987; Youngblood, Baysinger, & Mobley, 1985) have found that employees are more likely to quit their jobs when the unemployment rate is low. This suggests that people become less satisfied with their jobs in periods of high employment.

Huselid (1995) looked at the relationship between what he called *high performance work practices* and turnover, productivity, and corporate financial performance. High performance practices include a comprehensive recruitment and selection system, compensation based on incentives, performance management, extensive employee involvement, and training. Using financial and survey data from 986 firms, Huselid found that firms that used high performance practices did have significantly lower turnover, higher productivity, and stronger financial performance. In a similar study that focused on human resource practices in steel minimills, Arthur (1994) found companies that had human resource policies that emphasized employee commitment rather than managerial control had higher productivity, lower scrap rates, and lower turnover.

Krackhardt and Porter (1985a) hypothesized that turnover may be more related to group behavior—that is, a "turnover culture"—than to individual factors. Since most work settings require individuals to function as part of a group, the researchers predicted that turnover occurs in clusters among employees who perceive themselves as similar. In a study of fast-food workers in a company in which annual turnover was 200 percent, they found turnover did not occur randomly, but was concentrated in groups. Apparently the stability of those who remained behind was threatened by those who left. In a similar study (Krackhardt & Porter, 1985b), the researchers found that workers who decided to stay tended to have more positive attitudes toward their work after their friends left.

Finally, Hambrick and Cannella (1993) looked at the reasons why executives departed after their employers were acquired by another company. Although executive departure is often attributed to strategic and economic (pull) factors, these researchers looked at the social psychology of the workplace after a merger or acquisition. According to their study, executives are likely to leave when the merger results in lowered status at work:

> . . . some acquisitions result in very low relative standing for acquired executives—they feel inferior, the acquirers see them as inferior and themselves as superior, autonomy is removed, status is removed, and a climate of acrimony prevails. When these conditions exist, the rate of departure of acquired executives will be great.

Another factor that affects turnover is supervision. In a study of turnover among retail employees, for example, George and Bettenhausen (1990) found a relationship between the positive mood of the leader and turnover. Store managers who described themselves as more "active, strong, excited, enthusiastic, peppy, and elated" had lower turnover rates among their employees than managers who scored lower on these dimensions.

Individual Characteristics and Turnover A few studies have looked at the relationship between individual characteristics and turnover. In a meta-analysis of turnover research, Cotton and Tuttle (1986) found turnover was less common among employees who had more children and more common among women and better-educated employees.

Another study (Judge, 1993) looked at the relationship between having either a positive or a negative attitude toward life and turnover. Working with a group of nurses, lab technicians, and other medical personnel, the researcher found that among people who disliked their jobs, those with the most positive attitudes about life were most likely to quit. On the other hand, people with

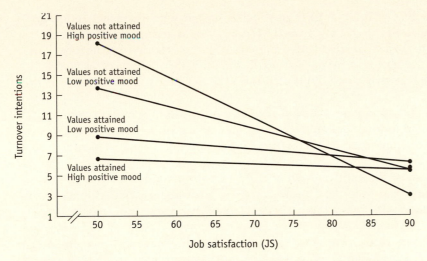

Source: George, J. M., and Jones, G. R. The experience of work and turnover intentions: Inter-active effects of value attainment, job satisfaction, and positive mood. *Journal of Applied Psychology,* 81, 318–325. Copyright © 1996 by the American Psychological Association. Reprinted by permission.

Figure 8.8 Mood and Absence
As you can see from the graph, people who attained their values and had either a high or low positive mood were less likely to turnover, regardless of their job satisfaction. When values were not attained, turnover intentions were higher for workers with both low posi-tive and high positive moods when job satisfaction was lower.

negative attitudes were much less likely to leave, even when they were dissatis-fied with their jobs. The study concluded that the likelihood of turnover might be predicted by a person's attitude toward life in general.

In a related study (George & Jones, 1996), 336 professional employees in the printing industry were asked about their values, mood, job satisfaction, and intention to quit. The reseachers hypothesized that people are least likely to quit when their jobs help them fulfill their values and they have a positive mood—that is, positive affectivity—about their work. Conversely, they are most likely to quit when their jobs do not help them fulfill their values and the mood at work is negative.

Results from the study confirmed the researchers' expectations. However, fulfillment of values proved to be a stronger predictor of job satisfaction and turnover than positive mood. This suggests that people will continue to work in jobs that do not cause them to have a positive mood if they believe these jobs are helping them reach their goals. Figure 8.8 illustrates the study results.

Some researchers have suggested that having the intention to quit is the best predictor of turnover. For example, one study (Dickter, Roznowski, & Harrison, 1996) found that employees who were highly satisfied with their jobs initially were less likely to quit over a longer period. Along the same lines, Steel and Ovalle (1984) found that having the intention of leaving pre-dicted turnover better than expressed feelings toward a job. In another study

(Doran, Stone, Brief, & George, 1991), workers who expressed an intention to quit at the time they started working at a department store were later found to be less satisfied with a number of facets related to their jobs. These studies suggest that asking job applicants directly about how long they intend to stay may provide information that can be used to reduce turnover cost.

The idea of asking candidates about their turnover intentions highlights a problem in turnover research, however. In a review of the turnover decisions of university employees, Campion (1991) looked at individual employment files, then asked supervisors and coworkers why specific individuals had quit. Although most turnover research is based on information in personnel records, apparently reasons for leaving are not always provided to the personnel department. Campion found the real reason for leaving was reported in the employee's personnel file only 25 percent of the time.

Another study of turnover among employed managers (Bretz, Boudreau, & Judge, 1994) found that people were most likely to leave when they were interested in having more time with their families and had higher levels of ambition. The researchers noted, however, that a considerable amount of job search behavior does not lead to turnover. That is, people may be looking for jobs, but that is no guarantee they will quit.

In recent years some researchers have suggested that our understanding of turnover would be enhanced by a greater emphasis on the cognitive factors involved in a withdrawal decision. For example, Lee and Mitchell (1994; Lee, Mitchell, Wise, & Fireman, 1996) proposed an "unfolding" model of turnover. In the unfolding model, the process of turnover begins with a "shock to the system"—an event that causes a person to evaluate his or her present job. The shock to the system can be positive or negative and can involve factors either inside or outside work.

The shock can cause an employee to quit without much deliberation, or it may begin a complex cognitive process. For some employees, the decision is whether to stay or leave their present place of work; for others, the decision is focused on the attractiveness of other companies as well. The major factor affecting either type of decision is compatibility or fit.

Finally, although researchers have argued that younger employees who are less psychologically committed to the organization are more likely to quit, this assumption has recently been challenged. In a meta-analysis that considered age and turnover (Healy, Lehman, & McDaniel, 1995), researchers concluded that age actually had little impact on turnover.

In summary, the evidence suggests that (1) turnover can be considered from either a push or a pull perspective; (2) factors in the work environment such as employment policies and group relations affect turnover; (3) women, the better educated, and people with positive attitudes are more likely to quit; and (4) age may not be related to turnover. With an understanding of these findings, personnel recruiters may be able to make inferences about who will be more likely to stay on the job.

Table 8.2   A TAXONOMY OF TARDINESS

Category	Characteristics	Antecedents of Tardiness
1. Increasing chronic	Nonrandom; frequency increases over time; length of absence increases over time	Low job satisfaction; low job involvement; low organizational commitment
2. Stable periodic	Nonrandom; both frequency and length of absence are stable over time	Leisure-income tradeoff; Work-family conflict
3. Unavoidable	Random	Transportation; Weather; Illness

Source: Blau, G. (1994). Developing and testing a taxonomy of lateness behavior. *Journal of Applied Psychology, 79,* 959–970. Copyright © 1994 by the American Psychological Association. Adapted by permission.

Tardiness

Tardiness is another form of withdrawal behavior related to job satisfaction. Although a source of significant organizational problems in terms of lost productivity, tardiness has not been widely studied by I/O psychologists. Recognizing this shortcoming in research relating to job satisfaction, Blau (1994) developed a taxonomy of tardiness (Table 8.2).

According to Blau, tardiness can be categorized as *increasing chronic,* in which an employee increases the frequency and duration of his or her tardiness because of a lack of job satisfaction; *stable periodic,* which refers to situations in which an employee doesn't necessarily dislike work but has other demands on his or her time; and *unavoidable,* which relates to ability to attend. Using attitude surveys and records of tardiness behaviors of 483 hospital employees and 619 bank employees, Blau found support for his model. Blau concluded that employers can deal more effectively with employee tardiness if they understand its causes. In addition, a recent study (Koslowsky, Sagie, Krausz, & Singer, 1997) found tardiness related to both absence and turnover, but more strongly to absence.

Deviant Behavior

Finally, dissatisfaction can take the form of deviant behavior—behavior that threatens the well-being of the organization. Deviant behavior is more serious than absenteeism and turnover because it can involve theft, embezzlement, sabotage, and vandalism (Harper, 1990). Interestingly, these kinds of behavior have been studied far less than withdrawal behaviors.

Two researchers (Robinson & Bennett, 1995) used a multidimensional scaling technique to develop a classification system for deviant behavior. They asked 70 individuals to describe incidents of deviant behavior they knew about,

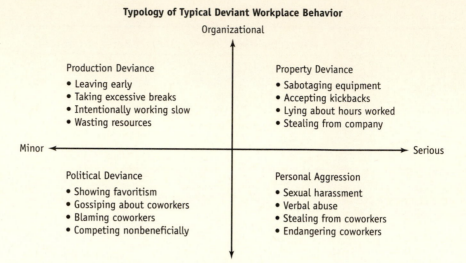

Typology of Typical Deviant Workplace Behavior

Source: Robinson, S. L., & Bennett, R. J. (1995). A typology of deviant workplace behaviors: A multidimensional scaling study. *Academy of Management Journal, 38,* 555–572. Copyright © 1995. Reprinted by permission of the Academy of Management.

Figure 8.9 Deviant Workplace Behavior

then analyzed these behaviors statistically. Results indicated that deviant workplace behavior could be classified along two dimensions: the seriousness of the act and whether it was directed against the organization or against other people. Figure 8.9 provides some examples of deviant workplace behavior placed within the researchers' dimensions.

Although this study did not consider the reasons behind worker deviance, it is easy to see how such behaviors are linked to both job satisfaction and motivation. When workers feel they are not being adequately rewarded for their efforts, for example, they may leave early, sabotage equipment, or steal. When they feel a supervisor is not treating workers equitably, they may undermine the work of others or harass coworkers. Interestingly, these behaviors clearly reflect dissatisfaction with some element of work, but they don't suggest that withdrawal is imminent.

Increasing Job Satisfaction

Compensation
Job Enlargement and
   Enrichment
Benefits

Although the relationship between productivity and job satisfaction is not straightforward, evidence suggests that dissatisfied employees are more likely than those who are satisfied to leave. As discussed in Chapter 3, turnover can be very expensive for an employer. Because of this, many employers have attempted to raise levels of job satisfaction in order to increase the tenures of their employees. For example, some researchers (Rodgers, Hunter, & Rogers, 1993) looked at the relationship between institution of a management by objectives (MBO) program and job satisfaction. MBO had a significant effect on job satisfaction only when managers demonstrated their commitment to the intervention. When the managers were indifferent or lackadaisical about MBO, job satisfaction did not increase. The researchers concluded from the study findings that management commitment to programs designed to raise job satisfaction is important to the program's success.

In terms of raising job satisfaction, more traditional approaches address compensation, job redesign, and benefits.

Compensation

No discussion of job satisfaction is complete without looking at the role of compensation. Although salary is an essential part of any job, its relationship to satisfaction depends on a variety of factors. For example, the two-factor theory of motivation suggests that salary is mostly a hygiene factor and not really as motivating as the work itself. On the other hand, it is hard to believe that migrant farmworkers are not motivated almost entirely by the wages they earn. Along the same lines, salary level may be valued less for its amount than for the status and prestige inherent in the level. So the satisfying effect of salary probably differs according to the situation.

We know, for example, that higher salaries result in higher rates of acceptance of job offers (Williams & Dreher, 1992), and that lower salaries lead to higher rates of turnover (Trevor, Gerhart, & Boudreau, (1997). We also know that satisfaction with compensation is only somewhat related to compensation amount (Heneman, Greenberger, & Strasser, 1988; Motowidlo, 1983). That is, higher-paid employees are not necessarily more satisfied with their salaries than lower-paid employees.

Industrial and organizational psychologists have developed a number of theories to explain this. **Discrepancy theory,** for example, suggests that employees compare their salaries with a personal standard of what they want, think they deserve, or see others receiving (Rice, Phillips, & McFarlin, 1990). According to this model, employees use a number of factors to decide how satisfied they are with their level of compensation.

Lawler (1971) proposed a model of pay satisfaction in which satisfaction depends on the relationship between what an employee thinks he or she should be paid and what he or she actually is paid. Dissatisfaction is likely to affect performance and other factors. For example, when employees of a manufacturing plant were forced to take a 15 percent pay cut because of business reversals, the amount of employee theft increased significantly (Greenberg, 1990).

Employees' feelings about compensation may also affect turnover and absenteeism. Although the evidence is not conclusive, most studies find that satisfaction or dissatisfaction with pay is an important consideration in any turnover decision.

Vroom (1964) proposed two models of pay decisions. In **compensatory models,** workers make trade-offs between job attributes and salary levels. This approach, based on expectancy theory, suggests that workers will demand more pay when they perceive a job to be unpleasant. Under the compensatory model, the frequent occurrence of sanitation workers being paid more than school-teachers is not illogical. Vroom's other model of pay decision is the **reservation wage model.** In this approach, workers set a bottom line wage, below which they will not work.

The Pay Satisfaction Questionnaire (PSQ) (Heneman & Schwab, 1985; Judge & Welbourne, 1994) is an 18-item measure of employee satisfaction with four areas related to compensation: current pay level, raises, structure of the compensation system, and benefits. Although results from the PSQ may be affected by job level, salaried versus hourly employees, or the general mental ability of respondents, the measure has been used to determine compensation satisfaction among nurses, law enforcement officials, teachers, and manufacturing employees (Carraher & Buckley, 1996; Scarpello, Huber, & Vandenberg, 1988).

Merit pay refers to salary increases based on an employee's performance, in which employees whose performances have been above average receive greater compensation than those whose performances have been average or below. Merit is often based on factors other than performance, however, including cost of living, merit pay budget, working conditions, and the tenure and level of the employee.

In recent years some employers have adopted **earnings-at-risk (EAR) plans.** In contrast with merit pay, which allows employees to earn bonuses above a fixed rate, EAR plans involve reductions in base pay so employees must earn their way back to a level that would have been guaranteed under a more traditional system (Wallace, 1990). EAR plans are becoming increasingly popular with employers because they offer an alternative to a fixed wage system.

In a longitudinal evaluation of employee attitudes toward EAR plans, 101 employees of a bank in the western United States were surveyed about their feelings about being placed on an EAR plan. Over time, the employees expressed less satisfaction with both their levels of pay and the pay process itself. They also expressed concern about greater effort being required for smaller rewards. Overall, their satisfaction with the compensation system declined (Brown & Huber, 1992).

Not surprisingly, supervisor characteristics can also affect pay increases. In a study of merit pay in a manufacturing plant, for example, two researchers (Heneman & Cohen, 1988) found that supervisors who received a large pay increase themselves were more likely to give large pay increases to their employees. In addition, organizational politics may affect raises, with some research suggesting that employees receive higher raises when their manager is dependent on their expertise, or when employees have connections to higher level managers (Bartol & Martin, 1989, 1990).

One of the most interesting aspects of compensation is the continuing discrepancy between male and female salaries. In general, this discrepancy can be traced to starting salary, where females are likely to be offered less than their male counterparts (Gerhart, 1990a). Although women are as likely as men to receive raises later, this initial gap in salary is hard to overcome. Results from a study of male and female MBAs entering the workforce suggest that although women attempt to negotiate higher salaries, they are less successful than men at raising initial compensation (Gerhart & Rynes, 1991).

As suggested above, some motivation theorists argue that pay is not a critical factor in determining performance. According to McClelland, for example, power, achievement, and social needs outweigh salary as motivators. Similarly, equity theory suggests that the fairness of the wage structure will be more important than the actual salary amount.

Another approach to understanding attitudes about pay is in terms of personality characteristics. Cable and Judge (1994), for example, looked at the relationship between personal values and pay systems among 171 college students looking for jobs. Students who scored high on a measure of materialism preferred jobs with higher levels of compensation; those who scored high on locus of control preferred benefit systems in which they could choose among options; and job seekers with high self-efficacy were more likely to pursue organizations with pay systems that rewarded individual performance rather than granting across-the-board raises. Finally, in comparison with other job applicants, risk-averse job seekers put less emphasis on pay level during their job search.

Another way of looking at compensation is in terms of business strategy regarding personnel. Companies can offer salaries that are higher, equal to, or lower than those offered by their competitors. Sometimes companies create compensation policies without evaluating the effectiveness of those policies. A hotel chain, for example, may pay its housekeeping staff wages that are higher than those of other chains and attract good employees. However, unless a careful analysis is performed, the quality of the employees may not be sufficient to compensate for the higher wages. That is, the hotel might get satisfactory performance at lower wages. For this reason, some researchers (Klass & McClendon, 1996) recommend using utility analysis to evaluate compensation policies.

What kind of companies pay best? Stroh, Brett, Baumann, and Reilly (1996) looked at factors that affected the size of bonuses of 309 managers who worked for Fortune 500 companies. The researchers found that managers whose tasks were fairly predictable were likely to receive lower bonuses than managers who described their responsibilities as being ill-defined and the results of their work as hard to measure, and who stated they had a lot of freedom to decide how to do their work. In addition, managers who worked in companies experiencing "turbulence"—defined as reductions in force, leveraged buyouts, mergers, acquisitions, and so forth—did not pay their managers more than nonturbulent companies. They did, however, offer more opportunities to earn bonuses.

Probably the safest generalization that can be made about pay is that it means different things to different people, and it certainly is not the most important motivator for many workers. Although few people are in positions to ignore the financial aspects of a job, many—if not most—choose their occupations on the basis of the work itself, rather than the financial rewards.

Job Enlargement and Enrichment

To help their employees cope with monotonous work—and perhaps to promote greater efficiency in the workplace—some employers have instituted programs of **job enlargement.** In this practice, jobs are combined or restructured so workers have opportunities to learn about other jobs in the company. In addition to regular duties, for example, Worker A learns to do part of Worker B's job. Occasionally, or even on a regular basis, Worker A will have the opportunity to vary his or her work activities by assuming B's duties. In a review of the literature on job enlargement, Lawler (1969) found that enlargement increased the quality but not the amount of production.

Although increased duties may enhance Worker A's job satisfaction, there is an obvious problem with the job enlargement approach to increasing worker satisfaction. Worker A may be expected to do more work without an increase in salary. Not surprisingly, many workers find this approach to making jobs more satisfying unacceptable.

Job enrichment, on the other hand, calls for restructuring jobs to make them more challenging (Hackman & Oldham, 1976). According to this model, today's employees are better educated and more interested in autonomy than previously, and employers need to design jobs with this in mind. Hackman and Oldham (1975) administered an instrument called the Job Diagnostic Survey (JDS) to hundreds of workers in a variety of jobs to identify aspects of jobs that affect satisfaction. From the survey, five key aspects were identified:

1. Skill variety: the different skills necessary to accomplish a job.
2. Task identity: the degree to which an individual completes a "whole" product or piece of work rather than just a small part.
3. Task significance: the impact that the work has on the lives of others.
4. Autonomy: the independence the employee has in planning and doing the job.
5. Feedback from the job itself: the manner in which the job provides feedback about employee performance.

Accordingly, if workers derive feelings of meaningfulness and responsibility and receive feedback on their performances, then they will experience high levels of satisfaction. In addition, workers will have high motivational levels, high-quality work performance, and low absenteeism and turnover.

The Job Characteristics Model—a model of facets that affect job satisfaction—can be used as an approach to motivation. Hackman and Oldham (1975) developed a formula for determining how motivating a job can be. Scores on skill variety, task identity, and task significance are averaged, and the average is multiplied with autonomy and feedback scores to equal the motivating potential score (MPS). Employers can use the Job Characteristics Model to motivate workers by "enriching" the values of each of the five job characteristics.

In an informal job enrichment strategy, a supervisor may assign some of his or her own duties to a subordinate so the subordinate has new opportunities for professional growth and achievement. In contrast with the job enlargement model, job enrichment focuses on the quality of the new duties, rather than on alleviating boredom simply by adding new duties. In a review of the literature on job enrichment and realistic job previews (Chapter 3), McEvoy and Cascio (1985) found that job enrichment was twice as effective at reducing turnover as realistic job previews.

Two researchers (Campion & McClelland, 1993) have suggested that job enlargement can be characterized as *task enlargement,* whereas job enrichment can be characterized as *knowledge enlargement.* In a study of the effects of task and knowledge enlargement among workers at a financial services firm, Campion and McClelland found increasing task knowledge had more long-term costs, such as lower satisfaction, efficiency, and customer service, and more errors, whereas knowledge enlargement had more benefits, such as higher satisfaction and customer service and fewer errors.

There are some considerations when applying a job enrichment strategy, however. First, as with job enlargement, the supervisor must be careful about simply adding more work without increased compensation of some kind. Second, employees have differing levels of need for growth and challenge. As suggested earlier, some workers are happy to fulfill their duties and look for satisfaction and growth outside the work environment. For these workers, changes in the workplace are unlikely to increase satisfaction. Finally, evidence supporting the Job Characteristics Model has been mixed. Factors such as individual differences and linkages among satisfaction, absence, and performance are unclear (Hackman & Oldham, 1976).

Benefits

Many employers have responded to the challenge of increasing job satisfaction by offering special benefits to their employees. Some typical benefits include flextime, flexible compensation systems, and employer-sponsored child care.

Flextime   For many years, psychologists have been aware of some of the negative effects of shiftwork. Common problems associated with working shifts other than daytime include sleep disruption, turnover, motor vehicle accidents,

accidents at work, and medical and psychiatric illnesses (Mardon, 1997). Rotating shifts, where working hours may vary from week to week, are particularly hard on workers. For example, a recent report from the Conference Board (Koretz, 1997) found that nurses who worked rotating shifts for six or more years had a 50 to 70 percent increased risk of heart attacks. Obviously, the hours employees work affect both health and performance.

Flextime (from flexible time) is a program in which workers have some autonomy in choosing their working hours. As long as they work a specific number of hours employees may choose when to come to work and when to leave. In a typical flextime arrangement, workers can arrive anytime between 7 A.M. and 9 A.M. and leave any time after 4 P.M., so long as the overall total of working hours per week is met. The flextime concept has been widely applied in the United States and by the late 1990s millions of employees were on flextime systems.

Obviously, not all jobs are compatible with a flextime approach. Production jobs that depend on the work of another person, for example, are poor candidates for flexible schedules. Supervisory and decision-making positions are also often difficult to adapt to flextime.

Although not many scientific studies have looked at the effects of flextime, there is some evidence that the approach does result in higher productivity. Flextime gives the workers more autonomy, allows them to meet nonwork demands—such as medical appointments—more easily, and permits them to work at times when their efficiency may be greatest.

In a study of flextime among programmers and data entry operators, Ralston, Anthony, and Gustafson (1985) found significantly higher productivity among programmers on the flextime system, but not among data entry operators. These authors concluded that flextime worked well when resources such as computers were shared among workers, but when employees worked independently, flextime did not improve performance. Nevertheless, the popularity of flextime among workers is expected to increase.

Flexible Compensation Systems   Flexible, or "cafeteria-style," **compensation systems** allow employees to choose from a variety of benefits offered by the company. For example, a company may offer an optional dental plan, mental health coverage, increased pension plan contributions, or similar benefits, and employees have the opportunity to select the benefits they prefer. In other words, benefits programs are adapted to the needs of the individual employee.

Flexible compensation systems are attractive to employees because they can be tailored to the needs of a diverse workforce, and they are popular with employers because they can be used to contain costs. Some evidence suggests they enhance job satisfaction in general, raise motivation and productivity, and increase attraction and retention of employees (Barber, Dunham, & Formisano, 1992; Beam & McFadden, 1988; Rosenbloom & Hallman, 1986).

In recent years some companies have designed benefits programs to appeal to "Generation X" employees just out of school. In addition to the usual medical and dental plans, companies such as Microsoft offer benefits such as special computer equipment, no dress codes, and individual offices with doors. Dell and CompuServe offer on-site fitness centers; other companies allow three weeks of vacation during the first year of employment (McShulskis, 1996b).

Although flexible programs have high start-up and administrative costs, some research (Gifford, 1984; Tane & Treacy, 1984) suggests companies save enough to cover the initial investment. Additionally, flexible compensation systems may help raise levels of employee motivation. For example, one study (Dreher, Ash, & Bretz, 1988) showed that employees are more satisfied with benefit plans in which employers assume a larger share of health care costs and dissatisfied when employees have to contribute more of these costs.

Child Care in the Workplace As suggested above, studies show that women with children are more likely to be absent than either men or women without children. With the increased numbers of women in the workforce since the 1950s, some employers have provided child care for their employees who have children. At Walt Disney World in Orlando, Florida, for example, 24-hour babysitting is available for all employees.

Although widely practiced during World War II, child care at the worksite has only recently become popular again in the United States. Such arrangements are commonplace in Europe and Russia, however. Many European and Russian factories have nurseries, and working mothers are allowed a half-hour break each morning and afternoon to spend with their children.

Aside from the benefit of lowered absenteeism, many employers feel that employer-sponsored child care improves employee attitudes, attracts job applicants, and has a favorable effect on community relations. Many claims as to cost savings have also been attributed to the establishment of day-care centers for the children of employees.

Although the idea that absenteeism might decrease if a child can be kept near its mother or father seems reasonable, this was not confirmed in a study of child care at a midwestern electronics company (Goff, Mount, & Jamison, 1990). Researchers found that parents who used the day-care facility were not absent less frequently than those who did not.

Nonetheless, other studies (Auerbach, 1988; Friedman, 1989) have suggested that on-site child care lowers turnover and increases job satisfaction (Goff et al., 1990; Shellenbarger, 1992). In a study evaluating the effect of on-site child care on job performance, researchers (Kossek & Nichol, 1992) studied the performance records of 155 hospital workers who placed their children in the company's child care center while they were working. Interestingly, the availability of child care had a positive effect on recruitment and retention, but it did not affect performance.

Additionally, extravagant claims about cost savings are almost certainly exaggerated. Although child care in the workplace may be a useful and humane social policy, there is presently no clear evidence that it improves productivity. In addition, most child care programs in the United States are established without a needs assessment. Child care programs can be quite expensive and organizations can waste resources if they establish child care facilities that will not be used by many employees (Kossek, 1990).

Chapter Summary

Despite the fact that many workers work under difficult conditions, the vast majority state that they are satisfied with their jobs. Job satisfaction is one of the most interesting areas of industrial and organizational psychology because research in this field may provide insights as to what the world of work will be like in the future. In addition, considerable research now shows a link between job satisfaction and life satisfaction.

In recent years, employers have become concerned about organizational commitment. When commitment is high, employees are likely to stay at their jobs longer and perhaps expend more effort than if their commitment is low. The relationship between commitment and performance, however, is not clear.

There are two approaches to measuring job satisfaction. The facet approach considers all of the factors that affect satisfaction; the global approach focuses on overall satisfaction. There are several well-known scales for measuring satisfaction.

Some theories of job satisfaction are need fulfillment, expectancy and equity approaches, social information processing, and genetic theory.

Common measures of dissatisfaction include absenteeism, turnover, tardiness, and deviant behavior. Absence is affected by both ability and motivation to attend. Women and employees with lower educational levels are absent more frequently and people with higher job satisfaction are absent less frequently. Absence rates are also affected by group norms.

Turnover can be considered from either a push or a pull perspective. Employment policies and group relations affect turnover, and women, the better educated, and people with more positive attitudes are more likely to quit. Currently the relationship between age and turnover is not clear.

Tardiness has not been widely studied by I/O psychologists, despite the fact that it is a major expense in terms of lost productivity. Deviant behavior, which refers to theft, embezzlement, sabotage, and vandalism, is another measure of dissatisfaction that has not been widely studied.

Salary is related to job satisfaction, but the relationship is usually so complex that few generalizations can be made. Merit pay refers to salary increases based on employee performance; earnings-at-risk is another model of performance-based pay. Salary is not the most important factor in job satisfaction for most people, however.

Strategies for increasing job satisfaction include job enrichment and job enlargement and the institution of benefits such as flextime and child care in the workplace.

Key Words and Concepts

ability to attend (p. 250)

affective commitment (p. 239)

attendance motivation (p. 250)

compensatory models (p. 262)

continuance commitment (p. 239)

discrepancy theory (p. 261)

earnings-at-risk (EAR) plans
  (p. 262)

facet approach (p. 241)

facet satisfaction theory (p. 247)

flexible compensation systems
  (p. 266)

flextime (p. 266)

genetic theory (p. 248)

global approach (p. 241)

job enlargement (p. 264)

job enrichment (p. 264)

job involvement (p. 238)

job satisfaction (p. 236)

life satisfaction (p. 236)

merit pay (p. 262)

need fulfillment theories (p. 0)

negative affectivity (p. 248)

normative commitment (p. 239)

organizational commitment
  (p. 238)

positive affectivity (p. 251)

reservation wage model (p. 262)

social information processing
  (p. 247)

value discrepancy theory (p. 247)

work centrality (p. 238)

Questions for Discussion

1. What's the best job you ever had? the worst? What made the job either the best or the worst?

2. What is the relationship between job satisfaction and life satisfaction? Which do you believe influences the other more?

3. What would it take for an employer to earn your commitment?

4. In your opinion, which is a better approach to measuring job satisfaction— the facet or the global approach? Why?

5. Which of the theories of job satisfaction makes the most sense to you? Do you believe genetics plays a role in satisfaction?

6. What kind of person is likely to be absent from work? As an employer, how would you address this problem?

7. What is an absence culture? Is there an absence culture at your college or among your friends? What are the norms of the absence culture?

8. What kind of person is likely to quit? As an employer, how would you address this problem?

9. What was the main factor in your decision to quit jobs you have left in the past?

10. Why is tardiness a problem? What do you think causes tardiness? How would you use some of the motivation theories discussed in Chapter 7 to respond to an employee who frequently had a problem with lateness?

11. Do you know someone who has performed a deviant act at work? In your opinion, why did he or she do it?

12. What is the relationship between compensation and job satisfaction? What are the dangers in relying on compensation to keep employees satisfied?

13. What are the benefits of flextime? of flexible benefits? of child care at work? Are these benefits worth their cost?

14. Given your knowledge of job satisfaction, what (within reason!) would make you want to stay at a job, perform at a high level, and never quit?

CHAPTER 9

Organizational Leadership

The Leadership Position

Personological Theories of Leadership

Behavioral Theories of Leadership

Cognitive Theories of Leadership

Leadership as Social Interaction

Chapter Summary

Key Words and Concepts

Questions for Discussion

In January 1991 the standoff between two of the world's most important leaders—President George Bush of the United States and President Saddam Hussein of Iraq—came to a head when Bush ordered the bombing of Iraq. The war that followed tested the wills of two extraordinary individuals.

Born into a privileged background, Bush had been the youngest pilot in the Navy during World War II. He flew 58 combat missions and was once shot down and rescued by submarine. After the war, Bush chose not to join his father's firm, instead founding his own successful oil business in Texas. Later he served two terms in the House of Representatives, chaired the Republican National Committee, and served as ambassador to the United Nations and to China, director of the CIA, and vice president during the Reagan administration.

Unlike George Bush, Saddam Hussein did not come from a wealthy background, but was born into a family of peasants who did not own their own land. In his youth Hussein became involved in politics, and in 1962 he joined the socialist Baath party, which gave him the secret mission of assassinating a prominent general. During the assassination attempt, Hussein was shot in the leg; as he fled to Syria on a donkey, he cut the bullet out of his leg with a knife. Hussein later studied law in Cairo, returned to Iraq, and participated in the overthrow of the government in 1972. Hussein ascended to the Iraqi presidency in 1979, and one of his first acts as president was to purge the Baath party by executing about 500 high-ranking members.

As a leader, George Bush relied on consensus, and during the period before the Gulf War he attempted to enlist the support of other world leaders. Hussein, on the other hand, was an authoritarian leader who took complete control of diplomatic and military affairs as Iraq prepared for war. Militarily, the war was a stunning success for the Americans and afterward, Bush received the highest popularity ratings of his presidency. Two years later, however, Bush was voted out of office by the American voters, whereas Hussein remained in power, vowing to rebuild his country and to fight again. After the election, Hussein continued to challenge President Bill Clinton, Bush's successor.

George Bush and Saddam Hussein represent two types of leaders—one who prefers to lead through consultation versus one who leads by commanding. Ironically, Bush's victory in the Gulf War did not displace Hussein from his leadership position; nor did it lead to Bush's reelection. To the American people, success in the war did not compensate for their concerns in domestic areas, and Bush was unable to persuade voters to share his vision of where the country should go. The ability to provide followers with a vision is a key element of successful leadership.

The outcome of the Gulf War illustrates the importance—and complexity—of studying leadership. Although Bush emerged as the victor, the American people doubted his leadership abilities overall. From a theoretical perspective, Bush was unable to translate his international success into a recognition of his competence in other areas. Consequently, many people began to regard him as an ineffective leader, and they began to look for someone to take his place.

Not surprisingly, many people regard leadership as one of the most important topics in the social sciences. Political and military scientists, sociologists, psychologists, and many others are interested in identifying the qualities, behaviors, and environments that affect leader performance and leadership development. Industrial and organizational psychologists are particularly interested in leadership as it affects the job performances and satisfaction of subordinates. Anthropologists argue that leadership is a universal phenomenon among humans, and even in groups in which decisions are made on a participative basis, leadership is a critical factor.

Leadership is also one of the most popular topics in the press, and hundreds of articles and books appear each year with advice on becoming an effective leader. In recent years, transformational leadership and empowerment have been two influential theories about leading effectively.

One researcher (Abrahamson, 1996) has referred to this fascination with leadership as "management fashion," which he defined as a transitory belief that one particular leadership or management technique is superior to all others. During the period when a fashion is popular, people rush to adopt the practice. Fashions change when the practice no longer meets the needs of the organization and when the practice is no longer highly regarded.

One important consideration in leadership research is the nature of the organization in which leadership occurs. In the military, for example, leadership is authoritarian, emphasizing absolute obedience and even the abrogation of civil rights (Smither & M. Houston, 1991). On the other hand, political leadership—at least in democracies—is based on influence, compromise, and the use of social skills to accomplish goals. Business leadership probably lies between the authoritarian and social skill perspectives, with authoritarian leadership more common in smaller businesses (Muczyk & Reimann, 1988). Although differences among these three types of environments—which are discussed below—affect leader behavior, few researchers have considered these aspects of leadership.

Another important consideration for leadership researchers is the difference between leadership emergence and leadership effectiveness. **Leadership emergence** refers to the qualities or behaviors that cause an individual to become a leader in the first place, whereas **leadership effectiveness** refers to making a group productive. Doing an excellent job at fulfilling one's duties, for example, may lead to emergence as a leader, but effectiveness depends on how well the leader motivates others to fulfill their duties. Emergence and effectiveness are important aspects of leadership, and recent thinking suggests they involve different behaviors and different aspects of personality.

In a study of leadership emergence and sex roles (Goktepe & Schneier, 1989), for example, researchers found that a person's gender did not affect emergence as a leader. That is, men and women were equally likely to be recognized as having leadership potential. On the other hand, men and women who emerged as leaders were rated as being more attractive and using more masculine—rather than feminine, androgynous, or undifferentiated—behavior during group interactions. Interestingly, the study results suggested that gender has less to do with leadership emergence than with qualities such as assertiveness, dominance, and competitiveness.

The Leadership Position

Participative Versus
  Authoritarian Leadership
Leadership and Power

In theory, at least, leadership is different from management (Holloman, 1984; Zaleznic, 1977). In most cases, managers are appointed to their positions by people above them in the hierarchy. These higher individuals define the manager's objectives and give the manager the formal authority to force subordinates to work toward those objectives.

In contrast, leadership occurs when the individuals below willingly comply with directions. Another way of looking at the difference is that leaders motivate followers to move toward organizational goals, whereas managers allocate human and material resources toward the accomplishment of goals. Additionally, managers sometimes create a wide social gap between themselves and their subordinates, whereas leaders often treat their subordinates as equals. Because of these differences, most organizations have some managers who are not leaders, and some leaders who are not managers. Nonetheless, most of the theories of leadership discussed in this chapter do not distinguish between leadership and management.

Few leaders are ever in a position to make decisions as important as those faced by George Bush and Saddam Hussein. Nonetheless, leaders in most organizations have similar obligations and experiences. In a survey of more than

200 chairmen, chief executives, and CEOs, for example, three researchers (Jonas, Fry, & Suresh, 1989) asked about the events that characterize a leadership career. Participants in the study identified five elements that were part of becoming a leader.

First, they spoke of having a dream early in their careers and needing to go beyond simply fulfilling their duties or providing a good income. In other words, they aspired to a leadership position long before they achieved it. Second, as they pursued their dreams, these leaders faced various trials and challenges that separated them from others less talented or less dedicated to their dreams.

Third, along the way to their positions, the leaders found someone who influenced them by providing a role model or by offering assistance. Fourth, after developing a dream, pursuing it, and being helped, the executives felt they were rewarded by achieving their dream or vision. In most cases, the salary associated with the leadership position was not the real reward, since by the time they reached their positions, they had been highly paid executives for some time.

In the final stage of the leader's career progression, the executives stated that being a leader provided them with certain meaningful experiences that affected their views on life and other people. In other words, being a leader meant more than simply fulfilling the goals of the organization—the experience made them look at life from a different perspective. The executives also agreed that leaders have three basic tasks: (1) creating an environment for change; (2) building employee commitment to, and psychological ownership of, the company; and (3) balancing the forces of innovation and stability, both of which are critical to the success of the organization.

In another study of what makes effective leadership, one researcher (Kotter, 1982) observed successful general managers in nine corporations over a five-year period. From his research he concluded that successful managers have a number of qualities and practices in common. Interestingly, successful managers spend almost all their time talking with other people about a wide range of topics, including families and sports activities. At least part of each exchange, however, is directed toward persuading people to take a certain course of action—rarely do effective executives simply tell their subordinates what to do. The researcher also noted that effective executives work long hours, typically 60 or more hours per week.

In another study (Borman, Hanson, Oppler, Pulakos, & White, 1993), researchers followed the careers of 570 second-tour soldiers, focusing on early supervisory experience and cognitive ability and their relationship to supervisor performance. Results from the study showed that soldiers high in cognitive ability were more likely to be given the opportunity to become supervisors early in their careers. Experience, in turn, led to higher levels of supervisor performance.

In another study of executive career success, researchers (Judge, Cable, Boudreau, & Bretz, 1995) found that educational level, quality, prestige, and degree type all predicted financial success. After analyzing the career progress of 1,388 executives, the researchers concluded:

The most objectively successful executive appears to be one who is a married, middle-aged, White man whose spouse does not work outside the home, who has impressive (high quality and prestigious) educational credentials, and who dislays a high commitment to his work. From the perspective of an individual who aspires to be a "successful" executive, it appears that educational credential and high commitment to work pay off.

(Executives are discussed in more detail in Chapter 10.)

Finally, two of the most fundamental tasks of any leader are, first, figuring out what to do in an uncertain environment, and, second, getting things done by relying on a large and diverse group of people, many of whom are outside the leader's direct control.

What kind of experiences are necessary to become a leader? Researchers at the Center for Creative Leadership (McCauley, Ruderman, Ohlott, & Morrow, 1994) collected data from 692 managers at various levels in their organizations about their experiences in rising to a leadership position. Specifically, the researchers were interested in establishing a scale to measure the developmental challenges that managers face.

Results from the research revealed that developmental experiences can be categorized into three broad areas: *job transitions,* which relates to finding oneself in a new and higher position; *task-related characteristics,* which refers to issues around planning, employee problems, and handling pressure; and *obstacles,* such as adverse business conditions or a difficult boss. Table 9.1 illustrates the 15 dimensions of leadership development identified by these researchers.

What are the differences between managers and nonmanagers? Carroll and Teo (1996) hypothesized that in comparison with nonmanagers, managers (1) were more likely to belong to social clubs; (2) interacted more frequently with coworkers; and (3) have discussion groups that include larger numbers of both coworkers and strangers. Using survey data from 270 managers and 366 nonmanagers, the researchers found that managers did belong to more social clubs, societies, and service clubs. In addition, they did interact with more people, and they included more strangers in their social networks. The researchers concluded their study supports the idea that managerial work consists chiefly of interacting with others. Another study (Tsui, Ashford, St. Clair, & Xin, 1995) found that managers who explained their actions and did not avoid dealing with discrepancies in employee expectations were perceived to be more effective.

Two researchers (Kilduff & Day, 1994) looked at the role of self-monitoring in managerial success. **Self-monitoring** (Snyder, 1974) refers to concern about the impression one makes. High self-monitors pay close attention to role expectations, whereas low self-monitors insist on being themselves without regard for social expectations. The researchers measured self-monitoring in a group of graduating MBAs, then followed up on the graduates' career success

Table 9.1   DIMENSIONS OF LEADERSHIP DEVELOPMENT

Dimensions	Description of scale	Sample item
Job Transitions		
Unfamiliar responsibilities	The manager must handle responsibilities that are new, very different, or much broader than previous ones	You have to manage something (e.g., a function, product technology, or market) with which you are unfamiliar
Proving yourself	The manager has added pressure to show others that he or she can handle the job	Most of the people reporting to you are more experienced than you are
Task-related Characteristics		
Creating change		
Developing new directions	The manager is responsible for starting something new, making strategic changes, carrying out a reorganization, or responding to rapid changes in the business environment	You have to make major strategic changes in the business—its direction, structure, or operations
Inherited problems	The manager has to fix problems created by the former incumbent or take over problem employees	You inherited at least one key direct report with serious performance problems
Reduction decisions	Decisions about shutting down operations or staff reductions have to be made	You have to lay off a significant number of your people
Problems with employees	Employees lack adequate experience, are incompetent, or are resistant	Your direct reports resist your initiatives
High level of responsibility		
High stakes	Clear deadlines, pressure from senior management, high visibility, and responsibility for key decisions make success or failure in this job clearly evident	You are being tested by top management
Managing business diversity	The scope of the job is large, with responsibilities for multiple functions, groups, products, customers, or markets	You are responsible for numerous different products or technologies or services

five years later. As the researchers had predicted, high self-monitors had received more promotions, changed employment, and changed geographical areas because of their jobs. The researchers concluded that the career strategies of high self-monitors were more successful than those of low self-monitors.

Table 9.1   *(Continued)*

Dimensions	Description of scale	Sample item
Job overload	The sheer size of the job requires a large investment of time and energy	This job requires you to put in long hours (60 or more hours a week)
Handling external pressure	External factors that impact the business (e.g., negotiating with unions or government agencies, working in a foreign culture, or coping with serious community problems) must be dealt with	This job requires dealing with foreign governments that can have a substantial impact on the business
Nonauthority relationships		
Influencing without authority	Getting the job done requires influencing peers, higher management, external parties, or other key people over whom the manager has no direct authority	To achieve your most important goals, you must influence peers at similar levels in other units, functions, divisions, and so on
Obstacles		
Adverse business conditions	The business unit or product line faces financial problems or difficult economic conditions	The business or a major product line faces intensely competitive markets
Lack of top management support	Senior management is reluctant to provide direction, support, or resources for current work or new projects	Resources are tight—you have to scrounge and "beg, borrow, or steal" to get the job done
Lack of personal support	The manager is excluded from key networks and gets little support and encouragement from others	It's difficult to find a supportive person to talk to in this job
Difficult boss	The manager's opinions or management style differs from those of the boss, or the boss has major shortcomings	Your boss is opposed to something you think is important to do

Source: McCauley, C. D., Ruderman, M. N., Ohlott, P. J. & Morrow, J. E. (1994). Assessing the developmental components of managerial jobs. *Journal of Applied Psychology, 79,* 544–560. Copyright © 1994 by the American Psychological Association. Adapted by permission.

From studies such as these, we know that being a leader is far more complex than simply making good decisions. Effective leaders must be able to judge situations accurately, inspire others, develop loyalty in subordinates, work long hours, and communicate effectively. Individuals may have authority to command based on their managerial positions, but leadership requires using that authority in ways that transcend simply ordering subordinates to follow a course of action.

One aspect of leadership that some leaders use to develop their subordinates is mentoring. **Mentoring** occurs when a more senior employee takes an interest in the career of a less senior employee and provides career guidance, special assignments, and increased visibility to higher management within the organization. In general, the mentor helps with two areas: career functions, which include promotions, desirable assignments, feedback, and protection from organizational enemies; and psychosocial functions, which include enhancing the younger employee's sense of competence and counseling the employee about problems that might arise (Kram, 1988; Olian, Giannantonio, & Carroll, 1985). Although the majority of mentoring relationships are informal, sometimes organizations assign mentors to younger employees.

In theory, mentoring is a useful practice, but not many researchers have attempted to evaluate its effects. Noe (1988), however, surveyed 139 educators and 43 mentors who were participating in a mentorship program about the benefits of the program. On average, mentors spent about four hours with each protégé during the six-month period covered by the study. Almost 22 percent of the mentors, however, spent no time with their protégés. Protégés reported more psychosocial than career benefits from their relationships and, interestingly, mentor–protégé relationships between the sexes were used more frequently than those of the same sex. Male mentor–male protégé relationships were less effective than either female–female or mixed gender mentor–protégé relationships.

Participative Versus Authoritarian Leadership

Leadership styles are sometimes classified by the way leaders use their power. For example, George Bush's style was earlier described as consultative, and Saddam Hussein's as authoritarian. Although all styles fluctuate occasionally, the behavior of most leaders can be described as being one of three types: authoritarian, participative, or laissez-faire.

Authoritarian leaders make the decisions, give orders, and take full responsibility for accomplishing organizational goals. In authoritarian environments, leaders emphasize hierarchies, status, rules, and procedures, and they may or may not use punishment to accomplish their goals. Although many people consider an authoritarian style ineffective, evidence on this point is not clear. Several researchers (Bass, 1990; Megargee & Carbonell, 1988; Smither, 1992) have pointed out that most employees are happier in a more participative environment, but this does not mean authoritarian leadership is always inappropriate. Particularly when goals are urgent, authoritarian leadership can be more effective than a participative leadership style.

Participative leaders, in contrast, engage their subordinates in the decision-making process and actively consult others before taking a course of action. Organizational theorist Rensis Likert (1961, 1967) produced a typology of organizations based on the amount of worker participation in decision making the managers allowed. Although many small businesses continue to operate on an authoritarian model, in recent years many organizations have adopted more participative leadership. Overall, participation appears to be more effective in larger organizations with strong corporate cultures (Muczyk & Reimann, 1988). Some forms of worker participation in decision making are discussed in Chapter 10.

Finally, some leaders use a laissez-faire style. Laissez-faire leadership refers to the practice of allowing subordinates to manage themselves, with the leader intervening only in unusual circumstances. Although no leadership style is appropriate in every situation, laissez-faire is almost always less effective than either authoritarian or participative leadership.

Leadership and Power

Power, the degree to which an individual can influence others, is a variable that applies to both leaders and managers. By definition, individual leaders and managers have power in varying degrees, depending on both the position an individual holds—referred to as position power—as well as the leader's personal characteristics or behavior in exercising that power—known as personal power. **Position power** can be the result of a person's position in either the management hierarchy or social networks within the company. **Personal power,** in contrast, refers to behaviors such as assertiveness, using logic to influence others, or forming coalitions (Brass & Burckhardt, 1993).

French and Raven (1959) suggested that power comes from one of five critical power bases. Leaders who have **reward power** are able to influence others through their ability to provide followers with something they desire. Typical rewards a leader may provide include attention, recognition, promotions, or salary increases.

Coercive power relies on threats and punishments to influence the behavior of subordinates. Effective use of coercive power by a leader requires constant surveillance, since followers are likely to comply with demands without accepting such demands internally. French and Raven suggested that leaders who use reward power are better liked than those who rely on coercive power. This point was supported in a study by Hinkin and Schriesheim (1989), in which undergraduates, employees of a psychiatric hospital, and MBA students expressed a strongly negative relationship between the use of coercive power and satisfaction with supervision.

Legitimate power refers to the right of the leader to command. That is, people recognize the authority of the individual or the position to be a leader (Kahn & Kram, 1994). This kind of power is inherent in a position and is particularly influential because it is a recognized component of the social order. In other words, workers follow the orders of supervisors simply because they recognize that the position of supervisor has legitimate power. Positions such as police officer, doctor, clergy, and professor also have certain legitimate powers attached, and individuals tend to obey these individuals because of the positions they hold in society.

When a leader provides an example that followers wish to emulate, the leader is exercising **referent power.** People look to this person for a model of how to behave, and by behaving as that person does, they hope to resemble the powerholder. A junior employee who works long hours because the boss does is probably being influenced by referent power.

Another way of looking at referent power is in terms of being linked to others who are powerful (Raia, 1985). In fact, some evidence (Kilduff & Krackhardt, 1994) suggests that simply having the reputation of being friends with someone powerful causes other workers to regard an individual's performance more highly.

Finally, when a leader demonstrates knowledge beyond that held by subordinates, the leader is exercising **expert power.** The leader does not need to have the actual knowledge; the power comes from subordinates attributing the expert knowledge to the leader. Many times leaders appear to be informed about aspects of the organization that are not accessible to subordinates. Subordinates consequently defer to the leader because of the leader's expert power. In a review of studies that used French and Raven's taxonomy of power, two researchers (Podsakoff & Schriescheim, 1985) found that effective managers had more expert and referent power than ineffective managers.

Over the years, researchers have expanded French and Raven's original list to include other sources of power. **Information power** (Raven, 1974) refers to holding information that other people need to do their work. **Persuasive power** (Aguinis, Nesler, Hosoda, & Tedeschi, 1994; Yukl, Kim, & Falbe, 1996) is the ability to persuade others to follow a course of action they might not normally follow; and **charismatic power** (Conger & Kanungo, 1987) attracts followers because the leader is perceived as being extraordinary in some way.

In a study of the types of power within a pharmaceutical company, a chemical and manufacturing company, and a financial services firm, Yukl and Falbe (1991) found support for information and persuasion as two types of power distinct from French and Raven's list; support for charismatic power was less certain. The researchers also found some support for the distinction between leadership and management. In this study, workers who had greater task commitment and rated their managers' performances higher attributed their ratings to the qualities of the individual manager rather than to the managerial position in general.

One researcher (Finkelstein, 1992) identified two other sources of power. **Ownership power** refers to power that comes from personal or family ownership of shares in a firm or from being a founder or relative of a founder. **Prestige power** comes from sitting on the boards of other corporations or nonprofit organizations or from having attended a prestigious university.

Finally, in a study of power tactics used by managers, two researchers (Falbe & Yukl, 1992) found distinct differences in the success of tactics managers used. Specifically, consulting with employees and making inspirational appeals were the most effective power tactics; relying on pressure or basing attempts to persuade on the manager's legitimacy were the least effective. Overall, "softer" tactics were more effective than "harder" tactics.

As suggested above, leadership is probably one of the most researched topics in the behavioral sciences. In general, the theories that have been developed explain leadership in one of three ways: (1) the personological approach, in which leadership is seen as a function of the unique qualities of individuals; (2) the behavioral approach, in which factors in the environment give rise to leadership; or (3) the cognitive approach, in which leadership is the result of understanding the perceptions of workers. A fourth approach, which looks at leadership from the perspective of the follower, has recently become popular among researchers. To help you understand the different theories of leadership, Box 9.1 highlights the major ideas of the various approaches to leadership.

Personological Theories of Leadership

Trait Theories
Need for Power and Leadership
Evaluating Personological Theories of Leadership

Most nonpsychologists believe there is something unique about individuals who become leaders. This approach to leadership is considered "personological" because it focuses on the personal characteristics of individuals. The two major varieties of personological leadership theories are trait theories and need theories.

Trait Theories

Trait theories start with the proposition that leaders have specific personality attributes that their followers do not. These attributes might include courage, foresight, intelligence, persuasiveness, and personal charisma. According to the specific theorist, these traits may be either genetic or acquired. The "Great Man" variety of trait theories, for example, suggests that from their birth, there was something unique about such people as Mao Tse-tung or Winston Churchill. Unfortunately, however, reviews of the trait literature show that leaders often have little in common. Adolf Hitler, Mohandas Gandhi, Fidel Castro, and Bill Clinton are all individuals who achieved high leadership positions, but the similarities in personal characteristics among these men are not immediately obvious.

Trait studies often take a retrospective approach. The backgrounds of leaders are studied to see what experiences can explain their achievements. Not surprisingly, the qualities that are identified are usually positive, since negative traits such as laziness or stupidity are disconfirming evidence to the trait theorist. Trait theories are also not very helpful in predicting who will become a

Box 9.1   FOUR APPROACHES TO UNDERSTANDING LEADERSHIP

Anthropologists tell us that leadership is a universal phenomenon that occurs in all cultures and groups. Over the years psychologists have developed various approaches to understanding leadership. The four major types of leadership theories used by psychologists are summarized below.

1. The Personological Approach. Most people believe that great leaders have special qualities that set them apart from the rest of us. These qualities are either inherited or develop in childhood, and they are the foundation for the leader's success later in life. In personological theories, the focus is on the *person,* not on the environment in which that person operates. Personological theories of leadership are deterministic—leadership qualities develop in childhood, and people who do not develop such qualities are unlikely to become leaders later. According to the personological approach, Abraham Lincoln was a great leader because he was honest, intelligent, compassionate, and persevering.

2. The Behavioral Approach. According to the behavioral approach, leadership is the product of what leaders *do,* not their personal attributes. Successful leadership results when a person in a leadership position acts to motivate subordinates to accomplish organizational goals. From a behavioral perspective, anyone who develops the ability to motivate—at any time in life—can be a leader. Most popular books on leadership take a behavioral perspective—that leadership results from behaving appropriately. According to behavioral theory, Lincoln was a great leader because he overcame his family's poverty to become a lawyer, then president; he appointed officials and military officers who could win the war for the Union; and he inspired the people with speeches such as the Gettysburg Address.

3. The Cognitive Approach. Over time, some theorists decided that appropriate behavior could result only if a leader *understands* the leadership situation, then acts. That is, the true basis of leadership is in the ability to evaluate and make decisions about a situation. Cognitive theorists are interested in how leaders make decisions and how they determine what motivates the people whom they hope to lead. According to this approach, Lincoln was a great leader because he understood what the people wanted, he knew when to consult them, and he knew how to persuade them to act in support of his goals.

4. The Social Interaction Approach. The personological, behavioral, and cognitive approaches to leadership all emphasize the qualities, behaviors, or cognitions of the leader separate from his or her subordinates. But social interaction theorists argue that leadership results from the social process that occurs between leaders and subordinates. That is, the actions of the leader influence the subordinates, and their reactions influence the leader. This approach holds that the personal characteristics, behaviors, and cognitions of *both* parties—leader and follower—create leadership. Social interaction theorists would argue that Lincoln was a great leader for a variety of reasons: because he knew which of the people around him he could rely on; the public felt he was extraordinary and so they were willing to do as he wished; or Lincoln's actions merely reflected the will of the people and his personal qualities had little to do with his success.

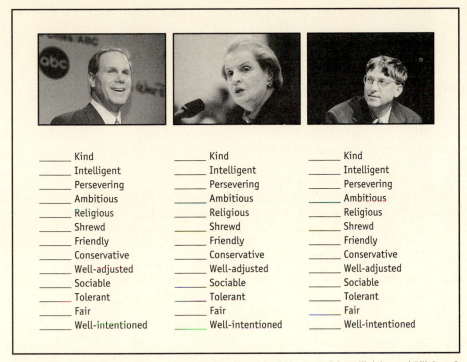

_____ Kind
_____ Intelligent
_____ Persevering
_____ Ambitious
_____ Religious
_____ Shrewd
_____ Friendly
_____ Conservative
_____ Well-adjusted
_____ Sociable
_____ Tolerant
_____ Fair
_____ Well-intentioned

_____ Kind
_____ Intelligent
_____ Persevering
_____ Ambitious
_____ Religious
_____ Shrewd
_____ Friendly
_____ Conservative
_____ Well-adjusted
_____ Sociable
_____ Tolerant
_____ Fair
_____ Well-intentioned

_____ Kind
_____ Intelligent
_____ Persevering
_____ Ambitious
_____ Religious
_____ Shrewd
_____ Friendly
_____ Conservative
_____ Well-adjusted
_____ Sociable
_____ Tolerant
_____ Fair
_____ Well-intentioned

Figure 9.1 Traits of the Leader   What traits describe Michael Eisner, Madelyn Allbright, and Bill Gates?

leader. An individual may have all the "right stuff" but fail to develop leadership skills. Virtually all trait approaches to leadership ignore factors in the environment that may affect leadership emergence.

One theory suggests it may be impossible to identify traits common to all leaders (see Figure 9.1), but there may be traits common to leader emergence (Kenny & Zaccaro, 1983). In other words, certain personality characteristics may motivate a person toward a leadership position, but whether the person maintains such a position depends more on behaviors than on traits. In a test of traits associated with leadership emergence, for example, Zaccaro, Foti, and Kenny (1991) had subjects lead different groups attempting different tasks. Results from the study found that the same subjects were identified as leaders regardless of group or task. In contrast with assertions that leadership is largely situational, the researchers concluded that leadership is more related to individual characteristics than to situational variables.

Reviews of the trait theory literature do suggest that there are some qualities often found in leaders. Stogdill (Bass, 1981) reported that leaders tend to have high energy levels, assertiveness, good judgment and good communication skills, the ability to cooperate, and tactfulness in dealing with their followers. Coming from a higher socioeconomic level is usually an advantage, but being at either extreme in intelligence is less helpful than being in the middle range.

Need for Power and Leadership

Chapters 7 and 8 discussed McClelland's theory of achievement motivation. In later years, McClelland modified his theory to include three different psychological needs: achievement, affiliation, and power. Although there are other needs, these three are the most relevant to performance in the workplace. Achievement needs relate to reaching a standard of excellence, whereas individuals whose chief motivation is affiliation are more concerned with the social aspects of work. People with strong power motivations focus on influencing others. According to McClelland, everyone has different levels of all three needs, but one need is likely to be dominant.

As you recall, individual levels of motivation can be assessed in a number of ways, but McClelland's studies rely on a projective personality measure called the Thematic Apperception Test (TAT). According to McClelland and Burnham (1976), the best managers have a higher than average need for affiliation and a higher than average need for power. Their TAT stories, however, typically describe situations in which powerful persons show restraint in exercising power.

McClelland called this configuration of responses—high social needs and high power needs that are restrained—the leadership motive pattern (LMP). A high level of need for achievement, which is important for success as entrepreneurs and small businesspeople, is not as important for success in larger organizations.

In a review of the TAT responses of employees who had participated in AT&T's Management Progress Study, McClelland and Boyatzis (1982) found that 16 years after the testing, 80 percent of the individuals who had high LMP scores had reached the top levels of AT&T management.

One important way in which McClelland's approach differs from trait theory is in the belief that need levels can be raised in adulthood. McClelland and his associates have developed a series of training programs—described in Chapter 7—designed to raise individual levels of need for achievement, affiliation, or power. Consequently, people can be groomed for leadership positions in the future, or need levels of incumbent managers can be raised.

Box 9.2 describes one theorist's view of Bill Clinton's changing psychological profile in terms of need theory.

Evaluating Personological Theories of Leadership

If nonpsychologists were asked what makes a good leader, quite likely they would give responses such as "intelligence," "communication skill," "vision," and so forth. Almost everyone has his or her own theory of leadership, and for most of us, these theories are personological in nature. (Popularity is not evidence for veracity, however.)

As widely held as personological theories may be, there are concerns about this approach. The following are four common concerns:

Box 9.2   CLINTON'S NEW PROFILE

In a study of 200 years of presidential speeches, psychologist David G. Winter looked for the themes of achievement, affiliation, and power. According to Winter, President Clinton's inaugural speech in 1993 contained many references to achievement. Historically, however, a presidential emphasis on achievement has sometimes led to disappointment. For example, Presidents Wilson, Lyndon Johnson, Nixon, and Carter also had achievement-themed inauguration speeches.

By the State of the Union address in 1996, however, Clinton's themes had changed. Reflecting a stronger power motive, the president directly challenged Republican colleagues at least a dozen times. Winter observed that this is also typical of politicians—as they become more comfortable in their office, they enjoy playing the "game" of politics. Looking at politics as a game, Winter says, can carry presidents through difficult periods of defeat and make them stronger leaders.

Source: Shea, C. (1996, November 1). Clinton said to adopt new psychological profile. *Chronicle of Higher Education,* p. A18.

1. These theories ignore the role of the environment in leadership. Quite possibly, talented individuals who are born in undesirable conditions never have the opportunity to show their leadership abilities.

2. Personological approaches are usually retrospective. In other words, individual leaders are identified and then their backgrounds are studied to identify qualities that made them leaders. With a retrospective approach, evidence that seems contradictory to the achievement of leadership is likely to be deemphasized in favor of confirming information.

3. Personological approaches take the position that experiences from early in life determine whether one becomes a leader. In some cases, it seems that an unhappy or deprived childhood is more desirable than a normal childhood. Research suggests, however, that leaders come from all types of backgrounds and that training can affect an individual's leadership abilities.

4. Finally, leadership emergence and leadership effectiveness are usually indistinguishable in personological theories. That is, the qualities that bring about an individual's emergence as a leader are thought to be the same as those that allow for effective performance in a leadership position. However, many people become leaders, only to fade into obscurity after a short time.

Behavioral Theories of Leadership

Ohio State Studies
Contingency Model
Situational Leadership
Reinforcement Theory
Evaluating Behavioral
  Approaches to
  Leadership

For all the reasons suggested above, many researchers concluded that personological approaches were inadequate for developing a general theory of leadership. In the period following World War II, psychologists turned to studying the behavior, rather than the personal qualities, of leaders. Among psychologists, the behavioral approach has dominated the study of leadership until quite recently. Four important behavioral approaches are the Ohio State studies, Fiedler's contingency model, situational leadership, and reinforcement theory.

Ohio State Studies

A general dissatisfaction with the trait approach to studying leadership led to the **Ohio State studies,** an influential program of research established by Shartle (1950), Hemphill (1950), and others at Ohio State University in the late 1940s. Taking the approach that behaviors could reveal more than traits about leadership, Hemphill and his associates developed a list of 1,800 characteristic leader behaviors. Factor analysis of this list identified two broad dimensions into which virtually every leader behavior could be classified: consideration and initiating structure. These two categories have been applied throughout the study of leadership and are still widely used today.

The dimension **consideration** relates to the ways a leader shows concern for the welfare of subordinates. Typical consideration behaviors include inquiring about a worker's family, expressing appreciation for a job well done, and spending time coaching the worker toward a higher level of performance. An extreme example of consideration comes from the American Civil War. After Pickett had failed to break through the Union lines at Gettysburg and the Confederate defeat appeared imminent, General Lee reportedly moved among his soldiers, reassuring each one, "All will come right in the end, we'll talk it over afterwards" (Ridgway, 1984).

Initiating structure refers to a focus on the tasks of a job. Leaders who emphasize structure are concerned with getting the work done efficiently and on time. They organize the work and give directions about how it is to be accomplished; production outweighs interpersonal concerns. When Grant wired Lincoln just before the Battle of Spottsylvania, "Our losses have been heavy, but so have those of the enemy. I propose to fight it out on this line if it takes all summer," he was indicating his orientation toward initiating structure.

One way of measuring a leader's consideration and structure is to have subordinates complete a version of the Leadership Behavior Description Questionnaire (LBDQ) (Hemphill, 1950), and have supervisors complete a form describing ideal leader behavior known as the Leadership Opinion Questionnaire (LOQ; Fleishman, 1957). The Ohio State studies and the voluminous research that followed showed that the two dimensions of leader behavior can have important consequences for worker performance.

In an often-cited study of leadership styles in a large insurance company (Morse & Reimer, 1956), for example, worker satisfaction was found to be greater when managers scored high on consideration. When managers scored high on structure, absenteeism and turnover were higher. Interestingly, both leadership styles resulted in higher productivity, suggesting that laissez-faire leadership is less desirable than either the participative or the authoritarian style. Stogdill (1965) found that neither consideration nor structure was consistently related to productivity, however.

The Ohio State studies and similar work done at the University of Michigan have provided an important framework for studying leader behavior that has been used by many researchers. Two aspects of the Ohio State approach that should be noted are (1) despite their focus on behavior rather than on traits, the Ohio State studies are still person-oriented rather than environment-oriented; and (2) although many, if not most, leader behaviors can be classified along these two dimensions, there are other leader activities that fall outside the categories.

Contingency Model

The contingency theory of leadership (Fiedler, 1967) grew out of research into the relationship between therapists and patients, and was later applied to leader–subordinate relationships. Specifically, Fiedler was interested in why both authoritarian and democratic approaches to leadership could be effective.

According to Fiedler (1965), leaders have individual styles of relating to both workers and tasks, and since these styles are based on individual personalities, they are difficult to change. Effective leadership occurs when there is a good match between individual style and factors in the environment. On the other hand, when style and environment are not a good match, Fiedler suggested that the better approach is to try to change the environment, since personal styles are so difficult to change. A person in a leadership position who is more inclined toward structure, for example, could arrange the environment by requiring that workers get the leader's approval before implementing changes in the workplace. On the other hand, a consideration-oriented leader could change the environment so that workers have more autonomy in making decisions.

The first step in developing effective leadership is to determine the leader's or manager's personal style. The manager is asked to think of a person with whom he or she would least like to work. Using a questionnaire called the Least Preferred Coworker (LPC), the manager identifies individual characteristics of this person. Results from the LPC are scored, and the manager's style is classified along the consideration/structure dimensions. High LPC scores indicate a human relations–consideration–orientation; low LPC scores suggest a task–structure–orientation.

The environment in which the leader operates is next evaluated along the dimensions of the quality of (1) leader–member relations; (2) task structure (i.e., the clarity of task requirements); and (3) the leader's position power. Having information about the leader's personal style and the environment in which the leader operates, the task becomes to change the environment so that it fits the personal style of the leader. Research suggests that low LPC leaders—those favoring structure—are more effective in situations of either high or low control, and that high LPC leaders—those favoring consideration—are more effective when the situation favors the leader.

The Leader Match Program (Fiedler & Chemers, 1977; Fiedler & Mahar, 1979) is a step-by-step method for changing a working environment to fit a manager's style. In a study of ROTC groups, for example, cadets who had experienced Leader Match training received higher ratings from both their superiors and their peers than those who had not.

The **contingency model of leadership** is based on the assumption that there is no one best way of leading. In this respect, contingency theory offers an advantage over the trait approach, in which leadership ability is based on childhood experience. In any theory, one of the defining qualities of a leader is that the leader can take control of the environment and make changes that optimize personal and group functioning. The contingency approach recognizes that different environments call for different behaviors, and the most effective leader will match the environment to his or her own personal style.

As is the case with all theories, however, there are additional considerations with regard to Fiedler's model. Some typical considerations include (1) the LPC questionnaire actually measures attitudes rather than behaviors and, as research in social psychology demonstrates, the linkage between attitudes and behavior is not strong; (2) the focus of the model is entirely on performance and not on worker satisfaction, which can also be an important component of leadership effectiveness; and (3) both high and low LPC leaders may be effective in leadership situations not necessarily predicted by the theory (Schriesheim, Tepper, & Tetrault, 1994).

Situational Leadership

Situational leadership (Hersey & Blanchard, 1969, 1982) is a behavioral theory that focuses on subordinate maturity as the factor that affects structure, consideration, and leader effectiveness. According to Hersey and Blanchard (1982), subordinate maturity refers to a worker's willingness to accept responsibility for directing his or her behavior. Maturity is of two types: psychological maturity and job maturity, referring, respectively, to being both committed and able to do the work.

When subordinate maturity is low, leaders need to focus on structure, but when maturity is high, structure can be deemphasized. The relationship between consideration and leader behavior is more complex. When maturity is low, leaders should put little effort into relationships, but as the workers mature, relationships become more important. After reaching a certain point in maturity, however, the importance of relationship begins to decline, and when maturity is at the highest level, relationship becomes unimportant again. Figure 9.2 illustrates proper leader behavior in relation to worker maturity.

Situational leadership has been intuitively appealing to managers, despite the fact that research supporting the model has been mixed (Hambleton & Gumpert, 1982; Vecchio, 1987). In a test of situational leadership among residence hall directors and resident advisors, for example, Blank, Weitzel, and Green (1990) measured leader behavior, psychological maturity, job maturity, performance, and job satisfaction. Overall, the model was not well supported by the research. Leader behavior was unrelated to any of the other variables except job satisfaction. When leaders were less task-oriented with low maturity workers, job satisfaction was low; when they were more task-oriented with low maturity workers, job satisfaction was high.

Despite these kinds of results, Hersey and Blanchard appear to have identified an important variable—subordinate maturity—that affects leadership effectiveness. However, the relationship between maturity and leadership needs further clarification.

Reinforcement Theory

As discussed in Chapter 7, **reinforcement** and related learning theories focus on shaping behavior by rewarding desired responses. Much of the behavior that occurs in the workplace is, intentionally or not, structured within a reinforcement framework. For example, workers receive bonuses for good performance, penalties are exacted for tardiness, paychecks appear at regular intervals, and so forth.

According to the behavioral approach, the job of the leader is to provide stimuli that evoke a desired response from a subordinate. These stimuli may take the form of economic incentives, threats, modeling behavior, or anything

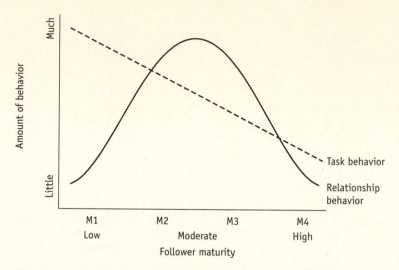

Source: Blank, W., Weitzel, J., & Green, S. (1990). A test of situational leadership theory. *Personnel Psychology, 43*(3) 582. Copyright © 1990. Reprinted by permission of the publisher.

Figure 9.2 Task and Relationship Behavior in the Situational Model of Leadership

else that motivates the worker to perform successfully. In sharp contrast with the personological theories of leadership, learning theories suggest that anyone who is sufficiently skilled in manipulating environments can become a leader.

Because work behaviors tend to be complex, however, relationships between reinforcers and behavior are not always straightforward. For example, Davis and Luthans (1979), two proponents of organizational behavior modification (Chapter 7), have suggested that leader-subordinate behavior in the workplace is actually interactive. That is, just as the leader shapes the behaviors of his or her followers, the followers also shape the behaviors of their leader. Behavior, much like communication, is sequenced in a fashion that makes identifying a beginning and an end difficult. When a leader behaves, almost certainly the response of subordinates will shape the leader's future behavior as well.

A more recent behavioral approach to leadership is cognitive social learning theory, which argues that behavior, cognition, and environment interact to create leadership (Wood & Bandura, 1989). Based on Bandura's (1986) social cognitive theory of personality, this approach uses self-efficacy, self-regulation, modeling, and goal setting to explain leadership. In other words, what a leader does is the product of cognitive factors, such as beliefs about the leader's abilities, workers' responses to the leader's actions, and factors in the environment in which the leader operates. This model, which integrates cognitive theory (discussed below) with behavioral theory, is more sophisticated than the reinforcement model.

Difficulties with the behavioral approach to leadership are the same as those with the application of reinforcement theory to motivation. To be successful, leaders must be knowledgeable about what is rewarding, and what is punishing, to a worker. Additionally, some leaders may object to calculated manipulation of the behavior of others. Finally, the notion that anyone can become a leader by successful use of behavioral principles is not credible. Certain individuals seem unlikely to become leaders regardless of how much they study the principles of reinforcement.

Evaluating Behavioral Approaches to Leadership

In one sense, behavioral approaches to understanding leadership represent an important step forward from the personological approaches. Specifically, behavioral theorists have demonstrated in a number of cases that environment very much affects leadership. This explains why so many leaders come from the same kinds of environments, and also why leaders who are successful in one setting may be less successful elsewhere. For example, retiring football coaches and military leaders often cannot make a successful transition to leadership in a business environment. When an individual can gain control of the environment, however, then perhaps leadership ability will emerge.

Another important advantage of the behavioral approach is its emphasis on learning. This approach holds that, given the right kinds of stimuli and training, almost anyone can become a leader. Although this claim may be extravagant, behavioral theorists have made it clear that at least some people can learn to be leaders. In a sense these theorists have "demystified" leadership: Individuals do not need to be born with great talents or be at the right historical moment to become a leader. All they need is the proper training.

Yet the question of training brings up a question similar to one that was raised with the personological approaches. If several individuals are given the same training, why do their leadership abilities differ? According to behavioral theories, the key to successful leadership is making a fit between behavior and environment. Nonetheless, some individuals are noticeably more perceptive than others when it comes to assessing a situation and acting appropriately.

Despite their advantages over other models, behavioral theories are not always useful in explaining individual differences and, as most researchers agree, individual differences are a critical factor in both leadership emergence and effectiveness.

Cognitive Theories of Leadership

Vroom-Yetton Decision-
   Making Model
Path-Goal Theory
Evaluating Cognitive
   Theories

In some respects, cognitive theories can be thought of as a compromise between the personological and behavioral approaches to leadership. As explained in Chapter 7, cognitive theories build on how workers perceive situations. From the cognitive perspective, leaders who understand this and act appropriately are likely to be more successful than those who do not. Two major cognitive approaches are the decision-making model and path-goal theory.

Vroom-Yetton Decision-Making Model

According to the **Vroom-Yetton decision-making model** (Vroom & Yetton, 1973), effective leadership results when a leader appropriately engages subordinates in decision making. The key word here is appropriate—effective leaders know when and how much their subordinates can participate in making decisions relevant to the workplace. This model is characterized by a decision tree (Figure 9.3, pp. 294–295) that informs leaders as to the appropriateness of a variety of actions.

For a leader to apply the decision-making model successfully, he or she needs to have an accurate understanding of the decision-making situation. Appraising the situation starts with a leader asking him- or herself questions about factors such as the necessary quality of the decision, the acceptability of a solution to subordinates, and the likelihood of conflict resulting from a decision. Vroom and Yetton identified ten possible approaches to solving these problems, ranging from the autocratic imposition of a decision to a laissez-faire approach.

Suppose, for example, the owner of a small business with ten employees must decide whether to expand company operations. The owner has enough information about the financial and marketing situation to make an informed decision, but she is not certain about employee acceptance. For example, employees may fear the expansion will result in more work without additional compensation. If the owner decides (1) that employee acceptance is important and (2) that the employees would resent her making the decision by herself, but (3) that their goals are not the same as hers, then the Vroom-Yetton model would prescribe approach CII: gathering the employees' ideas but making the decision herself.

The Vroom-Yetton model is prescriptive, where managers use a "hands-on" approach to solve real problems. The model provides explicit instructions about the actions a leader should take. In a study of 96 managers who were unfamiliar with the decision-making model, Vroom and Jago (1978) asked the managers to describe their behavior in various leadership situations. Of the 181 situations collected, the managers behaved as the model would have predicted in 117. Most of these behaviors were judged to be effective. On the other hand, among the 64 situations that did not fit the model, the majority of these were judged to be ineffective.

Some researchers (Heilman, Hornstein, Cage, & Herschlag, 1984) have raised interesting questions about the decision-making model and about evaluating the effectiveness of leader behavior. In some cases the Vroom-Yetton model prescribes autocratic or authoritarian behavior on the part of the manager. In a study of subordinates' perceptions of leader behavior, employees consistently found a participative management style to be at least as effective as an autocratic style. Even when the decision-making situation required the bosses to act autocratically, employees did not react favorably.

This suggests that the evaluation of leader effectiveness may be the result of the management style used and who—manager or subordinates—is doing the evaluating. In one study (Field & House, 1990), for example, the model was found to be valid when managers described their own decision-making processes; subordinate reports about the same decisions, however, disconfirmed the model. In recognition of these shortcomings, Vroom and Jago (1988) expanded the model to include situational variables.

Despite these questions, Vroom and Yetton have provided a model that greatly simplifies decision making. Leaders who follow the model will almost certainly approach the decision-making process in a rational and comprehensive fashion. However, we know that leaders spend little time actually making decisions. Following the Vroom-Yetton model may result in improved decision making, but in most cases, we cannot equate decision making and leadership. As evidenced by several of the preceding examples, leadership is counseling employees, motivating workers, providing an example of behavior, and so forth. As useful as the Vroom-Yetton model may be, it provides only for a narrow focus of leader behavior.

Confirming evidence for the Vroom-Yetton model as an effective tool for establishing leadership has not been particularly strong. Making an accurate assessment of the perceptions of another can be quite difficult, and if a leader misjudges a situation, the wrong actions may be taken. A related problem is the fact that some individuals can probably make a "wrong" decision work, whereas others will have trouble succeeding even with the right decision.

A final consideration with the decision-making model relates to establishing its validity. Decision-making theorists typically rely on the reports of managers as to whether a certain action was successful. These self-reports may be distorted by a manager's own perceptions and are not particularly useful as validity evidence. Overall, the decision-making model may be a useful tool, but it is unlikely that a leader can sustain his or her position solely on this kind of procedure.

Path-Goal Theory

Path-goal theory (Georgopoulos, Mahoney, & Jones, 1957; House, 1971; House & Mitchell, 1974) suggests that successful leadership results from successful manipulation of worker expectancies. Recall from Chapter 7 that expectancy theory argues that performance is a product of a worker's perceptions about the amount of effort necessary to achieve a desired goal. In the path-goal model, the job of the leader is to increase worker payoffs for performance. In other words, leaders identify goals for workers and enhance the paths to those goals. Some research (Keller, 1989) suggests the success of path-goal theory depends on the clarity of the employee's understanding of the task that leads to the goal.

In some respects, the path-goal framework is similar to reinforcement theory—leaders use a variety of techniques to bring about desired performances. This model differs from the reinforcement model in two important ways, however. First, as is typical of the cognitive approach, leader behavior depends on the perceptions of the workers; that is, effective managers or supervisors must first understand how workers view the present situation and what they expect in

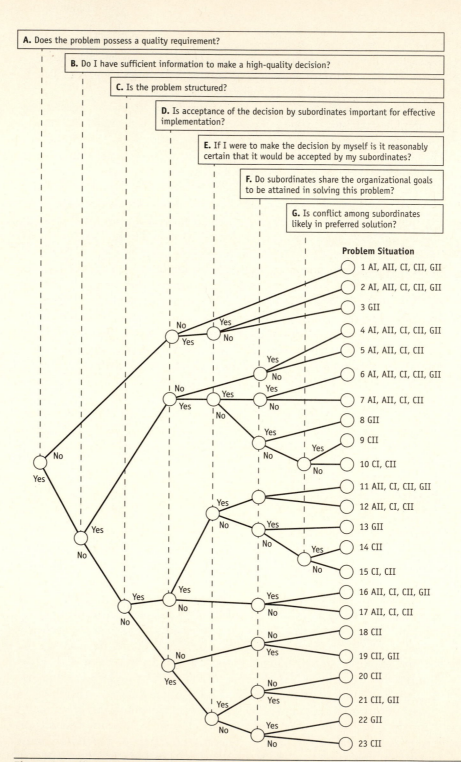

A. Does the problem possess a quality requirement?

B. Do I have sufficient information to make a high-quality decision?

C. Is the problem structured?

D. Is acceptance of the decision by subordinates important for effective implementation?

E. If I were to make the decision by myself is it reasonably certain that it would be accepted by my subordinates?

F. Do subordinates share the organizational goals to be attained in solving this problem?

G. Is conflict among subordinates likely in preferred solution?

Problem Situation

1 AI, AII, CI, CII, GII
2 AI, AII, CI, CII, GII
3 GII
4 AI, AII, CI, CII, GII
5 AI, AII, CI, CII
6 AI, AII, CI, CII, GII
7 AI, AII, CI, CII
8 GII
9 CII
10 CI, CII
11 AII, CI, CII, GII
12 AII, CI, CII
13 GII
14 CII
15 CI, CII
16 AII, CI, CII, GII
17 AII, CI, CII
18 CII
19 CII, GII
20 CII
21 CII, GII
22 GII
23 CII

Figure 9.3 The Vroom-Yetton Decision-Making Model

Decision Procedures for Group and Individual Problems
Group Problems
AI. You solve the problem or make the decision yourself, using information available to you at the time.
AII. You obtain the necessary information from your subordinates, then decide the solution to the problem yourself. You may or may not tell your subordinates what the problem is in getting the information from them. The role played by your subordinates in making the decision is clearly one of providing the necessary information to you rather than generating or evaluating alternative solutions.
CI. You share the problem with the relevant subordinates individually, getting their ideas and suggestions without bringing them together as a group. Then you make the decision, which may or may not reflect your subordinates' influences.
CII. You share the problem with your your subordinates as a group, obtaining their collective ideas and suggestions. Then you make the decision, which may or may not reflect your subordinates' influences.
GII. You share the problem with your your subordinates as a group. Together you generate and evaluate alternatives and attempt to reach agreement (consensus) on a solution. Your role is much like that of a chairman. You do not try to influence the group to adopt "your" solution, and you are willing to accept and implement any solution which has the support of the group.

Individual Problem
AI. You solve the problem or make the decision yourself, using information available to you at the time.
AII. You obtain the necessary information from your subordinate, then decide the solution to the problem yourself. You may or may not tell your subordinate what the problem is in getting the information from him. His role in making the decision is clearly one of providing the necessary information to you rather than generating or evaluating alternative solutions.
CI. You share the problem with your subordinate, getting his ideas and suggestions. Then you make a decision, which may or may or may not reflect his influence.
GI. You share the problem with your subordinate, and together you analyze the problem and arrive at a mutually agreeable solution.
DI. You delegate the problem to your subordinate, providing him with any relevant information that you possess but giving him responsibility for solving the problem by himself. You may not request him to tell you what solution he has reached.

Source: Reprinted from *Leadership and Decision-making,* by Victor H. Vroom and Philip W. Yetton, by permission of the University of Pittsburgh Press. © 1973 by University of Pittsburgh Press.

Figure 9.3 The Vroom-Yetton Decision-Making Model
In this model, successful leadership results from knowing when to involve subordinates in decision making. Leaders follow a decision tree as they ask themselves seven questions about the decision. Following the decision tree to its end will result in a prescription for handling the situation.

the future, then adjust their own behaviors accordingly. Second, the perceptions of both leader and subordinate are influenced by three kinds of moderating variables (House, 1972):

1. Task variables (e.g., amount of structure associated with performance or the interdependence of tasks);
2. Environmental variables, (e.g., the need to make decisions quickly); and
3. Individual differences among leaders and workers.

According to path-goal theory, leaders can adopt one of four styles: directive, supportive, achievement-oriented, or participative. In cases in which the task is highly structured—in an assembly line or automated environment, for example—a directive style may not be appropriate. On the other hand, among construction workers, where tasks are not structured, a style that is supportive and nondirective may be ineffective. In the path-goal model, adopting a leadership style inappropriate to the situation will result in lowered performance.

To be effective, the leader must consider the perceptions of workers with regard to the task to be accomplished. For example, if a worker seems to be motivated by the social aspects of a job—talking with coworkers, planning the company picnic, and so forth—then the leader uses those aspects as rewards for accomplishing goals.

Although the path-goal model seems straightforward, empirical testing of the theory has been difficult and results have often been contradictory. Path-goal theory can be conceptualized as having three elements: leader behavior, moderating variables, and worker performance. After reviewing studies designed to test the path-goal model, Schriesheim and Von Glinow (1977) concluded most research designs have not been able to encompass all three elements. Schriesheim and Schriesheim (1980) suggested that the lack of research as to the effects of environmental variables and individual differences has resulted in a lack of empirical validation for the model. Additionally, Staw and Ross (1980) found that leaders who adapted their styles to different situations were judged to be less effective than those who used one style consistently.

Evaluating Cognitive Theories

Cognitive theories start with the recognition that leader's or worker's perception of a situation is likely to influence behavior. In the case of the Vroom-Yetton decision-making model, the leader's perceptions determine the manner in which a decision is made, and path-goal theory explains leadership in terms of how effectively a manager matches employee goals with paths to achieve those goals.

A basic tenet of cognitive theory is that perceptions precede behavior, rather than vice versa. Cognitive theorists argue that understanding how individuals process information, make decisions, and come to conclusions provides a clearer picture of behavior in the workplace. Almost certainly, what workers *believe* is the case is more important than how things actually are.

Earlier it was suggested that bridging the gap from cognition to behavior is a diffficult process, and one in which our knowledge is not complete. What workers say and do are often unrelated. As promising as the cognitive approach may be, we need to be aware of this limitation. The cognitive approach will be much more useful when researchers are able to make this link.

An additional consideration with regard to cognitive theory, you will recall, is that there are substantial individual differences in ability to understand the perceptions of others. Why some individuals are so much better at judging others—as occurs with different employment interviewers, for example—is a matter of great theoretical and practical importance. Advances in this area will provide knowledge for use across a wide variety of fields.

Leader-Member Exchange
Charismatic Leadership
Transformational Leadership
Attributional Approaches to Leadership
Evaluating Social Influence Theories

Leadership as Social Interaction

Some researchers have focused on the role of subordinates in influencing leader behavior (Heilman et al., 1984; James & White, 1983; Sims & Manz, 1984). If leadership is a social process, then it seems reasonable that the actions of both

Table 9.2   THEORIES OF LEADERSHIP

Personological Theories of Leadership

Personological theories of leadership focus on personal characteristics of individuals. Two personological approaches to leadership are trait theories and need for power.

Trait Theory: Trait theory holds that there is something unique about leaders from early in life. These qualities are what make leaders different from everyone else.

Need for Power: Leadership results from a high need for power that develops in early childhood. Successful leadership also depends on the need for power being directed toward organizational goals and a strong need for affiliation.

Behavioral Theories of Leadership

Behavioral approaches to leadership emphasize what a leader does rather than his or her personal qualities. Until recently, behavioral approaches have been the most popular among leadership theorists.

Ohio State Studies: Leadership can be understood in terms of two broad dimensions of behavior: consideration and initiating structure. Consideration refers to behaviors that affect interpersonal relations; initiating structure refers to behaviors that affect accomplishing a task.

Contingency Model: Effective leadership occurs when there is a good match between a leader's individual style of behavior and factors in the environment. People become leaders by changing environments to fit their personal styles.

Situational Leadership: Leadership effectiveness results from how the leader deals with subordinates' maturity. When subordinates' maturity is low, the leader must emphasize structure and put little emphasis on consideration. When maturity is high, relationships become more important.

Reinforcement Theory: The job of the leader is to provide stimuli that bring about desired responses in subordinates. Consequently, leadership results from the successful manipulation of reinforcements.

the leader and the followers will influence each other. This final group of leadership theories looks at leadership as the product of the interaction between a leader and his or her subordinates.

Leader-Member Exchange

Leader-member exchange (LMX) (Graen & Scandura, 1987), a theory originally known as **vertical dyad linkage (VDL)** (Dansereau, Graen, & Haga, 1975), focuses on the quality of interaction between leader and subordinates. More than any of the theories discussed above, LMX sees leadership as the complex interplay of individual differences, group behavior, and situational

Table 9.2   *(continued)*

Cognitive Theories of Leadership

Cognitive approaches to leadership emphasize the leader's ability to understand when to involve subordinates in decision making or how to manipulate worker expectancies. Two major cognitive theories are the Vroom-Yetton decision-making model and path-goal theory.

Vroom-Yetton Decision-Making Model: Effective leadership results when a leader appropriately engages subordinates in decision making.

Path-Goal Theory: In the path-goal model, successful leadership results from manipulating worker expectancies, and the job of the leader is to increase worker payoffs for performance. In other words, leaders identify goals for workers and enhance the paths to those goals.

Social Interaction Theories of Leadership

Social interaction theories of leadership move beyond other approaches by emphasizing the role of the subordinate in leadership. According to these theories, subordinates influence leaders just as leaders influence subordinates.

Leader-Member Exchange: Leadership effectiveness is determined by the quality of the interaction between leader and subordinate. Leaders work with individual differences, group behavior, and situational constraints to motivate followers.

Charismatic Leadership: Leadership results from workers believing that an individual has vision, confidence, and the ability to inspire. In other words, subordinates believe their leader is extraordinary. Charismatic leadership differs from the trait approach because leaders need not have the traits the workers ascribe to them.

Transformational Leadership: Effective leaders recognize that many workplace situations are irrational and that workers must be motivated to transcend their self-interests. The goal of the transformational leader is to change worker goals.

Attributional Approaches to Leadership: Attributional approaches argue that qualities in the situation create leadership, and that individuals actually have little influence on the organization as a whole. People become leaders only because others agree to treat them as leaders.

constraints. As we know from research in personality and social psychology, individual behavior differs between being part of a group and acting independently. LMX theorists believe effective leaders recognize differences in behavior that result from group membership.

Leader-member exchange starts with the idea that leaders need to understand the individual differences among people. In any group setting, managers will find they have closer relationships with some employees than with others. These employees—referred to as the **Ingroup**—are closer to the source of power and are influential with the boss and their coworkers. Because the leader or manager feels these people can be trusted, he or she lessens control over their activities, offering them increased job latitude, influence in decision making, and open communication (Scandura & Graen, 1984). Workers who are less trustworthy—the **Outgroup**—require more structure, and so the manager deals more formally with them.

According to the LMX model, a leader must identify who among the workforce is committed to the company's goals, self-motivated, and able to handle some degree of autonomy—and who is not. The committed individuals constitute the Ingroup, and the leader and each subordinate form a vertical dyad. In any given work unit, the relationships between a leader and his or her subordinates consist of a series of vertical dyads. The relationship between a manager and a subordinate is referred to as a leader-member exchange (LMX). According to the theory, high-quality LMXs result in higher quality leadership, productivity, and job satisfaction.

Consider, for example, the manager of the cosmetics department in a large department store. Because cosmetics are typically sold on a commission basis, all successful employees need some degree of self-motivation. Nonetheless, the effective manager will be able to rely on some employees more than on others, allowing them to plan their own sales strategies, make displays, and introduce new products. According to LMX theory, these employees are the key to success for the department. They will have lower turnover, higher productivity, and better interpersonal relations with the manager than employees who depend on a more formal employment contract with the store.

The notion that the quality of the relationship between a manager and a subordinate affects performance seems logical, and it has been used as part of a number of the preceding theories. In a study of the success of 80 new recruits in a Japanese department store over seven years, for example, Wakabayashi and Graen (1984) found a positive relationship between career success and the quality of an employee's relationship with the manager; these results were replicated in a later follow-up study (Wakabayashi, Graen, Graen, & Graen, 1988).

Along the same lines, other researchers found a relationship between the quality of leader-member exchange, productivity, mentoring, and job satisfaction (Graen, Liden, & Hoel, 1982; Scandura & Schriesheim, 1994). In addition, two researchers (Seltzer & Numerof, 1988) found lower rates of job burnout among employees whose managers practiced consideration more than initiating structure. Another study (Bauer & Green, 1996) found delegation to be an important factor in the quality of leader–member exchange.

In an attempt to determine what affects the quality of the relationship between manager and subordinate, Wayne and Ferris (1990) proposed a model of how managers develop liking for their subordinates. According to the model (presented in Figure 9.4), employees manage the impressions they make on their managers so that the managers like them better. Performance appraisals are affected by objective criteria, but because the managers like these employees better, the employees receive higher ratings. How much a manager likes an employee, combined with the perceived quality of that employee's work, is what

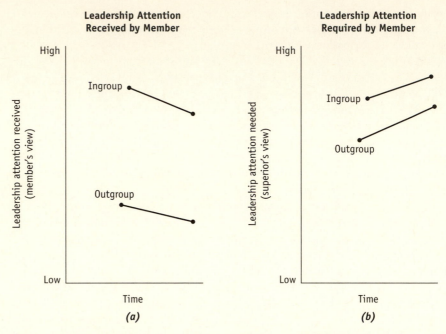

Source: Dansereau, F., Jr., Graen, G., & Haga, W. J. (1975). A vertical dyad linkage approach to leadership within formal organizations. *Organizational Behavior and Human Performance, 13,* 46–78. Copyright © 1975. Reprinted by permission of Academic Press, Inc.

Figure 9.4 Differences Between the Ingroup and the Outgroup in the Leader-Member Exchange Model
In graph *(a)*, the Ingroup feels it needs a high level of attention and the Outgroup feels it needs a low level of attention, and both groups feel they need less attention over time. In graph *(b)*, the leader feels both groups need more attention over time, but the Ingroup needs more attention than the Outgroup.

determines exchange quality. In a test of this model using bank employees, the researchers found that liking definitely influenced performance ratings, and that performance ratings affected leader-member exchange quality.

In an interesting study that looked at demographic variables and how much a supervisor liked an employee, Tsui and O'Reilly (1988) found that similarity of supervisor and subordinate had an important effect on the quality of the supervisor-employee relationship and on how the supervisor rated the employee's performance. For example, employees in same-gender dyads were rated higher than those in mixed-gender; older subordinates were liked less than younger; employees with more education than the supervisor were liked less than employees with less education; and subordinates with longer job tenure were liked better than those with shorter tenure. Results from this study support the idea that similarity greatly influences the quality of leader-member exchanges.

Some researchers (Liden, Wayne, & Stilwell, 1993) investigated leader-member exchanges among 166 newly hired university employees over a six-month period. Results from the study showed that leader expectations of members and members' expectations of leaders assessed within five days were predictive of expectations two weeks and six months later. Leader-member exchanges were also affected by the degree of similarity between the leader and the member. These findings suggest that the initial relationship between an employee and a supervisor can be an important predictor of their future relationship.

Two researchers (Phillips & Bedeian, 1994) studied the quality of leader-member exchanges in relation to similarity, introversion and extraversion, locus of control, and need for personal growth in a group of 130 registered nurses and their supervisors. The best predictor of quality leader-member exchanges was attitudinal similarity, followed by extraversion. Locus of control and need for personal growth were not related to exchange quality.

Some researchers (Kozlowski & Doherty, 1989) have pointed out that leader-member exchanges have an important bearing on organizational climate, which refers to worker perceptions about an organization. In a study that looked at climate and leadership in a manufacturing company, researchers found that workers who had high-quality leader-member exchanges had more positive perceptions about the climate, and that members of the Ingroup tended to agree with their supervisors in assessing the climate of the organization. (Organizational climate is discussed more fully in Chapter 12.)

Charismatic Leadership

Charisma is a Greek word meaning gift, and the German sociologist Max Weber used the term to describe authority based on the personal qualities of an individual. Some of the qualities of the charismatic leader include having a personal vision, behavior that instills confidence, an ability to inspire, a need to influence others, communication skills, and unconventional behavior (Conger & Kanungo, 1987). People who follow charismatic leaders typically accept the leaders' beliefs without question, trust and obey the leaders, feel affection for them, and identify with their goals. In this way, charisma is, at least in part, an attribution from the followers.

Although political scientists have studied this kind of leadership for some time, the charismatic model of leadership is relatively new in industrial and organizational psychology. Examples of business leaders who are considered charismatic are Lee Iacocca and H. Ross Perot.

Conger and Kanungo (1987) developed a model of **charismatic leadership** in industry. According to the model, charismatic leaders reject the status quo, do not hesitate to take high personal risks to achieve their vision, and attempt to accomplish their vision outside conventional channels. These leaders are assertive and self-confident, and they express concern for their followers' needs. Their power is expert and referent, rather than legitimate, coercive, or reward-based, and they rely more on setting an example than on consensus seeking. Charismatic leadership is usually linked with transformational leadership, which is described below.

Transformational Leadership

One of the newer approaches to leadership theory developed from path-goal theory and makes a distinction between transactional leadership and transformational leadership (Bass, 1985a). In **transactional leadership,** a term that covers most of the theories discussed in this chapter, the leader (1) recognizes what subordinates must do; (2) clarifies role and task requirements; and (3) recognizes subordinates' needs and how these needs will be satisfied when the job is done. In other words, leadership is based on a rational understanding of the task and leadership situation.

In contrast, **transformational leadership** recognizes the irrationality of many workplace situations. The goal of the transformational leader is not to clarify requirements and identify paths to goals that employees value, but rather, to motivate workers to transcend their own self-interests. By expanding their individual needs and by expressing confidence that workers can fulfill those needs, the transformational leader actually changes worker goals (Bass & Avolio, 1994).

In a survey of 70 chief executives, Bass (1985a) asked participants to name a transformational leader with whom they had worked. All of the respondents were able to name someone who had inspired them to work long hours and to do more than they ever expected, and who had acted as a model whom they wanted to emulate.

According to the chief executives, the transformational leader set high standards for performance; treated subordinates as equals; encouraged with advice, support, and recognition; and inspired the confidence of subordinates. At the same time, the transformational leader could also be firm and reprimanding when necessary. In another study (Howell & Avolio, 1993), the success of different units within a Canadian financial services firm was related to a transformational leadership style.

In a factor analytic study of leadership among military officers, Bass (1985b) identified five types of leader behaviors. Two of these were transactional. *Contingent reward* refers to the extent to which leaders provide rewards for their followers; *management-by-exception* refers to the extent to which subordinates hear from the leader only when problems occur.

More significantly, Bass identified three transformational qualities:

1. *Charisma*. The leader inspired the enthusiasm, faith, loyalty, and confidence of subordinates.
2. *Individualized consideration*. The leader recognized and encouraged the unique potentials and abilities of individuals.

3. *Intellectual stimulation*. The leader aroused an awareness of problems and new approaches to solving them.

In a related study of transformational leadership, researchers (Bycio, Hackett, & Allen, 1995) found that nurses were more likely to make an extra effort, express satisfaction with their leader, and regard the leader as more effective when they felt he or she was transformational. However, contingent rewards—such as raises—also significantly affected the nurses' attitudes toward their leader.

Two researchers (Kuhnert & Lewis, 1987) have proposed what they call a constructive/developmental approach to transformational leadership. According to this view, leadership operates at different levels, distinguished by how leaders view themselves and the people around them. At an early stage, a leader views the world solely from his or her own viewpoint and assumes everyone has similar motives. At the next level of development the leader appreciates that others have different views and priorities and emphasizes doing what is fair for everyone.

The leader's personal vision is paramount in the next stage. The leader takes an objective view of him- or herself and his or her subordinates, but maintains a goal or agenda that transcends interpersonal concerns. Conflicts are resolved in terms of values, not relationships with subordinates, and leaders at this stage are often able to persuade followers to their viewpoint. According to the researchers, the first two levels of leadership are transactional, but the third is transformational. In an experimental study of transformational leadership, two researchers (Kirkpatrick & Locke, 1996) found that the leader's vision was the most important factor in motivating subordinates. Another study (Pawar & Eastman, 1997) found that certain environmental characteristics influence the rise of transformational leadership.

In a comparison of transformational and transactional leadership at an air delivery company, Hater and Bass (1988) asked subordinates to describe the behavior of their managers. Overall, subordinates reported that top-performing managers were significantly higher in charismatic leadership and individualized consideration—two of the qualities of the transformational leader—than ordinary managers.

Transformational leadership is an attractive theory because it addresses a situation with which many of us are familiar. Most of us can remember a leader, manager, or teacher who inspired us to work harder than we had planned or to strive for goals that were not of our choosing. These individuals seemed to have something that led to higher achievement than we expected. In addition, some evidence (Bass, 1997) suggests that the transactional–transformational distinction occurs across different cultures.

Transformational leadership is a cognitive theory because it focuses on the perceptions of subordinates. In contrast with other approaches, the leader does not try to meet the expectations of workers; rather, the leader transforms those expectations. The leader's view of the situation quite clearly dominates the work environment and, for whatever reason, workers feel obliged to meet the expectations of their superiors.

Attributional Approaches to Leadership

Although leadership is a cultural universal and certainly one of the most studied topics in the social sciences, some researchers have asked whether leadership as it is presently defined really exists. These theorists question the difference between leadership and social influence (Kochan, Schmidt, & deCotiis, 1975) or the effect of leadership on performance (Hall, 1972; Sales, 1966). Some researchers (Meindl & Ehrlich, 1987) have even argued that leadership has become a "romantic" notion, in which people attribute heroic qualities to those who appear to be successful leaders.

Although people such as transformational and charismatic leadership researchers like to believe that leaders have unique qualities, attributional theorists argue that evidence supporting this view is scarce. Many "leader qualities" can be explained in terms of demographics, job characteristics, or the social network in which the individual is embedded (Davis-Blake & Pfeffer, 1989). Further, the dispositional qualities of leaders may have personal significance, but they probably have little significance when evaluated in terms of their impact on the organization as a whole.

Pfeffer (1977) has suggested that, overall, the effects of leaders on organizations are likely to be small for three reasons. First, leaders constitute a remarkably homogenous group—historically, they tend to be White males from higher socioeconomic classes. As leaders, these individuals select people like themselves to succeed them. Consequently, there is so little variance in leader performance that we cannot really determine the effectiveness of leaders.

Second, Pfeffer argues that the role of the leader is much more constrained than most leadership literature suggests. That is, even powerful leaders have much less control over organizational resources than may be expected. Additionally, organizational politics play a key role in leadership effectiveness. In fact, many of the decisions we attribute to individual leadership ability are probably determined more by factors in the environment that necessitate those decisions (Gunz & Jalland, 1996).

Third, many factors affecting leader performance are outside the leader's control. For example, labor markets, interest rates, and general economic conditions may be the critical variables in organizational performance. A leader could have made all the "right" decisions or performed all the appropriate behaviors according to any of the theories discussed above, yet still fail to accomplish the mission because of problems with external factors.

If we accept the argument that the actions of leaders are much less important than we usually consider them to be, then why is so much effort expended in studying, nurturing, and selecting leaders? According to Pfeffer, the answer has to do with the social system. In our system, people like to believe in meritocracy—that leadership positions are awarded to those who earn them. In fact, this is not the case, since individuals who have historically risen to leadership positions in the United States are White males with upper-class backgrounds (this is discussed in more detail in Chapter 11). Belief in the meritocratic approach to leadership does serve a useful social function, however:

> As long as persons believe that positions are allocated on meritocratic grounds, they are more likely to be satisfied with the social order and with their position in it. This satisfaction derives from the belief that occupational position results from application of fair and reasonable criteria, and that the opportunity exists for mobility if the person improves skills and performance. (Pfeffer, 1977)

Given this viewpoint, leadership becomes a process of attribution. Despite the fact that leaders themselves have little impact on performance, people attribute performance to the leader. In this framework, success as a leader comes from being associated with the successes of the organization and not associated with the failures. The role of the leader is not important in terms of organizational performance. Rather, the leader becomes a symbol of the social system.

Evaluating Social Interaction Theories

Social influence theories start with the assumption that the relationship between leader and subordinate—and not the traits or behaviors of the leader—is what defines leadership. This view is an interesting challenge to traditional psychological ideas about leadership.

Leader-Member Exchange Although one of the cornerstones of industrial and organizational psychology is the belief that social relations affect worker performance, LMX theory suggests that they *cause* worker performance. Good leaders are skilled at interacting on a personal basis with their subordinates, and if the quality of that relationship is high, then performances will be exemplary. On the other hand, leaders who are not good on an interpersonal level are likely to be ineffective.

One of the appealing aspects of LMX theory is its recognition of differences in workers. Whereas most leadership theories suggest that an effective leader can, given the right circumstances, motivate any employee, LMX recognizes that this may not always be the case. As suggested earlier, some individuals work solely for money or other reasons, and they are not interested in personal fulfillment through their work. Leader-member exchange suggests these people must be treated differently from members of the Ingroup, and that perhaps expending effort attempting to motivate these workers will not be cost or time effective. Virtually everyone who has been in a management position is familiar with this kind of worker.

LMX is a dynamic theory, suggesting that a leader's behaviors must change to fit the expectations of the worker with whom the leader is dealing. If a leader is limited to only one form of interaction, however, then the leader's effectiveness is going to be limited. In the LMX model, being participative all the time is just as bad as being authoritarian all the time.

One consideration about LMX that has been raised is the possibility that treating some employees more personally and allowing them more autonomy than others may result in dissatisfaction among other employees. Although this seems reasonable, research suggests that Outgroup members actually do not report differences in treatment from the leader (Duchon, Green, & Taber, 1986).

In the LMX framework, leader success depends almost entirely on social skills. This is probably an oversimplification of the leadership process. Certainly there are times when leaders must forget the social aspects of a job in order to accomplish an organizational goal. As important as social skills may be, more evidence is needed that these are the ultimate keys to effective leadership.

Nevertheless, in some ways LMX appears to approach the question of leadership in a more comprehensive fashion than the theories discussed earlier. LMX considers interpersonal relations too complex and too subtle to be dealt with by the direct application of a standardized formula for leadership effectiveness. Each leader and each employee is different, and leaders can be effective only so far as they understand their relations with each of their subordinates.

Charismatic and Transformational Leadership Charismatic and transformational theories are interesting because they appear to link social influence with personological approaches to leadership. In other words, the leader has certain traits, or behaves in certain ways, that persuade workers to accept his or her personal vision of organizational goals. In these models, personality factors and the quality of the relationship between leader and follower are more important than environment, task, or decision-making style. In some respects, charismatic and transformational approaches echo the "Great Man" theory of leadership mentioned earlier.

Not surprisingly, the effectiveness of charismatic and transformational approaches to leadership have not yet been well documented. Although these models have intuitive appeal, identifying what makes a person charismatic or transformational, and how these qualities affect organizational productivity, is not yet clear. Finally, an obvious question about these approaches is, Can anyone, with training, become charismatic or transformational, or are these styles so rooted in personality that they cannot be acquired later in life? If so, then effective leadership is destined to be practiced only by a lucky few.

Attribution In attributional theory, the actions of the leader are not nearly as important as the actions that subordinates or others attribute to the leader. Leader success is more related to organizational success than to any individual action—a position completely at odds with charismatic and transformational approaches. The idea that leader qualities or behaviors make little difference is an intriguing point of view, since it suggests that leadership theorists are studying the wrong aspects of leadership. Rather, researchers should be concentrating on the processes by which people choose their leaders and ascribe "leaderly" attributes to them.

Overall, evidence for an attributional point of view of leadership is weak, with only a few studies providing support for leadership being mostly attribution. Although attributional theory raises some important questions, its argument that individual leaders have little effect on performance is too simplified. Certainly there is evidence from history that individual leaders make a difference, and there is considerable evidence from psychological research as well.

In general, attribution theorists hold a view that is not unlike the sociological perspective—that situations create leaders. As suggested earlier, people who believe in individual differences—which includes most industrial and organizational psychologists—are not usually receptive to such viewpoints.

Chapter Summary

Leadership is a universal phenomenon among humans. As such, researchers from a variety of fields are interested in the topic. Industrial and organizational psychologists are particularly interested in leadership as it affects the job performances and satisfaction of subordinates. Additionally, some researchers are interested in the differences between leadership emergence and effectiveness.

Managers differ from leaders in that they are appointed, have their objectives defined by someone else, and rely on formal authority. Leadership occurs when subordinates willingly comply with their superior's directions. Both managers and leaders have power in varying degrees.

Studies suggest that people who achieve high leadership worked for their positions for many years, were assisted by others, and did not seek the position because of its financial rewards. Sometimes people become leaders through the practice of mentoring.

Leadership styles are often divided into three types—authoritarian, participative, or laissez-faire. Although authoritarian and participative can be effective, laissez-faire leadership seems to be the least effective.

Power is the degree to which an individual can influence others. Different kinds of power are reward, coercive, legitimate, referent, expert, information, persuasive, and charismatic. Two other kinds of power researchers have identified are ownership and prestige.

Personological theories of leadership start with the assumption that there is something inherently unique about individuals who become leaders. In these approaches, leadership ability is often rooted in childhood experience. Of the personological approaches, McClelland's need for power seems to generate the most research.

Behavioral approaches suggest that factors in the environment give rise to leadership. Leaders are disposed between initiating structure or consideration, and use of the appropriate behavior affects leader success. Behavioral theories suggest that controlling the environment will facilitate performance of subordinates.

Cognitive theories of leadership include the decision-making model and path-goal theory. The decision-making model prescribes behavior for leaders based on situational factors. Path-goal theory suggests that effective leadership consists of showing subordinates how they can reach their goals.

Social interaction theories focus on the relationship between the leader and the followers. Leader-member exchange theory, also known as vertical dyad linkage, is based on the quality of the social interaction between a leader and a subordinate. According to this approach, effective leadership is the product of a manager's understanding of how much autonomy to give an individual worker.

Charismatic and transformational leadership suggest that workers are motivated to follow a leader because of the attractiveness of the leader's personal qualities. Attribution, another social interaction theory, holds that leader behavior is seen as relatively unimportant. The real value of the leader is as a symbol of the social order.

Key Words and Concepts

attributional approaches to
    leadership (p. 304)
charismatic leadership (p. 301)
charismatic power (p. 280)
coercive power (p. 279)
consideration (p. 286)
contingency model of leadership
    (p. 288)
expert power (p. 280)
information power (p. 280)
Ingroup (p. 298)
initiating structure (p. 287)
leader-member exchange (LMX)
    (p. 297)
leadership effectiveness (p. 273)
leadership emergence (p. 273)
legitimate power (p. 279)
mentoring (p. 278)
need for power (p. 297)
Ohio State studies (p. 286)

Outgroup (p. 299)
ownership power (p. 280)
path-goal theory (p. 293)
personal power (p. 279)
persuasive power (p. 280)
position power (p. 279)
prestige power (p. 280)
referent power (p. 280)
reinforcement theory (p. 289)
reward power (p. 279)
self-monitoring (p. 275)
situational leadership (p. 289)
trait theories (p. 281)
transactional leadership (p. 302)
transformational leadership
    (p. 302)
vertical dyad linkage (VDL)
    (p. 297)
Vroom-Yetton decision-making
    model (p. 292)

Questions for Discussion

1. Whom do you consider a great leader? Why? Who has been a disappointing leader? Why?
2. What is the difference between leadership emergence and effectiveness?
3. What is the difference between leadership and management? What were some of the experiences leaders reported in rising to a leadership position?
4. Based on the studies reported in this chapter, which qualities and experiences are likely to create leaders?
5. What is power? What are the different kinds of power? When you want to influence someone, which type of power are you most likely to use? Which would be hardest for you to use?
6. What is the basic idea behind need theory approaches to leadership? What are the approaches' shortcomings?
7. What is the basic idea behind behavioral approaches? Which of the behavioral approaches seems most plausible to you?
8. Do you think the Vroom-Yetton model is really a theory of leadership? Do you think it would be effective in a work environment?
9. What is path-goal theory?
10. What is the basic idea behind social interaction approaches to leadership? Which of these approaches seems most plausible to you?
11. Of all the leadership theories mentioned in this chapter, which seems most plausible overall? Which kind of leadership would you practice, given the chance?

CHAPTER 10

Group Behavior in the Workplace

Studying Group Behavior

Types of Groups

Characteristics of Groups

Decision Making in Groups

Interpersonal Skills Groups

Employee Involvement Programs

Chapter Summary

Key Words and Concepts

Questions for Discussion

Since ancient times people have recognized that individuals change their behaviors when they join others in groups. Peaceful citizens who go to football games, teenagers who attend rock concerts, and young men who are sent into combat are examples of people who do things as a group that they probably would not do by themselves. Sociologists such as Emile Durkheim went so far as to suggest that a "group mind" arises out of social interaction, and that explaining individual behavior without considering the group is likely to be unsuccessful.

Even though such an astute observer as Freud had argued that group behavior differs from individual behavior, many psychologists strongly resisted Durkheim's notions. The social psychologist Floyd Allport, for example, argued that groups could not be the basic unit for studying human behavior, since only individuals are "real" (Allport, 1924).

By the 1930s, however, many psychologists had become convinced that groups are a legitimate area of study. For example, the Hawthorne research, and the bank wiring assembly study in particular (both discussed in Chapter 1), demonstrated that individual productivity was influenced by group norms. Although no researcher would dispute the importance of individual behavior in the workplace, today we recognize that group behavior is more than simply the sum of its parts. Industrial and organizational psychologists are particularly interested in what makes a group productive, how members make decisions, and who gains power in a group. This chapter provides an overview of current methods and research in group behavior, particularly as it applies to the workplace.

Studying Group Behavior

Groups are like communication: they are so pervasive that sometimes it is difficult to identify exactly what to study. Groups form along the lines of friendship, profession, proximity, race, gender, religion, or virtually any other category. They can consist of just a few people or of thousands.

Because of this, the researcher's first task is to identify the boundaries of the group to be studied. For example, a researcher may want to look at interpersonal relationships in an accounting department, or at the relationship between the accounting department and the marketing department. Typical approaches to studying groups are experiments, observations, sociometry, and case studies.

Experimental Approach Laboratory experiments have historically been the most common approach to studying groups, and a great deal of insight into human behavior has been developed through that method. As you may recall from Chapter 2, however, experimental research has some drawbacks. Specifically, we cannot be certain whether relationships among recruited participants resemble those of people who choose to belong to a group; we may wonder if the laboratory setting is affecting behavior; and there may be questions about generalizing the results from one small study to a large population. Regrettably, only a very small percentage of small-group studies has been done with real groups in real-life settings (Guzzo & Shea, 1992).

Two ways to make experimental results more certain, however, are to deal with intact groups—i.e., not recruited subjects—in the laboratory, or to do field experiments with intact groups. When intact groups are introduced into a laboratory setting, the researcher can control the environment, and existing relationships among group members are maintained.

Many industrial and organizational psychologists use field experiments in group research. Starting with an intact group in its naturalistic setting, the researcher introduces a change into the work environment, then records behavioral or attitudinal changes. The introduction of a female worker into an all-male group, for example, and the subsequent measure of changes in worker performance is an example of a field experiment (actually, this example would be a quasi-experiment). The researcher's findings have the advantage of being derived from actual behavior in the workplace but, as with all field experiments, a lack of control may undermine certainty about findings.

One problem that may occur when introducing experimental change to intact groups is disrupting the workplace. As a general rule, workers respond negatively to changes in the social environment, and changes that result from an experiment may be seen by management as undesirable. Additionally, experimental treatments introduced into a worksite typically must have a small impact. Managers are understandably hesitant to approve procedures that may result in changes in the work environment or in performance.

Observations Many social scientists use observation to study groups. For example, a researcher may join a group to study patterns of interaction, decision-making processes, or power relationships. In most cases, the observer does not intervene in the process, but simply keeps records about the way the group operates. At a later date, the researcher studies the data and makes conclusions about group functioning.

As suggested in Chapter 2, using this method successfully requires great skill on the part of the researcher. Although observation is likely to provide large amounts of data, the researcher must make every attempt to avoid bias in data collection. An additional consideration about observation is that without experimental control, the researcher can never be certain that data collected about one group can be generalized to others.

A third consideration about observation is that not everyone can do it well. Specifically, performing observational studies without a firm foundation in the theoretical aspects of group behavior may result in misleading conclusions.

Sociometry Sociometry is a technique developed by Moreno (1934) to determine the relationships among members of a group. Using this approach, individuals are asked to identify members with whom they would most and least like to work. Members are then rated as to their popularity with their coworkers.

From this measure, a map of the "psychological space" among group members can be drawn. In sociometry terms, popular workers are known as **stars.** **Isolates** are workers who are not particularly liked, and **pairs** are two people who have a reciprocal relationship. **Cliques** are groups of workers who like each other. Moreno believed that groups function more effectively if members are allowed to form their own structures rather than relying on an externally imposed framework. Figure 10.1 shows an example of the psychological space between members.

Case Studies Case studies focus on one group in depth; the researcher may observe the group function, interview members, or ask nonmembers about the group. The rationale behind the case study is that conclusions about one group can be generalized to others.

Recall from Chapter 2 that the advantages of a case study chiefly concern the scope of the information gathered. That is, a case study, like observation, provides more information about a group than other methods of study. In addition, case studies generally do not disrupt the workplace, and they are relatively easy to accomplish.

On the other hand, case studies focus on one group, and the researcher must always be aware that the group may be unusual and that findings from the case study may not apply to other groups. In addition, the researcher must be

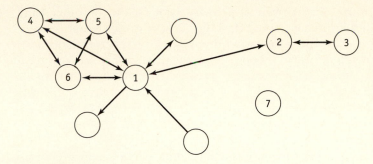

Worker 1: Star
Workers 2, 3: Pair
Workers 1, 4, 5, 6: Clique
Worker 7: Isolate

Figure 10.1 Sociometry of a Work Group

careful about his or her own biases. If, for example, the researcher believes participative decision making is the best way to organize a group, then the researcher is likely to find evidence supporting that view.

Finally, case studies do not yield information about causality. They may be rich in detail and make fascinating and insightful reading, but researchers must be cautious about the conclusions they draw from such studies.

Types of Groups

In U.S. society it is virtually impossible to avoid being a member of some group. People consider themselves citizens of a country, identify with ethnic minorities or religious groups, belong to professional associations, play on softball teams, associate with a circle of friends, and belong to extended and immediate families. At any given moment, some of these groups are more influential than others, and people usually adapt their behavior to fit the standards of the group with which they are identifying at that time.

Primary and Secondary
   Groups
Reference and Designated
   Groups

Primary and Secondary Groups

In the organizational setting and elsewhere, groups can be defined in terms of their structure. **Formal groups,** also known as **secondary groups,** appear on organizational charts and have their tasks and leaders chosen by higher management. These groups have specific rules of operation, and behavior is generally impersonal and unspontaneous.

Informal groups, also known as **primary groups,** on the other hand, typically arise outside organizational structure. These groups may use commonality of task as a basis for formation, but many other factors can lead to the establishment of informal groups. Informal groups may be organized along the lines of ethnic background, car-pool or day-care arrangements, organizational experience, or friendships. Primary groups are characterized by informality, shared values, and a concern for mutual friendship or welfare. Communication tends to be much faster in the informal or primary group than in formal groups.

Whereas a task is usually the basis for formation of the secondary group, friendship is more important for primary-group formation. Since research demonstrates that proximity, rather than shared values or personality, is the major determinant of friendship (Festinger, Schachter, & Back, 1950), it is not surprising that employees who work in the same area and who interact frequently are likely to form primary groups. Primary groups can affect productivity. For example, one study of coal miners found that groups of workers who knew each other better were more productive than workers who were unfamiliar with each other (Goodman & Leyden, 1991).

Although primary or informal groups do not appear on the organizational chart, they can have a powerful influence on organizational culture, employee morale, and worker productivity. In the bank wiring room and the Ahmedabad textile mills, discussed in Chapter 1, productivity was affected by group norms. Additionally, the dynamics of groups in the workplace also affect leadership effectiveness—a fact that many leadership theorists seem to ignore.

In recent years, industrial and organizational psychologists have become more interested in studying the effect of personality on work performance. One area of interest, extending from the organizational culture literature (discussed in Chapter 12), is how groups both reflect and influence the personalities of their members. According to the **attraction-selection-attrition (ASA) model** of organization (Schneider, 1987), individuals are attracted to certain kinds of organizations on the basis of personality factors. If their personalities resemble those of the organization's members they are more likely to be hired; if, after being hired, they find they do not fit, they will leave the organization. For this reason, members of specific organizations seem to have many qualities in common.

George (1990; George & James, 1993) looked at two personality qualities—positive and negative affectivity—among employees of a large department store in the northeastern United States. People with positive affectivity have a positive sense of well-being, generally enjoy what they are doing, and are usually in a good mood. Negative affectivity, on the other hand, refers to a tendency to feel nervous, tense, anxious, worried, and upset.

The department store employees, who belonged to 26 different work groups, completed personality and customer service behavior measures; in addition, the researcher collected absence data on the employees. Overall, the researcher found that people with similar personalities did belong to the same groups. In groups with a higher percentage of people with negative affectivity, members engaged in fewer positive acts of customer service. In groups with a higher level of positive affectivity, members were absent less frequently.

Reference and Designated Groups

Sometimes the behavior of an individual is not necessarily appropriate for the group with which the individual is associating, but is influenced by an abstraction referred to as a **reference group** (Hyman, 1942; Kelley, 1952). A reference group is a group with which an individual makes social comparisons. When people want to evaluate their economic well-being or status in the community, they are likely to think of the norms of groups with which they identify. Similarly, when confronted with an unfamiliar situation, a person may rely on a reference group for guidance as to how to behave. Although most people belong to many groups, only a few of these are used as reference groups.

For example, just as students think of what other students are wearing when buying clothes, executives also select their clothes on the basis of their own reference group—other executives. Religious people often consider what their religious organization teaches when confronted with a difficult situation; members of a work group may consider how their coworkers would respond when management asks them to do something out of the ordinary.

Reference groups are important because they can affect behavior in the workplace. For example, women typically receive lower salaries than men, yet their job dissatisfaction is not greater. One explanation for this is that most women use other women as a reference group when deciding about pay satisfaction (Major & Testa, 1989). One study (Crosby, 1982), in fact, found that women who were dissatisfied with their salaries used men, rather than women, as a reference group.

Some theorists (e.g., Levine & Moreland, 1987) have addressed the question of how workers choose reference groups. Basically, these theories argue that people choose reference groups on the basis of availability of knowledge about the group and the group's attractiveness. Other factors that affect reference choice are gender, race, position in the organization, and physical proximity (Kulik & Ambrose, 1992).

Another factor that apparently affects identification with a reference group is its perceived success or failure at accomplishing its goal. For example, Cialdini and colleagues (1976) found that when college football teams win, students are more likely to describe the game in terms of "we," but when they lose, students describe the game using "they." In a study of student union employees at a midwestern university, Riggs and Knight (1994) found that perceptions of group success affected beliefs about personal ability, the ability of one's group, job satisfaction, and organizational commitment.

Designated groups consist of people who are treated in a homogeneous fashion by others (Cartwright & Zander, 1968). In contrast with the reference group, in which identification is based on the individual, designated groups result from the attributions of others. For example, a supervisor may be a member of the designated group "management," even though, for the supervisor, management is not a significant reference group. Typical designated groups that—depending on the individual—may or may not be reference groups are top executives and blue-collar workers. Some characteristics of these designated groups are discussed in Chapter 11.

Formation of the Group
Task Versus Process
Deindividuation
Norms and Deviance
Group Cohesion and Social
   Support
Resolving Conflict in the
   Workplace

Characteristics of Groups

As suggested in previous chapters, people seem to have a biological need to congregate in groups. Humans, like other primates, are born in groups and depend on their group for survival. There are several characteristics and processes relevant to the study of groups. Some of these include the formation of the group, task versus process, deindividuation, the establishment of norms and the handling of deviance, the effects of group cohesion, and conflict resolution. These issues are discussed below.

Formation of the Group

When people come together in groups that have a formal purpose (i.e., secondary groups) there is usually a period in which patterns of interaction are established. As the group develops, two issues are confronted: the actual problem to be solved or issue to be addressed, and relations among members of the group (Bales, 1955; Bennis & Shepard, 1956). The question of relations among members forms an underlying agenda for group meetings and typically remains unresolved for a number of meetings.

One of the best-known models for understanding group process (Tuckman, 1965) suggests that all groups pass through four stages: forming, storming, norming, and performing. During the **forming stage,** members confront the issue of status since, in the first meetings of a group, status is likely to be unclear. For example, although most groups have a leader, real power may lie in other members. During the first stage of group formation, personal conversation and social interaction are usually limited as members focus mostly on the task to be accomplished.

As the group moves into the **storming stage,** some negative behavior occurs as members begin to establish positions of status and leadership. More objections to the ideas of others are voiced, and hostile exchanges may take place.

Certain individuals begin to establish themselves as leaders of the group, while other assertive members challenge their leadership. The storming stage lasts until the status hierarchy is relatively established.

Once the status of each member is determined, the group enters the **norming stage.** At this point, the group sets standards for behavior and develops ways of working together. Finally, the group moves toward **performing**—addressing the problem to be solved or task to be accomplished. As the group moves from the forming to the performing stage, the amount of purely informational communication declines and communication for social purposes increases. Interestingly, the more strongly members believe they will succeed at their task, the more likely it is they will be successful (Shea & Guzzo, 1987).

After they feel their task has been accomplished, members engage in considerably more social interaction than previously. In an update of the group performance literature (Tuckman & Jensen, 1977), Tuckman added a final stage—**adjourning.**

Although Tuckman's stages have influenced a great deal of small-group research, some researchers have suggested that they are not necessarily applicable to organizational groups. In other words, groups in organizations can form quickly and accomplish a task without passing through the five stages (Ginnett, 1990). For example, in a study of group effectiveness over time, Gersick (1988, 1989) developed an alternative model—referred to as *punctuated equilibrium*—of group process. After following eight groups over several months, Gersick identified three distinct phases of group development.

The first phase lasted exactly half the amount of time the group had to finish its task. During this period, group members were lethargic and lackadaisical about accomplishing their task. The next stage was characterized by a burst of activity, in which the group dropped old patterns, interacted more with people outside the group, took new perspectives on the task, and made dramatic progress. After this transition period, the group retreated into its state of inertia. The inertia continued as the group finished its task, but there was a sudden acceleration of activity at the last group meeting. Interestingly, Gersick found this exact pattern in groups with life spans ranging from seven days to six months.

Who becomes the leader of a group? Although considerable evidence suggests that individuals who talk the most are likely to be identified as leaders (Zander, 1979), expertise can be another important factor. In a study of "air time" versus expertise, Bottger (1984) found that group members who establish their credentials as experts were likely to be more influential than those who simply talk a lot. Nonetheless, a recent study (Barry & Stewart, 1997) found that extraverts affected group outcomes more than introverts.

By definition, the establishment of informal groups is much less structured. People who interact frequently often develop an identification with each other over time. As certain members leave the group, other members are likely to join. Although informal groups generally do not have formal leadership, issues of power and status are just as likely to affect interpersonal relations as in secondary groups.

Task Versus Process

Historically, group behavior has been studied in terms of two domains: task and process. Task variables focus on environmental factors such as group size or structure that affect performance. Process variables involve relations between group members. Most group researchers recognize the importance of both task and process. An effective group, for example, must have the expertise to solve a problem, but expertise alone cannot solve a problem unless members can work together effectively. In a typical model of group effectiveness (Prussia & Kinicki, 1996), for example, success at task performance is the result of group goals, the group's feelings of collective efficacy, and each member's feelings about his or her experiences.

One way of understanding the difference between task and process is through the concept of cues. *Task cues* include behaviors that imply ability, such as verbal fluency or a rapid rate of speech. *Dominance cues* imply control and include behaviors such as pointing or speaking loudly. Some evidence (Driskell, Olmstead, & Salas, 1993; Ridgeway & Diekema, 1989) suggests that others regard people who display task cues as more competent and they become more influential than people who rely on dominance cues.

Interestingly, women are generally seen as less effective than men in task-centered groups. In mixed groups, women are less active and influential, are interrupted more often, and are chosen as leaders less frequently than men (Ridgeway, 1988). Along the same lines, some research (Watson, 1988) suggests that female managers who use a dominant management style are more likely to be resisted than those who use a less dominant style.

Driskell, Olmstead, and Salas (1993) looked at the relationship among gender, task and dominance cues, and influence in task groups. For both males and females, task cues were more effective than dominance cues. That is, individuals who used task rather than dominance cues were more influential than those who relied on dominance cues.

In another study, Campion, Papper, and Medsker (1996) looked at work team characteristics and their relationship to effectiveness. Working with 357 employees, 93 managers, and the records of 60 teams in a financial services organization, Campion and his associates were interested in identifying predictors of satisfaction, employee and manager judgments about team effectiveness, and performance appraisal data. In this particular study, process variables, such as a belief in their effectiveness, social support, sharing of work, and good communication and cooperation, were most strongly related to team effectiveness.

Deindividuation

This chapter began by observing that group membership seems to change behavior. Why is it that individuals act differently when they are in groups? Social psychologists have argued that individuals in groups experience a phenomenon known as deindividuation (Festinger, Pepitone, & Newcomb, 1952). **Deindividuation** is a process by which some of the values and behaviors of individuals are modified to comply with the norms or standards of the group. That is, to have positive social interaction, members behave in ways that are acceptable or pleasing to others in the group.

Diffusion of responsibility is a quality related to deindividuation. Because several people are engaged in a task, individual members of the group are likely to feel less responsible for outcomes. Along the same lines, some group members may try to avoid responsibility and allow others to do the work of the group, a practice mentioned in Chapter 7 and known as *social loafing* (Latané, Williams, & Harkins, 1979).

Social loafing can occur when individuals are not interested in the group task, individual contributions to group outcomes are less identifiable, or workers feel the group can succeed without their input. In a study of social loafing in groups of salespeople, one researcher (George, 1992) found that task visibility—the likelihood the supervisor was going to know each worker's input—was the best predictor of social loafing. In a related study, Wagner (1995) found that small group size, high identifiability, and low shared responsibility were associated with greater cooperation between group members.

The effects of deindividuation can be either positive or negative. When group members compromise to accomplish a goal or to facilitate social interaction, the effects of deindividuation are likely to be positive. On the other hand, when deindividuation leads to avoiding responsibility—such as participation in a riot—its effects can be negative.

Norms and Deviance

One of the defining characteristics of both formal and informal groups is **norms,** which are standards and shared expectations that provide a range of acceptable behavior for group members. In formal groups, norms are usually delineated and known to their members. To become a member of the Mafia, for example, applicants had to swear to maintain secrecy about the organization and avoid romantic liaisons with other members' wives.

Norms for informal groups, on the other hand, are often unstated or unrecognized and are usually taken more seriously than those of the formal group (Hare, 1976). Typical unstated norms for work groups include not beginning to work early, not working while others are relaxing, and not doing such a good job that coworkers look bad. These kinds of unstated norms can have an important effect on behavior. One study (Rafaeli, Lutton, Harquail, & Mackie-Lewis, 1997), for example, found that female employees felt less stress when dressed "appropriately" rather than comfortably.

How do newcomers learn about the norms of an organization? Three researchers (Louis, Posner, & Powell, 1983) surveyed personnel officials, placement officers, and recent hires to obtain a list of common socialization experiences. Some of the experiences mentioned most often were the following:

- Formal onsite orientation;
- Information from other employees;
- A friendly relationship with a senior executive or mentor;
- Information from an immediate supervisor or support staff;
- Daily interactions with peers;
- Social and recreational activities with coworkers; and
- Business travel with coworkers.

In a second survey, of recently hired business school graduates, the researchers found that a friendly relationship with a senior executive, information from an immediate supervisor, and daily interactions with peers were the most useful ways of learning about the standards and norms of the organization.

In both formal and informal groups, norms serve a variety of useful functions. As in the example just cited, they provide guidelines for unsocialized individuals to fit into the ongoing group. Norms also provide standards for behavior that facilitate interaction among members and a means of identifying with one's peers. Norms are pervasive in groups, and they can often be quite subtle. For example, in many companies mode of dress is an important means of communicating the organizational level to which one belongs.

In most groups, however, there are individuals who reject group norms and behave independently. In the language of social science, these individuals are known as **deviants.** Typical examples of deviance that affect group behavior include being the only woman or minority in a work group, disregarding group norms about productivity, or refusing to participate in group activities, such as eating lunch together or socializing outside work. Strictly speaking, being deviant does not necessarily have a negative connotation—it simply means being different or behaving differently from other members of the group.

Groups, like society in general, are often intolerant of people who fail to live up to their standards or who do not behave in accordance with the norms of the group. "Scabs," for example, is the term used by union members for employees who continue to work during a strike. In highly structured authoritarian groups such as the military, deviance is taken seriously and almost certainly leads to ostracism or punishment. On the other hand, in less structured groups, such as a university faculty, deviance is more likely to be tolerated. Depending on the seriousness of the violation, members of informal groups can be lenient

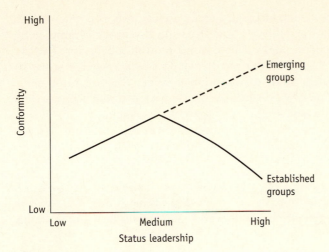

Source: Crosbie, P. V. (1975). *Interaction in Small Groups.* New York: Macmillan. Used by permission.

Figure 10.2 Group Status and Conformity
Groups that have low status tend to be low in conformity, and groups with medium status are the most conforming. Groups that are emerging as high status will also be high in conformity, but high-status groups that have been established for some time will be the least conforming.

or punishing. In the bank wiring room study discussed in Chapter 1, for example, employees who exceeded group norms for production were "binged," or hit forcefully on the arm.

With regard to norms, it is important to recognize that all groups have them and that individual violation of norms may lead to rejection by the group. The revolutionary who argues that the existing order is not so bad, for example, is as likely to feel the disapproval of his or her group as is the church member who advocates sexual promiscuity.

Crosbie (1975) has suggested an interesting relationship among status, conformity, and deviance. In both established and emerging groups, members who hold moderate status tend to be quite conforming, in contrast with low-status members, who tend to be quite deviant. In emerging groups, high-status members are the most conforming, but in established groups, high-status members are likely to be deviant. These relationships are illustrated in Figure 10.2.

Homans (1974) has suggested that although leaders have some latitude in deviating from unimportant norms, conformity to important norms must not be violated. Another explanation for the deviance among leaders is that they acquire **idiosyncrasy credits:** If members are accepted by other members, some deviance will be tolerated (Hollander, 1958).

As with group norms, deviance also serves useful purposes. The deviant demonstrates alternatives to established standards and also provides a means for group members to experience and evaluate nonconforming behavior. Particularly in science, deviance is often the route by which new knowledge is discovered or introduced. In their study of what they consider the best-run companies in America, Peters and Waterman (1982) suggested that a tolerance for deviance is an important characteristic of effective management.

In a review of the literature on group influences in organizations, one researcher (Hackman, 1992) identified five conditions in which deviant members will have the greatest impact on the majority.

1. The minority members offer an alternative to the majority position that is clear and unambiguous. By taking a position that differs sharply from the majority viewpoint, deviants force members to confront, rather than simply assimilate, other positions.

2. Minority members maintain their position consistently over time. Deviants who offer erratic and changing positions are usually ineffective. However, if a member agrees with the majority initially but later changes position, that member is likely to be even more influential.

3. Minority members stay together and present a united front to the rest of the group. Deviants who act without any support are likely to be ineffective; becoming influential requires the support of at least one other member.

4. Minority members succeed in avoiding rejection or institutionalization as the "group deviants." When dissenters from the group opinion take on the role of deviant (i.e., they are believed to be disagreeing for the sake of disagreeing), they are likely to be ignored by other group members.

5. The position advocated by the minority is consistent with dominant cultural values. Minorities will have greater influence when their positions fit with the dominant culture. That is, other group members will be more likely to be persuaded if the deviants advocate a position that is in keeping with the values and beliefs of the members who are in agreement.

Group Cohesion and Social Support

Group cohesion is one of the most studied topics in the behavioral sciences. Specifically, researchers are interested in why group members stick together or separate, as well as the effects of group cohesion on job satisfaction and productivity. Research suggests that the degree of group cohesion is affected by size (smaller groups are more cohesive), member homogeneity, stability of membership, the difficulty of entry (a long period of waiting before acceptance creates greater cohesiveness), and agreement about the relative status of each member (Wexley & Yukl, 1984).

Several studies have suggested that members of cohesive groups have higher job satisfaction and lower absenteeism and turnover. In a study of cohesion among members of basketball teams, for example, Peterson and Martens (1973) found that more cohesive teams had more interaction among members, evidenced more friendly and cooperative behavior, and were more satisfied with the group. In a meta-analysis of studies of group performance and cohesion, Evans and Dion (1991) found a strongly positive relationship.

Nonetheless, findings from research regarding productivity and cohesion are not completely clear. In laboratory studies, where most group research has taken place, cohesive groups are no more productive than noncohesive groups. On the other hand, evidence from field studies—those done in the workplace—suggest that higher levels of group cohesion do result in higher productivity (Shaw, 1976). In a study of cohesiveness and performance among research and development project groups (Keller, 1986), for example, highly cohesive teams produced higher quality work and met budget and schedule goals more effectively than less cohesive teams.

Some research (Hackman, 1992) suggests that when workers support company policies, cohesiveness raises productivity, but when workers are opposed, cohesion lowers productivity. Regardless of the scientific evidence, however, leaders such as military officers, coaches, and managers clearly regard group cohesion as important to success.

Cohesiveness is also affected by the attractiveness of individual group members. Although members are likely to communicate more with people they like, this pattern of interaction changes when the group is threatened. At that time, deviant members of the group receive more communication than conforming members (Nixon, 1979). In a study of social networks and conflicts, one researcher (Nelson, 1989) found that when different work units had frequent contact, conflict between them was lower. On the other hand, conflict was greater in organizations in which cohesive units had little external contact.

One quality of a cohesive group is that it offers social support to its members. As you may recall from Chapter 9, some researchers have been interested in the effect of social support on job performance and satisfaction. **Social support** is information that leads a person to believe he or she is valued by others in the organization (Cobb, 1976). In a study of feelings of social support among police officers and civilian radio dispatchers, Kirmeyer and Lin (1987) found that workers who interacted most frequently with their supervisors—about both work and nonwork matters—felt the most social support.

Resolving Conflict in the Workplace

In recent years, I/O researchers have begun to pay more attention to ways of resolving conflict in the workplace. Historically, managers have had authority to resolve disputes, but with greater latitude in decision making being given to groups, ways of handling conflict are not as clear as they once were. In addition, when individuals have tasks that are interdependent—as frequently occurs in groups—the potential for conflict increases (Saavedra, Earley, & Van Dyne, 1993).

Managers expend a surprising amount of effort—up to 20 percent of their time (Thomas, 1976)—resolving disputes. In general, conflicts are resolved in one of three ways: *forcing,* which involves dictating a resolution; *problem solving,* in which conflicting parties work together to resolve the difference; and *accommodating,* which usually refers to capitulation by one side of the disputing parties (van de Vliert, Euwema, & Huismans, 1995).

Not surprisingly, most researchers find problem solving to be a better strategy than forcing. In addition, when managers are concerned about morale, they are more likely to use a strategy of problem solving that involves giving disputants control over the situation than to rely on forcing a resolution (Pinkley, Brittain, Neale, & Northcraft, 1995).

One group of researchers (Weingart, Bennett, & Brett, 1993) looked at the role of individualism versus cooperation in group negotiations. In that simulation, MBA students were assigned to teams representing a grocery store, a liquor store, a florist, or a bakery and asked to consider opening a market together. Issues to be addressed included the temperature in the proposed market, procedures for hiring clerks, maintenance policies, advertising, and so forth.

The researchers were interested in whether groups addressed all the issues simultaneously or in sequence and whether the groups approached the problem from a cooperative or an individualistic stance. Interestingly, results from the study found that groups that considered the issues simultaneously and from a cooperative viewpoint made higher-quality decisions than other groups. Also, the least successful groups approached the problem from an individualistic and sequential perspective. Another study (Conlon & Ross, 1993) found that disputing parties resolved their disputes more quickly when they knew a third party was likely to impose a solution.

Finally, one study (Amason, 1996) looked at functional and dysfunctional conflict between management groups. Although conflict prevents consensus, many researchers believe some conflict in which a variety of viewpoints is presented is important for high-quality decisions. Working with management teams in the food processing and furniture manufacturing industries, Amason asked participants to describe a strategic decision and the process leading up to that decision. Interestingly, when the conflict was task-oriented and focused on the best way to achieve results—that is, a functional conflict—the conflict improved the quality of the decision. When the conflict was emotional—or dysfunctional—however, decision quality suffered. Amason concluded that managers should encourage conflict based on how to achieve a goal and discourage conflict based on emotions.

Decision Making in Groups

Group Decisions
Group Polarization
Groupthink
Delphi Method

In the 1980s, many employers moved to implement a team approach to decision making. This was an important step away from organizing work around individuals and focusing instead on larger units within the workplace. This change generated a great deal of research and our knowledge of how teams in the workplace operate is much greater than it was even a few years ago.

Most of the team research has focused on decision making. Remember that participation in decision making is a key element of sociotechnical systems (Chapter 2) and other areas of industrial and organizational psychology. Advocates of participative decision making believe workers will be more satisfied and more productive if they are allowed input as to how their jobs are structured and how work is performed. Despite the widespread movement toward involving workers more actively in decision making, evidence about the quality of group decisions is mixed. Some aspects of group decision making are discussed below.

Group Decisions

Decisions made by a group offer several advantages to employers. When large amounts of information need to be analyzed, groups are often more efficient than individuals. Most workplace groups have *distributed expertise,* with different members of the group having specialized knowledge about different aspects of the matters to be decided (Hollenbeck, Ilgen, Sego, Hedlund, Major, & Phillips, 1995). In addition, **subject matter experts (SMEs)** can contribute information not available to everyone that may save time and improve the quality of the decision.

Another advantage of group decisions is that involving workers in decision making is likely to make them more committed to the course of action decided on. In general, groups arrive at consensus or compromise positions that are more acceptable than if the decision were simply imposed by management. The group setting also offers opportunities to test decisions before implementing them. When an individual offers a solution to a problem, other members can identify potential problems and raise objections.

However, there are also disadvantages to the group decision-making process. Stopping work to hold discussions can seriously affect productivity. In addition, meetings are one of the most time-consuming activities of managers, and problem solving in groups may require more time than the workers can spare.

Although the broadening of viewpoints and sharing of knowledge likely to occur in a meeting may be advantageous, psychological research suggests there are limitations on the effectiveness of group problem solving. For example, groups, like individuals, are usually overconfident about the accuracy of their judgments (Plous, 1995). In addition, a single well-qualified decision maker will perform better than a group of decision makers (Wheeler & Janis, 1980). Making a group decision is actually a two-step process: The correct solution must be identified, and then it must be accepted by group members. Those who support a decision must be able to persuade group members to see their viewpoint (Laughlin, 1980; Laughlin & Adamopoulos, 1980).

Only when no one group member is clearly more competent than the others will group decisions be better than individual decisions. Additionally, some evidence suggests participative decision making results in more communication, but the quality of communication is not necessarily enhanced (Harrison, 1985).

When do groups make higher-quality decisions than individuals? Following 222 teams of organizational behavior students over a five-year period, Michaelsen, Watson, and Black (1989) found that 210 of the teams outperformed their best member on a decision-making task. Results of this study were further tested (Watson, Michaelsen, & Sharp, 1991) by measuring the quality of decision making in 50 different groups over time. Results from the second study showed that the importance of the contributions of the best member decreased as time passed, and that groups become more efficient at using everyone's knowledge the longer they worked together. These findings suggest that individuals are more likely to outperform the group if the group meets only once or twice, but that groups are more effective than individuals over longer periods. The researchers concluded that since workplace groups usually remain intact for longer periods, group decision making is likely to be more effective than individual decision making.

Another consideration regarding the quality of group decision making is the resources group members bring to the task. Although some researchers (Bottger & Yetton, 1987) have suggested that training in problem solving will enhance performance, others (Ganster, Williams, & Poppler, 1991) have suggested this is not necessarily the case. For example, participants working on a task in which they had to rank the importance of ten items of equipment for surviving a crash on the moon received training about factors that limit the quality of solutions to problems; however, they did not do better on the task than a group that had not been exposed to the training. The researchers concluded that the resources individuals bring to a group task do affect performance, but that training in problem solving is not all that useful.

Sometimes the quality of leadership can affect group decision making. Many times a problem requires a creative solution, but innovation is discouraged either by a fear of unfavorable responses from other group members or the leader, or by a simple willingness to conform to the leader's proposed solution.

In one study, four groups were presented with a problem and asked to come up with a solution. Results showed that the least creative solutions came from a management group, better solutions came from business students, but the best solutions came from students in an industrial psychology course (Maier

& Hoffman, 1961). The researchers concluded that the farther the problem solvers were removed from the situation, the better their solution, and that leaders have an important role in encouraging creativity in problem solving.

Other factors affecting the quality of group decisions are the relative status of members, group size, and member homogeneity. High-status members communicate more with other high-status members than they do with lower, and lower-status members also communicate with higher status more than with lower (Patten & Giffen, 1973). In large groups feedback is diminished, and assertive individuals may dominate the decision-making process. On the other hand, larger groups appear to be better for creative decision making (Gallupe, Dennis, Cooper, Valacich, Bastianutti, & Nunamaker, 1992).

In an interesting laboratory study of face-to-face decision making versus decision making by computer, Straus and McGrath (1994) hypothesized that tasks requiring more coordination between members would be performed more successfully through social interaction. Tasks requiring low coordination, on the other hand, were hypothesized to be performed more successfully by computer. Undergraduate psychology students performed decision-making tasks under both conditions. Results from the study showed little difference in the quality of decisions in either condition, but groups in which people worked face-to-face were more productive than the computer groups.

Finally, some evidence suggests that groups composed of members with different personalities perform better than groups whose members are similar. When members are dissimilar, solutions and decisions are more creative and of a higher quality (Guzzo, 1986).

Group Polarization

During the 1960s, social psychologists became aware of a phenomenon related to group decision making that was termed the **risky shift.** The risky shift phenomenon suggests that when individuals make decisions in groups, they often make riskier decisions than when deciding alone (Lamm & Myers, 1978). Although a substantial body of research confirms the existence of the risky shift, other factors that affect risk taking in decision making are the possibilities of gain or loss, past performance levels, and goals.

At the same time the risky shift was being investigated, some researchers also found evidence of a **cautious shift.** That is, certain groups recommended a more cautious plan of action than one that individual members had suggested. Risky and cautious shifts were explained by Myers and Lamm (1976) as being part of a **group polarization** process. According to these researchers, if individuals favor riskier actions before performing as a group, then the group as a whole will recommend a risky course. On the other hand, if individuals favor caution before they assemble as a group, then the group is likely to experience a cautious shift.

Although most decision-making theories assume people generally avoid risk, **prospect theory** (Kahneman & Tversky, 1979) suggests that people's tolerance of risk depends on possible outcomes. In other words, when people are confronted with a choice between losses, they are more likely to reach a risky decision. On the other hand, when people must choose between possible gains, they tend to be more risk averse. Prospect theory offers a possible explanation for why groups that have chosen a losing strategy often continue that strategy even as costs mount (Whyte, 1989).

One significance of group polarization is that members of groups often ignore evidence that challenges the positions they already hold, and they tend to make their positions even more extreme. An example of group polarization is the process known as groupthink.

Groupthink

Groupthink (Janis, 1972) refers to a situation in which the social concerns of a group outweigh concerns about the quality of a decision. That is, members choose to maintain the harmony of the group rather than express doubts about a course of action. The most famous example of groupthink was the decision to invade Cuba at the Bay of Pigs in 1961. After the failure of the invasion, President Kennedy ordered a review of the decision-making process to avoid such serious errors in judgment in the future.

Members of the group planning the invasion had developed such a high level of cohesion that dissension among members was suppressed. Expressing reservations about the plans was seen as being disloyal, and in a famous anecdote related by Arthur Schlesinger, Attorney General Robert Kennedy took Schlesinger aside at Mrs. Kennedy's birthday party and reproached him for his negative attitude toward the invasion. Although certain aspects of the plan were clearly unrealistic—for example, the notion that if the invasion failed, the surviving invaders would cross a swamp 20 miles wide and continue a guerilla movement from the mountains as Castro had—objections were seen as being unhelpful to the functioning of the group. In this case, quality of decision was sacrificed to maintain cohesion.

There are eight main characteristics of groupthink (Janis, 1982):

1. Group members have the illusion of invulnerability (i.e., they think they are incapable of making a poor decision).
2. Members feel they are acting on behalf of a higher moral purpose.
3. Members rationalize all their actions.
4. Members hold stereotyped views of people outside the group.
5. Members practice self-censorship (i.e., they do not say things that might threaten the cohesion of the group).
6. Members have the illusion of unanimity.
7. Members pressure dissidents to conform.

8. Members rely on others to help keep everyone in agreement. The cost of maintaining cohesiveness, however, is a loss of efficiency, reality testing, moral judgment, and decision-making quality.

Although groupthink can occur in any group, there are some precautions that can make groupthink less likely. Some of these include having all decisions made individually, then holding group meetings to compare solutions; inviting outsiders to meetings to lessen feelings of group cohesion; and listing both good and bad points of each idea. Other precautions include appointing someone to take a purely negative view of the solution and holding a follow-up meeting at which individuals can reconsider (Wheeler & Janis, 1980).

Delphi Method

The **Delphi method** (Helmer, 1967) is another means to avoid the interpersonal processes or process losses that may inappropriately affect decision making. Individuals are asked to state their views privately in writing about the nature of a problem and suggest possible solutions. These responses are collected and distributed without identification to everyone in the problem-solving group. Members whose views differ from the majority are asked to support their opinions in writing. These views are redistributed, and everyone again writes an opinion about the situation. The process of writing and distribution continues until a consensus is reached.

By requiring decision makers to act independently, the Delphi method avoids the dynamics of interpersonal interaction that may interfere with the quality of a decision. Individuals are able to use others' expertise without being exposed to the drawbacks of group decision making. The Delph method may not be useful, however, when a quick solution is needed or the importance of the issue at hand does not merit such a lengthy process.

Interpersonal Skills Groups

In some cases, work groups' performances may be hindered by problems among members. Managers may feel that productivity is being hampered by group members who refuse to cooperate, for example, or communication patterns may be disrupted when two departments are merged. Many times the approach taken to solve these kinds of problems is interpersonal skills training.

As discussed in Chapter 5, sensitivity groups were developed shortly after World War II as a method for improving communication among people who work together. These groups attempt to make group members aware of psychological factors that may affect communication.

Interpersonal skills groups start with the assumption that people bring patterns of interaction used in the workplace into group meetings. In other words, workers who are assertive will try to dominate a meeting, just as more timid workers will be reluctant to speak during group discussions. One purpose of a group meeting is to identify patterns or styles of interaction. Such identification is likely to lead to insights as to how individuals are being perceived by their coworkers.

Although the interpersonal skills group has an identified leader or trainer—generally someone from outside the work setting—the leader's role is usually not to direct the group, but to provide a model of behavior. The leader encourages members to share their feelings, to keep their focus on the communication processes that are occurring in the meeting, and to maintain confidentiality after the meeting is over. Additionally, the trainer assures members that what transpires during the meeting will not threaten the job security of any participant. After members agree to these conditions, the trainer typically says no more.

In the typical group meeting, participants quickly become dissatisfied and anxious about the lack of an agenda; the trainer has told them to talk and has not given them any guidelines about topics. At this point, an assertive member will usually suggest a topic that the group can discuss. This approach may be agreed on by the other participants, or it may be met with hostility by members who feel the suggesting member is trying to dominate the proceedings. When such objections are expressed, the initial spokesperson is often surprised that what he or she considered helpful behavior is perceived by others as domineering. Along the same lines, individuals who willingly agree to follow the agendas of others may find that others see them as compliant; people who listen but do not communicate may be seen as social loafers.

In the interpersonal skills group setting, members are free to explore their feelings about each other and ways relationships can be improved. Participants are encouraged not to be hostile or defensive, but to listen carefully to what others are saying. Advocates of this method believe this openness in communication will improve relations among group members.

Gist, Stevens, and Bavetta (1991) used training in self-efficacy as a means of improving interpersonal skills. Recall from Chapter 5 that self-efficacy refers to a belief in one's ability to accomplish a task. Researchers have shown self-efficacy to be related to absenteeism reduction (Latham & Frayne, 1989), as well as to learning to use computer software and to success in training (Gist, Schwoerer, & Rosen, 1989).

Because the majority of self-efficacy research has focused on cognitive skill, Gist and her associates wanted to see if self-efficacy was related to skill in negotiation, goal setting, and self-management. Self-efficacy did, in fact, appear to be related to successful performance in these areas—workers who received the self-efficacy training were more effective interpersonally. Gist and her colleagues regarded this as an important finding because it suggests that training people in self-efficacy will make training them in other skill areas more effective.

Employee Involvement Programs

Teams in the Workplace
Autonomous Work Groups
Matrix Management
Quality Circles and Total
    Quality Management
Other Participative
    Decision-Making Models
Improving Team Perfor-
    mance

One of the most important developments in the workplace in recent years has been **employee involvement programs** (EIPs), in which employees work together in teams and usually have the power to make and implement certain decisions. This use of teams in the workplace is not a new idea—autonomous work groups, as you will recall from Chapter 1, are the cornerstone of the sociotechnical school of organization design—but they have become increasingly popular in recent years. In general, such programs are not founded in the interest of workplace democracy; rather, companies use a team approach when they have a specific corporate objective they want to see accomplished (Magjuka & Baldwin, 1991).

For example, a large meat-packing plant in the Midwest instituted an employee involvement program to address human factors issues such as cumulative trauma disorders, improving employee productivity, and workplace redesign (human factors are discussed more fully in Chapter 14). Teams composed of employees, managers, medical staff, and maintenance workers participated in training in effective group discussion, effective feedback, brainstorming, and other team-building practices. In addition, they received training in identifying human factors problems in the workplace.

In the period after the teams began functioning, the numbers of both incidents of cumulative trauma disorders and referrals to physicians dropped significantly. The researchers concluded that the institution of the human factors teams saved the company almost $100,000 per year (May & Schwoerer, 1994).

Teams in the Workplace

Over the years, a variety of approaches to teamwork have evolved. In a review of articles concerning employee participation in decision making, a team of researchers (Cotton, Vollrath, Froggatt, Lengnick-Hall, & Jennings, 1988) identified the following six forms of employee participation:

1. Participation in work decisions. In this format, workers have a great deal of influence regarding the work itself, including how it is organized, what is done, who does what, and so forth.

2. Consultative participation. This format is similar to the participation in work decisions described above, but management determines which decisions will be implemented. Quality circles (which are also discussed in Chapter 12) usually fit in this category.

Box 10.1 COFFEE BREAKS AND PRODUCTIVITY IN THE AUTO INDUSTRY

Although most workers take a coffee break for granted, an interesting problem regarding breaks has arisen in the auto industry. Should all workers take their breaks at the same time, or should workers take individual breaks, with other workers stepping in to relieve them? This is an important question because allowing all workers to go on break requires shutting down the entire production line.

Industry experts argue that at the Saturn car plant in Spring Hill, Tennessee, for example, switching to a relief system could increase annual profits by as much as $75 million. Most plants have mass breaks, however, because of a belief that allowing workers to relax together will result in greater teamwork, productivity, and quality. This idea was originally adopted from Japanese car manufacturers.

Today, however, American auto companies want to produce more cars without having to build expensive plants. Any strategy that might lead to this—including altering the time-honored coffee break—is under consideration.

Source: Lucchetti, A. (1996, September 9). Detroit debates how to take a coffee break. *Wall Street Journal,* p. B1.

3. Short-term participation. This also resembles participation in work decisions, but rather than being an ongoing process, short-term participation focuses on a specific issue and rarely lasts more than a few days.

4. Informal participation. In this format, no formal procedures for employee participation exist, but employers occasionally convene meetings to ask employees for their opinions. Decision-making authority remains with management, however.

5. Employee ownership. In this form of organization, employees have the authority to make decisions about the organization.

6. Representative participation. Here, employees do not participate directly, but elect representatives to a governing body. In practice, representative participation resembles employee ownership, but without each employee being involved in decision making.

In recent years industrial and organizational psychologists and others have been particularly interested in forms 1 and 2. Typical teamwork structures in these forms are autonomous work groups, matrix management, quality circles, and participative decision making.

One group of researchers (Banker, Field, Schroeder, & Sinha, 1996) studied the impact of teams on productivity in an electromechanical assembly plant. Although the teams were not organized as autonomous work groups (described below), they had some decision-making authority and membership was determined by management. In addition, the teams had information on the company's budget and competitors' products to help them in their decision making. Not all managers supported the team concept, however. Following the teams over a 21-month period, the researchers nonetheless found that both quality and labor productivity improved over time.

Not everyone is enthusiastic about teams in the workplace. In particular, unions are suspicious that teams create illegal "company unions" where workers discuss workplace conditions directly with management (Rubis, 1996). In some unionized work environments, the team approach has been legally challenged and management has had to disband the teams.

Autonomous Work Groups

As you may recall from the Ahmedabad textile mill study (Chapter 1), one of the foundations of the sociotechnical approach to organizations is the **autonomous work group.** According to theory, participating in an autonomous group improves members' attitudes and job performance. Research investigating the theory, however, has not been completely supportive (Pearce & Ravlin, 1987). For example, one study (Wall, Kemp, Jackson, & Clegg, 1986) found that autonomous work groups did give employees feelings of empowerment and job satisfaction, but that they did not affect motivation, commitment, performance, or turnover.

Another study looked at autonomous work groups at a newly opened minerals processing plant in Australia (Cordery, Mueller, & Smith, 1991). The parent company had always used a traditional management style, but wanted to try a new approach. Workers were organized into ten autonomous work groups of 10 to 15 employees each. The groups' responsibilities included allocating work, maintaining safety and housekeeping standards, planning shift operations, determining priorities, and making recommendations about hiring. Workers' attitudes about their jobs were measured eight months after start-up, then again a year later. The study found that the organizational commitment of members of autonomous work groups declined over time, but it was still higher than that of workers in a traditional structure. Interestingly, however, the autonomous work groups had higher absenteeism and turnover rates than the traditional group.

Matrix Management

One team approach that encourages both horizontal and vertical communication is the matrix organization (Galbraith, 1971). **Matrix management** emphasizes both the functional and the product aspects of organization. For example, members of a product development team may need input from both the

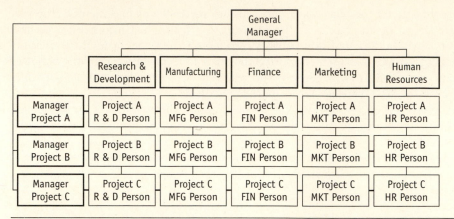

Figure 10.3 Matrix Management
In matrix management, personnel report to both a divisional head and a project manager. In this illustration, the Research and Development personnel who are working on Project A are responsible to both the project manager and the head of R & D.

product manager and individuals in advertising and sales. In the matrix organization, individuals are typically responsible to management in the functional area first, and to management in the product area second. This type of structure, often used in the aerospace industry, results in workers' being responsible to two supervisors. Figure 10.3 illustrates a matrix organization.

Two researchers (Burns & Wholey, 1993) studied the factors behind the adoption of matrix management among hospitals. Results from their research suggested that hospitals were more likely to move to a matrix model when task diversity was great and the hospital's prestige was high. In addition, hospitals were more likely to adopt matrix management when other hospitals in their area were doing so. In addition, hospitals with lower task diversity were more likely to adopt, then abandon, matrix management.

Although matrix management offers an expanded knowledge base, sometimes effectiveness is diminished because members do not share common concerns. Members of different departments are likely to see organizational goals differently and to have different ideas about priorities. Another problem that can occur in the matrix team is the confusion that comes from mixing horizontal and vertical reporting lines. For example, in most groups, communication with superiors is valued over communication with peers. Consequently, workers may pay more attention to managers than to their coworkers. On the other hand, managers may feel threatened if their subordinates are more effective at solving problems than they are. In this way, the status hierarchy of the organization may be challenged.

In recent years, some companies have become interested in cross-functional teams, a form of organizational design related to matrix management (Denison, Hart, & Kahn, 1996). **Cross-functional teams (CFTs)** are working groups that are created to make decisions lower in the organizational hierarchy and that overlay an existing organization (Galbraith, 1994). CFTs consist of members who come from different areas within the organization, and the task of the team is usually to bring about some form of organizational change. As a result, CFTs are often temporary.

Quality Circles and Total Quality Management

The modern interest in quality began early in World War II, when the U.S. Department of Defense established a sampling procedure to determine the acceptability of munitions (Reed, Lemak, & Montgomery, 1996). In the years following, theorists such as Philip Crosby, W. Edwards Deming, Joseph M. Juran, and others argued that reliability and quality assurance were essential for a firm's profitability. The quality movement has taken two major forms in American companies: quality circles and total quality management (TQM).

Quality circles (QCs) is an innovation widely applied in Japan. In the typical QC, members meet voluntarily for an hour to discuss problems in the workplace. Although QCs have been tried in the United States, they do not seem to be as successful as other approaches to teamwork. In a review of QC evaluation literature (Barrick & Alexander, 1987), two researchers found that QCs did not work well in the U.S. Department of Defense, that circles were more effective if members had greater experience, and that issues addressed in QCs in the United States were likely to focus on interpersonal relations, rather than on production and quality, as in Japan.

Along the same lines, another study that followed the progress of QCs in an electronics manufacturing company over three years (Griffin, 1988) found that job satisfaction, organizational commitment, and performance all increased over the first 18 months of the circle. After that period, however, satisfaction, commitment, and performance began to decline, and three years later, they were back to their original levels.

In recent years, more firms have become interested in **total quality management (TQM),** which refers to an organizational strategy that focuses on improving quality and productivity. As described by one researcher:

> TQM establishes quality enhancement as a dominant priority and one that is vital for long-term effectiveness and survival. It claims that improving quality can decrease rather than increase costs and facilitate attainment of other demands and objectives. (Spencer 1994)

Presently, over 50 percent of Fortune 500 firms use TQM (Persico & Tomasek, 1994). Although there is no agreement on a precise definition, typical features of a TQM program include a focus on the customer, continuous improvement of company operations, and teamwork. In recent years some researchers (e.g., Lengnick-Hall, 1996) have also become interested in how customers can contribute to quality.

Other Participative Decision-Making Models

As the shortcomings of the quality circle approach became more apparent, many employers moved to less formal participative decision-making models. In general, these models continue the practice of asking employees to make decisions in the workplace, and they continue to be popular in many organizational settings.

Although the arguments for participation seem reasonable—workers can make better decisions because they know their jobs better than managers, and decision making gives workers feelings of autonomy that lead to higher job satisfaction—results from research on the benefits of participation have not been impressive. For example, in an oft-cited review of research, Locke and Schweiger (1979) concluded that participation did not lead to higher productivity, and it led to only slightly higher job satisfaction.

In a meta-analysis of studies that considered participation, productivity, and satisfaction, Miller and Monge (1986) found support for Locke and Schweiger's conclusions. Specifically, participation is somewhat related to satisfaction; less so to productivity. Other findings from the meta-analysis were that (1) participation does not work better among managers than among lower-level employees, nor does it work better in certain kinds of industries; (2) working in a participative organizational climate is more satisfying than being asked to participate only occasionally; and (3) participation in goal setting does not raise productivity. These findings were largely supported in another meta-analytic study of the effects of participation on productivity and satisfaction by Wagner and Gooding (1987).

Finally, one researcher (Ancona, 1990) proposed that satisfaction with a team might come from factors outside the team environment. This hypothesis was contrary to most small-group research, where relations among members are considered the source of satisfaction or dissatisfaction. Working with groups of employees in a state education agency, the researcher identified three styles of interaction between teams and their external environments. One style was to focus on learning to work together effectively before extensive interaction with outsiders; the second style was to focus on internal team building at the same time the team interacted with outsiders; and the third style was to interact extensively with outsiders without spending much time on internal processes.

Interestingly, the team that focused primarily on internal team building had the least cohesion and the most dissatisfaction. In addition, top management gave this team the lowest performance ratings, labeling it "the classic case of what not to do." The second approach—in which members worked on team building at the same time they interacted externally—led to the highest job satisfaction and group cohesion. In terms of effectiveness, however, teams that did not spend time on internal processes, but instead went directly to interacting with outsiders, were rated as highly successful by top management. The researcher concluded that perhaps teams should attempt to be successful externally first, and wait for cohesion and satisfaction to follow.

Despite the popularity of the participative approach, research evidence clearly shows that it does not lead to higher productivity, nor does it affect satisfaction in a consistent and meaningful fashion. In addition, research suggests that teams lose their effectiveness over time, and that they should be disbanded and reconstituted occasionally to improve performance. Finally, some employees believe that working in teams prevents them from achieving management positions (Schellhardt, 1997).

Given these research findings, one might be tempted to conclude that employee participation in decision making might be another Hawthorne effect—benefits are the result of the attention paid to the employees. Nonetheless, many organizations moved to implement team approaches to decision making during the 1980s in the hope that teams would lead to more effective organizational functioning.

Improving Team Performance

Despite the lack of supportive research, many organizations continue to use teams for decision making. In a survey of administrators of employee involvement programs, Magjuka and Baldwin (1991) identified some characteristics necessary for a team to be successful. First, the team must have open and unrestricted access to information; managers must be willing to expend the resources to provide the team with data members consider necessary for making effective decisions.

Second, teams are more effective if they have a diverse composition. That is, teams consisting of managers, professionals, nonexempt workers, and hourly employees are more effective than teams composed of individuals from the same administrative level. Finally, these researchers found that larger teams are more effective than smaller. Table 10.1 summarizes the guidelines for making teams effective.

Finally, some researchers (Tesluk, Farr, Mathieu, & Vance, 1995) were interested in the impact of employee involvement training on the job setting. Participants in this study were employees in a large state transportation agency that offered 12 EIP training courses in problem solving, decision making, and communication skills. Not surprisingly, results from the study showed that employees who had the most experience with EIP and more organizational commitment were more likely to transfer their EIP training to their core job. Employees with cynical attitudes were less likely to transfer EIP training. The researchers concluded that organizations with highly cynical employees may be unsuccessful in motivating their employees to carry their EIP training back to the job.

Table 10.1 MAKING TEAMS EFFECTIVE

Successful implementation of an employee involvement program (EIP) requires careful planning. Factors that may affect the success of an EIP include:

Team Heterogeneity	When members of a team are similar, they may work together more effectively. On the other hand, too much similarity can stifle creativity.
Team Type	The effectiveness of the team may be affected by its identity. Is it a production team? a service team? Or does it support another unit and perhaps need input from that unit?
Information Access	In almost all cases, teams need access to information to be effective. Managers who implement a team approach need to plan for providing such information.
Problem Domain	Although teams can deal with a wide range of unspecified problems, if necessary, managers need to identify what requires immediate attention.
Financial Rewards	Team participants should be clear about any financial incentives connected with team performance.

Source: Adapted from Magjuka, R., & Baldwin, T. (1991). Team-based employee involvement programs: Effects of design and administration. *Personnel Psychology, 44*(4), 797. Used by permission.

Chapter Summary

Since ancient times it has been recognized that people change their behavior when they become members of groups. For many years psychologists resisted this notion, but the study of groups has become an important area of research. Approaches to studying groups include the laboratory experiment, the field experiment, observation, sociometry, and case studies.

Groups can be classified in several ways. Formal or secondary groups have rules of operation and a specific purpose for existence. Informal or primary groups form on the basis of friendship, proximity, experience, or other factors. Although much less organized than formal groups, informal groups can have a powerful influence on behavior. A reference group is a group with which an individual makes comparisons. Although an individual may belong to many groups, the individual typically uses only a few for reference. In contrast, a designated group consists of individuals who are treated in a homogeneous fashion by others. These individuals may or may not use the designated group as a reference group.

In the period in which a group is first forming, there is likely to be some conflict about status concerns, but eventually the group gets around to performing. Historically, group behavior has been studied in terms of task and process. Task variables focus on environmental factors; process variables involve relations between group members.

Most group members experience deindividuation, a process by which some of the values and behaviors of individuals are modified in order to comply with the norms or standards of the group. Deindividuation can have either positive or negative effects.

Groups establish norms, or rules, for behavior. Individuals who do not comply with these norms, known as deviants, may suffer ostracism from the group. Many groups develop a sense of cohesion. The effect of cohesion on productivity is unclear, but it does seem to be positively related to job satisfaction. Because many work sites now involve workers in decision making, managers have had to develop new methods for resolving conflict in the workplace.

Decisions made by groups are not always superior to individual decisions. Several researchers have studied the relationship between task and group performance. Overall, it appears that different types of tasks require different types of groups.

Group polarization refers to the tendency to favor extreme actions, in terms of either risk or caution. Groupthink is a phenomenon in which the way a decision is reached is more important than the quality of the decision. Groupthink can result in serious consequences. The Delphi method is a process for decision making that avoids groupthink.

Interpersonal skills groups have the goal of improving communication. Members are free to explore their feelings about each other and ways in which relationships can be improved. Methodological concerns and concerns about the transitory nature of the interpersonal group experience have been raised by researchers.

An important development in recent years has been the use of employee involvement programs, in which employees work together in teams and usually have the power to make certain decisions. Three approaches to employee involvement groups are autonomous work groups, matrix management, and quality circles.

Although the arguments for employee participation seem reasonable—workers can make better decisions because they know their jobs better than the managers, and decision making gives workers feelings of autonomy that lead to higher job satisfaction—findings from research on the benefits of participation have not been impressive. Nonetheless, more effective teams need access to information, they must have a diverse membership, and they should be larger, rather than smaller.

Key Words and Concepts

adjourning (p. 317)
attraction-selection-attrition (ASA) model (p. 314)
autonomous work groups (p. 333)
cautious shift (p. 327)

cliques (p. 312)
cross-functional teams (CFTs) (p. 334)
deindividuation (p. 319)
Delphi method (p. 329)

designated group (p. 316)
deviants (p. 320)
diffusion of responsibility (p. 319)
employee involvement programs
    (p. 331)
formal group (p. 313)
forming stage (p. 316)
group cohesion (p. 322)
group polarization (p. 327)
groupthink (p. 328)
idiosyncrasy credits (p. 321)
informal group (p. 314)
isolates (p. 312)
matrix management (p. 333)
norming stage (p. 317)
norms (p. 319)

pairs (p. 312)
performing (p. 317)
primary group (p. 314)
prospect theory (p. 328)
quality circles (QCs) (p. 335)
reference group (p. 315)
risky shift (p. 327)
secondary group (p. 313)
social support (p. 323)
sociometry (p. 312)
stars (p. 312)
storming stage (p. 316)
subject matter experts (SMEs)
    (p. 325)
total quality management (TQM)
    (p. 335)

Questions for Discussion

1. What are the different approaches to studying groups? Which would give the most accurate picture of group behavior?

2. What formal and informal groups do you belong to? Which do you enjoy more? Why?

3. What reference groups do you use to make comparisons? How might certain reference groups have a negative impact on a person's behavior?

4. What are the stages of group formation?

5. What is deindividuation? When might you experience deindividuation?

6. What are some of the norms that operate in your primary group? How might a member of your primary group become deviant?

7. How can a minority member of a group be effective?

8. When might group cohesion be negative?

9. Do individuals make better decisions than groups? What are the advantages of group decisions?

10. What is group polarization? groupthink? How can people avoid groupthink?

11. What is the purpose of an interpersonal skills group?

12. Why has there been such an emphasis on teamwork in recent years? Of the different forms of teamwork, which do you think would be most effective?

13. If you were putting together a team in the workplace, what would you do to make it successful?

CHAPTER 11

Special Populations in the Workplace: Women, Minorities, and Older Workers

Managing Diversity

Women in the Workplace

Minority Employees

Older Workers

Social Stratification in the Workplace

Chapter Summary

Key Words and Concepts

Questions for Discussion

After Congress passed the first Civil Rights Act in 1964, employers were suddenly faced with hundreds of legal challenges to their selection and promotion policies. Most people anticipated that the number of these challenges would subside over time but contrary to expectations, the number of employment discrimination cases has not declined in the last 35 years. Although the first challenges by women and minorities usually concerned hiring procedures, by the 1990s most employment discrimination suits concerned discrimination in firing (Hansen, 1991). The nature of unfair discrimination has changed, but apparently its incidence has not.

To the surprise of many, issues of race and gender in the workplace have proved to be too complex to be addressed simply through legislation. In the last three decades, demographic trends, civil rights legislation, improved selection procedures, global markets, and other factors began to change the nature and composition of people who were entering the American workforce. As more women, minorities, and people of other cultures became employees, companies were faced with managing a workforce of individuals different from the traditional White males who constituted the workforce of earlier decades.

As discussed in Chapter 1, population trends now suggest that the diversity of the workforce will continue to increase for the foreseeable future. From the present to about 2005, for example, two African-American workers will enter the labor force for every one who leaves, and one of every six new workers will be Hispanic (Exter, 1992).

At the same time the composition of the workforce is changing, projections suggest the growth rate of the workforce will decline over the next few decades—fewer workers will enter the workforce, and more baby boomers will retire. Consequently, the United States faces the prospect of a shortage of qualified workers in the near future. To get the workers they need, organizations will be forced to hire people of lower skill levels and provide them with training, and they will need to retain workers who have the option of retiring. In short, management will need to recruit, hire, train, and supervise a far more diverse workforce than has been the case.

Managing Diversity

Traditional theories of management are based on the assumption that everyone in the workplace is more or less similar in culture, experience, and personality. For example, two researchers (Mumby & Putnam, 1992) have argued that organizational theory has always been based in *bounded rationality* (Simon, 1976), an approach that emphasizes male-centered notions about the desirability of logic and the inappropriateness of emotional expression in the workplace.

Along the same lines, the researchers argue, economic theories typically regard workers as rational beings whose major motivation is to maximize their economic gains. After reviewing management theories from around the world, another theorist (Hofstede, 1993) concluded that American management theory has several features not found in other cultures. Three of the most obvious are U.S. management's emphasis on market processes, an orientation toward the individual rather than the group, and a focus on managers rather than on workers. As the workforce becomes increasingly diverse, however, traditional assumptions can no longer be taken for granted.

Managing diversity refers to directing employees of different cultures and backgrounds toward organizational goals. The diversity approach differs from traditional management because it does not focus solely on employee socialization to organizational values. In addition to the employee's socialization, diversity requires the organization to make some accommodation between its policies and procedures and the employee.

Historically, the Civil Rights Act and the legislation that followed forced many organizations to reconsider a broad range of personnel policies, particularly regarding women and ethnic and racial minorities. As described in Chapter 3, this was usually accomplished through affirmative action programs, where organizations developed plans for hiring women and minorities. One disadvantage of traditional affirmative action programs, however, is that they chiefly benefited people who were able to fit into an existing corporate culture without modifying that culture (Thomas, 1991). Opportunities for people who did not immediately fit into the culture were consequently limited.

Diversity programs take a different perspective from affirmative action, focusing instead on modifying the corporate culture so that different kinds of employees can make greater contributions to the organization. (Organizational culture is discussed more fully in Chapter 12.) Box 11.1 describes three major employers' diversity programs.

Although diversity is currently popular among many theorists and managers, not all researchers embrace the concept. In a critique of the ways organizational researchers have dealt with race, for example, Nkomo (1992) argued that diversity programs still operate on the assumption that the majority culture is the normal culture, and that separation of racial and ethnic groups is natural and not open to change. In addition, diversity programs often start with negative assumptions about the backgrounds, schooling, and experiences of minority employees.

Another criticism of the diversity movement is that it may be creating "social traps," which are situations in which people adopt seemingly beneficial behaviors that may have negative consequences over time or for a larger group (Barry & Bateman, 1996). Promoting differences is a different strategy from those used by managers in the past, so it is difficult to predict what the long-term outcome of managing diversity will be.

In addition, "celebrating differences" can be a superficial way to avoid confronting real issues of organizational power, salary differences, and group relations. Finally, anecdotal evidence suggests that sometimes participants in diversity programs have negative reactions when they perceive that such programs scapegoat other groups (Nemetz & Christensen, 1996).

Most researchers agree, however, that not being a part of the majority has a negative impact on individuals. As two researchers (Milliken & Martins, 1996) observed:

> In sum, the results of research on racial diversity in organizational groups suggest that people who are different from the majority race in an organization may not only experience less positive emotional responses to their employing organizations, but they are also likely to be evaluated less positively by their supervisors, and they are more likely to turn over. It seems likely that lower levels of attachment to the organization and lower performance ratings for minorities combine to drive minorities out of organizations at a faster rate than majority group members.

One researcher (Larkey, 1996) has developed a model of how a work group influences interactions between members. In this model, presented in Figure 11.1, work groups are considered on a continuum ranging from monolithic to multicultural. Within these work groups, workers perceive cultural differences in terms of *categorization,* in which stereotypes guide worker behavior, or *specification,* in which people do not rely on stereotypes when dealing with others.

Box 11.1 DIVERSITY AT THREE MAJOR EMPLOYERS

AT&T

Although AT&T had problems with unfair discrimination in the 1960s (see Chapter 3), by 1993 the percentage of women in the workforce had risen to 38 percent and of minorities to 18 percent. In 1993, however, a company magazine published drawings representing the cultures of different continents. African Americans were infuriated when African culture was represented by a monkey.

This incident led to a discontinuation of the magazine and a harder look at why women and minorities were not being promoted into management ranks. Using a team-building strategy (Chapter 13), AT&T created teams headed by senior executives charged with finding ways to move women and minority employees into management ranks. Today AT&T says that the number of women and minorities holding senior positions has doubled, to about 12 percent.

Xerox Corporation

At Xerox, the chairman appointed certain senior executives to take leading roles in addressing the concerns of women and minorities. In 1996, a group of African-American women warned a senior vice president that because there are so few African-American female engineering students, African-American women would always be at a disadvantage at Xerox. In response to their concerns, the vice president arranged a summer internship program specifically targeted at African-American female students.

Along the same lines, when it appeared that many talented females were resigning from Xerox to take jobs elsewhere, the company intervened with a special mentorship program. As part of the program, women with high potential were linked with high-level executives so they would have an "advocate" in the senior ranks of Xerox.

BankAmerica

Although BankAmerica has a 28-member diversity council run by a senior manager, with representatives from every division, each business unit also has its own diversity council. Diversity activities include workshops, articles in internal publications, and the establishment of networks for different groups.

Since 1994 female senior managers have increased from 18 percent to 25 percent and minority managers have increased from 9 percent to 11 percent. One particular goal of the diversity program at BankAmerica is to promote the empowerment of lower-level employees.

Source: Deutsch, C. H. (1996, November 20). Corporate diversity, in practice. *The New York Times,* p. C1.

This chapter looks at some groups that have challenged traditional assumptions about management and organizational culture. The influences of women, minorities, and older workers have grown in recent years and, given demo-

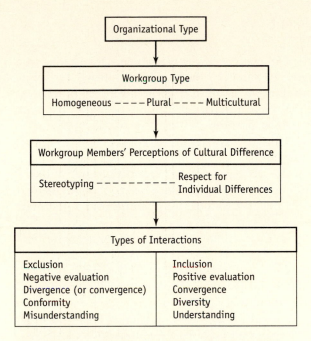

Source: Larkey, L. K. (1996). Toward a theory of communicative interactions in culturally diverse workgroups. *Academy of Management Review, 21,* 463–491. Copyright © 1996 Reprinted by permission of the Academy of Management.

Figure 11.1 How Culturally Diverse Work Groups Influence Their Members
As the figure above indicates, work groups can range from homogeneous to multicultural. In the extremes, they can use stereotypes when dealing with others or they can respect individual differences. Finally, the types of interactions between members will vary depending on the group's preference for homogeneity or diversity.

graphic trends and legislation, are likely to have an even greater impact in the decades to come (Fondas, 1997). The last part of the chapter looks at two more traditional groups in the workplace, top executives and blue-collar workers.

Women in the Workplace

Women in Management
Salary Issues
Work-Family Conflict
Sexual Harassment

During the last few years, many researchers have studied the role of women in the workplace. One reason for this interest is the growth rate of female workers. Between 1986 and 2000, for example, the number of White females working will increase 22 percent, compared with an 8 percent increase in the number of working White males. Although this growth is significant, it does not compare with the projected growth rate of working African-American females (33.2 percent), Asian females (83.3 percent), or Hispanic females (84.9 percent) (Thomas, 1991).

Women in Management

Women today comprise almost 50 percent of the workforce. Despite this gain in numbers, top management continues to be heavily dominated by White men, with women holding 30 percent of all managerial positions, but only 2 percent of senior executive positions (Kirkpatrick, 1996). Although far more women than men hold white-collar positions, 50 percent of these jobs are in clerical occupations. Table 11.1 presents the figures for women as a total percentage in selected white-collar jobs.

In general, women and minorities have made substantial progress into the ranks of middle management, but they have generally failed to reach higher executive levels. Some individuals have referred to this phenomenon as the **glass ceiling**—defined by one author as "invisible barriers, real or perceived, which appear to stymie advancement opportunities for women and minorities" (Dominguez, 1991).

In 1989 the U.S. Department of Labor launched its Glass Ceiling Initiative to examine how middle and upper management positions are filled in a variety of industries. Results from the study found that most companies have a level beyond which few women or minorities advance, and that these levels differ from company to company. In addition, the careers of minority employees appear to plateau at levels lower than those of women. This difficulty in advancing may be one reason why female workers currently join unions at a rate three times higher than male workers, despite the fact that union leadership remains overwhelmingly male (Mellor, 1995; Mellor, Mathieu, & Swim, 1994).

The Department of Labor study also found that few companies had an adequate strategy for dealing with the glass ceiling. Few were keeping records on the salaries, bonuses, and promotions of women and minorities in their companies. Although many organizations had programs for developing executive talent, women and minorities were often excluded from these programs. In addition, women and minorities were typically found in support, rather than in decision-making, positions.

Based on these findings, the secretary of labor announced a program to address the problem of the glass ceiling. Specifically, the secretary introduced an education program and special awards for companies that show initiative in dismantling the glass ceiling. Although information about the success of this program in the private sector is unclear, one study (Powell & Butterfield, 1994) found no differences in male and female promotion rates among high-level government employees.

Over the years, many authors have written about the problems women face when they attempt to advance into management ranks. Some have pointed out that women who aspire to higher leadership positions have had to fight for fair treatment at the same time they were learning the roles appropriate to management. In addition, some research (Morrison, White, & Van Velsor, 1987) suggests that women need more encouragement than men to reach executive levels. Another study (Tharenou, Latimer, & Conroy, 1994) found that company

Table 11.1   WOMEN AS A PERCENTAGE OF TOTAL EMPLOYMENT IN SELECTED WHITE-COLLAR JOBS

Occupation	Percentage Female
Accountants	51.2
Airplane pilots	3.4
Bank officials and financial managers	50.3
Bank tellers	90.1
Bookkeepers	92.8
Chemists	31.9
Clergy	11.1
Computer scientists	32.0
Economists	50.3
Editors and reporters	53.2
Engineers	8.4
File clerks	80.2
Lawyers	26.4
Librarians	83.9
Musicians and composers	37.3
Nurses	93.1
Painters and sculptors	50.1
Payroll clerks	92.8
Physicians	24.4
Psychologists	59.2
Real estate agents and brokers	50.7
Receptionists	96.5
Retail sales clerks	65.6
Secretaries	98.5
Social workers	67.9
Stockbrokers	31.3
Teachers, elementary	84.1
Teachers, secondary	57.0
Teachers, college and university	45.2
Telephone operators	88.4

Source: Adapted from U.S. Bureau of the Census (1996). Employed civilians, by occupation, sex, race, and Hispanic origin: 1983 and 1995. *Statistical Abstract of the United States,* 116th ed. Washington, DC: U.S. Government Printing Office.

training programs were more beneficial to men than to women, and that having a spouse and dependents at home reduced women's opportunities for training.

In the mid-1970s there was a veritable explosion of books and magazines offering advice to professional women. One major point of this literature is that women's experiences in organizations are often different from those of men.

For example, considerable evidence suggests that male workers regard female workers as different in attitudes and behaviors from other male workers. Overall, females are perceived as being less dedicated to their careers than males, their incomes and career opportunities are often considered secondary in importance to those of their spouses, and they, along with minorities, are regarded as a source of uncertainty or undependability in the workplace.

Among men, these kinds of attitudes toward women do not seem to change much over time. For example, researchers (Heilman, Block, Martell, & Simon, 1989) asked 268 male managers to choose adjectives that characterize men in general. Qualities associated with males included leadership ability, self-confidence, assertiveness, logic, steadiness, and emotional stability. Qualities the managers associated with females included curiosity, helpfulness, intuition, creativity, understanding, and neatness. The authors concluded that stereotypes about women "appear to be deeply rooted, widely shared, and remarkably resistant to change."

Along the same lines, a meta-analysis of studies dealing with sex differences in leadership (Dobbins & Platz, 1986) found that males and females did not differ significantly on such dimensions as choosing consideration (orientation toward people) or structure (orientation toward tasks) or subordinate satisfaction. Males were found to be better leaders only in studies done in laboratories.

Some researchers have pointed out that masculine characteristics are widely regarded as important, and feminine characteristics detrimental, for career success (Brenner, Tomkiewicz, & Schein, 1989; Heilman, Block, Martell, & Simon, 1989; Powell & Butterfield, 1989). In one study (Fagenson, 1989), men and women higher in the organizational structure described themselves with more masculine adjectives than those lower in the structure. Women with lower educational status used more feminine adjectives to describe themselves, but both older men and women used more feminine adjectives. Another study (Yammarino, Dubinsky, Comer, & Jolson, 1997) found that female leaders were more likely than males to form one-to-one relationships with both their female and male subordinates.

In an experimental study that looked at leadership in small groups, Kent and Moss (1994) found that students described by others as masculine or androgynous were more likely to emerge as leaders than students described as feminine. Another study (Lefkowitz, 1994a), however, found that males and females had similar reactions to handling job situations when the males and females were at the same levels of age, education, income, and occupation.

Other researchers (Blum, Fields, & Goodman, 1994) looked at the types of organizations in which women held a higher percentage of management jobs. After reviewing records at 297 work sites, the researchers found that women were more likely to achieve management positions in companies that encourage training and development and that had more women in nonmanagement jobs, more minorities in management positions, and a higher percentage of skilled and professional jobs. In addition, nonmanufacturing companies were more likely to promote women.

One study (Ohlott, Ruderman, & McCauley, 1994) focused on the rates of career success of 281 male and 226 female managers. This study found that men and women were being given opportunities for development at an equal rate. However, a closer analysis of the data revealed that men were receiving opportunities that related to higher levels of responsibility. Specifically, when stakes were high, businesses diverse, and external pressures great, men were more likely to be chosen for a management position.

Although there appear to be cracks in the glass ceiling, a report issued by the nonprofit organization Catalyst in 1996 reported that women still constitute only 10 percent of senior managers at the largest U.S. corporations (Himelstein, 1996). Among the highest executives, including CEO, president, and executive vice president, women constitute only 2.4 percent. Even though 50 percent of all accountants are women, females comprise only 13 percent of the partners in accounting firms (Koretz, 1997b).

Finally, of the top 2,500 salaries in the United States in 1996, only 50 went to women. Women are most likely to hold executive positions in service industries such as savings banks, publishing companies, financial companies, and food service organizations (Kirkpatrick, 1996).

Salary Issues

As the Catalyst study indicates, one area in which males and females are not equal is salary: In 1996 women were earning only 75.5 cents for every dollar men earned (Belknap, 1996), and 60 percent of full-time female employees were earning less than $25,000 annually (Micco, 1997). The only career in which men's and women's salaries were similar was sales.

This widespread disparity in pay occurs at both management and lower levels of the organizational hierarchy, and occurs irrespective of industry, experience, education, tenure, job performance, or job title (Gerhart, 1990a). In addition, a Department of Labor study found that women are more likely to be downsized than men and are more likely to find part-time jobs that pay less (Burkins, 1996). However, another study, by the Employee Benefit Research Institute, suggested that although the job tenure for males has declined recently, job tenure for women has remained relatively constant since 1983 (Koretz, 1997).

Psychological research suggests that how well a person expects to do has a significant effect on overall performance, and several studies found that women have lower expectations than men. For example, one group of researchers (Jackson, Gardner, & Sullivan, 1992) asked 447 college seniors to estimate the maximum pay in the occupations that they chose for after college. The differences between men and women were dramatic:

> Regardless of occupational field, women had lower expectations than men for career-peak pay and, with the exception of social science majors, for career-entry as well. Most dramatic was the gender gap in pay expectations in the male-dominated field of engineering, in which women expected to earn about $35,000 less at career peak than did men. However, even in female-dominated occupations, such as nursing and

education, women expected to earn about $20,000 less at career peak than did men.

Some evidence also suggests that workers who have gaps in their employment history (i.e., have taken time off from working full time) earn less than continuously employed individuals. One study (Schneer & Reitman, 1990), found that women were more likely to have experienced career interruptions, but the impact on their salaries was smaller than it was for men who had interrupted their careers.

Another study (Schneer & Reitman, 1993) considered the relationship between family structure and income. The researchers collected surveys from 925 people who had graduated from MBA programs between 1975 and 1980 asking about their jobs, income, families, and satisfaction. Interestingly, the researchers found that families with two working parents earned less than families in which the wife did not work. Single men, working couples with no children, and working couples with children all earned similar amounts. Contrary to findings from previous research, married women earned more than single women. Finally, working couples reported more career satisfaction than couples in which the wife did not work.

Aside from career gaps, another possible explanation for sex differences in salary is the availability of mentors. As you may recall from Chapter 8, mentors are individuals higher in the organizational structure who take an interest in, and often assist with, a junior employee's career progress. One study of female lawyers (Riley & Wrench, 1985), for example, found that women who had a mentor reported greater job success and more job satisfaction. Another study of female executives (Reich, 1986) found that women who had mentors reported greater self-confidence.

Because men dominate the upper strata of management, however, female mentors are rare (Betz & Fitzgerald, 1987; Noe, 1989; Ragins & Scandura, 1994), and so women are likely to have less assistance in obtaining promotions and pay raises. In a survey of 800 employees of research and development firms, two researchers (Ragins & Cotton, 1991) found that female employees felt they had a harder time finding mentors because (1) they had less access to possible mentors than men; (2) possible mentors were more likely to turn them down; or (3) the mentor or others in the organization would perceive an approach as a sexual advance. Nonetheless, women are more likely to have a male mentor than vice versa (Ragins, 1989; Tepper, 1995).

Dreher and Ash (1990) surveyed 320 business school graduates about their income, promotions, and experiences of mentoring in the years after they finished school. Interestingly, results from their survey indicated that women did not have fewer mentoring experiences than men—even though the men earned nearly $7,990 more annually than the women. Here again, job satisfaction may have affected income level: Despite the significant difference in salaries, males and females were not significantly different in their levels of satisfaction with pay.

In another study that looked at race, gender, and mentoring, Dreher and Cox (1996) asked 1,018 graduates of MBA programs about their career progress after graduation. Results from the survey showed that White MBAs were more likely than either minorities or women to form mentoring relationships with White male managers, although female MBAs were as likely as male MBAs to find a mentor. In addition, graduates who had White male mentors—irrespective of the graduate's race or gender—earned on average $22,454 more than those without mentors.

How does a person find a mentor? Turban and Dougherty 1994 looked at the personality characteristics of individuals who wanted to find a mentor. In that study, people who had a high internal locus of control, high self-monitoring (Chapter 9), and a high level of emotional stability were more likely to initiate and establish mentoring relationships. Individuals who established relationships with a mentor also attained more career success, regardless of gender.

Another explanation for the male-female wage gap is that women are less likely than men to choose their occupations on the basis of salary. In a study of applicants for a variety of jobs in a university (Hollenbeck, Ilgen, Ostroff, & Vancouver, 1987), researchers found that women were more likely to apply for the lower paying jobs, irrespective of their qualifications. Overall, women applicants placed a greater emphasis than men on having a sense of accomplishment from their work, control over work schedule, and ease of movement in and out of the workplace. Women did not regard pay as less important than the men, but they seemed to put more emphasis on flexibility in work arrangements.

Recall from Chapter 8 that negotiating skill also affects salary; some research suggests that women are less skilled than men in negotiating starting salaries. Even when provided with training in negotiation, one group of female MBAs still negotiated a salary averaging $1,350 less than a similar group of male MBAs (Stevens, Bavetta, & Gist, 1993).

Although expectations may contribute to career success, there are other factors that may explain the lower levels reached by women. It may be that women's expectations are grounded in a realistic understanding of how difficult it is to succeed in a male-dominated environment. For example, a study by the Women's Legal Defense Fund found that older women who sought legal recourse for age and sex bias generally lost their cases (Leonard, 1996).

Another factor that may affect level of aspiration is the fact that most career women continue to have more responsibility than men for the home and the children. Blumstein and Schwartz (1983) found, for example, that working women in the United States continue to do about 70 percent of the housework, and Kerblay (1983) found a similar statistic for working women in the former Soviet Union. A more recent study (Parasuraman, Greenhaus, Rabinowitz, Bedeian, & Mossholder, 1989) found that husbands of employed accountants reported lower levels of job satisfaction, marital adjustment, and quality of life than did husbands of housewives.

Comparable Worth Job evaluation refers to determining the "worth" of a job to an organization and setting a salary (Chapter 3). Policies toward setting wages are supposedly developed so that the organization has a rational system of salary scales, but some individuals maintain that part of the reason why females earn only 75 percent of what males earn is due to the present methods of job evaluation.

Take, for example, the practice of **exceptioning** (Fulgham, 1984). Exceptioning occurs when a job evaluation reveals the salary for a particular job is out of line with its responsibilities, but no steps are taken to bring the salary in line with prevailing standards. A good example of exceptioning is the job of nurse. Nurses have many responsibilities and duties similar to those of doctors, and they too have responsibility for the lives of their patients. Most likely a comparison of doctors' and nurses' job duties would suggest that, given their responsibilities, nurses are underpaid. Because hospitals simply cannot afford to pay nurses what they are worth, however, their salaries are exceptioned from the salary hierarchy.

In addition to exceptioning, another factor that may affect salaries is the sex-stereotyping of jobs. Despite 35 years of equal employment opportunity legislation, many jobs continue to be stereotyped by both employers and applicants as to sex suitability (e.g., secretaries should be women and truck drivers, men). Sex-stereotyping is particularly powerful when the job is primarily occupied by persons of one gender, when the applicant pool is primarily one gender, and when the organization is large and complex (Perry, Davis-Blake, & Kulik, 1994).

One result of this stereotyping is that many women have not progressed from the lower-paying jobs in society. Interestingly, one study of hiring practices found that African-American managers use sex stereotypes when making hiring decisions less often than White managers (McRae, 1994).

The **comparable worth** movement arose in part as a means of addressing discrepancies in pay rates based on sex. According to the Equal Pay Act of 1963, men and women performing the same *job* are to be paid equally. Comparable worth, however, does not focus on jobs, but on the *similarity of the tasks* that comprise the jobs. For example, suppose the job of data entry clerk is traditionally held by males and paid $2,000 more annually than the job of accounting clerk, which is traditionally held by females. A job analysis of the two positions reveals that filing, record keeping, and posting are the major tasks of both jobs. According to comparable worth, difference in salaries cannot be justified.

Although comparable worth has been discussed for a number of years, it is presently the position of the federal government that it will not take an active stance in pursuing the issue of comparable worth. Reasons for this position include (1) the institution of comparable worth legislation would require analyzing and evaluating all jobs in the economy; (2) jobs change so quickly that many parts of the evaluation would be useless as soon as they were finished; (3) instituting comparable worth legislation would cause major dislocations in the economy by causing wages to rise for virtually all jobs; and (4) salaries are often determined as much by the supply of workers in the economy as they are by job content. In general, the courts have accepted going market rates of pay as an acceptable defense for sex differences in salaries.

Work–Family Conflicts

In terms of job stress, women appear to be similar to men; that is, men and women experience stress at work equally (Martocchio & O'Leary, 1989). One area in which they may experience stress differently, however, is in the conflict between the demands of family and those of the job. This is an area of growing interest for researchers because such conflicts are a source of both job satisfaction and stress for women.

For example, paid employment for working mothers has been related to self-esteem, status, and life satisfaction (Gove & Zeiss, 1987; Kessler & McRae, 1982) on the one hand, and to stress, life dissatisfaction, and family tension (Cooke & Rousseau, 1984; Kandel, Davies, & Raveis, 1985) on the other. One explanation for this is that women who are required to fulfill multiple roles (e.g., wife, mother, manager) experience stress. In a study of work–family conflict in working mothers (Williams, Suls, Alliger, Learner, & Wan, 1991), researchers found that stress occurred when the demands of one role interrupted behaviors pertinent to another.

Work often interferes with the accomplishment of family duties because of the time demanded, and family duties—such as taking care of a sick child—often interfere with work (Gutek, Searle, & Klepa, 1991). In a study of work interference with family, for example, two researchers (Thomas & Ganster, 1995) found that more interference was associated with less job satisfaction and more depression and health complaints among health-care workers. Another study (Greenhaus, Bedeian, & Mossholder, 1987) found that more time spent at work correlated with more work–family conflict. This kind of work–family conflict is a problem for women in particular, who generally spend much more time than do men on family and household duties; men, in contrast, spend more time at work-related activities.

In one study (Frone, Russell, & Cooper, 1992), researchers interviewed 2,631 working adults about work interference with family and family interference with work. The researchers found that individuals who experienced family interference with their work were more likely to be depressed, but work interference with the family did not create depression. Another study of work–family conflict (Duxbury & Higgins, 1991) found that men were more upset when family roles interfered with work roles, whereas women were more upset when work roles interfered with family roles. Echoing a point made earlier in this chapter, the researchers commented that these findings "support the idea that there have been very few changes in society's perception of gender-specific work and family-role responsibilities over the past decades."

Some evidence (Adams, King, & King, 1996) suggests that a person's work–family relationship affects both job and life satisfaction. Also, higher job involvement is usually related to higher job satisfaction, but higher job involvement is also related to higher job interference with family.

Williams and Alliger (1994) looked at the carryover between unpleasant moods at home and work. The researchers used a sampling method in which participants were signalled by special wristwatches eight times per day to record their moods. In this study, work intrusions into family were not as disruptive as family intrusions into work. The results also showed that unpleasant moods spilled over from work to family and from family to work, but pleasant moods did not transfer from one setting to another. The researchers thus suggest that pleasant moods may be more transitory than unpleasant moods.

Doby and Caplan (1995) surveyed 102 accountants about stress at work and home, focusing on threats to reputation at work that affect home life negatively. In addition, the accountants completed a questionnaire about experiencing anxiety "while relaxing away from work." Results from this study suggested that when the accountants experienced a lack of feedback, inadequate training, role overload, and role ambiguity, they felt anxiety both at home and at work.

In contrast, some research (Ingram & Simons, 1995; Thomas & Ganster, 1995) suggests that "family-responsive" work environments have a positive impact on workers. In one study (Grover & Crooker, 1995), for example, organizational policies such as parental leave, flexible schedules, and child-care assistance increased organizational commitment and lowered employees' intentions to quit. In recent years eldercare, another family issue, has also become an important benefit for some employees (Goodstein, 1995). In an analysis of survey results from 1,239 organizations, Goodstein (1994) found that larger companies and companies with a higher percentage of female workers were more likely to adopt family-responsive policies.

Family-responsive policies apparently come at a price, however. In a comparison of companies with the highest number of female executives with a ranking of companies with the most family-responsive policies, there was little overlap (Dobrzynski, 1996). That is, in the companies in which women were advancing the fastest, policies were least responsive to the needs of families. In that study, variables considered related to family responsiveness included pay, the advancement of women, work schedule flexibility, child-care policies, and other benefits (Lublin, 1996b).

"Career-Primary" and "Career-and-Family" Women In 1989 Felice Schwartz, writing in the *Harvard Business Review,* made what many people considered a radical proposal. Pointing out that the cost of employing female managers is much higher than employing males because women leave the workforce 2.5 times more frequently than men, Schwartz attributed this turnover to women leaving to give birth and raise children. Certain women do not want the combined pressures of being an executive and a successful parent at the same time in their lives. In contrast with the **career-primary woman,** Schwartz referred to this group as the **career-and-family woman:**

The career-and-family woman is willing to trade off the pressures and demands that go with promotion for the freedom to spend more time with her children. She's very smart, she's talented, she's committed to her career, and she's satisfied to stay at the middle level, at least during the early child-rearing years. (1989)

Most companies, however, have only one career track for women—the usual increased responsibilities and opportunities leading directly to an executive position. According to Schwartz, women who want to spend time with their children usually end up being excluded from this path. At some point, virtually all women must make a decision—career or family—that most men do not have to make. In fact, 90 percent of male executives have children by age 40, but only 35 percent of female executives have children by that age.

Corporations lose talented women because they do not recognize the needs of women oriented to both family and career. Schwartz suggested that it is in the best interest of companies to develop a career path that accommodates the needs of these women by providing maternity leave, being flexible so the women can remain productive, and providing adequate child care.

Schwartz's proposal, which was nicknamed the **mommy track,** created a storm of controversy. Many women felt that developing a system of career progression that emphasized women's traditional role with children would simply perpetuate stereotypes and undermine the career progress of all women. In a study designed to determine women's feelings about a mommy track, for example, one company surveyed 26,500 managers in seven large corporations (Kelly, 1991). Results from the study found greater dissatisfaction with their career development among women than men, but only 9 percent of the women—compared with 26 percent of the men—stated that their intention to quit their jobs was related to children. The researchers concluded that Schwartz was misinterpreting the source of women's dissatisfaction, and attributing it to children, when in fact the dissatisfaction was more strongly correlated with age. Younger women, who happened to have younger children, tended to be more dissatisfied, as did younger men.

Sexual Harassment

One area of the psychology of work that has not been investigated until recently concerns sexual behavior. Researchers now know that such behavior—running the gamut from flirting to sexual harassment—is actually quite common, and that over half of all employees report having received some kind of sexual overture or comment from another employee (Gutek, 1985).

Nonharassing sexual behavior includes making sexual comments intended to be compliments, attempts to initiate dating, flirting, telling sexually oriented jokes, wolf whistling, and making comments that are annoying but not sufficiently offensive as to warrant a sexual harassment complaint. These kinds of behaviors increase when males and females have more contact in the workplace (Gutek, Cohen, & Konrad, 1990).

When such behaviors are offensive, however, workers may experience sexual harassment. According to the Equal Employment Opportunity Commission (EEOC Policy Guidance on Sexual Harassment Issues, 1990), **sexual harassment** consists of unwelcome sexual advances or requests for sexual favors that are explicitly or implicitly a condition of employment or that interfere with an employee's job performance. Sexual harassment takes two forms: *Quid pro quo* refers to demands for sexual favors in exchange for workplace benefits; *hostile environment* refers to creating an intimidating environment for the victim (Bennet-Alexander & Pincus, 1995). Hostile environment sexual harassment is much harder to demonstrate than quid pro quo.

Because sexual harassment is often a perception on the part of an employee, the concept is difficult to define precisely. In addition, much of the research in this area is based on convenience samples and questionable measurement instruments (Lengnick-Hall, 1995). Nonetheless, a survey of affirmative action officers (York, 1989) identified the following factors as the basis for a sexual harassment complaint: a negative reaction on the part of a victim; the existence of coercion; and job consequences relating to the incident. Less important are the victim's status or work history, where the incident took place, or the form of the harassment.

In a review of the outcomes of 81 sexual harassment complaints, two researchers (Terpestra & Baker, 1988) found that plaintiffs won their cases only 31 percent of the time. A follow-up study several years later (Terpestra & Baker, 1992) found complainants were successful in approximately the same percentage of cases, but that they won almost 100 percent of the cases in which the victim had witnesses and documents to support the allegation and when management had been notified but had taken no action.

Based on their review, the researchers recommended four steps for organizations to decrease the likelihood of sexual harassment lawsuits: (1) use training programs and severe penalties to encourage workers to refrain from such behavior; (2) develop a sexual harassment complaint system; (3) take immediate investigative action on learning of an incident; and (4) review sexual harassment lawsuits and settle out of court if the odds of losing the case are great.

Minority Employees

Hispanics in the Workplace

With the passage of the Civil Rights Act of 1964 and the following years of employment litigation, many minorities achieved positions in management that had not previously been open to them. This achievement was not without cost, however, and many people believe the movement of minorities into executive positions has been painfully slow. Although many White males believe equal employment policies have structured the workplace so that minorities receive a disproportionate share of rewards, minority workers often believe only White males get ahead.

Although there are many economic studies of minorities in the workplace that look at issues such as levels of income and labor force participation, there are very few *psychological* studies. Industrial and organizational researchers have addressed many issues of concern to women, but few have considered the effects of racial issues on organizations. In general, organizational researchers have ignored race and simply applied information from their studies of White employees to minorities (Nkomo, 1988, 1992).

Historically, research on race and its impact on organizational functioning first focused on finding ways for minorities to "fit into" the organization, but later theorists, such as diversity proponents, argued for cultural pluralism. In a review of articles concerning race in organizations between 1965 and 1989, Cox and Nkomo (1990) found five major content areas: affirmative action/equal employment opportunity; staffing and test validity; job satisfaction; motivation; and performance appraisal. Virtually all studies focused on differences between Whites and minorities, and hardly any considered racial issues from a historical perspective, or considered what racial issues meant to members of the majority culture. The researchers concluded that most studies looked at race in a superficial fashion, rather than addressing the more profound questions of power, authority, and dominance that characterize race relations in organizations.

One area in which minorities are likely to differ from the majority is in terms of the value they place on individualism (Triandis, 1989). Cross-cultural studies suggest that Western Europeans and North Americans tend to be more individualistic (Hofstede, 1980; Inkeles, 1983), whereas Asians, Hispanics, and Africans place a greater value on collectivism. Collectivist values include the strong role of family and the prevalence of personalism over achievement. Collectivists also emphasize cooperation and teamwork; individualists value competition and independent achievement (Diaz-Guerrero, 1984; Wagner & Moch, 1986).

Cox, Lobel, and McLeod (1991) tested this hypothesis by asking White, Asian, African-American, and Hispanic individuals to work on a task in which they could choose to cooperate or compete. Results showed that the minority participants were, in fact, more likely to cooperate, and the researchers observed that increased numbers of these groups in the workforce may influence organizations to take a more cooperative approach to work than they had previously.

Not all studies support the collectivist hypothesis, however. In another cross-cultural study (Chen, 1995), Chinese managers and workers were found to favor economic and social rewards for performance distributed on an individual basis. American managers and workers, in contrast, preferred that economic rewards be based on performance but that social rewards—friendliness from the boss, social interaction, and so forth—be distributed on an egalitarian basis.

In a further measure of the effects of collectivism versus individualism, Earley (1993) studied the performances of American, Chinese, and Israeli managers on an in-basket task. Managers completed a measure of collectivist or individualist orientation and then were assigned to work under one of three conditions: alone, as a member of an Ingroup, or as a member of an Outgroup. Participants assigned to the Ingroup were told that members of their group had been carefully selected, that they were all similar in terms of background, and that some members of the group might even be distantly related. Outgroup members, on the other hand, were told they were assigned randomly and that they probably had nothing in common with each other.

Results from the study showed that people with a collectivist Orientation had lower performances when they worked alone or as a member of an outgroup. Collectivists who were assigned to the Ingroup rated themselves higher on self-efficacy, and they performed better on the in-basket task. The researcher concluded that companies that place a heavy emphasis on individual gain may increase performance in collectivist cultures by stressing the social ties that bind workers to their groups.

Finally, one study (Watson, Kumar, & Michaelsen, 1993) looked at the impact of cultural diversity on group performance. Subjects in that study were assigned to either culturally homogeneous or culturally heterogeneous groups and asked to work on a number of problems for a 17-week period. Homogeneous groups consisted of people from the same nationality and ethnic background; heterogeneous groups consisted of one White American, one African American, one Hispanic American, and one foreign national from Asia, Africa, Latin America, or the Middle East.

Initially the heterogeneous groups did not perform as well as the homogeneous groups in terms of either process or problem solving. Both sets of groups improved in both process and problem solving over time, however, and by the end of four months, all groups were equal in performance. The researchers concluded that although heterogeneous groups may need longer to become effective, their performances improve more rapidly than those of homogeneous groups.

Many times minority workers feel they are excluded from the informal networks and social activities of White employees and that, like women, they must work harder to be accepted in the workplace. For example, one study (Greenhaus & Parasuraman, 1993) found that the successful job performances of White managers were generally attributed to ability, but that successful performances by African-American managers were often attributed to luck, job ease, and help from other workers.

Another study (Ibarra, 1995) looked at the informal networks of White and minority managers. Working with 63 middle-level managers (46 White managers, of whom 20 were women, and 17 minorities, of whom 5 were women), Ibarra and her associates asked respondents to complete a sociometric questionnaire and participate in a semistructured interview regarding their contacts with others. Results indicated that minority managers had more racially heterogeneous networks, but that high-potential minority managers had more same-race ties than lower-potential minorities. High-potential minorities also had wider social networks that included more lower-status individuals.

In another study (Cox & Nkomo, 1991), African-American MBAs had lower levels of job involvement than their White counterparts, were less satisfied with their jobs, and reported having less access to mentors and people higher up in the organization (Kram, 1988; Thomas, 1990). Lefkowitz (1994b) found that newly hired African-American employees were disproportionately assigned to African-American supervisors and that over time, African-American employees tended to remain with African-American supervisors.

As a result of these kinds of practices, minorities sometimes attempt to develop their own networks of colleagues. However, because minority colleagues are fewer in number, occupy lower positions in the organization, and are in their positions for shorter periods than White males, such networks tend to be unstable and not as useful as they are for other groups (Ibarra, 1993).

In another series of interviews with a broad spectrum of managers and employees, Jones (1986) found that a common perception among African-American males was that organizations often promoted White women rather than equally qualified African Americans—a perception supported by findings from the Department of Labor's Glass Ceiling Initiative, discussed above. In fact, the rate of promotion of African-American men appears to be lower than that of either White or African-American women, and African-American men are less satisfied than African-American women with their career progress (Nkomo & Cox, 1989). Nonetheless, one study of African-American managers found that male managers still earned higher salaries than female managers (McRae & Carter, 1992).

Table 11.2   PERCENTAGES OF MANAGERS AND PROFESSIONALS WHO ARE BLACK

Managers/Professionals	Percentage
Accountants and auditors	8.4
Actors and directors	9.8
Airline pilots and navigators	1.2
All executives and managers	7.2
Architects	2.5
College and university teachers	6.2
Editors and reporters	4.7
Engineers	4.7
Financial managers	4.0
Lawyers	3.6
Marketing, advertising, and public relations managers	2.2
Physicians	4.9
Public officials and administrators	13.6
Salespeople	7.8
Social workers	23.7
Percentage of Blacks in total work force	10.6

Source: U.S. Bureau of the Census, 1996.

One researcher (Shenhav, 1992) looked at promotional opportunities for African Americans in scientific and engineering occupations over time. According to that analysis, between 1982 and 1986, the promotion rate for African Americans was equal to or better than that for White males. In the public sector, in fact, African-American males had a distinct advantage over other groups. Another study (Powell & Butterfield, 1997), for example, found that race was less a factor in promotions in the public sector than minority applicants' limited experience.

Hispanics in the Workplace

Hispanic workers constitute one of the fastest growing segments of American society, yet very little is known about their experiences in the workplace (Knouse, Rosenfeld, & Culbertson, 1992). For example, the Hispanic civilian labor force grew by 52.4 percent between 1980 and 1989, whereas the non-Hispanic civilian labor force grew by only 17.3 percent (Cresce, 1992), but virtually no researchers have looked specifically at this group in terms of the psychology of work. In addition, few companies have taken steps to provide mentors for their Hispanic employees (Knouse, 1992). Possible reasons for this neglect include language differences, the low occupational status attained by most Hispanics, and divisions within the different Hispanic groups.

One study (Ferdman & Cortes, 1992), however, looked at the experiences of 27 Hispanic managers in a medium-sized corporation in New England. Using a case study approach and in-depth interviews, the researchers found that, in contrast with the bureaucratic style of the company, Hispanic managers put a greater emphasis on interpersonal relationships, and that they preferred a participatory rather than an autocratic leadership style.

In addition, the managers had a flexible attitude toward the organizational hierarchy, preferring to circumvent the hierarchy in order to accomplish a goal. The managers also felt strongly about their own autonomy and avoided becoming too dependent on their supervisors. Although it is difficult to generalize from this small sample to the experiences of Hispanic managers in general, this study may offer some support for the "collectivist" orientation mentioned earlier in this chapter.

Sanchez and Brock (1996) looked at perceived employment discrimination among Hispanic employees in Miami. Using a survey approach, researchers approached individuals at shopping malls and the motor vehicle bureau and asked them to complete questionnaires about issues such as role conflict, perceived discrimination, organizational commitment, and job satisfaction. Results from the survey suggested that perceived discrimination lowered organizational commitment and job satisfaction and increased feelings of tension. However, if a Hispanic individual had grown up in the United States, belonged to the largest Hispanic minority in the area (Cuban), and had a high salary, that individual perceived less unfair discrimination.

Table 11.3 PERCENTAGES OF MANAGERS AND PROFESSIONALS WHO ARE HISPANIC

Managers/Professionals	Percentage
Accountants and auditors	4.4
Actors and directors	3.0
Airline pilots and navigators	3.9
All executives and managers	4.8
Architects	5.8
College and university teachers	3.6
Editors and reporters	3.5
Engineers	3.3
Financial managers	5.7
Lawyers	3.1
Marketing, advertising, and public relations managers	3.3
Physicians	4.3
Public officials and administrators	4.7
Salespeople	6.9
Social workers	7.8
Percentage of Hispanics in total work force	8.9

Source: U.S. Bureau of the Census, 1996.

In earlier chapters we discussed a number of studies that looked at race as it affected selection and performance appraisal, but overall, researchers know little about the psychology of minority workers. Although some recent studies have considered the career progress of minorities—African-American workers in particular—very little research has addressed the impact of race on, for example, team performance, training, or organization development. This situation may change, however, with the current popularity of diversity programs. As the workforce changes, industrial and organizational psychologists will almost certainly be forced to consider race as an important organizational variable.

Older Workers

During the downsizing that occurred in the late 1980s and early 1990s, many older workers were offered early retirement. Because older workers usually earn more than younger workers, investors typically reacted favorably to turnover among older workers (Davidson, Worrell, & Fox, 1996). In recent years, in fact, average job tenure for males has been declining, with older men being particularly at risk for layoffs (Koretz, 1997a).

Nonetheless, the push toward early retirement may run contrary to other demographic trends, which suggest that people may be inclined to work longer. For example, the age at which a person becomes eligible for Social Security rises to 67 from 65 in the year 2000. In addition, mandatory retirement has been eliminated for virtually all jobs, legal protection against age discrimination encourages some people to work longer, and advances in health care may also allow people to work past age 65.

Finally, some people may be motivated to keep working for financial reasons, since research suggests the major reason workers choose to leave their jobs is financial—they simply find they have no need to work (Ruhm, 1989). On the other hand, when people are forced to retire for reasons not of their choosing, health, longevity, and life satisfaction are likely to be affected negatively (Cahill & Salomone, 1987; Herzog, House, & Morgan, 1991). Finally, workers increasingly do not retire completely, but find "bridge employment," such as part-time work or self-employment, before complete retirement begins (Feldman, 1994).

In recent years, some researchers have considered sex differences in retirement decisions. Talaga and Beehr (1995), for example, analyzed questionnaires from 368 employees of an office furniture manufacturing firm to determine factors that affected a decision to retire. Interestingly, the odds of men retiring decreased as the number of dependents living in their home increased; women, on the other hand, were more likely to retire if there were more dependents at home. Along the same lines, men were more likely to retire if their spouses were in poor health, whereas women retired more often when their spouses were in good health.

Although researchers have looked at older workers in terms of labor trends for many years, research into the psychological aspects of work and aging is relatively new. For example, researchers do not yet agree on the age at which a worker becomes "older," although the majority of studies choose age 55 (Ashbaugh & Fay, 1987).

With regard to job satisfaction, older workers consistently report higher levels than younger workers (Glenn & Weaver, 1985). This is not surprising, since younger workers typically earn less and have less authority and less desirable tasks to perform. Interestingly, however, some evidence suggests that although older male workers earn more than younger males, older female workers often earn less than their younger counterparts. This may be due to the fact that, unlike male workers, older female workers are often less well educated than younger women, and also that most women leave and reenter the workforce at least once in their lifetimes (Shaw, 1988).

Three researchers (Barnum, Liden, & DiTomaso, 1995) were interested in the relationship of age and race to salary. Using an interview methodology, they asked 240 nonmanagerial workers in a variety of firms about pay rates, education, race and ethnicity, and other variables. The researchers then used these data to develop a regression equation that would predict salary based on age and race.

Although salary differences were not significant among younger workers, the differences between White males and other groups became significant after

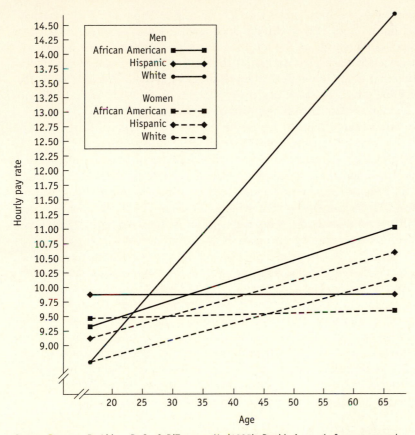

Source: Barnum, P., Liden, R. C., & DiTomaso, N. (1995). Double jeopardy for women and minorities: Pay differences with age. *Academy of Management Journal, 38,* 863–880. Copyright © 1995.

Figure 11.2 Relationship Among Salary, Age, Race-ethnicity, and Gender
As the chart indicates, all groups except African American women and Hispanic men earned more per hour as they got older, but White males earned significantly more than the other groups.

age 35. Interestingly, the equation predicted that salaries for White and African-American males would rise over time (though not at the same rate), but that salaries for Hispanic males were likely to remain unchanged. Along the same lines, salaries for White and Hispanic females were likely to rise, but those of African-American females were not. The most striking aspect of this study was the difference between White males salaries and those of other groups. Results from this study appear in Figure 11.2.

Another reason why older workers are more satisfied relates to the attraction-selection-attrition model discussed in Chapter 10—older workers have probably, over time, found that their personalities fit with their jobs. In addition, they are more committed to their jobs and absent less frequently (Martocchio, 1989).

Many people—younger males with less education in particular (Finkelstein, Burke, & Raju, 1995; Perry, Kulik, & Bourhis, 1996)—believe that older workers perform less well on the job than do other workers. Interestingly, virtually no evidence supports a decline in the performance of older workers, except in jobs that demand physical strength or speed (Avolio, Waldman, & McDaniel, 1990; McEvoy & Cascio, 1989). Between 1970 and 1977, for example, the Grumman Corporation laid off 13,000 people on the basis of performance rather than seniority. When the layoffs were completed, the average age of the workforce had risen from 37 to 45 (Knowles, 1988).

Although older workers experience some decline of sensory, intellectual, and physical abilities, these are usually so small as to be unnoticeable (Rabbitt, 1991). The greatest area of decrement is in information processing, resulting from changes in the nervous system, which may cause problems when it occurs in conjunction with low levels of deafness. Older workers do have higher benefit costs than younger employees, however.

Older workers have fewer accidents than younger workers. Nonetheless, when older workers do have accidents, they are likely to be more serious and more expensive to the employer (Dillingham, 1983). In addition, the death rate for injuries to workers age 50 or older is twice that of workers ages 21 to 24 (Root, 1981).

From the perspective of management, typical problems of older workers are a lack of meaningful involvement in their jobs, skill obsolescence, and increasing interest in activities outside work. Typical approaches to handling these problems include training opportunities, career counseling, mentoring, and involving older workers in special projects and task forces (Meier, 1988).

Table 11.4. describes some qualities of older workers.

Table 11.4   QUALITIES OF OLDER WORKERS

In a survey conducted by the American Association of Retired Persons, executives were asked their views on workers over age 50. The table below indicates the percentage of executives who rated the older workers as excellent or very good on the dimension.

Characteristic	Percentage
Good attendance and punctuality	86
Commitment to quality	82
Loyalty and dedication to company	79
Practical, not just theoretical, knowledge	79
Solid experience	74
Solid/reliable performance record	71
Someone to count on in a crisis	70
Ability to get along with coworkers	60
Emotional stability	59

Source: Meier, E. L. (1988) Managing an older workforce. In M. E. Borus, H. S. Parnes, S. H. Sandell, & B. Seidman (Eds.), *The older worker.* Madison, WI: Industrial Relations Research Association.

Social Stratification in the Workplace

Top Executives
Blue-Collar Workers

Although this chapter has focused on gender, age, and racial aspects of groups in the workplace, more traditional approaches to work groups focus on differences in *social stratification*—relative position in terms of status, responsibilities, and salary of employees. The final part of this chapter considers differences between the most extreme ends of the social structure—top executives and blue-collar workers.

As you may recall from Chapter 10, executives and blue-collar workers are examples of designated groups. Members do not necessarily choose to belong to a designated group; rather, *others* consider them members. There are important differences in the behaviors of designated groups in the workplace, and both top executives and blue-collar workers have constraints on their actions. For example, both groups have norms governing their dress, methods of communication, and work environments. Clearly, the designated group to which a worker belongs has an important effect on that worker's behavior in the workplace.

Top Executives

Just as in *The Great Gatsby* F. Scott Fitzgerald held that the rich are different from the nonrich, we can be certain that the top leaders of organizations differ from those below them. Although the motivations of top executives may be similar to those of individuals farther down the hierarchy, environments and behaviors of people at the top are usually quite distinct. Salaries are quite different, too. In 1995 the heads of the top companies in the United States earned 212 times the salary of the average American employee (Lublin, 1996a). In 1995 executive compensation increased an average of 10.4 percent, whereas average salaries increased only 2.9 percent.

Kanter (1977, 1980) used an observational approach to study how people at the top differ from other members of organizations. Probably more than any other stratum of management, corporate officers value conformity. Rules for behavior are strict and deviance is rarely tolerated. Top positions in the United States are almost routinely filled by White Protestant males who attended prestigious colleges. Top managers dress alike, have similar cars and homes, belong to the same social organizations, and are almost universally clean-shaven. Even the decor of executive offices is strictly regimented. Box 11.2 describes a typical corporate manager.

According to Kanter, the nature of decisions made at the top necessitates this compelling interest in conformity. Whereas jobs lower in the hierarchy are likely to be structured and duties clearly delineated, top managers have large degrees of discretion in their jobs. They must deal with uncertainties that are not generally a part of lower positions. Because of these uncertainties, managers

Box 11.2   PORTRAIT OF THE BOSS

Despite widespread interest in diversity, some people wonder if the workplace is really changing. In a survey of the qualities of the individuals who run the companies that comprise the *Business Week 1000,* every person at the top turned out to be male. He was 56 years old and had worked at the same company for more than 22 years.

As in the past, these leaders were White and predominantly Protestant, and 97 percent were married. The average number of children was three, which is one more than the national average. Most of the CEOs had majored in business at such universities as Princeton, Yale, and Harvard. Half went on to graduate school, and about half served in the military. The majority of these leaders had started their careers in finance, accounting, and, to a lesser extent, marketing. Typical annual income as head of the company was $868,000.

In college, 20 percent of these corporate leaders played varsity sports, most often football and, to a lesser degree, baseball or softball. Nearly all of the CEOs reported that they still played sports, most often golf or tennis.

Given the homogeneity of this group, it is easy to see how women and minorities may have trouble breaking through the glass ceiling.

Despite the prevalence of men in CEO positions, however, some women have achieved positions at vice presidential or higher levels. Among the women in senior management, 36 percent have four years of college or less, compared with 94 percent of all women age 25 and older. In addition, 31 percent of top female managers hold an MBA.

Among senior executive women, 91 percent are White, 3 percent are African American, and 1 percent are Hispanic. In terms of marital status, 72 percent are married, 11 percent never married, and 16 percent—a much higher percentage than among top male executives—are divorced or separated. Finally, senior executive women are most likely to be found in the finance, insurance, real estate, and manufacturing industries.

Sources: Roman, M., Mims, R., & Jespersen, F. (1991, November 25). A portrait of the boss. *Business Week,* 180–184; and Townsend, B. (1996, July). Room at the top for women. *American Demographics,* 28–37.

tend to rely on individuals of similar backgrounds because they feel they can communicate better with them. In many cases women and minorities are seen as deviants whose depth of commitment to the company is questionable.

Although such conformity may facilitate decision making, it may also create a kind of groupthink among managers. When executives tolerate only ideas similar to their own, they may lose touch with the realities of organizational functioning. Perhaps a classic example of this was the failure of top management at Chrysler Corporation to recognize changes in the marketplace in the 1970s, and similar situations at General Motors in the 1980s and IBM in the early 1990s. One study (Boeker, 1997), in fact, found that organizational change is more likely to occur when top management has had long tenure, there is diversity in tenure among the top management term, and organizational performance is poor.

In some respects, however, executives are no different from other workers. One group of researchers (Judge, Boudreau, & Bretz, 1994) studied the attitudes of almost 3,600 male executives regarding job and life satisfaction, job stress, and work–family conflict. Executives in the study averaged 46 years of age, earned $129,580 annually, and had been in their current positions for three years. Results from this study supported the finding of other studies discussed in Chapter 8 that job satisfaction and life satisfaction are related. In addition, job stress lowered job satisfaction, and job satisfaction was lowered when work interfered with family. However, family interference in work did not seem to lower job satisfaction among this group.

Blue-Collar Workers

Blue-collar workers are those who do manual rather than mental work. Although some blue-collar workers develop high levels of skill in certain areas, many are unskilled and semiskilled. Whereas the skilled blue-collar worker can earn more than lower-level managers, the unskilled and semiskilled are the lowest paid in the organizational hierarchy. The vast majority of skilled blue-collar jobs are held by men (Padavic, 1992; Rosen, 1987).

Although assembly line workers are often considered the prototypical blue-collar employees, this group has never constituted more than 6 percent of the American workforce (Drucker, 1974). Some broader examples of blue-collar jobs include agricultural work, construction, and electronics assembly.

There are several ways in which the careers of low-level employees differ from those of their counterparts elsewhere in the organization. Since these individuals are selling their labor rather than their expertise, management is often unwilling to provide training to improve their skills. Because the lack of training indicates a lack of commitment on either side, lower-level employees are unlikely to identify with their employers and, consequently, for them job change is easy and frequent. Additionally, lower-level employees are likely to reach the top of their salary ranges early in their careers. Professionals, on the other hand, expect to earn more as time passes.

Life at the bottom of an organization has many negative aspects. Since employees are paid the hour or the piece, there is no guarantee of income. Working conditions are rarely under the control of the employee. Automation controls the movements of the worker, and there is little opportunity for independent decision making (Ghidina, 1992). This lack of autonomy often makes jobs stressful. In a study of blue-collar women in textile mills (Rosen, 1987), however, workers complained that the fast pace and low wages of the piecework system were more stressful than boredom.

In the lower levels of organizations, the rates of both accidents and occupational diseases are much higher than elsewhere. Along the same lines, low-level employees are likely to evidence high proportions of personal or social handicaps (Mayes, Barton, & Ganster, 1991).

One researcher (Mechanic, 1980) described how the lowest-level employees can sometimes gain power within an organization. Although such individuals have virtually no authority, they use their positions to control the access of others to information, persons, or resources. Typical methods of achieving power from the bottom include developing expertise about an area that no one else is interested in, forming coalitions with other low-level employees so the formal structure can be circumvented when necessary, and knowing and applying the rules to further personal goals. An example of this occurs when union members seek to disrupt the workplace by adhering strictly to the rules and not doing anything beyond what is specified in the union contract.

Despite the negative aspects of blue-collar jobs, many individuals prefer this kind of work. As stated previously, some individuals do not desire autonomy and responsibility; the social and economic aspects of a job are sufficiently satisfying. Additionally, many workers want to avoid the stress associated with becoming a manager. As one blue-collar worker stated, "I wouldn't want to be in management because you never know when to quit. I wouldn't know when it was Miller time" (Blotnick, 1984).

Chapter Summary

Although some people felt employment discrimination issues in organizations would become less important after the passage of the Civil Rights Act of 1964, this has not been the case. In fact, these issues will become more important as the composition of the workforce changes in the next few decades. Management will need to recruit, hire, train, and supervise a far more diverse workforce than in the past.

Managing diversity refers to directing employees of different cultures and backgrounds toward organizational goals. Diversity emphasizes differences between groups. Not all theorists believe diversity is the best approach to management, however.

Women continue to enter the workforce in large numbers, but top management continues to be dominated by White males. The glass ceiling refers to the phenomenon of so few women and minorities actually making it to the top of organizations. Psychological research suggests that men's attitudes about women workers are remarkably resistant to change even though the behaviors of men and women who achieve management positions are similar.

Women continue to be paid less than men. This may be due to gaps in their employment history, a lack of mentors, or lower levels of aspiration.

Men and women experience job stress differently. When family interferes with work duties, men feel greater stress; when work interferes with family duties, women feel more stress. One proposal for dealing with women's stress regarding the work–family conflict was the so-called mommy track, which would allow women to stay at middle management while they raised their children.

Sexual harassment in the workplace has also become an important area of research.

Few studies have looked at race and the psychology of work. Some studies, however, suggest that minorities have a more collectivist attitude than White employees. Minorities also often feel that they are excluded from the informal networks that are necessary for success in complex organizations. In some respects, African-American women seem to be making greater career progress than do African-American men.

Although Hispanics constitute one of the fastest-growing segments of society, very little is known about their experiences in the workplace.

The role of older workers is likely to grow in the future. In general, older workers are more satisfied with their jobs than younger workers, and they perform as well or better than younger workers except in jobs requiring speed or physical strength. Older workers have fewer accidents, but their accidents are more serious.

Top executives place tremendous importance on conformity. Females and minorities may have had little success in making it to top positions because they are perceived as being too different from traditional male managers. One danger of such conformity is the likelihood of groupthink.

Blue-collar workers sell their labor rather than their skills. Consequently, blue-collar workers and their employers often have little commitment to each other. Blue-collar workers are typically paid by the hour or the piece, have no guaranteed income, and are under the control of a machine. Although they may have no authority, however, they can use their positions in the organization to control the access of others to information, individuals, or resources. Despite the negative aspects of blue-collar jobs, many individuals prefer this kind of work.

Key Words and Concepts

career-and-family woman (p. 354)

career-primary woman (p. 354)

comparable worth (p. 352)

exceptioning (p. 352)

glass ceiling (p. 346)

managing diversity (p. 342)

mommy track (p. 355)

sexual harassment (p. 356)

Questions for Discussion

1. What are some of the changes in the workforce expected in the next few decades? How will these changes affect you personally?
2. What are the advantages to a diversity approach to management? What are the disadvantages?
3. Why do women have difficulty advancing into the ranks of management? Do you think this will always be the case?

4. If you were a woman facing the challenge of succeeding as a manager today, what strategies would you use?

5. What are some of the reasons women receive lower salaries than men? Are any of these reasons justifiable?

6. What are mentors and why are they important?

7. How do men and women react differently to work–family conflicts? How do events at work affect home life? How does home life affect work?

8. Do you favor creating career-primary and career-and-family tracks for female employees? Why or why not?

9. What constitutes sexual harassment? How does a person win a sexual harassment case?

10. What is the difference between individualism and collectivism? Which do you think organizations value more? Are you personally more individualist or collectivist in your approach to life?

11. If you were a minority facing the challenge of succeeding in management today, what strategy would you use?

12. Why are older workers becoming increasingly important to organizations? Are the stereotypes about older workers accurate?

13. What is it like to be a top executive? Why are top executives as a group so homogeneous?

14. What is unique about blue-collar workers? How can people at the bottom of an organization gain power?

CHAPTER 12

The Nature of Organizations

Studying Organizations
Qualities of Organizations
Classical Organizational Theory
Human Relations Movement
Contingency Theories of Organization
Organizational Culture
Postmodern Organizations
Japanese Organization
Chapter Summary
Key Words and Concepts
Questions for Discussion

In this section of *The Psychology of Work* we shift our focus from the individual and group aspects of organizations and look at issues that affect the organization as a whole. These include organizational theory, organizational change, human factors and working conditions, and maintaining the health of workers.

Modern thinking recognizes organizations as *systems composed of interdependent parts.* Systems theorists believe that changes in one area of an organization bring about changes in other areas. Because of this, each part of the organization must be considered in terms of its impact on other parts. From a systems point of view, all of these aspects influence the overall functioning of the organization.

As you recall from Chapter 1, organizational psychology and organizational behavior both overlap and contrast with industrial psychology, in which independent parts of organizations are typically the focus of study. In general, the approach of industrial psychology is also much more quantitative than that of organizational psychology. Because the focus on systems multiplies the number of variables under consideration, quantitative analysis becomes much more difficult. Organizational theory, for example, is an area in which measurement has not been widely applied.

In terms of a definition, **organizational psychology** can be described as the study of groups established to accomplish specific goals. Typical goals of organizations include stopping people from operating automobiles while under the influence of alcohol (e.g., Mothers Against Drunk Driving), providing a forum for promoting world peace (e.g., the United Nations), or selling petroleum products (e.g., Mobil Oil). Some other areas of study for organizational psychologists include the impact of technology on the workplace, group behavior, power relationships, and the culture that forms the basis for the structure of the organization.

Many philosophers—including Marx and Freud—have argued that forming organizations is antithetical to human nature. That is, organizations typically suppress basic human motivations. According to Marx, organizations prevent the expression of positive human values and lead to the exploitation of individuals. Freud, on the other hand, felt that organizations are necessary to control the sexual and aggressive motives of individuals.

Although many organizations do create harmful environments, modern organizational researchers hold more positive views than did either Marx or Freud. Modern researchers recognize that, like all primates, humans are born and spend their entire lives in groups, and that the desire for organization seems to be a genetic predisposition. Living in organized groups requires certain behaviors to be controlled, but this is a sacrifice necessary for survival. Given these assumptions, the basic questions for organizational theorists become: (1) How do we study organizations? and (2) What structure most facilitates meeting organizational goals?

Studying Organizations

Just as psychologists have developed approaches such as behaviorism or psychoanalysis to study human behavior, organizational researchers have developed a variety of approaches for studying organizations. Astley and Van de Ven (1983) have classified these approaches into four categories, which are illustrated in Figure 12.1.

According to the **system-structural view,** the structure of an organization determines the behavior of its members. The characteristics of people who fill organizational roles are not as important as the duties assigned to the roles. The responsibilities of an airline pilot, for example, determine the pilot's behavior much more than the pilot's personal characteristics.

The **strategic choice approach** suggests that systems can exist because individuals within the system agree to have the system. In contrast with the system-structural, a strategic choice approach suggests that behavior causes the system. Organizations are political first and technical second, and they reflect the personalities and backgrounds of the people within them.

Perspectives and Debates

Natural-Selection Approach	Collective-Action Approach
Structure: Industrial structure is economically and technically determined.	*Structure:* Communities or networks of semiautonomous groups that interact to modify or construct their collective environment, rules, options. Through collective-action the organization controls, liberates, and expands individual action.
Change: A natural evolution, with the economic context determining the direction and extent of organizational growth.	
Behavior: Random, natural, or economic, environmental selection.	*Change:* Collective bargaining, conflict, negotiation, and compromise through exchanges with other groups.
Manager role: Inactive.	*Behavior:* Reasonable, collectively constructed, and politically negotiated orders.
	Manager role: Interactive.
System-Structural Approach	Strategic-Choice Approach
Structure: Roles and positions hiearchically arranged to achieve the function of the system efficiently.	*Structure:* People and their relationships organized and socialized to serve the choices and purposes of people in power.
Change: Divide and integrate roles to adapt subsystems to changes in environment, technology, size, and resource needs.	*Change:* Environment and structure are enacted and embody the meanings of action of people in power.
Behavior: Determined, constrained, and adaptive.	*Behavior:* Constructed, autonomous, and enacted; impression management.
Manager role: Reactive.	*Manager role:* Proactive.

Source: Astley, W., & Van de Ven, A. H. (1983). Central perspectives and debates in organization theory. *Administrative Science Quarterly, 28*(2), 245–273. Copyright © 1983 by Cornell University. Reprinted by permission of the publisher.

Figure 12.1 Four Approaches to Organizational Theory

The **natural selection approach** holds that society is composed of economic niches that organizations must fill, and structure is determined by economic factors and the need for efficiency. Under this approach, individuals or individual organizations have little power when faced with the laws of evolution or economics.

Finally, the **collective action approach** holds that organizations form interdependent networks to manipulate the environment. It is not the environment that determines the structure of the organization; rather it is organizations actively cooperating that determine the environment. Two examples of the collective action approach are the European Economic Community (EEC) and the Organization of Petroleum Exporting Countries (OPEC), both of which manipulate their environments to achieve specific goals.

Although each approach has value, psychologists are usually more interested in the system-structural view or the strategic choice perspective. Some researchers have found the natural science approach, with its emphasis on rationalism and empiricism, particularly difficult to apply to organizations. Psychology is, after all, the study of human behavior and cognition. Consequently, most—but certainly not all—psychologists believe that individual behavior is less the product of economic or collective action than it is the result of individuals interacting with their environments. The system-structural theories considered here include classical approaches and modern contingency theories; strategic choice perspectives include human relations, the sociotechnical system, and organizational culture. Before the various schools of organizational theory are described, however, it would be useful to look at some qualities common to all organizations.

Qualities of Organizations

Irrespective of theoretical framework, all organizations are formed to provide individuals with that which they cannot provide themselves. Certain individuals identify goals they want to see achieved, and they attract followers who assist in accomplishing these goals. The first quality of organizations is that they have a principle around which they are organized.

A second quality of organizations is an emphasis on survival. Organizations attempt to manipulate internal or external environments to maximize their chances of continuing to exist. Organizations whose existence is threatened may cut costs, introduce new products, change leadership, or try to attract new members. When the Chrysler Corporation appeared to be headed for bankruptcy, its management attempted to change the environment in which Chrysler did business by influencing Congress to obtain federal loans, asking workers for wage concessions, and firing many middle managers.

A third quality of organizations is that they have outputs; that is, they produce something that is regarded favorably by some constituency. The output may be products, such as consumer goods, or it may be something intangible, such as lobbying efforts to affect or change legislation. The outputs of organizations may be quite distant from their original purposes, and they may have evolved as attempts to adapt to changing environments. Outputs from Sears, Roebuck and Company, one of the world's largest retailers, for example, now include, in addition to retail sales, insurance, pest control, and securities trading.

A fourth quality of organizations is that they cannot exist without followers. If individuals stop believing in the goals of the organization, then the organization is likely to stop existing.

A fifth quality of organizations is the **psychological contract** between the employer and the employee. The psychological contract refers to a belief that employees will make certain contributions to an organization in return for benefits from the organization (Nicholson & Johns, 1985). Because the psychological contract is a perception on the part of the employee, it differs from a formal contract. Some research (Guzzo, Nelson, & Noonan, 1992; Guzzo, Noonan,

& Elron, 1994) suggests that the psychological contract is strengthened when employers have significant influence on employees' lives both on and off the job. Other research (Morrison & Robinson, 1997) suggests that employees feel anger when they feel the psychological contract has been broken.

In recent years some writers have argued that the psychological contract is dead—that employers and employees increasingly feel little loyalty toward each other. One study, in fact, found that over a two-year period, employees felt less obligation to their employer at the same time they felt their employer's obligations to them increase. The researchers (Robinson, Kraatz, & Rousseau, 1994) concluded that turnover may be more related to perceptions about obligations than to loyalty or job satisfaction. Perhaps reflecting society's concern about the decline of the psychological contract, some organizational researchers (Hosmer, 1995; Mayes, Davis, & Schoorman, 1995) have called for more research regarding trust within organizations.

In summary, organizations are organized around a goal; they emphasize survival; they have outputs and they have followers who believe in some form of psychological contract. As suggested above, these qualities are true of all organizations, regardless of theoretical perspective. The following sections discuss four major approaches to describing and understanding organizations—classical organizational theory, the human relations movement, contingency theories, and the organizational culture perspective.

Classical Organizational Theory

Weber's Bureaucracy
Fayol's Functionalism
Qualities of Formal Organizations
Evaluating Classical Theory

Classical organization theory arose as a response to changes in government in Europe at the end of the nineteenth century. As governments became more democratic and as the industrial revolution brought more workers into formal organizations, structures for administrating and controlling organizations also changed. Both researchers and managers became interested in identifying structures capable of meeting the increased needs of society.

Above all, classical organizational theory is characterized by an emphasis on **structure,** the framework that governs the interdependent parts of an organization. The classical theorists discussed here are Weber and Fayol. Scientific management, which is also considered a classical theory of organization, is discussed in Chapter 1.

Weber's Bureaucracy

Probably the first cohesive theory of how organizations function came from the German sociologist Max Weber (1864–1920). Weber observed that as European governments evolved to meet the increased demands of their citizens around the turn of the century, certain structural changes were also occurring.

Weber called these newly evolved structures bureaucracy, and he identified the ways they differed from older forms of organization. In essence, **bureaucracy** is the application of rationality and efficiency to organizational functioning. Although the word *bureaucracy* has a negative connotation today, Weber felt this kind of structure was a vast improvement over earlier forms of organization. The emphasis on universal rules and procedures that characterize the bureaucratic organization is intended to ensure that everyone is treated fairly and equally.

In Weber's time, as now, the stereotypic bureaucratic organization was the government agency, but bureaucracy is a common form of organization outside government as well. In comparison with other forms of organization, bureaucracies hire large numbers of semiskilled or unskilled people whose products or output are relatively simple.

Fayol's Functionalism

Henri Fayol (1841–1925) worked for many years in the French mining industry. In 1916, at the age of 75, Fayol published his ideas on organization, often referred to as **functionalism.** Although his work was not translated into English until 1949 (Weber's was not translated into English until 1947), Fayol's principles are still influential as a framework for understanding the structure of many organizations. Fayol's 14 principles of organization are as follows:

1. Division of work
2. Authority and responsibility
3. Discipline
4. Unity of command (everyone recognizes the leadership)
5. Unity of direction (everyone works for the same goals)
6. Subordination of individual interest to the general interest
7. Remuneration
8. Centralization
9. Scalar chain (line of authority)
10. Order
11. Equity (justice)
12. Stability of tenure
13. Initiative (enthusiasm about the task)
14. Esprit de corps

In one sense Fayol's principles are an elaboration of the principles of bureaucracy. Functionalism, as bureaucracy, recognizes the importance of structure, and these 14 criteria provide a framework for evaluating the efficiency of any organization. Fayol's schema is more psychological than Weber's, however, with such qualities as initiative and esprit de corps considered important for organizational functioning.

Given the applied nature of Fayol's principles, most researchers consider him the founding father of the field of management. Virtually all business students have been exposed to Fayol's five managerial functions: planning, organizing, staffing, coordinating, and controlling. Based on his own experience, Fayol believed that the manager's attention to each of the areas covered in the 14 principles would result in efficient and productive organizations.

Qualities of Formal Organizations

Classical approaches to organizational theory use a number of principles that describe qualities of the organization. Irrespective of theory—classical, human relations, contingency, or organizational culture—these terms are still widely applied by managers today.

The **functional principle** relates to the division of labor. Positions in an organization are determined by their functions, and each position has specific duties that contribute to accomplishing organizational goals. In one department of an organization, for example, work may be divided among accounts payable clerks, accounts receivable clerks, data entry operators, and supervisors. **Departmentalization** refers to grouping several positions doing similar work into departments or units. For example, based on the interrelationship of their duties, the positions listed above are grouped together in the accounting department.

The **scalar principle** is used to describe the chain of command in an organization. Work is delegated from the top downward. The board of directors delegates to the chief executive officer, who delegates to the president, who delegates to the vice presidents, and so forth. **Chain of command** refers to the different levels of management. At a small company, the chain of command may be quite short—the owner and nobody else. Figure 12.2 illustrates the scalar principle, departmentalization, and the functional principle.

Most management theorists believe that in the interest of efficiency, workers should be responsible to only one supervisor. This principle is known as **unity of command.** The **line-staff principle** refers to having authority based on position (line) or expertise (staff). Line positions generally make decisions based on support from staff. For example, the vice president of manufacturing, a line position, may do strategic planning based on recommendations from his or her staff. In formal organizational theory, staff can never control the line, and consequently, line positions are usually more powerful than staff positions.

Finally, **span of control** describes the number of workers a supervisor controls. In **tall organizational structures,** there are many layers of hierarchy, and managers typically control only a few employees directly. **Flat organizational structures** are characterized by fewer levels of hierarchy and larger spans of control. Tall and flat structures and spans of control are illustrated in Figure 12.3 (p. 379). Classical theory has a bias toward tall structures and short spans of control—eight or ten workers under one manager. In contrast, however, a modern Japanese supervisor can be responsible for 200 subordinates.

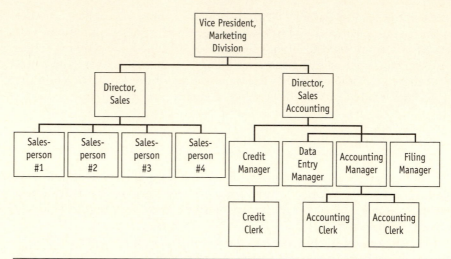

Figure 12.2 Scalar Principle, Departmentalization, and the Functional Principle
Scalar principle: The chain of command goes from the vice president to director to manager to clerk or from director to salesperson. *Departmentalization:* Because all of the positions support the marketing function, they are grouped together in the marketing division, and further delineated into sales and sales accounting departments. *Functional principle:* Each box in the organizational chart represents a unique position. Positions are grouped together on the basis of their similarities.

Although tall structures with smaller spans of control were originally thought to result in greater productivity, later researchers suggested that flatter structures were preferable. Flatter structures often result in better communication and higher levels of job satisfaction, but they do not necessarily result in higher levels of performance. In an era of downsizing and increased employee involvement in decision making, however, flatter structures have become more common.

Evaluating Classical Theory

Classical organizational theory was a first attempt to understand one of the most pervasive features of the modern world. In addition to understanding, classical theorists also offered suggestions about how organizations might be made more effective. As suggested earlier, the classical approach to organizations is still widely practiced today—particularly by the U.S. government, the United States' largest employer.

From a psychologist's perspective, one problem with classical theory is its emphasis on structure and order over individual differences. Classical theorists see structure and order as a way to remove uncertainty from organizational functioning and provide efficient management of people and situations. According to classical theory, a properly designed structure will accommodate any situation or person. In reality, however, this is rarely the case.

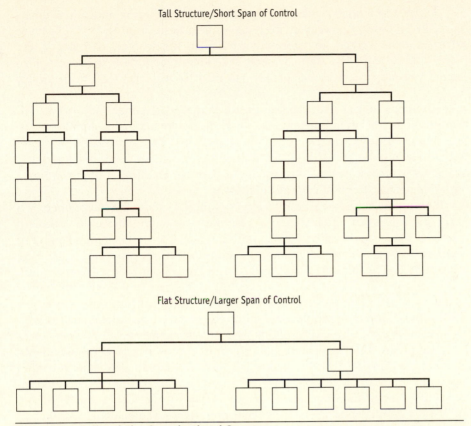

Tall Structure/Short Span of Control

Flat Structure/Larger Span of Control

Figure 12.3 Tall and Flat Organizational Structures

Classical models also assume an orderliness about organizational decision making that is unrealistic. Researchers (Cyert & March, 1963; March & Simon, 1958) have demonstrated that most organizational decision making is influenced by social factors as much as by reason. Because of this, the rationality that is the foundation of bureaucratic organizations is undermined by factors such as interpersonal relations, the importance of an issue to individual managers, and the time that individual managers can devote to resolving an issue. From a psychological persective, the bureaucratic model seems to be pursuing an ideal that, in reality, is unachievable.

In the bureaucratic organization, workers are socialized to conform to standards and procedures that have been developed by the organization, and those who do not cooperate are often criticized, isolated, or dismissed. "Whistleblowers" are employees who make public information about illegal or immoral practices in their organizations. In many cases, whistle-blowing results in the employee being ostracized by other members of the organization (Near & Miceli, 1995). The negative reactions of organizational members are a good example of a classical organization's response to a lack of socialization.

Today most organizational theorists feel that ignoring individual differences in the workplace is more likely to result in disruption than in efficiency. Most modern workers are more educated than the workers of Weber's and Fayol's days, and they often demand individual recognition for accomplishment. Valuing structure over people can lead to problems with both morale and productivity.

Another problem with classical theory is that it minimizes innovation. Although Weber believed bureaucracy would result in a rational system for meeting the needs of individuals, today bureaucracy has the connotation of depersonalized procedures. This is an inherent contradiction of bureaucracy—efficiency can come only at the expense of personal attention, but sometimes a lack of personal attention creates inefficiency.

Because the structure of the classical organization is so fully developed, it is often difficult for the organization to respond to changing demands. Although the ideal bureaucratic system would, in theory, have procedures for adapting to change, such a system has not been developed. Rather, procedures that have been formalized cannot be altered quickly, and the organization may have difficulty adapting to a changed environment. Along the same lines, the special needs or talents of employees cannot be easily integrated into the existing system. This is a common problem in highly structured environments such as government or banks, where promotions tend to come slowly.

Highly structured organizations also lower the responsibility of individuals. Because the division of labor makes jobs interdependent and there are rules and regulations to cover almost any event, individual responsibility for actions tends to be minimal. For example, when a consumer purchases a faulty product or the computer sends an incorrect bill, there is no one person to blame. In many cases, workers in classical organizations have little autonomy—they depend on their supervisors and on organizational history for determining their actions. Taking the responsibility for individual decision making often is not worth the risk.

Finally, classical theory seems to work better in organizations in which tasks are interdependent and high levels of coordination are necessary. On the other hand, in settings such as sales, advertising, or teaching, where individuals work more autonomously, a heavy reliance on structure can lower individual levels of motivation. Although structure is a critical aspect of organizations such as the military, for example, it simply is not efficient in others.

As suggested above, many researchers, and psychologists in particular, argue that there is an underlying contradiction in classical theory: Although structure is emphasized to heighten productivity, too much structure has the opposite effect. As evidenced in the Hawthorne studies or at the Ahmedabad textile mills discussed in Chapter 1, focusing on structure to the exclusion of the social aspects of the workplace can actually be counterproductive. In the period after World War II, some researchers responded to the shortcomings of classical theory by shifting their focus to the human—rather than structural—elements of the organization.

Human Relations Movement

Theory X and Theory Y
Four-Function Typology
Evaluating Human Rela-
tions Theories

In many respects the origin of the human relations movement can be traced to the **Hawthorne studies.** One of the most striking findings from Hawthorne is that individuals will circumvent, modify, or ignore aspects of the workplace structure they find objectionable. Work takes place in a social setting, and many times social factors override production considerations. In the bank wiring room study, for example, workers ignored a piecework system in order to maintain positive social relations; in the illumination study, worker production was more the result of receiving special treatment than the result of experimental manipulation of the lighting.

Human relations theorists felt that describing and managing organizations in terms of structure overlooked the most important aspect of any workplace: the individual and social psychology of the workers. These researchers, who typically came from social science backgrounds, sought to improve the structure of the workplace by improving social relations among workers, particularly between workers and management. Higher productivity—the goal of classical theory—was generally considered less important than providing a harmonious working environment, since higher production was believed to result from having satisfied workers. Two approaches of **human relations theory** to understanding organizations are McGregor's Theory X and Theory Y and Likert's four-function typology.

Theory X and Theory Y

One of the most damaging critiques of classical theory was proposed by Douglas McGregor (1960), whose theory of "X" and "Y" organizations continues to influence managers and social scientists. According to McGregor, **Theory X** organizations operate along the lines of the classical model. They see the functions of the organization to be those that Fayol identified—planning, organizing, staffing, coordinating, and controlling—and they do not give serious consideration to the individual psychology of each worker.

More specifically, the Theory X organization is defined by a set of beliefs about human nature. The first belief is that it is human nature to dislike work, so employees must be carefully controlled to be productive. Second, most workers also dislike autonomy, and they will attempt to avoid taking responsibility for their actions. Third, management must use external motivators—rewards and punishments—to control worker behavior.

The **Theory Y** organization, on the other hand, has a different view of human nature. In contrast with the authoritarian views of Theory X, Theory Y sees workers as trustworthy, open to new experiences, and willing to take responsibility for their actions. Theory Y holds that people naturally enjoy work and see it as an opportunity for personal growth. Consequently, offering individuals autonomy and challenge are two of the best strategies for motivating workers. Only when individuals are unchallenged or rigidly controlled do they lose their natural motivations to do a good job. According to McGregor, productivity is much higher in the Theory Y organization.

Four-Function Typology

In his work assessing the effectiveness of managers, Likert (1961) concluded that supervisors who focus most of their attention on getting the job done are less successful than those who put greater emphasis on human relations. "Job-centered" managers are concerned with schedules, instructions, and close supervision, whereas "employee-centered" managers work to build healthy relationships with employees. Although the job-centered managers may be successful in meeting production goals, their work groups experience higher levels of absenteeism, turnover, and worker hostility.

According to Likert, the style that management uses with its employees can be characterized as being one of four types that he termed the **four-function typology.** In what Likert calls **System 1 (exploitative authoritative),** decisions are made at the top, communications come from the top, and fear is used to motivate workers. **System 2 (benevolent authoritative)** allows some upward communication, both rewards and punishments are used to motivate workers, but decisions are still made at the top.

In **System 3 (consultative),** rewards are emphasized over punishments, communication upward is limited, but employees do influence decision making. Finally, in **System 4 (participative),** which is Likert's ideal type, employees are encouraged to reach high levels of achievement and satisfaction through their work, communication at all levels is open and honest, and workers have direct influence in making decisions. Differences among the four systems are illustrated in Table 12.1.

Likert's Systems 1 and 4 are similar to McGregor's Theory X and Theory Y. Just as McGregor preferred Theory Y organizations, Likert felt that System 4 was the ideal working environment.

Evaluating Human Relations Theories

As influential as the human relations movement became, the approach it developed to understanding organizations was never as comprehensive as that of the classical theorists. Although evidence that human relations are a critical aspect of organizational functioning is indisputable, human relations theory offers little beyond that particular insight. For this reason, the human relations movement had more or less died out among managers by the 1960s. Whereas the classical theorists had erred on the side of structure, the human relations theorists had erred on the side of the individual.

Table 12.1   LIKERT'S TYPOLOGY OF MANAGERIAL STYLES

| Operating Characteristics | Systems of Organization | | | |
	Exploitative Authoritative	Benevolent Authoritative	Consultative	Participative
Motivation	Fear, threats, punishment, and occasional rewards	Rewards and some actual or potential punishment	Rewards, occasional punishment, and some involvement	Economic rewards based on system developed through participation
Information flow	Downward	Mostly downward	Down and up	Down, up, and horizontally
Decision making	Bulk of decisions at top of organization	Policy at top, many decisions within prescribed framework made at lower levels	Broad policy and general decisions at top, more specific decisions at lower levels	Decision making widely done throughout organization
Productivity	Mediocre	Fair to good	Good	Excellent
Absenteeism and turnover	Tend to be high	Moderately high	Moderate	Low

Source: Adapted from Likert, R. (1961). *New patterns of management,* New York: McGraw-Hill.

Production, the basic function of any organization, was typically ignored in the writings of the human relations theorists. Emphasis on group relations, improved communication, and worker self-actualization was often given precedence over other areas more critical to organizational survival. It sometimes appears that, to the human relations movement, the quality of social interactions at work was more important than getting the work done.

A second problem with the human relations movement concerns measuring outcomes. For classical organizations, the quantity or quality of output is the measure of success; for the human relations movement, the quality of social relationships in the organization is a measure of success. Yet measuring output is much more straightforward than trying to assess the quality of relationships.

Human relations theories also have a tendentious nature that suggests that a specific approach is appropriate regardless of setting. Irrespective of the situation, Theory Y is better than Theory X, and System 4 is better than System 1, 2, or 3. In fact, these preferred approaches are counterproductive in some industries. In companies characterized by seasonal work, low skill levels among employees, and a high emphasis on production, for example, controlling and coordinating the activities of the workers are usually more appropriate than giving the workers autonomy (Smither, 1993). Although some individual initiative is valuable, certainly soldiers or football players cannot pursue individual autonomy at the expense of output.

A final consideration with regard to human relations theories is the assumption that virtually everyone is interested in psychological growth and the assumption of responsibility. Individuals who do not desire growth and responsibility are considered abnormal or psychologically handicapped. This view is simply not true. Many individuals find their satisfactions in areas of life other than work.

Despite these shortcomings, some evidence suggests that humanistic approaches to understanding organizations are again becoming popular with researchers. New interest in teamwork (discussed in Chapter 10) and intrinsic motivation and empowerment (Chapter 7) suggests that the human relations movement is showing signs of life. Stewardship theory (Davis, Schoorman, & Donaldson, 1997), for example, proposes that workers are motivated by higher-order needs—growth, achievement, self-actualization—rather than security and economic needs. In an interesting discussion of new directions in management thinking, one researcher (Aktouf, 1992) argued that modern theories of organization expect all employees to be active and intelligent participants in the organization. In the view of this researcher, only theories based in "radical humanism" can address the new issues in organizational life:

> There is a clear need to abandon management based on authority, on an order imposed by the organization, on the successive waves of scientism that have invaded the field (e.g., Taylorism, behavioral sciences, decision making, management information systems, office systems, and robotics). The solution is to open the way for managerial practices that will permit *development of the employee's desire to belong* and to use his or her intelligence to serve the firm. (Aktouf, 1992)

As discussed above, the human relations theorists' attempts to use communication to foster employee development were largely unsuccessful. Nonetheless, it may be possible that a combination of new factors—including challenges from a diverse workforce, an emphasis on teamwork and participation, and concern for more and more aspects of employees' lives outside the workplace—may revitalize the human relations movement in Western organizations.

Industrial Organization
  Model
Differentiation and Inte-
  gration
Mechanistic and Organic
  Systems
Sociotechnical Systems
Evaluating Contingency
  Theories

Contingency Theories of Organization

As mentioned at the beginning of this chapter, modern organizational theory considers the organization a *system* rather than a formalized structure or simply a network of social relations. Using analogies from the biological sciences, systems theorists believe that the modern organization exists in a symbiotic relationship with the environment in which it operates, and that both the organization and the environment continuously change as they influence each other.

Internally, the parts of the organization should not be rigid structures, but rather they should interact in an interdependent fashion. Like biological entities, organizations have cycles of growth, maturity, decline, and demise, and each stage has unique qualities. Historically, most organizational research has focused on studying the growth stage.

Some aspects of the growth and maturity stages of organizational life are presented in Table 12.2.

In contrast with both the classical and human relations schools, systems theorists reject universal principles of organization in favor of a **contingency approach to organization,** which holds that organizations must be studied in terms of the factors in their environments that affect the way they operate. Environments are constantly changing, and organizations must consequently be ready to adapt. Changes may come in the form of legislation, such as the passage of the Civil Rights Act, or they may be the product of current events, such as a downturn in the economy. One characteristic of virtually all environments is uncertainty, and effective structures are able to adapt to changing conditions.

Because environmental change seems to be a constant for modern organizations, managers often place great value on diagnostic skills in their employees. Departments such as strategic planning, management sciences, and operations research are considered critical in adapting to changing conditions. Organization development, the subject of Chapter 13, is the introduction of planned change into an organization.

All contingency theories share the qualities discussed above. Using Astley and Van de Ven's classification system, some emphasize the system-structural view, whereas others fall more clearly within the strategic choice perspective. Some influential contingency approaches to understanding the modern organization are discussed below.

Industrial Organization Model

Woodward (1965) studied approximately 100 British manufacturing firms to determine the relationship between organizational structure and company effectiveness. From her studies she concluded that these firms could be classified into three categories based on their organization.

Process production firms were characterized by a need to produce in anticipation of demand. Typical process production firms are found in the petroleum and light bulb industries. Since the production run in these kinds of firms is long and the product is uniform, the emphasis is on automation. Spans of control are low—typically 15 employees—since errors tend to be expensive. In the process production firm, the favored mode of organizational communication is verbal rather than written.

Table 12.2 STAGES OF ORGANIZATIONAL LIFE

Characteristics	Stage 1 Inception	Stage 2 High Growth	Stage 3 Maturity
Type of organizational structure	No formal structure	Centralized Formal	Decentralized Formal
Reward system	Personal Subjective	Systematic Impersonal	Impersonal Formal Totally objective
Communication process and planning	Informal Face-to-face Little planning	Moderately formal Budgets	Very formal Five-year plans Rules and regulations
Formalization adherence	Low adherence	High adherence	High formalization but low adherence
Method of decision making	Individual judgment Entrepreneurial	Professional management Analytical tools	Professional management Bargaining
Makeup of top level management staff	Generalists	Specialists	Strategists Planners
Organizational growth rate	Inconsistent but improving	Rapid positive growth	Growth slowing or declining
Organizational age and size	Young and small	Larger and older	Largest or once large and oldest

Note: Although these cycles are commonly accepted to describe private sector organizations, they seem less applicable to government agencies. Specifically, government agencies never seem to reach the demise stage. In a study of 175 governmental departments established in 1923, Kaufman (1976) found that 148 (85 percent) still existed in 1973! This survival rate is far greater than that for nongovernment organizations: Of the 100 largest corporations in the United States in 1917, only 30 were still in existence or among the largest in 1987.

Adapted from: Smith, K. G., Mitchell. T. R., & Summer, C. E. (1983). Top level management priorities in different stages of the organizational cycle. *Academy of Management Journal, 28,* 799–820. Used by permission.

In **large batch firms** or **mass production firms,** products are manufactured for inventory. This kind of structure, also referred to as *intermittent manufacturing,* is the most common in the United States and is typified by the automotive industry. Although products are standardized, the customer can order minor modifications.

The mass production firm also uses continuous production, based on demand and anticipation of demand. Typical problems with this approach include scheduling, predicting demands, and coordinating production. Since automation is used less frequently than in process production industries and errors are less disruptive, spans of control can be larger. Written communication is favored over verbal in this type of organization.

In the **unit production firm** or **small batch production firm,** products are manufactured on a job order basis. Firms in this category are typically found in aerospace and construction. Products are customized for individual customers, and production is a result of demand. In these firms, labor costs are very high, production runs are short, and there are fewer levels of hierarchy than in the process production or large batch types of organization. Verbal communication is favored over written, and spans of control are of moderate size.

Woodward concluded that the type of production that an organization used was the major determinant of structure. Deviance from the appropriate structure correlated with lower productivity and effectiveness. Overall, the most effective firms in each of the three categories represented the median with regard to the qualities found in that category. In other words, there seemed to be an optimal structure for each of the three kinds of manufacturing, and job order firms tended to need a more flexible structure than the process or mass production firms. Woodward's theory is known as the **industrial organization model.**

Woodward's work was among the first to suggest that no one theory of organization is applicable to all. The most successful firms in each category had evolved structures that met their particular needs and allowed for the necessary "fit" with the environment. Although Woodward's theory has been widely applied to understanding industrial organizations, there are some questions about its usefulness for studying nonindustrial or service firms, which constitute a large part of the U.S. economy. Nonetheless, the industrial organization approach clearly demonstrates a viable alternative to both classical and human relations theories.

Differentiation and Integration

If Woodward demonstrated that organizations evolve on the basis of their functions, then what about departments within organizations? Taking Woodward a step further, Lawrence and Lorsch (1967b) proposed that different departments within organizations must also be structured differently. These authors studied the impact of change on the organization of firms in rapidly changing, stable, and intermediately changing industries. More specifically, Lawrence and Lorsch focused their research on the manufacturing, sales, and research departments of firms within the three types of industry,

According to these authors, each part of an organization has a different view of the operation. The qualities considered important in the production department, for example, are not likely to be those considered important in sales. Whereas production is concerned with meeting goals and quotas and has an internal orientation overall, the sales department is concerned with immediate results and has an external orientation. Lawrence and Lorsch referred to the different views of departments within the same organization as **differentiation.**

Integration is the process by which these different points of view are brought together so the organization can function as a whole. Rather than relying on a rigid structure, various techniques and methods are used to bring about integration. Typical integrative mechanisms include committees and task forces, increased communication between departments, and individuals who serve as mediators between departments. Lawrence and Lorsch found that the individuals who understood the points of view of both sides were likely to be successful at integrating different functions.

Lawrence and Lorsch found that in rapidly changing environments, production, research, and sales were highly differentiated functions and that integration among departments was difficult. More organizational resources were required to integrate the various units. In less dynamic environments, differentiation was less and integration was easier to achieve.

As was the case with Woodward's study, Lawrence and Lorsch's results provided further evidence that different environments call for different structures and managerial styles. The approach that works successfully in a rapidly changing environment may work less well in less dynamic situations. In particular, methods for resolving conflict depend on the environment in which the organization operates.

In contrast with Woodward, however, Lawrence and Lorsch found that the external environment of the organization—and not the type of production—determines structure. For an organization to function smoothly, it is important for the overall structure and management style to be adaptive. Changes in the environment necessitate changes in the structure.

Mechanistic and Organic Systems

Burns and Stalker (1961) studied how electronics and other firms adapted to technological changes after World War II and found that success was a product of two factors: (1) technological breakthroughs and (2) management's ability to adapt to changing environments. From their research, Burns and Stalker identified two kinds of management styles, which they called mechanistic and organic systems.

The **mechanistic system** resembles classical organizational theory and seems to be most suitable for organizations in environments in which technology is unchanging. Precise role definitions, centralized control, and hierarchical communication between superiors and subordinates characterize the mechanistic approach. Management emphasizes directing and defining activities rather than consulting and negotiating with employees. Another quality of mechanistic systems is internal competition. Managers compete for resources and executives resolve disputes around resources.

The **organic system,** on the other hand, avoids a rigid hierarchy and is more flexible in dealing with its environment overall. The organic system emphasizes expertise over hierarchy, encourages lateral communication, emphasizes information and advice over instructions, and is willing to give authority to staff, as well as line, positions. In contrast with the mechanistic system, disputes are resolved by consulting knowledgeable employees. One study that compared communication in mechanistic and organic worksites found that organic managers were more likely to use question-and-answer formats to direct employees, whereas communications from managers at the mechanistic sites were more competitive, nonsupportive, and interruptive (Courtright, Fairhurst, & Rogers, 1989).

In recent years many organizations have moved more toward the organic model by encouraging informal rather than formal behavior among employees. Examples of informality include relaxed dress codes, the use of nonstandard furniture, informal language, and a deemphasis on organizational hierarchy and status. Technology firms often encourage informal behavior and even IBM, long known for its rigid rules of conduct, has relaxed its dress code.

The idea behind encouraging informality is that it promotes creativity (Morand, 1995). Other factors that appear to affect organizational creativity include participation, intrinsic rather than extrinsic rewards, information flow, training, and fewer levels of hierarchy (Woodman, Sawyer, & Griffin, 1993). One study of employees in a manufacturing environment found that creativity was greatest when jobs were complex and challenging and supervisors were supportive and noncontrolling (Oldham & Cummings, 1996).

In general, mechanistic systems seem to work better when there is little pressure to introduce new technology into the organization, and organic systems are better when confronting environments requiring technological change—a situation faced by most organizations at the end of the twentieth century.

Interestingly, Burns and Stalker's system provides a useful defense for bureaucracy and other classical models of organization. When environments are stable, it is good policy to develop procedures to handle all possibilities. Burns and Stalker felt that the important lesson is to recognize the appropriateness of either the mechanistic approach or the organic approach, and not to apply either indiscriminately.

Sociotechnical Systems

Chapter 1 looked at the application of psychology to the organization of the workplace of the Ahmedabad textile mills. As you may recall, the introduction of automated weaving equipment into the mills actually resulted in lower production. However, a review of the social relationships within the loom sheds eventually led to more worker control and higher productivity. The Ahmedabad study is one of the most famous projects of the Tavistock Institute of Human Relations. The Tavistock Institute is noted for, among other things, the development of the **sociotechnical systems** approach to organization.

The sociotechnical systems approach grew out of a classic study of technology and the coal mining industry in Great Britain after World War II (Trist & Bamforth, 1951). Historically miners had worked together in small teams, with each team being responsible for a specific section of a mine. Over time, these teams developed into cohesive units that affected social life outside working hours as well as on the job. Team members felt a bond not only with their coworkers, but also with their coworkers' families as well. For example, when an accident incapacitated a member of the team, coworkers would provide for that member's family.

With the introduction of modern technology, however, the teams were disbanded, and methods of production became much more standardized. Rather than having small teams responsible for short areas in the mine, the new technology operated as an assembly line. To the surprise of management, introducing technology into the mine had a disastrous effect on the workers. Social relationships were destroyed, autonomy and responsibility were reduced, and workers no longer took pride in their levels of skill. Outside the mine, social relationships within the mining community were also disrupted. In the opinion of the researchers, the social patterns that had developed for the mining job did not fit the new technology, and the result was greater absenteeism, heightened competition, and a lack of identification with work.

Both the coal mining and the textile weaving studies demonstrate the basic principle of the sociotechnical approach: Organizations are composed of two systems, the social and the technical, and technological change is likely to be disruptive if the social aspects of the workplace are not considered. According to Trist:

> The technical and social systems are *independent* of each other in the sense that the former follows the laws of the natural sciences while the latter follows the laws of the human sciences and is a purposeful system. Yet they are *corrective* in that one requires the other for the *transformation* of an input into an output, which comprises the functional task of a work system. (1981)

Important features of the technological system include the following:

- The materials being processed;
- The physical work setting;
- Spatial arrangement of the workplace;
- The level of automation;
- The essential, rather than optional, operations of production; and
- Repair and maintenance operations.

Important features of the social system, on the other hand, include the following:

- Whether work requires cooperation or competition;
- Whether workers take responsibility for output;
- The decision-making process;

- Individual work versus teamwork;
- The attractiveness of different jobs; and
- The personal goals of the workers.

According to the sociotechnical systems approach, the best organization is one in which management creates an environment that facilitates the functioning of **autonomous work groups.** Autonomous work groups are seen as a means for fulfilling both the production needs of management and the social needs of workers. Autonomous work groups differ from traditional groups because they give workers greater feelings of being in control, encourage group goals, produce higher satisfaction, and are adaptable to changing conditions. Table 12.3 compares the sociotechnical model with traditional models of organization.

The autonomous work group approach has been highly influential at companies such as Shell Oil, Cummins Engine, and Volvo (Trist, 1981). As you may recall from Chapter 10, two currently popular approaches to forming autonomous work groups are team building and the matrix organization. The sociotechnical systems approach is often credited with being one of the first applications of organization development to the workplace (Chapter 13).

Evaluating Contingency Theories

Contingency theories start with the assumptions that organizations are continually changing, and that they exist in environments that influence change. Because of this, contingency theories argue that there is no one best way to structure an organization. Developed as alternatives to classical theory's emphasis on structure and human relations theory's emphasis on personal relationships, contingency theories seem to offer a more comprehensive picture of the modern organization than do the other approaches. Table 12.4 (p. 393) summarizes the contingency approaches to organization discussed here.

Another feature of contingency theories is their emphasis on organizational effectiveness or productivity. Since the major function of most organizations is to produce something other than a hierarchy of command or rewarding social relations, contingency theory seems to be both more relevant and more useful for understanding modern organizations.

Despite the attractiveness of contingency theories, there are some drawbacks to this approach to organizational theory. First, most contingency theories of organization minimize the role of individual differences. Organizational behavior is seen as being a product of environmental influences—a system-structural view—and much less the result of actions taken by members. This may not always be the case, since a series of bad decisions by a manager can affect organizational structure. Along the same lines, the first part of this chapter suggested that the members of organizations actively attempt to manipulate the environment. Almost certainly a powerful personality like that of Henry Ford or H. Ross Perot affects organizational functioning.

Table 12.3 TRADITIONAL MODEL OF ORGANIZATION VS.
SOCIOTECHNICAL MODEL

Traditional	Sociotechnical
1. Technology first	1. Joint optimization of social/technical systems
2. People are extensions of machines	2. People complement machines
3. People are expendable spare parts	3. People are a resource to be developed
4. Tasks focus on simple, narrow skills	4. Tasks focus on grouping and multiple, broad skills
5. External controls: Procedures, supervisors, specialist staffs	5. Internal controls: Self-regulating subsystems
6. More organization levels, autocratic style: Unilateral goal setting, assignment of workers	6. Fewer levels, participative style: Bilateral goal setting, selection of workers
7. Competitive gamesmanship	7. Collaboration, collegiality
8. Organization's purposes only (often with poor understanding/ acceptance at lower levels)	8. Members' and society's purposes also (with good understanding/acceptance at lower levels): Shared vision and philosophy
9. Frequent alienation: "It's only a job"	9. Commitment: "It's *my* job, group, and organization"
10. Tendency toward low risk taking, maladaptation	10. Tendency toward innovation, adaptation
11. Less individual development opportunity and employment security	11. More individual development opportunity and employment security (Based on Trist, 1981)

Source: Fox, W. M. (1991). *A survey of sociotechnical system principles and guidelines.* Gainesville: University of Florida.

A second concern about contingency theories relates to their usefulness. If every situation calls for a unique fit between organization and environment, then it will be difficult to draw conclusions about the best structure. One of the basic rules in science is parsimony—we look for laws that explain the greatest number of phenomena or situations. Consequently, the viewpoint that each organization requires a unique approach does little to advance knowledge in this area.

Finally, the notion that there is no one best way to organize is not very helpful to individuals seeking guidance about structuring organizations. Should emphasis be placed on technology, integration, or autonomous work groups? Each approach has data to support a belief that one aspect is the most important to understanding organizational functioning. For an individual who has to develop a structural plan for an organization, the variety of contingency theories may be more confusing than helpful. Although the contingency approach is currently popular among organizational theorists, no one theory from this school has emerged as dominant.

Table 12.4   CONTINGENCY APPROACHES TO ORGANIZATION

The contingency approach to organization emphasizes that there is no one best way to organize. Each organization is unique, and structure should evolve to meet both internal and external demands on the organization. Some major aspects of the contingency theories are summarized below.

Theory	Rationale	Considerations
Industrial organization (Woodward, 1965)	Structure of a manufacturing firm depends on its product; deviating from the appropriate structure lowers productivity.	Research supports the theory when applied to manufacturing but the theory does not address service industries.
Differentiation and integration (Lawrence & Lorsch, 1967a)	Different parts of organizations require different kinds of structures; effectiveness depends on integrating the structures within organizations.	Research supports the idea that different environments— and not necessarily products— call for different structures.
Mechanistic and organic systems (Burns & Stalker, 1961)	Mechanistic systems work best in organizations in which technology is unchanging; organic systems work best when environments are changing.	In certain kinds of organizations, bureaucracy is preferable to more flexible systems.
Sociotechnical systems (Trist, 1981)	Organizations have two interrelated systems: social and technical.	Organizational success depends on effective integration of technology and social concerns.

Organizational Culture

During the 1980s, some theorists became interested in applying the concept of culture to understanding organizational structure or, more specifically, how organizations operate. One important influence on this approach to organizations was Peters and Waterman's (1982) best-selling book, *In Search of Excellence*. According to these authors, the most effective organizations in the United States had similar qualities that made them "America's best-run companies." Typical qualities included having a bias for action, being driven by values, using simple structures, and focusing on the key aspects of the business. In other words, excellent companies had cultures that made them highly effective organizations.

Organizational culture refers to the shared values and assumptions that organizations pass to newcomers through formal statements and informal patterns of behavior. For example, the culture of financial firms tends to be formal

Organizational Socialization
Organizational Citizenship Behavior
Organizational Climate
Evaluating Organizational Culture

and conservative; high-tech firms, on the other hand, often emphasize informality, creativity, and risk taking. Some of the dimensions that define an organization's culture are innovation, stability, respect for people, outcome orientation, detail orientation, team orientation, and aggressiveness (Chatman & Jehn, 1994).

Organizational culture is an interesting concept because it explains some other approaches to organization. Mechanistic firms, for example, have cultures different from those of organic firms; within the same firm, differentiated departments, such as accounting and marketing, are also likely to have different cultures.

Cultures are based on assumptions about customers, competitors, and society, and they can also be influenced by the background and personality of the company founder or leader (Gordon, 1991). In addition, cultures can change as companies evaluate past experiences, change the composition of their workforces, or make projections about the future (Hatch, 1993; Wilkins & Dyer, 1988). All American automobile companies, for example, have faced challenges to their corporate cultures by the loss of market share to the Japanese or the requirement for more fuel-efficient engines.

According to organizational culture theorists, organizations with strong cultures usually exhibit superior performances (Deal & Kennedy, 1982; Saffold, 1988; Vancouver, Millsap, & Peters, 1994). Theoretically this happens because these organizations emphasize a core set of values that, when shared by employees, reduces uncertainty and provides a common view of the organization and the external environment. In one study that considered the effect of work values on organizational culture (Meglino, Ravlin, & Adkins, 1989), the researchers found that when workers and supervisors shared similar values, job satisfaction and commitment to the organization were greater.

One approach to understanding the creation of organizational culture is through Schneider's (1987) attraction-selection-attrition (ASA) model, introduced in Chapter 10. In this model, organizational cultures are created by people who are attracted to the organization who, in turn, are drawn to work environments that most fit their personal characteristics (Holland, 1985). As a result, work environments attract people who are similar who then hire others who are similar to themselves.

The personality, attitudes, values, and goals of an organization's founder are major factors in creating an organizational culture. People considering joining an organization consider the similarity between their personal characteristics and the attributes of the organization (Schneider, Goldstein, & Smith, 1995). A founder's goals can include, for example, service, innovation, or profitability. Founders will choose top managers who reflect their goals.

A poor fit between an individual and an organization can have negative consequences. For example, a poor person-environment fit has been shown to cause psychological and physiological stress (Edwards & Harrison, 1993; French, Caplan, & Harrison, 1982). In addition, when people who are initially attracted to an organization eventually discover they do not fit and leave, the work environment becomes even more homogeneous. This can be a dangerous situation because the homogeneity of the workforce may prevent the organization from adapting to changes in the business environment. A major point of the ASA model is that most organizations should be careful about the kind of people they recruit.

In an interesting test of the person-organization fit hypothesis, three researchers (O'Reilly, Chatman, & Caldwell, 1991) developed an instrument to assess how well the values of an employee fit with the culture of the organization in which the employee worked. Informants familiar with the different organizations were first asked to rate their organizations on a variety of qualities that reflected different values. Participants in the study then described how important the same values were to them personally. The researchers found significant congruence between individual values and organizational culture, and satisfaction was higher among employees with stronger fit. In addition, the stronger the fit, the less likely the employee to leave.

In another test of organizational culture and fit, one researcher (J. Sheridan, 1992) followed 904 newly hired employees of six public accounting firms over a six-year period. The cultures of the accounting firms differed in their emphases on consideration or structure. Some firms emphasized a team orientation and respect for others; other firms emphasized rules, procedures, and accuracy in employees' work. Employees in the consideration-type culture typically stayed on the job 45 months, but those in the structured-type culture stayed only 31 months on average. According to Sheridan, the human resource costs associated with the shorter job tenure amounted to over $6 million. The effects of structure and retention are represented in Figure 12.4.

Organizational Socialization

Modern American workers typically hold eight different jobs during their careers (Wegmann, 1991). As workers move from job to job, they often discover that new positions require behaviors, attitudes, or values different from those required by previous jobs. **Organizational socialization** refers to the process by which members' values are brought into line with organizational values.

Organizations differ greatly in the amount of formal socialization they use, with the military having the most formal and comprehensive socialization programs. Ashforth and Saks (1996) looked at the socialization process ten months after a group of graduating business students had found jobs. Students who were working in companies that had more formal socialization programs reported lower role ambiguity and conflict, stress, and intentions to quit. They also reported higher job satisfaction, commitment, and identification with the organization where they worked.

Even though a worker may have job experience that relates to the new culture, such experience may not help in the socialization process (Adkins, 1995). Most people begin new jobs feeling they do not have sufficient information to

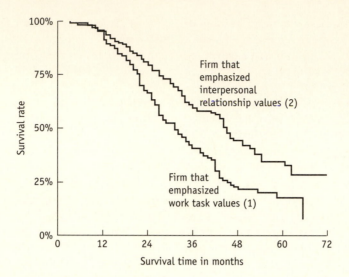

Source: Sheridan, J. E. (1992). Organizational culture and employee retention.
Academy of Management Journal, 35(5), 1049–1056. Copyright © 1992. Reprinted
by permission of the publisher.

Figure 12.4 Voluntary Survival Rates in Two Organizational Cultures
As you can see from the chart, job tenure in two accounting firms declined over a three-year
period. At the firm that emphasized interpersonal relationships (2), survival was higher, and it
stabilized at a level considerably higher than the survival rate for the task-centered firms (1).

be effective, so they engage in a variety of information-seeking behaviors to discover aspects of the culture that will help them be successful on the job. Some research (Bauer & Green, 1994; Morrison, 1993b) suggests that individuals who actively seek information about their new environment will be more effective on the job. In particular, individuals who have a strong need to be in control of their environment will be proactive in the socialization process (Ashford & Black, 1996).

Typical information-seeking strategies during socialization include the following:

- Asking questions of supervisors;
- Interacting with third parties to gain information;
- Testing the limits by trying new behaviors and seeing how supervisors react;
- Manipulating conversations to find out information—especially personal information about other workers—without asking directly;
- Observing the behavior of others to find a specific answer; and
- Observing the behavior of others to find general information that may be used later (Miller & Jablin, 1991).

One study (Morrison, 1995) looked at the ways that newly hired accountants learned information about their jobs and the organization. The accountants typically learned the answers to technical questions by asking others, but they learned about roles, norms, and values through observation. In addition, workers who more actively sought information had higher levels of satisfaction and job performance and lower intentions to leave at a later date.

Two researchers (Ostroff & Kozlowski, 1992) followed 151 new organizational members for almost four months to understand their socialization experiences. Findings from this study showed that newcomers rely chiefly on observing others to acquire information and, to a lesser degree, rely on supervisors and coworkers to supply information. However, the supervisor plays a critical role in successful socialization. The researchers made the interesting observation that companies might socialize their newcomers more effectively by spending fewer resources on formal orientation programs and more on training supervisors and coworkers to assist the newcomers in learning the tasks and roles of their positions. Results from another study that focused on socialization among new union members supported these results. Formal socialization experiences, such as orientation programs, were not as helpful in building commitment to the union as positive interactions with individual union members (Fullagar, Gallagher, Gordon, & Clark, 1995).

Finally, one group of researchers (Chao, O'Leary-Kelly, Wolf, Klein, & Gardner, 1994) followed the socialization experiences of a large sample of individuals who had graduated with degrees in engineering between 1956 and 1986. The researchers asked respondents to complete a questionnaire about six areas of organizational socialization: performance proficiency; people (relationships with others); politics (learning about power relationships); knowledge of both technical language and jargon unique to the organization; organizational goals and values; and history (traditions, myths, and rituals about the organization).

Results from the study indicated that, over time, people who changed jobs within the organization had experienced a decline in performance proficiency, language, and history. Individuals who left the organization altogether had experienced significant declines in performance proficiency, language, people, policies, and history. In other words, job changes became more likely as workers experienced a decline in their feelings of socialization.

Organizational Citizenship Behavior

Organizational citizenship behavior (OCB; Bateman & Organ, 1983) is a concept related to organizational culture that refers to "individual contributions in the workplace that go beyond role requirements and contractually rewarded job achievements" (Organ & Ryan, 1995). In other words, OCB occurs when members of an organization behave in ways that are not required by their job descriptions but benefit the organization. According to the theory, effective organizations have many members who do things that create a supportive environment for getting tasks done.

What causes organizational citizenship behavior? Two researchers (Organ & Bateman, 1995) performed a meta-analysis of studies to identify factors that predict OCB. Results from their analysis revealed that job satisfaction was related to OCB, as was perceived fairness, organizational commitment, and leader supportiveness. In other words, when workers feel that they are treated fairly, they believe their leaders are supportive, and they are committed to the organization, they are likely to perform behaviors outside their job duties that are helpful to the organization.

Another study (Settoon, Bennett, & Liden, 1996) found that hospital workers were more committed to the organization when they perceived its support, but they were more likely to engage in citizenship behaviors when they had a good relationship with a supervisor. Along the same lines, one study that followed graduating management and engineering students into the workplace (Ostroff & Kozlowski, 1992) found that good relationships with supervisors or team members helped overcome graduates' disappointments about unmet expectations.

In another study (McNeely & Meglino, 1994), researchers were interested in finding what motivated secretaries to perform behaviors that demonstrated "helping, sharing, donating, cooperating, and volunteering" (Brief & Motowidlo, 1986). Interestingly, when the secretaries helped other individuals, they were motivated by empathy and concern for others. Acts that benefitted the organization, however, were related to the secretaries' perceptions of fairness in terms of rewards and recognition for desirable behaviors. These findings suggest that the motivations behind organizational citizenship behavior depend on the beneficiary of the behavior.

Organizational Climate

In recent years, researchers have become increasingly interested in an aspect of organizations related to culture. **Organizational climate** is a loosely defined term that refers to how well workers' expectations about an organization are being met (Davis, 1984), the "mood" of an organization (Ott, 1989), or how employees perceive aspects of the organizational environment and interpret them in relation to their own well-being (Brown & Leigh, 1996). In other words, climate reflects how individuals feel about being a part of a particular organization.

The concept of climate comes from Kurt Lewin's studies of experimentally created social climates (Lewin, 1951; Lewin, Lippit, & White, 1939). One way of looking at the difference between culture and climate is in terms of perspective. Whereas culture tends to reflect the views of management, climate reflects the perceptions of workers (Denison, 1996):

Climate refers to a *situation* and its link to thoughts, feelings, and behaviors of organizational members. Thus, it is temporal, subjective, and often subject to direct manipulation by people with power and influence. Culture, in contrast, refers to an *evolved context* (within which a situation may be embedded).

Many theorists believe that when employees feel the organization has a positive climate, they become more committed to the work of the organization. Because climate is a perception, however, it varies from employee to employee. Typical aspects of organizational climate include role stress and lack of harmony; job challenge and autonomy; leadership facilitation and support; and work-group cooperation, friendliness, and warmth (James & James, 1989).

Climate has been studied in a number of ways, and it appears to be related to job satisfaction. The basic finding of this research is that workers are more satisfied in environments in which there is a positive organizational climate. For example, two researchers (Brown & Leigh, 1996) measured perceptions of organizational climate among sales representatives from three manufacturing companies. In this study, feelings that the organizational environment was safe and meaningful led to greater job involvement and commitment, which, in turn, led to superior performance.

Another group of researchers (Hershberger, Lichtenstein, & Knox, 1994) looked at factors that affected individuals' perceptions of organizational climate. Using data collected from a sample of twins who had been separated early in life, the researchers found that individual perceptions about the supportiveness of their work environment and "annoyance factors" such as odors, temperatures, and sanitation were influenced by genetic factors. Unlike other research (Chapter 8), however, this study found no evidence of a genetic factor in job satisfaction. Finally, one study of construction workers (Patterson, Payne, & West, 1996) found that the concept of climate had the most meaning when people worked in relatively isolated and defined physical locations.

Evaluating Organizational Culture

Organizational culture theorists have provided an interesting alternative to traditional models of organizational structure. In a sense, their model falls between the system-structural and the strategic choice views of organizations. People are attracted to certain companies on the basis of their personalities and backgrounds, they join the company, then their experiences socialize them so that their behavior and values are even more congruent with organizational norms. People who do not agree with the culture probably leave.

Culture theories are particularly appealing to psychologists because they explain organizations in terms of both environmental and individual difference factors. Further, they emphasize the traditional topics of social psychology—roles, norms, group behavior, and so forth. In a sense, organizational culture resembles the sociotechnical systems approach, although culture theorists generally spend little time considering the technological system. If the sociotechnical specialists are correct about the importance of technology, however, then organizational culture's emphasis on the social aspects of organizations may provide few insights beyond those developed by the human relations theorists. At this stage in its development, organizational culture does seem to overlook the importance of factors outside the social system of the organization.

In the social sciences, anthropologists and sociologists are generally considered the experts in studying culture. One continuing question in all cultural studies is how cultures change. If similar people are attracted to organizations, and dissimilar people are forced out, how can a culture adapt to new developments? What makes people want to change? In contrast with contingency models, organizational culture theorists do not yet have a good explanation for how cultures modify their norms and values.

Finally, organizational culture theory is not very clear about the relationship between culture and productivity. Culture exists because it serves some need of organizational members, who are socialized to view their world in a similar fashion. This need may have nothing to do with productivity or getting a job done, and people may, in fact, be socialized to values that are not useful for organizational survival.

For example, government insiders in Washington and auto executives in Detroit are often cited as examples of elites who have lost touch with the functions their organizations are supposed to fulfill. Culture theory has a bias toward accepting organizational norms as justifiable because members have developed them, but it generally fails to evaluate or explain these norms in terms of organizational output.

Although the organizational culture perspective has become popular in recent years, it has yet to be developed as fully as the other theories. Nonetheless, many aspects of organizational culture are intuitively appealing. As researchers gather more information about organizational culture in the future, we will be better able to evaluate the usefulness of this perspective for understanding how organizations operate.

Postmodern Organizations

In recent years some researchers have argued that the modern pace of change in organizations has made traditional theories no longer useful. Some of these researchers believe that *postmodernism,* an intellectual movement that began in the humanities, provides a framework for understanding organizations at the end of the twentieth century.

According to one postmodern theorist (Bergquist, 1993), for example, organizations have evolved through three stages. In the *premodern* organization, structures were simple, leadership was paternal or charismatic, and capital was based in land and reputation. *Modern* organizations, in contrast, have complex structures, leadership based on management principles, and capital based in building, money, and machines.

The **postmodern organization,** however, has a flexible structure, leadership that varies according to the situation, and an emphasis on information and expertise. Boundaries of the postmodern organization are unclear, which requires the organization to be clear about its mission. Whereas premodern organizations relied on oral communication and modern organizations on formal and written communication, postmodern organizations emphasize oral and electronic communication.

Another value of postmodernism is **constructivism,** which argues that people create their own social realities based on the culture in which they find themselves. Because of this there are no universal truths or principles (Hassard, 1993). One of the defining characteristics of postmodernism, in fact, is its skepticism about "truths" argued by other theories. In an interesting review of the motivation literature that fits with postmodern arguments, for example, Carter and Jackson (1993) argue that Vroom's expectancy theory is superior to Maslow's theory because expectancy theory takes the perspective of the individual worker into account.

In the postmodern world, the subjectivity of experience makes facts and figures less important and language, stories, and performances—which speak from an individual perspective—more important. From a postmodern perspective, organizations can best be described as collections of "fragmented" parts rather than the unified entities described by Weber or Fayol.

According to postmodern theorists (e.g., Boje, 1995; Boje, Gephart, & Thatchenkery 1996), the rapidity of change has made premodern and modern organizations ineffective. The most successful organizations of the future will be flexible, and postmodernism is a method that accommodates that need for flexibility. Table 12.5 compares premodern, modern, and postmodern organizations.

Not surprisingly, few industrial and organizational psychologists have adopted the postmodern perspective on organizations. The idea that organizations must be understood in terms of subjective beliefs does not yet fit well with the scientific method that is the foundation of modern I/O psychology. Nonetheless, the postmodern theorists have had an impact on organizational theory, particularly in the areas of diversity (Chapter 11) and organization development (Chapter 13). It will be interesting to see whether, in the years to come, the postmodern approach extends to traditional areas of I/O such as job analysis and performance appraisal.

Japanese Organization

Lifetime Employment
Quality Circles
Seven S Theory and
   Theory Z

One of the most interesting aspects of the study of organizations is that, until recently, all its major theorists have been from the United States and Western Europe. In addition to their geographic homogeneity, founders of the field also

Table 12.5 FEATURES OF PREMODERN, MODERN, AND POSTMODERN
ORGANIZATIONS

Feature	Premodern Organizations	Modern Organizations	Postmodern Organizations
Size	Small	Large	Small to moderate
Structure	Simple	Complex	Flexible
Mission	Unclear	Unclear or unnecessary	Clear
Boundaries	Unclear or unnecessary	Clear	Unclear
Leadership	Paternal or charismatic	Based on management principles	Changes based on time and situation
Growth	Nonexistent or organic	Primary criterion for success	Moderate
Communication	Oral	Formal/written	Oral and electronic
Primary focus of capital	Land and reputation	Building, money, and machines	Information and expertise

Source: Adapted from Bergquist, W. (1993). *The postmodern organization: Mastering the art of irreversible change.* San Francisco: Jossey-Bass.

studied the same kinds of organizations. Weber studied the German bureaucracy, Fayol was for many years an employee of the French mining industry, and Taylor worked at Bethlehem Steel.

The industrial success of postwar Japan, however, led to a new interest in alternative theories of organization. Millions of individuals around the world work in settings that are organized along lines different from the classical, human relations, or contingency approaches to organization. One model that has been particularly influential in the United States is the Japanese organization.

Because of Japan's impressive business performance, Western theorists and practitioners have carefully studied the organization of the Japanese workplace. In a number of respects, the Japanese model differs greatly from its Western counterparts. Of particular interest is the fact that the Japanese organization is, by Western standards, rigid, bureaucratic, and authoritarian—qualities that many theorists believe inhibit productivity in any system. Three areas of particular interest to researchers are lifetime employment, quality circles, and theories of organization.

Lifetime Employment

Probably the best known feature of the Japanese organization is its commitment to lifetime employment. This practice—though not as widespread as commonly believed in the West and also reserved only for male employees—gives the Japanese system a number of unique qualities.

For the majority of male Japanese workers, the lifetime commitment to employment works both ways. Typically, the employee starts at an entry-level position and through a slow (by Western standards) process, achieves promotions and salary increases on the basis of seniority. Because the company has assured the worker of job security, Japanese employees tend to be less threatened by the introduction of new technology or changes in management. Rewards in the Japanese system are based on a seniority system and consequently, Japanese workers are usually disinclined to quit their jobs and start at the bottom elsewhere. After a few years, it becomes virtually impossible to leave one job and start another.

Another aspect of lifetime employment is a different approach to recruitment and selection. Interestingly, large Japanese organizations usually limit their recruitment efforts to specific universities (Inohara, 1990). That is, certain firms recruit at specific universities. Because Japanese workers will undergo continuous training throughout their careers, entry-level skills are generally not regarded as important as the fit of the individual and the organization in terms of values and expectations. This contrasts sharply with the American system, in which students switch majors to ensure "employability" on graduation and organizations often expect their employees to move on to jobs in other companies.

Unlike most Western organizations, the Japanese firm expends considerable resources on socializing employees to company values. Socialization experiences may include singing company songs, doing calisthenics together at work, and having the company take an interest in the welfare of the worker's family.

The commitment to lifetime employment may also minimize conflict at work. Knowing they are going to be together a long time, employees and supervisors may make accommodations to avoid confrontation. At the same time, workers do not want to risk being dismissed, since they will probably have to start at the bottom at another company.

Finally, lifetime employment gives the employee an identity that is inextricably bound up with the company. If a Japanese worker fears that his or her employer is losing market share or competitiveness, the worker will often go to extreme lengths and make sacrifices for the company unheard of in the United States. Although these sacrifices may be out of loyalty to the company, they may also arise from a fear of becoming unemployed and perhaps unemployable.

Despite the tradition of lifetime employment, in recent years some Japanese employers have begun to move away from the practice. For example, some companies now use contract workers to avoid giving lifetime guarantees. Along the same lines, both Toyota and Honda recently introduced limited compensation programs based on performance rather than seniority (Kanabayashi, 1996).

Wiersma and Bird (1993) looked at the qualities of top managers in Japanese firms and their relationship to turnover. The researchers hypothesized that individual differences are more important in Japanese management teams than in American teams and that when members of Japanese teams were heterogeneous in terms of age, organizational tenure, team tenure, and prestige of university attended, turnover would be greater. Analyzing the turnover patterns of 220 Japanese executives in top management teams, the researchers found that turnover was most likely to occur when an executive's age and the prestige of the university he attended were most different from those of his fellow team members.

Quality Circles

In the Japanese management system, tremendous emphasis is placed on the quality of goods produced, and in many companies, a 1 percent error rate is considered unacceptable. Consequently, many Western managers have become interested in Japanese **quality circles.** As described in Chapter 10, quality circles refer to a small group of employees who meet regularly to discuss solutions to problems that arise in the workplace.

Quality circles build on the notion of participative decision making—that employees can take responsibility for their work and can make meaningful decisions about improving work quality. Although this idea originated in the West, it seems to have been more successfully applied in Japan. In a review of the quality circle literature, Munchus (1983) found that quality circles had been successful in a variety of cultures, but that their success in the United States had not been clearly demonstrated. Matsushita Electric, for example, uses quality circles in Japan, but does not use them with its workers in the United States.

As pointed out in Chapter 10, the participative nature of quality circles has had an important impact on the structure of many American organizations.

Seven S Theory and Theory Z

Although there are a variety of theories explaining the success of the Japanese business organization, two theories that have been particularly influential are the Seven S theory (Pascale & Athos, 1981) and Theory Z (Ouchi, 1981).

According to **Seven S theory,** all organizations are controlled by seven variables: superordinate goals, strategy, structure, systems, staff, skills, and style. These seven variables can be dichotomized into "hard Ss" and "soft Ss." Hard Ss are strategy, structure, and systems; according to Pascale and Athos, there is little difference between Japanese and American firms with regard to these areas. The important difference occurs in the soft Ss: staff, skills, and style. Whereas American management tends toward an explicit, open style, Japanese managers are much more adept at using ambiguity, trust, and subtle cues to accomplish organizational goals. Additionally, Japanese managers are often more open to learning about unfamiliar areas than are their American counterparts (Nonaka & Johansson, 1985).

The **Theory Z** organization (Ouchi, 1981) is a hybrid between Theory X and Theory Y. According to Ouchi, the model Japanese organization has the following features: lifetime employment, nonspecific career paths, slow promotions, participative decision making, collective responsibility, and holistic concern for employees. American organizations, on the other hand, have a different set of qualities: short-term employment, rapid advancement, specific career paths, individual decision making, individual responsibility, and limited concern for workers.

Although the Japanese model has its roots in the Japanese culture (Ouchi & Jaeger, 1978), the Japanese have transplanted their system to various overseas operations, including the United States. Successful transplant involves an approach Ouchi refers to as the Theory Z organization.

Theory Z stresses long, but not lifetime, employment, participative decision making with individual responsibility, slow promotions, moderately specific career paths, and a holistic concern for the employee. In a sense, it combines some elements of both the bureaucratic and human relations approaches to organization.

Although Western managers and management theorists are generally impressed by the Japanese model of organization, some critics have suggested that our understanding of these systems is too facile (Young, 1992). These critics argue that disregard of subtle cultural differences when adopting Japanese management practices may be counterproductive. Additionally, idealizing the Japanese system may overlook some of its shortcomings. In a survey of American and Japanese CEOs, Japanese managers were found to have higher levels of stress and lower levels of job satisfaction than their American counterparts (De-Frank, Matteson, Schweiger, & Ivancevich, 1985).

Sometimes theorists suggest that the Japanese model of organization will eventually become like its Western counterpart—that features such as lifetime employment and quality circles will become impractical and the Japanese will eventually adopt Western management strategies. On the other hand, in a review of the similarities between Japanese and American firms, one researcher (Dunphy, 1987) suggested that Japanese firms have a number of qualities that make them unlikely to adopt Western approaches to organization.

First, they have a different kind of relationship with government. Business leaders and the political system coordinate their activities to a greater degree than in the West. Second, Japanese firms focus on longer-term goals and, despite quality circles, they emphasize centralized power structures. Finally, personnel practices and decision-making procedures are different from those found in Western organizations. Because of these differences, Dunphy argued, Japanese firms will retain their unique character.

Chapter Summary

Organizational psychology is the study of groups established to accomplish specific goals. The formation of organizations seems to be a genetic predisposition in humans and is necessary for survival.

Some approaches to studying organizations include the system-structural, strategic choice, natural selection, and collective action models. Most organizational psychologists prefer system-structural and strategic choice models because they give greater importance to individual variables.

Qualities of organizations include an organizing principle, an emphasis on survival, the production of outputs, and a need for followers.

Classical organizational theory was developed around the turn of the century. Major proponents included Weber, Fayol, and Taylor. All classical approaches focus on developing formal structures that have policies and procedures for any situation.

The human relations approach to organization emphasized the importance of personal relationships in the workplace. Starting with the premise that satisfied workers will be more productive, human relations theorists attempted to improve the quality of interpersonal interaction. Their lack of interest in productivity, however, led to the end of the movement by about 1960.

Contingency theories of organization consider organizations as systems. Structures are not rigid, and there is no one best way to organize. Contingency theorists also use biological metaphors when studying organizations. Some contingency theories include Woodward's industrial organization, Lawrence and Lorsch's theory of differentiation and integration, and sociotechnical systems.

The organizational culture approach focuses on the behaviors, artifacts, creations, values, and basic assumptions of organizations. These create standards for behavior that are passed on to employees. According to the theory, organizations with stronger cultures exhibit superior performances.

Organizational socialization refers to the process by which members' values are brought into line with organizational values. When individuals enter organizations, they actively seek information about the culture. Organizational citizenship behavior refers to worker contributions to the workplace that go beyond formal job requirements.

In recent years some researchers have applied the principles of postmodernism to understanding organizations. Postmodern organizations have flexible structures, leadership that varies according to the situation, and an emphasis on information and expertise.

Most organizational theory has originated in the Western world, despite the fact that millions of individuals work in settings that are organized along different lines. Japanese models of organization, currently quite popular with Western business, are characterized by quality circles and lifetime employment. However, several researchers have pointed out that Western understanding of the Japanese system may be too facile.

Key Words and Concepts

autonomous work groups (p. 391)
bureaucracy (p. 376)
chain of command (p. 377)
classical organization theory
  (p. 375)

collective action approach (p. 373)
constructivism (p. 401)
contingency approach to
  organization (p. 385)
departmentalization (p. 377)

differentiation (p. 387)

flat organizational structures
  (p. 377)

four-function typology (p. 382)

functionalism (p. 376)

functional principle (p. 377)

Hawthorne studies (p. 381)

human relations theory (p. 381)

industrial organization model
  (p. 387)

integration (p. 388)

large batch or mass production
  firms (p. 386)

line-staff principle (p. 377)

mechanistic system (p. 388)

natural selection approach
  (p. 373)

organic system (p. 388)

organizational citizenship
  behavior (p. 397)

organizational climate (p. 406)

organizational culture (p. 393)

organizational psychology (p. 372)

organizational socialization
  (p. 395)

postmodern organization (p. 401)

process production firms (p. 385)

psychological contract (p. 374)

quality circles (p. 404)

scalar principle (p. 377)

Seven S theory (p. 404)

sociotechnical systems (p. 389)

span of control (p. 377)

strategic choice approach (p. 372)

structure (p. 375)

System 1 (exploitative
  authoritative) (p. 382)

System 2 (benevolent
  authoritative) (p. 382)

System 3 (consultative) (p. 382)

System 4 (participative) (p. 382)

system-structural view (p. 372)

tall organizational structures
  (p. 377)

Theory X (p. 381)

Theory Y (p. 381)

Theory Z (p. 404)

unit production or small batch
  production firm (p. 387)

unity of command (p. 377)

Questions for Discussion

1. What are some of the differences between industrial and organizational psychology?

2. What are the four theoretical perspectives on studying organizations described in this chapter? Which fits best with a psychological perspective?

3. What are some of the qualities of organizations?

4. What is the psychological contract? Do you think it is dead? From the perpective of an employer, would its demise be positive or negative? Would an employee share the same feeling?

5. What are the advantages and disadvantages of a classical approach to organization?

6. Why did human relations supplant classical theories? What are the advantages and disadvantages of human relations theories?

7. What is the basic idea behind contingency approaches to organization? Which of these approaches seems most plausible to you?

8. What is the organizational culture perspective? Does your school have a strong or a weak culture? What are some aspects of the culture?

9. If you were new to an organization, how would you learn about the culture?

10. What is climate? How does it differ from culture?

11. What is a postmodern organization? How does it differ from premodern and modern organizations? Do you think the postmodern perspective can be useful for I/O psychologists?

12. What are some of the features of Japanese organizations? Would you like to work in this kind of environment? Why or why not?

CHAPTER 13

Organization Development

Origins of Organization Development
Diagnosis and Analysis
Resistance to Organizational Change
Models of Planned Change
Organization Development Interventions
Evaluating Organization Development
The Future of Organization Development
Chapter Summary
Key Words and Phrases
Questions for Discussion

As every manager, employee, or I/O psychologist knows, change is one of the most pervasive qualities of organizations in the late twentieth century. Changing workforces, markets, and technology have challenged traditional ideas about organizational structures and ways of managing. For this reason, many organizations now actively attempt to manage, rather than simply respond to, change. **Organization development (OD)** is the area of industrial and organizational psychology that deals with managing change. **Interventions** are the techniques that OD practitioners use to deal with change.

According to OD theorist Warner Burke (1992), organizations today face five important challenges that probably cannot be handled effectively with traditional organizational structures and procedures. First, the movement toward growth that characterized American industry for much of this century has now changed toward consolidation. Consolidation typically means downsizing, layoffs, and restructuring, all of which create stress within an organization.

Second, organizations that used to move at moderate speeds now must move much more quickly. Technology and competition require organizations to respond to opportunities and challenges almost immediately. Third, organizations have become increasingly complex. Workforce diversity, new technology, and legislative initiatives, for example, have made managing the modern organization far more complicated than in the past.

Fourth, managers need quick answers to their problems. Since many of the practices of organization development have become accepted managerial behaviors, managers have little patience with OD specialists who rely on technical jargon and gimmicky interventions to bring about change. Managers want assistance they can understand and use immediately. Finally, organizations have shown a renewed interest in business ethics. Companies today pay more attention to the rights of their employees, and they want change strategies that fit with the ethical issues that arise in the workplace.

In addition to these changes, organizations face other challenges as they evolve through the stages of growth, maturity, decline, and demise (Freeman, 1990; Tushman & Romanelli, 1990). For example, typical problems in growing organizations—such as cellular communications or biotechnology firms—include the lessened control of leaders, confusion about goals, and the obsolescence of certain founding members. One retrospective study of organizational change (Lumpkin & Dess, 1995), for example, found that firms that concentrated on being strong in one area were more successful in their early years, but focusing on strength in only one area became detrimental as companies grew and matured.

In more stable, mature organizations—such as automobile manufacturers—challenges typically include inappropriate and inflexible policies and procedures, long-tenured management that is unable to respond to market changes, and the lack of a successor to top management.

Declining organizations—such as political campaigns and railroads—usually have problems with low morale, decreased professional status of the organization's members, and problems in recruiting talented individuals to take the places of those who leave before the demise stage.

The cornerstone of the contingency approach to organizational structure, you may recall, is that there is no one best way of organizing. For the modern organization, change is constant, and effective organizations—regardless of their developmental stage—develop methods for responding to change. Not only do effective organizations respond, but in many cases, they also actively introduce their own programs of planned change.

Consider, for example, the case of British Airways. Owned by the British government, British Airways had for many years been a model of inefficiency and financial loss. In 1982, the year the British government decided to sell the company, British Airways had required a $900 million subsidy from the government to remain solvent. That year, the government sold shares in the company to the public and introduced new management. The new managers hired organization development consultants to help change British Airways' bureaucratic structure and culture to a more modern, market-driven orientation.

One of the new managers' first steps was to reduce the workforce from 59,000 to 37,000 by cutting levels of hierarchy and giving more autonomy to employees. In the following year, virtually every performance indicator—on-time departures and arrivals, aircraft maintenance, customer satisfaction, number of lost bags, and so forth—improved. Working with the OD consultants, management also instituted a customer service training program so employees could become more customer-oriented.

Finally, peer support groups were established for managers, profit sharing for all employees was introduced, and a new compensation system rewarded workers on the basis of performance rather than seniority. Five years after the airline was sold to the public, British Airways made a profit of $435 million (Goodstein, 1990).

This chapter looks at the technique of organization development as a means of introducing change to an organization. OD is another relatively new area of organizational psychology, and is itself undergoing an evolution. At its most basic level, however, organization development is the process of using knowledge from the behavioral sciences—including sociology and anthropology, as well as psychology—to improve organizational functioning. Such knowledge may focus on leadership development, group processes, or any other areas that impact a company's effectiveness.

Organization development is very much an applied area of psychology. In the typical OD situation, management recognizes a problem and contracts the services of an OD specialist or consultant—sometimes referred to as a **change agent**—to study the situation and recommend or implement changes. More frequently, however, managers themselves act as change agents.

As is the case with any new area of social science, controversies about the theory, methods, and evaluation of OD are common. Nonetheless, OD practitioners have provided valuable services to many organizations and established their field as a legitimate area of organizational psychology. This chapter looks at the origins of OD, methods for diagnosing and responding to organizational problems, and some issues surrounding the effectiveness of an OD program.

Origins of Organization Development

Although organizational theory has existed for almost 100 years, the formal study of how change is introduced and what are the different methods of change is relatively new. Most OD practitioners trace the origins of their field to the Inter-Group Relations Workshop at the State Teachers College in New Britain, Connecticut, in 1946. At that workshop, leaders, groups, and individual participants received daily feedback on their performances. To the surprise of the individuals conducting the workshop, the feedback seemed to promote learning more than the lectures and seminars.

Because of intense interest in exploring further how feedback affects group members, leaders of the workshop organized the National Training Laboratories (NTL) in Group Development in Bethel, Maine, the following year. Over the years, NTL has continued to conduct training sessions for group facilitators and participants. The NTL method focuses on using the **T-** (for training) **group** to promote organizational change.

NTL programs, which are a form of sensitivity training (Chapter 5), are designed to help participants understand the ways they interact with others. From such understanding, communication, interpersonal relations, and an individual's psychological health often improve. Early participants in NTL programs were eager to apply the skills and insights they had developed to the organizational setting. In the years that followed, however, T-group enthusiasts discovered that introducing change into formal and complex organizations was more complicated than first believed. Consequently, the T-group approach has undergone a number of modifications in the years since its development.

Another important influence in the field of organization development was the work of Douglas McGregor, the creator of Theory X and Theory Y, who specifically addressed this problem of applying T-group skills to complex organizational settings. In 1957, McGregor, working with the management of Union Carbide, established an internal consulting group whose task was to use behavioral science knowledge to assist line managers.

At about the same time, Herbert Shepard launched three experiments in organization development at the Esso refineries at Bayonne, Baton Rouge, and Bayway. Techniques to bring about planned change in these environments included survey feedback (discussed below) followed by laboratory training and discussion, training activities that focused on intergroup and interpersonal relations, team development, and intergroup conflict resolution. Some OD specialists (French & Bell, 1984) believe the term "organization development" emerged from these studies at Esso.

Survey research was another important influence on the rise of organization development. In 1946, Rensis Likert founded the Survey Research Center at the University of Michigan. A year later Likert convinced the Detroit Edison Company that a survey of employee opinions and attitudes about the company could be useful in raising productivity. From that study researchers discovered that when survey results were given only to supervisors and not passed on to employees, little positive organizational change occurred. On the other hand, if findings were shared in group meetings, favorable changes were likely to result.

Finally, the work of the Tavistock Institute of Human Relations in London—which developed the sociotechnical systems approach discussed in Chapter 12—was another important influence on the development of OD. In both the study of the longwall method of coal getting and the Ahmedabad textile mill study, Tavistock researchers demonstrated that changing organizational structure at the same time technology is changed resulted in increased organizational effectiveness.

Interestingly, the work of the Tavistock Institute initially had little effect in either the United States or Great Britain. Rather, findings from the Tavistock studies were much more influential in the Scandinavian countries—Norway and Sweden in particular. Rather than focus on management development or enrichment of individual jobs—typical OD approaches in the United States—change in these countries usually occurred by fostering cooperation between management and the union. The application of the autonomous work group approach was successful at Volvo and Saab, and in later years was introduced into a number of American work settings, including the Gaines pet food plant of General Foods in Topeka, Kansas.

From these early beginnings, interest in organization development has increased dramatically. As suggested above, OD itself has been undergoing a change in recent years. From the beginning, OD practitioners usually focused on issues concerning interpersonal relations in the workplace, and the cornerstone practices of OD were team building, T-groups, survey feedback, and organizational diagnosis and feedback (Fagenson & Burke, 1990a).

By the 1990s, however, OD practitioners were spending less time on these issues and more time on management style enhancement and strategy development. In a survey of the direction in which OD specialists believe their field is headed, two researchers (Fagenson & Burke, 1990b) found that specialists expect future OD efforts to focus more on issues that affect the entire organization than on individual work groups. Issues likely to be important to future OD practitioners include strategy, reward systems, corporate culture, human resource development, executive coaching, and organizational culture. Some approaches to dealing with these issues are discussed later in this chapter.

Diagnosis and Analysis

Organization development interventions typically begin with a **diagnosis** that attempts to understand the different aspects of the organization and their relationship to the problem. The change agent begins the diagnosis by studying the **organizational architecture** (Nadler, 1992), a term that refers to the aspects of both the social and work systems that are part of a complex organization. From an OD perspective, working with an organization's formal structure or the ways that tasks are accomplished without considering the people within the organization will not lead to a successful resolution of a problem.

Although change agents use many different strategies to collect information, organizational diagnosis typically involves five steps:

1. Developing a sense of how the organization should ideally function;
2. Choosing an organizational model that reflects the ideal organization;
3. Comparing the actual processes of the organization to the model by collecting data on how the organization is functioning;
4. Identifying discrepancies to find problem areas; and
5. Developing interventions that will bring about changes to solve the problems (Smither, Houston, & McIntire, 1996).

Although this procedure seems straightforward, one of the hardest questions concerns how the organization should function ideally. During the diagnosis process, it often becomes clear that different parts of an organization have different goals and strategies for accomplishing those goals. The conflict in goals may limit an organization's effectiveness by creating conflict among its members.

During the diagnostic phase, the OD specialist works from a model of organization such as sociotechnical systems, contingency theory, or whatever model he or she finds most helpful. One of the newest models used for diagnosis (Porras & Robertson, 1992) looks at four factors that constitute the organizational work setting. *Organizing arrangements* refer to the formal aspects of the company—goals, strategies, administrative systems, and so forth. *Social factors* are characteristics of the people who belong to the organization, such as management style, informal networks and groups, and qualities of individuals.

Physical setting factors include lighting, heating, spatial arrangements, and so forth. Finally, *technology* refers to tools, job design, expertise, and technical systems. One way of diagnosing a problem is to see whether these factors fit

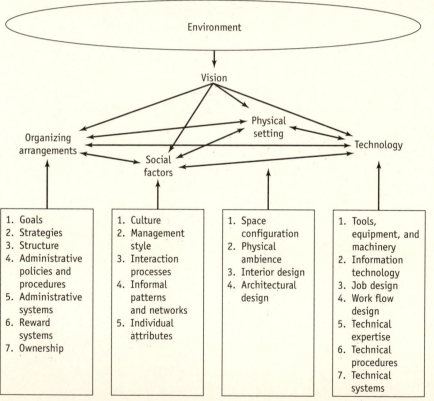

Figure 13.1 A Change-based Model of Organizations
As the figure indicates, an organization's environment affects its vision, which in turn affects the four categories of factors that constitute the work setting: organizing arrangements, social factors, physical setting, and technology. These also influence each other.

well with the vision of the organization. Porras and Robertson's framework is illustrated in Figure 13.1.

For example, an organization experiencing problems with productivity may ask an OD specialist to help with the problem. The OD specialist may discover that the company's vision stresses cooperation and teamwork, but that different parts of the organization stress competition. For example, tasks might be assigned to teams but rewards given to individuals; physical areas in which teams are required to work might be cramped and uncomfortable; and managers may be chosen on the basis of their technical expertise but not have much knowledge about how to facilitate teamwork. In this example it is easy to see how the organizational architecture may make accomplishing the vision impossible.

As the final stage of the diagnosis, the change agent identifies one or more interventions that will help the organization address its problem.

Resistance to Organizational Change

Barriers to Organizational Change
Overcoming Resistance to Change

Given both the rapid pace of change and its impact on organizational effectiveness, it seems reasonable that managers and workers would support the efforts of OD specialists. For a number of reasons, however, introducing planned change into an organization can be difficult. Often, organizations develop statements about how they value change—they state that they encourage risk taking and open communication, for example—but their reward systems encourage the status quo. In the example above, the architecture was in conflict with the organizational vision.

Organizational theorists Andrew Van de Ven and Marshall Poole (1995) developed a model that offers four theoretical explanations for why organizations change. According to *life cycle theory,* change is inevitable as an organization moves through the stages of growth, maturity, decline, and demise. *Teleological theory* suggests that organizations have goals, and that change occurs because the organization moves toward its goal. As goals are achieved, new goals take their place.

Dialectical theory, in contrast, holds that the struggle between different forces within an organization causes change. When one force becomes powerful, that force will confront and alter the status quo. Finally, *evolutionary theory* argues organizations change as different parts compete for scarce resources, and those parts that best fit the organization's environment are likely to force change. In the OD framework, the reason behind the change is less important than that the organization adapt successfully.

In one study (Kabanoff, Waldersee, & Cohen, 1995), researchers developed a taxonomy of organizations and their values and looked at how each type addressed organizational change. Working with annual reports, internal magazines, mission statements, and other documents, the researchers used computer-aided content analysis to identify how the different types of organizations reacted to change.

Box 13.1   A CONVERSATIONAL APPROACH TO CHANGE

Two researchers (Ford & Ford, 1995) proposed an interesting model that focuses on the role of conversation in a change effort once a diagnosis is finished. According to this model, change begins with an *initiative conversation*. Initiative conversations rely on assertions or directives to initiate a change effort. A manager may state, for example, that, based on his or her diagnosis, organizational members need more training in customer service.

Conversations for understanding are designed to help people understand the situation. During this part of the change effort, questions are raised, evidence is given, and people express their beliefs and feelings about the expressed need for more training in customer service. In the next stage, people engage in *conversations for performance*. These conversations are focused on producing results. They are designed to fulfill what was discussed in the initiative conversation.

Finally, *conversations for closure* are designed to bring an end to the change process. People comment that the change is complete or as complete as it can be, and they express satisfaction or regrets that the project is finished. Closure ends the change effort and restores equilibrium to the organization. Closure can also include ceremonies and rewards, and conversations during this stage of the change effort may focus on new possibilities.

In their study, *elite* organizations valued authority, performance, and rewards, and tended to regard change as something caused by negative factors. Along the same lines, elite organizations expressed concern about workers' abilities to cope with the changes.

In *meritocratic* organizations, in which teamwork, participation, commitment, performance, and reward were important values, change was viewed as a stressor that was likely to have a negative impact on organizational members.

Collegial organizations, in which teamwork, participation, and commitment are valued more than leadership, performance, or rewards, regarded change positively. Collegial organizations welcomed change and in their communications, the organizations expressed confidence that the changes would be dealt with successfully.

Finally, *leadership* organizations, in which authority, leadership, commitment, reward, and performance were important values and teamwork was not, viewed change negatively and as something that was imposed by conditions outside the organization. Not surprisingly, leadership organizations looked to their leaders to make the change successful.

In postmodern theory (Chapter 12), conversation is an important force for change. Box 13.1 describes the conversational approach to understanding organizational change.

Barriers to Organizational Change

In an account of the decline of the American auto industry, one researcher (Halberstam, 1986) argued that certain aspects of the manufacturers' culture were responsible for their failure to adapt to change. Specifically, Ford, GM, and Chrysler ignored their competitors, did not change their technologies, and clung to outdated strategies. In other words, the "homogeneity of beliefs" within the American auto industry made change almost impossible. The Big Three paid close attention to what the others were doing, but little attention to the Japanese (Abrahamson & Fombrun, 1994).

One lesson we know from social psychology is that people are usually more comfortable with the familiar than with the unfamiliar. Because the purpose of organization development is to implement change, sometimes workers automatically assume such changes will be for the worse. Others may have unpleasant memories of earlier efforts to change the organization or, as was the case with Taylor's subordinates (Chapter 1), fear management will exploit them. Failed efforts at organizational change also create cynicism that makes future changes difficult (Reichers, Wanous, & Austin, 1997).

On the other hand, management itself may be concerned that an OD project will disrupt normal work procedures, productivity will suffer, and the manager will be held responsible. Five typical barriers to change are listed below.

1. Disruption of personal relationships. One of the most disturbing events that can occur in the workplace is a change in the system of personal relationships. As illustrated by the experience of changing the teams of coal miners discussed in Chapter 12, disrupting social relations typically affects employee productivity and morale negatively at least initially. Not surprisingly, an OD consultant's recommendation that personnel reductions or changes in procedures will result in higher productivity are likely to be strongly resisted.

2. Perceived threats to status. Sometimes workers resist change because they feel changes will result in lowered status or in new and undesired job duties. Threats to status often result in defensiveness and are not conducive to the introduction of change. For example, many times workers resist the installation of new technology because they fear lowered skill requirements will cause lower responsibility and pay scales. Along the same lines, sometimes workers resist participating in quality circles or autonomous work groups because they feel they are being given greater responsibility without an increase in compensation.

3. Preference for the status quo. According to many theories, people become effective leaders by reducing uncertainty in the workplace. Although the goal of an OD intervention may be greater efficiency, change will probably bring uncertainty, at least initially. Not surprisingly, many managers are unwilling to introduce uncertainty into their areas of control. Particularly if problems are not pressing, they may see change as unnecessarily disruptive.

As suggested above, managers may feel they will be blamed by their superiors for any temporary decline in production caused by an OD intervention. Finally, managers may believe the necessity of change is an indication of some failure on their part and thus argue forcefully that the old system is satisfactory.

4. Economic factors. In addition to fearing a loss of status, workers sometimes resist change because they have the realistic fear that change will eliminate jobs. For example, workers are sometimes asked to participate in discussions about workplace problems so that production can be made more efficient. If production is made more efficient, however, some workers are likely to lose their jobs. From the perspective of many employees, change that improves efficiency is valuable only insofar as it does not threaten their status.

5. Problems with the OD specialist. In addition to the internal reasons for resistance to change, an OD specialist sometimes creates additional problems. By inadequately diagnosing the problem, for example, or by recommending an inappropriate change, a consultant may gain the hostility of people within the workplace. At the same time, the consultant may make a correct diagnosis but fail to prepare the organization for the recommendations for change. If management and workers do not agree with the consultant about the source of the problem, then the proposed solution is likely to be resisted.

A related problem occurs when the OD consultant takes too narrow a focus. Organization development has many different theories and techniques for dealing with problems. When a consultant rigidly subscribes to one particular approach—such as using T-groups to discuss workplace issues, for example—and attempts to impose this approach on a situation for which it is not appropriate, then problems are likely to occur. Both the specific change recommended and the change process in general may be resisted.

Finally, a similar problem sometimes occurs when a researcher attempts to design a change strategy that can be evaluated scientifically. In many cases, the application of scientific evaluation procedures to an organizational problem is not feasible, and insisting on methodological rigor may not always be appropriate. OD specialists need to remember that the primary goal of most organizations is productivity, and in most cases, this must come before research. Regrettably, OD and scientific research sometimes have antagonistic goals, and the OD consultant needs to be clear about which has priority.

Overcoming Resistance to Change

In many cases organizational procedures have a "taken-for-granted quality, in which actors unwittingly accept the prevailing template as appropriate, right, and the proper way of doing things" (Greenwood & Hinings, 1996). Because of this, changing a complex organization is not an easy task, and several steps must occur before an organization commits itself to changing. Harvey and Brown (1992) have identified four stages of organizational resistance during which the movement to change may end.

In the first stage, only a few people recognize organizational problems and the need for change. These people are often considered outside the organizational culture and are sometimes treated as deviants.

In the second stage of resistance, more people begin to recognize the need for change. The topic of change is talked about more openly, and management and workers explore and openly discuss issues involved in making organizational change. This usually leads to a showdown, the third stage. Those supporting the change confront those who are resistant, and a decision is reached regarding implementation. This part of overcoming resistance can result in open warfare between parts of the organization.

If those favoring change are victorious, people who continue to resist will be placed in the category of *deviant,* just as those favoring change were in the beginning of the process. In stage four, pockets of resistance remain, but they are seen as a nuisance to be overcome. In the fifth and final stage, virtually everyone supports the change.

OD specialists use a variety of techniques to convince people change is necessary. The most common approach is to encourage management and workers to become involved in the change process rather than merely being observers. In this way uncertainty—and possibly resistance—may be lessened. In addition, employees who will perform the work after the OD specialist has departed may make suggestions that can be incorporated into the change program. Also, informal worker evaluations of a program before it is fully implemented can often help identify problems that may occur in the future.

Another useful approach in overcoming resistance to change is to work through informal leaders in the workplace. If influential individuals can be convinced of the necessity of change then they are likely to convince others. Similarly, formal leaders should make clear to organizational members that they support the planned change and expect their subordinates to help implement the program. Managers must demonstrate unequivocally that they take the OD effort seriously.

Resistance also lessens when the consultant can demonstrate the need for change. When change can be shown to reduce workload or to make work more interesting, it is much more likely to be accepted. In an interesting study of organization development among miners, for example, Buller and Bell (1986) attempted to raise productivity by assigning workers to one of four treatment conditions: participation in both team-building and goal-setting activities; team building only; goal setting only; or no treatment.

Although none of the OD treatments resulted in increased productivity (the authors attribute this lack of success to problems with research design), the miners reported considerable satisfaction with simply having the opportunity to participate in the OD intervention. In this particular study, positive outcomes other than increased productivity were likely.

A final approach to overcoming resistance is by creating a vision of what the workplace could become. Although workers typically look to leaders to create visions, OD consultants have an important role to play in helping leaders communicate their visions. If the managers can inspire the workers, then workers are more likely to support the change process. If managers cannot inspire their subordinates, or cannot motivate them to become actively involved in the change effort, however, the OD effort will almost certainly fail.

Although it would seem logical that some people accept change more readily than others, few researchers have looked at the individual characteristics that influence openness to organizational change. In one study, however, people who had a high internal locus of control and were committed to the organization were more accepting of changes than people who scored lower on those dimensions (Lau & Woodman, 1995).

Lewin's Unfreezing-Moving-
  Freezing Model
Intervention Theory
Planned Change
Action Research
Organizational Transforma-
  tion
Punctuated Equilibrium
Evaluating Models of
  Change

Models of Planned Change

As a relatively new field, organization development lacks a long history of theory and research. One area of contention in the field concerns evaluation, with some theorists arguing that OD needs more rigorous research strategies so that more knowledge about organizational change can be gained (Bullock & Syvantek, 1987; Eden, 1986), whereas other theorists argue that OD research must be more innovative than the traditional scientific model (Beer & Walton, 1987; Porras, 1987; Woodman, 1989).

Despite attempts to impose scientific rigor on the field, much of OD remains "seat of the pants" responses to pressing organizational problems. Nonetheless, some models for responding to and implementing planned change have been developed.

Lewin's Unfreezing-Moving-Freezing Model

Kurt Lewin, an eminent social psychologist and one of the founders of the NTL workshops described above, suggested that the basic process of organizational change consists of a three-step process called **unfreezing, moving, and freezing** (Lewin, 1951, 1958). These three steps occur at the levels of both the individual worker and the system as a whole. Figure 13.2 illustrates the unfreezing, moving, and freezing model.

Figure 13.2 Lewin's Model of Change

Unfreezing refers to opening the organization to change by minimizing resistance. Organizations lessen resistance by promoting or terminating certain employees, developing new organizational structures, or providing experiential kinds of training. Whatever the practice, the goal of the unfreezing stage is to force members of the organization to confront the need for change and to make them more aware of their own behaviors.

Moving refers to making changes. In this stage people work to transform the organization and, according to Lewin, they display more trust and openness. Finally, freezing stabilizes the introduced changes. The goal of this stage is to ensure that changes are maintained. The structure may be redesigned to encourage change, new kinds of employees may be hired, or the reward system may be modified to reinforce behaviors that promote the changes.

Lewin's simple model of organizational change has been very popular with OD practitioners. Although the unfreezing-moving-freezing framework provides no guidelines for evaluating the success of an organization development intervention, OD specialists often use it as a guide for instituting organizational change. The models described below are more complex, but they still reflect Lewin's basic approach.

Intervention Theory

Developed by Argyris (1970), **intervention theory** starts with the assumption that, without assistance, organizations are unable to diagnose or solve their own problems. Because of the complexity and interdependence of organizational parts, participants often cannot see their situations clearly or act to change their situations. As suggested earlier, organizational statements about openness and trust are often contradicted by policies and behaviors. For example, a company may have a policy that encourages risk taking, but when risk takers fail, they are punished. In this situation, the policy is not supported by the outcome.

In most organizations, these kinds of contradictions are too subtle to be appreciated or addressed openly. Consequently, the job of the **intervenor**—the OD consultant—is to assist participants in gathering information to clarify their situations and to help them make decisions about change.

The intervenor first assists members as they gather data and develop alternative plans of action. But in keeping with Argyris's notion that not allowing workers to act in a mature and responsible fashion is harmful to both the individual and the organization, the intervenor never prescribes solutions. The intervenor only helps clarify situations and assists organizational members in making decisions. In this way the intervenor facilitates discussion but avoids giving advice, so that members come to their own conclusions about the situation. According to Argyris, organizational change succeeds only if it comes from within, rather than being imposed by some outside consultant or manager.

Given its nondirective nature, the theoretical basis for intervention theory is clearly humanistic psychology (Smither, Houston, & McIntire, 1996). Intervention theory assumes that, with a little assistance, organization members are the best source of information for implementing change. Consultants who are brought in to define problems and implement solutions are unlikely to be aware of the unique aspects of organizational culture that employees already recognize. Allowing employees to reach their own decisions is not only more efficient, but involving them in the change effort almost certainly lowers resistance.

Although Argyris's belief that change must come from within the organization may have merit, intervention theory can be a difficult strategy to implement. Sometimes situational demands, such as an organizational crisis, necessitate an OD consultant telling management what to do, rather than helping management discover its own plan for action. When conflict among members immobilizes an organization, for example, or when demise is certain if immediate action is not taken, intervention theory may be inappropriate.

Intervention theory also assumes that individuals in organizations can make good decisions if they have the necessary information. Two well-supported findings of modern cognitive research are that decision making is frequently—if not usually—an irrational process, and that translation of cognition into behavior is unpredictable. Consequently, the assumption that having knowledge will lead to good decisions appears to be unfounded. One of the most common criticisms of organization development consultants is that they focus on method and often ignore power issues and organizational politics (Beer & Walton, 1987; Greiner & Schein, 1989), which may be the real factors behind a decision.

Finally, modern OD practice typically has the consultant taking a more active role than is suggested in the intervention model. As is often the case, the OD consultant is summoned when an organization is operating in a crisis mode. In these cases, managers need quick answers and there may not be time for proper implementation of an intervention theory strategy.

Planned Change

The **planned change model** was developed by Lippit, Watson, and Westley (1958) and later modified by other researchers (Froham & Sashkin, 1970; Kolb & Froham, 1970; Schein, 1972; Schein & Bennis, 1965). Planned change is a seven-step process outlined below and illustrated in Figure 13.3.

In the first stage, an organization contacts the change agent, consultant, or OD practitioner about a problem occurring in the organization. The problem might be intergroup conflict, developing new performance standards, or confusion about organizational roles, for example. At this stage of the intervention, the organization assesses the qualifications of the change agent at the same time that the change agent is assessing the readiness of the organization for change.

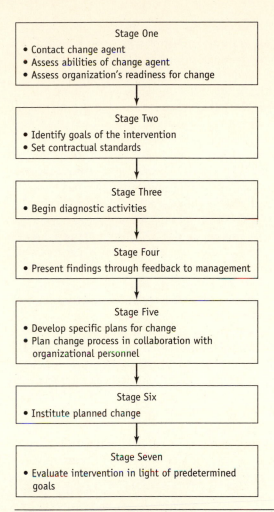

Figure 13.3 Planned Change Model

In the second stage of the process, the organization and the consultant agree on contractual standards. The consultant and the organization identify, usually within a broad framework, the goal of the OD activity. From an evaluation perspective the goal should be measurable, but many times goals are stated in vague and unquantifiable terms. For example, managers may feel the need to "improve communication" or to "raise worker morale." Although such goals are legitimate, evaluating the effectiveness of the OD program will be difficult if goals are not stated in a form conducive to measurement before the program begins.

In the planned change model, proper diagnosis of organizational problems is an essential step. In the third stage, the change agent begins diagnostic activities. The major strategies during this phase are interviews (the most popular approach), questionnaires (less costly and more easily quantifiable), observations, and the use of secondary data and unobtrusive measures such as turnover rates, profit and loss statements, and minutes of company meetings (Burke, 1982).

The next activity the consultant undertakes is to present findings through feedback. Generally, research results are first introduced to top management, then distributed more widely throughout the organization. During the fifth phase of the OD activity, plans for change are developed. Often these plans are made in collaboration with specific organizational members.

Stage six focuses on the intervention, the actual institution of the planned change. Typical interventions include job redesign, job enrichment, management by objectives, career development, team building, process consultation, and conflict resolution. In a review of change strategies reported in the literature in the early years of OD, Nicholas and Katz (1985) found job enlargement and sociotechnical approaches to be the most popular. During the 1980s, however, team building—which is discussed below—was the most popular form of intervention. Today OD practitioners predict strategy interventions will be the most popular in the years ahead.

In the final stage of the planned change process, results of the program are evaluated. Although the effects of some of the changes will be apparent immediately, others will be much more subtle and probably not obvious until some time later. During this phase it is important that management not expect immediate results. Also, as is the case with evaluating training programs, the evaluation should be done by someone other than the individuals who recommended and implemented the changes.

Two criticisms of the planned change model are that (1) in its focus on specific actions to solve specific problems, little diagnosis may be undertaken (Sashkin, Morriss, & Horst, 1973); and (2) the process of organization development is rarely as straightforward as the model suggests (Cummings & Huse, 1989).

Action Research

The third research strategy often used in organization development is action research. In contrast with the planned change model, in which existing behavioral science knowledge is applied to organizational problems, **action research** focuses on generating new knowledge at the same time that it works to solve an organization's problems. For this reason, action research emphasizes planning, diagnosis, and results that can be generalized to other settings.

The basic processes of action research are (1) data collection, (2) feedback of data to clients, and (3) action planning based on the data (Beckhard, 1969). Although action research and experimental research share the goal of generating new knowledge, they differ in a number of ways.

In general, it can be said that the methods of experimental research center on control: Variables and environments are controlled so that cause-and-effect relationships can be inferred. Although organizations occasionally use experimental or quasi-experimental research, most experiments are basic research, designed to gather knowledge without an immediate practical application. In contrast, action research focuses on solutions. Because the research program usually starts in a situation not created by the researcher, little control can be exercised.

Unlike experimental research, action research is almost always aimed at achieving concrete results that bring about change. Elegance of design is secondary to application of results. Although experimental research is more rigorous, action research usually provides information that is more relevant and useful to the manager (Aguinis, 1994).

Finally, unlike experiments, action research may not have a clear beginning and end. With the continuous feedback and modification that characterize action research, it is unlikely that clearly identifiable causal relationships can be determined. Additionally, action research recognizes that introducing changes at any one part of a complex system is likely to lead to unexpected changes elsewhere in the system. Figure 13.4 presents a model for doing action research.

Organizational Transformation

Organizational transformation (OT; Porras & Silvers, 1991), one of the newest models of planned change, focuses on radical change within an organization. OT developed as a response to corporate takeovers, mergers, and plant closings that resulted in downsizing, employee terminations, and large-scale restructuring. Unlike OD, which has historically focused on smaller-scale change, OT aims at changing entire systems, cultures, or ways of operating. For example, the reorientation of British Airways from a bureaucratic to a customer service organization described in the beginning of this chapter is an example of organizational transformation.

There are a number of characteristics that distinguish OT from OD. A key element in OT, for example, is the development of a vision of where the organization would like to be in the future. **Reframing** is an OT activity aimed at altering the way workers view the world. Reframing is designed to change attitudes and behaviors before implementing a transformation, and it may be accomplished through workshops, seminars, group discussions, or individual activities. **Industrial democracy,** in which workers have real responsibility for running the organization, is another example of organizational transformation.

Another interesting aspect of organizational transformation is that it is often directive rather than participative (Harvey & Brown, 1992). A senior manager in the organization articulates the need for change, then appoints individuals responsible for making the change happen. This approach is very different from the employee participation that characterizes most OD efforts. In general, transformation is based more on power relationships than on collaboration. This occurs because transformation often happens when an organization is under an external threat that demands an immediate response. In these kinds of situations, authoritarian, charismatic, or transformational leadership (Chapter 9) can be more effective than participative approaches.

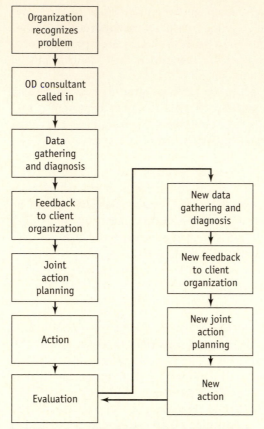

Figure 13.4 Action Research Model

Organizational transformation developed as a response to the large-scale organizational changes that began occurring in the 1980s. OT reflects a new concern with larger issues such as organizational culture and strategy, and pays less attention to the typical concerns of OD such as team building, survey feedback, and so forth. Because this approach is so new, it has not really been evaluated—or even articulated—in a systematic fashion. The next few years should reveal whether OT will supplant more traditional models of organizational change.

Punctuated Equilibrium

Punctuated equilibrium (Gersick, 1991; Miller & Friesen, 1984) is a model of organizational change that holds that organizations evolve through long periods of stability that are punctuated by revolutionary periods of short duration.

According to the theory, organizations establish a pattern of activity based on environmental conditions and management decisions made at the time of their founding. Organizational members have shared understandings that support continuance of the culture that eventually leads to inertia.

In the punctuated equilibrium model, inertia is the impetus for radical change. Because everyone is satisfied with the status quo, change can occur only if it is sudden and dramatic. Some factors that may provoke fundamental change are a severe crisis in organizational performance, major changes in the environment, or the succession of the chief executive officer.

In one study that looked at a punctuated equilibrium model of change (Romanelli & Tushman, 1994), researchers examined the histories of 25 minicomputer companies founded between 1967 and 1969. Information about organizational activities was collected from business press articles, financial reports, annual reports, and prospectuses. Organizational transformations were judged to occur whenever any firm had a substantial change in its strategy, structure, or power distribution.

Results from the study supported the punctuated equilibrium model. That is, revolutionary transformations greatly outnumbered incremental transformations.

Evaluating Models of Change

One weakness common to all models discussed above is that they are frequently applied in a nonscientific manner. Although it is unreasonable to expect OD practitioners to build laboratory control into their interventions, future development of the field will require some attention to building and improving on theory and knowledge. When studies are uncontrolled, their results may be misleading. In one review of organization development studies, for example, Terpestra (1981) found that as researchers relaxed their research standards, the frequency of positive OD outcomes increased. This problem of a "positive-findings bias" in OD—a tendency to find OD interventions successful—has not yet been resolved among researchers (Roberts & Robertson, 1992).

Historically, research in organization development has suffered from four problems (Beer & Walton, 1987). First, the research has copied the scientific model and aimed at identifying causation. Unfortunately, organizations and real-life situations are usually too complex to be studied with the experimental model. For example, one study focused on the effects of redesigning jobs and introducing participation in a unionized coal mine. When workers in the control group found out about the experimental group, they so resented the experimental group's advantages that they voted to stop any further changes in the workplace (Blumberg & Pringle, 1983).

Second, evaluation research in OD is usually based on a contradiction. Most OD practitioners argue that change will be subtle and will show up over time in many areas of the organization. Yet evaluation is usually done in terms of a specific variable at a specific time. In reality, organization development research should be longitudinal.

Third, OD research is often "flat"; that is, researchers identify their input or predictor variables and their outcome or criterion variables, but they often ignore in-depth description of the history of the group under consideration. In addition, important factors such as the environmental context of the intervention are overlooked.

Finally, the more rigorous the evaluation research, the less likely it will be useful to the user. As Beer and Walton (1987) commented:

> Good science may be antithetical to good action. More complex statistical techniques and more complex quasi-experimental designs, in attempts to achieve more precision and tighter scientific "proof," neglect the "social construction" of knowledge in the social sciences. The complexity of the subject material and the existence of nonrational responses to data will inhibit acceptance of even the most tightly controlled experiments.

It is obvious, then, that all methods of OD intervention must make trade-offs between scientific rigor and usefulness. Although organization development practitioners have been criticized for not being rigorous in their methodologies, more recent thinking suggests that traditional methods are simply inadequate for dealing with and evaluating organizational change. In this respect OD may be at a crossroads, where the field can advance only by developing new methods for evaluating the outcomes of interventions.

Meanwhile, there are guidelines on how to choose an intervention strategy. In cases in which the OD specialist has some discretion, for example, more scientifically rigorous approaches should be used when the problems are unclear or not urgent, when the researcher has little OD experience, or when there is a low level of trust in the organization. Less rigorous approaches should be taken when problems are critical and identifiable, and when the researchers have experience and are trusted.

Organization Development Interventions

Individual Interventions:
   Interpersonal Interaction
   and Disclosure
Interpersonal Interventions: Third-Party Interventions
Team Development Interventions: Team Building
Organizationwide Interventions: The Leadership Grid

As mentioned earlier in this chapter, the basic idea of organization development is to apply knowledge from the social sciences to bring about organizational change. Over the years, OD practitioners have developed a variety of interventions to bring about change. Interventions can be directed at individual workers, or they can be directed at the system as a whole. The following section looks at typical interventions at four levels of an organization.

Individual Interventions: Interpersonal Interaction and Disclosure

One of the values that are the foundation of organization development is the belief that every person desires psychological growth. When employers provide workers with opportunities for psychological development, OD theorists believe, both the organization and the worker will benefit.

One intervention at an individual level is to help people develop a better understanding of their own values and ways of communicating. The idea behind this intervention is that this kind of insight will make them more effective in the workplace.

The **Johari Window** is a widely used intervention designed to help people understand how they interact with others. In this activity people disclose personal information about themselves and receive feedback from others about their communication style. This openness often leads to greater personal insight and a better understanding of how one appears to others. Box 13.2 shows and explains the Johari Window.

Another individual intervention is measuring a person's style of perceiving the world and interacting with others. These activities are based on the notion that people can be categorized into different types or styles depending on their worldview. When workers understand each other's types, communication can be more effective.

Many OD specialists use tools such as the Myers-Briggs Type Indicator or the DISC test to identify a person's most comfortable way of interacting with others. In these interventions workers complete psychological instruments and participate in a series of activities designed to help them understand themselves and the people around them better. According to theory, when people have this kind of information, communication in the workplace can be more open and effective.

Interpersonal Interventions: Third-Party Interventions

Sometimes conflict in the workplace creates problems that become a barrier to productivity. When conflict escalates, communication can become impossible. In these situations, an OD practitioner may be called to intervene to resolve the conflict.

The intervenor usually begins by helping parties to the conflict understand how unresolved conflict escalates and perpetuates itself. Figure 13.5 (p. 431) illustrates a model of conflict developed by Richard Walton.

The first step in resolving the conflict is to diagnose the underlying issues that are the cause of the conflict. During this stage the intervenor has to perform a careful diagnosis of the situation because, in many cases, the underlying causes are different from the obvious causes. When the causes are apparent, the

Box 13.2   THE JOHARI WINDOW

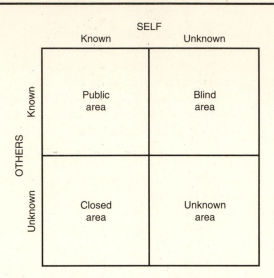

The Johari Window can be a useful intervention for finding out more about oneself. According to the theory, having more information in the public area also makes communication easier. This activity provides an opportunity to test the Johari intervention to see if it works for you. You will need a partner, who does not need to know you well.

1. Take a moment to think about how it would be to spend time with or be professional colleagues with your partner in this activity. Keep this information to yourself.

2. On a piece of paper, draw the four boxes of the Johari Window. In the first box (the public area), list some information about yourself that should be apparent to everyone.

3. Leave the second box of the window (the blind area) blank.

4. In the closed area, box 3, list some information about yourself that your partner probably does not know. Keep in mind that the depth of the information you disclose is an indication of how well you know and trust your partner.

5. In the fourth box of the Johari Window, the unknown area, write down some questions about yourself that probably neither you nor your partner can answer. These might be questions about how your family relationships affected the way you are today, how ethical you might be in a situation of great temptation, or possible unconscious reasons why you are taking a course in organization development.

6. After you have completed the three boxes of the Johari Window, take turns sharing the information with your partner. In the last part of the exercise, ask your partner for information that is obvious to him or her but not to you to put in your blind area.

7. After you have filled all four boxes of the Johari Window, think again about your feelings about your partner. Are your feelings more positive, negative, or just the same? What do you think your partner thinks of you?

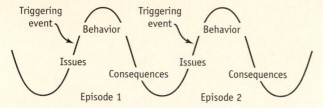

Source: Walton, R. (1987). *Managing Conflict,* 2nd ed. Copyright © 1987
by Addison Wesley Longman, Inc. Reprinted by permission of the publisher

---

Figure 13.5 A Model of Conflict
The cyclical model of conflict suggests that concerns about issues lead to conflict behavior
after a triggering event occurs. The behavior creates consequences that affect the issues,
which can lead to a second conflict episode.

intervenor next works to help the parties resolve their differences through compromise. At the same time, the intervenor works to defuse any negative emotions that have arisen because of the conflict.

In the next part of third-party intervention, the OD specialist helps the
conflicting parties understand what triggers conflict and how conflict can be
avoided in the future. Participants need to understand which of their own behaviors contribute to the conflict and they need to know how to avoid triggering new episodes.

In the final stage the intervenor helps parties understand both the feelings
that are generated by conflict and ways of coping with them.

Although managers often perform OD interventions themselves, managerial intervention is usually not appropriate for third-party situations. Because of
the emotions involved in conflict and the importance of having an intervenor
who appears unbiased, skilled professionals who understand the dynamics of
communication and conflict resolution are best suited for this activity.

Several studies (Sheppard & Lewicki, 1987; Sheppard, Lewicki, & Minton,
1986) provide support for the third-party intervention model. Another study
(Prein, 1984) found that third-party intervention works best when the intervenor
is directive and provides a structure for identifying and solving problems rather
than simply facilitating direct confrontation between the conflicting parties.

Team Development Interventions: Team Building

Team building is an intervention designed to enable workers to cooperate and
share skills so that work is completed more efficiently. Team building differs
from T-groups in its focus on task accomplishment rather than on interpersonal
processes. In a typical team-building situation, an organization has a problem
that requires the knowledge or experience of several individuals. Common
problems include lower production, confusion about assignments, apathy, lack
of initative, and poor customer service.

People who are affected by these problems or who may be able to contribute to a solution are brought together to form a team to address the problem. Teams may be temporary, or they may become a regular part of the organizational structure. Establishing a new team has been described (Dyer, 1987) as a five-step process:

1. Gaining the commitment to the team effort. The first step requires overcoming resistance and answering questions from team members about how the team members will operate, how long the team members will work together, and so forth.

2. Establishing the agenda. Team-building meetings are more effective if people know in advance what will be discussed. Typical agenda items include goals, strategic planning, expectations of participants, and strengths and weaknesses of the team.

3. Setting the team-building session. The first meeting should be for an extended period of time, typically two or three days. Also, the team meeting should be held away from the workplace so that distractions are minimized.

4. Establishing guidelines at the first session. The first task is to establish guidelines for the team meeting. Participants should discuss goals, review the agenda, and become familiar with the facilitator or consultant.

5. Keeping the team working at two levels. As the team begins its work, participants need to keep in mind that the team is operating at two levels. On the *task* level they are addressing issues, but on a *process* level they are learning how to work together. Effective team building usually requires participants to stop focusing on the task at some point and to discuss how the process aspects of the team building are working. Some considerations are that cooperation will be valued over competition, and that recognition will first be given to the team, and not to individual members.

As suggested above, the dynamics of the small group affect the activities of the team. Effective teams typically develop a strong sense of group identity and exhibit trust and openness in communications. Participants often emerge from a team-building experience with a better understanding of how authority, control, and power affect organizational decision making. Teams that do not develop a sense of trust and openness are likely to be limited in their effectiveness. In many cases participants find learning about small group processes even more valuable than solving specific organizational problems.

During the 1980s, team building became extremely popular among OD consultants. As more organizations moved toward implementing participative decision making, employees were forced to learn to work together to reach decisions. This was not always a straightforward process, and one review of conditions necessary for successful teamwork found that the most effective teams had training in leadership (Lawler & Mohrman, 1987).

Although the team-building approach will probably continue to be applied in many organizations, OD practice has moved away from teams toward dealing with larger organizational issues. Interpersonal processes will always be a critical aspect of any organization, but team building is unlikely to recapture the incredible popularity it enjoyed in the 1980s.

Organizationwide Interventions: The Leadership Grid®

The **Leadership Grid®** (previously known as the Managerial Grid®) is a copyrighted approach to organization development created by Blake and Mouton (1964) from activities in their social psychology classes at the University of Texas. The grid has been enormously popular with companies in the United States; Westinghouse, for example, trained 7,000 managers on grid techniques over a 15-year period (Harvey & Brown, 1992).

The Leadership Grid® emphasizes the importance of two basic leader behaviors: (1) a concern for others—consideration—and (2) a concern for production—initiating structure. Managers are rated on these dimensions along a scale of one (low emphasis) to nine (high emphasis). According to Blake and Mouton there are five basic leadership types, with the optimal style being an emphasis on both production and people. The five basic types are presented in Table 13.1.

The most recent version of the Leadership Grid® (Blake & McCanse, 1991) has two additional leadership styles. In *paternalistic management*, reward and approval are granted to people in return for loyalty and obedience; failure to comply leads to punishment. In *opportunistic management*, on the other hand, performance is considered a series of exchanges in which people expend effort only when others expend an equivalent amount. Managers change their styles to gain maximum advantage, and their styles reflect the styles of the people with whom they interact.

Figure 13.6 illustrates the Leadership Grid®.

Introducing the Leadership Grid® to an organization is a six-step process that takes five years to complete. *Laboratory-seminar training*, the first step of the process, introduces grid concepts to teams of managers and emphasizes the

Table 13.1   THE LEADERSHIP GRID®—FIVE BASIC TYPES OF LEADERSHIP

Basic Types	Emphasis On	
	Production	People
1,1 Impoverished Management	Low	Low
9,1 Authority Obedience	High	Low
1.9 Country Club Management	Low	High
5,5 Organization Man Management	Moderate	Moderate
9,9 Team Management	High	High

problem-solving aspects of every job. Throughout the course, the desirability of the 9,9 style is stressed. *Team development,* the second step, focuses on analyzing the management styles and operating methods of the individual managers. In step three, *intergroup development,* the consultant leads the group in activities designed to change a win-lose mentality toward problem solving into a more cooperative group focus.

In step four, *organizational goal setting,* major problems of the organization that need solutions are identified. *Goal attainment,* step five, requires teams of managers to work on the specific problems that have been identified in step four. In the last part of the process, *stabilization,* materials and styles are reviewed and critiqued so that the changes introduced will be continued.

The Leadership Grid® and similar programs have been widely accepted as organizationwide interventions. Evaluating the effectiveness of this approach is difficult, however, since it takes five years to implement and involves numerous steps and activities. One criticism has been that although the program has been effective in changing attitudes, changes in behavior have not been widely demonstrated (Gray & Starke, 1984).

Another criticism is that little evidence supports Blake and Mouton's belief that the 9,9 style is the most effective. As discussed in Chapter 9, the assumption that, regardless of situation, one leadership style is best is contrary to current thinking in leadership theory. In fact, it is hard to imagine that one approach to leadership will be appropriate in every managerial situation and with all different types of employees.

Total quality management (TQM) is another popular organizationwide intervention and was described in Chapter 10. Box 13.3 describes the application of the principles of TQM to a university setting.

Evaluating Organization Development

Ethical Issues in OD
Methodological Concerns

From the foregoing discussion it should be obvious that the field of organization development is probably less clearly defined than any other topic covered in this book. As a result, proper evaluation of the field and of specific OD interventions is not always a straightforward procedure. Some of the issues associated with the future of OD include concerns about ethics and methodology.

Ethical Issues in OD

The theory and practice of organization development contain several inherent contradictions that make ethical issues a matter of great importance to OD practitioners. For example, most approaches to OD recommend that consultants should, over time, teach organizations to solve their own problems.

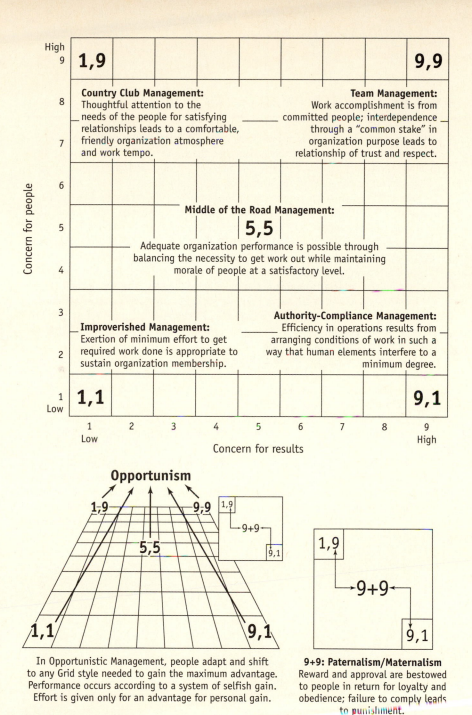

Figure 13.6 Leadership Grid®

In Opportunistic Management, people adapt and shift to any Grid style needed to gain the maximum advantage. Performance occurs according to a system of selfish gain. Effort is given only for an advantage for personal gain.

9+9: Paternalism/Maternalism Reward and approval are bestowed to people in return for loyalty and obedience; failure to comply leads to punishment.

Box 13.3 WHEN FACULTY TRY QUALITY

Although most quality interventions have occurred in private industry, some efforts have occurred at colleges and universities. At the University of Texas at Austin, for example, the Center for Teaching Effectiveness collaborated with the Quality Center in an experiment to support the application of quality principles to the classroom.

The effort began with an assessment of the needs of professors. Using a Delphi technique (Chapter 10), researchers found that faculty needed information about "what the quality concept is," "how quality principles might be applied in the classroom," and "how data can be used to improve teaching." After an exploratory conference, in which faculty were provided with information about quality concepts, several quality projects were designed. These projects were staffed by teams of professors.

One quality project team focused on involving students in teaching their classes. In human ecology and mechanical engineering classes, students were assigned to teach a component of the course. In both classes students put more effort into their learning, and the most highly rated learning format was when a professor acted as a discussant of a student presentation.

In another project, ten instructors from management, advertising, geology, zoology, and two foreign languages designed a curriculm to assess the impact of e-mail on student learning. In some cases the professors used e-mail to gather and distribute information and respond to student questions. Others used electronic journaling and peer editing. At the end of the class students expressed their satisfaction that their professors were available more frequently through e-mail than they were in person.

Finally, another quality project team considered better ways of providing feedback in large natural science classes. To determine which activities best promoted understanding they surveyed students after quizzes several times during the semester. As a result of the feedback, the instructors continuously modified their teaching methods throughout the semester. At the end of the term, students reported satisfaction with feedback and with the learning activities.

Source: Svinicki, M., & O'Reilly, M. (1996, November). When faculty try quality. *AAHE Bulletin, 49,* 10–13.

According to Argyris and others, it is not ethical for a consultant to foster a dependency relationship with an organization so that managers feel they must call on an outsider to address issues that arise in the workplace.

Ideally, in a typical intervention, the organization development consultant works him- or herself out of a job. At the end of the intervention, workers and managers should have the skills to handle many problems themselves. Yet for for many individuals who support themselves by practicing OD, keeping an organization dependent is a very real temptation.

Another ethical problem concerns making unpopular recommendations. When management wants the OD specialist to address issues the consultant feels are superficial, the consultant may feel an ethical obligation to disagree with the employer. Disagreement can lead to termination of the consultant's contract and the situation at the workplace will be no better. What is the proper course of action for the consultant: open disagreement with management, compliance with management's wishes, or overt compliance while maintaining a secret agenda for change?

Finally, OD consultants constantly face issues requiring a choice between organizational goals and worker goals. Although the humanistic nature of organization development suggests that concerns about people should outweigh productivity concerns, putting worker well-being first is often not realistic. OD consultants need to be clear about their values on this matter and willing to stand by their principles.

Methodological Concerns

In most cases OD specialists are called on to diagnose and solve problems that already exist in the workplace. Rarely can proper controls be applied so that results can be evaluated from a scientific standpoint.

Problems such as the multitude of confounding variables, the lack of control groups, little or no reliability or validity evidence about the measures applied in an OD intervention, and management pressure to achieve specific results sometimes make conclusions drawn from OD research questionable.

Because of these problems inherent in the situation, proper research design is usually impossible to achieve—and without proper design, the meanings of results can be uncertain. In the early days of OD, virtually all the evaluations used elementary and unsophisticated forms of statistical analysis to reach their conclusions. Although this lack of sophisticated analysis may be the result of poor design, it may also be the result of a lack of understanding of proper research techniques among some OD practitioners. In Nicholas and Katz's (1985) review of organization development research reported in the literature between 1948 and 1982, many studies were found to be uninterpretable because of poor design, analysis, or writing.

A review by Porras and Berg (1978) analyzed 35 of the most credible published reports of the outcomes of OD interventions. The analysis revealed that more than 50 percent of the interventions brought about positive change, and that the Leadership Grid® and survey feedback had the most impact. In another review (Neuman, Edwards, & Raju, 1989), a meta-analysis of 126 OD studies found that interventions had a positive impact on attitudes, and that group process interventions such as team building had the greatest impact on satisfaction.

Nonetheless, some OD specialists now argue that the traditional scientific model of evaluation is inappropriate for OD, and that new models must be developed. At the least, clients should become involved in the research; descriptions of context, systems, and personalities must be more detailed; and the effects of interventions should be studied over longer periods (Beer &

Walton, 1987). Finally, OD practitioners need to move beyond the simple statistical methods—frequencies, averages, and percentages—that characterize most of their research. Because OD deals with so many variables, more sophisticated analysis techniques, such as meta-analysis, time series, and multivariate methods, are probably more appropriate than other, simpler statistical methods.

The Future of Organization Development

Because of the sweeping changes in organizations at the end of the twentieth century, it is almost certain that organization development will continue to enjoy its current popularity. Increasingly, managers will turn to social scientists to help them deal with the challenges they face.

One group of OD theorists (Smither, Houston, & McIntire, 1996) identified some of the forces that will affect organizations in the future. In every case, OD specialists or managers will use the principles of OD to help organizations deal with the difficult process of change.

1. Changes in the organizational environment. As natural resources become more scarce, companies will have to develop policies and practices more sensitive to ecological concerns. At the same time, advances in communication and transportation will make trade between different geographic areas and nations easier.

2. Advances in technology. Given the advances in technology over the last 20 years, it is hard to imagine today what technology will be like 20 years from now. Nonetheless, we can expect more sophisticated voice input and output interfaces, natural language workstations, and greater reliance on virtual reality simulations.

3. Changes in the workforce. As discussed earlier in this book, minority women are the fastest-growing segment of the workforce, and older workers are staying on the job longer. Diversity makes workplaces more complex, and companies will need to develop new policies to accommodate different kinds of workers.

4. Increased emphasis on human values and ethics. Organizations of the future are expected to pay more attention to ethical issues. Increasingly, organizations are held accountable for actions that the public considers unethical. Some theorists (e.g., Axline, 1994; Mitroff, Mason, & Pearson, 1994) believe organizations of the future may have special departments that deal with ethics or codes of conduct that every employee must agree to uphold.

Finally, OD theorists believe that the process of change has become a fixed part of organizational life. Companies will not be returning to the bureaucratic structure identified by Weber, but will continue to develop flexible contingency-based models. In this scenario, OD will become a part of every organizational culture.

Chapter Summary

Almost every manager today recognizes that one of the most pervasive qualities of organizations is change. As organizations move through the different developmental stages they face challenges that often necessitate modifications to structure or changes in procedure. Organization development (OD) is the application of planned change. The field of OD has developed from the social sciences.

Some of the sources for the origin of OD include the T-groups developed at the National Training Laboratories, McGregor's Theory X and Theory Y, the use of survey research, and the work of the Tavistock Institute.

Organization development interventions begin with a diagnosis to understand different aspects of an organization and their relationship to the problem under consideration. During this stage of the intervention, OD specialists typically use a model of organization to guide their data collection.

Although it seems logical that workers would respond favorably to changes that facilitate organizational functioning, there are several sources of resistance to change. Workers often dislike any disruption of personal relationships, and they also often resist any changes that may threaten their status. Other sources of resistance include a preference for the status quo, economic factors, and problems with the organization development specialist.

OD practitioners use several models of change to guide their interventions. One of the most popular is the unfreezing-moving-freezing approach developed by Lewin. Intervention theory is another model of planned change in which the intervenor gathers information about the organization and helps its members to make decisions about change. Planned change is a seven-step process focusing on action to solve specific problems. Action research attempts to generate new knowledge at the same time it is introducing change into the organizational setting. A new OD technique, organizational transformation, aims to make radical changes in an organization's culture. Finally, punctuated equilibrium argues that change happens in spurts.

Some typical kinds of organization development activities include interpersonal interaction and disclosure, third-party interventions, team building, and the Leadership Grid®.

Because the field of organization development is less defined than other areas discussed in this book, proper evaluation of OD and its interventions is not always straightforward. Some concerns involve ethical issues and methodologies. Despite these concerns, OD is likely to continue to grow in the future becaues of changes in the organizational environment, advances in technology, changes in the workforce, and an increased emphasis on human values and ethics.

Key Words and Concepts

action research (p. 424)
change agent (p. 411)
diagnosis (p. 413)
industrial democracy (p. 425)
interpersonal interaction and
  disclosure (p. 429)
intervenor (p. 421)
intervention (p. 409)
intervention theory (p. 421)
Johari Window (p. 429)
Leadership Grid® (p. 433)
organizational architecture
  (p. 403)

organization development (OD)
  (p. 409)
organizational transformation
  (p. 425)
planned change model (p. 422)
punctuated equilibrium (p. 426)
reframing (p. 425)
team building (p. 431)
T-group (p. 411)
third-party interventions (p. 429)
unfreezing, moving, and freezing
  (p. 420)

Questions for Discussion

1. What are some of the changes you have seen occurring in organizations over the last few years? Has any particular change had a big impact on your life?
2. How did organization development originate? How is OD different from the traditional areas of I/O psychology?
3. What are some of the principles that guide diagnosis? How does diagnosis compare with other research strategies discussed elsewhere in this book?
4. What are some typical barriers to organizational change? What are some ways of overcoming these barriers?
5. If you were in charge of intervening to bring about change in a large company, which of the models of change would you use? If you were redesigning your college or university, which model would be most appropriate?
6. What is the purpose of individual interventions? What is the purpose of third-party interventions? Do you think one would be harder to accomplish successfully than the other? Why?
7. If you were put in charge of a team-building intervention, what would you do to make the intervention successful?
8. Why do you think the Leadership Grid® is so popular? Which leadership style best describes you? your friends? your professor?
9. What are the ethical problems that occur during interventions? Why are some people concerned about the methodologies used in OD? Do you think methodological questions are relevant to OD, or does the field need approaches different from the traditional methods used in I/O?
10. What are some of the factors that will affect organizations in the future? How do you think colleges and universities will be different in the future? Is there a role for OD in a university setting?

CHAPTER 14

Human Factors and Working Conditions

Fatigue and Performance
Origins of Human Factors
The Human-Machine System
Designing the Work Environment
Human Factors and Automation
Accidents and Safety
Chapter Summary
Key Words and Concepts
Questions for Discussion

In September 1991, workers were just beginning their day at the Imperial Food Products plant in Hamlet, North Carolina, when an overhead hydraulic line ruptured. The hydraulic lines ran above vats of hot oil 30 feet long and 3 feet wide used to cook chicken parts for sale to fast food restaurants. Under the vats were open flames, and when the flammable hydraulic fluid sprayed onto the floor, it was ignited by the fires under the huge frying vats. Suddenly, the plant was full of flames and thick yellow smoke.

Panicked employees who raced for emergency exits found them locked or obstructed. No exits signs were illuminated, employees had received no training about what to do in case of fire, and fire-fighting equipment was largely old and unuseable. Fifty-six of Imperial's employees were injured in the fire; 25 died in front of the blocked doorways or trapped in the freezer, where they had fled to escape the heat and smoke. Although federal regulations require employers to keep exit doors clear in case of emergencies, Imperial management had locked the doors to discourage employees from stealing chicken parts.

The 11-year-old Imperial plant had never been inspected for safety, despite the fact that poultry factories are among the most hazardous places to work. According to the National Institute for Occupational Safety and Health, 20 percent of all poultry workers have been seriously injured in the hands, wrists, or shoulders. These may not be the most damaging injuries, however:

> In addition to severe cuts, the most common problems are the chronic disabilities that go under the heading of repetitive-motion trauma. Line workers, who gut, clean, and divide hundreds of birds each day, typically perform the same movement from 60 to 90 times a minute, thousands of times a day. When the human body is pressed to imitate the tireless actions of a machine, it revolts. The result is chronic tendinitis and carpal-tunnel syndrome, a painful condition of the wrists and forearms that can leave a worker virtually crippled even after corrective surgery. (Lacayo, 1991)

In November 1992, three insurance companies agreed to pay $16.1 million to victims of the fire. Imperial Food Products declared bankruptcy, and the owner of the plant was sentenced to 19 years and 11 months in prison.

The deadly result of the fire at the Imperial Foods plant was a combination of poor workplace design and inadequate—or nonexistent—safety precautions. Although the poultry industry in particular is known for its dangerous conditions, many millions of Americans work in other poorly designed and unsafe environments. According to some estimates (Lacayo, 1991), 30 workers die from on-the-job accidents each day. Many other workers suffer injuries. Back injuries are the most common (28 percent of all injuries), with injuries to the wrists, hands, and fingers second most common (21 percent; Kumar, 1994).

One indication of how serious the problem of hand and wrist injuries has become is the number of cases filed against computer makers. For example, in 1996 a jury awarded nearly $6 million to three women who sustained injuries using keyboards made by Digital Equipment, one of the nation's largest makers of computer equipment. Interestingly, Digital had taken steps to protect its own workers from hand and wrist injuries but had not provided warnings to customers.

In response to the growing number of repetitive motion injuries, California passed a law requiring employers to provide injured workers with special training and to change their work procedures if necessary (Lohr, 1996). Along the same lines, the federal government has undertaken an initiative to set rules to prevent repetitive motion injuries at work.

Many times the cause of accidents at work are attributed to "human error." Human error, a nonspecific term used to explain accidents, often occurs when equipment is designed without consideration for the abilities of the people who use that equipment. When operating systems become highly sophisticated, tasks are complex, or workers feel time pressures or must perform multiple tasks, human sensory and motor abilities may be inadequate for operating the equipment safely (Murray & Caldwell, 1996; Urban, Weaver, Bowers, & Rhodenizer, 1996). Consequently, the probability of human error increases.

Human factors psychology, or **ergonomics,** is the study and design of human-machine systems that optimize human abilities while minimizing the probability of error. Human factors draws on experimental psychology, personnel psychology, physiology, anthropology, learning theory, cognitive science, engineering, and computer science to develop guidelines for designing equipment, tasks, workplaces, and environments so they match worker abilities and limitations. According to one of the founders of modern human factors (Chapanis, 1996), system design consists of five components: *personnel selection, personnel training, machine design, job design,* and *environmental design.* Although the traditional focus of human factors research has been on designing equipment and environments, researchers increasingly have focused on the decision-making processes involved in handling emergencies. Box 14.1 describes an emergency decision-making situation on an oil and gas production platform in the North Sea.

Fatigue and Performance

A particular area of interest for human factors researchers is the effect of fatigue on performance. One experimental study (Redfern & Chaffin, 1995), for example, looked at the effect of flooring on standing fatigue. For workers such as supermarket employees, whose jobs require them to stand in restricted areas for long periods of time, foot and back problems are common. The researchers asked employees of a manufacturing plant to perform their tasks on eight different kinds of floors including blown vinyl, corrugated vinyl, concrete, viscoelastic material with a shoe insert, and others. In general, the harder the floor, the more fatigue reported by the workers, but the shoe insert significantly lowered complaints of tiredness. Also, subjects with a history of low back pain reported the most discomfort with the harder floorings.

In another study of worker fatigue (Finkelman, 1994), the records of 3,705 employees who worked for a temporary agency were reviewed to identify predictors of fatigue associated with work. Interestingly, workers were more likely to experience fatigue when they had unchallenging jobs, poor quality supervision, little control over their work, and low pay. Also, workers experienced fatigue when they felt their jobs required little of them either physically or mentally.

Apparently physical factors are not the only consideration in fatigue, however. Another study (Duchon, Keran, & Smith, 1994) considered the switch from an 8- to a 12-hour workday in an underground metal mine in western Canada. Results showed that the workers were almost unanimous in their acceptance of the new schedule, and they reported improved sleep quality and no change or even a decrease in fatigue.

Many studies, however, have shown that shiftwork—and working at night in particular—has a negative effect on health. In recent years, in fact, many people are working longer days and fewer people are working the night shift (Kortez, 1997a).

One typical problem for night workers in all industries is a reduction in the number of hours slept. One study (Paley & Tepas, 1994) looked at the sleep patterns of firefighters. Firefighters on the afternoon and evening shift averaged

Box 14.1   EMERGENCY PROCEDURES ON AN OIL AND GAS PLATFORM

About 250,000 individuals work on offshore oil rigs around the world. Some of these rigs are portable, but others house as many as 300 people, who get there by helicopter and work 12-hour shifts for two or three weeks before being sent home for two or three weeks. The manager of an oil platform is called the offshore installation manager (OIM), and the OIM has responsibility for both day-to-day operations and emergencies.

Unlike emergencies on land, where help is available, fires or explosions on offshore oil rigs must be dealt with by the installation's own personnel. In the North Sea most oil rigs are located at least 100 miles from land, so even evacuating personnel by helicopter is not a simple task. At the same time, seas, which

426 minutes of sleep per day, whereas those working the day shift averaged 441 minutes. Firefighters on the night shift, however, averaged only 300 minutes of sleep per day, a difference of more than two hours.

Finally, one study (Summala & Mikkola, 1994) considered the relationship between fatigue and fatal car and truck accidents. Analysis of almost 1,800 accidents revealed that the proportion of fatigue-related accidents did not differ significantly among age groups, but time of the accident did differ. Specifically, 18- to 20-year-olds had more accidents between midnight and 6 A.M., whereas drivers 56 years and older had more accidents during the late afternoon.

Box 14.1   *(continued)*

typically swell 20 to 30 feet, make the use of lifeboats dangerous. So in many cases, the best way to survive is to stay on the oil rig and try to control the problem.

At 10 A.M. on July 6, 1988, the North Sea oil platform Piper Alpha exploded. The resulting fire spread rapidly, leading to explosions elsewhere on the platform. Over the next few hours, fires and explosions occurred throughout the rig. Of the 226 men aboard the installation, 165 died. In addition, two rescue personnel lost their lives.

Inquiries into the Piper Alpha incident indicated that the OIM had failed to take charge of the situation. According to reports of survivors:

> The OIM had been gone "a matter of seconds when he came running back" in what appeared . . . to be a state of panic. . . . One survivor said that at one stage people were shouting at the OIM and asking what was going on and what proce- dure to follow. He did not know whether the OIM was in shock or not but he did not seem able to come up with any answer.

The investigation concluded that managing an offshore oil rig is not like man- aging an ordinary drilling site. Given the importance of the decisions an OIM may be called on to make, the selection and training of OIMs is a critical function. A re- view revealed, however, that most OIMs were chosen on the basis of information in staff reports and annual appraisals rather than through a more targeted selection procedure.

As a result of the investigation, a more rigorous selection procedure was de- veloped. Most oil companies now assess the competencies of their managers in emergency command. Using simulations, OIM candidates are rated on their ability to handle disasters such as a helicopter crash onto the platform or a gas explosion. Candidates are typically rated on their ability to (1) evaluate an emergency situa- tion and anticipate needs; (2) maintain communications during the emergency; (3) delegate authority to others; and (4) deal with stress within themselves and others.

Source: Flin, R., Slaven, G., & Stewart, K. (1996). Emergency decision making in the offshore oil and gas industry. *Human Factors, 38,* 262–277.

Origins of Human Factors

Human factors psychologists often date the beginning of their discipline to Frederick W. Taylor's study of shovels at Bethlehem Steel in 1898 (Chapanis, 1965). To move materials, Bethlehem Steel used 400 to 600 full-time shovelers who furnished their own shovels and worked for $1.15 per day. Taylor experi- mented with shovel size and weight and concluded that lifting 21.5 pounds of material per shovelful produced maximum efficiency. Taylor designed different sizes and shapes of shovels for different jobs, and by using the appropriate shovel, Bethlehem Steel was able to cut its workforce of shovelers to 140.

Another example in the development of human factors is Frank B. Gilbreth's 1911 study of bricklaying. Typically, all bricklayers followed the inefficient procedure of bending over, picking up a brick, looking for its best side, scooping up and applying mortar, and then placing the brick. Gilbreth designed a scaffold that reduced the distance the bricklayer had to reach and allowed him to scoop mortar with his other hand at the same time he was picking up a brick. Bricks were also prepackaged so the best side was always forward. Gilbreth's method increased output from 120 to 350 bricks laid per hour.

In addition to emphasizing efficiency, however, the field of human factors also arose from a need to understand the causes of accidents. In the 1940s, increasingly sophisticated design was making aircraft more difficult to operate safely, and the probability of an accident occurring had become much greater. Studies of aircraft accidents during that period tended to blame mistakes on human error. In their landmark study of human error in aircraft accidents, however, Fitts and Jones (1961) demonstrated that the majority of pilot errors could be attributed to poor equipment design rather than to personal characteristics or behaviors of the pilots operating the planes.

By the 1960s, the U.S. Department of Defense was requiring all contractors to consider human factors in designing military equipment. The human factors approach was to be used in all areas in which design could be shown to be a possible source of error, or if improved design could prevent error. In modern Navy fighter planes, for example, pilots who are in danger from error or equipment malfunction are warned aurally by a computer using a digitized female voice. Since the vast majority of pilots, navigators, air traffic controllers, and military personnel are male, designers decided a female voice would more likely catch their attention. Another application of human factors in the military and elsewhere has been the use of anthropometrical measurement in planning workspace, clothing, consoles, and equipment. This has been particularly important, for example, in space research, where studies show that space travelers typically experience a temporary growth of about two inches during flight (Thornton, 1978). Consequently, equipment, environments, and clothing must be able to accommodate this growth. Box 14.2 describes some of the issues in applying the principles of human factors to missions in space.

Another important modern application of human factors in the military is in rapid deployment forces. Increasingly, the U.S. military depends on soldiers being quickly transported from the southeastern United States to trouble spots elsewhere in the world. Without much preparation, these soldiers may be confronted with frostbite, heat, dehydration, or altitude or seasickness. Ground soldiers are required to wear protective clothing that stores body heat, inhibits communication, and restricts visibility. In addition, they may be expected to fight using night vision and infrared devices. All of this is likely to occur in an environment of high stress and great uncertainty.

Box 14.2   HUMAN FACTORS IN THE MOST DIFFICULT WORKING ENVIRONMENT

Few environments could be more stressful for workers than space, where astronauts must deal with microgravity, motion sickness, confined living and working space, and high physical and mental demands related to job tasks. In addition to these demands, astronauts must deal with social stressors such as working in cramped quarters with others, little privacy, and isolation from family and friends. Some research (Grigoriev, Kozerenko, & Myasnikov, 1985) suggests that physical stressors can affect astronauts during any part of a space flight, but the social stressors tend to emerge after some weeks in space.

Interestingly, researchers have concentrated on the biomedical aspects of stress associated with working in space, but little is known about the psychological stressors and their impact on cognitive functioning. There are several reasons for this. First, replicating the space environment is so difficult that only small sample or single case studies are possible. Although information from these limited studies can be useful, there is no normative data from which to draw conclusions about probabilities.

Second, research about behavior in space tends to be reported anecdotally, so there is no way to judge the scientific methodology used to reach conclusions in the study being reported. Third, engineers may be able to design a simulator that has great physical fidelity, but psychological fidelity relating to a lengthy space trip is much harder to achieve.

Finally, some research (e.g., Gundel, Nalashiti, Reucher, Vejvoda, & Zulley, 1993) suggests that space flight causes sleep disruption in most astronauts. Sleep disruption may be a mediating variable that causes decrements in performance unrelated to the working environment. One study (Manzey, Lorenz, Schiewe, Finell, & Thiele, 1995), for example, found that astronauts were most likely to experience decrements in performance at either the very beginning or the very end of a flight.

Source: Manzey, D., Lorenz, B., Schiewe, A., Finell, G., & Thiele, G. (1994). Dual-task performance in space: Results from a single-case study during a short-term space mission. *Human Factors, 37,* 667–681.

The likelihood of women being used in combat, where many tasks are physical, complicates use of rapid deployment forces. Although there do not appear to be significant differences in cognitive ability between the sexes, there are important strength differences. Specifically, women's strength is about 65 percent of men's strength Thus the military has relied heavily on human factors researchers to help prepare for rapid deployment situations.

Today, human factors is one of the fastest growing areas in psychology. In addition to psychology, human factors specialists now come from areas such as engineering, communications, and biology. Current areas in which human factors specialists are likely to be involved include designing aerospace equipment, developing computer systems activated by voice or eye movements, and reviewing the safety of consumer products such as lawn mowers and microwave ovens. In the United States, human factors specialists now focus largely on human performance in relation to computer systems.

Human factors specialists have their own professional organization, the Human Factors and Ergonomics Society, and their own journal, *Human Factors*. Of all the psychological specialties, human factors is one of the most in demand. Given the increasing sophistication technology requires of its operators, human factors is likely to remain one of the most promising fields in the future.

The Human-Machine System

Human factors is often defined as the study of "human-machine systems." From a human factors perspective, the machine and its operator are a system that must be considered as a whole. For example, a pilot and a control panel, or a typist and a word processor, are actually systems with mutually interdependent parts designed to accomplish some goal. Aspects of both parts—operator and machine—affect production. Figure 14.1 illustrates a basic system model.

Although machines can increasingly regulate themselves and accomplish certain tasks more efficiently than humans, the human operator remains a critical component in any system. In many respects, human capabilities exceed those of machines. Van Cott and Warrick (1972), for example, concluded that the human sensing system is more reliable, consistent, precise, and less likely to fail than most electromechanical systems. Additionally, the authors concluded that human failure was usually due more to faulty equipment design than to human error.

Advantages of humans over machines include the following (Hutchinson, 1981):

- Humans are better than machines—including computers—at sensing unusual or low-probability events.

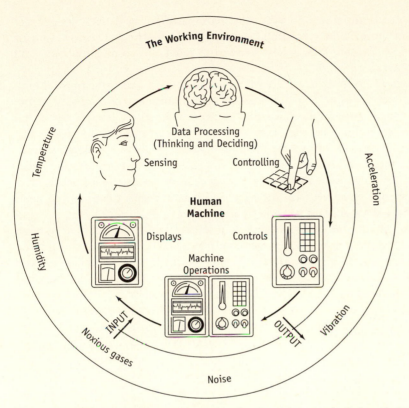

Source: Chapanis, A. (1965). *Man-machine Engineering.* Copyright © 1965 by Wadsworth, Inc. By permission of Brooks/Cole Publishing Company, Pacific Grove, CA 93950, a division of International Thomas Publishing, Inc.

Figure 14.1 A Basic Human-Machine System Model

- Humans can detect very low levels of energy, such as a weak light miles away in total darkness.
- Humans are good at detecting signals masked by other auditory stimuli. Parents, for example, can often hear their baby crying over other household noises.
- Humans can understand a variety of voices, dialects, and handwriting styles that machines cannot.
- Humans can store large amounts of data over long periods and access it quickly.
- Humans are good at solving problems through inductive reasoning.
- Although machines are likely to break down, humans will continue to work even when they are overloaded.

On the other hand, humans are not as good as machines in solving problems requiring deductive reasoning, such as math or logic, or in performing such operations quickly. Fiber-optic devices, for example, can transmit a billion bits of information per second over miles, compared to the 1,000 bits per second that the human eye can handle (Sanders & McCormick, 1993). Humans also have low abilities with regard to sensing radar, infrared, ultraviolet, and X-ray energies.

Humans are, of course, quite weak physically in comparison with machines. Reaction times are slow and performance varies among repetitions. Whereas machines can be programmed to react uniformly to stimuli, human reaction times vary widely. For example, humans react fastest to auditory and touch signals (0.15 seconds) and slowest to pain and taste signals (1.0 seconds). Similarly, humans react more quickly to green signals than to red or blue, and males can respond slightly faster than females. Reaction time with the human hand is also 20 percent faster than with the foot, and reaction with the preferred hand is 3 percent faster than with the nonpreferred.

Human factors psychologists use this kind of information in designing equipment and environments that facilitate performance. Ignoring the abilities and limitations of the human operator is likely to lead to errors, accidents, and diminished efficiency. Box 14.3 describes how human factors researchers improved the way the U.S. Postal Service sorts mail.

The following sections look at the application of human factors psychology to design of the workplace, workplace automation, and robotics.

Designing the Work Environment

Illumination
Temperature
Noise and Vibration
Automatic Speech
  Recognition Systems
Space Arrangements

To provide a comfortable and safe environment that enhances performance, human factors psychologists are routinely involved in designing work environments that consider the physical and psychological limitations of workers. For example, human factors specialists have designed seating that optimizes comfort and stairs that minimize accidents. Specifications for seat design are pictured in Figure 14.2 (p. 452).

Some typical concerns for human factors designers include illumination, temperature, noise and vibration, speech recognition systems, and space arrangements.

Illumination

From the theoretical perspective of human factors efficiency, having windows in the workplace is usually poor design. Windows lose energy; provide inadequate lighting; let in noise, odors, dirt, and burglars; encourage daydreaming; and waste space. However, virtually all workers express a preference for working in environments with windows, so windows may be necessary to maintain worker satisfaction.

In terms of energy efficiency, direct lighting, such as ceiling fixtures, is best, but direct lighting also tends to cause glare, contrast, and shadows. Different types of lights have different effects on vision. Objects that are orange, yellow,

Box 14.3   CHANGES AT THE U.S. POSTAL SERVICE

For almost 200 years postal sorting in the United States was done by delivering trays of letters to sorters who would pick up a batch of letters, read each address, and stick each letter into a given compartment, depending on its destination. When U.S. Postal Service planners predicted that the volume of mail would soon make this practice impossible, human factors designers were consulted about designing a new system.

The tasks of sorters identified during the consultation included the following:

■ Emptying incoming sacks of mail
■ Sorting mail by size
■ Arranging letters in trays with the stamp in the upper-right corner

■ Deciding whether the amount of postage was correct
■ Reading the address
■ Distributing letters according to zip codes

After studying the functions, designers concluded a machine could do all of these except determine whether the amount of postage was correct. Although a machine could determine if the postage was appropriate for the weight, it could not determine if the mail was from a tax-exempt organization or was going overseas, functions that cannot be performed without reading the address.

Although the human factors analysis of mail-sorting tasks began almost 50 years ago, no one has yet figured out a way to automate the two functions of reading the address to determine if the postage is appropriate. Today, trays of letters are delivered to sorters who sit in front of a keyboard. A mechanical arm places a letter in front of a sorter, who has six-tenths of a second to read the address and four-tenths of a second to key in the zip code. The arm then takes away the letter and sorts it automatically. Although this system is much more efficient, from a human factors standpoint, the boring and monotonous nature of the job indicates it still needs redesign.

Source: Chapanis, A. (1996). *Human Factors in Systems Engineering.* New York: Wiley.

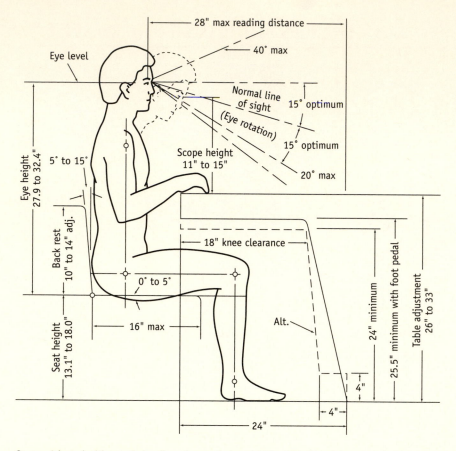

Source: Adapted with permission from *Human Factors, 15*(2), 1973. Copyright © 1973 by the Human Factors and Ergonomics Society, Inc. All rights reserved.

Figure 14.2 Seat Design

or blue, for example, are more visible under fluorescent lights, whereas incandescent lights are better for seeing red (Wotton, 1986). Overall, fluorescent lights minimize shadows, thereby improving visual and manipulative performance, and they also provide better diffusion of light. Painting workplace walls pastel colors or light gray also improves illumination.

Illumination has been related to performance in a number of studies. In general, better lighting improves performance up to a certain point, where, depending on the level of detail, performance levels off (Sanders & McCormick, 1993). Some evidence also suggests that accidents occur less frequently during the night shift than during the day or swing shift because of greater reliance on artificial lighting. Along the same lines, most accidents occur at dusk while the transition to artificial lighting is being made.

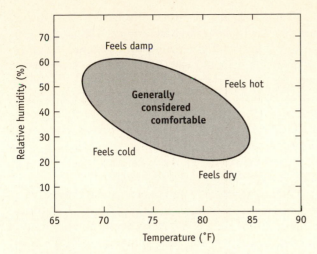

Source: Bailey, R. W. *Human performance engineering: A guide for system designers,* p. 500. Copyright © 1989. Reprinted by permission of Prentice-Hall, Inc., Englewood Cliffs, NJ.

Figure 14.3 Temperature and Performance

Too much illumination can have negative effects on performance, however. In one study (Sanders, Gustanski, & Lawton, 1974), noise was measured in a hallway in which 20 fluorescent panels were lit. When two-thirds of the panels were turned off, noise levels dropped 21 percent.

Temperature

Not surprisingly, temperature and humidity have a critical effect on performance. In general, the amount of work performed decreases as humidity increases. Most people are comfortable between 70 and 80 degrees with 70 percent humidity. At 85 degrees and 90 percent humidity, however, discomfort begins. Temperatures above 92 degrees with 90 percent humidity increase body temperature, pulse and breathing rates, and can lead to heat exhaustion. For doing light work, the maximum allowable body temperature is 102 degrees; for heavy work, the maximum allowable is 104 degrees. Accidents tend to be rarest in temperatures around 68 to 70 degrees. Figure 14.3 illustrates the relationship between temperature and work performance.

Another important factor in dealing with temperature is length of exposure. Both the health and the productivity of workers exposed to long periods of high humidity and temperature are likely to suffer. For employees who work under these conditions, some period of adjustment—typically 12 to 14 days—is likely to be necessary. One factor that affects heat tolerance is physical fitness.

Consequently, older workers and workers who are overweight are at greater risk for heat stroke and other illnesses (Sanders & McCormick, 1993). Because males are, on average, more physically fit than females, they generally tolerate heat better (Burse, 1979). Nonetheless, in all cases, heat tolerance is impaired by odors, fatigue, lack of sleep, alcohol, anxiety, smoke, and illness.

Short exposure to high temperatures may not affect performance, however. Hammer (1976) found that brief exposure to temperatures of 160 degrees, 200 degrees, and 235 degrees did not decrease subjects' abilities to solve math problems. In general, however, physical performance begins to decline at temperatures above 84 degrees (Wyndham, 1974), and complex tasks become more difficult in higher temperatures (Ramsey & Kwon, 1988).

Cold temperatures also affect performance, particularly in the oil and gas extraction, trucking, and protection services industries (Sinks, Mathias, Halpern, Timbrook, & Newman, 1987). In a cold environment, the minimum allowable body temperature is 95 degrees. When body temperature falls below 95 degrees tissue damage results; survival is threatened when the body temperature drops below 82 degrees. Overall, acclimation to cold is much more difficult to achieve than acclimation to heat.

When workers must perform complex tasks, cold can be a stressor. For example, one group of researchers (Van Orden, Benoit, & Osga, 1996) designed a simulated war game in which participants had to make decisions in a room with a temperature of 22 or 4 degrees Celsius (72 or 39 degrees Fahrenheit). In the cold condition, participants were more liberal with their missile fire and more conservative in responding to commands. The researchers also concluded that cold interferes with short-term memory.

In addition to effects on the body, another problem with temperature is its effects on materials that are handled. In extreme situations, such materials can injure workers. For example, employees cannot be expected to handle equipment or materials whose temperatures are over 108 degrees or under 32 degrees, since both will result in pain and tissue damage.

One area often overlooked in controlling workplace climate is floor temperatures. Floors conduct both heat and cold to the feet, and maximally comfortable floor temperature is between 64.4 degrees and 84.2 degrees. Foot skin temperature is the lowest in the body, with normal male temperature being 91.9 degrees and female 88.2 degrees, the only area in the body where temperature varies between sexes.

Some evidence suggests temperature can affect society in general. In an interesting cross-national study of role overload, which was defined as "an individual's lack of the personal resources needed to fulfill commitments, obligations, or requirements" (Peterson et al., 1995), researchers compared role overload with variables such as the average daytime temperature of a nation's capital, percentage of people engaged in agriculture, number of workplace strikes, safety and working conditions, and many other variables. Results from the study indicated a positive relationship between role overload and temperature. That is, the hotter the average temperature, the more people felt they lacked the personal resources to fulfill the demands being made on them (Van de Vliert & Van Yperen, 1996).

Noise and Vibration

Noise is an important factor in both the working and nonworking environments. Table 14.1 shows some typical noise levels for different activities. Although research shows that noise requires additional concentration for doing mental work, there is no firm evidence that physical labor suffers in a noisy environment.

Noise is a serious problem because noise-induced hearing damage is irreversible. Hearing loss begins when noise levels exceed 67 dB (in the A frequency range) (Kryter, 1970), although there are individual differences in noise tolerance. Federal regulations require that workers be exposed to no more than 90 dBA over an eight-hour period. Given this level of exposure, 20 percent of workers will suffer sufficient hearing loss to qualify for workers' compensation after 10 years. At noise levels over 105 dBA, all individuals suffer hearing loss. Additionally, impulsive noises, such as explosions, are more dangerous than continuous noises.

Several studies (Ewigman, Kivlahan, Hosokawa, & Horman, 1990; Gassaway, 1987) have supported the use of hearing protection devices in reducing noise exposure, but not all workers will agree to wear such devices, particularly when they interfere with communication with other workers, lower the intelligibility of radio communication, or reduce the effectiveness of team coordination (Gower & Casali, 1994).

One study (Lusk, Ronis, & Kerr, 1995) looked at predictors of protective device use among a group of 504 manufacturing employees. Results from this study indicated workers were more likely to wear devices when they scored high in self-efficacy, perceived the benefits of hearing protection use, and did not focus on barriers to device use.

Some work environments have recorded music in the background designed to contribute to productivity. The idea behind background music is that it relieves the fatigue and boredom that accompany repetitive tasks. Since alertness is governed by the reticular activating system in the brain, tasks that do not stimulate the reticular system lead to underarousal and inefficiency. Theoretically, background music will provide additional arousal and improve worker performance.

Some evidence (Oldham, Cummings, Mischel, Schmidtke, & Zhou, 1996) suggests that introducing background music in the work environment raises productivity about 5 percent. However, music in the work setting should not be continuous—as such, it becomes just another background noise and loses its effectiveness. Background music is more effective if it is played during periods

Table 14.1 LEVELS AND EFFECTS OF COMMON SOUNDS IN THE ENVIRONMENT

Common Sounds	Noise Levels (Decibels)	Effects
Carrier deck jet operation Air raid siren	140	Painfully loud (blurring vision, nausea, dizziness)
Jet takeoff (200 feet) Thunderclap	130	Begin to "feel" the sound
Discotheque Auto horn (3 feet)	120	Hearing becomes uncomfortable
Pile drivers	110	Cannot speak over the sound
Garbage truck	100	
Heavy truck (50 feet) City traffic	90	Very annoying
Alarm clock (2 feet) Hair dryer	80	Annoying
Noisy restaurant Freeway traffic Man's voice (3 feet)	70	Telephone use difficult
Air conditioning unit (20 feet)	60	Intrusive
Light auto traffic (10 feet)	50	Quiet
Living room Bedroom Quiet office	40	
Library Soft whisper (15 feet)	30	Very quiet
Broadcasting studio	20	
	10	Just audible
	0	Hearing begins

Source: Bailey, R. W. *Human Performance Engineering: A Guide for System Designers* (p. 494). © 1982. Reprinted by permission of Prentice-Hall, Inc.; Englewood Cliffs, NJ.

of the day when workers report the highest levels of fatigue and boredom. Some research (Oldham et al., 1996) suggests that the use of stereo headsets also increases productivity. Results from this study appear in Figure 14.4.

Vigilance refers to the ability to maintain attention to a task over an uninterrupted period. Vigilance is important in many jobs, but a number of studies have shown that vigilance tends to decline after about 30 minutes (Warm & Jerison, 1984). At that time, researchers believe, boredom occurs and performance typically declines. Although many people experience boredom, some

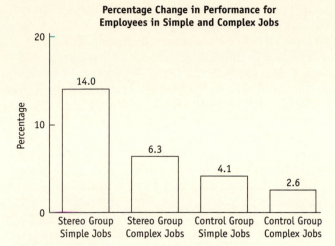

Percentage Change in Performance for Employees in Simple and Complex Jobs

Figure 14.4 Stereo Headsets and Productivity
As you can see from the graph, workers with headsets peforming both simple and complex jobs outperformed those without headsets. *Source:* Oldham, G. R., Cummings, A., Mischel, L. J., Schmidtke, J. M., & Zhou, J. (1996, April). Can personal stereos improve productivity? *HRMagazine,* 95–99.

recent research (Sawin & Scerbo, 1995) suggests that there are individual differences in susceptibility to boredom. In other words, certain workers are better at vigilance tasks than others.

Vibration Although individuals differ in the amount of vibration they can endure, exposure to prolonged vibration has serious consequences for all workers. Under vibrating conditions, body parts are moving against each other, large organs are pulling on the ligaments, and the small organs may be crushed by other parts of the body.

Aside from duration, the frequency (i.e., speed) of vibration can also affect worker health. Electric drills, jackhammers, screwdrivers, and other vibrating equipment can cause motion sickness and nausea, blurred vision, and spinal damage (Oborne, 1982). Frequency damages tend to affect the peripheral blood and nervous system rather than the organs. Although the evidence is strong that vibration has an adverse effect on visual and motor performance, no good evidence exists that vibration affects mental abilities, and some research (Poulton, 1978) suggests vibration can heighten alertness.

Automatic Speech Recognition Systems

In recent years, advances in technology have made simulated speech more common in the workplace. Although simulated speech has been available for some time, researchers have been challenged to make it recognizable to most people.

Researchers are aware that in its current state of development, simulated speech is harder to understand than natural language speech, but simulated speech systems vary in their intelligibility (Paris, Gilson, Thomas, & Silver, 1995).

A related use of speech is the operation of equipment by voice command. Today, however, **automatic speech recognition (ASR)** technology—in which equipment responds to commands from a human voice—is suffciently advanced to be applied in factory control systems, telephone menu systems, and wheelchair operations (Noyes & Frankish, 1992).

An obvious problem with the application of voice systems is background noise, but vibration and acceleration, as in an aircraft cockpit, also create problems for ASR systems. When a speaker is experiencing vibration or acceleration, his or her voice is affected. Along the same lines, stress has been shown to alter the range and frequency of a person's voice, increasing the probability of error.

Finally, ASR systems generally require the use of specific vocabulary, but in stressful situations, operators may not be able to recall the necessary commands to control the system (Baber, 1996). Although earlier ASR systems relied on specific prompting words, newer research suggests that a "word spotting" technique—in which a system is able to recognize a key word in a series of words—can lessen the importance of specific vocabulary (Brems, Rabin, & Waggett, 1995).

Space Arrangements

Modern offices are increasingly laid out so that desks are placed in a large, open space. This approach to office design has a number of advantages, including more useable space; better light, acoustics, and climate; the ability to exchange information quickly; ease in communication among employees; and greater flexibility in reorganizing the office. DuPont, for example, is spending $35 million to change from private offices to cubicles to promote teamwork (Milford, 1997). Disadvantages of the open space layout, however, include a greater amount of noise and distraction, a decreased interest in work, and a general lack of confidentiality. In addition, workers in open-plan offices report more health complaints (Hedge, 1984).

With regard to space requirements, workers have very definite spatial needs that must be considered in the design of any work environment. In general, the need for personal space can be categorized into four types: intimate distance, personal space, social distance, and public distance.

Intimate distance is from 0 to 6 inches in its close range and from 6 to 18 inches in its far range. When other individuals enter intimate space, there is no way to ignore them. Sensory stimulation is great, and intrusion into this area is usually accompanied by physical contact. Entering the intimate space of another individual is taboo in many cultures.

Personal space (close: 18 to 30 inches; far: 30 to 77 inches) is used for most social contact. Good friends are welcomed into the close area of personal space, and most normal social contact occurs in the farther area of personal space.

On the job, most people prefer to interact in **social distance,** which is 40 to 80 inches in the close range (overlapping with personal space), and 80 to 140 inches in the far range. This is a little beyond arm's length, and it is the range found during interactions at most social gatherings. By standing at the far end of the social distance area, however, people can make interactions more formal. **Public distance** (close: 12 to 24 feet; far: beyond 24 feet) involves no social contact.

Numerous studies have shown that violation of personal space leads to tension, discomfort, and, in extreme cases, flight. Needs for personal space are affected by several different variables, including age, sex, culture, and status. Patterson and Sechrest (1970) found that extraverts need less personal space than introverts; Hall (1976) found that Germans need a larger personal space than Americans, but that Latin Americans, French, and particularly Arabs need less. Given the variety of factors affecting need for personal space, design of the office environment may require some attention to these relationships.

Human Factors and Automation

Computers in the Office
Telecommunications
Virtual Reality Simulations
Robotics

Although the initial application of human factors principles focused mainly on the design of the industrial environment, human-machine interactions are obviously important within the office setting as well. Typical office concerns for human factors specialists include computers, office communication systems, virtual reality simulations, and robotics.

Computers in the Office

Until about 1970, most research about computers focused on designing hardware and programming languages; little attention was directed toward investigating the human skills necessary to operate computers. In the 1980s, however, computers became part of everyday technology—in microwave ovens, telephones, and automobiles—as well as the most common office machine. By this time, "human-computer interaction" had become one of the largest research areas in human factors (Boehm-Davis, 1995). Although the office computer does not usually change the tasks that must be accomplished, its main advantage is in eliminating paper.

An important aspect of computerizing any office is the person expected to operate the computers. Although many human factors designers have specified the optimal arrangement of computer equipment, real-life users rarely follow these guidelines (Sanders & McCormick, 1993). Therefore, the basic principle of workstation design is that components should be easily adjustable. In a study of productivity and satisfaction among workers in three different types of workstations, two researchers (Dressel & Francis, 1987) found that using newer furniture and a special "ergonomic" chair increased productivity 20.6 percent over a control condition.

Considerable controversy has arisen about the effect of long hours spent in front of a visual display terminal (VDT). Proper use of the VDT requires consideration of several factors. First, lighting must be regulated in relation to the VDT screen. If the screen is considerably darker than the work surface, the eye muscles must adjust each time they focus. This continual focusing and refocusing throughout the workday leads to fatigue and poor concentration. When characters on the screen are too bright against a dark background, the VDT screen will produce glare. Glare is also produced by improper placement of the VDT so that room lighting bounces off the screen.

Although color on VDT screens can be useful, colors must be chosen carefully. Red, orange, and blue are most fatiguing to the eye, whereas buff, ivory, cream, light green, and pale yellow are least fatiguing. For overall reading speed, the worst colors are red and blue backgrounds, whereas the best are white or yellow backgrounds with black print. In general, colors that contrast most with screen background are easiest to read (Lippert, 1986).

Another office automation issue that concerns human factors specialists is the design of the user-computer software interface, sometimes referred to as **software psychology.** As the population of computer users becomes more diverse, people are likely to have specific software needs that must be addressed. "User-friendly" systems are designed to meet these specialized needs.

A user-friendly system guides users through the interactions, has helpful and directive error messages, and also has a good "help" system. The commands of menu items are written to make sense to nonspecialists; that is, the meaning of the command words reflects what they are meant to do. The best software systems are designed so that they can change as their users become more experienced. For example, a good system can lead a naive user through an interaction but also be adaptable to shortcuts as the user gains more experience.

Telecommunications

Probably the most important activity of any manager is communicating with other employees. Since managers use most of their time for communication, automating this function increases productivity.

One common office communication problem is the telephone call. In an interesting study of telephone usage, Knopf (1982) found the vast majority of calls are unsuccessful: The person called is out of the office 50 percent of the time, 18 percent of the time the telephone line is busy, and 14 percent of the time the person called is in an ongoing meeting. The high probability of making an unsuccessful call results in substantially decreased productivity.

There are several methods by which telephone communication can be made more efficient. One method is **voice mail**—the recording of a message that will be transmitted by telephone at a specified time. Two researchers (Lind & Zmud, 1995) investigated the impact of a voice mail system on a manufacturing firm and its network of dealerships. Results from the study indicated that dealerships in regions that used voice mail had higher sales than dealerships in regions that did not have voice mail. In addition, sales managers who relied on voice mail were more satisfied with the performances of their field representatives than managers who did not rely on voice mail.

Another strategy to facilitate communication is to use teleconferences rather than face-to-face meetings. Teleconferences can be effective when the distance between participants is great, discussions are expected to be short, information to be discussed is not too complex, the parties know each other, and the topic is noncontroversial (Helander, 1985). Another study (Kahai, Sosik, & Avolio, 1997) found a participative leadership style more effective than a directive style in an electronic meeting system environment.

Videocommunication refers to telecommunication with sound and picture. One advantage of videocommunication is that it allows transmission of nonverbal behaviors—such as smiling, frowning, shrugging, and so forth—that are important in communication. Another advantage of videocommunication is that it allows participants to see objects such as pictures or graphics. Interestingly, one of the problems of videocommunication is dealing with eye contact—users are sometimes uncomfortable because they don't know whether to look into a camera or at another individual when speaking. Some research (Muhlbach, Bocker, & Prussog, 1995) suggests, however, that this awkwardness can be overcome by restricting the angles at which eye contact can occur.

E-mail E-mail is a medium in which a user can communicate with one or many other people by typing a message at a computer terminal (Culnan & Markus, 1987; Federico & Bowley, 1996). Although e-mail does not offer the "richness" of telecommunication in terms of visual information, it has several unique attributes that make it different from speech communication (Sproull & Kiesler, 1991). First, e-mail has *multiple addressability*—information can reach many people at one time—a characteristic not shared by telephone communication. Second, e-mail is *externally recorded,* which means that a copy of the message exists outside the sender and the receiver. Finally, e-mail relies on *computer-processable memory,* which means that the information in the message can be searched, sorted, or analyzed in ways that voice communication cannot. Other advantages of e-mail are that the message can be any length; recipients can read, save, edit, delete, or forward messages; and recipients can reply to the sender. In addition, e-mail messages can be printed and filed. A disadvantage of e-mail (and other electronic communication systems) is a lack of management control and organizational liability for employee misuse (Townsend, Aalberts, & Whitman, 1997).

In one study of the way managers use e-mail (Markus, 1994), effective senior managers were found to use e-mail frequently and to send electronic messages to all levels of the organization. Another study of communication patterns in a large telecommunications firm (Hinds & Kiesler, 1995) found that technical personnel used e-mail more frequently, whereas managers were more likely to use the telephone.

Finally, one study (Allen, 1995) looked at gender differences in the use of an e-mail system at the headquarters of the Public Broadcasting System (PBS). Results from the study indicated that female employees found e-mail more efficient, effective, and easier to use than male employees. In addition, the females were more likely to rely on coworkers for information about using the system than were the males.

Virtual Reality Simulations

One of the newest human factors applications is virtual reality, which is a sophisticated form of simulation. **Virtual reality** refers to a computer-generated environment in which a person can interact with portrayed entities (Wells, 1992). The U.S. Air Force uses virtual reality in some of its flight simulators. For example, one simulator requires the user to wear a helmet-mounted display that causes images to move as the user moves his or her head. The image gives the appearance of viewing the world through the window of a cockpit.

Because virtual reality is a system composed of computer technology and the human operator, human factors principles are used to design and evaluate the effectiveness of virtual reality simulations. Effective virtual reality simulations exhibit the "three Is": They are *immersive*—the user experiences being surrounded by the simulation; *interactive*—the user has some control over the simulation; and *intuitive*—the user communicates with the simulation by using familiar and obvious actions. Virtual reality simulators use sounds, odors, and other stimuli to heighten the perceived fidelity of the activity.

One of the most interesting aspects of virtual reality simulations is their ability to create motion sickness without the individual actually moving. This occurs so frequently in military simulators that guidelines have been developed to reduce its occurrence (Kennedy, Berbaum, Lilenthal, Dunlap, Mulligan, & Funaro, 1987). Until this problem is solved, the effectiveness of virtual reality for training pilots will be limited.

Many people have hypothesized that virtual reality simulations will be a new form of leisure activity, with people participating in simulated championship tennis matches, flying aircraft combat missions, or skydiving. Although the technology exists to create such simulations, presently the main use of virtual reality is in training applications, and in flying military aircraft in particular.

Robotics

The increased use of robots to perform jobs previously done by humans is also an area of interest to human factors psychologists. The study of **robotics** generally addresses two questions: (1) What functions currently being performed by humans could be better performed by robots? and (2) How can the operating system for the robot best utilize human abilities?

Most researchers agree that the development of robotic technology has been hampered by the "anthropomorphization" of robots. In other words, robotic technology was hindered for many years by the notion that the robot should resemble a human. This is illogical, since the methods by which humans accomplish tasks are efficient only in light of human abilities and physiology. Modern robotics is the design of equipment that accomplishes the tasks of humans more efficiently, and in actuality, few modern robots have any resemblance to humans.

In most respects, robots can be considered computers with expanded input/output systems; that is, the robotic system has more capabilities for both determining and performing its tasks than does a standard computer. Despite these expanded abilities, however, virtually all robotic systems still require human operators for initial programming, adjustment, and control, and typically a human factors specialist will be involved in some aspect of the design process.

For example, the Nordson Corporation submitted its design for a spray-painting robot to a human factors expert to ensure its "user-friendliness." The human factors specialist suggested modifications in the control panel for ease of operation, changes in the training arm grip by which the computer is programmed or "taught" how to paint, and development of specialized software commands that decrease the chances for error (Shulman & Olex, 1985). Although the use of robotic technology is not yet well developed, researchers have established standards for deciding when to adopt robotics (Nof, 1985).

Not surprisingly, worker attitudes toward robotics in the workplace are mixed. In a study of worker perceptions toward implementing robotic technology, Chao and Kozlowski (1986) found that low-skill employees reacted negatively toward robotics, whereas high-skill employees reacted more favorably. Although the low-skill employees considered robots a threat to their job security, higher-skill workers believed the implementation of robots would provide opportunities to improve their own skills.

Accidents and Safety

Causes of Accidents
Reducing Accidents

Studies by the U.S. Department of Labor's Bureau of Labor Statistics (1989) suggest that the number of injuries on the job in the United States is increasing. This is a serious problem that many employers address through safety programs. Although both employers and the public believe that safety programs are expensive to implement, these expenses are usually less than the costs associated with accidents and injuries. The National Safety Council (NSC) estimates the annual costs of accidents is in excess of $30 billion; the Department of Labor believes the NSC's estimate to be too low and puts the cost of accidents at about ten times that amount.

Whatever the actual figure, from any point of view—social, economic, or psychological—the cost of accidents is tremendous. Direct costs include insurance settlements, workers' compensation, pain and suffering, legal liabilities, and increased insurance premiums. Indirect costs include investigation time and support, medical center costs, payments to the injured party, replacement of the injured worker, cost of time of other employees who assist the injured party and who are involved in the accident investigation, loss of production, equipment damage, and time spent adjudicating the case.

Causes of Accidents

Defining exactly what constitutes an accident is often a problem, since many companies—and many workers—are reluctant to admit the occurrence of an accident. Two defining qualities of an accident, however, are its unexpectedness and the resulting injury or damage to a person or system (Meister, 1987). Also, company guidelines are often unclear as to how serious an incident must be to be classified as an accident. The instance of a worker being cut on the hand by machinery, then returning to the job after a bandage is applied, for example, may or may not be counted as an accident.

Establishing what exactly is an accident often seems to be an arbitrary procedure that varies from workplace to workplace. One study of industrial injuries at Southern California Edison (Dieterly, 1995), for example, used the following classification system for accidents that occurred on the job:

first aid—injuries treated by a nonphysician;

nonlost time/recordable—injuries requiring treatment by a physician but resulting in less than one day's work lost;

lost time—injuries resulting in one or more days off from work; and

restricted duty—injuries that required the employee to be placed on restricted duty for one or more days.

In that study, costs were calculated three ways: medical, nonmedical, and lost productivity. Average annual costs of injuries was $13 million, of which $11 million was attributable to lost time. Meter readers incurred the greatest number of injuries, with an average cost of $3,305. Injuries to managers were less frequent but more serious, with an average cost of $13,433.

Although accidents are often blamed on workers, some researchers have tried to determine the percentage of accidents actually caused by human error. Although researchers do not agree on this percentage, one review of accident cases (Sanders & Shaw, 1988) found a median of 35 percent of accidents attributable to human error. In a review of 338 underground mining accidents, the researchers found no case in which an accident was solely the result of human error.

With regard to the causes of accidents, many people believe in the notion of the "accident-prone" person. This idea was first introduced in 1919 by statisticians who were studying accidents in munitions factories in England during World War I. These researchers found that a small minority of workers had the majority of accidents. Most researchers admit, however, that evidence for the accident-prone worker does not bear up under scrutiny. Although there may be individuals who have more accidents, this may be related more to the kind of work they do, rather than to their particular personalities. For example, one study (Porter & Corlett, 1989) found that individuals who considered themselves accident prone paid less attention to the environment when performing a particular task.

One model of accident causation (Oborne, 1982) has been based on learning theory. Safe behavior is often not reinforcing since it is more time-consuming, requires special equipment and procedures, and is sometimes regarded as "unmanly" by other workers. Unsafe behavior, on the other hand, can be reinforcing. It is often quicker, more comfortable, and more socially acceptable. Safe behavior is reinforced only when an accident occurs as a result of unsafe behavior. Accidents do not occur often enough to promote safe behavior.

Age and experience are also important factors in accidents, with most accidents occurring among workers in their teens and early 20s. Between the mid-20s and the mid-50s, accident rates remain stable. Although experience has some effect on accident rates, even experienced young workers have more accidents than older workers. Possible explanations for the high rate of accidents for young workers include impulsivity, inattentiveness, and the lack of family responsibilities. Accidents among older workers are often attributable to declining capacities, especially in speed and perception.

One study (Guide & Gibson, 1991) looked at the effects of age and experience on flight safety. In 1960, the Federal Aviation Administration formulated its "Age 60 Rule," which states that no person over age 60 can serve as pilot or co-pilot of a commercial airliner. The basis of the Age 60 Rule was a belief that age-related declines in a pilot's physical abilities would create danger for passengers, and that older pilots were at risk for "sudden incapacitation" from events such as heart attacks. A review of accident data revealed, however, that sudden incapacitation is a rare event most frequently associated with food poisoning rather than age. The researchers also found that the highest accident rate was among pilots ages 20 to 24, and lowest among the 45 to 49 age group. Accident rates for pilots ages 55 to 59 were similar to those of pilots ages 35 to 39. The researchers concluded that experience may compensate for any decline in physical abilities, and that the Age 60 Rule is open to challenge.

Overall, older workers have fewer accidents than younger workers; however, their accidents are more serious and more likely to result in death (Dillingham, 1983; Root, 1981). Interestingly, African American workers have fewer accidents than Whites, but on-the-job accidents among African Americans are likely to be more serious (Wagener & Winn, 1991).

Some other theories of accidents include the following: (1) **adjustment-to-stress theory,** which argues that accidents occur more frequently when workers are experiencing psychological or physiological stress; (2) **arousal-alertness theory,** which predicts that accidents occur whenever a worker's state of arousal is either too high or too low; and (3) **goals-freedom-alertness theory,** which maintains that workers who have the autonomy to set realistic performance goals are less likely to have accidents (Sanders & McCormick, 1993).

In addition to qualities of workers, accidents are caused by factors in the environment. Noise, temperature, poorly designed equipment, productivity demands, and communication among workers are all factors that can cause accidents.

Finally, accident rates vary among industries, with the highest rates in trucking, transit, meat products, shipbuilding, and lumber products. The lowest accident rates are found in the chemical, aircraft, communication, pipeline transportation, and textile industries (National Safety Council, 1982).

Reducing Accidents

Employers can take a number of steps to lessen the probability of an accident occurring. One method is to use checklists when completing a specified routine. This approach is commonly used in the aircraft industry and the military. Checklists help employees to make certain they have not left out a critical step when performing an operation.

Another approach is safety training, which is one of the best ways to prevent accidents. To be effective, however, such training must (1) focus on learning safe behavior rather than on avoiding unsafe acts; (2) allow for practice that has a high degree of fidelity with actual work conditions; and (3) have goals and provide feedback to employees (Cohen, Smith, & Anger, 1979).

One laboratory study (Zeitlin, 1994) looked at the relationship among safety training, experience, and compliance with safety instructions. Groups of male participants were separated on the basis of their knowledge of using a chain saw, given a lecture of chain saw safety, then assigned a task. During task completion compliance with safety instructions for the inexperienced was 70 percent, but the experienced group complied with the instructions only 41 percent of the time. The researcher concluded that safety training alone is not enough to encourage compliance and that training must also emphasize the dangers associated with not following instructions.

Incentive programs, in which workers receive bonuses, promotions, and special privileges for safe behavior, are another approach to promoting safety. Effective use of incentives may be tricky, however, since workers are likely to expect larger rewards over time.

Another approach is to involve employees in workplace redesign. At a large meat-packing plant in the Midwest, management established employee involvement teams to look at ways of changing the workplace to reduce cumulative trauma disorders. As illustrated by the example that opened this chapter, cumulative trauma disorders involve damage to the tendons and related bones and muscles, and often result from repeated movements.

Team members included employees, management, medical staff, and maintenance workers. Teams had the authority to implement low-cost solutions to ergonomic problems but had to obtain clearance for more extensive changes. In the meetings, medical staff provided information about trauma disorders for particular jobs, and teams asked employees for suggestions about changes in the workplace. At the end of several months the number of cumulative trauma disorders had decreased, and cases referred to physicians outside the plant decreased. The researchers (May & Schwoerer, 1994) concluded that involving employees in ergonomic teams can have a significant impact on employee health.

Finally, companies can raise the consciousness of employees to be more aware of safety issues. One researcher (Hammer, 1976) outlined a five-part program that is more comprehensive than a typical safety training program. First, employees must be instructed in the company rules, emergency procedures, potential hazards, location of the medical office, and means of reporting hazards in the work environment. Second, management must demonstrate its commitment to safety by holding meetings in which old procedures are reviewed and new procedures are introduced.

Third, specific individuals should be trained in specialized safety procedures such as cardiopulmonary resuscitation (CPR), first aid, and fire prevention. Fourth, employee awareness of safety programs must be maintained over time. Signs reminding workers of specific safe procedures—as opposed to general messages such as "Be Careful"—should be posted in entryways and lunchrooms. Workers can be provided with folders and booklets, and safety messages can be included in paycheck envelopes. Additionally, rewards or recognition should be given to departments and individuals with low rates of accidents or injuries.

Finally, management should establish a safety committee that considers suggestions from workers about safe behavior. As suggested above, membership on the committee must be taken seriously, since workers will not be concerned about safety if management fails to make safety a serious issue.

Chapter Summary

One of the most serious problems facing employers is accidents. Accidents cause a great deal of human suffering, and as technology becomes more sophisticated, accidents become more likely. Human factors psychology, or ergonomics, is the study and design of human-machine systems to increase efficiency, productivity, and safety.

The human factors approach considers the operator and the equipment as a system, and each aspect of the system is designed with the capabilities and limitations of the human operator in mind. One area in which human factors psychologists have focused their attention is relieving fatigue that affects performance.

The field of human factors also arose from a need to understand the concept of "human error." From the human factors viewpoint, human error is more likely the result of faulty equipment design than personality factors or behavior. As machines and equipment become increasingly complex, engineers need to consider possible sources of error when designing equipment for human use.

Despite the growing capabilities of machines—and computers in particular—humans can still do many things better than machines. Humans are better at inductive reasoning and they can continue to work when they are overloaded. Machines, on the other hand, are much better at deductive problems, they are much faster and capable of handling more information, and they are physically much stronger than humans.

In the work environment, human factors considerations are used to increase productivity and optimize worker performance. Some areas of human factors applications include illumination, temperature, noise, vibration, speech recognition, and space arrangements.

One area of growing interest is office automation, where human factors principles have been applied to user-computer interactions. Of particular interest is the controversy about the effects of prolonged exposure to VDTs on worker health. In addition, developments in telecommunications and e-mail have affected worker performance in the office. Virtual reality and robotics are other promising areas of human factors research.

Worker safety is another area of growing concern to the industrial psychologist, particularly with the passage of the Occupational Safety and Health Act of 1970. The act empowers federal inspectors to fine industries where conditions are found to be unsafe. Overall, the burden of the act seems to fall more heavily on the smaller companies in which most accidents occur.

In general, accidents can be said to be a product of unsafe acts in unsafe conditions. Often it is difficult to define what constitutes an accident, so accident statistics are not precise. Although the concept of the "accident prone" worker continues to be popular, most researchers feel that it does not bear up under scientific study. Some other explanations for causes of accidents include type of occupation, compatibility with other workers, a lack of positive reinforcement for safe behavior, age and experience, and time of day.

One of the best ways of preventing accidents seems to be the institution of safety programs. By heightening employee awareness of safety procedures, accidents can be minimized. The success of such programs depends, to a large extent, on management's commitment to providing a safe working environment.

Key Words and Concepts

adjustment-to-stress theory (p. 465)

arousal-alertness theory (p. 465)

automatic speech recognition (ASR) (p. 458)

e-mail (p. 461)

ergonomics (p. 442)

goals-freedom-alertness theory
(p. 466)

human factors psychology
(p. 442)

intimate distance (p. 458)

personal space (p. 458)

public distance (p. 459)

robotics (p. 462)

social distance (p. 459)

software psychology (p. 460)

videocommunication (p. 461)

vigilance (p. 456)

virtual reality (p. 462)

voice mail (p. 460)

Questions for Discussion

1. Can you think of some dangerous places on your campus? How could a human factors approach make the environment safer?

2. If you redesigned your classroom along the principles of human factors, what would it look like? Would you change the hours of the class? the instructional method?

3. What happens when workers become fatigued? What are some defenses employers can take against fatigue?

4. What was the significance of Taylor's studies at Bethlehem Steel and Gilbreth's study of bricklaying? Why is it important to study the causes of accidents when they are attributed to human error?

5. What can machines do better than humans? humans better than machines? When are you part of a human-machine system?

6. How do illumination and temperature affect performance?

7. What are some guidelines for creating the best human-computer system?

8. Do you know someone who might be described as "accident prone"? What makes that person accident prone?

9. What are some reasons people have accidents? Who is most likely to have an accident?

10. What are some ways of reducing accidents?

CHAPTER 15

I/O Psychology and Worker Health

Issues in Worker Health

Addictive Behavior in the Workplace

Stress

Violence in the Workplace

AIDS in the Workplace

Health Promotion in the Workplace

Models of Employee Assistance Programs

Evaluating Employee Assistance Programs

Worker Health and the Future

Chapter Summary

Key Words and Concepts

Questions for Discussion

During the 1970s and 1980s, the role of psychology in the workplace took a new direction. Employers turned to psychologists in increasing numbers to address employees' personal problems that hindered performance. Specifically, management began to recognize that problems with alcohol, drugs, stress, and other areas were affecting productivity, and that many times such problems could be treated effectively in the workplace. Although employee counseling, especially for alcohol-related problems, had existed since before World War II, the 1970s saw a rapid increase in both the number and scope of **employee assistance programs (EAPs).** Today, virtually every Fortune 500 company provides some form of counseling for employees.

Typical problems seen in EAPs include stress, anxiety, depression, and substance abuse. Recent estimates (Blum & Roman, 1995) suggest that aproximately 25 percent of an organization's workforce will use an EAP over a five-year period, and 7.5 percent will receive services for drug or alcohol problems.

As suggested in Chapter 1, employee assistance programs are not a traditional area of industrial and organizational psychology. EAPs are usually staffed with individuals with backgrounds in social work, counseling, or clinical psychology. Nevertheless, the negative relationship between performance and personal problems has long been recognized by I/O psychologists. Although an I/O psychologist without special training would not be involved in counseling workers, it is likely that the psychologist would help design the EAP, redesign jobs and environments that create employee problems, and evaluate the success of the EAP. This chapter looks at problems that affect worker health and hinder job performance.

Issues in Worker Health

Historical Background
Employee Assistance
Programs

Although the idea of counseling in the workplace may not be new, modern employers have different views about, and approaches to, dealing with employee health problems. Today employers are much more aware of the high cost of both physical and mental health problems on productivity. For example, the cost of replacing a top executive who dies of a heart attack was estimated in the 1980s to be between $250,000 and $500,000 (Naditch, 1984). Along the same lines, General Motors spent $800 million per year on employee health in the 1980s (Matteson & Ivancevich, 1988). Given these kinds of statistics, promoting healthy behavior in employees would seem to be good business sense.

Historical Background

One of the first programs designed to help troubled employees began at the famous Hawthorne plant of the Western Electric Company in the years after the research program. Nonprofessional counselors at the plant used the nondirective method of psychological counseling developed by Carl Rogers to help employees with their problems.

Although the Hawthorne program was a pioneer attempt in this area, it was terminated when evaluation of its success proved to be impossible. Specifically, when management attempted to determine how many people were being seen and the nature of their problems, the counselors refused to disclose such information, arguing that providing such data would violate the guarantee of confidentiality given to clients. Because of their refusal to keep records, the program could not justify its existence and was consequently phased out (Levinson, 1983).

Despite this early effort, most modern EAPs owe their existence to the alcoholism treatment programs established at companies such as DuPont, Eastman Kodak, and Kemper Insurance in the 1940s. These programs were staffed by recovering alcoholics who counseled individuals, typically in the last stages of alcoholism. Employees seen in these programs had received repeated warnings from their supervisors, were frequently absent, and had problems with both their families and their health because of alcoholism.

Overall success of these programs was limited, since they relied on supervisors for referrals. In many cases, supervisors were reluctant to make a diagnosis in an area for which they had no training, and they often waited until a problem became severe before making a referral. Consequently, workers who were referred to the programs were often in the terminal stages of alcoholism, and treatment was rarely successful.

Another problem limiting the success of early alcoholism programs was their focus on blue-collar workers. Because supervisors were responsible for making referrals, alcoholic executives usually went undetected. Over the years, this belief that alcoholism is a blue-collar problem has eventually given way to a recognition that alcoholism is more commonly an executive problem. Estimates now place the percentage of alcoholics who are blue-collar workers at 30 percent, white-collar workers at 25 percent, and professionals and managers at 45 percent (Palisano, 1980).

Alcoholism programs were expanded in the 1960s because of a recognition of two factors. First, alcoholism typically led to other problems—for example, alcoholic workers often had financial and marital problems. At the same time, management recognized that providing counseling only for alcoholic employees was not fair to other workers. Typically, mental health and financial counseling were added to the alcoholism program.

In 1970, the precedent-setting comprehensive Alcohol Abuse and Alcoholism Prevention, Treatment, and Rehabilitation Act (the Hughes Act) established the National Institute of Alcohol Abuse and Alcoholism and mandated that programs for alcoholism be established in every federal agency. This act was amended in 1972 to include the establishment of programs for drug abuse as well.

By the 1970s an important philosophical change in employee treatment programs had occurred. In most programs, emphasis shifted from a focus on treating alcoholism and drug abuse to treating any condition that impairs job performance. Additionally, supervisors were no longer required to diagnose substance abuse, but were simply to identify employees whose performances were substandard. Specific employee problems such as attendance were targeted for counseling. At General Motors, for example, employees whose absences are more than 15 percent above the number justified are required to see a counselor; at the Social Security Administration, supervisors of employees with too many absences are notified by computer to refer the individuals for counseling.

Employee Assistance Programs

In the late 1970s, several important demographic factors converged to make the issue of employee health problems significant for employers. One important

factor was the incredible growth in the cost of medical treatment for employees; another was the substantial evidence that providing psychotherapy or counseling for workers lowers health care costs significantly.

In a landmark study of individuals who used physicians' services at the Kaiser-Permanente Medical Center in San Francisco, Follette and Cummings (1967) found that providing counseling greatly lessened medical complaints over time. In this study, randomly selected participants were divided into four treatment conditions: one counseling session only, brief therapy (an average of 6.2 sessions), long-term therapy (an average of 33.9 sessions), or no psychotherapy.

The effect of counseling on medical services usage was surprising even to the researchers. In the five years following the initial study, people who had received only one counseling session used medical services 60 percent less than members who received no therapy. People who had received two to three sessions of counseling also reduced their visits to the doctor, as much as 75 percent compared with the control group (Cummings & Follette, 1976). Although usage of outpatient medical services did not decline among long-term therapy patients, incidence of hospitalization did decline. Since psychotherapy costs are generally much lower than medical treatment costs, this research seemed to indicate that mental health treatment can be a significant factor in controlling health care expenditures.

Another factor affecting the proliferation of EAP programs is related to the change in labor force composition during the 1970s. Specifically, the number of young people (ages 25 to 44) working increased from 30 million in 1965 to 39 million in 1975, and had reached over 60.5 million individuals by 1990. Statistically, this group is particularly at risk for alcohol and drug problems.

A final factor in the development of the EAP movement has been legal considerations. Whereas legislation providing for some compensation to workers injured on the job had existed in the United States since 1908, court decisions in recent years have increasingly held employers liable for psychological, as well as physical, injury to workers.

In one case, for example, the director of security for a department store, who had been experiencing a tremendous amount of stress, committed suicide in his office. His secretary, who had been forced to take on some of his duties, experienced a severe depression that required hospitalization. The court held that the secretary's depression was job related and that the employer was liable for workers' compensation claims.

Increasingly, psychological issues are being included in state workers' compensation codes. As evidence accumulated that psychological considerations such as workplace stress are related to heart disease, migraine, and ulcers, employers developed programs to help control these kinds of problems. In addition, recent court cases have questioned whether, under the Americans with Disabilities Act, employers cannot legally limit the amount of mental health coverage for employees (Jeffrey, 1997).

Alcoholism
Drug Use
Gambling

Addictive Behavior in the Workplace

Although the newer employee counseling programs offer a wide variety of services—the International Ladies Garment Workers Union Local 23-25 in New York City, for example, counsels members with immigration problems—alcohol- and drug-related problems still constitute the bulk of the work for EAP counselors. Problems of drug use in the workplace had been recognized since the 1960s, but in the mid-1980s, the seriousness of the problem led to a new emphasis on the screening of employees. At the same time, the recognition that gambling can be classified as an addictive behavior that leads to problems with employee theft also led to the development of counseling programs.

Alcoholism

Alcoholism has been the historical basis of most employee counseling problems and continues to be a serious problem in the United States. There are at least 13 million problem drinkers in this country, of whom 3 million are teenagers. Alcoholism is estimated to cost employers $60 billion annually in lost productivity (Faley, Kleiman, & Wall, 1988).

Obvious costs of alcohol-related problems are absenteeism, sick leave, accidents, and health benefits claims. Hidden costs include poor decisions, thefts, decreased work quality, early retirement, and higher workers' compensation claims. Health problems related to alcohol abuse include cirrhosis, gastritis, pancreatitis, hypertension, and cancer of the mouth, tongue, throat, esophagus, liver, pancreas, and bowel.

Alcoholics are typically ages 35 to 50, hold full-time jobs, and are usually white-collar workers and professionals. Some evidence suggests that better educated workers—White males in particular—are most at risk for alcoholism (Delaney & Ames, 1995; French, Zarkin, & Bray, 1995). Whereas alcohol abuse among lower-level employees typically results in absenteeism and tardiness, identification of the alcoholic executive is usually much more difficult. Of all alcoholics, however, only 15 percent ever receive treatment (Stuart, 1991a).

Sherman (1984) has identified the progression of a typical case of alcoholism in executives. As executives become less able to accomplish their jobs, secretaries and other subordinates often do more of their work while the executive's boss begins to give him or her less to do. If the boss senses alcohol may be a problem, he or she may talk with the alcoholic employee and suggest that the employee do something about the situation. After each conversation with the boss, the performance of the alcoholic employee is likely to improve, but improvement rarely lasts. The secretary, boss, and coworkers engage in a conspiracy of silence, pretending that the drinking is not really a problem.

In most cases, the boss eventually loses patience and threatens to fire the manager. Interestingly, the threat of being fired is often effective in motivating the manager to do something about drinking problems. The loss of job and income is more threatening to alcoholic employees than the loss of their families. Figure 15.1 illustrates the progression of alcoholism in executives.

Two common—and erroneous—beliefs of alcoholic executives is that they can still accomplish their jobs satisfactorily and that no one knows they are drinking. The threat of job loss on the basis of poor performance, rather than on the basis of drinking, is often sufficient to move an individual into a treatment program.

There is some evidence alcoholism differs between males and females. Whereas males are likely to drink because of stress and emotional isolation, females are more likely to start drinking in response to specific life situations (Masi, 1984; Sherman, 1984). Males are more likely to abuse alcohol in social situations; females are likely to begin their drinking problems alone or in conjunction with an alcoholic partner. Although alcoholism occurs more frequently in men (Steffy & Laker, 1991), women are more likely to abuse other drugs at the same time they abuse alcohol. Overall, female alcoholics have poorer prognoses than male alcoholics, and they are more likely to commit suicide.

Treatment As mentioned earlier, alcoholism has historically been the major counseling problem in organizations. Supervisors were charged with identifying and referring employees to counseling programs. In most cases these programs failed because of supervisors' unwillingness to refer and the lack of an effective treatment modality. Counseling in early alcohol programs usually consisted of a moral appeal simply to stop drinking. For individuals in advanced stages of alcoholism, such an appeal had little effect.

During the 1960s, however, a new model for handling alcoholism in the workplace was introduced. Rather than relying on a diagnosis of alcoholism as a basis for referral to an EAP, employers began to require counseling for any form of diminished performance. In other words, the focus of the counseling became the problem—absenteeism or tardiness, for example—rather than its suspected cause. Under this new approach, supervisors were no longer required to make psychological diagnoses, and alcoholics were referred for treatment before the problem became terminal.

Traditionally, alcoholic employees were referred by employers to 28-day inpatient treatment programs. With the current popularity of HMOs, however, more and more alcohol treatment is outpatient and provided outside of working hours. This new approach is much less costly, but some questions about its effectiveness have been raised (McShulskis, 1996a).

Although programs for treating alcoholism have existed for decades, surprisingly little scientific research has evaluated their effectiveness. In reviewing the literature on alcoholism in the workplace, Weiss (1987) concluded that specialists in the alcoholism field have overstated both the severity of the problem

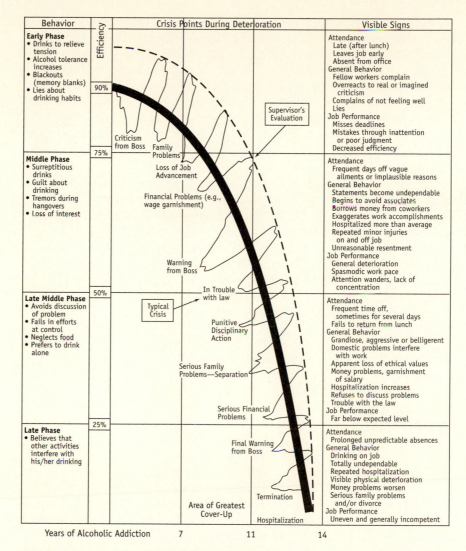

Behavior	Efficiency	Crisis Points During Deterioration	Visible Signs

Early Phase
• Drinks to relieve tension
• Alcohol tolerance increases
• Blackouts (memory blanks)
• Lies about drinking habits
	90%
	
	75%
		Criticism from Boss — Family Problems
		Loss of Job Advancement
		Supervisor's Evaluation
			Attendance
			  Late (after lunch)
			  Leaves job early
			  Absent from office
			General Behavior
			  Fellow workers complain
			  Overreacts to real or imagined criticism
			  Complains of not feeling well
			  Lies
			Job Performance
			  Misses deadlines
			  Mistakes through inattention or poor judgment
			  Decreased efficiency

Middle Phase
• Surreptitious drinks
• Guilt about drinking
• Tremors during hangovers
• Loss of interest
		Financial Problems (e.g., wage garnishment)
		
		Warning from Boss
			Attendance
			  Frequent days off vague ailments or implausible reasons
			General Behavior
			  Statements become undependable
			  Begins to avoid associates
			  Borrows money from coworkers
			  Exaggerates work accomplishments
			  Hospitalized more than average
			  Repeated minor injuries on and off job
			  Unreasonable resentment
			Job Performance
			  General deterioration
			  Spasmodic work pace
			  Attention wanders, lack of concentration

Late Middle Phase
• Avoids discussion of problem
• Fails in efforts at control
• Neglects food
• Prefers to drink alone
	50%	Typical Crisis
		In Trouble with law
		Punitive Disciplinary Action
		Serious Family Problems—Separation
		Serious Financial Problems
			Attendance
			  Frequent time off, sometimes for several days
			  Fails to return from lunch
			General Behavior
			  Grandiose, aggressive or belligerent
			  Domestic problems interfere with work
			  Apparent loss of ethical values
			  Money problems, garnishment of salary
			  Hospitalization increases
			  Refuses to discuss problems
			  Trouble with the law
			Job Performance
			  Far below expected level

Late Phase
• Believes that other activities interfere with his/her drinking
	25%	Final Warning from Boss
		Termination
		Area of Greatest Cover-Up
		Hospitalization
			Attendance
			  Prolonged unpredictable absences
			General Behavior
			  Drinking on job
			  Totally undependable
			  Repeated hospitalization
			  Visible physical deterioration
			  Money problems worsen
			  Serious family problems and/or divorce
			Job Performance
			  Uneven and generally incompetent

Years of Alcoholic Addiction   7   11   14

Source: MacDonnell, F. J. Alcoholism in the workplace: Differential diagnosis. *EAP Digest,* 1(4) (May/June 1981): 26–40. Copyright © 1981 by Performance Resource Press, Inc., Troy, MI.

Figure 15.1 The Alcoholic Executive

and the effectiveness of their treatment programs. Nonetheless, whereas most earlier treatment programs for alcoholics failed, some researchers now report recovery rates of 50 percent and better (Sherman, 1984). Today researchers also recognize that the majority of alcoholics recover without professional treatment—they simply stop drinking.

Drug Use

During the 1980s, employers became increasingly concerned about the use of drugs among employees. Specifically, employers worried that drug-abusing workers would steal, their performances would be unsatisfactory, and they would entice other employees to drug use.

In a study that looked at preemployment drug use and job performance (McDaniel, 1988), for example, people who had never used drugs made better employees than those who had. People who had been arrested for a drug offense were far more likely to be discharged than those who had never been arrested—irrespective of whether they were convicted. In another study (Normand, Salyards, & Mahoney, 1990), employees who used drugs had a 60 percent higher absenteeism rate and a 47 percent rate of involuntary termination.

In 1994, the National Research Council estimated that 10 percent of the full-time workforce has used illicit drugs in the past year (Norman, Lempert, & O'Brien, 1994). According to NIDA, 66 percent of drug abusers are currently employed. In terms of lost productivity, product defects, thefts, absenteeism, accidents, and health care claims, it is estimated that substance abuse costs employers $140 billion annually (Oliver, 1994). Although illegal drug use tends to concentrate in younger employee groups, the abuse of prescription drugs is found in older groups, particularly among women.

In addition, drug use among higher-level employees tends to be more hidden because they have more resources to cope with a drug problem. Not only do higher-level employees have access to private physicians rather than emergency rooms or the EAP, but their levels of responsibility and lifestyles require them to keep their drug problem under control. For these reasons, drug use statistics about middle-class employees are almost certainly underestimates (Granfield & Cloud, 1996; Sterk-Elifson, 1996).

In some respects, drug abuse is a more serious problem than alcoholism for the employer. Unlike the alcoholic, who generally tries to keep the drinking a secret, drug users often support their habits by selling to other employees. Some evidence suggests the major source of income for drug users is shoplifting, and for this reason, many drug users are attracted to the retail industry. In addition, the prices of cocaine and heroin dropped significantly between the early 1980s and the early 1990s (Rhodes, Hyatt, & Scheiman, 1996), which made these drugs accessible to more people.

What causes an employee to use illicit drugs? Although research in this area has historically focused on personal characteristics of the employee, some studies have suggested that environmental factors may also cause employees to drink or use drugs. In one study (Lehman, Farabee, Holcom, & Simpson, 1995), 1,325 municipal employees completed questionnaires about a variety of factors believed to be related to substance abuse. Results from the study found that individual characteristics were better predictors of drug abuse, and that young, single males who did not attend religious services regularly and had low

self-esteem, an arrest history, and family or friends who used drugs were most at risk for substance abuse. Work-related predictors included stress and low levels of satisfaction, faith in management, job involvement, and organizational commitment.

Klaas and Dell'omo (1991) looked at managerial responses to drug use on the job. In their study of almost 3,000 disciplinary actions taken against employees, these researchers found that the majority of managers determined the severity of discipline in terms of the seriousness of the offense. In other words, when the employee using drugs jeopardized workplace safety or productivity, the punishment was likely to be harsher. Possible responses to employee drug use are termination, suspension, referral to an EAP, written warning, and informal counseling.

Treatment Historically, employers have taken little interest in rehabilitating drug users, and the knowledge that an applicant has a history of drug use usually disqualified the applicant for employment. Almost all early treatment programs focused on individuals addicted to narcotics—opium, morphine, and heroin. These treatment programs emphasized total abstinence, and they usually attempted to instill a phobia of drugs in program participants. Not surprisingly, these programs were often ineffective and employers remained skeptical and resistant to hiring ex-addicts.

During the 1960s, however, two important changes among drug users occurred. First, the development of methadone programs allowed many addicts to function effectively in the community and to hold regular jobs. Second, there was a tremendous increase in the use of other kinds of drugs—both legal and illegal—throughout society. The use of drugs had become so widespread that employers could no longer automatically refuse to hire applicants they suspected of drug use. Hiring problems were further complicated by the fact that many addictions seemed to be based on prescriptions for legal drugs written by physicians. Table 15.1 lists some controlled substances and their effects on performance.

Today about 63 percent of all medium-size and large organizations do drug testing (Harris & Heft, 1992), but only about 3 percent of small businesses—which constitute 93 percent of all businesses in the United States—test for drugs (Hayghe, 1991). The vast majority of these tests are conducted "for cause"—that is, after an accident or suspicious behavior—rather than randomly (Axel, 1990). According to the *Wall Street Journal* (O'Boyle, 1985), 12 percent to 20 percent of job applicants who are screened for drug use fail those tests.

One particular problem with regard to the employee abusing drugs is differences in behavior patterns caused by different drugs. Whereas cocaine tends to cause increased alertness, for example, marijuana use is likely to result in relaxed behavior. Typical behaviors of individuals using drugs in the workplace include increased absenteeism, unexplained absences from the work area, lengthy trips to the restroom, falling asleep on the job, and serious financial problems. Because accusing an employee of drug use is accusing the employee of criminal activity, employers must be very careful about making false accusations.

Table 15.1 DRUGS FOUND IN THE WORKPLACE

Drugs	Often Prescribed Brand Names	Usual Methods of Administration	Possible Effects
Narcotics			
Heroin	None	Injected, sniffed	Euphoria, drowsiness, respiratory depression, constricted pupils, nausea
Methadone	Dolophine, Methadone, Methadose	Oral, injected	
Depressants			
Barbiturates	Amytal, Butisol, Nembutal, Phenobarbital, Seconal, Tuinal	Oral, injected	Slurred speech, disorientation, drunken behavior without odor of alcohol
Methaqualone	Optimil, Parest, Quaalude, Somnafac, Sopor	Oral	
Tranquilizers	Equanil, Librium, Miltown, Serax, Tranxene, Valium	Oral	
Stimulants			
Cocaine	Cocaine	Injected, sniffed	Increased alertness, excitation, euphoria, dilated pupils, increased pulse rate and blood pressure, insomnia, loss of appetite
Amphetamines	Benzedrine, Biphetamine, Desoxyn, Dexedrine	Oral, injected	
Cannabis			
Marijuana Hashish Hashish Oil	None	Oral, smoked	Euphoria, relaxed inhibitions, increased appetite, disoriented behavior

Source: Myers, D. W. (1984). *Establishing and building employee assistance programs* (pp. 314–315). Westport, CT: Quorum Books, a division of Greenwood Press, Inc. Used by permission.

One technique some employers use for identifying drug users is urinalysis. Problems associated with urinalysis, however, include the substitution of the urine of someone else by the abusing employee, the need for test procedures to be administered properly, and accusations by employees that the employer is violating their privacy. Interestingly, some researchers (Ostrov & Cavanaugh,

1987; Rosse & Ringer, 1991) have attempted to determine drug use through paper-and-pencil measures, although this form of drug testing is not yet well developed.

One issue drug testing does not address is the frequency of use. Employers may wish to discriminate between employees who use drugs infrequently and those who have a serious addiction. As they are presently constituted, most drug-testing programs could not make such a distinction. Some research (Stein, Newcomb, & Bentler, 1988), for example, shows that quantity of drug use is a better predictor of disruptive behavior than frequency of use.

As pointed out in Chapter 3, drug testing often has an impact on employee and applicant attitudes. Not surprisingly, individuals who are heavy users of drugs are likely to oppose employee drug-testing programs (Murphy, Thornton, & Reynolds, 1990). Applicants may also object to a drug test because they feel such tests invade their privacy, or they may fear results from the test will prevent their being hired. One study found that workers were more favorably disposed toward drug testing that came after advance notice and that would result in referral to an EAP rather than termination (Stone & Kotch, 1989). In another study of employee attitudes toward drug testing, Konovsky and Cropanzano (1991) found that assurance of fair procedures affected employee attitudes more than outcome of the procedures.

Finally, in a survey comparing groups of adults taking university courses and traditional college students, Murphy, Thornton, and Prue (1991) found a high level of agreement about the acceptability of drug testing. Specifically, both groups strongly favored drug testing for jobs that might create danger for the worker or coworkers—sometimes referred to as "safety-sensitive jobs." Respondents also favored drug testing for jobs that are routine, require a high level of awareness of the environment, and involve infrequent contact with clients or the public. Table 15.2 presents some of the results of this study.

Gambling

Another addiction that affects performance is gambling. In recent years, gambling has been recognized as the major cause of white-collar crime, with 85 percent of the compulsive gamblers in treatment admitting they stole from their employers (Stuart, 1991b). Of the 80 million to 100 million gamblers in the United States, 6 percent are considered compulsive—that is, unable to control their gambling behavior. Gamblers Anonymous (GA) estimates that $100 billion is gambled in the United States annually; this figure rises to $300 billion if stock market activity is included. When casinos opened in Atlantic City, New Jersey, GA membership in Maryland, Pennsylvania, New Jersey, and Delaware increased by 200 percent.

Traditionally a male problem, gambling has become widespread among female employees as well. GA estimates that the gambling debts of women in its therapy groups average $45,000. In addition, some evidence (Stuart, 1991b)

Table 15.2   JOBS AND DRUG TESTING

Three researchers (Murphy, Thornton, & Prue, 1991) asked a group of adults about the acceptability of drug testing in a variety of jobs. A rating of 7 indicated a high acceptance of testing; a rating of 1 indicated a low acceptance. Results from their study appear in the table below. Not surprisingly, drug testing was most acceptable for jobs that related to danger.

	Acceptability Rating
Job	**Mean**
Janitor	4.39
Photographer	4.33
Salesperson	4.42
Farmworker	4.69
Clerk	4.45
Market research analyst	4.65
Waiter/waitress	4.14
Computer programmer	4.91
Laborer	4.75
Cook	4.76
Priest	4.73
Reporter	4.83
Accountant	4.77
Professor	4.87
Game warden	5.21
Personnel manager	5.00
Welder	5.48
Stockbroker	4.83
Mechanic	5.32
Miner	5.69
Construction worker	5.63
Electrician	5.50
Electrical engineer	5.13
Machinist	5.05
Fork lift operator	5.74
Truck driver	6.10
Firefighter	6.00
Nurse	6.16
Nuclear engineer	6.08
Train conductor	6.13
Surgeon	6.22
Day care attendant	5.96
Police officer	6.21
Air traffic controller	6.37
Airline pilot	6.40

Source: Murphy, K. R., Thornton, G. C., III, & Prue, K. (1991). Influence of job characteristics on the acceptability of employee drug testing. *Journal of Applied Psychology, 76*(3), 447–453. Used by permission.

suggests compulsive gamblers are attracted to occupations such as stockbroker, insurance agent, banker, and salesperson, in all of which they are in a position to handle money.

Because of the need for a constant cash flow, many gamblers hang on to their jobs tenaciously. In most cases, gambling has a devastating effect on both employee and employer. In a study of the causes of employee theft over an 18-year period, gambling debt was cited as the number one motivation for stealing from an employer. Other causes of theft in order of frequency were drug and alcohol use, extramarital affairs with support of two households, economic needs, and following the boss's example (Beck, 1981).

Because compulsive gamblers, unlike alcoholics or drug users, do not exhibit physiological symptoms, they are often difficult to detect. Research shows, however, that the typical compulsive gambler is above average in intelligence, has a high need for achievement, has a reputation for enjoying gambling, and has problems at home related to gambling (Stuart, 1991b).

Some employees who have been prosecuted for embezzling or stealing from an employer to pay gambling debts have attempted to claim an insanity defense. In several decisions, however, the courts have ruled that pathological gambling is insufficient for claiming insanity.

Characteristics of Stress
Environmental Stressors
Dispositional Stress
Stress and Type A Behavior
Stress Management
  Programs

Stress

Job burnout (Lee & Ashforth, 1990; Maslach, 1982) is a syndrome in which a worker feels emotionally exhausted, treats others as objects rather than people, and experiences diminished feelings of accomplishment. Interestingly, some research (Anderson & Iwanicki, 1984; Russell, Altmaier, & Van Velzen, 1987) suggests that married workers and workers with children express less burnout than single or childless workers.

Two key elements in burnout are the frequency of interpersonal contact and the intensity or emotion associated with that contact (Cordes & Dougherty, 1993).

Characteristics of Stress

Job burnout is also associated with stress, and probably the fastest growing area in EAP treatment of nonaddictive behaviors is stress management. In general, **stress** can be defined as a physiological or psychological response to demands made on an individual. Hans Selye (1976) is generally recognized as the first researcher to identify the pattern of physiological responses that occurs when the body experiences a stressful situation. These responses include elevated heart rate, higher blood pressure, increased respiration, and such conditions as hyper-

tension, heart disease, or ulcer. Psychological reactions to stress include headaches, insomnia, anxiety, and fear. According to an analysis of disability cases conducted by Northwestern Mutual Life Insurance, the average cost of rehabilitating an employee disabled because of stress was $1,925. If the employee is not rehabilitated, costs rise to an average of $73,270 per employee ("The costs of stressed workers to employers," 1996).

Although early research on stress suggested that the condition is usually dysfunctional, more recent studies have emphasized both the positive and negative aspects of experiencing stress. For example, one group of researchers (Schaubroeck, Ganster, & Fox, 1992) argued that stress should not be studied alone, but along with the coping mechanisms that employees develop to handle stress. Overall, most researchers now agree that stress facilitates performance up to a certain level, but beyond that level, additional stress results in a decline in performance.

One approach to studying stress is to look at the person-environment (P-E) fit. This approach considers both conditions in the environment that cause stress as well as characteristics of the individual who may experience stress. One researcher (Edwards, 1996) hypothesized that stress can be studied from the P-E perspective in two ways. *Supplies-values* fit refers to the amount, frequency, and quality of environmental attributes that fulfill a person's values. *Demands-abilities* fit, on the other hand, refers to both the physical and socially constructed requirements placed on an individual. Poor fit from either perspective is a cause of stress.

One study of person-environment fit and stress (Xie & Johns, 1995) looked at the role of *job scope,* defined as the set of job-related activities performed by a job holder. In this study, 418 employees representing 143 different jobs completed questionnaires about stress. Results indicated a curvilinear relationship between job scope and stress. That is, stress—defined as emotional exhaustion—was greatest when job scope was either very small or very large. Individuals who perceived a misfit between their abilities and job demands experienced higher stress. Along the same lines, some research suggests that role ambiguity contributes to stress. **Role ambiguity** refers to uncertainty about such job areas as work method, scheduling, and performance criteria (Breaugh & Colihan, 1994).

Interestingly, stress occurs in both pleasant and unpleasant situations. Being promoted may be just as stressful as being fired, and some researchers have found that men who receive promotions have more heart attacks than those who do not (Jenkins, Rosenman, & Friedman, 1966). Along the same lines, individual responses to stress vary greatly. Whereas some individuals perform best when racing to meet deadlines or handling multimillion-dollar deals, others experience extreme anxiety when faced with making a sales call or a presentation to coworkers.

Aside from psychological states, factors such as genetics, race, sex, age, and diet also affect how an individual responds to a stressful situation. Stress can be considered in terms of either factors in the environment or dispositional qualities in the individual worker.

| **Box 15.1** | **NATIONAL INSTITUTE OF OCCUPATIONAL SAFETY AND HEALTH'S RANKING OF 12 MOST STRESSFUL JOBS** |

1. Laborer
2. Secretary
3. Inspector
4. Clinical Lab Technician
5. Office Manager
6. Supervisor
7. Manager/Administrator
8. Waitress/Waiter
9. Machine Operator
10. Farm Owner
11. Miner
12. Painter

Environmental Stressors

Although some research suggests that environment is a factor in individual levels of stress, one study found coal miners to have stress levels no higher than workers in less dangerous jobs (Althouse & Harrell, 1977). Nevertheless, some jobs are generally accepted as being more stressful than others. Box 15.1 lists some of the most stressful occupations.

Apparently, operating a public transit vehicle is one of the most stressful jobs in modern society. Bus drivers have higher rates of cardiovascular disease, hypertension, gastrointestinal disorders, and absenteeism than many in other occupations (Long & Perry, 1985; Winkleby, Ragland, Fisher, & Syme, 1988). For bus drivers, stress comes from being required to keep on a schedule and be polite to passengers, and from having little latitude in making decisions.

In a study of bus drivers in Los Angeles, the main predictor of stress was the amount of traffic congestion the bus driver experienced (Evans & Carrere, 1991). Results from this study also suggest that traffic congestion may be a cause of stress for commuters in general.

Does having a social support system at work lower stress levels? Research on this point is unclear, with some studies suggesting that social support helps protect individuals from the negative effects of stress (Manning, Jackson, & Fusilier, 1996; Vitkovic & Koslow, 1994). In two other studies, however, social support from peers was found to have no relationship to feelings of stress; support from a supervisor, on the other hand, did seem to lower stress levels (Ganster, Fusilier, & Mayes, 1986; Kaufmann & Beehr, 1986).

Social support may be important in times of great stress, however, as when a worker loses a job. One study (Caplan, Vinokur, Price, & van Ryn, 1989) followed 928 unemployed individuals who either attended workshops on how to find a job or received a self-help booklet on the same subject. People who attended the workshops found higher-quality jobs in terms of earnings and job satisfaction than those who had received only the booklet. In addition, those who had found reemployment were significantly less anxious, depressed, and angry than those who remained unemployed.

However, even the workshop participants who did not find jobs were more motivated to continue job seeking than those who had received only the book-

---

Box 15.2   JAPAN SAYS AN EXECUTIVE WORKED HIMSELF TO DEATH

TOKYO, July 15 (Reuters)—A Japanese executive who spent one day out of every three on the road last year has been officially certified as working himself to death.

In a rare ruling affecting white-collar workers, the Labor Standards Inspection Office ruled that 47-year-old Jun Ishii, an official of Mitsui & Company, a trading company, died from overwork, the labor office said today.

Each year about 30 deaths are officially recognized as resulting from overwork, which means the Government compensates the families of the deceased. But most such "karoshi" cases deal with blue-collar workers; only rarely is a karoshi death of a white-collar worker recognized.

Mr. Ishii was found dead in a hotel room in the central city of Nagoyain on July 15, 1990. A Russian speaker, he had been escorting four Russian clients for his company. His widow, Sachiko, 48, applied to the labor standards office in November of that year for compensation on the ground that he died of overwork. In the year before his death, Mrs. Ishii's husband spent a total of 115 days abroad on business trips.

The Labor Standards Inspection Office said it took into account Mr. Ishii's long work hours in the week just before he died, when he was unable to take a day off, and ruled that compensation should be paid. Mitsui has already paid the family 30 million yen (about $240,000) and cooperated with the widow's application.

The National Defense Council for Victims of Karoshi says that as many as 10,000 Japanese work themselves to death every year.

Source: "A Case of White Collar 'Karoshi' Japan Says an Executive Worked Himself to Death," *The New York Times,* July 16, 1992. Copyright © 1992. Reprinted by permission of Reuters Information.

---

let. The researchers concluded that the workshop intervention was more successful because it helped to "establish trust, engender skills and the motivation to use them, inoculate against setbacks, and provide social support."

Box 15.2 describes an extreme case of stress, in which an executive worked himself to death.

Dispositional Stress

Another line of stress research considers dispositional factors, and negative affectivity in particular. Researchers (Brief, Burke, George, Robinson, & Webster, 1988), for example, surveyed 497 managers and professionals earning an average of $47,000 concerning stress, job satisfaction, negative affectivity, and other factors. People with high negative affectivity scores were more depressed, less satisfied with their jobs and lives in general, and more stressed at home and at work.

In contrast, however, Chen and Spector (1991) found that physical strains, as indicated by absence, doctor visits, and physical symptoms, were more predictive of stress than was negative affectivity. Finally, George (1991) found that positive affectivity was related to customer service behavior and sales productivity among workers at a large clothing and household products store.

Two researchers (Schaubroeck & Williams, 1993) considered the relationship between Type A behavior (discussed below) and **escalating commitment,** which refers to persistence in a course of behavior. The researchers hypothesized that people with Type A behavior are motivated to justify their previous failed decisions by escalating their commitment to a course of action. In a laboratory study that tested this hypothesis, the researchers found that Type As (defined on the next page) who held high-responsibility positions were more likely to continue the same course of action than Type As who held low-responsibility positions. Researchers attributed this finding to the high achievement motivation of Type As and to their belief in their own personal competency, which led them to persist at failed actions.

Some research has considered the role of *private self-consciousness* (PSC; Carver & Scheier, 1981) in mediating stress. PSC refers to the degree to which a person pays attention to his or her own emotional experiences and bodily sensations. According to one theory (Nelson & Quick, 1985), people who are high in PSC are more likely to notice they are stressed and take corrective action.

In a study of PSC and stress among blue-collar workers, Frone and McFarlin (1989) found that people who scored high on a measure of PSC—that is, were more attentive to their internal states—were more stressed than those with low private self-consciousness. The researchers concluded that increasing self-focused attention among employees who are exposed to stress is likely to make the problem worse. Apparently, workers will be less stressed if they do not think about stress.

Results from another study (Parkes, 1990) suggest that the effects of job stress may be lessened by coping with, rather than suppressing, stress. Student teachers who were experiencing stress completed a measure of how they dealt with it. Teachers who took an active role in confronting and dealing with stressors described themselves as being in better health than teachers who tried the strategy of ignoring stressors. Interestingly, female student teachers were more likely to take an active coping strategy, whereas males were more likely to attempt to suppress their feelings of stress.

One study (Jones, Barge, Steffy, Fay, Kunz, & Wuebker, 1988) looked at the impact of stress on hospitals. In a series of studies looking at the relationship between stress and medical malpractice, hospitals reporting higher levels of organizational stress also had more malpractice claims. When several of these hospitals instituted an organizationwide stress management program, the number of malpractice claims dropped significantly from the number occurring at a matched set of hospitals without a stress management program.

Another study of stressful job demands among nurses (Fox, Dwyer, & Ganster, 1993) looked at perceived control of job demands and blood pressure. Not surprisingly, low perceptions of control were related to higher blood pressure. More intriguing was the finding that elevated blood pressure continued after individuals left work, suggesting that feelings of low job control may affect health outside of work.

Two researchers (Nelson & Sutton, 1990) collected data about new employees' stress levels before they assumed their new positions and for nine months afterward. Interestingly, workers who reported higher levels of stress at the end of the nine-month period had reported higher levels of stress before assuming their new jobs. The researchers concluded that a person's tendency to feel stress off the job is likely to be an important determinant of how much stress that person feels on the job.

Finally, one group of researchers (James, Lovato, & Khoo, 1994) looked at the effects of stress on minority employees. Participants in the study were Mexican Americans, African Americans, Asian Americans, Native Americans, and mixed heritage. In this study, lower self-esteem, perceptions of prejudice or discrimination, and value differences with supervisors were related to elevated blood pressure among participants.

Stress and Type A Behavior

In 1974, Friedman and Rosenman described a pattern of behavior linked to coronary heart disease. These authors suggested that most individuals could be classified into what they referred to as "Type A" or "Type B" behavior patterns. **Type A** individuals are characterized by a chronic sense of time urgency, a distaste for idleness, impatience with any thing or person they see as a barrier to accomplishing their goals, hostility, and competitiveness. Type As experience heightened arousal of the autonomic nervous system, muscle tension, and often use rapid and emphatic speech patterns. In terms of personality, they tend to be extraverted, have high levels of job involvement, and have a strong need for power (Ganster, Schaubroeck, Sime, & Mayes, 1991).

Type Bs, on the other hand, are typically easygoing, relaxed, satisfied, and unhurried. Type As are more likely to be found in industrialized and densely populated urban areas and Type Bs in smaller, rural communities (Rosenman & Chesney, 1982).

In recent years, some researchers have questioned some of the elements originally associated with Type A behavior. For example, one group of researchers (Booth-Kewley & Friedman, 1987) suggest that the focus of Type A research should be on the "AHA!" syndrome (anger, hostility, and aggression), whereas others (Conte, Landy, & Mathieu, 1995; Landy, Rastegary, Thayer, & Colvin, 1991) argue that the role of time urgency in Type A is not clear.

Being a Type A, however, does not automatically lead to stress. What typically causes stress is being a Type A working in a Type B environment, or being a Type B working in a Type A environment. In other words, ambitious, hard-charging individuals who are required to work in challenging environments are likely to feel less stress than if they are required to work in a relaxed and uneventful workplace. Type Bs are likely to be stressed if they must work in a hard-charging, rather than a more relaxed environment. Nevertheless, the personality characteristics of the Type A lead these individuals to seek situations that are likely to create stress.

In a study of Type A and the high-pressure job of police dispatcher, Kirmeyer (1988) considered the number of times a dispatcher was in the difficult position of having simultaneous demands for a response. Regardless of the actual number of response demands, Type A individuals were more likely to report themselves as being overloaded at work. This finding suggests that individual perception of overload and stress may be more important than objective measures.

Considerable research has demonstrated that Type A individuals are at significantly greater risk for heart attack and stroke than Type B individuals. One study of police and fire department employees (Schaubroeck, Ganster, & Kemmerer, 1994), for example, found the incidence of cardiovascular disorder in Type A individuals in complex jobs increased over time, but did not increase among individuals with low Type A ratings.

Because the success of an organization may depend on Type A behavior in certain of its employees, many companies have instituted programs to deal with the stress that Type As often experience. Typical organizational responses to managing stress in workers include redesigning jobs, eliminating work overloads, moving workers around to maximize the person/environment fit, and allowing more employee participation in decision making.

Some researchers have raised questions about the relationship between Type A behavior and coronary heart disease (Booth-Kewley & Friedman, 1987; Matthews, 1988), as well as its measurement (Edwards, Baglioni, & Cooper, 1990; Landy, Rastegary, Thayer, & Colvin, 1991). Some research suggests Type A behavior may be similar to job satisfaction in terms of being measurable at both the global and the facet levels. In a study of Type A among 756 executives attending a summer executive program at a university, for example, Edwards and Baglioni (1991) found that measuring the facets associated with Type A was more predictive of blood pressure, heart rate, anxiety, and depression than relying on global measures of Type A.

One particularly important question about Type A behavior is its weak relationship to job performance (Lee, Earley, & Hanson, 1988; Lee & Gillen, 1989). Some researchers (Bluen, Barling, & Burns, 1990) have suggested that Type A can be better understood if it is considered in terms of two dimensions—achievement strivings and impatience-irritability—typical of the Type A personality. In a sample of 222 life insurance brokers, Type As who were high on achievement strivings had higher sales performance and greater job satisfaction. Brokers who scored high on a measure of impatience-irritability, on the other hand, were less satisfied with their jobs and more likely to be depressed. The researchers concluded that both aspects of Type A behavior affect job success—achievement strivings in a positive direction and impatience-irritability negatively.

Stress Management Programs

During the 1980s, many companies introduced programs to lower stress in the workplace. Equitable Life Assurance, for example, has the Emotional Health Program, which uses a clinical psychologist, a physician, a psychology intern, and a counselor to teach employees relaxation techniques. Typical interventions in stress management programs include teaching employees goal setting and time management, advising on exercise and meditation, and helping workers clarify values concerning their fit in the organization.

Despite the growth in stress management programs, few companies have attempted to evaluate their impact scientifically (Ivancevich, Matteson, Freedman, & Phillips, 1990). When evaluation occurs, it usually focuses on the individual worker, and not on the benefits of the stress management program to the organization as a whole. Although important strides are being made in this area, little firm evidence about the impact of stress management programs is yet available.

Violence in the Workplace

In recent years violence at work has become a serious problem for employers. In 1994, for example, 1,071 Americans were murdered on the job; close to 600 of these workers died during robberies of small retail stores (Micco, 1997). Although transportation accidents are the number one cause of death at work, homicide is second; for women, homicide is the leading cause of death at work (Bensimon, 1994; Rigdon, 1994).

Murder is, of course, only the most extreme form of workplace violence. During an 18-month period, the Postal Service recorded 500 cases of employee violence toward a supervisor and 200 cases of supervisor violence toward an employee (Kurland, 1993). In terms of frequency, violence occurs most often in the health care and social service sectors. In most industries, the incidence of violence is 3 cases per 10,000 workers; in health care and social services, however, the rate is 38 cases per 10,000 workers ("OSHA Finalizes Workplace Violence Guidelines," 1996).

In 1996, OSHA issued guidelines for preventing violence directed at health care and social service employees. The guidelines have four basic elements: (1) work site analysis to identify high-risk situations; (2) hazard prevention and control through engineering, administrative, and task controls to limit risk; (3) training and education so workers know about risks; and (4) management commitment and employee involvement in a program to prevent violence. Employers who do not implement the guidelines may be found guilty of an OSHA violation and fined up to $7,000 per day (Yarborough, 1995).

Not surprisingly, violence has a terrible effect on both workers and productivity. Employees who experience violence, as well as employees who witness violence in their workplace, report stress, lower productivity, and greater amount of lost work time. In terms of legal costs, a workplace death results in an average jury verdict of $2.2 million; a rape that occurs on business property averages $1.8 million (Woo, 1993).

One model of workplace violence (O'Leary-Kelly, Griffin, & Glew, 1996) suggests that some companies create climates of aggression that increase the likelihood of organizational violence. For example, companies that mistreat their employees, allow supervisors or others to model aggressive behavior, reward intense competition, or create a stressful environment may contribute to employee violence.

At the same time, some individuals are likely to be more predisposed toward violent behavior. Researchers have had little success in identifying people who are likely to become violent—other than in terms of gender, age, and previous aggressive behavior (i.e., younger males with histories of violence). Some research (Johnson & Indvik, 1994) suggests that violent workers typically do not fit a criminal profile, but they tend to be loners, often angry, depressed, or paranoid, and have a fascination with weapons. Another report (Waxman, 1995) described people with a tendency toward violence as follows:

> These persons blame others for their problems. They lack insight about the role they play in their own predicament. They believe they have nothing to lose. They are on the verge of becoming depressed but are defending against that depression by being angry and attacking those around them. . . .
>
> Behavioral signs that a person is in turmoil include lateness and absence from work, taking up an inordinate amount of the supervisor's time with complaints or concerns, low productivity, poor relations with colleagues, threats against the supervisor, frequent accidents, deterioration in hygiene or appearance, peculiar behavior, inappropriate remarks, evidence of drug or alcohol abuse, and evidence of a crisis in the worker's personal life.

Other hypothesized reasons for violence include emotional abuse on the job that resembles emotional abuse from a parent early in life; severance of the psychological contract by the employer; authoritarian work environments; and hopelessness about economic conditions.

AIDS in the Workplace

During the 1980s, employers confronted a new problem affecting many areas of the psychology of work—acquired immune deficiency syndrome (AIDS). AIDS affects one in every 300 workers in the United States, and 90 percent of the individuals infected with HIV are working (Breuer, 1995). AIDS affects selection, motivation, and group performance, and it occurs most frequently in the health care, pharmaceutical, broadcasting, communications, recreation, and food service industries (Backer, 1988b).

The American Medical Association estimates that treatment of an AIDS case from infection to death costs $120,000 (Breuer, 1995). Because of this high cost, many employers attempt to persuade workers to modify their behavior to minimize the chances of contracting AIDS. Industrial and organizational psychologists are sometimes asked to design AIDS education programs for other employees, review AIDS policies for compliance with fairness and nondiscrimination legislation, and help develop procedures for dealing with the concerns of noninfected employees.

Probably the most immediate problem regarding AIDS in the workplace is the fear of noninfected employees that they will contract the disease. Because the AIDS virus is transmitted only through sexual contact or contact with another person's blood, the probability of infection at most workplaces is minimal. Nonetheless, the belief that working with someone with AIDS increases risk of infection is widespread (Vest, O'Brien, & Vest, 1991).

One of the most effective strategies for dealing with concerns about AIDS infection is through an AIDS education program. This has become increasingly important as advances in research have made the life span of HIV-infected workers much longer. Consequently, these individuals are likely to remain in the workplace longer than previously.

Steps toward instituting a training program include creating a task force to formulate the organization's approach to problems concerning AIDS in the workplace; including AIDS as part of routine discussions of disability benefits; providing information to dispel incorrect beliefs about AIDS; and, so far as possible, treating the illness as any other (Breuer, 1995).

Some researchers (Vest, O'Brien, & Vest, 1991) recommend that AIDS training start with a needs assessment. Specifically, managers should conduct a survey to determine level of employee understanding about AIDS. Box 15.4 presents some statements used to measure employee opinions about the impact of AIDS on the workplace. Once the organization knows the areas of greatest concern, training programs that address these areas can be developed.

Some research, however, suggests that education alleviates the concerns of some, but not all, employees. In one study (Pryor, Reeder, & McManus, 1991), people who held a negative view of homosexuality continued to be concerned about contracting AIDS after viewing an AIDS education film, whereas people without such an attitude were more reassured. This kind of research suggests that AIDS education is helpful, but that it does not solve all the problems connected with AIDS in the workplace.

One group of researchers (George, Reed, Ballard, Colin, & Fielding, 1993) looked at the effects of taking care of AIDS patients on a group of nurses. Specifically, nurses who were required to care for AIDS patients reported more negative affectivity as the time they spent with such patients increased. Interestingly, however, nurses who felt organizational and social support—that is, they felt valued and cared about by their employer and coworkers—felt significantly less negative affectivity.

The Human Interaction Research Institute has developed guidelines for employers to use in managing AIDS at work. These guidelines include the following (Backer, 1988a):

1. Top management must be committed to providing leadership and resources to the AIDS education program.
2. An employee advisory committee should plan the program.

Box 15.3   PERCEIVED CONSEQUENCES OF EMPLOYING PEOPLE WITH AIDS

Three researchers (Vest, O'Brien, & Vest, 1991) developed a scale to measure what employers might perceive as problems relating to hiring workers with AIDS and surveyed 248 managers in manufacturing, mining, and public administration positions. The researchers found that the factor that most concerned the employers was disruption of the workplace, especially the possibility that some workers might refuse certain job assignments, morale might be lowered, and perhaps even violence might occur.

To a lesser extent, employers were concerned about the possibility of a decline in revenues due to the loss of customers or damage to the company's image. Interestingly, the area of least concern was increased labor costs due to insurance premiums and claims.

Some of the items from the scale were as follows:

I believe that allowing AIDS victims to work at our facility will . . .

cause some employees to refuse job assignments.

increase the number of grievances and complaints.

diminish the ability of other employees to concentrate on their work.

result in lost sales.

undermine our ability to provide service to clients.

increase our cost of disability payments.

Increase the cost of our unemployment insurance.

According to the researchers, an effective AIDS information program needs to address three areas of concern—disruption of the workplace, lost revenues, and higher insurance premiums.

3. External resources—such as social service agencies—should be involved in the program.
4. The company must be aware of both internal and external attitudes about AIDS.
5. Organizational policies about AIDS must be in writing.
6. Education and prevention activities must be available for all employees.
7. Benefits must be revised to deal with AIDS-related illnesses.
8. The work environment should be modified, if necessary, to protect employees from injury or infection.
9. Support services should be available for infected workers.
10. The employer should provide community outreach programs.

It is important for employers to remember that AIDS is covered under the Americans with Disabilities Act (ADA). When an employer is notified that an individual has HIV/AIDS, the organization is required to protect the rights of that applicant or employee. Specifically, the employer is required to make reasonable accommodations to meet the job-related needs of the individual and also to make sure that the work environment is accepting of the worker (Slack, 1996).

Health Promotion in the Workplace

During the 1980s, some researchers became interested in the effects of exercise on individuals. For example, in a study of almost 17,000 men, researchers (Paffenbarger, Hyde, Wing, & Hsieh, 1986) found that physically active individuals had significantly lower mortality rates than those who had sedentary lifestyles. Even when the physically active smoked cigarettes, were overweight, and had a hereditary disposition toward early death, they were still healthier than the nonactive. The survival rates of men expending more or less than 2,000 calories weekly in physical activity are presented in Table 15.3.

Table 15.3   SURVIVAL RATES OF ACTIVE AND SEDENTARY MEN

As the figures below indicate, physically active men live almost 10 years longer than physically inactive men.

Age (Years)	Percentage Surviving with Physical Activity Index of[a]	
	More than 2,000	Less than 2,000
35–39	68.2	57.8
40–44	68.5	58.2
45–49	69.0	59.2
50–54	69.9	59.8
55–59	71.1	61.0
60–64	73.0	63.4
65–69	76.4	67.6
70–74	82.4	74.6
75–79	91.8	85.0
35–79[b]	69.7	59.8

[a]Based on kilocalories expended per week in walking, climbing stairs, and playing sports, adjusted for differences in blood pressure status, cigarette smoking, net gain in body mass index since college, and age of parental death.
[b]Weighted average.

Source: Adapted from Paffenburger, R. S., Jr., Hyde, R. T., Wing, A. L., & Hsieh, C. C. (1986). Physical activity, all-cause mortality, and longevity of college alumni. *New England Journal of Medicine, 314,* 605–613. Reprinted by permission of the *New England Journal of Medicine.*

During the 1970s and 1980s, many companies attempted to control health care and workers' compensation claims by establishing in-house medical and mental health programs aimed at improving health and longevity by changing behavior. Health promotion programs are designed to prevent problems before they occur.

Health promotion programs typically come in three forms (O'Donnell, 1986). At the first level, management tries to raise awareness of health issues by sending newsletters, holding health fairs, and offering classes about health. Health promotion at the second level provides specific programs to employees on an ongoing basis. Companies may offer fitness classes, pay for memberships at local health clubs, or hold discussions about ways of doing physically demanding work. At the third level, the organization takes an active role in helping people sustain a healthy lifestyle. This may include providing an in-house fitness facility, healthy foods in the company cafeteria, and special programs that keep employees informed about health. In reality, however, most health promotion programs are aimed at minimizing physical and mental health problems (level one) rather than at changing workers' lifestyles (Stokols, Pelletier, & Fielding, 1996).

Typical health promotion programs in industry include smoking cessation, weight control, nutrition, and fitness and exercise. In a controlled study of job satisfaction, body image, and absenteeism among employees, Der-Karabetian and Gebharbp (1986) found that employees enrolled in exercise programs experienced higher levels of satisfaction, more positive body images, and lower absence rates than a control group.

In many cases, corporate response to the health promotion concept has been quite positive. At Pepsi headquarters in Purchase, New York, for example, employees are offered four programs that begin with a physical exam, a fitness profile, and the development of a personalized exercise program. Kimberly-Clark spent $2.5 million on a health facility staffed by 15 full-time personnel, and employees at McDonald's corporate headquarters use biofeedback to deal with stress. Although such programs have traditionally been reserved for corporate executives, more programs are being made available for lower-level employees.

Although many employers have assumed employee fitness programs have a positive impact on productivity and job satisfaction, this belief has rarely been evaluated in a scientific fashion (Falkenberg, 1987). Erfurt, Foote, and Heirich (1992), however, considered the effects of different types of wellness programs on the comprehensive health of employees at four different sites. The first site used the most common type of wellness program—a health education program, consisting of lectures, pamphlets, blood pressure testing, and so forth. The second site relied on a physical fitness facility to promote employee health.

The third site used a health education program similar to that at the first site, but at this facility, trained counselors contacted employees with health risks every six months to encourage and assist them in controlling their health problems. That site had no physical facilities, but relied chiefly on interpersonal contact for health promotion. The fourth site had the most comprehensive health promotion program. In addition to health education and interpersonal counseling, that program relied on a buddy system to encourage healthful activities, formed a wellness committee to organize companywide activities and programs, and promoted health by developing a mile-long walking course within the plant.

In terms of controlling high blood pressure, weight loss, and smoking cessation, programs at sites three and four—both of which relied on interpersonal contact to motivate healthy behavior—were the most successful over a three-year period. Overall participation in on-site physical fitness activities was greatest at sites two and four, but workers used the physical facilities at site two less frequently over time.

In terms of cost, the health education program (site one) was the least expensive; the physical facilities (site two) the most expensive. In addition, the health education program and the physical facilities approach were equally effective in encouraging healthy behavior. Sites three and four were similar in their benefits, and both were more effective in promoting employee health. The researchers concluded that the most cost-effective health programs have follow-up outreach and counseling, and they offer employees a variety of health promotion activities.

Establishing a health promotion program does not guarantee employees will use the program. In one study of employee motivation to achieve exercise goals (Harrison & Liska, 1994), researchers looked at the role of goal commitment. Results from the study showed that employees were more likely to exercise if they were committed to their goal, and they were more likely to be committed if they found the goal attractive and had higher self-efficacy. Employees who complained more about their health, took more sick leave, smoked, or were obese all perceived less efficacy and more barriers to achieving the exercise goal.

In a review of employee fitness and wellness programs, two researchers (Gebhardt & Crump, 1990) identified four elements that contribute to successful employer-sponsored health promotion programs. First, goals and objectives of the program should be developed through consultation with management, employees, health and fitness specialists, psychologists, and labor officials. These goals must be achievable, quantifiable, and congruent with the organization's goals.

Second, management must demonstrate its long-term commitment to a health promotion program, and quality staff must be available to provide services. In fact, quality of staff is the factor that promotes adherence to a health promotion activity (Iverson, Fielding, Crow, & Christenson, 1985).

Third, the health promotion program should have an evaluation strategy. Management needs to know the cost of such programs, as well as the benefits that come from employee participation. The progress of each participant in the program should be carefully recorded.

Finally, the health promotion program must provide outreach to the employees. Incentives must be available so that workers who are most at risk for health-related problems will participate in the program. Almost certainly, one program will not fit all employees, so the offerings of the health promotion program must appeal to people with diverse lifestyles.

Smoking, of course, has long been recognized by most people as injurious to health, with some studies showing that smokers require expenditures of $2,000 to $5,000 annually (Colosi, 1988). One study (Greenberg, 1994) followed the reactions of 732 clerical employees to a smoking ban. Reactions differed between smokers and nonsmokers. Smokers were more accepting of the ban if they had received large amounts of information about the ban delivered in a sensitive manner than if they had received little information or information delivered in an insensitive manner. Nonsmokers, on the other hand, supported the ban regardless of the way it was announced to them.

Although the initial evaluation of health promotion programs is promising, employers should be cautious about indirect effects that can result from such programs. In an interesting study of the outcome of a smoking cessation program at a chemical company and a health insurance company, Manning, Osland, and Osland (1989) found that employees who had recently stopped smoking reported more tension and less job satisfaction and were absent more frequently. Other changes included increased depression and anxiety, poorer eating habits, and weight gain. The researchers concluded that smoking cessation may result in decreased employee health costs and absenteeism in the long run, but that such programs may have hidden costs initially.

Models of Employee Assistance Programs

Although the employee assistance program model has been widely adopted in the last two decades, it would be incorrect to assume that it has been accepted universally. For various reasons, the establishment of an in-house employee counseling program has sometimes met with resistance. Some typical objections to EAPs include the lack of confidentiality, the belief that short-term therapy is not effective, and the fact that most users of EAPs are low-level employees.

Manuso (1984) developed some demographic data about EAP users. For example, males and females use EAPs in proportion to their numbers in the workforce, but typically the problems of males require more counseling sessions than those of female. Male employees also tend to wait until problems become more serious before seeking counseling. Manuso suggested that the most "at-risk group" for psychological problems are White or Hispanic married males ages 20 to 30. These males have typically been with the company for more than five years and hold premanagerial positions. Before an employee uses an EAP, the employee will typically want to know about costs, availability during working hours, use of drugs in treatment, and confidentiality (Sonnenstuhl, 1990).

In response to the varieties of employee needs and company resources, several models of employee assistance programs have been developed. These models can be characterized as external, where counseling occurs only outside the workplace, or in-house.

Typical external models include the hot line, consortium, and contractor. Under the hot-line model, callers are referred to telephone service providers outside the company. Advantages of this approach to providing employee assistance are that it is confidential, anonymous, and economical. Disadvantages include the difficulties in making diagnoses and referrals over the telephone, as well as the inability to follow up to see whether the caller received proper treatment.

The consortium model is typically a nonprofit organization funded by government agencies. Treatment is often based on ability to pay and occurs away from the workplace. Although accessibility may be lower, confidentiality is high. This model may be used by companies that do not have the resources or do not feel the need to establish their own in-house programs.

The final external model is the outside contractor. In this situation, companies hire firms that specialize in providing EAP services to employers. Employees are referred to treatment off site. The contracting model is probably the most popular external program, and presently hundreds of EAP firms provide counseling services for employers.

In the in-house EAP model, supervisors refer employees, or employees refer themselves, to counselors who interview, diagnose, and treat or refer individuals. Under this model treatment is easily accessible, but fears about confidentiality or anonymity are commonplace. The in-house EAP is likely to be more expensive than other models, and other problems for the employer include legal liability and the necessity of providing qualified staff. One of the most serious criticisms of EAPs in general is a lack of quality control with regard to the training and expertise of the individuals hired to do counseling.

The union EAP differs from the other models in several regards. First, it is usually run by union members who volunteer their services. Second, referrals are usually identified by other workers, not by supervisors or by the employee. Third, the union model is the only program that seems to be universally acceptable to union management.

Evaluating Employee Assistance Programs

Although employee assistance programs have enjoyed considerable popularity in recent years, there is surprisingly little scientific research about their effectiveness. What research does exist has typically been done by the individuals and institutions that have an interest in maintaining such programs, and it has almost all been done at large companies.

Nonetheless, some studies suggest that EAPs can create dramatic savings for companies. An evaluation of the EAP at McDonnell-Douglas Corporation (Smith & Mahoney, 1989), for example, suggested the company had saved

$5.1 million by offering workers treatment in-house. Employees who sought treatment for alcohol or drug dependency at the McDonnell-Douglas EAP had a turnover rate of 7.5 percent over a four-year period; employees who sought treatment for the same problems elsewhere had a turnover rate of 40 percent for the same period.

At Campbell Soup (Yandrick, 1992), an evaluation showed that mental health care costs declined 28 percent one year after implementation of an EAP. Along the same lines, 88 percent of alcoholic employees treated at the American Airlines EAP were not drinking two years after treatment and 67 percent of the cocaine-using employees had not relapsed (Saylor, 1993).

One study (Milne, Blum, & Roman, 1994) looked at factors that influenced an employee's decision to use an EAP. Researchers collected survey data from 1,987 employees of a large communications company about their feelings toward an EAP program. Not surprisingly, employees were more likely to use the EAP if they had confidence in it. Confidence, in turn, was the result of familiarity with the EAP, perceptions of accessibility, and a belief in management's support of the program.

Another study (Capece & Akers, 1995) looked at the factors that prompted supervisors to refer employees to an EAP. Interestingly, supervisors were most likely to make referrals when they expected social approval from other supervisors. This was true even if the supervisor expressed little faith in the EAP treatment program.

Evaluation of an EAP needs to proceed along two lines. First, the program should be evaluated in terms of accomplishing its mission. Typical questions to be addressed include the following: Is it reaching the individuals who need assistance? Is it providing the services that those individuals need? What is its "success" rate?

Second, evaluation should focus on the costs and benefits of providing such services. Although there may be substantial benefits in providing an EAP, management needs to know if such benefits are worth the costs. Typical questions here include the following: Are there fewer absences and higher levels of performance since the program became available? Are there fewer disciplinary problems? Is morale higher? Information from these kinds of evaluations can help an employer determine whether such services are needed and, if so, the best form of providing them.

One group of researchers (French, Zarkin, & Bray, 1995) developed a model for evaluating the effectiveness of an EAP. Noting that scientific evaluations of EAPs are rare, the researchers suggested four components for an evaluation strategy:

1. A process description of the structure, operating environment, and goals of the EAP;
2. A cost analysis to identify and estimate the full range of EAP costs;
3. An outcomes analysis to estimate the effectiveness of the EAP for employees and the impact of the EAP on employee performance; and

4. An economic evaluation to estimate cost-effectiveness ratios, dollar benefits, and net benefits of the EAP.

The problems that make evaluation difficult, however, are those associated with any therapy outcome research. First, the data are probably not kept in a form amenable to scientific evaluation. Case histories and anecdotal reports are notoriously inaccurate when assessing treatment outcomes. Second, counselors and clients may object to evaluation on the grounds that confidentiality will be breached. Many employees are likely to have problems they do not want their bosses or coworkers to know about, and any evaluation increases the risks that such information could become public.

Third, most treatment programs are unclear about their objectives. Defining successful treatment of an alcoholic executive, for example, is difficult: Should it be defined in terms of fewer bad decisions or number of days without drinking? Is successful referral to an Alcoholics Anonymous program comparable to several months of in-house therapy?

Finally, making a clear identification of the effect of treatment programs is also difficult. For example, linking improved performance and marital counseling provided by the in-house EAP is virtually impossible in many cases. Although the counselor may take credit for the improvement, the employee's supervisor may attribute the change to his or her own managerial skills. These differences in perspective also make proper evaluation difficult.

Worker Health and the Future

In a sense, the effectiveness of an EAP may be irrelevant to its existence. Increasingly, workers see employee assistance programs as a benefit and a possible facet of job satisfaction. Even employees who do not use the EAP may regard it as a resource and a useful part of a working environment. As suggested earlier, employment is increasingly seen as having important effects on other areas of life. Given this viewpoint, providing counseling services in the workplace seems altogether appropriate.

Along the same lines, it seems that society increasingly expects the employer to provide counseling, rehabilitative, and health promotion services for employees. Whereas employers were not even legally responsible for physical injuries on the job until early in this century, modern trends increasingly hold the employer accountable for many aspects of the worker's physical and emotional health. Employers are expected to pay for such services and to make them available to the healthy, as well as to those who have problems.

Given these kinds of considerations, it seems likely that the role of employers in providing physical and mental health services for employees is likely to increase in the coming years.

Chapter Summary

During the 1970s and 1980s, psychology in the workplace took on an added dimension as more employers became involved in helping employees with personal problems. Although this is not a traditional area of involvement for industrial and organizational psychologists, the I/O psychologist may be involved in the design and evaluation of the EAP.

Early employee assistance programs centered on rehabilitating the alcoholic employee. Typically staffed with recovering alcoholics and counseling individuals in the last stages of alcoholism, these programs were rarely successful. Such programs were expanded in the 1960s, however, as it became evident that alcoholics had problems other than drinking, and nonalcoholics may have problems as well. During this period, the focus of such programs shifted from treating alcoholism to improving performance.

Some of the reasons for the increased interest in EAPs include significant increases in health care costs, evidence that psychological counseling limits medical facility usage, changes in labor force composition, and legal issues.

Alcoholism remains the major area of activity for most employee assistance programs. Alcoholic executives tend to experience work shrinkage and have their staffs cover for them. Patterns of alcoholism are different between males and females. Recovery rates for alcoholics who receive professional treatment may be as high as 50 percent. The majority of workers who stop drinking do so without receiving any formal treatment.

Drug use has become a serious problem in the workplace. Drug abuse is often considered more serious than alcoholism because users typically try to support their habit by selling drugs to other employees. Although employers have usually tried to avoid hiring drug users, the proliferation of drug use in society has made this virtually impossible. Many employees and applicants react negatively to drug testing by employers.

Gambling is another addictive behavior that often leads to employee theft.

Stress is a physiological or psychological response to demands made on the individual. Stress can be either functional or dysfunctional, and it occurs in both pleasant and unpleasant situations. Type A refers to a pattern of behavior among individuals at increased risk for heart attack. Type As are usually valuable to employers, and some efforts should be made to assist such employees in dealing with stress.

Environmental stressors include having little decision-making authority and a lack of social support from a supervisor. Dispositional factors involved in stress include negative affectivity, private self-consciousness, and coping skills.

A new problem regarding employee health is violence in the workplace. Murder is the leading cause of death at work for women. Violence is a particular danger in small retail stores and in the health care and social service industries. OSHA has recently begun to issue guidelines on the responsibilities of employers in preventing violence.

In recent years employers have developed programs to deal with AIDS in the workplace. The most immediate problem is the fear of infection, and employers use AIDS education programs to try to minimize workers' concerns.

Health promotion refers to encouraging employees toward positive health behavior by preventing problems before they occur.

Models of employee assistance programs include hot-line, consortium, contractor, in-house, and union. Little formal research into the effectiveness of such programs has been conducted. Problems associated with EAP evaluation include questionable data, confidentiality issues, unclear objectives, and identification of outcomes. Whatever the outcome of evaluation, however, it seems that society will continue to expect employers to provide more employee assistance programs.

Key Words and Concepts

employee assistance programs (EAPs) (p. 470)
escalating commitment (p. 486)
health promotion programs (p. 494)
job burnout (p. 482)

role ambiguity (p. 483)
stress (p. 482)
Type A (p. 487)
Type B (p. 487)
violence in the workplace (p. 489)

Questions for Discussion

1. Why would worker health become an area of interest for industrial and organizational psychologists?
2. What factors are responsible for the growth in the number of employee assistance programs?
3. What are the major dangers of alcoholism on the job? Who is most at risk for alcoholism at work? Does treatment work?
4. Why did employer attitudes toward substance abuse change in the 1960s? How do you feel about drug testing programs?
5. What causes you to feel stress? When can stress be positive?
6. Do you consider yourself a Type A or a Type B? Which would you prefer to be?
7. Why is violence suddenly a problem in the workplace? Have you ever experienced violence at work? Who is likely to become violent?
8. From the employer's perspective, what is the major problem with AIDS in the workplace? How can an employer deal with this problem?
9. What is health promotion? What kind of health promotion program would be most appealing to you? What does your college or university do to promote the health of employees or students?
10. What are the considerations in evaluating an employee assistance program?
11. Overall, do you agree with the idea that employee health is the responsibility of employers?

Glossary

abilities Foundation on which skills are built.

ability to attend Factor affecting absence rates.

achievement motivation theory Explanation for motivation based on a psychological need for achievement.

action research In organization development, a research strategy designed to generate new knowledge at the same time that organizational problems are being addressed.

act-on-Other Strategy for resolving inequity.

adjourning Last stage of group interaction.

adjustment-to-stress theory Theory holding that accidents occur when employees are stressed.

adverse impact According to the *Uniform Guidelines,* adverse impact occurs when the selection ratio for a protected group is less than 80 percent of that for the group with the highest selection ratio.

affective commitment Organizational commitment based on emotional ties to the organization.

affirmative action Hiring plans that give preferential treatment to certain groups.

after-only with a control group A strategy for evaluating training effectiveness.

altering the object of comparison Strategy for resolving inequity.

alter inputs Strategy for resolving inequity.

alter outcomes Strategy for resolving inequity.

analysis of covariance A sophisticated analysis of variance model.

analysis of variance Statistical method used to determine the significance of results from experimental studies.

applied science Research to be used in a real-life setting.

applied setting Location in which research results will be applied to solving a specific problem.

appraisal interview An interview in which the supervisor and employee discuss performance.

apprenticeship Learning a trade from the teaching of a skilled craftsperson.

aptitude An ability to learn.

arousal-alertness theory Theory holding that inappropriate levels of arousal cause accidents.

assessment center Program in which participants are evaluated on a number of individual or group exercises constructed to simulate important activities at the organizational level to which those participants aspire.

attendance motivation Factor composed of job satisfaction and pressures to attend that affects absence rates.

attraction-selection-attrition (ASA) model States that similar people are attracted to similar organizations.

attributional approaches to leadership The idea that leadership is the result of attributions by others rather than the qualities or behaviors of an individual.

audiovisual methods Methods of training using films, slide presentations, videotapes, closed circuit television, and so on.

automatic speech recognition systems Systems that allow equipment to respond to human voice commands.

autonomous work groups Method of organization associated with the sociotechnical approach in which groups of workers are given responsibility for planning and accomplishing their work.

base rate The frequency of an occurrence.

behaviorally anchored rating scales (BARS) Performance appraisal method that uses descriptions of behavior at different levels of effectiveness.

behavioral observation scale (BOS) Method of performance appraisal focusing on the frequency of a behavior.

behavioral performance appraisal Performance appraisal based on employee behaviors rather than traits.

behavior descriptions in interviews Interviews in which applicants describe how they would perform in certain situations.

behavior modeling Method of training in which trainees observe and then practice a desired behavior.

biodata Information about educational background, interests, work experience, and other areas.

biographical inventory Expanded application blank covering areas such as recreational activities, values, and health.

bona fide occupational qualification (BFOQ) Standards that are necessary to perform a job successfully.

Brogden-Cronbach-Gleser model Statistical model for determining the dollar value of performance.

bureaucracy According to Weber, the application of the principles of rationality and efficiency to the design of organizational structure.

career-and-family woman Woman who attempts to balance career and family.

career-primary woman Woman who places greater emphasis on career than on family.

case study Research method in which an individual case is analyzed in order to arrive at general principles to be applied to other cases.

causality The reason something occurs.

cautious shift Tendency of certain individuals when making decisions in groups to make more cautious recommendations than when deciding alone.

central tendency errors In performance appraisal, giving everyone mediocre ratings with no one being rated as exceptionally good or bad.

chain of command Different levels of management in an organization.

change agent Individual who is responsible for introducing planned change into an organization.

charismatic leadership A style of leadership based on personal vision, confident behavior, inspiration, and unconventional behavior.

charismatic power Power that comes from being perceived as extraordinary.

checklist Format of performance appraisal. The *weighted* checklist has differing values assigned to the various job tasks; the *forced-choice* checklist requires the rater to choose one of four statements relevant to employee performance.

Civil Rights Act of 1964 First major federal law prohibiting discrimination on the basis of race, color, religion, sex, or national origin.

Civil Rights Act of 1991 Legislation designed to strengthen provisions of the original Civil Rights Act.

classical organization theory Theories of organization that emphasize the importance of structure in organizational functioning.

cliques Groups of workers who like each other.

coercive power Power based on threats and punishments.

cognitive ability test Used to measure the different aspects of intelligence, such as inductive and deductive reasoning, memory, and mathematical reasoning.

collective action approach Theory maintaining that organizations form interdependent networks to manipulate the environment.

comparable worth Refers to equal pay for individuals who hold different jobs but perform work that is comparable in terms of knowledge required or level of responsibility.

compensatory model Model of pay decision where potential employees make trade-offs between job attributes and salary levels.

computer-adaptive testing (CAT) Method of computer testing in which questions automatically adjust to the level of proficiency of the test taker.

computer-assisted instruction (CAI) Training method in which trainees work at computer terminals on material that is appropriate to their levels of knowledge or ability.

computerized interview Interview in which applicants are asked and respond to questions via computer.

concurrent validity A form of criterion-related validity that is demonstrated by comparing scores on a measure with scores of individuals known to have the qualities being measured and using their scores as standards for selection.

conference A training method where people with specialized knowledge are brought together.

consideration Leader behaviors that focus on the concerns of subordinates.

construct equivalence Administration of experimental measures at the same time applicants are taking measures known to be valid.

construct validity Refers to the accuracy of the hypothesis being addressed in a research study; also, a strategy for demonstrating validity in which a hypothetical concept is shown to be related to a criterion.

constructivism A belief that people create their realities based on the culture in which they find themselves.

content validity Method of validating a selection procedure where job applicants are tested on their abilities to perform tasks that are representative of actual job tasks.

context errors In performance appraisal, ratings of an employee's performance based on comparisons to other employees or to the employee's previous performance.

contingency approach to organization The belief that organizations should be studied in terms of the factors in their environment that affect the way they operate.

contingency model of leadership Theory holding that there is no one best way to lead, and the leader should structure the environment to fit his or her personal style.

continuance commitment Organizational commitment based on investments in the organization.

control group Group similar to the treatment group in an experiment but that does not receive the treatment.

controlled environment Environment in which extraneous factors that may affect results are controlled.

correlation Measure of the extent to which two variables are related, not necessarily causally.

correlation coefficient Numerical expression of the degree of relationship between two variables.

criterion Standard by which performance is judged; analogous to the dependent variable in an experiment.

criterion contamination Occurs when extraneous and nonrelevant factors are used in performance appraisal.

criterion deficiency Occurs when the standard by which performance is judged does not contain all the elements necessary for success.

criterion-related validity Strategy for demonstrating validity in which applicant scores on a measure are compared with some other criterion score of job performance.

criterion relevance Those aspects of performance standards that are relevant to evaluation.

critical incidents Research method in which employees are asked to describe real incidents of ineffective and effective job performance.

cross-functional teams (CFTs) Working groups created to make decisions lower in the organizational hierarchy.

customer service Meeting customer expectations to generate customer satisfaction.

cytogenetic monitoring Testing employees to see if chromosomal damage is occurring because of conditions in the workplace.

defamation Occurs when an employer makes a statement that is injurious to an employee.

deindividuation Process in which the values and behaviors of individuals are modified in order to comply with the norms of the group.

Delphi method Method of decision making designed to control for social influences.

departmentalization Grouping of individuals doing similar work.

dependent variable Outcome variables or results of a study; that which is expected to change after the treatment is applied.

designated group Individuals who are treated in a homogeneous fashion by others.

deviance Rejection of group norms.

diagnosis An attempt to understand the different aspects of the organization and their relationship to organizational problems.

differentiation Qualities that cause different part of organizations to develop different viewpoints, values, and priorities.

diffusion of responsibility Lowered feelings of responsibility within individual group members.

discrepancy theory Theory that employees determine pay satisfaction by comparing what they receive with a personal standard of what they want, deserve, or see others receiving.

disparity studies Studies used to justify programs for minorities.

dissonance The tension that occurs when a person holds contradictory beliefs.

dissonance theory Theory holding that tension occurs when a person holds beliefs that contradict each other.

downsizing A reduction of the workforce.

earnings-at-risk (EAR) plans Compensation systems in which employees must earn their way to a base pay rate.

e-mail Communication via computer.

employee assistance program (EAPs) Employer-sponsored programs that provide for the physical and mental health of workers.

employee involvement programs Employees work together in teams and have some decision-making authority.

empowerment Workers' feelings of competence.

Equal Employment Opportunity Commission (EEOC) Federal agency responsible for enforcing Title VII of the Civil Rights Act of 1964.

equity theory Theory of motivation holding that performance is a product of worker perceptions about fairness in the workplace.

equivalent forms reliability Reliability determined by creating two measures from a large pool of items.

ergonomics Study of human-machine systems; also known as *human factors psychology*.

escalating commitment Persistence in a course of behavior.

evaluation essay Unstructured form of performance appraisal in which a supervisor describes an employee's strengths and weaknesses.

expectancy The probability of an outcome occurring.

experiment Research method in which the researchers attempt to control factors in the environment that may influence results.

exceptioning Practice of allowing disproportions in compensation and level of responsibility.

exchanges In equity theory, effort a worker expends expecting to get something in return.

existence, relatedness, and growth (ERG) A theory of motivation.

expectancy theory Model of motivation that states that a worker's level of motivation depends on the worker's expectations with regard to outcomes, the desirability of outcomes, and the level of effort needed to achieve outcomes.

experimental group Participants in an experiment who receive the treatment.

expert power Power based on knowledge being attributed to a leader.

ex post facto study Study in which the researcher does not manipulate variables but simply observes what occurs after changes in an environment; similar to a natural experiment.

external validity Generalizability of a study or a measure to other factors.

extinction Removal of a behavior by non-reinforcement.

facet approach Approach to job satisfaction based on factors related to the job.

face validity Apparent validity of a measure.

facet satisfaction theory The application of equity theory to determining job satisfaction.

factor analysis Method for determining an underlying structure in data.

field experiment Experiment conducted outside the laboratory, usually in the setting where the results are likely to be applied.

five-factor theory Approach to personality based on the idea that personality can be described in terms of five specific factors.

flat organizational structures Organizational structures with few levels of hierarchy and large spans of control.

flexible compensation systems Compensation systems where workers can choose from a variety of benefits.

flextime System of flexible work hours where employees determine what hours they will be working so long as they meet a required number per day or week.

focus groups A group of people who discuss a topic of interest to a researcher.

force In expectancy theory, the motivation to act.

forced-choice checklist Method of performance appraisal designed to control leniency on the part of the rater.

forced distribution System of performance appraisal in which the supervisor is required to rate a certain percentage of employees as superior, average, or below average.

formal groups Groups that have their tasks and leaders chosen by higher management; same as *secondary groups*.

forming stage Period of group formation.

four-function typology Likert's system of organizational types.

frame-of-reference training A method for training people to do performance appraisals.

F ratio Numerical expression of the differences in the between-group and within-group scores in an analysis of variance.

free riding Obtaining the benefits of group membership without expending a proportional amount of effort.

frequencies Number of times a response occurs.

functionalism Framework of organization developed by Fayol; often considered the foundation of management.

functional principle Principle of organization in which jobs are defined by their functions.

games A method of training based on responding to scenarios.

genetic screening Testing applicants for constitutional factors that may affect performance.

genetic theory An approach that argues that job satisfaction has a genetic basis.

glass ceiling Invisible barriers that limit the career progress of women and minorities.

global approach Approach to job satisfaction based on workers' feelings of satisfaction with the job in general.

goal setting Theory of worker motivation holding that setting goals for employees improves performance.

goals-freedom-alertness theory Theory holding that allowing workers to set their own goals will lead to fewer accidents.

graphic rating scale Method of performance appraisal in which employee performance is rated on a continuum.

group characteristic bias Occurs when characteristics of a group obscure the accuracy of performance appraisal.

group cohesion Feelings of loyalty to the group.

group polarization Tendency of a group to take a more extreme position than individuals would normally have taken when acting alone.

groupthink Refers to a situation where social considerations and the process of decision making become more important than the quality of the decision.

halo effect When raters judge performance as being good or bad solely on the basis of one factor.

Hawthorne studies Series of research studies at the Hawthorne plant of the Western Electric Company that is considered one of the cornerstones of modern industrial and organizational psychology.

health promotion programs Movement in many organizations aimed at preventing illness among employees through such programs as aerobics, smoking cessation, and stress management.

hierarchy of needs Theory of motivation developed by Maslow maintaining that humans have five levels of needs, with the highest being a need for self-actualization.

human factors Study and design of human-machine systems that optimize human abilities while minimizing error; also called *ergonomics.*

human relations theory Organizational theory maintaining that interpersonal relations is the most important factor in organizational functioning.

hypothesis Statement of a belief.

hygiene factors According to the two-factor theory, hygiene factors are conditions that occur in the working environment.

idiosyncrasy credits Tolerance of the deviance of accepted group members.

in-basket activity Simulation requiring an applicant to organize and respond to items typically found in a manager's in-basket.

independent variable Factor manipulated by a researcher.

individual assessment Practice of one psychologist evaluating an individual applicant in depth.

industrial and organizational psychology Application of the principles of psychology to the workplace.

industrial democracy Occurs when workers have real responsibility for decision making.

industrial organization model Theory that organizational outputs should determine structure.

inferences Predictions about a larger group based on research with a smaller group that is similar to the larger one.

informal groups Groups that operate outside organizational structures; same as *primary groups.*

information power Power based on holding information that people need to do their jobs.

Ingroup In vertical dyad linkage theory, the workers who are influential with the leader.

initiating structure Leader behaviors that are focused on task accomplishment.

inputs In equity theory, that which is brought to the exchange.

integration Process by which differentiated parts of an organization are brought together so that the organization can function as a whole.

integrity testing Assessment of an applicant's honesty.

interest measures Psychological measures used in assessing vocational interests.

internal consistency reliability Form of reliability in which the interrelationships between responses to items are calculated and an average reliability coefficient is determined.

internal referencing A training evaluation strategy that uses only one group of participants.

internal validity Accuracy of a study or a measure in measuring what it is supposed to measure.

interval scales Scales that reflect identity and magnitude of differences between variables.

intervenor Individual who is responsible for introducing change into a system.

intervention A method for introducing planned change.

intervention theory Theory of organization development maintaining that the task of the change agent is to help organizations solve their own problems.

intimate distance Six to eight inches; the space in which the most intimate interpersonal interactions occur.

intrinsic motivation Theory holding that such factors as need for achievement, feelings of responsibility, or enjoyment of work affect levels of motivation.

isolates Individuals who are not well liked.

job analysis Procedure for identifying the duties or behaviors that define a job.

job burnout Syndrome in which a worker feels emotionally exhausted, treats others as objects, and experiences diminished feelings of accomplishment.

job description Information about all aspects of a job.

job enlargement Method of job redesign in which jobs are combined or restructured so workers can learn about other jobs in the organization.

job enrichment Method of job redesign in which responsibilities are reassigned so that work becomes more challenging.

job evaluation Procedure for determining salary levels.

job involvement Person's psychological identification with a job.

job rotation Method of job redesign in which individuals change jobs so they can learn the skills associated with other jobs in the organization.

job sample Method of applicant screening in which the employer makes an assessment based on samples of the applicant's past work.

job satisfaction Study of what makes a job satisfying to a worker.

job specifications Knowledge, skills, and abilities necessary to accomplish a job.

knowledge of predictor bias Occurs when supervisors allow their evaluations of employees to be biased by some knowledge about the employee.

laboratory experiment Experiment done in a laboratory so the researcher can maximize control over the environment.

large batch or mass production firms According to industrial organization theory, firms that produce items for inventory.

leader-member exchange (LMX) Also known as *vertical dyad linkage;* the relationship between a leader and an individual worker.

leadership effectiveness Leadership that makes a group productive.

leadership emergence Process by which an individual becomes a leader.

Leadership Grid® Copyrighted system of organization development focusing on developing leadership skills in managers.

leave the field Strategy for resolving inequity.

lecture A training method in which information is presented orally to an audience.

legitimate power Power based on a recognized right to command.

leniency/severity errors Errors in which all employees are rated at the extremes of scales.

life satisfaction Satisfaction with aspects of an individual's life.

line-staff principle Principle of classical organizational theory in which jobs are dichotomized in terms of decision-making functions (line) and support (staff) functions.

log-linear modeling Statistical technique for analyzing data when variables have quantitative properties.

management by objectives (MBO) System in which managers identify objectives to be achieved by specific dates.

managing diversity Directing employees of different cultures and backgrounds toward organizational goals.

matrix management Form of organizational structure in which individuals who have specialized knowledge join in project teams and are responsible to more than one supervisor.

mean Average.

mechanistic system Organizational structure similar to the classical model.

mentoring Occurs when a senior employee provides career guidance to a junior employee.

merit pay Salary increases based on performance.

meta-analysis Statistical technique by which data from several research studies can be combined and analyzed in one study.

mixed-standard scales (MSS) Method of performance appraisal designed to control for leniency and halo errors.

mommy track Career path that allows women executives to devote more time to their families.

motivated distortion Faking on an assessment instrument.

motivation Force that drives people to perform their jobs.

motivators In two-factor theory, opportunities for advancement, professional growth, and satisfaction.

multimedia training Training that uses computers, CD-ROMS, and the World Wide Web.

multiple regression Statistical technique based on the correlations of several predictors with a single criterion; the factors are given differential weighting as to the degree to which they explain the variance in predicting the criterion; sometimes referred to as *multiple correlation.*

multirater feedback Appraisal method where individuals receive feedback from a variety of sources.

multivariate analysis of variance Analysis of variance where there are several dependent variables.

narrative methods Qualitative approaches to performance appraisal.

natural experiment Kind of study in which a researcher has no control and simply makes observations after changes in the environment occur: similar to an ex post facto study.

natural selection Theory of organization holding that the structure of an organization is determined by economic factors.

Naylor-Shine model Model of utility analysis.

need for achievement Concept developed by McClelland maintaining that motivation results from a drive to compete with a standard of perfection.

need for affiliation Concept developed by McClelland maintaining that motivation results from an intrinsic need for social interaction.

need for power Concept developed by McClelland maintaining that motivation results from an intrinsic need to control and influence situations and individuals.

need theory Approach to job satisfaction stating that jobs that fulfill psychological needs will be satisfying.

negative affectivity Refers to having a generally negative self-concept and attitude toward life.

negative correlation A relationship in which more of one variable is associated with less of another.

negative reinforcement Reinforcement that strengthens a response because it removes an unpleasant stimulus or allows the subject to avoid it.

negligent hiring Occurs when an employer puts an employee into a situation where he or she may harm another person.

nominal scales Scales based on categories.

normal distribution Occurs when most people score near the mean on a variable and fewer score at the extremes.

normative commitment Organizational commitment based on feelings of obligation.

norming Period in which a group develops methods for working together.

norms Accepted standards of behavior and expectations.

objective criteria Output measures used in performance appraisal.

objective personality measures Measures of personality in which both the stimulus and the response are structured.

observational studies A research method based on the observation of behavior.

Ohio State studies Series of studies that identified consideration and initiating structure as the main dimensions of leadership.

OJT On-the-job training.

open learning A method of employee training in which materials are made available for employees to proceed at their own pace.

operant conditioning Form of learning in which behavior is linked with its consequences.

opportunity bias Occurs when workers have different opportunities for success.

ordinal scales Scales that reflect identity and magnitude.

organic system Organizational structure that emphasizes flexibility.

organizational analysis Analysis of the needs of the organization in order to develop training programs.

organizational architecture Aspects of both the social and work systems that are part of a complex organization.

organizational behavior Study of groups established to accomplish goals, usually with particular attention to the qualities of the groups and organizations within which individuals perform.

organizational behavior modification (OBM) Use of the principles of reinforcement to shape workplace behavior.

organizational citizenship behavior Behaviors that go beyond job requirements.

organizational climate Refers to how well worker expectations about an organization are being met.

organizational commitment Belief in the organization's goals and values, a willingness to expend effort on behalf of the organization, and a desire to stay in the organization.

organizational culture Shared values and assumptions of an organization.

organizational psychology Study of groups established to accomplish goals, usually with a particular focus on the behavior of individuals within those groups.

organizational socialization Process by which an individual's values are brought in line with organizational values.

organizational transformation Process of changing entire cultures or systems.

organization development (OD) Use of knowledge from the behavioral sciences to bring about organizational change.

Other In equity theory, any individual with whom Person is in an exchange relationship.

outcomes In equity theory, the result of an employee's actions.

outdoor experiential training (OET) Training held outdoors to encourage employee creativity and trust.

Outgroup In leader-member exchange theory, the less trustworthy workers.

overlearning Continuous practice of a behavior after it is acquired.

ownership power Power that comes from personal or family ownership of a firm.

paired comparisons Ranking method of performance appraisal in which each employee is compared with every other.

pairs In sociometry, individuals in a reciprocal relationship.

participants Individuals who take part in a research study.

path-goal theory Model maintaining that leadership is the successful manipulation of worker expectancies.

Pearson product moment Formula most frequently used to calculate a correlation coefficient.

peer ratings Performance appraisal based on ratings from coworkers.

performance appraisal Evaluation of employee performance in light of predetermined standards.

performing Period in which a group addresses the problem to be solved.

Person Major actor in equity theory.

personality A person's distinctive interpersonal characteristics.

personal power Power based on an individual's personal characteristics or behavior.

personal space Eighteen to 77 inches; the space within which most social interaction occurs.

person analysis Analysis of the abilities of the individual workers expected to perform a job in order to develop a training program.

persuasive power Power based on the ability to persuade others to follow a course of action they would not normally follow.

physical fidelity Refers to training equipment and environments that are physically similar to the site where the actual work will be performed.

piecework System in which wages are determined by output.

planned change model Seven-step program for introducing change into an organization.

population Larger group to which results from a study will be applied.

position power Power based on the position an individual holds.

positive affectivity A positive self-concept and attitude toward life.

positive correlation A relationship in which more of one variable is associated with more of another.

positive reinforcement Reinforcement that strengthens a response because the response is followed by a pleasant stimulus.

postmodern organization An organization characterized by a flexible structure, flexible leadership, and an emphasis on expertise and communication.

predictive validity Degree to which some measure can be used to make accurate predictions about job performance.

predictor Factor believed to be related to a criterion; analogous to an independent variable in an experiment.

prestige power Power based on being associated with prestigious institutions.

pretest-posttest Research design in which an experimental group is measured on a behavior or a characteristic, administered a treatment, and then measured again.

pretest-posttest with a control group A method for evaluating a training program.

primary groups Groups that arise outside the organizational structure; same as *informal groups.*

process production firms According to industrial organization theory, firms that produce products in anticipation of demand.

programmed instruction (PI) Training material developed so that trainees can proceed at their own pace; previous material must be mastered before the trainees can advance to another section of the material.

projective personality measures Measures of personality in which both the stimulus and the response are unstructured.

prospect theory Theory linking risk tolerance with the possibility of outcomes.

proximity errors and logical errors Errors in performance appraisal due to the proximity of names on a performance rating form.

psychological contract A belief that workers contribute to an organization in return for certain benefits.

psychological fidelity Occurs in a training situation when the trainee experiences cognitions, emotions, and perceptions similar to those occurring on the actual job.

psychology The scientific study of behavior and cognition.

public distance Distance between people involving no social contact.

punctuated equilibrium Theory holding that organizations evolved through periods of stability punctuated by revolutionary periods of short duration.

punishment The application of an aversive stimulus.

Pygmalion effect Occurs when a person communicates expectations that cause a change in another person's behavior.

qualitative research Nonstatistical research.

quality circles Small groups of employees that meet regularly to discuss solutions to problems that arise in the workplace.

quantitative research Research that uses statistics.

quasi-experiment Research design in which subjects are not assigned randomly to groups.

random sample A randomly chosen group that is representative of a larger group.

ranking system Method of performance appraisal in which employees are ranked from best to worst.

rating scales Method of performance appraisal in which employees are rated along a number of dimensions believed to be relevant to job success.

ratio scales Scales that reflect identity, magnitude, equal intervals, and have a true zero point.

realistic job previews (RJPs) Practice of providing applicants with both positive and negative information about jobs.

realistic recruitment Approach to recruitment maintaining that employees will stay longer on the job if they are given a realistic, rather than an idealized, preview of what the job is like.

recruitment Procedures used to induce individuals to consider or apply for positions with a particular employer.

reference group Group with which an individual makes social comparisons.

referent power Power based on providing a model of behavior that followers wish to emulate.

reframing A part of organizational transformation that attempts to change how workers view their situation.

reinforcement theory Theory used in both leadership and motivation research that focuses on shaping behavior through reinforcement.

reliability Stability of scores on a measure; replicability of a measure.

representative Used to describe a sample in which members have the same qualities as members of the population.

reservation wage model Model used in compensation decisions in which the individual determines the lowest wage he or she is willing to accept.

restriction in range Occurs when a sample is not representative of the full range of scores found in the population.

reverse discrimination Refers to a situation in which a member of a nonprotected group feels his or her rights have been violated in favor of members of a protected group.

reward power Power based on the ability to provide followers with something they desire.

risky shift Tendency of individuals in groups to make recommendations that are riskier than the recommendations they would make when deciding alone.

robotics Computer systems with enhanced input/output features.

role ambiguity Uncertainty about what behavior is expected.

sample Small group that participates in a research study.

scalar principle Principle of organization maintaining that work is delegated from the top downward.

scientific management System of management developed by Taylor that focuses on determining the most efficient method of performing specific jobs.

scientific theory A set of related propositions designed to explain a phenomenon that can be tested empirically.

scientist-practitioner model Model often applied in industrial and organizational psychology in which members of the profession both develop and apply new knowledge.

score banding Practice of considering all scores that fall within a certain range equal.

secondary groups Groups that have their tasks and leaders chosen by higher management; same as *formal groups*.

selection ratio Percentage of the total number of applicants who are hired.

self-actualization Performance at one's highest potential.

self-assessments Performance appraisal ratings based on a worker's judgment of his or her own performance.

self-efficacy Individual's belief in his or her ability to accomplish a task.

self-monitoring Concern about the impression one makes.

semistructured interview Interview in which broad areas and categories are used as a basis for questions.

sensitivity training Training programs that focus on interpersonal communication skills.

Seven S theory Theory maintaining that organizations are controlled by seven variables: superordinate goals, strategy, structure, systems, staff, skills, and style.

sexual harassment Experience of receiving unwanted sexual advances.

shirking Withholding effort.

similar-to-me errors Errors in performance appraisal where the rater judges a subordinate's performance on the basis of its similarity to the rater's performance.

simulation Method of training that focuses on creating a training environment that is as similar to the actual job site as possible.

situational leadership Behavioral theory of leadership that focuses on worker maturity.

situational specificity Said to occur when a predictor for a particular job appears to be valid only in a particular employment setting and the validity of that predictor elsewhere cannot be inferred.

skewed distribution A distribution in which most scores lie at the extreme.

social distance Forty to 140 inches; the space in which most on-the-job interaction occurs.

social influence errors Occur when interpersonal factors affect performance appraisal.

social information processing Theory maintaining that motivation is the product of factors in a worker's immediate environment.

social loafing Avoiding responsibility within groups.

social support Feelings of being valued by others in the organization.

sociometry Technique for measuring patterns of attraction between group members.

sociotechnical systems Approach to organization in which the effects of changing technology on the social structure of an organization are considered.

software psychology Design of user-computer software interface.

Solomon four-group design Research design that controls for effects from pretesting.

span of control Number of employees a supervisor controls.

standard deviation Measure of the ranges in which most responses occur.

stars Popular individuals.

statistical inference validity In research, accuracy based on the size of statistical significance.

storming Second stage in group development in which members exhibit some negative behavior as they establish positions of status and leadership.

strategic choice approach Theory of organization maintaining that systems exist only because the individuals within a system agree to have the system.

stress Physiological or psychological responses to demands made on the individual.

stress interview Interview in which the interviewer tries to determine how the candidate performs in difficult situations.

structure The framework that governs the parts of an organization.

structured interview Procedure in which all applicants are asked the same questions.

subgroup norming Practice of using different norms on a predictor to make decisions about different groups of applicants.

subject matter experts (SMEs) In job analysis, those who are most knowledgeable about a specific job.

surveys Method of research in which people are asked their opinions about a topic.

synthetic validity Method of determining validity in which parts of several measures known to be valid are combined into a separate measure.

System 1 (exploitative authoritative Organizational structure based on authoritarian exploitation of workers.

System 2 (benevolent authoritative) Organizational structure allowing some upward feedback from workers.

System 3 (consultative) Organizational structure where workers influence decisions.

System 4 (participative) Organizational structure emphasizing open and honest communication.

system-structural view Structure of an organization determines the behavior of its members.

tall organizational structures Organizational structures with many layers of hierarchy and short spans of control.

task analysis Part of the training program development process that focuses on the tasks that are to be performed.

Taxonomies Methods of classification.

Taylor-Russell tables Used to determine how many employees must be hired to attain a satisfactory level of performance.

team building Organization development approach in which managers cooperate and share skills in order to solve organizational problems.

test bias Said to occur when minority job applicants score lower on employment screening measures but whose job performances are equal to those of the majority.

test of significance Statistical test to determine if results from research are due to chance factors.

test-retest A measure of reliability based on correlating results from one administration of a measure with results from a second administration.

T-groups Interpersonal skills groups.

theoretical science Research designed to advance knowledge without consideration of practical application.

theory Set of related propositions used to explain a particular phenomenon.

Theory X View of human nature maintaining that individuals need control and will work only if properly rewarded and punished.

Theory Y View of human nature maintaining that individuals naturally seek fulfillment through work.

Theory Z Theory developed by Ouchi maintaining that the best form of organization is a hybrid between McGregor's Theory X and Theory Y organizations.

third-party intervention An intervention designed to resolve conflict between two parties.

third-variable problem Occurs when two unrelated variables are related to a third variable.

360° feedback "Full-circle" feedback in which information from supervisors, peers, direct reports, and customers are compared with self assessments.

time-and-motion study Analysis of workers' movements to determine the most efficient way to perform a task.

Title VII That part of the Civil Rights Act of 1964 prohibiting unfair discrimination in employment.

total quality management (TQM) An organizational strategy focused on improving quality and productivity.

traditional interview Interview in which interviewer focuses on any topic of interest.

traits Qualities ascribed to an individual's personality.

trait theories A belief that leadership is based on the personal qualities of an individual.

transactional leadership Occurs when leader exchanges something the worker desires for a certain level of performance.

transfer of training Transfer of skills learned in a training program to performance on the job.

transformational leadership Leaders and followers raise each other to higher levels of motivation and morality.

t test Method of determining the significance of differences in scores between two groups.

two-factor theory Theory of motivation focusing on hygiene factors and motivators.

Type A personality Pattern of behavior characterized by a chronic sense of time urgency, distaste for idleness, impatience with any thing or person seen as a barrier to goal accomplishment, and competitiveness.

Type B personality Pattern of behavior in which such individuals are seen as being easygoing, relaxed, satisfied, and unhurried.

Type I error Occurs when a researcher mistakenly concludes significant differences exist.

Type II error Occurs when a researcher mistakenly concludes significant differences do not exist.

ultimate criterion Standard that contains all possible determinants of job success.

unfreezing-moving-freezing Lewin's model of organizational change.

unit production firms According to industrial organization theory, firms that produce goods on a job order basis.

unity of command Principle of organization maintaining that workers should be responsible to only one supervisor.

upward feedback Appraisal method where subordinates rate their supervisors.

utility analysis Technique used to determine the institutional gain or loss anticipated from various courses of action.

valence Perceived value.

validity Correspondence between the measurement of a phenomenon and the actual phenomenon.

validity generalization Degree to which inferences from test scores can be transported across situations.

value discrepancy Job satisfaction theory that focuses on workers' values.

variability Degree to which the scores on a measure differ from the mean score.

vertical dyad linkage (VDL) Model of leadership that focuses on the quality of relationships between a leader and subordinates; also known as *leader-member exchange theory*.

vestibule training Training that takes place outside the actual work area in which the workers operate the same machines they will be expected to use later.

video-based assessment Use of video simulations in applicant screening.

videocommunication Telecommunication with sound and pictures.

vigilance The ability to maintain attention to a task over an uninterrupted period.

virtual reality Computer-generated interactive environment.

voice mail The recording of a message to be transmitted by telephone at a specified time.

Vroom-Yetton decision-making model Model maintaining that leadership occurs when subordinates are appropriately engaged in decision making.

weighted application blank Application in which areas most predictive of performance are given greater significance.

weighted checklist Method of performance appraisal in which the different aspects of jobs have varying weights in proportion to their importance.

work centrality The degree of importance that work plays in a person's life.

work restriction Putting limits on the amount of work accomplished in a certain period.

zero correlation A numerical expression of the lack of relationship between two variables.

References

Abrahamson, E. (1996). Management fashion. *Academy of Management Review, 21,* 254–285.

Abrahamson, E., & Fombrun, C. J. (1994). Macrocultures: Determinants and consequences. *Academy of Management Review, 19,* 728–755.

Adams, G. A., King, L. A., & King, D. W. (1996). Relationships of job and family involvement, family social support, and work-family conflict with job and life satisfaction. *Journal of Applied Psychology, 81,* 411–420.

Adams, J. A. (1989). *Human factors engineering.* New York: Macmillan.

Adams, J. S. (1965). Inequity in social exchange. In L. Berkowitz (Ed.), *Advances in experimental social psychology* (Vol. 2). New York: Academic Press.

Adams, J. S., & Freedman, S. (1976). Equity theory revisited: Comments and annotated bibliography. In L. Berkowitz & E. Walster (Eds.), *Advances in experimental social psychology* (Vol. 9). New York: Academic Press.

Adkins, C. (1995). Previous work experience and organizational socialization: A longitudinal analysis. *Academy of Management Journal, 38,* 839–862.

Adkins, C. L., Russell, C. J., & Werbel, J. D. (1994). Judgments of fit in the selection process: The role of work value congruence. *Personnel Psychology, 47,* 605–623.

Aguinis, H. (1994). Action research and scientific method: Presumed discrepancies and actual similarities. *Journal of Applied Behavioral Sciences, 29,* 416–431.

Aguinis, H., Nesler, M. S., Hosoda, M., & Tedeschi, J. T. (1994). The use of influence tactics in persuasion. *The Journal of Social Psychology, 134,* 429–438.

Aktouf, O. (1992). Management and theories of organizations in the 1990s: Toward a critical radical humanism? *Academy of Management Review, 17,* 407–431.

Albanese, R., & Van Fleet, D. D. (1985). Rational behavior in groups: The free-riding tendency. *Academy of Management Review, 10,* 244–255.

Alderfer, C. P. (1972). *Existence, relatedness, and growth: Human needs in organizational settings.* New York: Free Press.

Allen, B. J. (1995). Gender and computer-mediated communication. *Sex Roles, 32,* 557–563.

Allport, F. H. (1924). *Social psychology.* Boston: Houghton Mifflin.

Althouse, R., & Harrell, J. (1977). *An analysis of job stress in coal mining* (U.S. Dept. of Health, Education and Welfare [NIOSH] Publication No. 77-2 17). Washington, DC: U.S. Government Printing Office.

Amason, A. C. (1996). Distinguishing the effects of functional and dysfunctional conflict on strategic decision making: Resolving a paradox for top management teams. *Academy of Management Journal, 39,* 123–148.

American Psychological Association. (1996). *Salaries in psychology: Report of the 1995 APA salary survey.* Washington, DC: APA Research Office.

American Psychological Association. (1997, March/April). Task force on statistical inference identifies change and produces report. *Psychological Science Agenda,* 9–10.

Anastasi, A. (1988). *Psychological testing* (6th ed.). New York: Macmillan.

Ancona, D. G. (1990). Outward bound: Strategies for team survival in an organization. *Academy of Management Journal, 33,* 334–365.

Anderson, C. D., Warner, J. L., & Spencer, C. C. (1984). Inflation bias in self-assessment examinations. *Journal of Applied Psychology, 69,* 574–580.

Anderson, D. C., Crowell, C. R., Doman, M., & Howard, G. S. (1988). Performance posting, goal setting and activity-contingent praise as applied to a university hockey team. *Journal of Applied Psychology, 73,* 87–95.

Anderson, M. B. G., & Iwanicki, E. F. (1984). Teacher motivation and its relationship to burnout. *Educational Administration Quarterly, 20,* 109–132.

Antonioni, D. (1994). The effects of feedback accountability on upward appraisal ratings. *Personnel Psychology, 47,* 349–356.

Argyris, C. (1970). *Intervention theory and method.* Reading, MA: Addison-Wesley.

Arthur, J. B. (1994). Effect of human resource systems on manufacturing performance and turnover. *Academy of Management Journal, 37,* 670–687.

Arthur, W., Jr., & Bennett, W., Jr. (1995). The international assignee: The relative importance of factors perceived to contribute to success. *Personnel Psychology, 48,* 99–114.

Arvey, R. D. (1979a). *Fairness in selecting employees.* Reading, MA: Addison-Wesley.

Arvey, R. D. (1979b). Unfair discrimination in the employment interview: Legal and psychological aspects. *Psychological Bulletin, 86,* 736–765.

Arvey, R. D., Bouchard, T. J., Jr., Segal, N. L., & Abraham, L. M. (1989). Job satisfaction: Environmental and genetic components. *Journal of Applied Psychology, 74,* 187–192.

Arvey, R. D., Landon, T. E., Nutting, S. M., & Maxwell, S. E. (1992). Development of physical ability tests for police officers: A construct validity approach. *Journal of Applied Psychology, 77,* 996–1013.

Arvey, R. D., Maxwell, S. E., & Salas, E. (1992). The relative power of training evaluation designs under different cost configurations. *Journal of Applied Psychology, 77,* 155–160.

Arvey, R. D., Miller, H. E., Gould, R., & Burch, P. (1987). Interview validity for selecting sales clerks. *Personnel Psychology, 40,* 1–12.

Arvey, R. D., Strickland, W., Drauden, G., & Martin, C. (1990). Motivational components of test taking. *Personnel Psychology, 43,* 695–716.

Ashbaugh, D. L., & Fay, C. H. (1987). The threshold for aging in the workplace. *Research on Aging, 9,* 417–427.

Asher, J. J. (1972). The biographical item: Can it be improved? *Personnel Psychology, 25,* 251–269.

Ashford, S. J., & Black, J. S. (1996). Proactivity during organizational entry: The role of desire for control. *Journal of Applied Psychology, 81,* 199–214.

Ashford, S. J., Lee, C., & Bobko, P. (1989). Content, causes, and consequences of job insecurity: A theory-based measure and substantive test. *Academy of Management Journal, 32,* 803–829.

Ashforth, B. E., & Saks, A. M. (1996). Socialization tactics: Longitudinal effects on newcomer adjustment. *Academy of Management Journal, 39,* 149–178.

Astley, W. G., & Van de Ven, A. H. (1983). Central perspectives and debates in organization theory. *Administrative Science Quarterly, 28,* 245–273.

Atwater, L., Roush, P., & Fischthal, A. (1995). The influence of upward feedback on self- and follower ratings of leadership. *Personnel Psychology, 48,* 35–59.

Audia, G., Kristof-Brown, A., Brown, K. G., & Locke, E. A. (1996). Relationship of goals and microlevel work processes to performance on a multipath manual task. *Journal of Applied Psychology, 81,* 483–497.

Auerbach, J. D. (1988). *In the business of child care: Employer initiatives and working women.* New York: Praeger.

Austin, J. T., Humphreys, L. G., & Hulin, C. L. (1989). Another view of dynamic criteria: A critical reanalysis of Barrett, Caldwell, and Alexander. *Personnel Psychology, 42,* 583–596.

Avolio, B. J., Waldman, D. A., & McDaniel, M. A. (1990). Age and work performance in nonmanagerial jobs: The effects of experience and occupational type. *Academy of Management Journal, 33,* 407–422.

Axel, H. (1990). *Corporate experiences with drug testing programs.* New York: The Conference Board.

Axline, L. L. (1994). Business ethics & OD: Organization development or decay? In D. W. Cole, J. C. Preston, & J. S. Finlay (Eds.), *What is new in organization development.* Chesterland, OH: The Organization Development Institute.

Baba, V. V. (1990). Methodological issues in modeling absence: A comparison of least squares and Tobit analyses. *Journal of Applied Psychology, 75,* 428–432.

Baba, V. V., & Harris, M. J. (1989). Stress and absence: A cross-cultural perspective. In K. Rowland, A. Nedd, & G. Ferris (Eds.), *Research in personnel and human resources management.* Greenwich, CT: JAI Press.

Babbie, E. R. (1979). *The practice of social research* (2nd ed.). Belmont, CA: Wadsworth.

Baber, C. (1996). Automatic speech recognition in adverse environments. *Human Factors, 38,* 142–155.

Backer, T. E. (1988a). Managing AIDS at work. *American Psychologist, 43,* 983–987.

Backer, T. E. (1988b). Managing AIDS at work. *Healthy Companies,* 22–27.

Baldwin, T. T., & Ford, K. J. (1988). Transfer of training: A review and directions for future research. *Personnel Psychology, 41,* 63–105.

Baldwin, T. T., Magjuka, R. J., & Lohrer, B. T. (1991). The perils of participation: Effects of choice of training on trainee motivation and learning. *Personnel Psychology, 44,* 51–65.

Bales, R. F. (1955). How people interact in conferences. *Scientific American, 34,* 31–35.

Balzer, W. K., & Sulsky, L. M. (1992). Halo and performance appraisal research: A critical examination. *Journal of Applied Psychology, 77,* 975–985.

Bandura, A. (1969). *Principles of behavior modification.* New York: Holt, Rinehart, and Winston.

Bandura, A. (1977). *Social learning theory.* Englewood Cliffs, NJ: Prentice-Hall.

Bandura, A. (1986). *Social foundations of thought and action: A social cognitive theory.* Englewood Cliffs, NJ: Prentice-Hall.

Banker, R. D., Field, J. M., Schroeder, R. G., & Sinha, K. K. (1996). Impact of work teams on manufacturing performance: A longitudinal field study. *Academy of Management Journal, 39,* 867–890.

Banker, R. D., Lee, S-Y., Potter, G., & Srinivasan, D. (1996). Contextual analysis of performance impacts of outcome-based incentive compensation. *Academy of Management Journal, 39,* 920–948.

Barber, A. E., Daly, C. L., Giannantonio, C. M., & Phillips, J. M. (1994). Job search activities: An examination of changes over time. *Personnel Psychology, 47,* 739–765.

Barber, A. E., Dunham, R. B., & Formisano, R. A. (1992). The impact of flexible benefits on employee satisfaction: A field study. *Personnel Psychology, 45,* 55–75.

Barber, A. E., Hollenbeck, J. R., Tower, S. L., & Phillips, J. M. (1994). The effects of interview focus on recruitment effectiveness: A field experiment. *Journal of Applied Psychology, 79,* 886–896.

Barber, A. E., & Roehling, M. V. (1993). Job postings and the decision to interview: A verbal protocol analysis. *Journal of Applied Psychology, 78,* 845–856.

Barling, J., & Beattie, R. (1983). Self-efficacy beliefs and sales performance. *Journal of Organizational Behavior Management, 5,* 41–51.

Barnes-Farrell, J. L., & Weiss, H. M. (1984). Effects of standard extremity on mixed standard scale performance ratings. *Personnel Psychology, 37,* 301–316.

Barnum, P., Liden, R. C., & DiTomaso, N. (1995). Double jeopardy for women and minorities: Pay differences with age. *Academy of Management Journal, 38,* 863–880.

Barrett, B., Phillips, J., & Alexander, R. (1981). Concurrent and predictive validity designs: A critical re-analysis. *Journal of Applied Psychology, 66,* 1–6.

Barrett, G. V., Caldwell, M. S., & Alexander, R. A. (1985). The concept of dynamic criteria: A critical reanalysis. *Personnel Psychology, 38,* 41–56.

Barrett, G. V., & Depinet, R. L. (1991). A reconsideration of testing for competence rather than intelligence. *American Psychologist, 46,* 1012–1024.

Barrett, P. M. (1996, September 26). Courts attack studies used for set-asides. *Wall Street Journal,* p. B1.

Barrick, M. R., & Alexander, R. A. (1987). A review of quality circle efficacy and the existence of positive-findings bias. *Personnel Psychology, 40,* 579–592.

Barrick, M. R., & Mount, M. K. (1991). The Big Five personality dimensions and job performance: A meta-analysis. *Personnel Psychology, 44,* 1–26.

Barrick, M. R., & Mount, M. K. (1993). Autonomy as a moderator of the relationship between the Big Five personality dimensions and job perforrmance. *Journal of Applied Psychology, 78,* 111–118.

Barrick, M. R., & Mount, M. K. (1996). Effects of impression management and self-deception on the predictive validity of personality constructs. *Journal of Applied Psychology, 81,* 261–272.

Barrick, M. R., Mount, M. K., & Strauss, J. P. (1993). Conscientiousness and performance of sales representatives: Test of the mediating effects of goal setting. *Journal of Applied Psychology, 78,* 715–722.

Barrick, M. R., Mount, M. K., & Strauss, J. P. (1994). Antecedents of involuntary turnover due to a reduction in force. *Personnel Psychology, 47,* 515–535.

Barry, B., & Bateman, T. S. (1996). A social trap analysis of the management of diversity. *Academy of Management Review, 21,* 757–790.

Barry, B., & Stewart, G. L. (1997). Composition, process, and the role of performance in self-arranged groups: The role of personality. *Journal of Applied Psychology, 82,* 62–78.

Bartol, K. M., & Martin, D. C. (1989). Effects of dependence, dependency threats, and pay secrecy on managerial pay allocations. *Journal of Applied Psychology, 74,* 105–113.

Bartol, K. M., & Martin, D. C. (1990). When politics pays: Factors influencing managerial compensation decisions. *Personnel Psychology, 43,* 599–614.

Bass, B. M. (1981). *Stogdill's handbook of leadership.* New York: Free Press.

Bass, B. M. (1985a, Winter). Leadership: Good, better, best. *Organizational Dynamics, 14,* 26–40.

Bass, B. M. (1985b). *Leadership and performance beyond expectations.* New York: Free Press.

Bass, B. M. (1990). *Bass & Stogdill's Handbook of Leadership* (3rd ed.). New York: Free Press.

Bass, B. M. (1997). Does the transactional-transformational leadership paradigm transcend organizational and national boundaries? *American Psychologist, 52,* 130–139.

Bass, B. M., & Avolio, B. J. (Eds.). (1994). *Improving organizational effectiveness through transformational leadership.* Thousand Oaks, CA: Sage.

Bateman, T. S., & Organ, D. W. (1983). Job satisfaction and the good soldier: The relationship between affect and employee "citizenship." *Academy of Management Journal, 26,* 587–595.

Bauer, T. N., & Green, S. G. (1994). Effect of newcomer involvement in work-related activities: A longitudinal study of socialization. *Journal of Applied Psychology, 79,* 211–223.

Bauer, T. N., & Green, S. G. (1996). Development of a leader-member exchange: A longitudinal test. *Academy of Management Journal, 39,* 1538–1567.

Baumgartel, H., Reynolds, J. I., & Pathan, R. Z. (1984). How personality and organizational climate variables moderate the effectiveness of management development programmes: A review and some recent research findings. *Management and Labour Studies, 9,* 1–16.

Beam, B., & McFadden, J. (1988). *Employee benefits* (2nd ed.). Homewood, IL: Richard D. Irwin.

Beck, S. (1981). How to cope with the corporate crook. *Journal of Risk Insurance, 42,* 14.

Becker, B. E. (1989). The influence of labor markets on human resource utility estimates. *Personnel Psychology, 42,* 531–546.

Becker, T. E. (1992). Foci and bases of commitment: Are they distinctions worth making? *Academy of Management Journal, 35,* 232–244.

Becker, T. E., Billings, R. S., Eveleth, D. M., & Gilbert, N. L. (1996). Foci and bases of employee commitment: Implications for job performance. *Academy of Management Journal, 39,* 464–482.

Becker, T. E., & Colquitt, A. L. (1992). Potential versus actual faking of a biodata form: An analysis along several dimensions of item type. *Personnel Psychology, 45,* 389–406.

Beckhard, R. (1969). *Organization development: Strategies and models.* Reading, MA: Addison-Wesley.

Beer, M., & Walton, A. E. (1987). Organization change and development. *Annual Review of Psychology, 38,* 339–367.

Begley, T. M., & Czajka, J. M. (1993). Panel analysis of the moderating effects of commitment on job satisfaction, intention to quit, and health following organizational change. *Journal of Applied Psychology, 78,* 552–556.

Belknap, T. (1996, October 28). Is the grumble gap shrinking? *Business Week,* 8.

Benedict, M. E., & Levine, E. L. (1988). Delay and distortion: Tacit influences on performance appraisal effectiveness. *Journal of Applied Psychology, 74,* 507–514.

Bennet-Alexander, D. D., & Pincus, L. B. (1995). *Employment law for business.* Chicago: Richard D. Irwin.

Bennis, W. G., & Shepard, H. A. (1956). A theory of group development. *Human Relations, 9,* 415–437.

Bensimon, H. F. (1994, January). Violence in the workplace. *Training and Development Journal,* 27–32.

Bergquist, W. (1993). *The postmodern organization: Mastering the art of irreversible change.* San Francisco: Jossey-Bass.

Bernardin, H. J. (1989). Innovative approaches to personnel selection and performance appraisal. *Journal of Management Systems, 1,* 25–36.

Bernardin, H. J., & Buckley, M. R. (1981). A consideration of strategies in rater training. *Academy of Management Review, 6,* 205–212.

Bernardin, H. J., & Cooke, D. K. (1993). Validity of an honesty test in predicting theft among convenience store employees. *Academy of Management Journal, 36,* 1097–1108.

Bertrand, K. (1989, November). Is sales turnover inevitable? *Business Marketing, 26.*

Betz, N. E., & Fitzgerald, L. F. (1987). *The career psychology of women.* Orlando, FL: Academic Press.

Bible, J. D. (1990). When employers look for things other than drugs: The legality of AIDS, genetic, intelligence, and honesty testing in the workplace. *Legal Law Journal, 41,* 195–213.

Bigoness, W. J. (1976). Effect of applicant's sex, race, and performance on employers' performance ratings: Some additional findings. *Journal of Applied Psychology, 61,* 80–84.

Binning, J. F., Goldstein, M. A., Garcia, M. F., & Scattaregia, J. H. (1988). Effects of preinterview impressions on questioning strategies in same- and opposite-sex employment interviews. *Journal of Applied Psychology, 73,* 30–37.

Blake, R. R., & McCanse, A. A. (1991). *Leadership dilemmas—Grid solutions.* Houston: Gulf.

Blake, R. R., & Mouton, J. S. (1964). *The Managerial Grid.*® Houston: Gulf.

Blakley, B. R., Quiñones, M. A., Crawford, M. S., & Jago, I. A. (1994). The validity of isometric strength tests. *Personnel Psychology, 47,* 247–274.

Blank, W., Weitzel, J. R., & Green, S. G. (1990). A test of the situational leadership theory. *Personnel Psychology, 43,* 579–597.

Blanz, F., & Ghiselli, E. E. (1972). The mixed standard scale: A new rating system. *Personnel Psychology, 25,* 185–199.

Blau, F. D., & Beller, A. H. (1992). Black-White earnings over the 1970s and 1980s: Gender differences in trends. *Review of Economics and Statistics, 74,* 276–286.

Blau, G. (1993). Further exploring the relationship between job search and voluntary individual turnover. *Personnel Psychology, 46,* 313–330.

Blau, G. (1994). Developing and testing a taxonomy of lateness behavior. *Journal of Applied Psychology, 79,* 959–970.

Blau, G. (1995). Influence of group lateness on individual lateness: A cross-level examination. *Academy of Management Journal, 38,* 1483–1496.

Blau, G. J., & Boal, K. B. (1989). Using job involvement and organizational commitment interactively to predict turnover. *Journal of Management, 15,* 115–127.

Bloom, B. S. (1976). *Human characteristics and school learning.* New York: McGraw-Hill.

Blotnick, S. (1984). *The corporate steeplechase: Predictable crises in a business career.* New York: Facts on File.

Bluen, S. D., Barling, J., & Burns, W. (1990). Predicting sales performance, job satisfaction, and depression by using the achievement strivings and impatience-irritability dimensions of Type A behavior. *Journal of Applied Psychology, 75,* 212–216.

Blum, M. L., & Naylor, J. C. (1968). *Industrial psychology: Its theoretical and social foundations.* New York: Harper & Row.

Blum, T. C., Fields, D. L., & Goodman, J. S. (1994). Organization-level determinants of women in management. *Academy of Management Journal, 37,* 241–268.

Blum, T. C., & Roman, P. M. (1995). *Cost-effectiveness and preventive implications of employee assistance programs.* Rockville, MD: Center for Substance Abuse Prevention, U. S. Department of Health and Human Services.

Blumberg, M., & Pringle, C. D. (1983). How control groups can cause loss of control in action research. *Journal of Applied Behavioral Science, 19,* 409–425.

Blumstein, P., & Schwartz, P. (1983). *American couples.* New York: Morrow.

Bobko, P., & Colella, A. (1994). Employee reactions to performance standards: A review and research propositions. *Personnel Psychology, 47,* 1–29.

Boehm-Davis, D. A. (1995). Human-computer interaction techniques. In J. Weimer (Ed.), *Research techniques in human engineering.* Englewood Cliffs, NJ: Prentice-Hall.

Boeker, W. (1997). Strategic change: The influence of managerial characteristics and organizational growth. *Academy of Management Journal, 40,* 152–170.

Boje, D. M. (1995). Stories of the storytelling organization: A postmodern analysis of Disney as "*Tamara*-land." *Academy of Management Journal, 38,* 997–1035.

Boje, D. M., Gephart, R. P., Jr., & Thatchenkery, T. J. (Eds.). (1996). *Postmodern management and organization theory.* Thousand Oaks, CA: Sage.

Bommer, W. H., Johnson, J. L., Rich, G. A., Podsakoff, P. M., & MacKenzie, S. B. (1995). On the interchangeability of objective and subjective measures of employee performance: A meta-analysis. *Personnel Psychology, 48,* 587–605.

Booth-Kewley, S., & Friedman, H. S. (1987). Psychological predictors of heart disease: A quantitative review. *Psychological Bulletin, 101,* 343–362.

Borman, W. C. (1979). Individual differences correlates of accuracy in evaluating others' performance effectiveness. *Applied Psychological Measurement, 3,* 103–115.

Borman, W. C., & Cox, G. L. (1996, April). Who's doing what: Patterns in the practice of I/O psychology. *The Industrial-Organizational Psychologist, 21*–29.

Borman, W. C., Dorsey, D., & Ackerman, L. (1992). Time-spent responses as time allocation strategies: Relations with sales performance in a stockbroker sample. *Personnel Psychology, 45,* 763–777.

Borman, W. C., & Dunnette, M. D. (1975). Behavior based versus trait oriented performance ratings: An empirical study. *Journal of Applied Psychology, 60,* 561–565.

Borman, W. C., Hanson, M., & Hedge, J. (1997). Personnel selection. *Annual Review of Psychology, 48,* 299–337.

Borman, W. C., Hanson, M. A., Oppler, S. H., Pulakos, E. D., & White, L. A. (1993). Role of early supervisory experience in supervisor performance. *Journal of Applied Psychology, 78,* 443–449.

Borman, W. C., White, L. A., & Dorsey, D. W. (1995). Effects of ratee task performance and interpersonal factors on supervisor and peer performance ratings. *Journal of Applied Psychology, 801,* 168–177.

Borman, W. C., White, L. A., Pulakos, E. D., & Oppler, S. H. (1991). Models of supervisory job performance ratings. *Journal of Applied Psychology, 76,* 863–872.

Bottger, P. C. (1984). Expertise and air time as bases of actual and perceived influence in problem-solving groups. *Journal of Applied Psychology, 69,* 214–221.

Bottger, P. C., & Yetton, P. W. (1987). Improving group performance by training in individual problem solving. *Journal of Applied Psychology, 72,* 651–657.

Bouchard, T. J., Jr., Arvey, R. D., Keller, L. M., & Segal, N. L. (1992). Genetic influences on job satisfaction: A reply to Cropanzano and James. *Journal of Applied Psychology, 77,* 89–93.

Bramel, D., & Friend, R. (1981). Hawthorne, the myth of the docile worker, and class bias in psychology. *American Psychologist, 36,* 867–878.

Brannick, M. T., Michaels, C. E., & Baker, D. P. (1989). Construct validity of in-basket scores. *Journal of Applied Psychology, 74,* 957–963.

Brass, D. J., & Burkhardt, M. E. (1993). Potential power and power use: An investigation of structure and behavior. *Academy of Management Journal, 36,* 441–470.

Breaugh, J. A., & Colihan, J. P. (1994). Measuring facets of job ambiguity: Construct validity evidence. *Journal of Applied Psychology, 79,* 191–202.

Brems, D. J., Rubin, M. D., & Waggett, J. L. (1995). Using natural language conventions in the user interface design of automatic speech recognition systems. *Human Factors, 37,* 265–282.

Brenner, O. C., Tomkiewicz, J., & Schein, V. E. (1989). The relationship between sex role stereotypes and requisite management characteristics revisited. *Academy of Management Journal, 32,* 662–689.

Bretz, R. D., Jr., Boudreau, J. W., & Judge, T. A. (1994). Job search behavior of employed managers. *Personnel Psychology, 47,* 275–301.

Breuer, N. L. (1995). Emerging trends for managing AIDS in the workplace. *Personnel Journal, 74,* 125–134.

Brief, A. P., Burke, M. J., George, J. M., Robinson, B. S., & Webster, J. (1988). Should negative affectivity remain an unmeasured variable in the study of job stress? *Journal of Applied Psychology, 73,* 193–198.

Brief, A. P., & Motowidlo, S. J. (1986). Prosocial organizational behavior. *Academy of Management Review, 11,* 710–725.

Briggs, K. C., Myers, I. B., & McCaulley, M. H. (1985). Myers-Briggs Type Indicator. Palo Alto, CA: Consulting Psychologists Press.

Broadwell, M. M., & Dietrich, C. B. (1996, February). How to get trainees into the action. *Training,* 52–56.

Brogden, H. (1949). When testing pays off. *Personnel Psychology, 2,* 171–185.

Brooke, P. P., Jr. (1986). Beyond the Steers and Rhodes model of employee attendance. *Academy of Management Review, 11,* 345–361.

Brown, B. K., & Campion, M. A. (1994). Biodata phenomenology: Recruiters' perceptions and use of biographical information in resume screening. *Journal of Applied Psychology, 79,* 897–908.

Brown, K. A., & Huber, V. L. (1992). Lowering floors and raising ceilings: A longitudinal assessment of the effects of an earnings-at-risk plan on pay satisfaction. *Personnel Psychology, 45,* 279–311.

Brown, S. P., & Leigh, T. W. (1996). A new look at psychological climate and its relationship to job involvement, effort, and performance. *Journal of Applied Psychology, 81,* 358–368.

Browning, R. C. (1968). Validity of reference ratings from previous employers. *Personnel Psychology, 21,* 389–393.

Buller, P. F., & Bell, C. H., Jr. (1986). Effects of team building and goal setting on productivity: A field experiment. *Academy of Management Journal, 29,* 305–328.

Bullock, R. J., & Svyantek, D. J. (1987). The impossibility of using random strategies to study the organization development process. *Journal of Applied Behavioral Science, 23,* 255–262.

Burke, M. J. (1984). Validity generalization: A review and critique of the correlation model. *Personnel Psychology, 37,* 93–115.

Burke, M. J., & Day, R. R. (1986). A cumulative study of the effectiveness of managerial training. *Journal of Applied Psychology, 71,* 232–245.

Burke, W. W. (1982). *Organization development.* Boston: Little, Brown.

Burke, W. W. (1992 August). *The changing world of organizational change.* Paper presented at the annual meeting of the American Psychological Association, Washington, DC.

Burkins, G. (1996, October 8). Women get hurt most in downsizing, study finds. *Wall Street Journal,* p. A1.

Burns, L. R., & Wholey, D. R. (1993). Adoption and abandonment of matrix management programs: Effects of organizational characteristics and interorganizational networks. *Academy of Management Journal, 36,* 106–138.

Burns, T., & Stalker, C. M. (1961). *The management of innovation.* London: Tavistock.

Burse, R. (1979). Sex differences in human thermoregulatory response to heat and cold stress. *Human Factors, 21,* 687–699.

Butcher, J. N. (1979). Use of the MMPI in personnel selection. In J. N. Butcher (Ed.), *New developments in the use of the MMPI.* Minneapolis: University of Minnesota Press.

Bycio, P., Hackett, R. D., & Allen, J. S. (1995). Further assessments of Bass's (1985) conceptualization of transactional and transformational leadership. *Journal of Applied Psychology, 80,* 468–478.

Cable, D. M., & Judge, T. A. (1994). Pay preferences and job search decisions: A person-organization fit perspective. *Personnel Psychology, 47,* 317–347.

Cahill, M., & Salomone, P. R. (1987). Career counseling for work life extension: Integrating the older worker in the labor force. *Career Development Quarterly, 35,* 188–196.

Caldwell, D. F., & O'Reilly, C. A., III. (1990). Measuring person-job fit with a profile-comparison process. *Journal of Applied Psychology, 75,* 648–657.

Campion, J. E., & Arvey, R. D. (1989). Unfair discrimination in the employment interview. In R. W. Eder & G. R. Ferris (Eds.), *The employment interview: Theory, research, and practice.* Newbury Park, CA: Sage.

Campion, M. A. (1991). Meaning and measurement of turnover: Comparison of alternative measures and recommendations for research. *Journal of Applied Psychology, 76,* 199–217.

Campion, M., A., & Campion, J. E. (1987). Evaluation of an interviewee skills training program in a natural field experiment. *Personnel Psychology, 40,* 675–692.

Campion, M. A., Campion, J. E., & Hudson, J. P., Jr. (1994). Structured interviewing: A note on incremental validity and alternative question types. *Journal of Applied Psychology, 79,* 998–1002.

Campion, M. A., Cheraskin, L., & Stevens, M. J. (1994). Career-related antecedents and outcomes of job rotation. *Academy of Management Journal, 37,* 1418–1524.

Campion, M. A., & McClelland, C. L. (1993). Follow-up and extension of the interdisciplinary costs and benefits of enlarged jobs. *Journal of Applied Psychology, 78,* 339–351.

Campion, M. A., Papper, E. M., & Medsker, G. J. (1996). Relations between work team characteristics and effectiveness: A replication and extension. *Personnel Psychology, 49,* 429–464.

Capece, M., & Akers, R. (1995). Supervisor referrals to employee assistance programs: A social learning perspective. *Journal of Drug Issues, 25,* 341–361.

Caplan, R. D., Vinokur, A. D., Price, R. H., & van Ryn, M. (1989). Job seeking, reemployment, and mental health: A randomized field experiment in coping with job loss. *Journal of Applied Psychology, 74,* 759–769.

Carlson, R. M., & Sperduto, W. A. (1982). Improving attendance and punctuality within a behavioral consultation model. In R. M. O'Brien, A. M. Dickinson, & M. P. Rosow (Eds.), *Industrial behavior modification.* New York: Pergamon.

Carraher, S. M., & Buckley, M. R. (1996). Cognitive complexity and the perceived dimensionality of pay satisfaction. *Journal of Applied Psychology, 81,* 102–109.

Carrier, M. R., D'Alessio, A. T., & Brown, S. H. (1990). Correspondence between estimates of content and criterion-related validity values. *Personnel Psychology, 43,* 85–100.

Carroll, G. R., & Teo, A. C. (1996). On the social networks of managers. *Academy of Management Journal, 39,* 421–440.

Carsten, J. M., & Spector, P. E. (1987). Unemployment, job satisfaction, and employee turnover: A meta-analytic test of the Muchinsky model. *Journal of Applied Psychology, 72,* 374–381.

Carter, P. & Jackson, N. (1993). Modernism, postmodernism and motivation, or why expectancy theory failed to come up to expectation. In J. Hassard & M. Parker (Eds.), *Postmodernism and organizations.* London: Sage.

Cartwright, D., & Zander, A. (1968). *Group dynamics* (3rd ed.). New York: Harper & Row.

Carver, C. S., & Scheier, M. F. (1981). *Attention and self-regulation: A control theory approach to human behavior.* New York: Springer-Verlag.

Cascio, W. F. (1982). *Costing human resources: The financial impact behavior in organizations.* Boston: Kent.

Cascio, W. F., Outtz, J., Zedeck, S., & Goldstein, I. L. (1991). Statistical implications of six methods of test score use in personnel selection. *Human Performance, 4,* 233–264.

Cascio, W. F., & Silbey, V. (1979). Utility of the assessment center as a selection device. *Journal of Applied Psychology, 64,* 107–118.

Cash, T. F., Gillen, B., & Burns, D. W. (1977). Sexism and "beautyism" in personnel consultant decision making. *Journal of Applied Psychology, 62,* 301–307.

Cattell, R. B., Eber, H. W., & Tatsuoka, M. M. (1970). *Handbook for the Sixteen Personality Factor Questionnaire (16PF).* Champaign, IL: Institute for Personality and Ability Testing.

Cellar, D. F., Miller, M. L., Doverspike, D. D., & Klawsky, J. D. (1996). Comparison of factor structures and criterion-related validity coefficients for two measures of personality based on the five-factor model. *Journal of Applied Psychology, 81,* 694–784.

Chan, D., & Schmitt, N. (1997). Video-based versus paper-and-pencil method of assessment in situational judgment tests: Subgroup differences in test performance and face validity perceptions. *Journal of Applied Psychology, 82,* 143–159.

Chao, G. T., & Kozlowski, S. W. J. (1986). Employee perceptions on the implementation of robotic manufacturing technology. *Journal of Applied Psychology, 71,* 70–75.

Chao, G. T., O'Leary-Kelly, A. M., Wolf, S., Klein, H. J., & Gardner, P. D. (1994). Organizational socialization: Its contents and consequences. *Journal of Applied Psychology, 79,* 730–743.

Chapanis, A. (1965). *Man-machine engineering.* Monterey, CA: Brooks/Cole.

Chapanis, A. (1996). *Human factors in systems engineering.* New York: Wiley.

Chatman, J. A., & Jehn, K. A. (1994). Assessing the relationship between industry characteristics and organizational culture: How different can you be? *Academy of Management Journal, 37,* 522–553.

Chen, C. C. (1995). New trends in rewards allocation preferences. *Academy of Management Journal, 38,* 408–428.

Chen, P. Y., & Spector, P. E. (1991). Negative affectivity as the underlying cause of correlations between stressors and strains. *Journal of Applied Psychology, 76,* 398–407.

Christiansen, N. D., Goffin, R. D., Johnston, N. G., & Rothstein, M. G. (1994). Correcting the 16PF for faking: Effects on criterion-related validity and individual hiring decisions. *Personnel Psychology, 47,* 847–860.

Cialdini, R. B., Borden, R., Thorne, A., Walker, M., & Freeman, S. (1976). Basking in reflected glory: Three (football) field studies. *Journal of Personality and Social Psychology, 34,* 366–375.

Cleveland, J. N., Murphy, K. R., & Williams, R. E. (1989). Multiple uses of performance appraisal: Prevalence and correlates. *Journal of Applied Psychology, 74,* 130–135.

Cobb, S. (1976). Social support as a moderator of life stress. *Psychosomatic Medicine, 38,* 300–314.

Cohen, A. (1993). Organizational commitment and turnover: A meta-analysis. *Academy of Management Journal, 36,* 1140–1157.

Cohen, A., Smith, M. J., & Anger, W. K. (1979). Self-protective measures against workplace hazards. *Journal of Safety Research, 11,* 121–131.

Cohen, S. L., & Bunker, K. A. (1975). Subtle effects of sex role stereotypes in recruiters' hiring decisions. *Journal of Applied Psychology, 60,* 566–572.

Collins, J. M., & Muchinsky, P. M. (1993). An assessment of the construct validity of three job evaluation methods: A field experiment. *Academy of Management Journal, 36,* 895–904.

Collins, J. M., & Schmidt, F. L. (1993). Personality, integrity, and white-collar crime: A construct validity study. *Personnel Psychology, 46,* 295–311.

Colosi, M. (1988, April). Do employees have the right to smoke? *Personnel Journal, 72,* 70.

Conger, J. A., & Kanungo, R. N. (1987). Toward a behavioral theory of charismatic leadership in organizational settings. *Academy of Management Review, 12,* 637–647.

Conger, J. A., & Kanungo, R. N. (1988). The empowerment process: Integrating theory and practice. *Academy of Management Review, 13,* 471–482.

Conlon, D. E., & Ross, W. H. (1993). The effects of partisan third parties on negotiator behavior and outcome perceptions. *Journal of Applied Psychology, 78,* 280–290.

Conte, J. M., Landy, F. J., & Mathieu, J. E. (1995). Time urgency: Conceptual and construct development. *Journal of Applied Psychology, 80,* 178–185.

Conway, J. M., Jako, R. A., & Goodman, D. F. (1995). A meta-analysis of interrater and internal consistency reliability of selection interviews. *Journal of Applied Psychology, 80,* 565–579.

Cooke, R. A., & Rousseau, D. M. (1984). Stress and strain from family roles and work-role expectations. *Journal of Applied Psychology, 69,* 252–260.

Cordery, J. L., Mueller, W. S., & Smith, L. M. (1991). Attitudinal and behavioral effects of autonomous group working: A longitudinal field study. *Academy of Management Journal, 34,* 464–476.

Cordes, C. L., & Dougherty, T. W. (1993). A review and an intergration of research on job burnout. *Academy of Management Review, 18,* 621–656.

Cortina, J. M., Doherty, M. L., Schmitt, N., Kaufman, G., & Smith, R. G. (1992). The "Big Five" personality factors in the IPI and MMPI: Predictors of police performance. *Personnel Psychology, 45,* 119–140.

Cotton, J. L., & Tuttle, J. M. (1986). Employee turnover: A meta-analysis and review with implications for research. *Academy of Management Review, 11,* 55–70.

Cotton, J. L., Vollrath, D. A., Froggatt, K. L., Lengnick-Hall, M. L., & Jennings, K. R. (1988). Employee participation: Diverse forms and different outcomes. *Academy of Management Review, 13,* 8–22.

Courtright, J. A., Fairhurst, G. T., & Rogers, L. E. (1989). Interaction patterns in organic and mechanistic systems. *Academy of Management Journal, 32,* 773–802.

Cox, T., Jr., & Nkomo, S. M. (1990). Invisible men and women: A status report on race as a variable in organizational behavior research. *Journal of Organizational Behavior, 11,* 419–431.

Cox, T. H., Lobel, S. A., & McLeod, P. L. (1991). Effects of ethnic group cultural differences on cooperative and competitive behavior on a group task. *Academy of Management Journal, 34,* 827–847.

Cox, T. H., & Nkomo, S. M. (1991). A race and gender-group analysis of the early career experience of MBAs. *Work and Occupations, 18,* 431–446.

Crant, J. M. (1995). The Proactive Personality Scale and objective job performance among real estate agents. *Journal of Applied Psychology, 80,* 532–537.

Crant, J. M., & Bateman, T. S. (1990). An experimental test of the impact of drug-testing programs on potential job applicants' attitudes and intentions. *Journal of Applied Psychology, 75,* 127–131.

Cresce, A. R. (1992). Hispanic work force characteristics. In S. Knouse, P. Rosenfeld, & A. L. Culbertson (Eds.), *Hispanics in the workplace.* Newbury Park, CA: Sage.

Cronbach, L., & Gleser, G. (1965). *Psychological tests and personnel decisions.* Urbana: University of Illinois Press.

Cropanzano, R., & Folger, R. (1989). Referent cognitions and task decision autonomy: Beyond equity theory. *Journal of Applied Psychology, 74,* 293–299.

Cropanzano, R., & James, K. (1990). Some methodological considerations for the behavioral genetic analysis of work attitudes. *Journal of Applied Psychology, 75,* 433–439.

Crosbie, P. V. (Ed.). (1975). *Interaction in small groups.* New York: Macmillan.

Crosby, F. J. (1982). *Relative deprivation and working women.* New York: Oxford University Press.

Culnan, M. J., & Markus, M. L. (1987). Information technologies. In F. M. Jablin, K. H. Roberts, L. L. Putnam, & L. W. Porter (Eds.), *Handbook of organizational communication: An interdisciplinary perspective.* Newbury Park, CA: Sage.

Cummings, N. A., & Follette, W. T. (1976). Brief psychotherapy and medical utilization: An eight-year follow-up. In H. Dorken & Associates (Eds.), *The professional psychologist today: New developments in law, health, insurance, and health practice.* San Francisco: Jossey-Bass.

Cummings, T. G., & Huse, E. F. (1989). *Organization development and change* (4th ed.). St. Paul, MN: West.

Cunningham, M. R., Wong, D. T., & Barbee, A. P. (1994). Self-presentation dynamics on overt integrity tests: Experimental studies of the Reid Report. *Journal of Applied Psychology, 79,* 643–658.

Cyert, R., & March, J. (1963). *A behavioral theory of the firm.* Englewood Cliffs, NJ: Prentice-Hall.

Dalessio, A. T., & Silverhart, T. A. (1994). Combining biodata test and interview information: Predicting decisions and performance criteria. *Personnel Psychology, 47,* 303–315.

Dalton, D. R., & Enz, C. A. (1988). New directions in the management of employee absenteeism: Attention to policy and culture. In R. S. Schuler & S. A. Youngblood (Eds.), *Readings in personnel and human resource management.* St. Paul, MN: West.

Dalton, D. R., & Mesch, D. J. (1991). On the extent and reduction of avoidable absenteeism: An assessment of absence policy provisions. *Journal of Applied Psychology, 76,* 810–817.

Dansereau, F., Graen, G., & Haga, W. J. (1975). A vertical dyad linkage approach to leadership within formal organizations. *Organizational Behavior and Human Performance, 13,* 46–78.

Davidson, W. N., Worrell, D. L., & Fox, J. B. (1996). Early retirement programs and firm performance. *Academy of Management Journal, 39,* 970–984.

Davis, B. L., & Mount, M. K. (1984). Effectiveness of performance appraisal training using computer assisted instruction and behavior modeling. *Personnel Psychology, 37,* 439–452.

Davis, J. H., Schoorman, F. D., & Donaldson, L. (1997). Toward a stewardship theory of management. *Academy of Management Journal, 22,* 20–47.

Davis, S. M. (1984). *Managing corporate culture.* Cambridge, MA: Ballinger.

Davis, T. R. V., & Luthans, F. (1979). Leadership reexamined: A behavioral approach. *Academy of Management Review, 4,* 237–248.

Davis-Blake, A., & Pfeffer, J. (1989). Just a mirage: The search for dispositional effects in organizational research. *Academy of Management Review, 14,* 385–400.

Day, D. V., & Silverman, S. B. (1989). Personality and job performance: Evidence of incremental validity. *Personnel Psychology, 42,* 25–36.

Day, D. V., & Sulsky, L. M. (1995). Effects of frame-of-reference training and information configuration on memory organization and rating accuracy. *Journal of Applied Psychology, 81,* 158–167.

Deadrick, D. L., & Madigan, R. M. (1990). Dynamic criteria revisited: A longitudinal study of performance stability and predictive validity. *Personnel Psychology 43,* 717–744.

Deal, T., & Kennedy, A. (1982). *Corporate cultures: The rites and rituals of corporate life.* Reading, MA: Addison-Wesley.

Dean, R. A., & Wanous, J. P. (1984). Effects of realistic previews on hiring bank tellers. *Journal of Applied Psychology, 69,* 61–68.

Deaux, J. E., & Taynor, J. (1973). Evaluation of male and female ability: Bias works two ways. *Psychological Reports, 32,* 261–262.

Deci, E. L. (1975a). Notes on the theory and metatheory of intrinsic motivation. *Organizational Behavior and Human Performance, 15,* 130–145.

Deci, E. L. (1975b). *Intrinsic motivation.* New York: Plenum.

Deci, E. L., Connell, J. P., & Ryan, R. M. (1989). Self-determination in a work organization. *Journal of Applied Psychology, 74,* 580–590.

Deci, E. L., & Ryan, R. M. (1985). *Intrinsic motivation and self-determination in human behavior.* New York: Plenum.

Decker, P. J. (1983). The effects of rehearsal group size and video feedback in behavior modeling training. *Personnel Psychology, 36,* 763–773.

DeFrank, R. S., Matteson, M. T., Schweiger, D. M., & Ivancevich, J. M. (1985, Spring). The impact of culture on the management practices of Japanese and American CEOs. *Organizational Dynamics, 13,* 62–70.

Delaney, W. P., & Ames, G. (1995). Work team attitudes, drinking norms, and workplace drinking. *Journal of Drug Issues, 25,* 275–290.

DeNisi, A. S., & Peters, L. H. (1996). Organization of information in memory and the performance appraisal process: Evidence from the field. *Journal of Applied Psychology, 81,* 717–737.

Denison, D. R. (1996). What *is* the difference between organizational culture and organizational climate? A native's point of view on a decade of paradigm wars. *Academy of Management Review, 21,* 619–654.

Denison, D. R., Hart, S. L., Kahn, J. A. (1996). From chimneys to cross-functional teams: Developing and validating a diagnostic model. *Academy of Management Journal, 39,* 1005–1023.

Der-Karabetian, A., & Gebharbp, N. (1986). Effect of a physical fitness program in the workplace. *Journal of Business and Psychology, 1,* 51–58.

DeShon, R. P., Brown, K. G., & Greenis, J. L. (1996). Does self-regulation require cognitive resources? Evaluation of resource allocation models of goal setting. *Journal of Applied Psychology, 81,* 595–608.

Diaz-Guerrero, R. (1984). La psicologia de los Mexicanos: Un paradigma. *Revista Mexicana de Psicologia, 1,* 95–104.

Dickter, D. N., Roznowski, M., & Harrison, D. A. (1996). Temporal tempering: An event history analysis of the process of voluntary turnover. *Journal of Applied Psychology, 81,* 703–716.

Diehl, A. E., & Ryan, L. E. (1977, February). *Current simulator substitution practices in flight training.* Orlando, FL: U.S. Navy, Training Analysis and Evaluation Group.

Dieterly, D. L. (1995). Industrial injury cost analysis by occupation in an electric utility. *Human Factors, 37,* 591–595.

Digman, J. M. (1990). Personality structure: Emergence of the five-factor model. *Annual Review of Psychology, 41,* 417–440.

Dillingham, A. (1983). Demographic and economic change and the costs of workers' compensation. In J. Worrall (Ed.), *Safety and the work force.* Ithaca, NY: Cornell University Press.

Dobbins, G. H., & Platz, S. J. (1986). Sex differences in leadership: How real are they? *Academy of Management Review, 11,* 118–127.

Dobbins, G. H., & Russell, J. M. (1986). The biasing effects of subordinate likeableness on leaders' responses to poor performers: A laboratory and a field study. *Personnel Psychology, 39,* 759–777.

Dobrzynski, J. H. (1996, November 6). Somber news for women on corporate ladder. *The New York Times,* p. C1.

Doby, V. J., & Caplan, R. D. (1995). Organizational stress as threat to reputation: Effects on anxiety at work and at home. *Academy of Management Journal, 38,* 1105–1123.

Doerr, K. H., Mitchell, T. R., Klastorin, T. D., & Brown, K. A. (1996). Impact of material flow policies and goals on job outcomes. *Journal of Applied Psychology, 81,* 142–152.

Dominguez, C. M. (1991). The glass ceiling and Workforce 2000. *Labor Law Journal, 42,* 715–717.

Doran, L. I., Stone, V. K., Brief, A. P., & George, J. M. (1991). Behavioral intentions as predictors of job attitudes: The role of economic choice. *Journal of Applied Psychology, 76,* 40–45.

Dossett, D. L., & Hulvershorn, P. (1983). Increasing technical training efficiency: Peer training via computer-assisted instruction. *Journal of Applied Psychology, 68,* 552–558.

Dougherty, T. W., Ebert, R. J., & Callender, J. C. (1986). Policy capturing in the employment interview. *Journal of Applied Psychology, 71,* 9–15.

Dougherty, T. W., Turban, D. B., Callender, J. C. (1994). Confirming first impressions in the employment interview: A field study of interviewer behavior. *Journal of Applied Psychology, 79,* 659–665.

Dreher, G. F., & Ash, R. A. (1990). A comparative study of mentoring among men and women in managerial, professional, and technical positions. *Journal of Applied Psychology, 75,* 539–546.

Dreher, G. F., Ash, R. A., & Bretz, R. D. (1988). Benefit coverage and employee cost: Critical factors in explaining compensation satisfaction. *Personnel Psychology, 41,* 237–254.

Dreher, G. F., Ash, R. A., & Hancock, P. (1988). The role of the traditional research design in underestimating the validity of the employment interview. *Personnel Psychology, 41,* 315–327.

Dreher, G. F., & Cox, T. H., Jr. (1996). Race, gender, and opportunity: A study of compensation attainment and the establishment of mentoring relationships. *Journal of Applied Psychology, 81,* 297–308.

Dreher, G. F., & Sackett, P. R. (1981). Some problems with applying content validity evidence to assessment center procedures. *Academy of Management Review, 6,* 551–560.

Dressel, D., & Francis, J. (1987). Office productivity: Contributions of the workstation. *Behaviour and Information Technology, 6,* 279–284.

Driskell, J. E., Copper, C., & Moran, A. (1994). Does mental practice enhance performance? *Journal of Applied Psychology, 81,* 481–492.

Driskell, J. E., Olmstead, B., & Salas, E. (1993). Task cues, dominance cues, and influence in task groups. *Journal of Applied Psychology, 78,* 51–60.

Driskell, J. E., Willis, R. P., & Copper, C. (1992). Effect of overlearning on retention. *Journal of Applied Psychology, 77,* 615–622.

Drucker, P. F. (1954). *The practice of management.* New York: Harper & Row.

Drucker, P. F. (1974). *Management: Tasks, responsibilities, practices.* New York: Harper & Row.

Duarte, N. T., Goodson, J. R., & Klich, N. R. (1994). Effects of dyadic quality and duration on performance appraisal. *Academy of Management Journal, 37,* 499–521.

DuBois, C. L. Z., Sackett, P. R., Zedeck, S., & Fogli, L. (1993). Further exploration of typical and maximum performance criteria: Definitional issues, prediction, and White Black differences. *Journal of Applied Psychology, 81,* 205–211.

Duchon, D., Green, S. G., & Taber, T. D. (1986). Vertical dyad linkage: A longitudinal assessment of antecedents, measures, and consequences. *Journal of Applied Psychology, 71,* 56–60.

Duchon, D., & Jago, A. G. (1981). Equity and performance of major league baseball players: An extension of Lord & Hohenfeld. *Journal of Applied Psychology, 66,* 728–732.

Duchon, J. C., Keran, C. M., & Smith, T. J. (1994). Extended workdays in an underground mine: A work performance analysis. *Human Factors, 36,* 258–268.

Duesbury, R. T., & O'Neil, H. F., Jr. (1996). Effect of type of practice in a computer-aided design environment in visualizing three-dimensional objects from two-dimensional orthographic projections. *Journal of Applied Psychology, 81,* 249–260.

Dunbar, S. B., & Novick, M. R. (1988). On predicting success in training for men and women: Examples from Marine Corps clerical specialties. *Journal of Applied Psychology, 73,* 545–550.

Dunham, R. B., Grube, J. A., & Castañeda, M. B. (1994). Organizational commitment: The utility of an integrative definition. *Journal of Applied Psychology, 79,* 370–380.

Dunham, R. B., & Herman, J. B. (1975). Development of a female faces scale for measuring job satisfaction. *Journal of Applied Psychology, 60,* 629–631.

Dunn, W. S., Mount, M. K., Barrick, M. R., & Ones, D. S. (1996). Relative importance of personality and general mental ability in managers' judgments of applicant qualifications. *Journal of Applied Psychology, 81,* 500–509.

Dunphy, D. (1987). Convergence/divergence: A temporal review of the Japanese enterprise and its management. *Academy of Management Review, 12,* 445–459.

Duxbury, L. E., & Higgins, C. A. (1991). Gender differences in work-family conflict. *Journal of Applied Psychology, 76,* 60–74.

Dyer, W. G. (1987). *Team building: Issues and alternatives* (2nd ed.). Reading, MA: Addison-Wesley.

Earley, P. C. (1993). East meets West meets Mideast: Further explorations of collectivistic and individualistic work groups. *Academy of Management Journal, 36,* 319–348.

Earley, P. C., Northcraft, G. B., Lee, C., & Lituchy, T. R. (1990). Impact of process and outcome feedback on the relation of goal setting to task performance. *Academy of Management Journal, 33,* 87–105.

Edelman, L. B. (1992). Legal ambiguity and symbolic structures: Organizational mediation of civil rights law. *American Journal of Sociology, 997,* 1531–1576.

Eden, D. (1986). OD and self-fulfilling prophecy: Boosting productivity by raising expectations. *Journal of Applied Behavioral Science, 22,* 1–13.

Eden, D., & Aviram, A. (1993). Self-efficacy training to speed reemployment: Helping people to help themselves. *Journal of Applied Psychology, 78,* 352–360.

Eden, D., and Zuk, Y. (1996). Seasickness as a self-fulfilling prophecy: Raising self-efficacy to boost performance at sea. *Journal of Applied Psychology, 81,* 628–635.

Eder, R., & Buckley, M. (1988). The employment interview: An interactionist perspective. In K. Rowland & G. Ferris (Eds.), *Research in personnel and human resources management.* Greenwich, CT: JAI Press.

Edwards, J. R. (1996). An examination of competing versions of the person-environment fit approach to stress. *Academy of Management Journal, 39,* 292–339.

Edwards, J. R., & Baglioni, A. J., Jr. (1991). Relationship between Type A behavior pattern and mental and physical symptoms: A comparison of global and component measures. *Journal of Applied Psychology, 76,* 276–290.

Edwards, J. R., Baglioni, A. J., Jr., & Cooper, C. L. (1990). Examining the relationships between self-report measures of the Type A behavior pattern: The effects of dimensionality, measurement error, and differences in underlying constructs. *Journal of Applied Psychology, 75,* 440–454.

Edwards, J. R., & Harrison, R. V. (1993). Job demands and worker health: Three-dimensional reexamination of the relationship between person-environment fit and strain. *Journal of Applied Psychology, 78,* 628–648.

EEOC Policy Guidance on Sexual Harassment Issues. (1990, March 19). *EEOC Compliance Manual.* New York: Commerce Clearing House.

Eichel, E., & Bender, H. E. (1984). *Performance appraisal.* New York: American Management Association.

Eisenberger, R., & Cameron, J. (1996). Detrimental effects of reward: Reality or myth? *American Psychologist, 51,* 1153–1166.

Eisenberger, R., Fasolo, P., & Davis-LaMastro, V. (1990). Perceived organizational support and employee diligence, commitment, and innovation. *Journal of Applied Psychology, 75,* 51–59.

Elangovan, A. R. (1995). Managerial third-party dispute intervention: A prescriptive model of strategy selection. *Academy of Management Review, 20,* 800–830.

Ellis, R. A., & Taylor, M. S. (1983). Role of self-esteem within the job search process. *Journal of Applied Psychology, 68,* 632–640.

Elmes, D. G., Kantowitz, B. H., & Roediger, H. L., III. (1992). *Research methods in psychology* (4th ed.). St. Paul, MN: West.

Equal Employment Opportunity Commission et al. (1978). Uniform guidelines on employee selection procedures. *Federal Register, 43,* 38295–38309.

Erfurt, J. C., Foote, A., & Heirich, M. A. (1992). The cost-effectiveness of worksite wellness programs for hypertension control, weight loss, smoking cessation, and exercise. *Personnel Psychology, 45,* 5–27.

Evans, C. R., & Dion, K. L. (1991). Group cohesion and performance: A metaanalysis. *Small Group Research, 22,* 175–186.

Evans, G. W., & Carrere, S. (1991). Traffic congestion, perceived control, and psychophysiological stress among urban bus drivers. *Journal of Applied Psychology, 76,* 658–663.

Ewigman, B. G., Kivlahan, C. H., Hosokawa, M. C., & Horman, D. (1990). Efficacy of an intervention to promote use of hearing protection devices by firefighters. *Public Health Reports, 105,* 53–59.

Exter, T. G. (1992). In and out of work. *American Demographics, 14,* 63.

Fagenson, E. A. (1989). The mentor advantage: Perceived career/job experiences of protégés versus non-protégés. *Journal of Organizational Behavior, 10,* 309–320.

Fagenson, E. A., & Burke, W. W. (1990a). Organization development practitioners' activities and interventions in organizations during the 1980s. *Journal of Applied Behavioral Science, 26,* 285–297.

Fagenson, E. A., & Burke, W. W. (1990b). The activities of organization development practitioners at the turn of the decade of the 1990s. *Group & Organization Studies, 15,* 366–380.

Falbe, C. M., & Yukl, G. (1992). Consequences for managers of using single influence tactics and combinations of tactics. *Academy of Management Journal, 35,* 638–652.

Faley, R., Kleiman, L., & Wall, P. (1988). Drug testing in the public and private sector workplaces: Technical and legal issues. *Journal of Business and Psychology, 3,* 154–186.

Falkenberg, L. E. (1987). Employee fitness programs: Their impact on the employee and the organization. *Academy of Management Review, 12,* 511–522.

Farh, J., Dobbins, G. H., & Cheng, B. (1991). Cultural relativity in action: A comparison of self-ratings made by Chinese and U.S. workers. *Personnel Psychology, 44,* 129–147.

Farkas, A. J., & Tetrick, L. E. (1989). A three-wave longitudinal analysis of the causal ordering of satisfaction and commitment on turnover decisions. *Journal of Applied Psychology, 74,* 855–868.

Farr, J. L. (1973). Response requirements and primacy-recency effects in a simulated selection interview. *Journal of Applied Psychology, 57,* 228–233.

Farr, J. L. (1976). Task characteristics, reward contingency, and intrinsic motivation. *Organizational Behavior and Human Performance, 16,* 294–307.

Fay, C. H., & Latham, G. P. (1982). Effects of training and rating scales on rating errors. *Personnel Psychology, 35,* 105–116.

Fayol, H. (1949). *General and industrial management.* New York: Pitman.

Fear, R. A. (1984). *The evaluation interview* (3rd ed.). New York: McGraw-Hill.

Federico, R. F., & Bowley, J. M. (1996, January). The great e-mail debate. *HRMagazine,* 67–72.

Fedor, D. B., Rensvold, R. B., & Adams, S. M. (1992). An investigation of factors expected to affect feedback seeking: A longitudinal field study. *Personnel Psychology, 45,* 779–805.

Feldman, D. C. (1994). The decision to retire early: A review and conceptualization. *Academy of Management Review, 19,* 285–311.

Feldman, R. A. (1969). Group integration and intense personal disliking. *Human Relations, 22,* 405–413.

Ferdman, B. M., & Cortes, A. C. (1992). Culture and identity among Hispanic managers in an Anglo business. In S. Knouse, P. Rosenfeld, & A. L. Culbertson (Eds.), *Hispanics in the workplace.* Newbury Park, CA: Sage.

Ferris, G. R., Yates, V. L., Gilmore, D. C., & Rowland, K. M. (1985). The influence of subordinate age on performance ratings and causal attributions. *Personnel Psychology, 38,* 545–557.

Festinger, L. (1957). *A theory of cognitive dissonance.* Stanford, CA: Stanford University Press.

Festinger, L., Pepitone, A., & Newcomb, T. (1952). Some consequences of deindividuation in a group. *Journal of Abnormal and Social Psychology, 47,* 382–389.

Festinger, L., Schachter, S., & Back, K. (1950). *Social pressure in informal groups.* New York: Harper & Row.

Feuer, D. (1985). Training at Three Mile Island: Six years later. *Training, 22,* 26–40.

Fiedler, F. E. (1965). Engineer the job to fit the manager. *Harvard Business Review, 43,* 115–122.

Fiedler, F. E. (1967). *A theory of leadership effectiveness.* New York: McGraw-Hill.

Fiedler, F. E., & Chemers, M. M., with Mahar, L. (1977). *Improving leadership effectiveness: The leader match concept* (rev. ed.). New York: Wiley.

Fiedler, F. E., & Mahar, L. (1979). The effectiveness of contingency model training: A review of the validation of leader match. *Personnel Psychology, 32,* 45–62.

Field, R. H. G., & House, R. J. (1990). A test of the Vroom-Yetton model using manager and subordinate reports. *Journal of Applied Psychology, 75,* 362–366.

Fine, S. A., Holt, A. M., & Hutchinson, M. F. (1974). *Functional job analysis: How to standadize task statements.* Kalamazoo, MI: Upjohn Institute for Employment Research.

Finkelman, J. M. (1994). A large database study of the factors associated with work-induced fatigue. *Human Factors, 36,* 232–243.

Finkelstein, L. M., Burke, M. J., & Raju, N. S. (1995). Age discrimination in simulated employment contexts: An integrative analysis. *Journal of Applied Psychology, 80,* 652–663.

Finkelstein, S. (1992). Power in top management teams: Dimensions, measurement, and validation. *Academy of Management Journal, 35,* 505–538.

Finney, M. I. (1996, December). Playing a different tune: Using the hidden assets of employees. *HRMagazine,* 70–75.

Fisher, C. W., Berliner, D. C., Filby, N. N., Marliave, R., Cahen, L., & Dishaw, M. M. (1980). Teaching behaviors, academic learning time, and student achievement: An overview. In C. Denham & A. Lieberman (Eds.), *Time to learn.* Washington, DC: National Institute of Education.

Fitts, P. M., & Jones, R. E. (1961). Analysis of factors contributing to 460 "pilot-error" experiences in operating aircraft controls. In H. W. Sinaiko (Ed.), *Selected papers on human factors in the design and use of control systems.* New York: Dover.

Flanagan, J. C. (1954). The critical incident technique. *Psychological Bulletin, 51,* 327–358.

Fleishman, E. A. (1957). The Leadership Opinion Questionnaire. In R. M. Stogdill & A. E. Coons (Eds.), *Leader behavior: Its description and measurement.* Columbus: Ohio State University, Bureau of Business Research.

Fleishman, E. A. (1975). Toward a taxonomy of human performance. *American Psychologist, 30,* 1127–1149.

Fleishman, E. A., & Hogan, J. C. (1978). *A taxonomic method for assessing the physical requirements of jobs.* Washington, DC: Advanced Research Resources Organization.

Fleishman, E. A., & Quaintance, M. K. (1984). *Taxonomies of human performance: The description of human tasks.* New York: Academic Press.

Fogli, L., Hulin, C. L., & Blood, M. R. (1971). Development of first level behavioral job criteria. *Journal of Applied Psychology, 55,* 3–8.

Follette, W. T., & Cummings, N. A. (1967). Psychiatric services and medical utilization in a prepaid health plan setting. *Medical Care, 5,* 25–35.

Fondas, N. (1997). Feminization unveiled: Management qualities in contemporary writings. *Academy of Management Review, 22,* 257–282.

Ford, J. D., & Ford, L. W. (1995). The role of conversations in producing intentional change in organizations. *Academy of Management Review, 20,* 541–570.

Ford, J. K., & Noe, R. A. (1987). Self-assessed training needs: The effects of attitudes towards training, managerial level, and function. *Personnel Psychology, 40,* 39–53.

Ford, J. K., Quiñones, M. A., Sego, D. J., & Sorra, J. S. (1992). Factors affecting the opportunity to perform trained tasks on the job. *Personnel Psychology, 45,* 511–527.

Ford, J. K., Smith, E. M., Sego, D. J., & Quiñones, M. A. (1993). Impact of task experience and individual factors on training-emphasis ratings. *Journal of Applied Psychology, 78,* 583–590.

Forsythe, S., Drake, M. F., & Cox, C. E. (1985). Influence of applicant's dress on interviewer's selection decisions. *Journal of Applied Psychology, 70,* 374–378.

Fox, M. L., Dwyer, D. J., & Ganster, D. C. (1993). Effects of stressful job demands and control on physiological and attitudinal outcomes in a hospital setting. *Academy of Management Journal, 36,* 289–318.

Frayne, C. A., & Latham, G. P. (1987). Application of social learning theory to employee self-management of attendance. *Journal of Applied Psychology, 72,* 387–392.

Freeman, J. (1990). Organizational life cycle and natural selection. In B. M. Staw & L. L. Cummings (Eds.), *The evolution and adaptation of organizations.* Greenwich, CT: JAI Press.

Freeman, R. B., & Medoff, J. L. (1982). Substitution between production labor and other inputs in unionized and nonunionized manufacturing. *Review of Economics and Statistics, 64,* 220–233.

French, J. R. P., Jr., Caplan, R. D., & Harrison, R. V. (1982). *The mechanisms of job stress and strain.* New York: Wiley.

French, J. R. P., Jr., & Raven, B. (1959). The bases of social power. In D. Cartwright (Ed.), *Studies in social power.* Ann Arbor: University of Michigan, Institute for Social Research.

French, M. T., Zarkin, G. A., & Bray, J. W. (1995). A methodology for evaluating the costs and benefits of employee assistance programs. *Journal of Drug Issues, 25,* 451–470.

French, W. L., & Bell, C. H., Jr. (1978, 1984). *Organization development: Behavioral science interventions for organization improvement* (2nd & 3rd eds.). Englewood Cliffs, NJ: Prentice-Hall.

Fried, Y., & Tiegs, R. B. (1995). Supervisors' role conflict and role ambiguity differential relations with performance ratings of subordinates and the moderating effect of screening ability. *Journal of Applied Psychology, 80,* 282–291.

Friedman, D. E. (1989). Impact of child care on the bottom line. In Commission on Workforce Quality and Labor Market Efficiency, *Investing in people: A strategy to address America's workforce crisis* (vol. 2, pp. 1427–1476). Washington, DC: U.S. Department of Labor.

Friedman, M., & Rosenman, R. (1974). *Type A behavior and your heart.* New York: Knopf.

Frohman, M. A., & Sashkin, M. (1970, October). The practice of organizational development: A selective review [Technical Report]. Ann Arbor: University of Michigan, Institute for Social Research.

Frone, M. R., & McFarlin, D. B. (1989). Chronic occupational stressor, self-focused attention, and well-being: Testing a cybernetic model of stress. *Journal of Applied Psychology, 74,* 876–883.

Frone, M. R., Russell, M., & Cooper, M. L. (1992). Antecedents and outcomes of work-family conflict: Testing a model of the work-family interface. *Journal of Applied Psychology, 77,* 65–78.

Fulgham, J. B. (1984). The newest balancing act: A comparable worth study. *Personnel Journal, 63,* 32–38.

Fullagar, C. J. A., Gallagher, D. G., Gordon, M. E., & Clark, P. F. (1995). Impact of early socialization on union commitment and participation: A longitudinal study. *Journal of Applied Psychology, 80,* 147–157.

Galagan, P. A. (1991, December). Training delivers results to Federal Express. *Training & Development,* 27–33.

Galbraith, J. R. (1971). Matrix organization designs: How to combine functional and project forms. *Business Horizons, 8,* 29–40.

Galbraith, J. R. (1994). *Competing with flexible lateral organizations* (2nd ed.). Reading, MA: Addison-Wesley.

Gallupe, R. B., Dennis, A. R., Cooper, W. H., Valacich, J. S., Bastianutti, L. M., & Nunamaker, J. F., Jr. (1992). Electronic brainstorming and group size. *Academy of Management Journal, 35,* 350–369.

Ganster, D. C., Fusilier, M. R., & Mayes, B. T. (1986). Role of social support in the experience of stress at work. *Journal of Applied Psychology, 71,* 102–110.

Ganster, D. C., Schaubroeck, J., Sime, W. E., & Mayes, B. T. (1991). The nomological validity of the Type A personality among employed adults. *Journal of Applied Psychology, 76,* 143–168.

Ganster, D. C., Williams, S., & Poppler, P. (1991). Does training in problem solving improve the quality of group decisions? *Journal of Applied Psychology, 76,* 479–483.

Ganzach, Y. (1995). Negativity (and positivity) in performance evaluation: Three field studies. *Journal of Applied Psychology, 81,* 491–499.

Gassaway, D. (1987, December). Noise reduction ratings describe current hearing protection devices. *Occupational Health & Safety, 42–50.*

Gatewood, R. D., Gowan, M. A., & Lautenschlager, G. J. (1993). Corporate image, recruitment image, and initial job choice decisions. *Academy of Management Journal, 36,* 414–427.

Gaugler, B. B., Rosenthal, D. B., Thornton, G. C., III, & Bentson, C. (1987). Meta-analyses of assessment center validity. *Journal of Applied Psychology, 72,* 493–511.

Gebhardt, D. L., & Crump, C. E. (1990). Employee fitness and wellness programs in the workplace. *American Psychologist, 45,* 262–272.

Gellatly, I. R. (1996). Conscientiousness and task performance: Test of a cognitive process model. *Journal of Applied Psychology, 81,* 474–482.

George, J. M. (1989). Mood and absence. *Journal of Applied Psychology, 74,* 317–324.

George, J. M. (1990). Personality, affect, and behavior in groups. *Journal of Applied Psychology, 75,* 107–116.

George, J. M. (1991). State or trait: Effects of positive mood on prosocial behaviors at work. *Journal of Applied Psychology, 76,* 299–307.

George, J. M. (1992). Extrinsic and intrinsic origins of perceived social loafing in organizations. *Academy of Management Journal, 35,* 191–202.

George, J. M., & Bettenhausen, K. (1990). Understanding prosocial behavior, sales performance, and turnover: A group-level analysis in a service context. *Journal of Applied Psychology, 75,* 698–709.

George, J. M., & James, L. R. (1993). Personality, affect, and behavior in groups revisited: Comment on aggregation, levels of analysis, and a recent application of within and between analysis. *Journal of Applied Psychology, 78,* 798–804.

George, J. M., & Jones, G. R. (1996). The experience of work and turnover intentions: Interactive effects of value attainment, job satisfaction, and positive mood. *Journal of Applied Psychology, 81,* 318–325.

George, J. M., Reed, T. F., Ballard, K. A., Colin, J., & Fielding, J. (1993). Contact with AIDS patients as a source of work-related distress: Effects of organizational and social support. *Academy of Management Journal, 36,* 157–171.

Georgopoulos, B. S., Mahoney, G. M., & Jones, N. W. (1957). A path-goal approach to productivity. *Journal of Applied Psychology, 41,* 345–353.

Gerhart, B. (1987, August). *The prediction of voluntary turnover using behavioral intentions, job satisfaction, and area unemployment rates.* Paper presented at the meeting of the National Academy of Management, New Orleans.

Gerhart, B. (1990a). Gender differences in current and starting salaries: The role of performance, college major, and job title. *Industrial and Labor Relations Review, 43,* 418–433.

Gerhart, B. (1990b). Voluntary turnover and alternative job opportunities. *Journal of Applied Psychology, 75,* 467–476.

Gerhart, B., & Rynes, S. (1991). Determinants and consequences of salary negotiations by male and female MBA graduates. *Journal of Applied Psychology, 76,* 256–262.

Gersick, C. J. G. (1988). Time and transition in work teams: Toward a new model of group development. *Academy of Management Journal, 31,* 9–41.

Gersick, C. J. G. (1989). Marking time: Transitions in task groups. *Academy of Management Journal, 32,* 274–309.

Gersick, C. J. G. (1991). Revolutionary change theories: A multilevel exploration of the punctuated equilibrium paradigm. *Academy of Management Review, 16,* 10–36.

Ghidina, M. J. (1992). Social relations and the definition of work: Identify management in a low-status occupation. *Qualitative Sociology, 15,* 73–85.

Ghiselli, E. E. (1966). The validity of a personnel interview. *Personnel Psychology, 19,* 389–395.

Ghiselli, E. E. (1973). The validity of aptitude tests in personnel selection. *Personnel Psychology, 26,* 461–477.

Gifford, D. (1984, May). The status of flexible compensation. *Personnel Administrator,* 19–25.

Giles, W. F., & Mossholder, K. W. (1990). Employee reactions to contextual and session components of performance appraisal. *Journal of Applied Psychology, 75,* 371–377.

Gilliland, S. W. (1993). The perceived fairness of selection systems: An organizational justice perspective. *Academy of Management Review, 18,* 694–734.

Ginnett, R. C. (1990). The airline cockpit crew. In J. R. Hackman (Ed.), *Groups that work (and those that don't): Increasing conditions for effective teamwork.* San Francisco: Jossey-Bass.

Gist, M. E. (1989). The influence of training method on self-efficacy and idea generation among managers. *Personnel Psychology, 42,* 787–805.

Gist, M. E., Bavetta, A. G., & Stevens, C. K. (1990). Transfer training method: Its influence on skill generalization, skill repetition, and performance level. *Personnel Psychology, 43,* 501–523.

Gist, M. E., & Mitchell, T. R. (1992). Self-efficacy: A theoretical analysis of its determinants and malleability. *Academy of Management Review, 17,* 183–211.

Gist, M. E., Schwoerer, C., & Rosen, B. (1989). Effects of alternative training methods on self-efficacy and performance in computer software training. *Journal of Applied Psychology, 74,* 884–891.

Gist, M. E., Stevens, C. K., & Bavetta, A. G. (1991). Effects of self-efficacy and post-training intervention on the acquisition and maintenance of complex interpersonal skills. *Personnel Psychology, 44,* 837–861.

Glass, G. V. (1976). Primary, secondary, and meta-analysis of research. *Educational Researcher, 5,* 3–8.

Glenn, N. D., & Weaver, C. N. (1985). Age, cohort, and reported job satisfaction in the United States. In A. S. Blau (Ed.), *Current perspectives on aging and the life cycle. A research annual* (Vol. 1). Greenwich, CT: JAI Press.

Goff, S. J., Mount, M. K., & Jamison, R. L. (1990). Employer supported child care, work/family conflict and absenteeism: A field study. *Personnel Psychology, 43,* 793–809.

Goffin, R. D., Rothstein, M. G., & Johnston, W. G. (1996). Personality testing and the assessment center: Incremental validity for managerial selection. *Journal of Applied Psychology, 81,* 746–756.

Goktepe, J. R., & Schneier, C. E. (1989). Role of sex, gender roles, and attraction in predicting emergent leaders. *Journal of Applied Psychology, 74,* 165–167.

Goldstein, I. L. (1986, 1992). *Training* (2nd & 3rd eds.). Monterey, CA: Brooks/Cole.

Goodale, J. G. (1989). Effective employment interviewing. In R. W. Eder & G. R. Ferris (Eds.), *The employment interview: Theory, research, and practice.* Newbury Park, CA: Sage.

Goodman, P. S., & Garber, S. (1988). Absenteeism and accidents in a dangerous environment: Empirical analysis of underground coal mines. *Journal of Applied Psychology, 73,* 81–86.

Goodman, P. S., & Leyden, D. P. (1991). Familiarity and group productivity. *Journal of Applied Psychology, 76,* 578–586.

Goodstein, J. (1996). Employer involvement in eldercare: An organizational adaptation perspective. *Academy of Management Journal, 38,* 1657–1671.

Goodstein, J. D. (1994). Institutional pressures and strategic responsiveness: Employer involvement in work-family issues. *Academy of Management Journal 37,* 350–382.

Goodstein, L. D. (1990). A case study in effective organization change toward high involvement management. In D. B. Fishman & C. Cherniss (Eds.), *The human side of corporate competitiveness.* Newbury Park, CA: Sage.

Gordon, G. G. (1991). Industry determinants of organizational culture. *Academy of Management Review, 16,* 396–415.

Gough, H. G. (1975). *Manual for the California Psychological Inventory.* Palo Alto, CA: Consulting Psychologists Press.

Gove, W. R., & Zeiss, C. (1987). Multiple roles and happiness. In F. Crosby (Ed.), *Spouse, parent, worker.* New Haven, CT: Yale University Press.

Gower, D. W., Jr., & Casali, J. G. (1994). Speech intelligibility and protective effectiveness of selected active noise reduction and conventional communications headsets. *Human Factors, 36,* 350–367.

Graen, G. B., Liden, R., & Hoel, W. (1982). Role of leadership in the employee withdrawal process. *Journal of Applied Psychology, 67,* 868–872.

Graen, G. B., & Scandura, T. A. (1987). Toward a psychology of dyadic organizing. In L. L. Cummings & B. M. Staw (Eds.), *Research in organizational behavior* (Vol. 9). Greenwich, CT: JAI Press.

Granfield, R., & Cloud, W. (1996). The elephant that no one sees: Natural recovery among middle-class addicts. *Journal of Drug Issues, 26,* 45–61.

Graves, L. M., & Powell, G. N. (1988). An investigation of sex discrimination in recruiters' evaluations of actual applicants. *Journal of Applied Psychology, 73,* 20–29.

Graves, L. M., & Powell, G. N. (1995). The effect of sex similarity on recruiters' evaluations of actual applicants: A test of the similarity-attraction paradigm. *Personnel Psychology, 48,* 85–98.

Gray, J. L., & Starke, F. A. (1984). *Organizational behavior: Concepts and applications* (3rd ed.). Columbus, OH: Charles E. Merrill.

Greenberg, J. (1988). Equity and workplace status: A field experiment. *Journal of Applied Psychology, 73,* 606–613.

Greenberg, J. (1989). Cognitive reevaluation of outcomes in response to underpayment equity. *Academy of Management Journal, 32,* 174–184.

Greenberg, J. (1990). Employee theft as a reaction to underpayment inequity: The hidden costs of pay cuts. *Journal of Applied Psychology, 75,* 561–568.

Greenberg, J. (1994). Using socially fair treatment to promote acceptance of a work site smoking ban. *Journal of Applied Psychology, 79,* 288–297.

Greenberg, J., & Ornstein, S. (1983). High status job title as compensation for underpayment: A test of equity theory. *Journal of Applied Psychology, 68,* 285–297.

Greenhaus, J. H., Bedeian, A. G., & Mossholder, K. (1987). Work experiences, job performance, and feelings of personal and family well-being. *Journal of Vocational Behavior, 31,* 200–215.

Greenhaus, J. H., & Parasuraman, S. (1993). Job performance attributions and career advancement prospects: An examination of gender and race effects. *Organizational Behavior and Human Decision Processes, 55,* 273–297.

Greenhaus, J. H., Parasuraman, S., & Wormely, W. M. (1990). Effects of race on organizational experiences, job performance evaluations, and career outcomes. *Academy of Management Journal, 33,* 64–86.

Greenwood, R., & Hinings, C. R. (1996). Understanding radical organizational change: Bringing together the old and the new institutionalism. *Academy of Management Review, 21,* 1022–1054.

Greiner, L. E., & Schein, V. E. (1989). *Power and organization development.* Reading, MA: Addison-Wesley.

Griffeth, R. W., Vecchio, R. P., & Logan, J. W. (1989). Equity theory and interpersonal attraction. *Journal of Applied Psychology, 74,* 394–401.

Griffin, R. W. (1988). Consequences of quality circles in an industrial setting: A longitudinal assessment. *Academy of Management Journal, 31,* 338–356.

Grigoriev, A. I., Kozerenko, O. P., & Myasnikov, V. I. (1985). *Selected problems of prolonged space flights.* Paper presented at the 36th International Astronautical Federation Congress, Stockholm, Sweden.

Grover, S. L., & Crooker, K. J. (1995). Who appreciates family-responsive human resource policies: The impact of family-friendly policies on the organizational attachment of parents and non-parents. *Personnel Psychology, 48,* 271–288.

Guide, P. C., & Gibson, R. S. (1991). An analytical study of the effects of age and experience on flight safety. *Proceedings of the Human Factors Society 35th Annual Meeting.* Santa Monica, CA: Human Factors Society.

Guilford, J. P. (1954). *Psychometric methods* (2nd ed.). New York: McGraw-Hill.

Guion, R. M. (1965). *Personnel testing.* New York: McGraw-Hill.

Guion, R. M. (1991). Personnel assessment, selection, and placement. In M. D. Dunnette & L. M. Hough (Eds.), *Handbook of industrial and organizational psychology* (2nd ed., Vol. 2). Palo Alto, CA: Consulting Psychologists Press.

Guion, R. M., & Cranny, C. J. (1982). A note on concurrent and predictive validity designs: A critical reanalysis. *Journal of Applied Psychology, 67,* 239–244.

Guion, R. M., & Gottier, R. J. (1965). Validity of personality measures in personnel selection. *Personnel Psychology, 18,* 135–164.

Gundel, A., Nalashiti, V., Reucher, E., Vejvoda, M., & Zulley, J. (1993). Sleep and circadian rhythm during a short space mission. *Clinical Investigator, 71,* 718–724.

Gunz, H. P., & Jalland, R. M. (1996). Managerial careers and business strategies. *Academy of Management Journal, 21,* 716–756.

Gutek, B. A. (1985). *Sex and the workplace: The impact of sexual behavior and harassment on women, men, and organizations.* San Francisco: Jossey-Bass.

Gutek, B. A., Cohen, A. G., & Konrad, A. M. (1990). Predicting social-sexual behavior at work: A contract hypothesis. *Academy of Management Journal, 33,* 560–577.

Gutek, B. A., Searle, S., & Klepa, L. (1991). Rational versus gender role explanations for work-family conflict. *Journal of Applied Psychology, 76,* 560–568.

Guthrie, J. P., & Olian, J. D. (1991). Does context affect staffing decisions? The case of general managers. *Personnel Psychology, 44,* 263–292.

Guzzo, R. A. (1986). Group decision making and group effectiveness in organizations. In P. S. Goodman (Ed.), *Designing effective work groups.* San Francisco: Jossey-Bass.

Guzzo, R. A., Nelson, G. L., & Noonan, K. A. (1992). Commitment and employer involvement in employees' nonwork lives. In S. Zedeck (Ed.), *Work, families, and organizations.* San Francisco: Jossey-Bass.

Guzzo, R. A., Noonan, K. A., & Elron, E. (1994). Expatriate managers and the psychological contract. *Journal of Applied Psychology, 79,* 617–626.

Guzzo, R. A., & Shea, G. P. (1992). Group performance and intergroup relations in organizations. In M. D. Dunnette & L. M. Hough (Eds.), *Handbook of industrial and organizational psychology* (2nd ed., Vol. 3). Palo Alto, CA: Consulting Psychologists Press.

Haccoun, R. R., & Hamtiaux, T. (1994). Optimizing knowledge tests for inferring learning acquisition levels in single group training evaluation designs: The internal referencing strategy. *Personnel Psychology, 47,* 593–604.

Hackett, R. D., Bycio, P., & Hausdorf, P. A. (1994). Further assessments of Meyer and Allen's (1991) three-component model of organizational commitment. *Journal of Applied Psychology, 79,* 15–23.

Hackett, R. D., & Guion, R. M. (1985). A reevaluation of the absenteeism–job satisfaction relationship. *Organizational Behavior and Human Decision Processes, 35,* 340–381.

Hackman, J. R. (1992). Group influence on individuals in organizations. In M. D. Dunnette & L. M. Hough (Eds.), *Handbook of industrial and organizational psychology.* Palo Alto, CA: Consulting Psychologists Press.

Hackman, J. R., & Oldham, G. R. (1975). Development of the Job Diagnostic Survey. *Journal of Applied Psychology, 60,* 159–170.

Hackman, J. R., & Oldham, G. R. (1976). Motivation through the design of work: Test of a theory. *Organizational Behavior and Human Performance, 16,* 250–279.

Halberstam, D. (1986). *The reckoning.* New York: Morrow.

Hall, E. T. (1976). The anthropology of space: An organising model. In H. M. Proshansky, H. H. Littleson, & L. G. Rivlin (Eds.), *Environmental psychology* (2nd ed.). New York: Holt, Rinehart and Winston.

Hall, R. H. (1972). *Organizations: Structure and process.* Englewood Cliffs, NJ: Prentice-Hall.

Hambleton, R. K., & Gumpert, R. (1982). The validity of Hersey and Blanchard's theory of leader effectiveness. *Group and Organization Studies, 7,* 225–242.

Hambrick, D. C., & Cannella, A. A., Jr. (1993). Relative standing: A framework for understanding departures of acquired executives. *Academy of Management Journal, 36,* 733–762.

Hammer, W. (1976). *Occupational safety management and engineering.* Englewood Cliffs, NJ: Prentice-Hall.

Hamner, W. C., Kim, J. S., Baird, L., & Bigoness, N. J. (1974). Race and sex as determinants of ratings by potential employers in a simulated work sampling task. *Journal of Applied Psychology, 59,* 705–711.

Hanisch, K. A., & Hulin, C. L. (1994). Two-stage sequential selection procedures using ability and training performance: Incremental validity of behavioral consistency measures. *Personnel Psychology, 47,* 767–785.

Hansen, M. (1991, May). Study shows job bias changing. *ABA Journal,* 34–35.

Harder, J. W. (1991). Equity theory versus expectancy theory: The case of Major League Baseball free agents. *Journal of Applied Psychology, 76,* 458–464.

Hare, A. P. (1976). *Handbook of small group research* (2nd ed.). New York: Free Press.

Harper, D. (1990). Spotlight abuse—save profits. *Industrial Distribution, 79,* 47–51.

Harris, M. (1981). *America now.* New York: Simon & Schuster.

Harris, M. M. (1989). Reconsidering the employment interview: A review of recent literature and suggestions for future research. *Personnel Psychology, 42,* 691–726.

Harris, M. M., Becker, A. S., & Smith, D. E. (1993). Does the assessment center scoring method affect the cross-situational consistency of ratings? *Journal of Applied Psychology, 78,* 675–678.

Harris, M. M., & Heft, L. L. (1992). Alcohol and drug use in the workplace: Issues, controversies, and directions for future research. *Journal of Management, 18,* 239–266.

Harris, M. M., & Schaubroeck, J. (1988). A meta-analysis of self-supervisor, self-peer, and peer-supervisor ratings. *Personnel Psychology, 41,* 43–62.

Harris, M. M., Smith, D. E., & Champagne, D. (1995). A field study of performance appraisal purpose: Research- versus administrative-based ratings. *Personnel Psychology, 48,* 151–160.

Harrison, D. A., & Liska, L. Z. (1994). Promoting regular exercise in organizational fitness programs: Health-related differences in motivational building blocks. *Personnel Psychology, 47,* 47–71.

Harrison, D. A., & Shaffer, M. A. (1994). Comparative examinations of self-reports and perceived absenteeism norms: Wading through Lake Woebegon. *Journal of Applied Psychology, 79,* 240–251.

Harrison, T. M. (1985). Communication and participative decision making: An exploratory study. *Personnel Psychology, 38,* 93–116.

Hartel, C. E. J. (1993). Rating format research revisited: Format effectiveness and acceptability depend on rater characteristics. *Journal of Applied Psychology, 81,* 212–217.

Harvey, D. F., & Brown, D. R. (1992). *An experiential approach to organization development.* Englewood Cliffs, NJ: Prentice-Hall.

Hassard, J. (1993). Postmodernism and organizational analysis: An overview. In J. Hassard and M. Parker (Eds.), *Postmodernism and organizations.* London: Sage.

Hatch, M. J. (1993). The dynamics of organizational culture. *Academy of Management Review, 18,* 657–693.

Hater, J. J., & Bass, B. M. (1988). Superiors' evaluations and subordinates' perceptions of transformational and transactional leadership. *Journal of Applied Psychology, 73,* 695–702.

Hathaway, S. R., & McKinley, J. C. (1940). A multiphasic personality schedule (Minnesota): I. Construction of the schedule. *Journal of Psychology, 10,* 249–254.

Hauenstein, N. M. A., & Foti, R. J. (1989). From laboratory to practice: Neglected issues in implementing frame-of-reference rater training. *Personnel Psychology, 42,* 359–378.

Hayghe, H. V. (1991, April). Anti-drug programs in the workplace: Are they here to stay? *Monthly Labor Review, 114,* 26–29.

Hazer, J. T., & Highhouse, S. (1997). Factors influencing managers' reactions to utility analysis: Effects of *SD,* method, information frame, and focal intervention. *Journal of Applied Psychology, 82,* 104–112.

Healy, M. C., Lehman, M., & McDaniel, M. A. (1995). Age and voluntary turnover: A quanitative review. *Personnel Psychology, 48,* 335–345.

Hedge, A. (1984). Ill health among office workers: An examination of the relationship between office design and employee well-being. In E. Grandjean (Ed.), *Ergonomics and health in modern offices.* London: Taylor & Francis.

Hedge, J. W., & Kavanagh, M. J. (1988). Improving the accuracy of performance evaluations: Comparison of three methods of performance appraiser training. *Journal of Applied Psychology, 73,* 68–73.

Heilman, M. E., Block, C. J., Martell, R. F., & Simon, M. C. (1989). Has anything changed? Current characterizations of men, women, and managers. *Journal of Applied Psychology, 74,* 935–942.

Heilman, M. E., Block, C. J., & Stathatos, P. (1997). The affirmative action stigma of incompetence: Effects of performance information ambiguity. *Academy of Management Journal, 40,* 603–625.

Heilman, M. E., Hornstein, H. A., Cage, J. H., & Herschlag, J. K. (1984). Reactions to prescribed leader behavior as a function of role perspective: The case of the Vroom-Yetton model. *Journal of Applied Psychology, 69,* 50–60.

Heilman, M. E., McCullough, W. F., & Gilbert, D. (1996). The other side of affirmative action: Reactions of nonbeneficiaries to sex-based preferential selection. *Journal of Applied Psychology, 81,* 346–357.

Heilman, M. E., Rivero, J. C., & Brett, J. F. (1991). Skirting the competence issue: Effects of sex-based preferential selection on task choices of women and men. *Journal of Applied Psychology, 76,* 99–105.

Heilman, M. E., & Saruwatari, L. R. (1979). When beauty is beastly: The effects of appearance and sex on evaluations of job applicants for managerial and nonmanagerial jobs. *Organizational Behavior and Human Performance, 23,* 360–372.

Helander, M. G. (1985). Emerging office automation systems. *Human Factors, 27,* 3–20.

Helmer, O. (1967). *Analysis of the future: The delphi method.* Santa Monica, CA: Rand.

Hemphill, J. K. (1950). Leader behavior description [mimeo]. Columbus: Ohio State University, Bureau of Educational Research.

Henderson, R. (1980). *Performance appraisal: Theory to practice* (1st ed.). Reston, VA: Reston Publishing.

Heneman, H. G., Schwab, D. P., Fossum, J. A., & Dyer, L. D. (1986). *Personnel/human resource management* (3rd ed.). Homewood, IL: Richard D. Irwin.

Heneman, R. L., & Cohen, D. J. (1988). Supervisory and employee characteristics as correlates of employee salary increases. *Personnel Psychology, 41,* 345–360.

Heneman, R. L., Greenberger, D. B., & Anonyuo, C. (1989). Attributions and exchanges: The effects of interpersonal factors on the diagnosis of employee performance. *Academy of Management Journal, 32,* 466–476.

Heneman, R. L., Greenberger, D. B., & Strasser, S. (1988). The relationship between pay-for-performance perceptions and pay satisfaction. *Personnel Psychology, 41,* 745–759.

Heneman, R. L., & Schwab, D. P. (1985). Pay satisfaction: Its multidimensional nature and measurement. *International Journal of Psychology, 20,* 129–141.

Henriques, D. B. (1996, December 10). Big award in keyboard injury case. *The New York Times,* p. C1.

Hequet, M. (1996, September). Video shakeout. *Training,* 44–50.

Hersey, P., & Blanchard, K. (1969). Life cycle theory of leadership. *Training and Development Journal, 2,* 6–34.

Hersey, P., & Blanchard, K. (1982). *Management of organizational behavior* (4th ed.). Englewood Cliffs, NJ: Prentice-Hall.

Hershberger, S. L., Lichtenstein, P., & Knox, S. S. (1994). Genetic and environmental influences on perceptions of organizational climate. *Journal of Applied Psychology, 79,* 1–24.

Herzberg, F. (1966). *Work and the nature of man.* Cleveland, OH: World.

Herzberg, F., Mausner, B., & Snyderman, B. (1959). *The motivation to work.* New York: Wiley.

Herzog, A. R., House, J. S., & Morgan, J. A. (1991). Relation of work and retirement to health and well-being in older age. *Psychology and Aging, 6,* 202–211.

Hicks, W. D., & Klimoski, R. J. (1987). Entry into training programs and its effects on training outcomes: A field experiment. *Academy of Management Journal, 30,* 542–552.

Himmelein, L. (1996, October 28). Shatterproof glass ceiling. *Business Week,* 55.

Hinds, P., & Kiesler, S. (1995). Communication across boundaries: Work, structure, and use of communication technologies at a large organization. *Organization Science, 6,* 373–393.

Hinkin, T. R., & Schriesheim, C. A. (1989). Development and application of new scales to measure the French and Raven (1959) bases of social power. *Journal of Applied Psychology, 74,* 561–567.

Hitt, M. A., & Barr, S. H. (1989). Managerial selection decision models: Examination of configural cue processing. *Journal of Applied Psychology, 74,* 53–61.

Hochshild, A. R. (1983). *The managed heart.* Berkeley: University of California Press.

Hoffman, C. C. (1995). Applying range restriction corrections using published norms: Three case studies. *Personnel Psychology, 48,* 913–923.

Hofmann, D. A., Jacobs, R., & Gerras, S. J. (1992). Mapping individual performance over time. *Journal of Applied Psychology, 77,* 185–195.

Hofstede, G. (1980). *Culture's consequences.* Beverly Hills, CA: Sage.

Hofstede, G. (1993). Cultural constraints in management theories. *Academy of Management Executive, 7,* 81–94.

Hogan, J., & Hogan, R. (1989). How to measure employee reliability. *Journal of Applied Psychology, 74,* 273–279.

Hogan, J., & Hogan, R. (1993). Ambiguities of conscientiousness. Paper presented at the annual meeting of the Society of Industrial and Organizational Psychologists, San Francisco.

Hogan, J., & Quigley, A. M. (1986). Physical standards for employment and the courts. *American Psychologist, 41,* 1193–1217.

Hogan, J. C. 1991. Physical abilities. In M. D. Dunnette & L. M. Hough (Eds.), *Handbook of industrial/organizational psychology* (rev. ed., Vol. 2). Palo Alto, CA: Consulting Psychologists Press.

Hogan, J. C. (1991). Structure of physical performance in occupational tasks. *Journal of Applied Psychology, 76,* 495–507.

Hogan, J. C., Zenke, L. L., & Thompson, C. (1985). Dollar-value utility of alternative procedures for selecting school principals. Tulsa, OK: University of Tulsa Press.

Hogan, R. (1985, 1992). *The Hogan Personality Inventory: User's manual* (1st & 2nd eds.). Minneapolis: National Computer Systems.

Hogan, R., Carpenter, B. N., Briggs, S. R., & Hansson, R. O. (1984). Personality assessment and personnel selection. In H. J. Bernardin & D. A. Bownas (Eds.), *Personality assessment in organizations.* New York: Praeger.

Hogan, R., Hogan, J., & Roberts, B. W. (1996). Personality measurement and employment decisions: Questions and answers. *American Psychologist, 51,* 469–477.

Holland, J. L. (1966). *The psychology of vocational choice: A theory of personality types and model environments.* Waltham, MA: Blaisdell.

Holland, J. L. (1979). *The Self-Directed Search professional manual.* Palo Alto, CA: Consulting Psychologists Press.

Holland, J. L. (1985). *Making vocational choices: A theory of careers.* Englewood Cliffs, NJ: Prentice-Hall.

Hollander, E. P. (1958). Conformity, status, and idiosyncrasy credit. *Psychological Review, 65,* 117–127.

Hollenbeck, J. R., Ilgen, D. R., Ostroff, C., & Vancouver, J. B. (1987). Sex differences in occupational choice, pay, and worth: A supply-side approach to understanding the male-female wage gap. *Personnel Psychology, 40,* 715–743.

Hollenbeck, J. R., Ilgen, D. R., Sego, D. J., Hedlund, J., Major, D. A., & Phillips, J. (1995). Multilevel theory of team decision making: Decision performance in teams incorporating distributed expertise. *Journal of Applied Psychology, 80,* 292–316.

Hollenbeck, J. R., Ilgen, D. R., Tuttle, D. B., & Sego, D. J. (1995). Team performance on monitoring tasks: An examination of decision errors in contexts requiring sustained attention. *Journal of Applied Psychology, 80,* 685–696.

Hollenbeck, J. R., Klein, H. J., O'Leary, A. M., & Wright, P. M. (1989). Investigation of the construct validity of a self-report measure of goal commitment. *Journal of Applied Psychology, 74,* 951–956.

Hollenbeck, J. R., Williams, C. R., & Klein, H. J. (1989). An empirical examination of the antecedents of commitment to difficult goals. *Journal of Applied Psychology, 74,* 18–23.

Holloman, C. R. (1984). Leadership and headship: There is a difference. In R. L. Taylor & W. E. Rosenbach (Eds.), *Military leadership: In pursuit of excellence.* Boulder, CO: Westview Press.

Hom, P. W., Caranikas-Walker, F., Prussia, G. E., & Griffeth, R. W. (1992). A meta-analytical structural equations analysis of a model of employee turnover. *Journal of Applied Psychology, 77,* 890–909.

Homans, G. C. (1974). *Social behavior: Its elementary forms* (rev. ed.). New York: Harcourt Brace Jovanovich.

Hont, C. R., Raskin, D. C., & Kircher, J. C. (1994). Mental and physical countermeasures reduce the accuracy of polygraph tests. *Journal of Applied Psychology, 80,* 252–259.

Hosmer, L. T. (1995). Trust: The connecting link between organizational theory and philosophical ethics. *Academy of Management Review, 20,* 379–403.

Hough, L. M., Eaton, N. K., Dunnette, M. D., Kamp, J. D., & McCloy, R. A. (1990). Criterion-related validities of personality constructs and the effect of response distortion on those validities. *Journal of Applied Psychology, 75,* 581–595.

Hough, L. M., & Schneider, R. J. (1996). Personality traits, taxonomies, and applications in organizations. In K. R. Murphy (Ed.), *Individual differences and behavior in organizations.* San Francisco: Jossey-Bass.

House, R. J. (1971). A path-goal model of leader effectiveness. *Administrative Science Quarterly, 16,* 321–338.

House, R. J. (1972). Some new applications and tests of the path-goal theory of leadership. *Proceedings of the National Organizational Behavior Conference.*

House, R. J., & Mitchell, T. R. (1974). Path-goal theory of leadership. *Journal of Contemporary Business, 3,* 81–97.

House, R. J., Shane, S. A., & Herold, D. M. (1996). Rumors of the death of dispositional research are vastly exaggerated. *Academy of Management Review, 21,* 203–224.

Houston, J. M., & Smither, R. D. (1992, August). *What do managerial potential scales measure?* Paper presented at the annual meeting of the American Psychological Association, Washington, DC.

Howard, A., Byham, W. C., & Hauenstein, P. (1994). *Multirater assessment and feedback: Applications, implementation, and implications.* Pittsburgh: Development Dimensions International.

Howard, L. W., & Miller, J. L. (1993). Fair pay for fair play: Estimating pay equity in professional baseball with data envelopment analysis. *Academy of Management Journal, 36,* 882–894.

Howell, J. M., & Avolio, B. J. (1993). Transformational leadership, transactional leadership, locus of control, and support for innovation: Key predictors of consolidated-business-unit performance. *Journal of Applied Psychology, 78,* 891–902.

Huber, V. L. (1991). Comparison of supervisor-incumbent and female-male multidimensional job evaluation ratings. *Journal of Applied Psychology, 76,* 115–121.

Huffcutt, A. I., & Arthur, W., Jr. (1994). Hunter and Hunter (1984) revisted: Interview validity for entry-level jobs. *Journal of Applied Psychology, 79,* 184–190.

Huffcutt, A. I., Roth, P. L., & McDaniel, M. A. (1996). A meta-analytic investigation of cognitive ability in employment interview evaluations: Moderating characteristics and implications for incremental validity. *Journal of Applied Psychology, 81,* 459–473.

Hughes, G. L., & Prien, E. P. (1986). An evaluation of alternative scoring methods for the mixed standard scale. *Personnel Psychology, 39,* 839–847.

Hulin, C. L., Dragow, F., & Parsons, C. K. (1983). *Item response theory: Application to psychological measurement.* Homewood, IL: Dow Jones-Irwin.

Hulin, C. L., Roznowski, M., & Hachiya, D. (1985). Alternative opportunities and withdrawal decisions: Empirical and theoretical discrepancies and an integration. *Psychological Bulletin, 97,* 233–250.

Hunt, S. D., & Morgan, R. M. (1994). Organizational commitment: One of many commitments or key mediating construct? *Academy of Management Journal, 37,* 1568–1587.

Hunt, S. T. (1996). Generic work behavior: An investigation into the dimensions of entry-level, hourly job performance. *Personnel Psychology, 49,* 51–83.

Hunter, J. E. (1983). A causal analysis of cognitive ability, job knowledge, job performance, and supervisor ratings. In F. Landy, S. Zedeck, & J. Cleveland (Eds.), *Performance measurement and theory.* Hillsdale, NJ: Erlbaum.

Hunter, J. E., & Hunter, R. F. (1984). Validity and utility of alternative predictors of job performance. *Psychological Bulletin, 96,* 72–98.

Hunter, J. E., Schmidt, F. L., & Jackson, G. B. (1982). *Meta-analysis: Cumulating research findings across studies.* Beverly Hills, CA: Sage.

Huselid, M. A. (1995). The impact of human resource management practices on turnover, productivity, and corporate financial performance. *Academy of Management Journal, 38,* 635–672.

Huseman, R. C., Hatfield, J. D., & Miles, E. W. (1987). A new perspective on equity theory: The equity sensitivity construct. *Academy of Management Review, 12,* 222–234.

Hutchinson, R. D. (1981). *New horizons for human factors in design.* New York: McGraw-Hill.

Hyman, H. H. (1942). The psychology of status. *Archives of Psychology* (No. 269).

Ibarra, H. (1993). Personal networks of women and minorities in management: A conceptual framework. *Academy of Management Review, 18,* 56–87.

Ibarra, H. (1995). Race, opportunity, and diversity of social circles in managerial networks. *Academy of Management Journal, 38,* 673–703.

Industry Report, 1996. (1996, October). *Training,* 37–61.

Ingram, P., & Simons, T, (1995). Institutional and resource dependence determinants of responsiveness to work-family issues. *Academy of Management Journal, 38,* 1466–1482.

Inkeles, A. (1983). The American character. *Center Magazine, 16,* 25–39.

Inohara, T. (1990). *Human resource development in Japanese companies.* Tokyo: Asian Productivity Organization.

Ivancevich, J. M., Matteson, M. T., Freedman, S. M., & Phillips, J. S. (1990). Worksite stress management interventions. *American Psychologist, 45,* 252–261.

Iverson, D. C., Fielding, J. E., Crow, R. S., & Christenson, G. M. (1985). The promotion of physical activity in the United States population: The status of programs in medical, worksite, community, and school settings. *Public Health Reports, 100,* 212–224.

Jackson, L. A., Gardner, P. D., & Sullivan, L. A. (1992). Explaining gender differences in self-pay expectations: Social comparison standards and perceptions of fair pay. *Journal of Applied Psychology, 77,* 651–663.

Jacobs, R., Hofmann, D. A., & Kriska, S. D. (1990). Performance and seniority. *Human Performance, 3,* 107–121.

Jacobs, R., Kafry, D., & Zedeck, S. (1980). Expectations of behaviorally anchored rating scales. *Personnel Psychology, 33,* 595–640.

Jamal, M. (1981). Shift work related to job attitudes, social participation, and withdrawal behavior. *Personnel Psychology, 34,* 535–548.

James, K., Lovato, C., & Khoo, G. (1994). Social identity correlates of minority workers' health. *Academy of Management Journal, 37,* 383–396.

James, L. A., & James, L. R. (1989). Integrating work environment perceptions: Explorations into the measurement of meaning. *Journal of Applied Psychology, 74,* 739–751.

James, L. R., Demaree, R. G., Mulaik, S. A., & Ladd, R. T. (1992). Validity generalization in the context of situational models. *Journal of Applied Psychology, 77,* 3–14.

James, L. R., & White, J. R., III. (1983). Cross-situational specificity in managers' perceptions of subordinate performance, attributions, and leader behaviors. *Personnel Psychology, 36,* 809–856.

Janis, I. L. (1972). *Victims of groupthink.* Boston: Houghton Mifflin.

Janis, I. L. (1982). *Groupthink.* Boston: Houghton Mifflin.

Janz, J. T., Hellervik, L., & Gilmore, D. C. (1986). *Behavior description interviewing.* Boston: Allyn & Bacon.

Janz, T. (1989). The patterned behavior description interview: The best prophet of the future is the past. In R. W. Eder & G. R. Ferris (Eds.), *The employment interview: Theory, research, and practice.* Newbury Park, CA: Sage.

Jaros, S. J., Jermier, J. M., Koehler, J. W., & Sincich, T. (1993). Effects of continuance, affective, and moral commitment on the withdrawal process: An evaluation of eight structural equation models. *Academy of Management Journal, 36,* 951–995.

Jeffrey, N. A. (1997, January 22). Mental-health ruling alarms employers and insurers. *Wall Street Journal,* p. B10.

Jenkins, C. D., Rosenman, R., & Friedman, M. (1966). Components of the coronary-prone behavior pattern: Their relation to silent myocardial infarction and blood lipids. *Journal of Chronic Diseases, 19,* 599–609.

Johns, G. (1994a). How often were you absent? A review of the use of self-reported absence data. *Journal of Applied Psychology, 79,* 574–591.

Johns, G. (1994b). Absenteeism estimates by employees and managers: Divergent perspectives and self-serving perceptions. *Journal of Applied Psychology, 79,* 229–239.

Johnson, B. T., Mullen, B., & Salas, E. (1995). Comparison of three major meta-analytic approaches. *Journal of Applied Psychology, 80,* 94–106.

Johnson, J. W. (1996). Linking employee perceptions of service climate to customer satisfaction. *Personnel Psychology, 49,* 831–851.

Johnson, P. R., & Indvik, J. (1994). Workplace violence: An issue of the nineties. *Public Personnel Management, 23,* 515–523.

Johnson, R. H., Ryan, A. M., and Schmit, M. J. (1994, April) Employee attitudes and branch performance at Ford Motor Credit. In N. Rotchford (Chair), *Linking employee survey data to organizational outcome measures.* Paper presented at the Ninth Annual Conference at the Society of Industrial and Organizational Psychology, Nashville, TN.

Jonas, H. S., III, Fry, R. E., & Suresh, S. (1989). The person of the CEO: Understanding the executive experience. *Academy of Management Executive, 3,* 205–215.

Jones, E. W., Jr. (1986). Black managers: The dream deferred. *Harvard Business Review, 64,* 84–93.

Jones, G. R. (1984). Task visibility, free riding, and shirking: Explaining the effect of structure and technology on employee behavior. *Academy of Management Review, 9,* 684–695.

Jones, J. W., Barge, B. N., Steffy, B. D., Fay, L. M., Kunz, L. K., & Wuebker, L. (1988). Stress and medical malpractice: Organizational risk assessment and intervention. *Journal of Applied Psychology, 73,* 727–735.

Jones, R. G., & Whitmore, M. D. (1995). Evaluating developmental assessment centers as interventions. *Personnel Psychology, 48,* 377–388.

Jourden, F. J., & Heath, C. (1996). The evaluation gap in performance perceptions: Illusory perceptions of groups and individuals. *Journal of Applied Psychology, 81,* 369–379.

Joyce, L. W., Thayer, P. W., & Pond, S. B. III. (1994). Managerial functions: An alternative to traditional assessment center dimensions? *Personnel Psychology, 47,* 109–121.

Judge, T. A. (1993). Does affective disposition moderate the relationship between job satisfaction and voluntary turnover? *Journal of Applied Psychology, 78,* 395–401.

Judge, T. A., Boudreau, J., & Bretz, R. (1994). Job and life attitudes of male executives. *Journal of Applied Psychology, 80,* 767–782.

Judge, T. A., Cable, D. M., Boudreau, J. W., & Bretz, R. D., Jr. (1995). An empirical investigation of the predictor of executive career success. *Personnel Psychology, 48,* 485–519.

Judge, T. A., & Ferris, G. R. (1993). Social context of performance evaluation decisions. *Academy of Management Journal, 36,* 80–105.

Judge, T. A., & Locke, E. A. (1993). Effect of dysfunctional thought processes on subjective well-being and job satisfaction. *Journal of Applied Psychology, 78,* 939–948.

Judge, T. A., & Watanabe, S. (1993). Another look at the job satisfaction-life satisfaction relationship. *Journal of Applied Psychology, 78,* 939–948.

Judge, T. A., & Welbourne, T. M. (1994). A confirmatory investigation of the dimensionality of the Pay Satisfaction Questionnaire. *Journal of Applied Psychology, 79,* 461–466.

Jung, C. G. (1921 [1971]). *Psychological types.* Princeton, NJ: Princeton University Press.

Kabanoff, B., Waldersee, R., & Cohen, M. (1995). Espoused values and organizational change themes. *Academy of Management Journal, 38,* 1075–1104.

Kacmar, K. M., & Ferris, G. R. (1989). Theoretical and methodological considerations in the age-job satisfaction relationship. *Journal of Applied Psychology, 74,* 201–207.

Kahai, S. S., Sosik, J. J., & Avolio, B. J. (1997). Effects of leadership style and problem structure on work group process and outcomes in an electronic meeting system environment. *Personnel Psychology, 50,* 121–146.

Kahn, L. M. (1991). Discrimination in professional sports: A survey of the literature. *Industrial and Labor Relations Review, 44,* 395–418.

Kahn, W. A. (1990). Psychological conditions of personal engagement and disengagement at work. *Academy of Management Journal, 33,* 692–724.

Kahn, W. A., & Kram, K. E. (1994). Authority at work: Internal models and their organizational consequences. *Academy of Management Review, 18,* 17–50.

Kahneman, D., & Tversky, A. (1979). Prospect theory: An analysis of decisions under risk. *Econometrika, 47,* 263–291.

Kanabayashi, M. (1996, August 20). Work in Japan. *Wall Street Journal,* p. A1.

Kandel, D. B., Davies, M., & Raveis, V. H. (1985). The stressfulness of daily social roles from women: Marital, occupational, and household roles. *Journal of Health and Social Behavior, 26,* 64–78.

Kane, J. S., Bernardin, H. J., Villanova, P., & Peyrefitte, J. (1995). Stability of rater leniency: Three studies. *Academy of Management Journal, 38,* 1036–1051.

Kanfer, R., Crosby, J. V., & Brandt, D. M. (1988). Investigating behavioral antecedents of turnover at three job tenure levels. *Journal of Applied Psychology, 73,* 331–335.

Kanter, R. M. (1977). *Men and women of the corporation.* New York: Basic Books.

Kanter, R. M. (1980). How the top is different. In H. J. Leavitt, L. R. Pondy, & D. M. Boje (Eds.), *Readings in managerial psychology* (3rd ed.). Chicago: University of Chicago Press.

Kanungo, R. N. (1982). *Work alienation.* New York: Praeger.

Katzell, R. A. (1979). Changing attitudes toward work. In C. Kerr & J. M. Rosow (Eds.), *Work in America: The decade ahead.* New York: Van Nostrand Reinhold.

Katzell, R. A. (1994). Contemporary meta-trends in industrial and organizational psychology. In H. C. Triandis, M. D. Dunnette, & L. M. Hough (Eds.), *Handbook of industrial and organizational psychology* (2nd ed., Vol. 4). Palo Alto, CA: Consulting Psychologists Press.

Kaufman, H. (1976). *Are government institutions immortal?* Washington, DC: Brookings Institution.

Kaufmann, G. M., & Beehr, J. A. (1986). Interactions between job stressors and social support: Some counterintuitive results. *Journal of Applied Psychology, 71,* 522–526.

Keller, L. M., Bouchard, T. J., Jr., Arvey, R. D., Segal, N. L., & Dawis, R. V. (1992). Work values: Genetic and environmental influences. *Journal of Applied Psychology, 77,* 79–88.

Keller, R. T. (1986). Predictors of the performance of project groups in R & D organizations. *Academy of Management Journal, 29,* 715–726.

Keller, R. T. (1989). A test of the path-goal theory of leadership with need for clarity as a moderator in research and development organizations. *Journal of Applied Psychology, 74,* 208–212.

Kelley, H. H. (1952). Two functions of reference groups. In G. E. Swanson, T. M. Newcomb, & E. L. Hartley (Eds.), *Readings in social psychology* (2nd ed.). New York: Holt.

Kelly, R. M. (1991). *The gendered economy.* Newbury Park, CA: Sage.

Kennedy, R. S., Berbaum, K. S., Lilenthal, M. G., Dunlap, W. P., Mulligan, E. E., & Funaro, J. F. (1987). *Guidelines for the alleviation of simulator sickness symptomatology* (Technical Report No. 87007). Orlando, FL: Naval Training Systems Center.

Kenny, D. A., & Zaccaro, S. J. (1983). An estimate of variance due to traits in leadership. *Journal of Applied Psychology, 68,* 678–685.

Kent, R. L., & Moss, S. E. (1994). Effects of sex and gender role on leader emergence. *Academy of Management Journal, 37,* 1335–1346.

Kerblay, B. (1983). *Modern Soviet society.* New York: Pantheon.

Kessler, R. C., & McRae, J. A., Jr. (1982). The effects of wives' employment on the mental health of married men and women. *American Sociological Review, 47,* 216–227.

Kidwell, R. E., Jr., & Bennett, N. (1993). Employee propensity to withhold effort: A conceptual model to intersect three avenues of research. *Academy of Management Review, 16,* 429–456.

Kilduff, M., & Day, D. V. (1994). Do chameleons get ahead? The effects of self-monitoring on managerial careers. *Academy of Management Journal, 37,* 1047–1060.

Kilduff, M., & Krackhardt, D. (1994). Bringing the individual back in: A structural analysis of the internal market. *Academy of Management Journal, 37,* 87–108.

Kingstrom, P. O., & Bass, A. R. (1981). A critical analysis of studies comparing behaviorally anchored rating scales (BARS) and other rating formats. *Personnel Psychology, 34,* 263–289.

Kinicki, A. J., Hom, P. W., Trost, M. R., & Wade, K. J. (1995). Effects of category prototypes on performance-rating accuracy. *Journal of Applied Psychology, 81,* 354–370.

Kinicki, A. J., Lockwood, C. A., Hom, P. W., & Griffeth, R. W. (1990). Interviewer predictions of applicant qualifications and interviewer validity: Aggregate and individual analyses. *Journal of Applied Psychology, 75,* 477–486.

Kirkpatrick, D. D. (1996, October 18). Women occupy few top jobs, a study shows. *Wall Street Journal,* p. A7A.

Kirkpatrick, D. L. (1959a). Techniques for evaluating training programs. *American Society of Training Directors Journal, 13,* 3–9.

Kirkpatrick, D. L. (1959b). Techniques for evaluating training programs. Part 2—learning. *American Society of Training Directors Journal, 13,* 21–26.

Kirkpatrick, D. L. (1960a). Techniques for evaluating training programs. Part 3—behavior. *American Society of Training Directors Journal, 14,* 13–18.

Kirkpatrick, D. L. (1960b). Techniques for evaluating training programs. Part 4—results. *American Society of Training Directors Journal, 14,* 28–32.

Kirkpatrick, D. L. (1978, September). Evaluating inhouse training programs. *Training and Development Journal,* 6–9.

Kirkpatrick, S. A., & Locke, E. A. (1996). Direct and indirect effects of three core charismatic leadership components on performance and attitudes. *Journal of Applied Psychology, 81,* 36–51.

Kirmeyer, S. L. (1988). Coping with competing demands: Interruption and Type A pattern. *Journal of Applied Psychology, 73,* 621–629.

Kirmeyer, S. L., & Lin, T-R. (1987). Social support: Its relationship to observed communication with peers and superiors. *Academy of Management Journal, 30,* 138–151.

Kirnan, J. P., Farley, J. A., & Geisinger, K. (1989). The relationship between recruiting source, applicant quality, and hire performance: An analysis by sex, ethnicity, and age. *Personnel Psychology, 42,* 293–308.

Klaas, B. S., & Dell'omo, G. G. (1991). The determinants of disciplinary decisions: The case of employee drug use. *Personnel Psychology, 44,* 813–835.

Klaas, B. S., & DeNisi, A. S. (1989). Managerial reactions to employee dissent: The impact of grievance activity on performance ratings. *Academy of Management Journal, 32,* 705–717.

Klaas, B. S., & McClendon, J. A. (1996). To lead, lag, or match: Estimating the financial impact of pay level policies. *Personnel Psychology, 49,* 121–141.

Kleiman, L. S., & Faley, R. H. (1988). Voluntary affirmative action and preferential treatment: Legal and research implications. *Personnel Psychology, 41,* 481–496.

Klein, H. J., & Wright, P. M. (1994). Antecedents of goal commitment: An empirical examination of personal and situational factors. *Journal of Applied Social Psychology, 24,* 95–114.

Kleinmann, M. (1993). Are rating dimensions in assessment centers transparent for participants? *Journal of Applied Psychology, 78,* 988–993.

Kluger, A. N., & Collela, A. (1993). Beyond the mean bias: The effect of warning against faking on biodata item variances. *Personnel Psychology, 46,* 763–780.

Knopf, C. (1982). Proceedings of Probe research seminar on voice technology. New Brunswick, NJ: Probe Research.

Knouse, S. B. (1983). The letter of recommendation: Specificity and favorability of information. *Personnel Psychology, 36,* 331–341.

Knouse, S. B. (1989). Impression management and the letter of recommendation. In R. A. Giacalone & P. Rosenfeld (Eds.), *Impression management in the organization.* Hillsdale, NJ: Erlbaum.

Knouse, S. B. (1992). The mentoring process for Hispanics. In S. B. Knouse, P. Rosenfeld, & A. L. Culbertson (Eds.), *Hispanics in the workplace.* Newbury Park, CA: Sage.

Knouse, S. B., Rosenfeld, P., & Culbertson, A. L. (1992). Hispanics and work: An overview. In S. B. Knouse, P. Rosenfeld, & A. L. Culbertson (Eds.), *Hispanics in the workplace.* Newbury Park, CA: Sage.

Knowles, D. E. (1988). Dispelling myths about older workers. In H. Axel (Ed.), *Employing older Americans: Opportunities and constraints.* New York: The Conference Board.

Kochan, T. A., Schmidt, S. M., & deCotiis, T. A. (1975). Superior-subordinate relation. Leadership and headship. *Human Relations, 28,* 279–294.

Kolb, D. A., & Frohman, A. (1970). An organization development approach to consulting. *Sloan Management Review, 12,* 51–65.

Konovsky, M. A., & Cropanzano, R. (1991). Perceived fairness of employee drug testing as a predictor of employee attitudes and job performance. *Journal of Applied Psychology, 76,* 698–707.

Konrad, A. M., & Linnehan, F. (1995). Formalized HRM structures: Coordinating equal employment opportunity or concealing organizational practices? *Academy of Management Journal, 38,* 787–820.

Koretz, G. (1997a, January 20). The moribund graveyard shift. *Business Week,* 20.

Koretz, G. (1997b, January 27). Job mobility, American-style. *Business Week,* 20.

Koretz, G. (1997c, February 17). Truly tying pay to performance. *Business Week,* 25.

Koretz, G. (1997d, March 10). Perils of the graveyard shift. *Business Week,* 22.

Koslowsky, M., Sagie, A., Krausz, M., & Singer, A. D. (1997). Correlates of employee lateness: Some theoretical considerations. *Journal of Applied Psychology, 82,* 79–88.

Kossek, E. E. (1990). Diversity in child care assistance needs: Employee problems, preferences, and work-related outcomes. *Personnel Psychology, 43,* 769–791.

Kossek, E. E., & Nichol, V. (1992). The effects of on-site child care on employee attitudes and performance. *Personnel Psychology, 45,* 485–509.

Kotter, J. P. (1982, November–December). What effective general managers really do. *Harvard Business Review,* 156–167.

Kozlowski, S. W. J., & Doherty, M. L. (1989). Integration of climate and leadership: Examination of a neglected issue. *Journal of Applied Psychology, 74,* 546–553.

Krackhardt, D., & Porter, L. W. (1985a). The snowball effect: Turnover embedded in communication networks. *Journal of Applied Psychology, 71,* 50–55.

Krackhardt, D., & Porter, L. W. (1985b). When friends leave: A structural analysis of the relationship between turnover and stayers' attitudes. *Administrative Science Quarterly, 30,* 242–261.

Kraiger, K., & Ford, J. K. (1985). A meta-analysis of ratee race effects in performance appraisal. *Journal of Applied Psychology, 70,* 56–65.

Kraiger, K., Ford, J. K., & Salas, E. (1993). Application of cognitive, skill-based, and affective theories of learning outcomes to new methods of training evaluation. *Journal of Applied Psychology, 78,* 311–328.

Kram, K. E. (1988). *Mentoring at work: Developmental relationships in organizational life.* New York: University Press of America.

Kraut, A. I. (1975). Predicting turnover of employees from measured job attitudes. *Organizational Behavior and Human Performance, 13,* 233–243.

Kravitz, D. A., & Balzer, W. K. (1992). Context effects in performance appraisal: A methodological critique and empirical study. *Journal of Applied Psychology, 77,* 24–31.

Kravitz, D. A., & Platania, J. (1993). Attitudes and beliefs about affirmative action: Effects of target and of respondent sex and ethnicity. *Journal of Applied Psychology, 78,* 928–938.

Kriska, S. D. (1995, January). Comments on banding. *The Industrial-Organizational Psychologist, 32,* 93–94.

Kristof, A. L. (1996). Person-organization fit: An integrative review of its conceptualizations, measurement, and implications. *Personnel Psychology, 49,* 1–49.

Kryter, K. D. (1970). *The effects of noise on man.* New York: Academic Press.

Krzystofiak, F., Cardy, R., & Newman, J. (1988). Implicit personality and performance appraisal: The influence of trait inferences on evaluations of behavior. *Journal of Applied Psychology, 73,* 515–521.

Kuder, C. F. (1964). *Kuder General Interest Survey: Manual.* Chicago: Science Research Associates.

Kuhnert, K. W., & Lewis, P. (1987). Transactional and transformational leadership: A constructive/developmental analysis. *Academy of Management Review, 12,* 648–657.

Kulik, C. T., & Ambrose, M. L. (1992). Personal and situational determinants of referent choice. *Academy of Management Review, 17,* 212–237.

Kulik, C. T., & Ambrose, M. L. (1993). Category-based and feature-based processes in performance appraisal: Integrating visual and computerized sources of performance data. *Journal of Applied Psychology, 81,* 821–830.

Kumar, S. (1994). A conceptual model of overexertion, safety, and risk of injury in occupational settings. *Human Factors, 36,* 197–209.

Kunin, T. (1955). The construction of a new type of attitude measure. *Personnel Psychology, 8,* 65–78.

Kurland, O. (1993). Workplace violence. *Risk Management, 40,* 76–77.

Lacayo, R. (1991, September 16). Death on the shop floor. *Time,* 28–29.

Lamm, H., & Myers, D. G. (1978). Group-induced polarization of attitudes and behavior. In L. Berkowitz (Ed.), *Advances in experimental social psychology* (Vol. 11). New York: Academic Press.

Landy, F. J. (1986). Stamp collecting versus science. *American Psychologist, 41,* 1183–1192.

Landy, F. J., & Farr, J. L. (1980). Performance rating. *Psychological Bulletin, 87,* 72–107.

Landy, F. J., Rastegary, H., Thayer, J., & Colvin, C. (1991). Time urgency: The construct and its measurement. *Journal of Applied Psychology, 76,* 644–657.

Larkey, L. K. (1996). Toward a theory of communicative interactions in culturally diverse workgroups. *Academy of Management Review, 21,* 463–491.

Larson, J. R., Jr. (1989). The dynamic interplay between employees' feedback seeking strategies and supervisors' delivery of performance feedback. *Academy of Management Review, 14,* 408–422.

Latack, J. C., Kinicki, A. J., & Prussia, G. E. (1995). An integrative process model of coping with job loss. *Academy of Management Review, 20,* 311–342.

Latané, B., Williams, K., and Harkins, S. (1979). Many hands make light the work: The causes and consequences of social loafing. *Journal of Personality and Social Psychology, 37,* 822–832.

Latham, G. P. (1989). The reliability, validity, and practicality of the situational interview. In R. W. Eder & G. R. Ferris (Eds.), *The employment interview: Theory, research, and practice.* Newbury Park, CA: Sage.

Latham, G. P., & Frayne, C. A. (1989). Self-management training for increasing job attendance: A follow-up and a replication. *Journal of Applied Psychology, 74,* 411–416.

Latham, G. P., & Locke, E. A. (1979). Goal setting—A motivational technique that works. *Organizational Dynamics, 8,* 68–80.

Latham, G. P., & Saari, L. M. (1982). The importance of union acceptance for productivity improvement through goal setting. *Personnel Psychology, 35,* 781–787.

Latham, G. P., & Saari, L. M. (1984). Do people do what they say? Further studies on the situational interview. *Journal of Applied Psychology, 69,* 569–573.

Latham, G. P., & Wexley, K. N. (1977). Behavioral observation scales for performance appraisal purposes. *Personnel Psychology, 30,* 255–268.

Latham, G. P., & Whyte, G. (1994). The futility of utility analysis. *Personnel Psychology, 47,* 31–46.

Latham, V. M., & Leddy, P. M. (1987). Source of recruitment and employee attitudes: An analysis of job involvement, organizational commitment, and job satisfaction. *Journal of Business and Psychology, 1,* 230–235.

Lau, Chung-Ming, & Woodman, R. W. (1995). Understanding organizational change: A schematic perspective. *Academy of Management Journal, 38,* 537–554.

Laughlin, P. R. (1980). Social combination processes of cooperative problem solving groups on verbal intellective tasks. In M. Fishbein (Ed.), *Progress in social psychology.* Hillsdale, NJ: Erlbaum.

Laughlin, P. R., & Adamopoulos, J. (1980). Social combination processes and individual learning for six-person cooperative groups on an intellective task. *Journal of Personality and Social Psychology, 38,* 941–947.

Law, K. S., Schmidt, F. L., & Hunter, J. E. (1994). A test of two refinements in procedures for meta-analysis. *Journal of Applied Psychology, 79,* 978–986.

Lawler, E. E., III. (1969). Job design and employee motivation. *Personnel Psychology, 22,* 426–435.

Lawler, E. E., III. (1971). *Pay and organizational effectiveness: A psychological view.* New York: McGraw-Hill.

Lawler, E. E. III. (1973). *Motivation in work organizations.* Pacific Grove, CA: Brooks/Cole.

Lawler, E. E., III, & Mohrman, S. A. (1987, Spring). Quality circles: After the honeymoon. *Organizational Dynamics,* 42–54.

Lawrence, B. S. (1988). New wrinkles in the theory of age: Demography, norms, and performance ratings. *Academy of Management Journal, 31,* 309–337.

Lawrence, P. R., & Lorsch, J. W. (1967a). *Developing organizations: Diagnosis and action.* Reading, MA: Addison-Wesley.

Lawrence, P. R., & Lorsch, J. W. (1967b). *Organization and environment: Managing differentiation and integration.* Cambridge, MA: Harvard Graduate School of Business Administration.

Lawshe, C. H. (1952). Employee selection. *Personnel Psychology, 5,* 31–34.

Lee, C. (1991, October). Who gets trained in what. *Training,* 47–59.

Lee, C., & Bobko, P. (1994). Self-efficacy beliefs: Comparison of five measures. *Journal of Applied Psychology, 79,* 364–369.

Lee, C., Earley, P. C., & Hanson, L. A. (1988). Are Type As better performers? *Journal of Organizational Behavior, 9,* 263–269.

Lee, C., & Gillen, D. J. (1989). Relationship of Type A behavior pattern, self-efficacy perceptions on sales performance. *Journal of Organizational Behavior, 10,* 75–81.

Lee, R. T., & Ashforth, B. E. (1990). On the meaning of Maslach's three dimensions of burnout. *Journal of Applied Psychology, 75,* 743–747.

Lee, T. W., & Mitchell, T. R. (1994). An alternative approach: The unfolding model of voluntary employee turnover. *Academy of Management Review, 19,* 51–89.

Lee, T. W., Mitchell, T. R., Wise, L., & Fireman, S. (1996). An unfolding model of voluntary employee turnover. *Academy of Management Journal, 39,* 5–36.

Lefkowitz, J. (1994a). Sex-related differences in job attitudes and dispositional variables: Now you see them. . . . *Academy of Management Journal 37,* 323–349.

Lefkowitz, J. (1994b). Race as a factor in job placement: Serendipitous findings of "ethnic drift." *Personnel Psychology, 47,* 497–513.

Lehman, W. E. K., Farabee, D. J., Holcom, M. L., & Simpson, D. D. (1995). Prediction of substance use in the workplace: Unique contributions of personal background and work environment variables. *Journal of Drug Issues, 25,* 253–274.

Lengnick-Hall, C. A. (1996). Customer contributions to quality: A different view of the customer-oriented firm. *Academy of Management Review, 21,* 791–824.

Lengnick-Hall, M. L. (1995). Sexual harassment research: A methodological critique. *Personnel Psychology, 48,* 841–864.

Lenin, V. I. (1965). The immediate tasks of the Soviet government. *Collected works, 27,* 259.

Levin, I., & Stokes, J. P. (1989). Dispositional approach to job satisfaction: Role of negative affectivity. *Journal of Applied Psychology, 74,* 752–758.

Levine, J. M., & Moreland, R. L. (1987). Social comparison and outcome evaluation in group contexts. In J. C. Masters & W. P. Smith (Eds.), *Social comparison, justice, and relative deprivation: Theoretical, empirical, and policy perspectives.* Hillsdale, NJ: Erlbaum.

Levinson, H. (1983). Clinical psychology in organizational practice. In J. S. J. Manuso (Ed.), *Occupational clinical psychology.* New York: Praeger.

Lewin, K. (1951). *Field theory in social science.* New York: Harper & Bros.

Lewin, K. (1958). Group decision and social change. In E. E. Maccoby, T. M. Newcomb, & E. L. Hartley (Eds.), *Readings in social psychology.* New York: Holt.

Lewin, K., Lippit, R., & White, R. (1939). Patterns of behavior in experimentally created "social climates." *Journal of Social Psychology, 10,* 271–299.

Liden, R. C., Martin, C. L., & Parsons, C. K. (1993). Interviewer and applicant behaviors in employment interviews. *Academy of Management Journal, 36,* 372–386.

Liden, R. C., Wayne, S. J., & Stilwell, D. (1993). A longitudinal study on the early development of leader-member exchanges. *Journal of Applied Psychology, 78,* 662–674.

Likert, R. (1961). *New patterns of management.* New York: McGraw-Hill.

Likert, R. (1967). *The human organization.* New York: McGraw-Hill.

Lind, M. R., & Zmud, R. W. (1995). Improving interorganizational effectiveness through voice mail facilitation of peer-to-peer relationships. *Organization Science, 6,* 445–461.

Lindsley, D. H., Brass, D. J., & Thomas, J. B. (1995). Efficacy-performance spirals: A multilevel perspective. *Academy of Management Review, 20,* 645–678.

Lippert, T. (1986). Color difference prediction of legibility for raster CRT imagery. *Society of Information Displays Digest of Technical Papers, 16,* 86–89.

Lippit, R., Watson, J., & Westley, B. (1958). *The dynamics of planned change.* New York: Harcourt, Brace & World.

Locke, E. A. (1976). The nature and causes of job satisfaction. In M. D. Dunnette (Ed.), *Handbook of industrial and organizational psychology.* Chicago: Rand McNally.

Locke, E. A. (1982). The ideas of Frederick W. Taylor: An evaluation. *Academy of Management Review, 7,* 14–24.

Locke, E. A., & Henne, D. (1986). Work motivation theories. In C. L. Cooper & I. Robertson (Eds.), *International review of industrial and organizational psychology: 1986.* New York: Wiley.

Locke, E. A., & Latham, G. P. (1990). *A theory of goal setting and task performance.* New York: Prentice-Hall.

Locke, E. A., Latham, G. P., & Erez, M. (1988). The determinants of goal commitment. *Academy of Management Review, 13,* 23–39.

Locke, E. A., & Schweiger, D. M. (1979). Participation in decision-making: One more look. *Research in Organizational Behavior, 1,* 265–339.

Lohr, S. (1996, November, 16). California approves first law on repetitive motion injuries. *The New York Times,* p. Y11.

London, M., & Smither, J. W. (1995). Can multi-source feedback change perceptions of goal accomplishment, self-evaluations, and performance-related outcomes? Theory-based applications and directions for research. *Personnel Psychology, 48,* 803–839.

London, M., & Wohlers, A. J. (1991). Agreement between subordinate and self-ratings in upward feedback. *Personnel Psychology, 44,* 375–390.

Long, L., & Perry, J. (1985). Economic and occupational causes of transit operator absenteeism: A review of research. *Transport Reviews, 5,* 247–267.

Lord, R. G., DeVader, C. L., & Alliger, G. M. (1986). A meta-analysis of the relation between personality traits and leadership perceptions: An application of validity generalization procedures. *Journal of Applied Psychology, 71,* 402–410.

Lord, R. G., & Hohenfeld, J. A. (1979). Longitudinal field assessment of equity effects on the performance of major league baseball players. *Journal of Applied Psychology, 64,* 19–26.

Louis, M. L., Posner, B. Z., & Powell, G. N. (1983). The availability and helpfulness of socialization practices. *Personnel Psychology, 36,* 857–866.

Love, K. G., Bishop, R. C., Heinisch, D. A., & Montei, M. S. (1994). Selection across two cultures: Adapting the selection of American assemblers to meet Japanese job performance demands. *Personnel Psychology, 47,* 837–846.

Lublin, J. S. (1996a, April 11). The great divide. *Wall Street Journal,* p. R1.

Lublin, J. S. (1996b, July 18). Family-friendly Wall Street? Policies of Merrill, Bankers Trust win praise. *Wall Street Journal,* p. B7.

Lumpkin, G. T., & Dess, G. G. (1995). Simplicity as a strategy-making process: The effects of stage of organizational development and environment on performance. *Academy of Management Journal, 38,* 1386–1407.

Lusk, S. L., Ronis, D. L., & Kerr, M. J. (1995). Predictors of hearing protection use among workers: Implications for training programs. *Human Factors, 37,* 635–640.

Luthans, F., & Kreitner, R. (1985). *Organizational behavior modification* (2nd ed.). New York: Scott, Foresman.

Macan, T. H., Avedon, M. J., Paese, M., & Smith, D. E. (1994). The effects of applicants' reactions to cognitive ability tests and an assessment center. *Personnel Psychology, 47,* 715–738.

Macan, T. H., & Dipboye, R. L. (1990). The relationship of interviewers' preinterview impressions to selection and recruitment outcomes. *Personnel Psychology, 43,* 745–768.

Mael, F. A., & Ashforth, B. E. (1995). Loyal from day one: Biodata, organizational identification, and turnover among newcomers. *Personnel Psychology, 48,* 309–333.

Mael, F. A., Connerley, M., & Morath, R. A. (1996). None of your business: Parameters of biodata invasiveness. *Personnel Psychology, 49,* 613–650.

Magjuka, R. J., & Baldwin, T. T. (1991). Team-based employee involvement programs: Effects of design and administration. *Personnel Psychology, 44,* 793–812.

Maier, N. R. F., & Hoffman, L. R. (1961). Organization and creative problem solving. *Journal of Applied Psychology, 45,* 277–280.

Major, B., & Testa, M. (1989). Social comparison processes and judgments of entitlement and satisfaction. *Journal of Experimental Social Psychology, 25,* 101–120.

Malcolm, S. E. (1992, August). Reengineering corporate training. *Training,* pp. 57–61.

Malos, S. (1996, July). The commentators speak: Emerging trends in the legal analysis of affirmative action. *The Industrial-Organizational Psychologist, 34,* 33–39.

Mann, F. C., & Likert, R. (1952). The need for research on communicating research results. *Human Organization, 11,* 15–19.

Mann, R. D. (1959). A review of the relationship between personality and performance in small groups. *Psychological Bulletin, 56,* 241–270.

Manning, M. R., Jackson, C. N., & Fusilier, M. R. (1996). Occupational stress, social support, and the costs of health care. *Academy of Management Journal, 39,* 738–750.

Manning, M. R., Osland, J. S., & Osland, A. (1989). Work-related consequences of smoking cessation. *Academy of Management Journal, 32,* 606–621.

Manuso, J. S. J. (1981). Psychological services and health enhancement: A corporate model. In A. Broskowski (Ed.), *Linking health and mental health: Coordinating care in the community* (Vol. 2). Beverly Hills, CA: Sage.

Manuso, J. S. J. (1984). The metamorphosis of a corporate emotional health program. In J. S. J. Manuso (Ed.), *Occupational clinical psychology.* New York: Praeger.

Manzey, D., Lorenz, B., Schiewe, A., Finell, G., & Thiele, G. (1995). Single-case study during a short-term space mission. *Human Factors, 37,* 667–681.

March, J. G., & Simon, H. A. (1958). *Organizations.* New York: Wiley.

Mardon, S. (1997, January). Screen applicants for shift compatibility. *HRMagazine,* 53–55.

Markham, S. E., Dansereau, F., Jr., & Alutto, J. A. (1982). Female vs. male absence rates: A temporal analysis. *Personnel Psychology, 35,* 371–382.

Markham, S. E., & McKee, G. H. (1991). Declining organizational size and increasing unemployment rates: Predicting employee absenteeism from within- and between-plant perspectives. *Academy of Management Journal, 34,* 952–965.

Markham, S. E., & McKee, G. H. (1995). Group absence behavior and standards: A multilevel analysis. *Academy of Management Journal, 38,* 1174–1190.

Markus, M. L. (1994). Electronic mail as the medium of managerial choice. *Organization Science, 5,* 502–527.

Marlowe, C. M., Schneider, S. L., & Nelson, C. E. (1996). Gender and attractiveness biases in hiring decisions: Are more experienced managers less biased? *Journal of Applied Psychology, 81,* 11–21.

Marsh, R. M., & Mannari, H. (1981). Technology and size as determinants of the organizational structure of Japanese factories. *Administrative Science Quarterly, 26,* 33–57.

Martell, R. F., & Borg, M. R. (1993). A comparison of the behavioral rating accuracy of groups and individuals. *Journal of Applied Psychology, 81,* 43–50.

Martell, R. F., Guzzo, R. A., Willis, C. E. (1995). A methodological and substantive note on the performance-cue effect in ratings of work-group behavior. *Journal of Applied Psychology, 81,* 191–195.

Martin, C. L., & Nagao, D. H. (1989). Some effects of computerized interviewing on job applicant responses. *Journal of Applied Psychology, 74,* 72–80.

Martin, D. C., & Bartol, K. M. (1987). Potential libel and slander issues involving discharged employees. *Employee Relations Law Journal, 13,* 43–60.

Martocchio, J. J. (1989). Age-related differences in employee absenteeism: A meta-analysis. *Psychology and Aging, 4,* 409–414.

Martocchio, J. J. (1992). Microcomputer usage as an opportunity: The influence of context in employee training. *Personnel Psychology, 45,* 529–552.

Martocchio, J. J. (1994). Effects of conceptions of ability on anxiety, self-efficacy, and learning in training. *Journal of Applied Psychology, 79,* 819–825.

Martocchio, J. J., & Dulebohn, J. (1994). Performance feedback effects in training: The role of perceived controllability. *Personnel Psychology, 47,* 357–373.

Martocchio, J. J., & O'Leary, A. M. (1989). Sex differences in occupational stress: A meta-analytic review. *Journal of Applied Psychology, 74,* 495–501.

Martocchio, J. J., & Webster, J. (1992). Effects of feedback and cognitive playfulness on performance in microcomputer software training. *Personnel Psychology, 45,* 553–578.

Masi, D. A. (1984). *Designing employee assistance programs.* New York: AMACOM.

Maslach, C. (1982). *Burnout: The cost of caring.* New York: Prentice-Hall.

Maslow, A. (1954). *Motivation and personality.* New York: Van Nostrand Reinhold.

Mathieu, J. E. (1991). A cross-level nonrecursive model of the antecedents of organizational commitment and satisfaction. *Journal of Applied Psychology, 76,* 607–618.

Mathieu, J. E., & Kohler, S. S. (1990a). A test of the interactive effects of organizational commitment and job involvement on various types of absence. *Journal of Vocational Behavior, 36,* 33–44.

Mathieu, J. E., & Kohler, S. S. (1990b). A cross-level examination of group absence influences on individual absence. *Journal of Applied Psychology, 75,* 217–220.

Mathieu, J. E., & Leonard, R. L., Jr. (1987). Applying utility concepts to a training program in supervisory skills: A time-based approach. *Academy of Management Journal, 30,* 316–335.

Mathieu, J. E., Martineau, J. W., & Tannenbaum, S. I. (1993). Individual and situational influences on the development of self-efficacy: Implications for training effectiveness. *Personnel Psychology, 46,* 125–127.

Mathieu, J. E., Tannenbaum, S. I., & Salas, E. (1992). Influences of individual and situational characteristics on measures of training effectiveness. *Academy of Management Journal, 35,* 828–847.

Mathieu, J. E., & Zajac, D. (1990). A review and meta-analysis of the antecedents, correlates, and consequences of organizational commitment. *Psychological Bulletin, 108,* 171–194.

Matteson, M. T., & Ivancevich, J. M. (1988). Health promotion at work. In C. L. Cooper and I. Robertson (Eds.), *International review of industrial organizational psychology.* New York: Wiley.

Matthews, K. A. (1988). Coronary heart disease and Type A behaviors: Update on an alternative to the Booth-Kewley and Friedman (1987) quantitative review. *Psychological Bulletin, 91,* 293–323.

Maurer, S. D., & Fay, C. (1988). Effect of situational interviews, conventional, structured interviews, and training on interview rating agreement: An experimental analysis. *Personnel Psychology, 41,* 329–344.

Maurer, S. D., Howe, V., & Lee, T. W. (1992). Organizational recruiting as marketing management: An interdisciplinary study of engineering graduates. *Personnel Psychology, 45,* 807–833.

Maurer, T. J., Palmer, J. K., & Ashe, D. K. (1993). Diaries, checklists, evaluations, and contrast effects in measurement of behavior. *Journal of Applied Psychology, 81,* 226–231.

Maurer, T. J., & Tarulli, B. A. (1994). Investigation of perceived environment, perceived outcome, and person variables in relationship to voluntary development activity by employees. *Journal of Applied Psychology, 79,* 3–14.

Maxwell, S. E., & Arvey, R. D. (1993). The search for predictors with high validity and low adverse impact: Compatible or incompatible goals? *Journal of Applied Psychology, 78,* 433–437.

May, D. R., & Schwoerer, C. E. (1994). Employee health by design: Using employee involvement teams in ergonomic job redesign. *Personnel Psychology, 47,* 861–876.

May, K. E. (1996, April). Work in the 21st century: Implications for job analysis. *The Industrial-Organizational Psychologist, 33,* 98–100.

Mayer, R. C., Davis J. H., & Schoorman, F. D. (1995). An integrative model of organizational trust. *Academy of Management Review, 20,* 709–734.

Mayes, B. T., Barton, M. E., & Ganster, D. C. (1991). An exploration of the moderating effect of age on job stressor-employee strain relationships. *Journal of Social Behavior and Personality, 6,* 289–308.

Mayfield, E. C. (1964). The selection interview—A re-evaluation of published research. *Personnel Psychology, 17,* 239–260.

Mayfield, E. C., Brown, S. H., & Hamstra, B. W. (1980). Selection interviewing in the life insurance industry: An update of research and practice. *Personnel Psychology, 33,* 725–740.

Mayo, E. (1939). Preface. In F. J. Roethlisberger & W. J. Dickson, *Management and the worker.* Cambridge, MA: Harvard University Press.

McCauley, C. D., Ruderman, M. N., Ohlott, P. J., & Morrow, J. E. (1994). Assessing the developmental components of managerial jobs. *Journal of Applied Psychology, 79,* 544–560.

McClelland, D. C. (1961). *The achieving society.* New York: Van Nostrand Reinhold.

McClelland, D. C. (1975). *Power: The inner experience.* New York: Irvington.

McClelland, D. C., & Boyatzis, R. E. (1982). The leadership motive pattern and long-term success in management. *Journal of Applied Psychology, 67,* 737–743.

McClelland, D. C., & Burnham, D. (1976). Power is the great motivator. *Harvard Business Review, 25,* 159–166.

McCormick, E. J. (1959). The development of processes for indirect or synthetic validity: III. Application of job analysis to indirect validity. A symposium. *Personnel Psychology, 12,* 402–413.

McCormick, E., DeNisi, A., & Staw, J. (1979). Use of the Position Analysis Questionnaire for establishing the job component validity of tests. *Journal of Applied Psychology, 64,* 51–56.

McCormick, E. J., Jeanneret, P. R., & Mecham, R. C. (1972). A study of job characteristics as based on the Position Analysis Questionnaire (PAQ). *Journal of Applied Psychology, 56,* 347–368.

McDaniel, M. A. (1988). Does pre-employment drug use predict on-the-job suitability? *Personnel Psychology, 41,* 717–729.

McDaniel, M. A., Whetzel, D. L., Schmidt, F. L., & Maurer, S. D. (1994). The validity of employment interviews: A comprehensive review and meta-analysis. *Journal of Applied Psychology, 79,* 599–616.

McEvoy, G. M., & Beatty, R. W. (1989). Assessment centers and subordinate appraisals of managers: A seven-year examination of predictive validity. *Personnel Psychology, 42,* 37–52.

McEvoy, G. M., & Buller, P. F. (1988). User acceptance of peer appraisals in an industrial setting. *Personnel Psychology, 40,* 785–797.

McEvoy, G. M., & Cascio, W. F. (1985). Strategies for reducing employee turnover: A meta-analysis. *Journal of Applied Psychology, 70,* 342–353.

McEvoy, G. M., & Cascio, W. F. (1989). Cumulative evidence of the relationship between employee age and job performance. *Journal of Applied Psychology, 74,* 11–17.

McGregor, D. (1960). *The human side of enterprise.* New York: McGraw-Hill.

McIntire, S. A., & Thomas, J. (1990). Adapting a video selection test for use in another culture. Paper presented at the International Congress of Applied Psychology, Kyoto, Japan.

McManus, M. A., & Brown, S. H. (1995). Adjusting sales results measures for use as criteria. *Personnel Psychology, 48,* 391–400.

McNeely, B. L., & Meglino, B. M. (1994). The role of dispositional and situational antecedents in prosocial organizational behavior: An examination of the intended beneficiaries of prosocial behavior. *Journal of Applied Psychology, 79,* 836–844.

McRae, M. (1994). Influence of sex role stereotypes on personnel decisions of Black managers. *Journal of Applied Psychology, 29,* 306–309.

McRae, M., & Carter, R. T. (1992). Occupational profiles of Blacks in management: Implications for career counseling. *Journal of Employment Counseling, 29,* 2–4.

McShulskis, E. (1996a, December). Less is less when it comes to substance abuse treatment. *HRMagazine,* 24–25.

McShulskis, E. (1996b, August). New benefits for a new generation. *HRMagazine,* 24.

Mechanic, D. (1980). Sources of power of lower participants in complex organizations. In H. J. Leavitt, L. R. Pondy, & D. M. Boje, *Readings in managerial psychology* (3rd ed.). Chicago: University of Chicago Press.

Megargee, E. I., & Carbonell, J. L. (1988). Evaluating leadership with the CPI. In C. D. Spielberger & J. N. Butcher (Eds.), *Advances in personality assessment* (Vol. 7). Hillsdale, NJ: Erlbaum.

Meglino, B. M., DeNisi, A. S., & Ravlin, E. C. (1993). Effects of previous job exposure and subsequent job status on the functioning of a realistic job preview. *Personnel Psychology, 46,* 803–822.

Meglino, B. M., DeNisi, A. S., Youngblood, S. A., & Williams, K. J. (1988). Effects of realistic job previews: A comparison using an enhancement and reduction preview. *Journal of Applied Psychology, 73,* 259–266.

Meglino, B. M., Ravlin, E. C., & Adkins, C. L. (1989). A work values approach to corporate culture: A field test of the value congruence process and its relationship to individual outcomes. *Journal of Applied Psychology, 74,* 424–432.

Meier, E. L. (1988). Managing an older workforce. In Industrial Relations Association, *The older worker.* Madison, WI: Author.

Meindertsma, D. C. (1996, Fall). Implications of the new job reference immunity statutes. *Legal Report.* Alexandria, VA: Society for Human Resource Management.

Meindl, J. R., & Ehrlich, S. B. (1987). The romance of leadership and the evaluation of organizational performance. *Academy of Management Journal, 30,* 91–109.

Meister, D. (1987). *Behavioral analysis and measurement methods.* New York: Wiley.

Melamed, S., Ben-Avi, I., Luz, J., & Green, M. S. (1995). Objective and subjective work monotony: Effects of job satisfaction, psychological distress, and absenteeism in blue-collar workers. *Journal of Applied Psychology, 80,* 29–42.

Mellor, S. (1995). Gender composition and gender representation in local unions: Relationships between women's participation in local office and women's participation in local activities. *Journal of Applied Psychology, 80,* 706–720.

Mellor, S., Mathieu, J. E., & Swim, J. K. (1994). Cross-level analysis of the influence of local union structure on women's and men's union commitment. *Journal of Applied Psychology, 79,* 203–210.

Mento, A. J., Locke, E. A., & Klein, H. J. (1992). Relationship of goal level to valence and instrumentality. *Journal of Applied Psychology, 77,* 395–405.

Mento, A. J., Steel, R. P., & Karren, R. J. (1987). A meta-analytic study of the effects of goal setting on task performance: 1966–1984. *Organizational Behavior and Human Decision Processes, 39,* 52–83.

Mero, N. P., & Motowidlo, S. J. (1995). Effects of rater accountability on the accuracy and the favorability of performance ratings. *Journal of Applied Psychology, 81,* 517–524.

Messick, S. (1995). Validity of psychological assessment. *American Psychologist, 50,* 741–749.

Meyer, H. H., & Raich, M. S. (1983). An objective evaluation of a behavioral modeling training program. *Personnel Psychology, 36,* 755–761.

Meyer, J. P., Allen, N. J., & Gellatly, I. R. (1990). Affective and continuance commitment to the organization: Evaluation of measures and analysis of concurrent and time-lagged relations. *Journal of Applied Psychology, 75,* 710–720.

Meyer, J. P., Allen, N. J., & Smith, C. A. (1993). Commitment to organizations and occupations: Extension and test of a three-component conceptualization. *Journal of Applied Psychology, 78,* 538–551.

Micco, L. (1997, January). Debate flares over OSHA's night retail guidelines. *HR News,* 3.

Michaelsen, L. K., Watson, W. E., & Black, R. H. (1989). A realistic test of individual versus group consensus decision making. *Journal of Applied Psychology, 74,* 834–839.

Milford, M. (1997, February 22). DuPont shuts the door on private offices. *The New York Times,* p. Y31.

Miller, D., & Friesen, P. H. (1984). Structural change and performance: Quantum vs. piecemeal-incremental approaches. *Academy of Management Journal, 25,* 867–892.

Miller, K. I., & Monge, P. R. (1986). Participation, satisfaction, and productivity: A meta-analytic review. *Academy of Management Journal, 29,* 727–753.

Miller, L. E., & Grush, J. E. (1988). Improving predictions in expectancy theory research: Effects of personality, expectancies, and norms. *Academy of Management Journal, 31,* 107–122.

Miller, V. D., & Jablin, F. M. (1991). Information seeking during organizational entry: Influences, tactics, and a model of the process. *Academy of Management Review, 16,* 92–120.

Milliken, F. J., & Martins, L. L. (1996). Searching for common threads: Understanding the multiple effects of diversity in organizational groups. *Academy of Management Review, 21,* 402–433.

Milne, S. H., Blum, T. C., & Roman, P. M. (1994). Factors influencing employees' propensity to use an employee assistance program. *Personnel Psychology, 47,* 123–145.

Miner, J. B. (1988). *Organizational behavior: Performance and productivity.* New York: Random House.

Miner, J. B., Smith, N. R., & Bracker, J. S. (1989). Role of entrepreneurial task motivation in the growth of technologically innovative firms. *Journal of Applied Psychology, 74,* 554–560.

Miner, J. B., Smith, N. R., and Bracker, J. S. (1994). Role of entrepreneurial task motivation in the growth of technologically innovative firms: Interpretations from follow-up data. *Journal of Applied Psychology, 79,* 627–630.

Mitra, A., Jenkins, G. D., Jr., & Gupta, N. (1992). A meta-analytic review of the relationship between absence and turnover. *Journal of Applied Psychology, 77,* 879–889.

Mitroff, I. I., Mason, R. O., & Pearson, C. M. (1994). Radical surgery: What will tomorrow's organizations look like? *Academy of Management Executive, 8,* 11–21.

Mohrman, A. M., Mohrman, S. A., Cooked, R., & Duncan, R. (1977). Survey feedback and problem-solving intervention in a school district: "We'll take the survey but you can keep the feedback." In P. Mirvis & D. Berg (Eds.), *Failures in organization development and change.* New York: Wiley.

Mone, M. A., Mueller, G. C., & Mauland, W. (1996). The perceptions and usage of statistical power in applied psychology and management research. *Personnel Psychology, 49,* 103–120.

Morand, D. A. (1995). The role of behavioral formality and informality in the enactment of bureaucratic versus organic organizations. *Academy of Management Review, 20,* 831–872.

Moreno, J. L. (1934). *Who shall survive?* Washington, DC: Nervous and Mental Diseases Publishing Co.

Morris, J. A., & Feldman, D. C. (1996). The dimensions, antecedents, and consequences of emotional labor. *Academy of Management Review, 21,* 986–1010.

Morrison, A. M., White, R. P., & Van Velsor, E. (1987, August). *Psychology Today,* 18–26.

Morrison, E. W. (1993a). Newcomer information seeking: Exploring types, modes, sources, and outcomes. *Academy of Management Journal, 36,* 557–589.

Morrison, E. W. (1993b). Longitudinal study of the effects of information seeking on newcomer socialization. *Journal of Applied Psychology, 78,* 173–183.

Morrison, E. W., & Robinson, S. L. (1997). When employees feel betrayed: A model of how psychological contract violation develops. *Academy of Management Review, 22,* 226–256.

Morrison, R. F., & Brantner, T. M. (1992). What enhances or inhibits learning a new job? A basic career issue. *Journal of Applied Psychology, 77,* 926–940.

Morrow, C. C., Jarrett, M. Q., & Rupiniski, M. T. (1997). An investigation of the effect and economic utility of corporate-wide training. *Journal of Applied Psychology, 50,* 91–119.

Morse, N. C., & Reimer, E. (1956). The experimental change of a major organizational variable. *Journal of Abnormal Social Psychology, 51,* 120–129.

Mossholder, K. W., & Arvey, R. D. (1984). Synthetic validity: A conceptual and comparative review. *Journal of Applied Psychology, 69,* 322–333.

Motowidlo, S. J. (1983). Predicting sales turnover from pay satisfaction and expectation. *Journal of Applied Psychology, 68,* 484–489.

Motowidlo, S. J., & Van Scotter, J. R. (1994). Evidence that task performance should be distinguished from contextual performance. *Journal of Applied Psychology, 81,* 475–480.

Mount, M. K. (1983). Comparisons of managerial and employee satisfaction with a performance appraisal system. *Personnel Psychology, 36,* 99–110.

Mount, M. K. (1984). Psychometric properties of subordinate ratings of managerial performance. *Personnel Psychology, 37,* 687–702.

Mount, M. K., Barrick, M. R., & Strauss, J. P. (1994). Validity of observer ratings of the Big Five personality factors. *Journal of Applied Psychology, 79,* 272–280.

Mount, M. K., Sytsma, M. R., Hazucha, J. F., & Holt, K. E. (1997). Rater-ratie race effects in developmental performance ratings of managers. *Personnel Psychology, 50,* 51–69.

Muchinsky, P. M. (1979). The use of reference reports in personnel selection: A review and evaluation. *Journal of Occupational Psychology, 52,* 287–297.

Muczyk, J. P., & Reimann, B. C. (1988, November). The case for directive leadership. *Academy of Management Executive,* 301–311.

Muhlbach, L., Bocker, M., & Prussog, A. (1995). Telepresence in videocommunications: A study on stereoscopy and individual eye contact. *Human Factors, 37,* 290–305.

Multimedia Training in the *Fortune* 1,000. (1996, September). *Training,* pp. 53–60.

Mumby, D. K., & Putnam, L. L. (1992). The politics of emotion: A feminist reading of bounded rationality. *Academy of Management Review, 17,* 465–486.

Mumford, M. D. (1983). Social comparison theory and the evaluation of peer evaluations: A review and some applied implications. *Personnel Psychology, 36,* 867–881.

Mumford, M. D., Costanza, D. P., Connelly, M. S., & Johnson, J. F. (1996). Item generation procedures and background data scales: Implications for construct and criterion-related validity. *Personnel Psychology, 49,* 361–398.

Mumford, M. D., & Stokes, G. S. (1992). Developmental determinants of individual action: Theory and practice in the application of background data measures. In M. D. Dunnette & L. M. Hough (Eds.), *Handbook of industrial and organizational psychology* (2nd ed., Vol. 3). Palo Alto, CA: Consulting Psychologists Press.

Mumford, M. D., Weeks, J. L., Harding, J. L., & Fleishman, E. A. (1988). Relations between student characteristics, course content, and training outcomes: An integrative modeling effort. *Journal of Applied Psychology, 73,* 443–456.

Munchus, G. (1983). Employer-employee based quality circles in Japan: Human resource policy implications for American firms. *Academy of Management Review, 8,* 255–261.

Murphy, K. R. (1993). *Honesty in the workplace.* Belmont, CA: Brooks/Cole.

Murphy, K. R. (1994). Potential effects of banding as a function of test reliability. *Personnel Psychology, 47,* 477–495.

Murphy, K. R., & Balzer, W. K. (1986). Systematic distortions in memory-based behavior ratings and performance evaluations: Consequences for rating accuracy. *Journal of Applied Psychology, 71,* 39–44.

Murphy, K. R., & Balzer, W. K. (1989). Rater errors and rating accuracy. *Journal of Applied Psychology, 74,* 619–624.

Murphy, K. R., Balzer, W. K., Lockhart, M. C., & Eisenman, E. J. (1985). Effects of previous performance on evaluations of present performance. *Journal of Applied Psychology, 70,* 72–84.

Murphy, K. R., & Cleveland, J. N. (1991). *Performance appraisal.* Needham Heights, MA: Allyn & Bacon.

Murphy, K. R., Jako, R. A., & Anhalt, R. L. (1993). Nature and consequences of halo error: A critical analysis. *Journal of Applied Psychology, 78,* 218–225.

Murphy, K. R., & Reynolds, D. H. (1988). Does true halo affect observed halo? *Journal of Applied Psychology, 73,* 235–238.

Murphy, K. R., Thornton, G. C., III, & Prue, K. (1991). Influence of job characteristics on the acceptability of employee drug testing. *Journal of Applied Psychology, 76,* 447–453.

Murphy, K. R., Thornton, G. C., III, & Reynolds, D. H. (1990). College students' attitudes toward employee drug testing programs. *Personnel Psychology, 43,* 615–631.

Murray, H. M., et al. (1938). *Explorations in personality.* New York: Oxford University Press.

Murray, S. A., & Caldwell, B. S. (1996). Human performance and control of multiple systems. *Human Factors, 38,* 323–329.

Myers, D. G., & Lamm, H. (1976). The group polarization phenomenon. *Psychological Bulletin, 83,* 602–627.

Naditch, M. P. (1984). The StayWell Program: Health enhancement at work. In J. S. J. Manuso (Ed.), *Occupational clinical psychology.* New York: Praeger.

Nadler, D. A. (1992). *Organizational architecture: Designs for changing organizations.* San Francisco: Jossey-Bass.

Nathan, B. R., & Tippins, N. (1990). The consequences of halo "error" in performance ratings: A field study of the moderating effect of halo on test validation results. *Journal of Applied Psychology, 75,* 290–296.

National Safety Council. (1982). *Accident facts.* Chicago.

Naylor, J., & Shine, L. (1965). A table for determining the increase in mean criterion score obtained by using a selection device. *Journal of Industrial Psychology, 3,* 33–42.

Naylor, J. C., Pritchard, R. D., & Ilgen, D. R. (1980). *A theory of behavior in organizations.* New York: Academic Press.

Near, J. P., & Miceli, M. P. (1995). Effective whistle-blowing. *Academy of Management Review, 20,* 679–708.

Nedelsky, L. (1954). Absolute grading standards for objective tests. *Educational and Psychological Measurement, 14,* 3–19.

Nelson, D. L., & Quick, J. C. (1985). Professional women: Are stress and disease inevitable? *Academy of Management Review, 10,* 206–218.

Nelson, D. L., & Sutton, C. (1990). Chronic work stress and coping: A longitudinal study and suggested new directions. *Academy of Management Journal, 33,* 859–869.

Nelson, R. E. (1989). The strength of strong ties: Social networks and intergroup conflict in organizations. *Academy of Management Journal, 32,* 377–401.

Nemetz, P. L., & Christensen, S. L. (1996). The challenge of cultural diversity: Harnessing a diversity of views to understand multiculturalism. *Academy of Management Review, 21,* 434–462.

Neuman, G. A., Edwards, J. E., & Raju, N. S. (1989). Organizational development interventions: A meta-analysis of their effects on satisfaction and other attitudes. *Personnel Psychology, 42,* 461–489.

Nicholas, J. M., & Katz, M. (1985). Research methods and reporting practices in organization development: A review and some guidelines. *Academy of Management Review, 10,* 737–749.

Nicholson, N., & Johns, G. (1985). The absence culture and the psychological contract—Who's in control of absence? *Academy of Management Review, 10,* 397–407.

Nixon, H. L., II. (1979). *The small group.* Englewood Cliffs, NJ: Prentice-Hall.

Nkomo, S. M. (1988). Race and sex: The forgotten case of the Black female manager. In S. Rose & L. Larwood (Eds.), *Women's careers: Pathways and pitfalls.* New York: Praeger.

Nkomo, S. M. (1992). The emperor has no clothes: Rewriting "race in organizations." *Academy of Management Review, 17,* 487–513.

Nkomo, S. M., & Cox, T., Jr. (1989). Gender differences in the upward mobility of Black managers: Double whammy or double advantage? *Sex Roles, 21,* 825–839.

Noe, R. A. (1988). An investigation of the determinants of successful assigned mentoring relationships. *Personnel Psychology, 41,* 457–479.

Noe, R. A. (1989). Women and mentoring: A review and research agenda. *Academy of Management Review, 13,* 65–78.

Noe, R. A., & Schmitt, N. (1986). The influence of trainee attitudes on training effectiveness: Test of a model. *Personnel Psychology, 39,* 497–523.

Nof, S. (1985). Robot ergonomics: Optimizing robot work. In S. Nof (Ed.), *Handbook of industrial robotics.* New York: Wiley.

Nonaka, I., & Johansson, J. K. (1985). Japanese management: What about the "hard" skills? *Academy of Management Review, 10,* 181–191.

Normand, J., Lempert, R. O., & O'Brien, C. P. (1994). *Under the influence? Drugs and the American work force.* Washington DC: National Academy Press.

Normand, J., Salyards, S., & Mahoney, J. (1990). An evaluation of pre-employment drug testing. *Journal of Applied Psychology, 75,* 629–639.

Nowack, K. M. (1993, January). 360–degree feedback: The whole story. *Training and Development,* 69–72.

Noyes, J. M., & Frankish, C. R. (1992). Speech recognition technology for individuals with disabilities. *Augmentative and Alternative Communication, 8,* 297–303.

Oborne, D. J. (1982). *Ergonomics at work.* Norwich, England: Wiley.

O'Boyle, T. F. (1985, August 8). More firms require drug tests. *Wall Street Journal,* p. 6.

Occupational Outlook Quarterly. (1996, Spring). Washington, DC: U.S. Department of Labor, Bureau of Labor Statistics.

O'Donnell, M. P. (1986). *Design of workplace health promotion programs.* Royal Oak, MI: American Journal of Health Promotion.

Ohlott, P. J., Ruderman, M. N., & McCauley, C. D. (1994). Gender differences in managers' developmental job experiences. *Academy of Management Journal, 37,* 46–67.

Oldham, G. R., & Cummings, A. (1996). Employee creativity: Personal and contextual factors at work. *Academy of Management Journal, 39,* 607–634.

Oldham, G. R., Cummings, A., Mischel, L. J., Schmidtke, J. M., & Zhou, J. (1996, April). Can personal stereos improve productivity? *HRMagazine,* 95–99.

Olea, M. M., & Ree, M. J. (1994). Predicting pilot and navigator criteria: Not much more than *g. Journal of Applied Psychology, 79,* 845–851.

O'Leary-Kelly, A. M., Griffin, R. W., & Glew, D. J. (1996). Organization-motivated aggression: A research framework. *Academy of Management Review, 21,* 225–253.

O'Leary-Kelly, A. M., Martocchio, J. J., & Frink, D. D. (1994). A review of the influence of group goals on group performance. *Academy of Management Journal, 37,* 1285–1301.

Olian, J. D. (1984). Genetic screening for employment purposes. *Personnel Psychology, 37,* 423–438.

Olian, J. D., Giannantonio, C. M., & Carroll, S. J., Jr. (1985). *Managers' evaluations of the mentoring process: The protege's perspective.* Paper presented at the Midwest Academy of Management meeting, St. Louis.

Oliver, B. (1994, May). Fight drugs with knowledge. *Training & Development,* 105–109.

Olson-Buchanan, J. B. (1996). Voicing discontent: What happens to the grievance filer after the grievance? *Journal of Applied Psychology, 81,* 52–63.

Ones, D. S., Viswesvaran, C., & Schmidt, F. L. (1993). Comprehensive meta-analysis of integrity test validities: Findings and implications for personnel selection and theories of job performance. *Journal of Applied Psychology, 78,* 679–703.

O'Reilly, C. A., III, Chatman, J., & Caldwell, D. F. (1991). People and organizational culture: A profile comparison approach to assessing person-organization fit. *Academy of Management Journal, 34,* 487–516.

Organ, D. W., & Ryan, K. (1995). A meta-analytic review of attitudinal and dispositional predictors of organizational citizenship behavior. *Personnel Psychology, 48,* 775–802.

Orlansky, J., & String, J. (1977). *Cost effectiveness of flight simulator for military training: 1. Use and effectiveness of flight simulators* (IDA Paper P-1275). Arlington, VA: Institute for Defense Analyses.

Orpen, C. (1985). Patterned behavior description interviews versus unstructured interviews: A comparative validity study. *Journal of Applied Psychology, 70,* 774–776.

Orr, J. M., Sackett, P. R., & Mercer, M. (1989). The role of prescribed and nonprescribed behaviors in estimating the dollar value of performance. *Journal of Applied Psychology, 74,* 34–40.

OSHA finalizes workplace guidelines. (1996, May). *Occupational Hazards, 58,* 25–26.

Ostroff, C. (1991). Training effectiveness measures and scoring schemes: A comparison. *Personnel Psychology, 44,* 353–374.

Ostroff, C. (1992). The relationship between satisfaction, attitudes, and performance: An organizational level analysis. *Journal of Applied Psychology, 77,* 963–974.

Ostroff, C., & Kozlowski, S. W. (1992). Organizational socialization as a learning process: The role of information acquisition. *Personnel Psychology, 45,* 849–874.

Ostrov, E., & Cavanaugh, J. L., Jr. (1987). Validation of police officer recruit candidates' self-reported drug use. *Journal of Forensic Sciences, 32,* 496–502.

Ott, J. S. (1989). *The organizational culture perspective.* Pacific Grove, CA: Brooks/Cole.

Ouchi, W. C. (1981). *Theory Z: How American business can meet the Japanese challenge.* Reading, MA: Addison-Wesley.

Ouchi, W. C., & Jaeger, A. M. (1978). Type Z organization: Stability in the midst of mobility. *Academy of Management Review, 3,* 305–314.

Overton, R. C., Harris, H. J., Taylor, L. R., & Zickar, M. J. (1997). Adapting to adaptive testing. *Personnel Psychology, 50,* 171–185.

Owenby, P. H. (1992, January). Making case studies come alive. *Training,* 43–46.

Paajanen, G. E. (1986). *Development and validation of the PDI Employment Inventory.* Paper presented at the annual meeting of the American Psychological Association, Washington, DC.

Paajanen, G. E., Hansen, T. L., & McLellan, R. A. (1993). *PDI Employment Inventoory and PDI Customer Service Inventory Manual.* Minneapolis: Personnel Decisions, Inc.

Padavic, I. (1992). White-collar work values and women's interest in blue collar jobs. *Gender & Society, 6,* 215–230.

Paffenbarger, R. S., Jr., Hyde, R. T., Wing, A. L., & Hsieh, C. (1986). Physical activity, all-cause mortality, and longevity of college alumni. *New England Journal of Medicine, 314,* 605–613.

Paley, M. J., & Tepas, D. I. (1994). Fatigue and the shift-worker: Firefighters working on a rotating shift level. *Human Factors, 36,* 269–284.

Palisano, P. (1980, September). Alcoholism: Industry's $15 billion hangover. *Occupational Hazards,* 55.

Parasuraman, S., Greenhaus, J. H., Rabinowitz, S., Bedeian, A. G., & Mossholder, K. W. (1989). Work and family variables as mediators of the relationship between wives' employment and husbands' well-being. *Academy of Management Journal, 32,* 185–201.

Paris, C. R., Gilson, R. D., Thomas, M. H., & Silver, N. C. (1995). Effect of synthetic voice intelligibility on speech comprehension. *Human Factors, 37,* 335–340.

Parish, D. C. (1989). Relation of the pre-employment drug testing result to employment status: A one year follow-up. *Journal of General Internal Medicine, 4,* 44–47.

Parkes, K. R. (1990). Coping, negative affectivity, and the work environment: Additive and interactive predictors of mental health. *Journal of Applied Psychology, 75,* 399–409.

Parsons, H. M., (1974). What happened at Hawthorne? *Science, 183,* 922–932.

Pascale, R. T., & Athos, A. G. (1981). *The art of Japanese management.* New York: Simon & Schuster.

Patten, B. R., & Giffen, K. (1973). *Problem-solving group interaction.* New York: Harper & Row.

Patterson, M., Payne, R., & West, M. (1996). Collective climates: A test of their sociopsychological significance. *Academy of Management Journal, 39,* 1675–1691.

Patterson, M. L., & Sechrest, L. B. (1970). Interpersonal distance and impression formation. *Journal of Personality, 38,* 161–166.

Paullay, I. M., Alliger, G. M., & Stone-Romero, E. F. (1994). Construct validation of two instruments designed to measure job involvement and work centrality. *Journal of Applied Psychology, 79,* 224–228.

Pawar, B. S., & Eastman, K. K. (1997). The nature and implications of contextual influences on transformational leadership: A conceptual examination. *Academy of Management Review, 22,* 80–109.

Pearce, J. A., & Ravlin, E. C. (1987). The design and activation of self-regulating work groups. *Human Relations, 40,* 751–782.

Performance Research Associates, Inc., & Questar Data Systems, Inc. (1988). *Service management practices inventory users manual.* Eagan, MN: Questar Data Systems, Inc.

Perry, E. L., Davis-Blake, A., & Kulik, C. T. (1994). Explaining gender-based selection decisions: A synthesis of contextual and cognitive approaches. *Academy of Management Review, 19,* 786–820.

Perry, E. L., Kulik, C. T., & Bourhis, A. C. (1996). Moderating effects of personal and contextual factors in age discrimination. *Journal of Applied Psychology, 81,* 628–647.

Persico, J., & Tomasek, H. (1994). Organizational development toward continual quality improvement. In D. W. Cole, J. C. Preston, & J. S. Finlay (Eds.), *What is new in organization development.* Chesterland, OH: The Organization Development Institute.

Personnel Selection Inventory. (1987). Park Ridge, IL: London House Press.

Peters, L. H., O'Connor, E. J., Weekley, J., Pooyan, A., Frank, B., & Erenkrantz, B. (1984). Sex bias and managerial evaluations: A replication and extension. *Journal of Applied Psychology, 69,* 349–352.

Peters, T. J., & Waterman, R. H., Jr. (1982). *In search of excellence.* New York: Warner Books.

Peterson, J. A., & Martens, R. (1973). Success and affiliation as determinants of team cohesiveness. *Research Quarterly, 43,* 62–76.

Peterson, M. F., Smith, P. B., Akande, A., Ayestaran, S., Bochner, S., Callan, V., Cho, N. G., Jesuino, J. C., D'Amorim, M., Francois, P. H., Hofmann, K., Koopman, P., Leung, K., Lim, T. K., Mortazavi, S., Munene, J., Radford, M., Ropo, A., Savage, G., Setiadi, B., Sinha, T. N., Sorenson, R., & Viedge, C. (1995). Role conflict, ambiguity, and overload: A 21–nation study. *Academy of Management Journal, 38,* 429–452.

Peterson, N. G., Mumford, M. D., Borman, W. C., Jeanneret, P. R., & Fleishmann, E. A. (1995). *Development of a prototype Occupational Information Network (O*NET) content model* (Vols. 1, 2). Salt Lake City: Utah Deptment of Employee Security.

Pfeffer, J. (1977). The ambiguity of leadership. *Academy of Management Review, 2,* 104–112.

Phillips, A. P., & Dipboye, R. L. (1989). Correlational tests of predictions from a process model of the interview. *Journal of Applied Psychology, 74,* 41–52.

Phillips, A. S., & Bedeian, A. G. (1994). Leader-follower exchange quality: The role of personal and interpersonal attributes. *Academy of Management Journal, 37,* 990–1001.

Pingitore, R., Dugoni, B. L., Tindale, R. S., & Spring, B. (1994). Bias against overweight job applicants in a simu-

lated employment interview. *Journal of Applied Psychology,
79,* 909–917.

Pinkley, R. L., Brittain, J., Neale, M. A., & Northcraft, G. B.
(1995). Managerial third-party dispute intervention: An inductive analysis of intervenor strategy selection. *Journal of
Applied Psychology, 80,* 386–402.

Plous, S. (1995). A comparison of strategies for reducing interval overconfidence in group judgments. *Journal of Applied Psychology, 80,* 443–454.

Podsakoff, P. M., & Schriescheim, C. A. (1985). Field studies of French and Raven's bases of power: Critique, reanalysis, and suggestions for future research. *Psychological Bulletin, 97,* 387–411.

Porras, J. I. (1987). *Stream analysis: A powerful new way to diagnose and manage change.* Reading, MA: Addison-Wesley.

Porras, J. I., & Berg, P. O. (1978). The impact of organization development. *Academy of Management Review, 3,*
249–266.

Porras, J. I., & Robertson, P. J. (1992). Organizational development: Theory, practice, and research. In M. Dunnette
& L. Hough (Eds.), *Handbook of industrial and organizational psychology* (2nd ed., Vol. 3). Palo Alto, CA: Consulting Psychologists Press.

Porras, J. I., & Silvers, R. C. (1991). Organization development
and transformation. *Annual Review of Psychology, 42,* 51–78.

Porter, C. H., & Corlett, E. N. (1989). Performance differences of individuals classified by questionnaire as accident
prone or non-accident prone. *Ergonomics, 32,* 317–333.

Poulton, E. (1978). Increased vigilance with vertical vibration at 5 HZ: An alerting mechanism. *Applied Ergonomics,
9,* 73–76.

Powell, G. N., & Butterfield, D. A. (1989). "The good manager": Did androgyny fare better in the 1980s? *Group and
Organization Studies, 14,* 216–233.

Powell, G. N., & Butterfield, D. A. (1994). Investigating the
"glass ceiling" phenomenon: An empirical study of actual
promotions to top management. *Academy of Management
Journal, 37,* 68–86.

Powell, G. N., & Butterfield, D.A. (1997). Effect of race on
promotion to top management in a federal department.
Academy of Management Journal, 40, 112–128.

Prein, H. C. M. (1984). A contingency approach to conflict
management. *Group and Organization Studies, 9,* 81–102.

Premack, S. L., & Wanous, J. P. (1985). A meta-analysis of
realistic job preview experiments. *Journal of Applied Psychology, 70,* 706–719.

Prewett-Livingston, A. J., Feild, H. S., Veres, J. G., III, &
Lewis, P. M. (1996). Effects of race on interview ratings in
a situational panel interview. *Journal of Applied Psychology,
81,* 178–186.

Primoff, E. S. (1955). *Test selection by job analysis: The J-
Coefficient, what it is, how it works* (Test Technical Series
No. 20). Washington, DC: U.S. Civil Service Commission,
Standards Division.

Primoff, E. S. (1975). *Has to prepare and conduct job element
examinations.* Personnel Research and Development Center. U.S. Civil Service Commission. Washington, DC: U.S.
Government Printing Office.

Prussia, G. E., & Kinicki, A. J. (1996). A motivational investigation of group effectiveness using social-cognitive theory. *Journal of Applied Psychology, 81,* 187–198.

Pryor, J. B., Reeder, G. D., & McManus, J. A. (1991). Fear
and loathing in the workplace: Reactions to AIDS-infected
co-workers. *Personality and Social Psychology Bulletin, 17,*
133–139.

Pulakos, E. D., & Schmitt, N. (1995). Experience-based and
situational interview questions: Studies of validity. *Personnel Psychology, 48,* 289–308.

Pulakos, E. D., Schmitt, N., & Ostroff, C. (1986). A warning about the use of a standard deviation across dimensions
within ratees to measure halo. *Journal of Applied Psychology, 71,* 29–32.

Pulakos, E. D., Schmitt, N., Whitney, D., & Smith, M.
(1996). Individual differences in interviewer ratings: The
impact of standardization, consensus discussion, and sampling error on the value of a structured interview. *Personnel
Psychology, 49,* 85–102.

Pulakos, E. D., White, L., Oppler, S. H., & Borman, W. C.
(1989). Examination of race and sex effects on performance ratings. *Journal of Applied Psychology, 74,* 770–780.

Punnett, B. J. (1986). Goal-setting: An extension of the research. *Journal of Applied Psychology, 71,* 171–172.

Quiñones, M. A. (1995). Pretraining context effects: Training assignment as feedback. *Personnel Psychology, 45,* 226–
238.

Quiñones, M. A., Ford, J. K., & Teachout, M. S. (1995).
The relationship between work experience and job perfor-
mance: A conceptual and meta-analytic review. *Personnel
Psychology, 48,* 887–910.

Rabbitt, P. (1991). Management of the working population.
Ergonomics, 34, 775–790.

Rafaeli, A., Dutton, J., Harquail, C. V., & Mackie-Lewis, S.
(1997). Navigating by attire: The use of dress by female
administrative employees. *Academy of Management Journal, 40,* 5–45.

Rafaeli, A., & Pratt, M. G. (1993). Tailored meanings: On
the meaning and impact of organizational dress. *Academy
of Management Review, 18,* 32–55.

Ragins, B. R. (1989). Barriers to mentoring: The female
manager's dilemma. *Human Relations, 42,* 1–22.

Ragins, B. R., & Cotton, J. L. (1991). Easier said than done:
Gender differences in perceived barriers to gaining a mentor. *Academy of Management Journal, 34,* 939–951.

Ragins, B. R., & Scandura, T. A. (1994). Gender differences
in expected outcomes of mentoring relationships. *Academy
of Management Journal, 37,* 957–971.

Raia, A. (1985). Power, politics, and the human resource professional. *Human Resource Planning, 8,* 201–207.

Rajagopalan, N., & Datta, D. K. (1996). CEO characteristics: Does industry matter? *Academy of Management Journal, 39,* 197–215.

Raju, N. S., Burke, M. J., & Normand, J. (1990). A new approach for utility analysis. *Journal of Applied Psychology, 75,* 3–12.

Ralston, D. A., Anthony, W. P., & Gustafson, D. J. (1985). Employees may love flextime, but what does it do to the organization's performance? *Journal of Applied Psychology, 70,* 272–279.

Ramsey, J., & Kwon, Y. (1988). Simplified decision rules for predicting performance loss in the heat. *Proceedings on heat stress indices.* Luxembourg: Commission of the European Communities.

Randall, D. M. (1987). Commitment and the organization: The organization man revisited. *Academy of Management Review, 12,* 460–471.

Raven, B. H. (1974). The comparative analysis of power and power preference. In J. T. Tedeschi (Ed.), *Perspectives on social power.* Chicago: Aldine.

Raza, S., & Carpenter, B. (1987). A model of hiring decisions in real employment interviews. *Journal of Applied Psychology, 72,* 596–603.

Redfern, M. S., & Chaffin, D. B. (1995). Influence of flooring on standing fatigue. *Human Factors, 37,* 570–581.

Ree, M. J., Carretta, T. R., & Teachout, M. S. (1995). Role of ability and prior job knowledge in complex training performance. *Journal of Applied Psychology, 80,* 721–730.

Ree, M. J., & Earles, J. A. (1991). Predicting training success: Not much more than *g. Personnel Psychology, 44,* 321–332.

Ree, M. J., Earles, J. A., & Teachout, M. S. (1994). Predicting job performance: Not much more than *g. Journal of Applied Psychology, 81,* 518–524.

Reed, R., Lemak, D. J., & Montgomery, J. C. (1996). Beyond process: TQM content and firm performance. *Academy of Management Review, 21,* 173–202.

Reeves, C. A., & Bednar, D. A. (1994). Defining quality: Alternatives and implications. *Academy of Management Review, 19,* 419–445.

Reich, M. H. (1986). The mentor connection. *Personnel, 63,* 50–56.

Reichers, A. E., Wanous, J. P., & Austin, J. T. (1997). Understanding and managing cynicism about organizational change. *Academy of Management Executive, 11,* 48–59.

Reilly, R. R., & Chao, G. T. (1982). Validity and fairness of some alternative employee selection procedures. *Personnel Psychology, 35,* 1–62.

Rhodes, S. R., & Steers, R. M. (1990). *Managing employee absenteeism.* Reading, MA: Addison-Wesley.

Rhodes, W., Hyatt, R., & Scheiman, P. (1994). The price of cocaine, heroin, and marijuana. *Journal of Drug Issues, 24,* 383–402.

Rice, A. K. (1953). Productivity and social organization in an Indian weaving shed. *Human Relations, 6,* 297–329.

Rice, R. W., McFarlin, D. B., & Bennett, D. E. (1989). Standards of comparison and job satisfaction. *Journal of Applied Psychology, 74,* 591–598.

Rice, R. W., Phillips, S. M., & McFarlin, D. B. (1990). Multiple discrepancies and pay satisfaction. *Journal of Applied Psychology, 75,* 386–393.

Richman, W. L., & Quiñones, M. A. (1996). Task frequency rating accuracy: The effect of task engagement and experience. *Journal of Applied Psychology, 81,* 512–524.

Ridgeway, C. L. (1988). Gender differences in task groups: A status and legitimacy account. In M. Webster and M. Foschi (Eds.), *Status generalization: New theory and research.* Stanford, CA: Stanford University Press.

Ridgeway, C. L., & Diekema, D. (1989). Dominance and collective hierarchy formation in male and female task groups. *American Sociological Review, 54,* 79–93.

Ridgway, M. B. (1984). Leadership. In R. L. Taylor & W. E. Rosenbach (Eds.), *Military leadership: In pursuit of excellence.* Boulder, CO: Westview Press.

Rigdon, J. E. (1994, April 12). Companies see more workplace violence. *Wall Street Journal,* p. B1.

Riggs, M. L., & Knight, P. A. (1994). The impact of perceived group success-failure on motivational beliefs and attitudes: A causal model. *Journal of Applied Psychology, 79,* 755–766.

Riley, S., & Wrench, D. (1985). Mentoring among women lawyers. *Journal of Applied Social Psychology, 15,* 374–386.

Ritchie, R. J., & Moses, J. L. (1983). Assessment center correlates of women's advancement into middle management: A 7–year longitudinal analysis. *Journal of Applied Psychology, 68,* 227–231.

Robbins, T. L., & DeNisi, A. S. (1994). A closer look at interpersonal affect as a distinct influence on cognitive processing in performance evaluations. *Journal of Applied Psychology, 81,* 341–353.

Roberts, D. R., & Robertson, P. J. (1992). Positive-findings bias, and measuring methodological rigor, in evaluations of organization development. *Journal of Applied Psychology, 77,* 918–925.

Robertson, I. T., & Down, S. (1989). Work-sample tests of trainability: A metaanalysis. *Journal of Applied Psychology, 74,* 402–410.

Robertson, P. J., Roberts, D. R., & Porras, J. I. (1993). Dynamics of planned organizational change: Assessing empirical support for a theoretical model. *Academy of Management Journal, 36,* 619–634.

Robinson, S. L., & Bennett, R. J. (1995). A typology of deviant workplace behaviors: A multidimensional scaling study. *Academy of Management Journal, 38,* 555–572.

Robinson, S. L., Kraatz, M. S., & Rousseau, D. M. (1994). Changing obligations and the psychological contract: A longitudinal study. *Academy of Management Journal, 37,* 137–152.

Rodgers, R., Hunter, J. E., & Rogers, D. L. (1993). Influence of top management commitment on management program success. *Journal of Applied Psychology, 78,* 151–155.

Roethlisberger, F. J., & Dickson, W. J. (1939). *Management and the worker.* Cambridge, MA: Harvard University Press.

Romanelli, E., & Tushman, M. L. (1994). Organizational transformation as punctuated equilibrium: An empirical test. *Academy of Management Journal, 37,* 1141–1166.

Romzek, B. S. (1989). Personal consequences of employee commitment. *Academy of Management Journal, 32,* 649–661.

Root, N. (1981). Injuries at work are fewer among older employees. *Monthly Labor Review, 104,* 30–34.

Rosen, E. I. (1987). *Bitter choices: Blue-collar women in and out of work.* Chicago: University of Chicago Press.

Rosenbloom, J. S., & Hallman, G. V. (1986). *Employee benefit planning* (2nd ed.). Englewood Cliffs, NJ: Prentice-Hall.

Rosenman, R. H., & Chesney, M. A. (1982). Stress, Type A behavior, and coronary disease. In L. Goldberger & S. Breznitz (Eds.), *Handbook of stress.* New York: Free Press.

Rosenthal, R., & Rubin, D. B. (1978). Interpersonal expectancy effects: The first 345 studies. *Behavioral and Brain Sciences, 3,* 377–415.

Rosse, J. G., Miller, J. L., & Ringer, R. C. (1996). The deterrent value of drug and integrity testing. *Journal of Business and Psychology, 10,* 477–485.

Rosse, J. G., Miller, J. L., & Stecher, M. D. (1994). A field study of job applicants' reactions to personality and cognitive ability testing. *Journal of Applied Psychology, 79,* 987–992.

Rosse, J. G., & Ringer, R. C. (1991). *Applicant reactions to paper-and-pencil forms of drug testing.* Paper presented at the annual meeting of the Society for Industrial and Organizational Psychology. St. Louis.

Rosse, J. G., Ringer, R. C., & Miller, J. L. (1996). Personality and drug testing: An exploration of the perceived fairness of alternatives to urinalysis. *Journal of Business and Psychology, 10,* 459–485.

Roth, P. L., BeVier, C. A., Switzer, F. S., III, & Schippmann, J. S. (1996). Meta-analyzing the relationship between grades and job performance. *Journal of Applied Psychology, 81,* 548–556.

Rothstein, H. R. (1990). Interrater reliability of job performance ratings: Growth to asymptote level with increasing opportunity to observe. *Journal of Applied Psychology, 75,* 322–327.

Rowe, P. M. (1989). Unfavorable information and interview decisions. In R. W. Eder & G. R. Ferris (Eds.), *The employment interview: Theory, research and practice.* Newbury Park, CA: Sage.

Rubis, L. (1996, August). TEAM Act sent to Clinton. *HR News,* p. 1. Alexandria, VA: Society for Human Resource Management.

Ruhm, C. J. (1989). Why older Americans stop working. *The Gerontologist, 29,* 294–299.

Russell, C. J. (1987). Person characteristic versus role congruency explanations for assessment center ratings. *Academy of Management Journal, 30,* 817–826.

Russell, C. J., Mattson, J., Devlin, S. E., & Atwater, D. (1990). Predictive validity of biodata items generated from retrospective life experience essays. *Journal of Applied Psychology, 75,* 569–580.

Russell, C. J., Settoon, R. P., McGrath, R. N., Blanton, A. E., Kidwell, R. E., Lohrke, F. T., Scifres, E. L., & Danforth, G. W. (1994). Investigator characteristics as moderators of personnel selection research: A meta-analysis. *Journal of Applied Psychology, 79,* 163–170.

Russell, D. W., Altmaier, E., & Van Velzen, D. (1987). Job-related stress, social support, and burnout among classroom teachers. *Journal of Applied Psychology, 72,* 269–274.

Ryan, A. M., Daum, D., Bauman, T., Grisez, M., Mattimore, K., Nalodka, T., & McCormick, S. (1995). Direct, indirect, and controlled observation on rating accuracy. *Journal of Applied Psychology, 80,* 664–670.

Ryan, A. M., & Lasek, M. (1991). Negligent hiring and defamation: Areas of liability related to pre-employment inquiries. *Personnel Psychology, 44,* 293–319.

Ryan, A. M., & Sackett, P. R. (1987). Exploratory study of individual assessment practices: Interrater reliability and judgments of assessor effectiveness. *Journal of Applied Psychology, 74,* 568–579.

Ryan, A. M., & Sackett, P. R. (1992). Relationships between graduate training, professional affiliation, and individual psychological assessment practices for personnel decisions. *Personnel Psychology, 45,* 363–387.

Ryan, A. M., & Schmit, M. J. (1996). Calculating EEO statistics in the temporary help industry. *Personnel Psychology, 49,* 167–180.

Rynes, S. L. (1991). Recruitment, job choice, and post-hire consequences: A call for new research directions. In M. D. Dunnette & L. M. Hough (Eds.), *Handbook of industrial and organizational psychology* (2nd ed., Vol. 2). Palo Alto, CA: Consulting Psychologists Press.

Rynes, S. L., & Boudreau, J. W. (1986). College recruiting in large organizations: Practice, evaluation, and research implications. *Personnel Psychology, 39,* 729–757.

Rynes, S. L., Bretz, R. D., & Gerhart, B. (1991). The importance of recruitment in job choice: A different way of looking. *Personnel Psychology, 44,* 487–521.

Rynes, S. L., & Gerhart, B. (1990). Interviewer assessments of applicant "fit": An exploratory investigation. *Personnel Psychology, 43,* 13–35.

Rynes, S. L., Heneman, H. G., III, & Schwab, D. P. (1980). Individual reactions to organizational recruiting: A review. *Personnel Psychology, 33,* 529–542.

Saal, F. E., & Moore, S. C. (1993). Perceptions of promotion fairness and promotion candidates' qualifications. *Journal of Applied Psychology, 78,* 105–110.

Saavedra, R., Earley, P. C., & Van Dyne, L. (1993). Complex interdependence in task-performing groups. *Journal of Applied Psychology, 78,* 61–72.

Saavedra, R., & Kwun, S. K. (1993). Peer evaluation in self-managing work groups. *Journal of Applied Psychology, 78,* 450–462.

Sackett, P. R., & DuBois, C. L. Z. (1991). Rater-ratee effects on performance evaluation: Challenging meta-analytic conclusions. *Journal of Applied Psychology, 76,* 873–877.

Sackett, P. R., DuBois, C. L. Z., & Noe, A. W. (1991). Tokenism in performance evaluation: The effects of work group representation on male-female and White-Black differences in performance ratings. *Journal of Applied Psychology, 76,* 263–267.

Sackett, P. R., & Mullen, E. J. (1993). Beyond formal experimental design: Towards an expanded view of the training evaluation process. *Personnel Psychology, 46,* 613–627.

Sackett, P. R., & Ostgaard, D. J. (1994). Job-specific applicant pools and national norms for cognitive ability tests: Implications for range restriction corrections in validation research. *Journal of Applied Psychology, 79,* 680–684.

Sackett, P. R., & Roth, L. (1996). Multi-stage selection strategies: A Monte Carlo investigation of effects on performance and minority hiring. *Personnel Psychology, 49,* 549–572.

Sackett, P. R., & Wanek, J. E. (1996). New developments in the use of measures of honesty, integrity, conscientiousness, dependability, trustworthiness, and reliability for personnel selection. *Personnel Psychology, 49,* 787–829.

Sackett, P. R., & Wilk, S. L. (1994). Within-group norming and other forms of score adjustment in preemployment testing. *American Psychologist, 49,* 929–954.

Saffold, G. S., III. (1988). Culture traits, strength, and organizational performance: Moving beyond "strong culture." *Academy of Management Review, 13,* 546–558.

Sagie, A., & Koslowsky, M. (1993). Detecting moderators with meta-analysis: An evaluation and comparison of techniques. *Personnel Psychology, 46,* 629–640.

Saks, A. M. (1995). Longitudinal field investigation of the moderating and mediating effects of self-efficacy on the relationship between training and newcomer adjustment. *Personnel Psychology, 45,* 211–225.

Salancik, G. R., & Pfeffer, J. (1977). An examination of need-satisfaction models of job attitudes. *Administrative Science Quarterly, 22,* 427–456.

Salancik, G. R., & Pfeffer, J. (1978). A social information processing approach to job attitudes and task design. *Administrative Science Quarterly, 23,* 224–253.

Sales, S. M. (1966). Supervisory style and productivity: Review and theory. *Personnel Psychology, 19,* 275–286.

Salgado, J. F. (1997). The five-factor model of personality and job performance in the European community. *Journal of Applied Psychology, 82,* 30–43.

Salkind, N. J., (1997). *Exploring research* (3rd ed.). Upper Saddle River, NJ: Prentice-Hall.

Sample, J., & Hylton, R. (1996, May). Falling off a log—and landing in court. *Training,* 66–69.

Sanchez, J. I. (1994). From documentation to innovation: Reshaping job analysis to meet emerging business needs. *Human Resource Management Review, 4,* 51–74.

Sanchez, J. I., & Brock, P. (1996). Outcomes of perceived discrimination among Hispanic employees: Is diversity management a luxury or necessity? *Academy of Management Journal, 39,* 704–719.

Sanchez, J. I., & De La Torre, P. (1996). A second look at the relationship between rating and behavioral accuracy in performance appraisal. *Journal of Applied Psychology, 81,* 3–10.

Sanchez, J. I., & Fraser, S. L. (1994). An empirical approach to identify job duty—KSA linkages in managerial jobs: A case example. *Journal of Business & Psychology, 8,* 309–325.

Sanders, M., & Shaw, B. (1988). *Research to determine the contribution of system factors in the occurrence of underground injury accidents.* Pittsburgh, PA: Bureau of Mines.

Sanders, M. S., Gustanski, J., & Lawton, M. (1974). Effect of ambient illumination on noise level of groups. *Journal of Applied Psychology, 59,* 527–528.

Sanders, M. S., & McCormick, E. J. (1993). *Human factors in engineering and design* (7th ed.). New York: McGraw-Hill.

Sashkin, M., Morriss, W., & Horst, L. (1973). A comparison of social and organizational change models: Information flow and data use processes. *Psychological Review, 80,* 510–526.

Sawin, D. A., & Scerbo, M. W. (1995). Effects of instruction type and boredom proneness in vigilance: Implications for boredom and workload. *Human Factors, 37,* 752–765.

Saylor, J. S. (1993). American Airline's EAP bucks trend, proves value of inpatient care. *Employee Assistance Professional Report, 3,* 3–4.

Scandura, T. A., & Graen, G. B. (1984). Moderating effects of initial leader-member exchange status on the effects of a leadership intervention. *Journal of Applied Psychology, 69,* 428–436.

Scandura, T. A., & Schriesheim, C. A. (1994). Leader-member exchange and supervisor career mentoring as complementary constructions in leadership research. *Academy of Management Journal, 37,* 1588–1602.

Scarpello, V., & Campbell, J. P. (1983). Job satisfaction: Are all the parts there? *Personnel Psychology, 36,* 577–600.

Scarpello, V., Huber, V., & Vandenberg, R. J. (1988). Compensation satisfaction: Its measurement and dimensionality. *Journal of Applied Psychology, 73,* 163–171.

Schaubroeck, J., Ganster, D. C., & Fox, M. L. (1992). Dispositional affect and work-related stress. *Journal of Applied Psychology, 77,* 322–335.

Schaubroeck, J., Ganster, D. C., & Kemmerer, B. E. (1994). Job complexity, "Type A" behavior, and cardiovascular disorder: A prospective study. *Academy of Management Journal, 37,* 426–439.

Schaubroeck, J., & Williams, S. (1993). Type A behavior pattern and escalating commitment. *Journal of Applied Psychology, 78,* 862–867.

Schein, E. H. (1972). *Professional education: Some new directions.* New York: McGraw-Hill.

Schein, E. H., & Bennis, W. G. (1965). *Personal and organizational change through group methods.* New York: Wiley.

Schellhardt, T. D. (1996, November 19). It's time to evaluate your work, and all involved are groaning. *Wall Street Journal,* p. A1.

Schellhardt, T. D. (1997, February 13). Race-bias suit at S. C. Johnson raises some worker-team issues. *Wall Street Journal,* p. B7.

Schippmann, J. S., Prien, E. P., & Katz, J. A. (1990). Reliability and validity of in-basket performance measures. *Personnel Psychology, 43,* 837–859.

Schmidt, F. L. (1991). Why all banding procedures in personnel selection are logically flawed. *Human Performance, 4,* 265–278.

Schmidt, F. L., & Hunter, J. E. (1977). Development of a general solution to the problem of validity generalization. *Journal of Applied Psychology, 62,* 529–540.

Schmidt, F. L., & Hunter, J. E. (1981). Employment testing: Old theories and new research findings. *American Psychologist, 36,* 1128–1137.

Schmidt, F. L., & Hunter, J. E. (1995). The fatal internal contradiction in banding: Its statistical rationale is logically inconsistent with its operational procedures. *Human Performance, 8,* 203–214.

Schmidt, F. L., Hunter, J. E., McKenzie, R. C., & Muldrow, T. W. (1979). Impact of valid selection procedures on work force productivity. *Journal of Applied Psychology, 64,* 609–626.

Schmidt, F. L., Hunter, J. E., Outerbridge, A. N., & Trattner, M. H. (1986). The economic impact of job selection methods on size, productivity, and payroll costs of the federal work force: An empirically based demonstration. *Personnel Psychology, 39,* 1–29.

Schmidt, F. L., Law, K., Hunter, J. E., Rothstein, H. R., Pearlman, K., & McDaniel, M. (1993). Refinements in validity generalization methods: Implications for the situational specificity hypothesis. *Journal of Applied Psychology, 78,* 3–12.

Schmidt, F. L., & Ones, D. S. (1992). Personnel selection. *Annual Review of Psychology, 43,* 627–670.

Schmidt, F. L., Ones, D. S., & Hunter, J. E. (1992). Personnel selection. *Annual Review of Psychology, 43,* 627–670.

Schmidt, F. L., Pearlman, K., & Hunter, J. E. (1980). The validity and fairness of employment and educational tests for Hispanic Americans: A review and analysis. *Personnel Psychology, 33,* 705–724.

Schmidt, F. L., Pearlman, K., Hunter, J. E., & Hirsch, H. R. (1985). Forty questions about validity generalization and meta-analysis. *Personnel Psychology, 38,* 697–798.

Schmit, M. J., Amel, E. L., & Ryan, A. M. (1993). Self-reported assertive job-seeking behaviors of minimally educated job hunters. *Personnel Psychology, 46,* 105–124.

Schmit, M. J., & Ryan, A. M. (1993). The Big Five in personnel selection: Factor structure in applicant and nonapplicant populations. *Journal of Applied Psychology, 78,* 966–974.

Schmit, M. J., Ryan, A. M., Stierwalt, S. L., & Powell, A. B. (1995). Frame-of-reference effects on personality scale scores and criterion-related validity. *Journal of Applied Psychology, 80,* 607–620.

Schmitt, N., Gilliland, S. W., Landis, R. S., & Devine, D. (1993). Computer-based testing applied to selection of secretarial applicants. *Personnel Psychology, 46,* 149–165.

Schmitt, N., Gooding, R. Z., Noe, R. A., & Kirsch, M. (1984). Metaanalyses of validity studies published between 1964 and 1982 and the investigation of study characteristics. *Personnel Psychology, 37,* 407–422.

Schmitt, N., & Hill, T. (1977). Sex and race composition of assessment center groups as a determinant of peer and assessor ratings. *Journal of Applied Psychology, 62,* 261–264.

Schmitt, N. W., & Klimoski, R. J. (1991). *Research methods in human resources management.* Cincinnati: South-Western.

Schneer, J. A., & Reitman, F. (1990). Effects of employment gaps on the careers of M.B.A.'s: More damaging for men than for women? *Academy of Management Journal, 33,* 391–406.

Schneer, J. A., & Reitman, F. (1993). Effects of alternate family structures on managerial career paths. *Academy of Management Journal, 36,* 830–843.

Schneider, B. (1985). Organizational behavior. *Annual Review of Psychology, 36,* 573–611.

Schneider, B. (1987). The people make the place. *Personnel Psychology, 40,* 437–452.

Schneider, B., & Bowen, D. E. (1995). *Winning the service game.* Boston: Harvard Business School Press.

Schneider, B., Goldstein, H. W., & Smith, D. B. (1995). The ASA framework: An update. *Personnel Psychology, 48,* 747–773.

Schneider, J. R., & Schmitt, N. (1992). An exercise design approach to understanding assessment center dimension and exercise constructs. *Journal of Applied Psychology, 77,* 32–41.

Schriesheim, C. A., & Kerr, S. (1977). Theories and measures of leadership: A critical reappraisal of current future directions. In J. G. Hunt & L. L. Larson (Eds.), *Leadership: The cutting edge.* Carbondale: Southern Illinois University Press.

Schriesheim, C. A., Tepper, B. J., & Tetrault, L. A. (1994). Least Preferred Co-Worker score, situational control, and leadership effectiveness: A meta-analysis of contingency model performance predictions. *Journal of Applied Psychology, 79,* 561–573.

Schriesheim, C. A., & Von Glinow, M. A. (1977). Tests of the path-goal theory of leadership. *Academy of Management Journal, 20,* 398–405.

Schriesheim, J. F., & Schriesheim, C. A. (1980). A test of the path-goal theory of leadership and suggested directions for future research. *Personnel Psychology, 33,* 349–370.

Schwartz, F. N. (1989, January–February). Management women and the new facts of life. *Harvard Business Review,* pp. 65–76.

Scott, D. R., McIntire, S. A., & Burroughs, W. A. (1992). *Improving performance and retention through video assessment: A longitudinal study.* Paper presented at the annual meeting of the American Psychological Association, Washington, DC.

Scott, K. D., & Taylor, G. S. (1985). An examination of conflicting findings on the relationship between job satisfaction and absenteeism: A meta-analysis. *Academy of Management Journal, 28,* 599–612.

Scott, W. E., Jr. (1975). The effects of extrinsic rewards on "intrinsic motivation." *Organizational Behavior and Human Performance, 15,* 117–129.

Scott, W. E., Jr., & Erskine, J. A. (1980). The effects of variations in task design and monetary reinforcers on task behavior. *Organizational Behavior and Human Performance, 25,* 311–335.

Segal, J. A. (1996, December). Take applicants for a test drive. *HRMagazine,* 120–122.

Seltzer, J., & Numerof, R. E. (1988). Supervisory leadership and subordinate burnout. *Academy of Management Journal, 31,* 439–446.

Selye, H. (1976). *The stress of life* (2nd ed.). New York: McGraw-Hill.

Semple, C. A., Hennessy, R. T., Sanders, M. S., Cross, B. K., Beith, B. J., & McCauley, M. E. (1981). Aircrew training devices: Fidelity features (Technical Report No. AFHRL-TR-80-36). Brooks Air Force Base, TX: Air Force Human Resources Laboratory, Air Force Systems Command.

Settoon, R. P., Bennett, N., & Liden, R. C. (1996). Social exchange in organizations: Perceived organizational support, leader-member exchange, and employee reciprocity. *Journal of Applied Psychology, 81,* 219–227.

Shaffer, G. S., Saunders, V., & Owens, W. A. (1986). Additional evidence for the accuracy of biographical data: Long-term retest and observer ratings. *Personnel Psychology, 39,* 791–809.

Shalley, C. E. (1995). Effects of coaction, expected evaluation, and goal setting on creativity and productivity. *Academy of Management Journal, 38,* 483–503.

Shartle, C. L. (1950). Studies of leadership by interdisciplinary methods. In H. Guetzkow (Ed.), *Groups, leadership, and men.* Pittsburgh: Carnegie Press.

Shaw, L. B. (1988). Special problems of older women workers. In Industrial Relations Research Association, *The older worker.* Madison, WI: Author.

Shaw, M. E. (1976). *Group dynamics: The psychology of small group behavior* (2nd ed.). New York: McGraw-Hill.

Shea, G. P., & Guzzo, R. A. (1987). Group effectiveness: What really matters? *Sloan Management Review, 28,* 25–31.

Shellenbarger, S. (1992, January 20). Work and family: Work-family plans cut absenteeism and stress. *Wall Street Journal,* p. B1.

Shenhav, Y. (1992). Entrance of Blacks and women into managerial positions in scientific and engineering occupations: A longitudinal analysis. *Academy of Management Journal, 35,* 889–901.

Sheppard, B. H., & Lewicki, R. J. (1987). Toward a general principle of managerial fairness. *Social Justice Research, 1,* 161–176.

Sheppard, B. H., Lewicki, R. J., & Minton, J. (1986). A new view of organizations: Some retrospective comments. In R. J. Lewicki, B. H. Sheppard, & M. Bazerman (Eds.), *Research on negotiation in organizations.* Stamford, CT: JAI Press.

Shepperd, J. A. (1993). Productivity loss in performance groups: A motivation analysis. *Psychological Bulletin, 113,* 67–81.

Sheridan, D. (1992, February). Off the road again: Training through teleconferencing. *Training,* 63–68. .

Sheridan, J. E. (1992). Organizational culture and employee retention. *Academy of Management Journal, 35,* 1036–1056.

Sherman, P. A. (1984). The alcoholic executive. In J. S. J. Manuso (Ed.), *Occupational clinical psychology.* New York: Praeger.

Shore, L. M., Barksdale, K., & Shore, T. H. (1995). Managerial perceptions of employee commitment to the organization. *Academy of Management Journal, 38,* 1593–1615.

Shore, L. M., & Wayne, S. J. (1993). Commitment and employee behavior: Comparison of affective commitment and continuance with perceived organizational support. *Journal of Applied Psychology, 78,* 774–780.

Shore, T. H., Shore, L. M., & Thornton, G. C., III. (1990). Construct validity of self and peer evaluations of performance dimensions in an assessment center. *Journal of Applied Psychology, 77,* 42–54.

Shore, T. H., Thornton, G. C., III, & Shore, L. M. (1990). Construct validity of two categories of assessment center dimension ratings. *Personnel Psychology, 43,* 101–116.

Shulman, H. G., & Olex, M. B. (1985). Designing the user-friendly robot: A case history. *Human Factors, 27,* 91–98.

Simon, H. (1976). *Administrative behavior* (3rd ed.). New York: Free Press.

Simon, S. J., & Werner, J. M. (1996). Computer training through behavior modeling, self-paced, and instructional approaches: A field experiment. *Journal of Applied Psychology, 81,* 648–659.

Sims, H. P., Jr., & Manz, C. C. (1984). Observing leader verbal behavior: Toward reciprocal determinism in leadership theory. *Journal of Applied Psychology, 69,* 222–232.

Sinks, T., Mathias, C., Halpern, W., Timbrook, C., & Newman, S. (1987). Surveillance of work-related cold injuries using worker's compensation claims. *Journal of Occupational Health and Safety, 29,* 505–509.

Slack, J. D. (1996). Workplace preparedness and the Americans with Disabilities Act: Lessons from municipal governments' management of HIV/AIDS. *Public Administration Review, 56,* 159–167.

Smith, D. C., & Mahoney, J. J. (1989). *McDonnell Douglas Corporation employee assistance program financial offset study, 1985–1988.* Paper presented at the EAPA Annual Conference, Baltimore, MD.

Smith, P. C. (1976). Behaviors, results, and organizational effectiveness: The problem of criteria. In M. D. Dunnette (Ed.), *Handbook of industrial and organizational psychology.* Chicago: Rand McNally.

Smith, P. C., & Kendall, L. M. (1963). Retranslation of expectations: An approach to the construction of unambiguous anchors for rating scales. *Journal of Applied Psychology, 47,* 149–155.

Smith, P. C., Kendall, L. M., & Hulin, C. L. (1969). *The measurement of satisfaction in work and retirement.* Chicago: Rand McNally.

Smith, R. A., & Davis, S. F. (1997). *The psychologist as detective.* Upper Saddle River, NJ: Prentice-Hall.

Smith-Jentsch, K. A., Jentsch, F. G., Payne, S. C., & Salas, E. (1996). Can pretraining experiences explain individual differences in learning? *Journal of Applied Psychology, 81,* 110–116.

Smither, J. W., Barry, S. R., & Reilly, R. R. (1989). An investigation of the validity of expert true score estimates in appraisal research. *Journal of Applied Psychology 74,* 143–151.

Smither, J. W., London, M., Vasilopoulos, N. L., Reilly, R. R., Millsap, R. E., & Salvemini, N. (1995). An examination of the effects of an upward feedback program over time. *Personnel Psychology, 48,* 1–34.

Smither, J. W., Reilly, R. R., Millsap, R. E., Pearlman, K., & Stoffey, R. W. (1993). Applicant reactions to selection procedures. *Personnel Psychology, 46,* 49–76.

Smither, R. D. (1984). *Competitors and comrades: Personality, economics, and culture.* New York: Praeger.

Smither, R. D. (1988). *The psychology of work and human performance.* New York: Harper & Row.

Smither, R. D. (1989). *Using social psychology to make quality circles more effective.* Winter Park, FL: Rollins College. (ERIC Document Reproduction Service No. ED 314 673.)

Smither, R. D. (1990, November). The return of the authoritarian leader. *Training,* pp. 40–44.

Smither, R. D. (1993). Authoritarianism, dominance, and social behavior: A perspective from evolutionary personality psychology. *Human Relations, 46,* 23–43.

Smither, R. D., & Houston, J. M. (1991, August). *What do managerial potential scales measure?* Paper presented at the annual meeting of the American Psychology Association, Washington, DC.

Smither, R. D., Houston, J. M., & McIntire, S. A. (1996). *Organization development: Strategies for changing environments.* New York: HarperCollins.

Smither, R.D., & Houston, M. R. (1991). Racial discrimination and forms of redress in the military. *Journal of Intercultural Relations, 15,* 459–468.

Smither, R. D., & Lindgren, H. C. (1978). Salary, age, sex, and need for achievement in bank employees. *Psychological Reports, 42,* 334.

Snell, A. F., Stokes, G. S., Sands, M. M., & McBride, J. R. (1994). Adolescent life experiences as predictors of occupational attainment. *Journal of Applied Psychology, 79,* 131–141.

Snow, R. E., & Lohman, D. F. (1984). Toward a theory of cognitive aptitude for learning from instruction. *Journal of Educational Psychology, 76,* 347–376.

Snyder, M. (1974). The self-monitoring of expressive behavior. *Journal of Personality and Social Psychology, 30,* 526–537.

Sonnenstuhl, W. J. (1990). Help-seeking and helping processes within the workplace: Assisting alcoholic and other troubled employees. In P. M. Roman (Ed.), *Alcohol problem intervention in the workplace.* New York: Quorum Books.

Spencer, B. A. (1994) Models of organization and Total Quality Management: A comparison and critical evaluation. *Academy of Management Review, 19,* 446–471.

Spera, S. P., Buhrfeind, E. D., & Pennebaker, J. W. (1994). Expressive writing and coping with job loss. *Academy of Management Journal, 37,* 722–733.

Spitz, C. (1992, June). Multimedia training at Hewlett-Packard. *Training & Development,* 39–41.

Spreitzer, G. M. (1995). Psychological empowerment in the workplace: Dimensions, measurement, and validation. *Academy of Management Journal, 38,* 1442–1465.

Spreitzer, G. M. (1996). Social structural characteristics of psychological empowerment. *Academy of Management Journal, 39,* 483–504.

Springbett, B. M. (1958). Factors affecting the final decision in the employment interview. *Canadian Journal of Psychology, 12,* 13–22.

Sproull, L., & Kiesler, S. (1991). *Connections: New ways of working in the networked organization.* Cambridge, MA: MIT Press.

Spychalski, A. C., Quiñones, M. A., Gaugler, B. B., & Pohley, K. (1997). A survey of assessment center practices in organizations in the United States. *Personnel Psychology, 50,* 71–90.

Stahl, M. J. (1983). Achievement, power, and managerial motivation: Selecting managerial talent with the job choice exercise. *Personnel Psychology, 36,* 775–789.

Stamoulis, D. T., & Hauenstein, N. M. A. (1993). Rater training and rating accuracy: Training for dimensional accuracy versus training for ratee differentiation. *Journal of Applied Psychology, 81,* 994–1003.

Stamps, D. (1996, October). Relaxed fit. *Training,* 90–100.

Stanton, J. M., & Barnes-Farrell, J. L. (1996). Effects of electronic performance monitoring on personal control, task satisfaction, and task performance. *Journal of Applied Psychology, 81,* 738–745.

Staw, B. M. (1982). Motivation in organizations: Toward synthesis and redirection. In B. M. Staw & G. R. Salancik (Eds.), *New directions in organizational behavior.* Chicago: St. Clair Press.

Staw, B. M., & Ross, J. (1980). Commitment in an experimenting society: A study of the attribution of leadership from administrative scenarios. *Journal of Applied Psychology, 65,* 249–260.

Steel, R. P. (1996). Labor market dimensions as predictors of the reenlistment decisions of military personnel. *Journal of Applied Psychology, 81,* 421–428.

Steel, R. P., & Ovalle, N. K., II. (1984). A review and meta-analysis of research on the relationship between behavioral intentions and employee turnover. *Journal of Applied Psychology, 69,* 673–686.

Steel, R. P., & Rentsch, J. R. (1995). Influence of cumulation strategies on the long-range prediction of absenteeism. *Academy of Management Journal, 38,* 1616–1634.

Steers, R. M., & Rhodes, S. R. (1978). Major influences on employee attendance. *Journal of Applied Psychology, 63,* 391–407.

Steffy, B. D., & Grimes, A. J. (1986). A critical theory of organization science. *Academy of Management Review, 11,* 322–336.

Steffy, B. D., & Laker, D. R. (1991). Workplace and personal stresses antecedent to employees' alcohol use. *Journal of Social Behavior and Personality, 6,* 115–126.

Stein, J. A., Newcomb, M. D., & Bentler, P. M. (1988). Structure of drug use behaviors and consequences among young adults: Multitrait-multimethod assessment of frequency, quantity, work site, and problem substance use. *Journal of Applied Psychology, 73,* 595–605.

Stein, J. A., Smith, G. M., Guy, S. M., & Bentler, P. M. (1993). Consequences of adolescent drug use on young adult job behavior and job satisfaction. *Journal of Applied Psychology, 78,* 463–474.

Steiner, D. D., & Gilliland, S. W. (1996). Fairness reactions to personnel selection techniques in France and the United States. *Journal of Applied Psychology, 81,* 134–141.

Steiner, D. D., & Rain, J. S. (1989). Immediate and delayed primacy and recency effects in performance evaluation. *Journal of Applied Psychology, 74,* 136–142.

Steiner, D. D., Rain, J. S., & Smalley, M. M. (1993). Distributional ratings of performance: Further examination of a new rating format. *Journal of Applied Psychology, 78,* 438–442.

Sterk-Elifson, C. (1996). Just for fun: Cocaine use among middle-class women. *Journal of Drug Issues, 26,* 63–76.

Stevens, C. K., Bavetta, A. G., & Gist, M. E. (1993). Gender differences in the acquisition of salary negotiation skills: The role of goals, self-efficacy, and perceived control. *Journal of Applied Psychology, 78,* 723–735.

Stevens, C. K., & Kristof, A. L. (1995). Making the right impression: A field study of applicant impression management during job interviews. *Journal of Applied Psychology, 80,* 587–606.

Stewart, G. L. (1996). Reward structure as a moderator of the relationship between extraversion and sales performance. *Journal of Applied Psychology, 81,* 619–627.

Stewart, G. L., Carson, K. P., & Cardy, R. L. (1996). The joint effects of conscientiousness and self-leadership training on employee self-directed behavior in a service setting. *Personnel Psychology, 49,* 143–164.

Stogdill, R. M. (1965). *Managers, employees, organizations.* Columbus: Ohio State University, Bureau of Business Research.

Stokes, G. S., Hogan, J. B., & Snell, A. F. (1993). Comparability of incumbent and applicant samples for the development of biodata keys: The influence of social desirability. *Personnel Psychology, 46,* 739–762.

Stokes, G. S., Mumford, M. D., & Owens, W. A. (1994). *Biodata handbook: Theory, research, and use of biographical information in selection and performance prediction.* Palo Alto, CA: Consulting Psychologists Press.

Stokols, D., Pelletier, K. R., & Fielding, J. E. (1996). The ecology of work and health: Research and policy directions for the promotion of employee health. *Health Education Quarterly, 23,* 137–158.

Stone, D. L., & Colella, A. (1996). A model of factors affecting the treatment of disabled individuals in organizations. *Academy of Management Review, 21,* 352–401.

Stone, D. L., & Kotch, D. A. (1989). Individuals' attitudes toward organizational drug testing policies and practices. *Journal of Applied Psychology, 74,* 518–521.

Straus, S. G., & McGrath, J. E. (1994). Does the medium matter? The interaction of task type and technology on group performance and member reactions. *Journal of Applied Psychology, 79,* 87–97.

Stroh, L. K., Brett, J. M., Baumann, J. P., & Reilly, A. H. (1996). Agency theory and variable pay compensation strategies. *Academy of Management Journal, 39,* 751–767.

Strong, E. K., & Campbell, D. P. (1966). *Manual for the Strong Vocational Interest Blank.* Stanford, CA: Stanford University Press.

Stuart, P. (1991a, June). The chemical dependency care package. *Personnel Journal, 20,* 94–101.

Stuart, P. (1991b, November). The hidden addiction. *Personnel Journal, 20,* 103–108.

Sulsky, L. M., & Balzer, W. K. (1988). Meaning and measurement of performance ratings accuracy: Some methodological and theoretical concerns. *Journal of Applied Psychology, 73,* 497–506.

Sulsky, L. M., & Day, D. V. (1994). Effects of frame-of-reference training on rater accuracy under alternative time delays. *Journal of Applied Psychology, 81,* 535–543.

Sumer, H. C., & Knight, P. A. (1996). Assimilation and contrast effects in performance ratings: Effects of rating the previous performance on rating subsequent performance. *Journal of Applied Psychology, 81,* 436–442.

Summala, H., & Mikkola, T. (1994). Fatal accidents among car and truck drivers: Effects of fatigue, age, and alcohol consumption. *Human Factors, 36,* 315–326.

Summers, T. P., & Hendrix, W. H. (1991). Development of a turnover model that incorporates a matrix measure of valence-instrumentality-expectancy perceptions. *Journal of Business and Psychology, 6,* 227–245.

Sutcliffe, K. M. (1994). What executives notice: Accurate perceptions in top management teams. *Academy of Management Journal, 37,* 1360–1378.

Sutton, C. D., & Woodman, R. W. (1989). Pygmalion goes to work: The effects of supervisor expectations in a retail setting. *Journal of Applied Psychology, 74,* 943–950.

Swaroff, P. G., Barclay, L. A., & Bass, A. R. (1985). Recruiting sources: Another look. *Journal of Applied Psychology, 70,* 720–728.

Sweeney, P. D., McFarlin, D. B., & Inderrieden, E. J. (1990). Using relative deprivation theory to explain satisfaction with income and pay level: A multistudy examination. *Academy of Management Journal, 33,* 423–436.

Tabachnik, B. G., & Fidell, L. S. (1989). *Using multivariate statistics* (2nd ed.). New York: Harper & Row.

Tait, M., Padgett, M. Y., & Baldwin, T. T. (1989). Job and life satisfaction: A reevaluation of the strength of the relationship and gender effects as a function of the date of the study. *Journal of Applied Psychology, 74,* 502–507.

Talaga, J. A., & Beehr, T. A. (1995). Are there gender differences in predicting retirement decisions? *Journal of Applied Psychology, 80,* 16–28.

Tane, L. D., & Treacy, M. E. (1984, April). Benefits that bend with employees' needs. *Nation's Business,* 80–82.

Tarullo, G. M. (1992, August). Making outdoor experiential training work. *Training,* 47–52.

Taylor, F. W. (1907). *On the art of cutting metals.* New York: ASME.

Taylor, F. W. (1947). Testimony before the Special House Committee. In *Scientific Management.* New York: Harper & Row.

Taylor, H., & Russell, J. (1939). The relationship of validity coefficients to the practical effectiveness of tests in selection: Discussion and tables. *Journal of Applied Psychology, 23,* 565–578.

Taylor, M. S., Locke, E. A., Lee, C., & Gist, M. E. (1984). Type A behavior and faculty research productivity: What are the mechanisms? *Organizational Behavior and Human Decision Processes, 34,* 402–418.

Tellegen, A. (1982). *Brief manual for the Differential Personality Questionnaire.* Minneapolis: University of Minnesota Press.

Tepper, B. (1995). Upward maintenance tactics in supervisory mentoring and nonmentoring relationships. *Academy of Management Journal, 38,* 1191–1205.

Terpstra, D. E. (1981). Relationship between methodological rigor and reported outcomes in organization development evaluation research. *Journal of Applied Psychology, 66,* 541–543.

Terpstra, D. E., & Baker, D. D. (1988). Outcomes of sexual harassment charges. *Academy of Management Journal, 31,* 185 –194.

Terpstra, D. E., & Baker, D. D. (1992). Outcomes of federal court decisions on sexual harassment. *Academy of Management Journal, 35,* 181–190.

Terpstra, D. E., & Rozell, E. J. (1993). The relationship of staffing practices to organizational level measures of performance. *Personnel Psychology, 46,* 27–48.

Terris, W. (1986). *The development and validation of EP1-3.* Park Ridge, IL: London House Press.

Tesluk, P. E., Farr, J. L., Mathieu, J. E., & Vance, R. J. (1995). Generalization of employee involvement training to the job setting: Individual and situational effects. *Personnel Psychology, 48,* 607–632.

Tett, R. P., Jackson, D. N., & Rothstein, M. (1991). Personality measures as predictors of job performance: A meta-analytic review. *Personnel Psychology, 44,* 703–742.

Tett, R. P., & Meyer, J. P. (1993). Job satisfaction, organizational commitment, turnover intention, and turnover: Path analyses based on meta-analysis findings. *Personnel Psychology, 46,* 259–293.

Tharenou, P., Latimer, S., & Conroy, D. (1994). How do you make it to the top? An examination of influences on women's and men's managerial advancement. *Academy of Management Journal, 37,* 899–931.

The costs of stressed workers to employers. (1996, August). *Working Age, 12,* 5.

Thomas, D. A. (1990). The impact of race on managers' experiences of developmental relationships (mentoring and sponsorship): An intra-organizational study. *Journal of Organizational Behavior, 2,* 479–492.

Thomas, K. M., & Mathieu, J. E. (1994). Role of causal attributions in dynamic self-regulation and goal processes. *Journal of Applied Psychology, 79,* 812–818.

Thomas, K. W. (1976). Conflict and conflict management. In M. Dunnette (Ed.), *Handbook of industrial and organizational psychology.* Chicago: Rand McNally.

Thomas, K. W., & Velthouse, B. A. (1990). Cognitive elements of empowerment: An "interpretive" model of intrinsic task motivation. *Academy of Management Review, 15,* 666–681.

Thomas, L. T., & Ganster, D. C. (1995). Impact of family-supportive work variables on work-family conflict and strain: A control perspective. *Journal of Applied Psychology, 80,* 6–15.

Thomas, R. R., Jr. (1991). *Beyond race and gender.* New York: AMACOM.

Thorndike, R. L. (1949). *Personnel selection.* New York: Wiley.

Thornton, W. (1978). Anthropometric changes in weightlessness. In Anthropology Research Staff (Eds.), *Anthropometric source book (Vol. 1: Anthropometry for designers)* (NASA RP- 1024). Houston, TX: National Aeronautics and Space Administration.

Townsend, A. M., Aalberts, R. J., & Whitman, M. E. (1997, January). Danger on the desktop. *HRMagazine,* 82–85.

Tracey, J. B., Tannenbaum, S. I., & Kavanagh, M. J. (1995). Applying trained skills on the job: The importance of the work environment. *Personnel Psychology, 45,* 239–252.

Trevor, C. O., Gerhart, B., & Boudreau, J. W. (1997). Voluntary turnover and job performance: Curvilinearity and the moderating influences of salary growth and promotions. *Journal of Applied Psychology, 82,* 44–61.

Triandis, H. C. (1989). Cross-cultural studies of individualism-collectivism. In J. J. Berman (Ed.), *Nebraska Symposium on Motivation: Cross-cultural perspectives* (Vol. 37). Lincoln: University of Nebraska Press.

Trist, E. L. (1981). The evolution of sociotechnical systems as a conceptual framework and as an action research program. In A. H. Van de Ven & W. F. Joyce (Eds.), *Perspectives on organization and behavior.* New York: Wiley.

Trist, E. L., & Bamforth, K. W. (1951). Some social and psychological consequences of the longwall method of coal-getting. *Human Relations, 4,* 1–38.

Tsui, A. S., Ashford, S. J., St. Clair, L., & Xin, K. R. (1995). Dealing with discrepant expectations: Response strategies and managerial effectiveness. *Academy of Management Journal, 38,* 1515–1543.

Tsui, A. S., & O'Reilly, C. A., III. (1988). Beyond simple demographic effects: The importance of relational demography in superior-subordinate dyads. *Academy of Management Journal, 32,* 402–423.

Tubbs, M. E. (1986). Goal setting: A meta-analytic examination of the empirical evidence. *Journal of Applied Psychology, 71,* 474–483.

Tubbs, M. E. (1993). Commitment as a moderator of the goal-performance relation: A case for clearer construct definition. *Journal of Applied Psychology, 78,* 86–97.

Tubbs, M. E. (1994). Commitment and the role of ability in motivation: Comment on Wright, O'Leary- Kelly, Cortina, Klein, and Hollenbeck (1994). *Journal of Applied Psychology, 79,* 804–811.

Tubbs, M. E. (1995). Commitment as a moderator of the goal-performance relation: A case for clearer construct definition. *Journal of Applied Psychology, 78,* 86–97.

Tubbs, M. E., Boehne, D. M., and Dahl, J. G. (1993). Expectancy, valence, and motivational force functions in goal-

setting research: An empirical test. *Journal of Applied Psychology, 78,* 361–373.

Tubbs, M. E., & Dahl, J. G. (1991). An empirical comparison of self-report and discrepancy measures of goal commitment. *Journal of Applied Psychology, 76,* 708–716.

Tubbs, M. E., & Ekeberg, S. E. (1991). The role of intentions in work motivation: Implications for goal-setting theory and research. *Academy of Management Review, 16,* 180–199.

Tuckman, B. W. (1965). Development sequences in small groups. *Psychological Bulletin, 63,* 384–399.

Tuckman, B. W., & Jensen, M. (1977). Stages of small-group development. *Group and Organizational Studies, 2,* 419–427.

Turban, D. B., & Dougherty, T. W. (1992). Influences of campus recruiting on applicant attraction to firms. *Academy of Management Journal, 35,* 739–765.

Turban, D. B., & Dougherty, T. W. (1994). Role of protégé personality in receipt of mentoring performance and turnover. *Academy of Management Journal, 37,* 688–702.

Turban, D. B., Sanders, P. A., Francis, D. J., & Osbrun, H. G. (1989). Construct equivalence as an approach to replacing validated cognitive ability selection tests. *Journal of Applied Psychology, 74,* 62–71.

Turnage, J. J., & Muchinsky, P. M. (1984). A comparison of the predictive validity of assessment center evaluations versus traditional measures in forecasting supervisory job performance: Interpretive implications of criterion distortion for the assessment paradigm. *Journal of Applied Psychology, 69,* 595–602.

Tushman, M. L., & Romanelli, E. (1990). Organizational evolution: A metamorphosis model of convergence and reorientation. In B. M. Staw & L. L. Cummings (Eds.), *The evolution and adaptation of organizations.* Greenwich, CT: JAI Press.

Tuzzolino, F., & Armandi, B. R. (1981). A need-hierarchy framework for assessing corporate social responsibility. *Academy of Management Review, 6,* 21–28.

Tziner, A., & Kopelman, R. (1988). Effects of rating format on goal-setting dimensions: A field experiment. *Journal of Applied Psychology, 73,* 323–326.

U.S. Department of Labor. (1989). *Handbook of labor statistics.* Washington, DC: U.S. Government Printing Office.

U.S. Department of Labor. (1989, November 15). BLS reports on survey of occupational injuries and illnesses in 1988. *News from the United States Department of Labor.* Washington DC: Bureau of Statistics.

U.S. Department of Labor. (1991, Fall). Outlook: 1990–2005. *Occupational outlook quarterly.* Washington, DC: Bureau of Labor Statistics.

Urban, J. M., Weaver, J. L., Bowers, C. A., & Rhodenizer, L. (1996). Effects of workload and structure on team processes and performance: Implications for complex team decision making. *Human Factors, 38,* 300–310.

Vance, R. J., & Colella, A. (1990). Effects of two types of feedback on goal acceptance and personal goals. *Journal of Applied Psychology, 75,* 68–76.

Van Cott, H. P., & Warrick, M. J. (1972). Man as a system component. In H. P. Van Cott & R. G. Kinkade (Eds.), *Human engineering guide to equipment design* (rev. ed.). Washington, DC: U.S. Government Printing Office.

Vancouver, J. B., Millsap, R. E., & Peters, P. A. (1994). Multilevel analysis of organizational goal congruence. *Journal of Applied Psychology, 79,* 666–679.

Vandenberg, R. J., & Scarpello, V. (1990). The matching model: An examination of the processes underlying realistic job previews. *Journal of Applied Psychology, 75,* 60–67.

Van de Ven, A. H., & Poole, M. S. (1995). Explaining development and change in organizations. *Academy of Management Review, 20,* 510–540.

Van de Vliert, E., Euwema, M. C., & Huismans, S. E. (1995). Managing conflict with a subordinate or a superior: Effectiveness of conglomerated behavior. *Journal of Applied Psychology, 80,* 271–281.

Van de Vliert, E., & Van Yperen, N. W. (1996). Why cross-national differences in role overload? Don't overlook ambient temperature! *Academy of Management Journal, 39,* 986–1004.

Van Eerde, W., & Thierry, H. (1996). Vroom's expectancy models and work-related criteria: A meta-analysis. *Journal of Applied Psychology, 81,* 575–586.

Van Orden, K. F., Benoit, S. L., & Osga, G. A. (1996). Effects of cold air stress on the performance of a command and control task. *Human Factors, 38,* 130–141.

Van Scotter, J. R., & Motowidlo, S. J. (1996). Interpersonal facilitation and job dedication as separate facets of contextual performance. *Journal of Applied Psychology, 81,* 525–531.

Vecchio, R. (1987). Situational leadership theory: An examination of a prescriptive theory. *Journal of Applied Psychology, 72,* 444–451.

Vecchio, R. P. (1982). Predicting worker performance in inequitable settings. *Academy of Management Review, 7,* 470–481.

Veroff, J., Atkinson, J. W., Feld, S. C., & Guinn, G. (1974). The use of thematic apperception to assess motivation in a nationwide study. In J. W. Atkinson, S. W. Raynor et al., *Motivation and achievement.* Washington, DC: Winston.

Vest, J. M., O'Brien, F. P., & Vest, M. J. (1991, December). AIDS training in the workplace. *Training & Development,* 59–64.

Villanova, P., Bernardin, H. J., Johnson, D. L., & Dahmus, S. A. (1994). The validity of a measure of job compatibility in the prediction of job performance and turnover of motion picture personnel. *Personnel Psychology, 47,* 73–90.

Viswesvaran, C., Barrick, M. R., & Ones, D. S. (1993). How definitive are conclusions based on survey data: Estimating robustness to nonresponse. *Personnel Psychology, 46,* 551–567.

Viswesvran, C., & Ones, D. S. (1995). Theory testing: Combining psychometric meta-analysis and structural equations modeling. *Personnel Psychology, 48,* 865–885.

Viswesvaran, C., Ones, D. S., & Schmidt, F. L. (1996). Comparative analysis of the reliability of job performance ratings. *Journal of Applied Psychology, 81,* 557–574.

Viswesvaran, C., & Schmidt, F. L. (1992). A meta-analytic comparison of the effectiveness of smoking cessation methods. *Journal of Applied Psychology, 77,* 554–561.

Vitkovic, L., & Koslow, S. H. (Eds.) (1994). *Neuroimmunology and mental health* (DHHS publication no. [NIH] 94–3774). Rockville, MD: U.S. Department of Health and Human Services.

Vroom, V. H. (1964). *Work and motivation.* New York: Wiley.

Vroom, V. H., & Jago, A. G. (1978). On the validity of the Vroom-Yetton model. *Journal of Applied Psychology, 63,* 151–162.

Vroom, V. H., & Jago, A. G. (1988). *The new leadership: Managing participation in organizations.* Englewood Cliffs, NJ: Prentice-Hall.

Vroom, V. H., & Yetton, P. W. (1973). *Leadership and decision-making.* New York: Wiley.

Wagener, D. K., & Winn, D. W. (1991). Injuries in working populations: Black-White differences. *American Journal of Public Health, 81,* 1408–1414.

Wagner, J. A., III. (1995). Studies of individualism-collectivism: Effects on cooperation in groups. *Academy of Management Journal, 38,* 152–172.

Wagner, J. A., III, & Gooding, R. Z. (1987). Shared influence and organizational behavior: A meta-analysis of situational variables expected to moderate participation-outcome relationships. *Academy of Management Journal, 30,* 524–541.

Wagner, J. A., III, & Moch, M. K. (1986). Individualism-collectivism: Concept and measure. *Group and Organization Studies, 11,* 280–304.

Wagner, R. J., & Roland, C. C. (1992, July). How effective is outdoor training? *Training & Development,* 61–66.

Wahba, M. A., & Bridwell, L. T. (1976). Maslow reconsidered: A review of research on the need hierarchy theory. *Organizational Behavior and Human Performance, 15,* 212–240.

Wakabayashi, M., & Graen, G. B. (1984). The Japanese career progress study: A 7-year follow-up. *Journal of Applied Psychology, 69,* 603–614.

Wakabayashi, M., Graen, G., Graen, M., & Graen, M. (1988). Japanese management progress: Mobility into middle management. *Journal of Applied Psychology, 73,* 217–227.

Waldman, D. A., & Avolio, B. J. (1986). A meta-analysis of age differences in job performance. *Journal of Applied Psychology, 71,* 33–38.

Waldman, D. A., & Avolio, B. J. (1991). Race effects in performance evaluations: Controlling for ability, education, and experience. *Journal of Applied Psychology, 76,* 897–901.

Wall, T. D., Kemp, N. J., Jackson, P. R., & Clegg, C. W. (1986). Outcomes of autonomous workgroups: A long-term field experiment. *Academy of Management Journal, 29,* 280–304.

Wallace, M. (1990). *Rewards and renewal: America's search for competitive advantage.* Scottsdale, AZ: American Compensation Association.

Wanberg, C. R., Watt, J. D., & Rumsey, D. J. (1996). Individuals without jobs: An empirical study of job-seeking behavior and reemployment. *Journal of Applied Psychology, 81,* 76–87.

Wanous, J. P. (1980). *Organizational entry.* Reading, MA: Addison-Wesley.

Wanous, J. P. (1989). Installing a realistic job preview: Ten tough choices. *Personnel Psychology, 42,* 117–134.

Wanous, J. P. (1992). *Organizational entry: Recruitment, selection, orientation, and socialization of newcomers* (2nd ed.). Reading, MA: Addison-Wesley.

Wanous, J. P., & Zwany, A. (1977). A cross-sectional test of need hierarchy theory. *Organizational Behavior and Human Performance, 18,* 78–97.

Warm, J. S., & Jerison, H. J. (1984). The psychophysics of vigilance. In J. S. Warm (Ed.), *Sustained attention in human performance.* Chichester, England: Wiley.

Warr, P., & Bunce, D. (1995). Trainee characteristics and the outcomes of open learning. *Personnel Psychology, 48,* 347–375.

Watson, C. (1988). When a woman is the boss: Dilemmas in taking charge. *Group and Organizational Studies, 13,* 163–181.

Watson, W. E., Kumar, K., & Michaelsen, L. K. (1993). Cultural diversity's impact on interaction process and performance: Comparing homogeneous and diverse task groups. *Academy of Management Journal, 36,* 590–602.

Watson, W. E., Michaelsen, L. K., & Sharp, W. (1991). Member competence, group interaction, and group decision making: A longitudinal study. *Journal of Applied Psychology, 76,* 803–809.

Waxman, H. S. (1995, September). Putting workplace violence in perspective. *Security Management,* 123–126.

Wayne, S. J., & Ferris, G. R. (1990). Influence tactics, affect, and exchange quality in supervisor-subordinate interactions: A laboratory experiment and field study. *Journal of Applied Psychology, 75,* 487–499.

Wayne, S. J., & Liden, R. C. (1995). Effects of impression management on performance ratings: A longitudinal study. *Academy of Management Journal, 38,* 232–260.

Webster, E. C. (1982). *The employment interview: A social judgment process.* Schomberg, Ontario: S.I.P. Publications.

Weekley, J. A., & Gier, J. A. (1989). Ceilings in the reliability and validity of performance ratings: The case of expert raters. *Academy of Management Journal, 32,* 213–222.

Weekley, J. A., & Jones, C. (1997). Video-based situational testing. *Personnel Psychology, 50,* 25–49.

Wegmann, R. G. (1991). From job to job. *Journal of Employment Counseling, 28,* 8–12.

Weingart, L. R. (1992). Impact of group goals, task component complexity, effort, and planning on group performance. *Journal of Applied Psychology, 77,* 682–693.

Weingart, L. R., Bennett, R. J., & Brett, J. M. (1993). The impact of consideration of issues and motivational orientation group negotiation and outcome. *Journal of Applied Psychology, 78,* 504–517.

Weisner, W. H., & Cronshaw, S. F. (1988). A meta-analytic investigation of the impact of interview format and degree of structure on the validity of the employment interview. *Journal of Occupational Psychology, 61,* 275–290.

Weiss, D. J., Dawis, R. V., England, G. W., & Lofquist, L. H. (1967). Manual for the Minnesota Satisfaction Questionnaire. *Minnesota Studies in Vocational Rehabilitation,* Bulletin No. 22.

Weiss, R. M. (1987). Writing under the influence: Science versus fiction in the analysis of corporate alcoholism programs. *Personnel Psychology, 40,* 341–356.

Wells, D. L., & Muchinsky, P. M. (1985). Performance antecedents of voluntary and involuntary managerial turnover. *Journal of Applied Psychology, 70,* 329–336.

Wells, M. J. (1992). Virtual reality: Technology, experience, assumptions. *Human Factors Society Bulletin, 35,* 1–3.

Welsh, D. H. B., Luthans, F., & Sommer, S. M. (1993). Managing Russian factory workers: The impact of U.S.-based behavioral and participative techniques. *Academy of Management Journal, 36,* 58–79.

Wiersema, M. F., & Bird, A. (1993). Organizational demography in Japanese firms: Groups heterogenity, individual dissimilarity, and top management team turnover. *Academy of Management Journal, 36,* 996–1025.

Werner, J. M. (1994). Dimensions that make a difference: Examining the impact of in-role and extra-role behaviors on supervisory ratings. *Journal of Applied Psychology, 81,* 98–107.

Werner, J. M., & Bolino, M. C. (1997). Explaining U.S. Court of Appeals decisions involving performance appraisal: Accuracy, fairness, and validation. *Personnel Psychology, 50,* 1–24.

Wexley, K. N., & Latham, G. P. (1981). *Developing and training human resources in organizations.* Glenview, IL: Scott, Foresman.

Wexley, K. N., & Yukl, G. A. (1977). *Organizational behavior and personnel psychology.* Homewood, IL: Richard D. Irwin.

Wexley, K. N., & Yukl, G. A. (1984). *Organizational behavior and personnel psychology.* Homewood, IL: Richard D. Irwin.

Wheeler, D. D., & Janis, I. L. (1980). *A practical guide for making decisions.* New York: Free Press.

White, J. B., & Lublin, J. S. (1996, September 27). Some companies try to rebuild loyalty. *Wall Street Journal,* p. B1.

White, M., Tansey, R., Smith, M., & Barnett, T. (1993). Log-linear modeling in personnel research. *Personnel Psychology, 46,* 667–686.

White, S. E., & Mitchell, T. R. (1976). Organization development: A review of research content and research design. *Academy of Management Review, 1,* 57–73.

Whitney, D. J., & Schmitt, N. (1997). Relationship between culture and responses to biodata items. *Journal of Applied Psychology, 82,* 113–129.

Whyte, G. (1989). Groupthink reconsidered. *Academy of Management Review, 14,* 40–56.

Wiersma, M. F., & Bird, A. (1993). Organizational demography in Japanese firms: Group heterogeneity, individual dissimilarity, and top management turnover. *Academy of Management Journal, 36,* 996–1025.

Wilk, S. L., & Sackett, P. R. (1996). Longitudinal analysis of ability-job complexity fit and job change. *Personnel Psychology, 47,* 937–967.

Wilkins, A. L., & Dyer, W. G., Jr. (1988). Toward culturally sensitive theories of culture change. *Academy of Management Review, 13,* 522–533.

Williams, C. R., & Livingstone, L. P. (1994). Another look at the relationship between performance and voluntary turnover. *Academy of Management Journal, 37,* 269–298.

Williams, J. R., & Levy, P. E. (1992). The effects of perceived system knowledge on the agreement between self-ratings and supervisor ratings. *Personnel Psychology, 45,* 835–847.

Williams, K. D., & Karau, S. J. (1991). Social loafing and social compensation: The effects of expectations of co-worker performance. *Journal of Personality and Social Psychology, 61,* 570–581.

Williams, K. J., & Alliger, G. M. (1994). Role stressors, mood spillover, and perceptions of work-family conflict in employed parents. *Academy of Management Journal, 37,* 837–868.

Williams, K. J., Suls, J., Alliger, G. M., Learner, S. M., & Wan, C. K. (1991). Multiple role juggling and daily mood states in working mothers: An experience sampling study. *Journal of Applied Psychology, 76,* 664–674.

Williams, L. J., & Hazer, J. T. (1986). Antecedents and consequences of satisfaction and commitment in turnover models: A reanalysis using latent variable structural equation methods. *Journal of Applied Psychology, 71,* 219–231.

Williams, M. L., & Dreher, G. F. (1992). Compensation system attributes and applicant pool characteristics. *Academy of Management Journal, 35,* 571–595.

Winkleby, M., Ragland, D., Fisher, J., & Syme, S. L. (1988). Excess risk of sickness and disease in bus drivers: A review and synthesis of epidemiological studies. *International Journal of Epidemiology, 17,* 255–262.

Winkler, H., & Sheridan, J. (1989). *An examination of behavior related to drug use at Georgia Power Company.* Paper presented at the National Institute on Drug Abuse Conference on Drugs in the Workplace: Research and Evaluation Data, Bethesda, MD.

Woehr, D. J. (1994). Understanding frame-of-reference training: The impact of training on the recall of performance information. *Journal of Applied Psychology, 81,* 525–534.

Woehr, D. J., & Feldman, J. (1993). Processing objective and question order effects on the causal relation between memory and judgment in performance appraisal: The tip of the iceberg. *Journal of Applied Psychology, 81,* 232–241.

Wong, C-S., & Campion, M. A. (1991). Development and test of a task level model of motivational job design. *Journal of Applied Psychology, 76,* 825–837.

Woo, J. (1993, September 1). Businesses find suits on security hard to defend. *Wall Street Journal,* p. 81.

Wood, R., & Bandura, A. (1989). Social cognitive theory of organizational management. *Academy of Management Review, 14,* 361–384.

Woodman, R. W. (1989). Evaluation research on organizational change: Arguments for a "combined paradigm" approach. In R. W. Woodman & W. A. Pasmore (Eds.), *Research in organizational change* (Vol. 1). Greenwich, CT: JAI Press.

Woodman, R. W., Sawyer, J. E., & Griffin, R. W. (1993). Toward a theory of organizational creativity. *Academy of Management Review, 18,* 293–321.

Woodward, J. (1965). *Industrial organization: Theory and practice.* London: Oxford University Press.

Wotton, E. (1986). Lighting the electronic office. In R. Lueder (Ed.), *The ergonomics payoff, designing the electronic office.* Toronto: Holt, Rinehart and Winston.

Wright, P. A., George, J. M., Farnsworth, S. R., & McMahan, G. C. (1993). Productivity and extra-role behavior: The effects of goals and incentives on spontaneous helping. *Journal of Applied Psychology, 78,* 374–381.

Wright, P. M. (1990). Operationalization of goal difficulty as a moderator of the goal difficulty-performance relationship. *Journal of Applied Psychology, 75,* 227–234.

Wright, P. M., Lichtenfels, P. A., & Pursell, E. D. (1989). The structured interview: Additional studies and a meta-analysis. *Journal of Occupational and Organizational Psychology, 62,* 191–199.

Wright, P. M., O'Leary-Kelly, A. M., Cortina, J. M., Klein, H. J., & Hollenbeck, J. R. (1994). On the meaning and measurement of goal commitment. *Journal of Applied Psychology, 79,* 795–803.

Wyndham, C. (1974). Research in the human sciences in the gold mining industry. *American Industrial Hygiene Association Journal,* 113–136.

Xie, J. L., & Johns, G. (1995). Job scope and stress: Can job scope be too high? *Academy of Management Journal, 38,* 1288–1309.

Yammarino, F. J., & Dubinsky, A. J. (1994). Transformational leadership theory: Using levels of analysis to determine boundary conditions. *Personnel Psychology, 47,* 787–811.

Yammarino, F. J., Dubinsky, A. J., Comer, L. B., & Jolson, M. A. (1997). Women and transformational and contingent reward leadership: A multiple-levels-of-analysis perspective. *Academy of Management Journal, 40,* 205–222.

Yammarino, F. J., & Waldman, D. A. (1993). Performance in relation to job skill importance: A consideration of rater source. *Journal of Applied Psychology, 81,* 242–249.

Yandrick, R. (1992). Taking inventory. *EAPA Exchange, 22,* 22–29.

Yang, H., Sackett, P. R., & Arvey, R. D. (1996). Statistical power and cost in training evaluation: Some new considerations. *Personnel Psychology, 49,* 651–668.

Yarborough, M. H. (1995). OSHA now assesses employer liability. *HR Focus, 72,* 7.

York, K. M. (1989). Defining sexual harassment in workplaces: A policy-capturing approach. *Academy of Management Journal, 32,* 830–850.

Young, S. M. (1992). A framework for successful adoption and performance of Japanese manufacturing practices in the United States. *Academy of Management Review, 17,* 677–700.

Youngblood, S. A. (1984). Work, nonwork, and withdrawal. *Journal of Applied Psychology, 69,* 106–117.

Youngblood, S. A., Baysinger, B. D., & Mobley, W. H. (1985). The role of unemployment and job satisfaction on turnover: A longitudinal study. Paper presented at the meeting of the National Academy of Management, Boston.

Youngblood, S. A., Mobley, W. H., & Meglino, B. M. (1983). A longitudinal analysis of the turnover process. *Journal of Applied Psychology, 68,* 507–516.

Yu, J., & Murphy, K. R. (1993). Modesty bias in self-ratings of performance: A test of the cultural relativity hypothesis. *Personnel Psychology, 46,* 357–363.

Yukl, G., & Falbe, C. M. (1990). Influence tactics and objectives in upward, downward, and lateral relations. *Journal of Applied Psychology, 75,* 132–140.

Yukl, G., & Falbe, C. M. (1991). Importance of different power sources in downward and lateral relations. *Journal of Applied Psychology, 76,* 416–423.

Yukl, G., Kim, H., & Falbe, C. M. (1996). Antecedents of influence outcomes. *Journal of Applied Psychology, 81,* 309–317.

Zaccaro, S. J., Foti, R. J., & Kenny, D. A. (1991). Self-monitoring and trait-based variance in leadership: An investigation of leader flexibility across multiple group situations. *Journal of Applied Psychology, 76,* 308–315.

Zalesny, M. (1990). Rater confidence and social influence in performance appraisal. *Journal of Applied Psychology, 75,* 274–289.

Zaleznick A. (1977, May–June). Managers and leaders: Are they different? *Harvard Business Review.*

Zander, A. (1979). The psychology of group processes. *Annual Review of Psychology, 30,* 417–451.

Zedeck, S., & Blood, M. R. (1974) *Foundations of behavioral science research in organizations.* Monterey, CA: Brooks/Cole.

Zedeck, S., Cascio, W., Goldstein, I., & Outtz, J. (1994, January). Assessing fairness requires understanding the issues. *The Industrial-Organizational Psychology, 31,* 74–75.

Zedeck, S., Tziner, A., & Middlestadt, S. E. (1983). Interviewer validity and reliability: An individual analysis approach. *Personnel Psychology, 36,* 355–370.

Zeitlin, L R. (1994). Failure to follow safety instructions: Faulty communication or risky decisions? *Human Factors, 36,* 172–181.

Zeitz, K. (1991). Employer genetic testing: A legitimate screening device or another method of discrimination? *Labor Law Journal, 41,* 230–238.

Zemke, R. (1991, September). Shell scores with interactive video. *Training,* 33–38.

Zemke, R. (1992, April). Second thoughts about the MBTI. *Training,* 43–47.

Zickar, M. & Taylor, R. (1996, January). Income of SIOP members in 1994. *The Industrial-Organizational Psychologist, 33,* 63–70.

Name Index

Aalberts, R. J., 461
Abraham, L. M., 248
Abrahamson, E., 417
Ackerman, L., 71
Adamopoulos, J., 326
Adams, G. A., 353
Adams, J. A., 149
Adams, J. S., 211–212, 214, 216
Adams, S. M., 169
Adkins, C. L., 84, 394–395
Aguinis, H., 280, 425
Akers, R., 498
Aktouf, O., 384
Albanese, R., 205
Alderfer, C. P., 207
Alexander, R. A., 100, 185, 335
Allen, B. J., 462
Allen, N. J., 239, 303
Alliger, G. M., 238, 353–354
Allport, F., 310
Althouse, R., 484
Altmaier, E., 482
Alutto, J. A., 253
Amason, A. C., 324
Ambrose, M. L., 190, 315
Amel, E. L., 74
Ames, G., 474
Anastasi, A., 126
Ancona, D. G., 336
Anderson, D. C., 229
Anderson, M. B. G., 482
Anger, W. K., 466
Anhalt, R. L., 187
Anonyuo, C., 184
Anthony, W. P., 266
Antonioni, D., 198
Argyris, C., 421–422, 436
Armandi, B. R., 210
Arthur, J. B., 256
Arthur, W., 41, 83
Arvey, R. D., 60, 82, 85, 99, 105,
   107, 113, 161–162, 248–249

Ash, R. A., 83, 267, 350
Ashbaugh, D. L., 362
Ashe, D. K., 190
Asher, J. J., 80
Ashford, S. J., 240, 275, 396
Ashforth, B. E., 78, 395, 482
Astley, W. G., 372–373, 385
Athos, A. G., 404
Atkinson, J. W., 210
Atwater, D., 78
Atwater, L., 198
Audia, G., 228
Auerbach, J. D., 267
Austin, J. T., 185, 417
Avedon, M. J., 105, 118
Aviram, A., 156
Avolio, B. J., 185, 191, 302, 364,
   461
Axel, H., 478
Axline, L. L., 438

Baba, V. V., 250–251
Babbie, E. R., 47
Baber, C., 458
Back, K., 314
Backer, T. E., 490–491
Baglioni, A. J., Jr., 488
Bahnsen, E., 81
Bailey, R. W., 453, 456
Baird, L., 191
Baker, D. P., 123, 356
Baldwin, T. T., 136, 157, 237,
   331, 337–338
Bales, R. F., 316
Balzer, W. K., 187, 189–190, 244
Bamforth, K. W., 390
Bandura, A., 145, 218, 226, 290
Banker, R. D., 221, 332
Barbee, A. P., 120
Barber, A. E., 74, 83, 266
Barclay, L. A., 75
Barge, B. N., 486

Barksdale, K., 239
Barling, J., 218, 488
Barnes-Farrell, J. L., 177, 190
Barnett, T., 39
Barnum, P., 362
Barr, S. H., 81
Barrett, B., 66, 100
Barrett, G. V., 111, 185
Barrick, M. R., 48, 116–117, 229,
   254, 335
Barry, B., 317, 343
Barry, S. R., 192
Bartol, K. M., 89, 262
Barton, M. E., 367
Bass, A. R., 75
Bass, B. M., 278, 283, 302–303
Bastianutti, L. M., 327
Bateman, T. S., 90, 343, 397–398
Bauer, T. N., 299, 396
Baumann, J. P., 263
Baumgartel, H., 157
Baretta, A. G., 137, 330, 351
Baysinger, B. D., 255
Beam, B., 266
Beattie, R., 218
Beatty, R. W., 123
Beck, S., 482
Becker, A. S., 124
Becker, B. E., 109
Becker, T. E., 78, 239
Beckhard, R., 424
Bedeian, A. G., 301, 351, 353
Beehr, T. A., 362
Beer, M., 420, 422, 427–428, 437
Begley, T. M., 240
Beith, B. J., 149
Belknap, T., 349
Bell, C. H., 412, 419
Ben-Avi, I., 252
Bender, H. E., 177
Benedict, M. E., 191
Bennet-Alexander, D. D., 356

Bennett, D. E., 241
Bennett, N., 205, 398
Bennett, R. J., 259–260, 324
Bennett, W., 41
Bennis, W. G., 316, 422
Benoit, S. L., 454
Bensimon, H. F., 489
Bentler, P. M., 90, 480
Benton, C., 123–124
Berbaum, K. S., 462
Berg, P. O., 437
Bergquist, W., 400, 402
Berliner, D. C., 158
Bernadin, H. J., 120, 188, 193, 243–244
Bertrand, K., 253
Bettenhausen, K., 256
Betz, N. E., 350
BeVier, C. A., 60
Bible, J. D., 125
Bigoness, N. J., 191
Billings, R. S., 239
Binet, A., 184
Binning, J. F., 80
Bird, A., 403
Bishop, R. C., 67
Black, J. S., 396
Black, R. H., 326
Blake, R. R., 433–435
Blakely, B. R., 112
Blanchard, K., 289
Blank, W., 289–290
Blanton, A. E., 104
Blanz, F., 177
Blau, G., 238, 252, 258
Block, C. J., 67, 348
Blood, M. R., 178, 188
Bloom, B. S., 158
Blotnick, S., 368
Bluen, S. D., 488
Blum, M. L., 108, 174
Blum, T. C., 348, 470, 498
Blumberg, M., 427
Blumstein, P., 351
Boal, K. B., 238
Bobko, P., 199, 218, 240
Bocker, M., 461
Boehm-Davis, D. A., 459
Boehne, D. M., 228
Boeker, W., 366

Boje, D. M., 401
Bolino, M. C., 171
Bommer, W. H., 185
Booth-Kewley, S., 487
Borg, M. R., 196
Borman, W. C., 17, 70–71, 112, 114, 184, 189, 191, 193, 274
Borus, M. E., 364
Bottger, P. C., 317, 326
Bouchard, T. J., 248–249
Boudreau, J. W., 73, 258, 261, 274, 367
Bourhis, A. C., 364
Bowen, D. E., 38
Bowers, C. A., 442
Bowley, J. M., 461
Boyatzis, R. E., 284
Bracker, J. S., 209–210
Bradley, M. T., 119
Bramel, D., 14, 45
Brannick, M. T., 123
Brass, D. J., 218, 279
Braus, P., 236
Bray, D. W., 122
Bray, J. W., 474, 498
Breaugh, J. A., 483
Brems, D. J., 458
Brenner, O. C., 348
Brett, J. F., 66
Brett, J. M., 263, 324
Bretz, R. D., 73–74, 258, 267, 274, 367
Breuer, N. L., 490–491
Bridwell, L. T., 210
Brief, A. P., 258, 398, 485
Briggs, K. C., 116
Briggs, S. R., 95
Brittain, J., 324
Broadwell, M. M., 143
Brock, P., 360
Brogden, H., 108–109
Brooke, P. P., 250
Brown, B. K., 77
Brown, D. R., 419, 425, 433
Brown, K. A., 229, 262
Brown, K. G., 228
Brown, S. H., 80, 84, 102, 174
Brown, S. P., 398–399
Browning, R. C., 88
Bucklan, M. A., 69

Buckley, M. R., 83, 193, 262
Buhrfeind, E. D., 254
Buller, P. F., 196, 419
Bullock, R. J., 420
Bunce, D., 152
Bunker, K. A., 82
Burch, P., 85
Burckhardt, M. E., 279
Burke, M. J., 104, 109, 143, 364, 485
Burke, W. W., 409, 413, 424
Burnham, D., 210, 284
Burns, D. W., 82
Burns, L. R., 334
Burns, T., 388–389, 393
Burns, W., 488
Burroughs, W. A., 127
Burse, R., 454
Burtt, H. E., 113
Bush, George, 271–273, 278
Butcher, J. N., 115
Butterfield, D. A., 346, 348, 360
Bycio, P., 239, 303
Byham, W. C., 197–198

Cable, D. M., 263, 274
Cage, J. H., 292, 296
Cahen, L., 158
Cahill, M., 362
Caldwell, B. S., 442
Caldwell, D. F., 84, 395
Caldwell, M. S., 185
Callender, J. C., 82
Cameron, J., 225
Campbell, D. P., 121
Campbell, J. P., 241
Campbell, R. J., 122
Campion, J. E., 82, 85, 160
Campion, M. A., 77, 85, 142, 160, 204, 258, 265, 318
Cannella, A. A., 256
Capece, M., 498
Caplan, R. D., 354, 394, 484
Caranikas-Walker, F., 255
Carbonell, J. L., 115, 278
Cardy, R. L., 156, 184
Carle, S. B., 119
Carlson, R. M., 220
Carpenter, B. N., 81, 95
Carraher, S. M., 262

Carrere, S., 484
Carretta, T. R., 153
Carrier, M. R., 102
Carroll, G. R., 275, 278
Carson, K. P., 156
Carsten, J. M., 255
Carter, P., 401
Carter, R. T., 359
Cartwright, D., 316
Carver, C. S., 486
Casali, J. G., 455
Cascio, W. F., 74, 106, 108–109, 265, 364
Cash, T. F., 82
Castañeda, M. B., 239
Cattell, James McKeen, 95
Cattell, R. B., 115
Cavanaugh, J. L., 479
Cellar, D. F., 117
Chaffin, D. B., 443
Champagne, D., 168
Chan, D., 127
Chao, G. T., 88, 397, 463
Chapanis, A., 443, 449, 451
Chatman, J. A., 394–395
Chemers, M. M., 288
Chen, C. C., 357
Chen, P. Y., 485
Cheng, B., 196
Cheraskin, L., 142
Chesney, M. A., 487
Christensen, S. L., 343
Christenson, G. M., 495
Christiansen, N. D., 116
Cialdini, R. R., 315
Clark, P. F., 397
Clegg, C. W., 333
Cleveland, J. N., 169, 194
Clinton, Bill, 272, 284–285
Cloud, W., 477
Cobb, S., 323
Cohen, A., 240, 466
Cohen, A. G., 355
Cohen, D. J., 262
Cohen, M., 415
Cohen, S. L., 82
Colella, A., 78, 199, 228
Colihan, J. P., 483
Collins, J. M., 67, 120
Colosi, M., 496

Colquitt, A. L., 78
Colvin, C., 487–488
Conger, J. A., 280, 301
Conlon, D. E., 324
Connell, J. P., 224
Connelly, M. S., 78
Connerley, M., 78
Conroy, D., 346
Conte, J. M., 487
Conway, J. M., 83
Cooke, D. K., 120
Cooke, R. A., 353
Cooper, M. L., 353
Cooper, W. H., 327
Copper, C., 159
Cordery, J. L., 333
Cordes, C. L., 482
Corlett, E. N., 465
Corner, L. B., 348
Cortes, A. C., 360
Cortina, J. M., 115, 228
Costanza, D. P., 78
Cotton, J. L., 256, 331, 350
Courtright, J. A., 389
Cox, C. E., 82
Cox, G. L., 17
Cox, T. H., 351, 357, 359
Cranny, C. J., 100
Crant, J. M., 90, 117
Crawford, M. S., 112
Cresce, A. R., 360
Cronbach, L., 108–109
Cronshaw, S. F., 84
Crooker, K. J., 354
Cropanzano, R., 216, 248, 480
Crosbie, P. V., 321
Crosby, F. J., 315
Crosby, P., 335
Cross, B. K., 149
Crow, R. S., 495
Crowell, C. R., 229
Crump, C. E., 495
Culbertson, A. L., 360
Culnan, M. J., 461
Cummings, A., 389, 455–457
Cummings, N. A., 473
Cummings, T. G., 424
Cunningham, M. R., 120
Cyert, R., 379
Czajka, J. M., 240

Dahl, J. G., 228
Dahmus, S. A., 243–244
D'Alessio, A. T., 83, 102
Dalton, D. R., 249–250
Daly, C. L., 74
Danforth, G. W., 104
Dansereau, F., 253, 297, 300
Darwin, Charles, 32
Datta, D. K., 84
Davidson, W. N., 361
Davies, M., 353
Davis, B. L., 192
Davis, J. H., 375, 384
Davis, S. F., 27
Davis, S. M., 398
Davis, T. R. V., 290
Davis-Blake, A., 304, 352
Davis-LaMastro, V., 240, 252
Dawis, R. V., 242, 246, 249
Day, D. V., 115, 193, 175
Day, R. R., 143
Deadrick, D. L., 186
Deal, T., 394
Dean, R. A., 74
Deaux, J. E., 190
Deci, E. L., 223–225
Decker, P. J., 146
DeCotiis, T. A., 304
DeFrank, R. S., 405
Delaney, W. P., 474
De La Torre, P., 189
Dell'omo, G. G., 478
Demaree, R. G., 102
Deming, W. E., 335
DeNisi, A. S., 32, 74–75, 190, 192
Denison, D. R., 334, 398
Dennis, A. R., 327
Depinet, R. L., 111
Der-Karabetian, A., 494
DeShon, R. P., 228
Dess, G. G., 410
Deutsch, C. H., 344
Devine, D., 126
Devlin, S. E., 78
Diaz-Guerrero, R., 357
Dickson, W. J., 13, 15
Dickter, D. N., 257
Diehl, A. E., 149
Diekema, D., 318

Dieterly, D. L., 463
Dietrich, C. B., 143
Digman, J. M., 116
Dillingham, A., 364, 465
Dion, K. L., 323
Dipboye, R. L., 82–83
Dishaw, M. M., 158
DiTomaso, N., 362
Dobbins, G. H., 188, 196, 348
Dobrzynski, J. H., 94, 354
Doby, V. J., 354
Doerr, K. H., 229
Doherty, M. L., 115, 301
Dole, Bob, 65
Doman, M., 229
Dominguez, C. M., 346
Donaldson, L., 384
Doran, L. I., 258
Dorsey, D., 71
Dossett, D. L., 147
Dougherty, T. W., 82, 351, 482
Doverspike, D. D., 117
Down, S., 157
Drake, M. F., 82
Drauden, G., 99
Dreher, G. F., 83, 101, 261, 267, 350–351
Dressel, D., 459
Driskell, J. E., 159, 318
Drucker, P., 180, 367
Duarte, N. T., 189
Dubinsky, A. J., 348
DuBois, C. L. Z., 186, 191
Duchon, D., 213, 306
Duchon, J. C., 443
Duesbury, R. T., 99
Dugoni, B. L., 82
Dulebohn, J., 156
Dunbar, S. B., 155
Dunham, R. B., 239, 242, 245, 266
Dunlap, W. P., 462
Dunn, W. S., 117
Dunnette, M. D., 117, 184
Dunphy, D., 405
Dutton, J., 320
Durkheim, E., 310
Duxbury, L. E., 353
Dwyer, D. J., 486

Dyer, L. D., 80
Dyer, W. G., 394, 432

Earles, J. A., 157, 184
Earley, P. C., 226, 324, 357, 488
Eastman, K. K., 303
Eaton, N. K., 117
Eber, H. W., 115
Ebert, R. J., 82
Edelman, L. B., 66
Eden, D., 156, 218, 420
Eder, R., 83
Edwards, J. E., 437
Edwards, J. R., 394, 483
Ehrlich, S. B., 304
Eichel, E., 177
Eisenberger, R., 225, 240, 252
Ekeberg, S. E., 228
Ellis, R. A., 73
Elmes, D. G., 36
Elron, E., 375
England, G. W., 242, 246
Enz, C. A., 249
Erenkrantz, B., 190
Erez, M., 228
Erfurt, J. C., 494
Erskine, J. A., 225
Euwema, M. C., 324
Evans, C. R., 323
Evans, G. W., 484
Eveleth, D. M., 239
Ewigman, B. G., 455
Exter, T. G., 342

Fagenson, E. A., 348, 413
Fairhurst, G. T., 389
Falbe, C. M., 280–281
Faley, R. H., 66, 474
Falkenberg, L. E., 494
Farabee, D. J., 477
Farh, J., 196
Farkas, A. J., 238
Farley, J. A., 72
Farnsworth, S. R., 228–229
Farr, J. L., 80, 179, 184, 192, 225, 337
Farrell, E. E., 203
Fasolo, P., 240, 252
Fay, C. H., 82, 179, 362

Fay, L. M., 486
Fayol, H., 376–377, 380, 401–402
Fear, R. A., 82
Federico, R. F., 461
Fedor, D. B., 169
Feild, H. S., 82
Feld, S. C., 210
Feldman, D. C., 43, 362
Feldman, J., 189
Ferdman, B. M., 360
Ferris, G. R., 191, 194–195, 242–243, 299
Festinger, L., 211, 314, 319
Feuer, D., 149
Fidell, L. S., 27
Fiedler, F. E., 287–288
Field, J. M., 332
Field, R. H. G., 292
Fielding, J. E., 494–495
Fields, D. L., 348
Filby, N. N., 158
Filipczak, B., 145
Fine, S. A., 70
Finell, G., 447
Finkelman, J. M., 443
Finkelstein, L. M., 364
Finkelstein, S., 280
Finney, M. I., 84
Fireman, S., 258
Fischer, Cheryl Ann, 58–59
Fischthal, A., 198
Fisher, C. W., 158
Fisher, J., 484
Fitts, P. M., 446
Fitzgerald, F. Scott, 365
Fitzgerald, L. F., 350
Flanagan, J. C., 70
Flavey, J., 45
Fleishman, E. A., 70–71, 112, 153, 287
Flin, R., 445
Fogli, L., 178, 186
Folger, R., 216
Follette, W. T., 473
Fombrun, C. J., 417
Fondas, N., 345
Foote, A., 494
Ford, Henry, 391

Ford, J. D., 416
Ford, J. K., 135–137, 160, 182, 191–192
Ford, L. W., 416
Formisano, R. A., 266
Forsythe, S., 82
Fossum, J. A., 80
Foti, R. J., 195, 283
Fox, J. B., 361
Fox, M. L., 483, 486
Fox, W. M., 392
Francis, D. J., 102
Francis, J., 459
Frank, B., 190
Frankish, C. R., 458
Frayne, C. A., 218, 250, 330
Freedman, S., 214
Freedman, S. M., 489
Freeman, J., 410
French, J. R. P., 279–280, 394
French, M. T., 474, 498
French, W. L., 412
Freud, S., 372
Fried, Y., 192
Friedman, D. E., 267
Friedman, H. S., 487
Friedman, M., 483, 487
Friend, R., 14, 45
Friesen, P. H., 426
Frink, D. D., 226
Froggart, K. L., 331
Froham, M. A., 422
Frone, M. R., 353, 486
Fry, R. E., 274
Fulgham, J. B., 352
Fullagar, C. J. A., 397
Funaro, J. F., 462
Fusilier, M. R., 484

Galagan, P. A., 148
Galbraith, J. R., 333, 335
Gallagher, D. G., 397
Gallupe, R. B., 327
Ganster, D. C., 326, 353–354, 367, 483, 486–488
Ganzach, Y., 188
Garber, S., 249
Garcia, M. F., 80
Gardner, P. D., 349, 397

Gassaway, D., 455
Gatewood, R. D., 73
Gaugler, B. B., 123–124
Gebharbp, N., 494
Gebhardt, D. L., 495
Geisinger, K., 72
Gellatly, I. R., 218, 239
George, J. M., 228–229, 251, 256–258, 314, 319, 485
Georgopoulos, B. S., 293
Gephart, R. P., 401
Gerhart, B., 73–74, 84, 255, 261, 263, 349
Gerras, S. J., 186–187
Gersick, C. J. G., 317, 426
Ghidina, M. J., 367
Ghiselli, E. E., 102–103, 114, 177
Giannantonio, C. M., 74, 278
Gibson, R. S., 465
Gier, J. A., 168
Giffen, K., 327
Gifford, D., 267
Gilbert, D., 67
Gilbert, N. L., 239
Gilbreth, F. B., 446
Giles, W. F., 175
Gillen, B., 82
Gillen, D. J., 488
Gilliland, S. W., 105, 126
Gilmore, D. C., 87, 191
Gilson, R. D., 458
Ginnett, R. C., 317
Gist, M. E., 137, 143, 146, 218, 330, 351
Glass, G. V., 40
Glenn, N. D., 362
Gleser, G., 108–109
Glew, D. J., 489
Goff, S. J., 267
Goffin, R. D., 116, 124
Goktepe, J. R., 273
Goldstein, H. W., 394
Goldstein, I. L., 106, 136, 153, 173
Goldstein, M. A., 80
Goodale, J. G., 86
Gooding, R. Z., 100, 126, 336
Goodman, D. F., 83
Goodman, J. S., 348
Goodman, P. S., 249, 314

Goodson, J. R., 189
Goodstein, J. D., 354
Goodstein, L. D., 411
Gordon, G. G., 394
Gordon, M. E., 397
Gottier, R. J., 114
Gough, H. G., 115
Gould, R., 85
Gove, W. R., 353
Gowan, M. A., 73
Gower, D. W., 455
Graen, G., 297, 299–300
Graen, M., 299
Granfield, R., 477
Grant, Ulysses S., 287
Graves, L. M., 73
Gray, J. L., 434
Green, M. S., 252
Green, S., 289–290
Green, S. G., 299, 306, 396
Greenberg, J., 213, 215, 261, 496
Greenberger, D. B., 184, 261
Greenhaus, J. H., 191, 351, 353, 358
Greenis, J. L., 228
Greenwood, R., 418
Greiner, L. E., 422
Griffeth, R. W., 82, 215, 255
Griffin, R. W., 335, 389, 489
Grigoriev, A. I., 447
Grover, S. L., 354
Grube, J. A., 239
Grush, J. E., 217
Guide, P. C., 465
Guilford, J. P., 186
Guinn, G., 210
Guion, R. M., 100, 114, 126, 185, 188, 253
Gumpert, R., 289
Gundel, A., 447
Gunz, H. P., 304
Gupta, N., 253
Gustafson, D. J., 266
Gustanski, J., 453
Gutek, B. A., 353, 355
Guthrie, J. P., 84
Guy, S, M., 90
Guzzo, R. A., 189, 311, 317, 327, 374

Haccoun, R. R., 164
Hachiya, D., 255
Hackett, R. D., 239, 253, 303
Hackman, J. R., 264–265, 322–323
Haga, W. J., 297, 300
Halberstam, D., 417
Hall, E. T., 459
Hall, R. H., 304
Hallman, G. V., 266
Halperin, W., 454
Hambleton, R. K., 289
Hambrick, D. C., 256
Hammer, W., 454, 467
Hamner, W. C., 191
Hamstra, B. W., 80, 84
Hamtiaux, T., 164
Hancock, P., 83
Hanisch, K. A., 112
Hansen, M., 341
Hansen, T. L., 71
Hanson, L. A., 488
Hanson, M., 112, 124, 274
Hansson, R. O., 95
Harder, J. W., 217
Harding, J. L., 153
Hare, A. P., 319
Harkins, S., 319
Harper, D., 259
Harquail, C. V., 320
Harrell, J., 484
Harris, H. J., 126
Harris, M. J., 250
Harris, M. M., 82, 124, 168, 195,
    478
Harrison, D. A., 250, 257, 495
Harrison, R. V., 394
Harrison, T. M., 326
Hart, S. L., 334
Hartel, C. E. J., 175
Harvey, D. F., 419, 425, 433
Hassard, J., 401
Hatch, M. J., 394
Hater, J. J., 303
Hatfield, J. D., 213
Hathaway, S. R., 115
Hauerstein, N. M. A., 193, 195,
    197–198
Hausdorf, P. A., 239
Hayghe, H. V., 478

Hazer, J. T., 109, 238
Hazucha, J. F., 191
Healy, M. C., 258
Heath, C., 30
Hedge, A., 458
Hedge, J., 112, 124, 193
Hedlund, J., 325
Heft, L. L., 478
Heilman, M. E., 66, 82, 292, 296,
    348
Heinisch, D. A., 67
Heirich, M. A., 494
Helander, M. G., 461
Hellervik, L., 87
Helmer, O., 329
Hemphill, J. K., 286–287
Hendrix, W. H., 219
Heneman, H. G., 74, 80
Heneman, R. L., 184, 261–262
Henne, D., 216
Hennessy, R. T., 149
Hequet, M., 143–144
Herman, J. B., 242, 245
Herschlag, J. K., 292, 296
Hersey, P., 289
Hershberger, S. L., 399
Herzberg, F., 205, 207–208, 218,
    246
Herzog, A. R., 362
Hicks, W. D., 157
Higgins, C. A., 353
Highhouse, S., 109
Hill, T., 191
Himelstein, L., 349
Hinds, P., 461
Hinings, C. R., 418
Hinkin, T. R., 279
Hirsch, H. R., 104, 186
Hitt, M. A., 81
Hochshild, A. R., 43
Hoel, W., 299
Hoffman, C. C., 99
Hoffman, L. R., 327
Hofmann, D. A., 185–187
Hofstede, G., 342, 357
Hogan, J., 113–114, 120
Hogan, J. B., 78
Hogan, J. C., 108, 112, 184
Hogan, R., 95, 114–115, 120

Hohenfeld, J. A., 213
Holcom, M. L., 477
Holland, J. L., 121, 394
Hollander, E. P., 321
Hollenbeck, J. R., 83, 228, 325,
    351
Holloman, C. R., 273
Holt, A. M., 70
Holt, K. E., 191
Hom, P. W., 82, 189, 255
Homans, G. C., 321
Honts, C. R., 119
Horman, D., 455
Hornstein, H. A., 292, 296
Horst, L., 424
Hosmer, L. T., 375
Hosoda, M., 280
Hosokawa, M. C., 455
Hough, L. M., 117
House, J. S., 362
House, R. J., 292–293, 295
Houston, J. M., 123, 224, 413,
    422, 438
Houston, M. R., 272
Howard, A., 197–198
Howard, G. S., 229
Howard, L. W., 214
Howe, V., 74
Howell, J. M., 302
Hsieh, C. C., 493
Huber, V., 196, 262
Hudson, J. R., 85
Huffcutt, A. I., 83
Hughes, G. L., 177
Huismans, S. E., 324
Hulin, C. L., 112, 178, 185, 242,
    244, 255
Hulvershorn, P., 147
Humphreys, L. G., 185
Hunt, S. D., 239
Hunt, S. T., 71
Hunter, J. E., 40, 78, 88, 96,
    103–104, 106–108, 126,
    193, 261
Hunter, R. F., 88, 126
Huse, E. F., 424
Huselid, M. A., 255–256
Huseman, R. C., 213
Hussein, Saddam, 271–273, 278

Hutchinson, M. F., 70
Hutchinson, R. D., 448
Hyatt, R., 477
Hyde, R. T., 493
Hylton, R., 151
Hyman, H. H., 315

Iacocca, Lee, 301
Ibarra, H., 358–359
Ilgen, D. R., 219, 325, 351
Indvik, J., 490
Ingram, P., 354
Inkeles, A., 357
Inohara, T., 403
Ishii, Jun, 485
Ivancevich, J. M., 405, 471, 489
Iverson, D. C., 495
Iwanicki, E. F., 482

Jablin, F. M., 396
Jackson, C. N., 484
Jackson, D. N., 114
Jackson, G. B., 40
Jackson, L. A., 349
Jackson, N., 401
Jackson, P. R., 333
Jacobs, R., 179, 185–187
Jaeger, A. M., 405
Jago, A. G., 213
Jago, I. A., 112, 292–293
Jako, R. A., 83, 187
Jalland, R. M., 304
James, K., 248, 487
James, L. A., 399
James, L. R., 102, 296, 314, 399
Jamison, R. L., 267
Janis, I. L., 326, 328–329
Janz, J. T., 87
Jaros, S. J., 239
Jarrett, M. Q., 164
Jeanneret, P. R., 70
Jeffrey, N. A., 473
Jehn, K. A., 394
Jenkins, C. D., 483
Jenkins, G. D., 253
Jennings, K. R., 331
Jensen, M., 317
Jentsch, F. G., 157
Jerison, H. J., 456

Jermier, J. M., 239
Jesperson, F., 366
Johns, G., 250, 252, 483
Johnson, B. T., 40
Johnson, D. L., 243–244
Johnson, J. F., 78
Johnson, J. L., 185
Johnson, J. W., 38
Johnson, P. R., 490
Johnson, R. H., 238
Johnston, N. G., 116
Johnston, W. G., 124
Jolson, M. A., 348
Jonas, H. S., 274
Jones, C., 128
Jones, E. W., 359
Jones, G. R., 205, 257
Jones, J. W., 486
Jones, N. W., 293
Jones, R. E., 446
Jones, R. G., 124
Jourden, F. J., 30
Judge, T. A., 194–195, 236–237,
    256, 258, 262–263, 274, 367
Jung, C. G., 116
Juran, J. M., 335

Kabanoff, B., 415
Kacmar, K. M., 242–243
Kafry, D., 179
Kahai, S. S., 461
Kahn, J. A., 334
Kahn, L. M., 68
Kahn, W. A., 239, 279
Kahneman, D., 328
Kamp, J. D., 117
Kanabayashi, M., 403
Kandel, D. B., 353
Kane, J. S., 188
Kanter, R. M., 365
Kantowitz, B. H., 36
Kanungo, R. N., 238, 280, 301
Karren, R. J., 225
Karau, S. J., 205
Katz, J. A., 123
Katz, M., 424, 437
Katzell, R. A., 78
Kaufman, G., 115
Kavanaugh, M. J., 137, 193

Keller, L. M., 248–249
Keller, R. T., 293, 323
Kelley, H. H., 315
Kelly, R. M., 355
Kemmerer, B. E., 488
Kemp, N. J., 333
Kendall, L. M., 177, 242, 244
Kennedy, A., 394
Kennedy, John, 328
Kennedy, R. S., 462
Kenny, D. A., 283
Kent, R. L., 348
Keran, C. M., 443
Kerblay, B., 351
Kerr, M. J., 455
Kessler, R. C., 353
Khoo, G., 487
Kidwell, R. E., 104, 205
Kiesler, S., 461
Kilduff, M., 275, 280
Kim, H., 280
Kim, J. S., 191
King, D. W., 353
King, L. A., 353
Kinicki, A. J., 81, 189, 318
Kircher, J. C., 119
Kirkpatrick, D. L., 160
Kirkpatrick, S. A., 303, 346, 349
Kirmeyer, S. L., 323, 488
Kirnan, J. P., 72
Kirsch, M., 100, 126
Kivlahan, C. H., 455
Klaas, B. S., 192, 263, 478
Klastorin, T. D., 229
Klawsky, J. D., 117
Kleiman, L. S., 66, 474
Klein, H. J., 219, 228, 397
Kleinmann, M., 124
Klepa, L., 353
Klich, N. R., 189
Klimoski, R. J., 52, 157
Kluger, A. N., 78
Knight, P. A., 189, 315
Knopf, C., 460
Knouse, S. B., 88–89, 360
Knowles, D. E., 364
Knox, S. S., 399
Kochan, T. A., 304
Koehler, J. W., 239

Kohler, S. S., 238, 252
Kolb, D. A., 422
Konovsky, M. A., 480
Konrad, A. M., 355
Kopelman, R., 228
Koretz, G., 13, 266, 349, 361, 443
Koslow, S. H., 484
Koslowsky, M., 40, 259
Kossek, E. E., 267–268
Kotch, D. A., 480
Kotter, J. P., 274
Kozerenko, O. P., 447
Kozlowski, S. W. J., 301, 397–398, 463
Kraatz, M. S., 375
Krackhardt, D., 256, 280
Kraiger, K., 160, 191–192
Kram, K. E., 278–279, 359
Krausz, M., 259
Kraut, A. I., 194
Kravitz, D. A., 67, 189
Kravitz, D. E., 244
Kreitner, R., 219
Kriska, S. D., 185
Kristof, A. L., 73, 84
Kristof-Brown, A., 228
Kryter, K. D., 455
Krzystofiak, F., 184
Kuder, C. F., 121
Kuhnert, K. W., 303
Kulik, C. T., 190, 315, 352,364
Kumar, K., 358, 442
Kunin, T., 242, 245
Kunz, L. K., 486
Kurland, O., 489
Kwon, Y., 454
Kwun, S. K., 195

Lacayo, R., 442
Ladd, R. T., 102
Laker, D. R., 475
Lamm, H., 327
Landis, R. S., 126
Landon, T. E., 113
Landy, F. J., 98, 100, 178–179, 184, 192, 487–488
Larkey, L. K., 343, 345
Larson, J. R., 169
Lasek, M., 89

Latané, B., 319
Latham, G. P., 87, 111, 147, 179, 218, 225–226, 228, 250, 330
Latham, V. M., 72
Latimer, S., 346
Lau, C. M., 420
Laughlin, P. R., 326
Lautenschlager, G. J., 73
Law, K. S., 40, 104
Lawler, E. E., 247, 261, 264, 432
Lawrence, B. S., 192
Lawrence, P. R., 387–388, 393
Lawshe, C. H., 105
Lawton, M., 454
Learner, S. M., 353
Leddy, P. M., 72
Lee, C., 170, 218, 226, 240, 488
Lee, R. T., 482
Lee, Robert E., 286
Lee, S. Y., 221
Lee, T. W., 74, 254, 258
Lefkowitz, J., 348, 359
Lehman, M., 258
Lehman, W. E. K., 477
Leigh, T. W., 398–399
Lemak, D. J., 335
Lempert, R. O., 477
Lengnick-Hall, M. L., 331, 336, 356
Lenin, V. I., 12
Leonard, R. L., 164
Levin, I., 248
Levine, E. L., 191
Levine, J. M., 315
Levinson, H., 471
Levy, P. E., 196
Lewicki, R. J., 431
Lewin, K., 398, 420–421
Lewis, P., 303
Lewis, P. M., 82
Leyden, D. P., 314
Lichtenfels, P. A., 84
Lichtenstein, P., 399
Liden, R. C., 81, 188, 299, 301, 362, 398
Likert, R., 279, 382–383, 412
Lilenthal, M. G., 462
Lin, T. R., 323
Lincoln, Abraham, 282, 287

Lind, M. R., 460
Lindgren, H. C., 209
Lindsley, D. H., 218
Lippert, T., 460
Lippit, R., 398, 422
Liska, L. Z., 495
Litchy, T. R., 226
Livingstone, L. P., 254
Lobel, S. A., 357
Locke, E. A., 13, 216, 218–219, 225–226, 228, 236, 241, 247, 303, 336
Lockwood, C. A., 81
Lofquist, L. H., 242, 246
Logan, J. W., 215
Lohman, D. F., 155
Lohr, S., 442
Lohrer, B. T., 157
Lohrke, F. T., 104
London, M., 194, 196–197
Long, L., 484
Lord, R. G., 213
Lorenz, B., 447
Lorsch, J. W., 387–388, 393
Louis, M. L., 320
Lovato, C., 487
Love, K. G., 67
Lublin, J. S., 238, 354, 365
Lucchetti, A., 332
Lumpkin, G. T., 410
Lusk, S. L., 455
Luthans, F., 31, 219–220, 290
Luz, J., 252

Macan, T. H., 82–83, 105, 118
MacDonnell, F. J., 476
MacKenzie, S. B., 185
Mackie-Lewis, S., 320
MacLaren, V. V., 119
Madigan, R. M., 186
Mael, F. A., 78
Magjuka, R. J., 157, 331, 337–338
Mahar, L., 288
Mahoney, G. M., 293
Mahoney, J. J., 477, 497
Maier, N. R. F., 326
Major, B., 315
Major, D. A., 325
Malor, S., 67

Manning, M. R., 484, 496
Manuso, J. S. J., 496
Manz, C. C., 296
Manzey, D., 447
March, J., 379
Mardon, S., 266
Markham, S. E., 252–253
Markus, M. L., 461
Marliave, R., 158
Marlowe, C. M., 82
Martell, R. F., 189, 196, 348
Martens, R., 323
Martin, C., 99
Martin, C. L., 81, 88
Martin, D. C., 89, 262
Martineau, J. W., 156
Martins, L. L., 343
Martocchio, J. J., 138, 156, 226, 353, 363
Marx, K., 10, 372
Masi, D. A., 475
Maslow, A. H., 205–207, 211, 218, 246, 401
Mason, R. O., 438
Mathias, C., 454
Mathieu, J. E., 156–157, 164, 218, 238–239, 252, 337, 346, 487
Matteson, M. T., 405, 471, 489
Mattson, J., 78
Mauland, W., 33
Maurer, S. D., 74, 82–83
Maurer, T. J., 152, 190
Mausner, B., 207
Maxwell, S. E., 107, 113, 162
May, D. R., 331, 467
May, K. E., 71
Mayes, B. T., 367, 487
Mayes, R. C., 375
Mayfield, E. C., 80, 84
Mayo, Elton, 13, 15
McBride, J. R., 78, 79
McCause, A. A., 433, 435
McCauley, C. D., 275, 348
McCauley, M. E., 149
McCaulley, M. H., 116
McClelland, D., 205, 209–210, 246, 263, 265, 284
McClendon, J. A., 263
McCloy, R. A., 117

McCormick, E. J., 32, 70, 105, 450, 452, 454, 459, 466
McCullough, W. F., 67
McDaniel, M. A., 83, 104, 185, 258, 364, 477
McEvoy, G. M., 74, 123, 196, 265, 364
McFadden, J., 266
McFarlin, D. B., 241, 261, 486
McGrath, J. E., 327
McGrath, R. N., 104
McGregor, D., 381–382, 412
McIntire, S. A., 69, 127, 224, 413, 422, 438
McKee, G. H., 252
McKenzie, R. C., 108
McKinley, J. C., 115
McLellan, R. A., 71
McLeod, P. L., 357
McMahon, G. C., 228–229
McManus, J. A., 491
McManus, M. A., 174
McNeely, B. L., 398
McRae, M., 352–353, 359
McShulskis, E., 267, 475
Mecham, R. C., 70
Mechanic, D., 368
Medsker, G. J., 318
Megargee, E. I., 15, 278
Meglino, B. M., 74–75, 255, 394, 398
Meier, E. L., 364
Meindertsma, D. C., 89
Meindl, J. R., 304
Meister, D., 464
Melamed, S., 252
Mellor, S., 346
Mento, A. J., 219, 225
Mercer, M., 109
Mero, N. P., 192
Mesch, D. J., 250
Messick, S., 101
Meyer, H. H., 146
Meyer, J. P., 238–239
Micco, L., 349, 489
Michaels, C. E., 123
Michaelsen, L. K., 326, 358
Michelin, M. P., 379
Middlestadt, S. E., 80

Mikkola, T., 444
Milbank, D., 140
Miles, E. W., 213
Milford, M., 458
Miller, D., 426
Miller, H. E., 85
Miller, J. L., 90, 118, 214
Miller, K. I., 336
Miller, L. E., 217
Miller, M. L., 117
Miller, V. D., 396
Milliken, F. J., 343
Millsap, R. E., 105, 118, 197, 394
Milne, S. H., 498
Mims, R., 366
Miner, J. B., 209–210
Minton, J., 431
Mischel, L. J., 455–457
Mitchell, T. R., 218, 229, 254, 258, 293, 386
Mitra, A., 253
Mitroff, I. I., 438
Mobley, W. H., 255
Moch, M. K., 357
Mohrman, S. A., 432
Mone, M. A., 33
Monge, P. R., 336
Montei, M. S., 67
Montgomery, J. C., 335
Moore, S. C., 67
Morand, D. A., 389
Morath, R. A., 78
Moreland, R. L., 315
Moreno, J. L., 312
Morgan, J. A., 362
Morgan, R. M., 239
Morris, J. A., 43
Morrison, A. M., 346
Morrison, E. W., 375, 396–397
Morriss, W., 424
Morrow, C. C., 164
Morrow, J. E., 275
Morse, N. C., 287
Moses, J. L., 124
Moss, S. E., 348
Mossholder, K. W., 105, 175, 351, 353
Motowidlo, S. J., 190, 192, 261, 398

Mount, M. K., 116–117, 191–192, 194, 229, 254, 267
Mouton, J. S., 433–435
Muchinsky, P. M., 67, 88, 124
Muczyk, J. P., 273, 279
Mueller, G. C., 33
Mueller, W. S., 333
Muhlbach, L., 461
Mulaik, S. A., 102
Muldrow, T. W., 108
Mullen, B., 40
Mullen, E. J., 164
Mulligan, E. E., 462
Mumby, D. K., 342
Mumford, M. D., 70, 77–78, 153, 194
Munchus, G., 404
Munsterberg, H., 1–2
Murphy, K. R., 106, 118, 169, 186–187, 190, 194, 197, 480–481
Murray, H. M., 210
Murray, S. A., 442
Myart, Leon, 60
Myasnikov, V. I., 447
Myers, D. G., 327
Myers, D. W., 479
Myers, I. B., 116

Naditch, M. P., 471
Nadler, D. A., 413
Nagao, D. H., 88
Nalashiti, V., 447
Nathan, B. R., 187
Naylor, J. C., 108–109, 174, 219
Neale, M., A., 324
Near, J. P., 379
Nelson, C. E., 82
Nelson, D. L., 486–487
Nelson, G. L., 374
Nelson, R. E., 323
Nemetz, P. L., 343
Nesler, M. S., 280
Neuman, G. A., 437
Newcomb, M. D., 480
Newcomb, T., 319
Newman, J., 184
Newman, S., 454

Nichol, V., 267
Nicholas, J. M., 424, 437
Nicholson, N., 252
Nixon, H. L., 323
Nkomo, S. M., 343, 357, 359
Noe, R. A., 100, 126, 135, 191, 278, 350
Nof, S., 463
Noonan, K. A., 374
Normand, J., 109, 477
Northcraft, G. B., 226, 324
Novick, M. R., 155
Nowack, K. M., 197
Noyes, J. M., 458
Numerof, R. E., 299
Nunamaker, J. F., 327
Nutting, S. M., 113

Oborne, D. J., 457, 465
O'Boyle, T. F., 478
O'Brien, C. P., 477
O'Brien, F. P., 491–492
O'Connor, E. J., 190
O'Donnell, M. P., 494
Ohlott, P. J., 275, 348
Oldham, G. R., 264–265, 389, 455–457
Olea, M. M., 184
O'Leary-Kelly, A. M., 226, 228, 353, 397, 489
Olex, M. B., 463
Olian, J. D., 84, 278
Oliver, B., 477
Olmstead, B., 318
Olson-Buchanan, J. B., 254
O'Neil, H. F., 99
Ones, D. S., 40, 48, 78, 111, 117, 120, 196
Oppler, S. H., 191, 193, 274
O'Reilly, C. A., 84, 300, 395
O'Reilly, M., 436
Organ, D. W., 397–398
Orlansky, J., 149
Ornstein, S., 215
Orpen, C., 88
Orr, J. M., 109
Osburn, H. G., 102
Osga, G. A., 454

Osland, A., 496
Osland, J. S., 496
Ostgaard, D. J., 99
Ostroff, C., 160, 186, 238, 351, 397–398
Ostrov, E., 479
Ott, J. S., 398
Ouchi, W. C., 404–405
Outerbridge, A. N., 104
Outtz, J., 106
Ovalle, N. K., 257
Overton, R. C., 126
Owenby, P. H., 150
Owens, W. A., 77–78

Paajanen, G. E., 71, 120
Padavic, I., 367
Padgett, M. Y., 237
Paese, M., 105, 118
Paffenbarger, R. S., 493
Paley, M. J., 443
Palisano, P., 472
Palmer, J. K., 190
Papper, E. M., 318
Parasuraman, S., 191, 351, 358
Paris, C. R., 458
Parish, D. C., 89
Parkes, K. R., 486
Parnes, H. S., 364
Parson, C. K., 81
Parsons, H. M., 14
Pascale, R. T., 404
Pathan, R. Z., 157
Patten, B. R., 327
Patterson, M., 399
Patterson, M. L., 459
Paullay, I. M., 238
Pawar, B. S., 303
Payne, R., 399
Payne, S. C., 157
Pearce, J. A., 333
Pearlman, K., 104–105, 118
Pearson, C. M., 438
Pelletier, K. R., 494
Pennebaker, J. W., 254
Pepitone, A., 319
Perot, H. Ross, 301, 391
Perry, E. L., 352, 364

Perry, J., 484
Persico, J., 335
Peters, L. H., 190
Peters, P. A., 394
Peters, T. J., 322, 393
Peterson, J. A., 323
Peterson, M. F., 454
Peterson, N. G., 70
Peyrefitte, J., 188
Pfeffer, J., 211, 247, 304–305
Phillips, A. P., 83
Phillips, A. S., 301
Phillips, J., 100, 325
Phillips, J. M., 74, 83
Phillips, J. S., 489
Phillips, S. M., 261
Pickett, George, 286
Pincus, L. B., 356
Pingitore, R., 82
Pinkley, R. L., 324
Platania, J., 67
Platz, S. J., 348
Plous, S., 326
Podsakoff, P. M., 185, 280
Pohley, K., 124
Poole, M., 415
Pooyan, A., 190
Poppler, P., 326
Porras, J. I., 414–415, 420, 425,
    437
Porter, C. H., 465
Porter, L. W., 256
Posner, B. Z., 320
Potter, G., 221
Poulton, E., 457
Powell, A. B., 116
Powell, G. N., 73, 320, 346, 348,
    360
Pratt, M. G., 82
Prein, H. C. M., 431
Premack, S. L., 75
Prewett-Livingston, A. J., 82
Price, R. H., 484
Prien, E. P., 123, 177
Primoff, E. S., 70, 105
Pringle, C. D., 427
Pritchard, R. D., 219
Prue, K., 480–481

Prussia, G. E., 255, 318
Prussog, A., 461
Pryor, J. B., 491
Pulakos, E. D., 83, 85, 186, 191,
    193, 274
Punnett, B. J., 226
Pursell, E. D., 84
Putnam, L. L., 342

Quaintance, M. K., 71
Quick, J. C., 486
Quigley, A. M., 113–114
Quiñones, M. A., 112, 124, 135,
    137, 155, 182, 192

Rabbitt, P., 364
Rabin, M. D., 458
Rabinowitz, S., 351
Rafaeli, A., 82, 320
Ragins, B. R., 350
Ragland, D., 484
Raia, A., 280
Raich, M. S., 146
Rain, J. S., 179, 189
Rajagopalan, N., 84
Raju, N. S., 109, 364, 437
Ralston, D. A., 266
Ramsey, J., 454
Randall, D. M., 240
Raskin, D. C., 119
Rastegary, H., 487–488
Raveis, V. H., 353
Raven, B., 279–280
Ravlin, E. C., 74–75, 333, 394
Raza, S., 81
Reagan, Ronald, 119
Redfern, M. S., 443
Ree, M. J., 153, 157, 184
Reed, R., 335
Reeder, G. D., 491
Reich, M. H., 350
Reichers, A. E., 417
Reilly, A. H., 263
Reilly, R. R., 88, 105, 118, 192,
    197
Reimann, B. C., 273, 279
Reimer, E., 287
Reitman, F., 350

Rensvold, R. B., 169
Rentsch, J. R., 251
Reucher, E., 447
Reynolds, D. H., 186, 480
Reynolds, J. I., 157
Rhodenizer, L., 442
Rhodes, S. R., 250–251
Rhodes, W., 477
Rice, A. K., 15
Rice, R. W., 241, 261
Rich, G. A., 185
Richman, W. L., 192
Rigdon, J. E., 489
Ridgeway, C. L., 318
Ridgway, M. B., 286
Riggs, M. L., 315
Riley, S., 350
Ringer, R. C., 90, 480
Ritchie, R. J., 124
Rivero, J. C., 66
Robbins, T. L., 192
Roberts, B. W., 114
Roberts, D. R., 427
Robertson, I. T., 157
Robertson, P. J., 414–415, 427
Robinson, S. L., 259–260, 375,
    485
Rodgers, R., 261
Roediger, H. L., 36
Roehling, M. V., 74
Roethlisberger, F. J., 13, 15
Rogers, C., 471
Rogers, D. L., 261
Rogers, L. E., 389
Roland, C. C., 151
Roman, M., 366
Roman, P. M., 470, 498
Romanelli, E., 410, 427
Romzek, B. S., 238
Ronis, D. L., 455
Root, N., 364, 465
Rosen, B., 146, 330
Rosen, E. I., 367
Rosenbloom, J. S., 266
Rosenfeld, P., 360
Rosenman, R., 483, 487
Rosenthal, D. B., 123–124
Rosenthal, R., 194

Ross, J., 296
Ross, W. H., 324
Rosse, J. G., 90, 118, 480
Roth, P. L., 60, 83
Rothstein, H. R., 104
Rothstein, M. G., 114, 116, 124
Roush, P., 198
Rousseau, D. M., 353, 375
Rowe, P. M., 80
Rowland, K. M., 191
Rozell, E. J., 58
Roznowski, M., 255, 257
Rubin, D. B., 194
Rubis, L., 333
Ruderman, M. N., 275, 348
Ruhm, C. J., 362
Rupinski, M. T., 164
Russell, C. J., 78, 84, 104, 123
Russell, D. W., 482
Russell, J. M., 188
Russell, J. T., 108–110
Russell, M., 353
Ryan, A. M., 61, 74, 89,
    116–117, 120–121, 238
Ryan, K., 397
Ryan, L. E., 149
Ryan, R. M., 223–224
Rynes, S. L., 72–74, 84, 263

Saal, F. E., 67
Saari, L. M., 88, 226
Saavedra, R., 195, 324
Sackett, P. R., 32, 65, 99, 101,
    112, 120–121, 161, 164,
    186, 191
Saffold, G. S., 394
Sagie, A., 40, 259
St. Clair, L., 275
Saks, A. M., 156, 395
Salancik, G. R., 211, 247
Salas, E., 40, 157, 160, 162, 318
Sales, S. M., 304
Salgado, J. F., 116
Salkind, N. J., 27
Salomone, P. R., 362
Salvemini, N., 197
Salyards, S., 477
Sample, J., 151

Sanchez, J. I., 189
Sanchez, J. I., 70, 360
Sandell, H., 364
Sanders, M. S., 149, 450,
    452–454, 459, 464, 466
Sanders, P. A., 102
Sands, M. M., 78–79
Saruwatari, L. R., 82
Sashkin, M., 422, 424
Saunders, V., 78
Sawin, D. A., 457
Sawyer, J. E., 389
Saylor, J. S., 498
Scandura, T. A., 297, 299, 350
Scarpello, V., 74, 241, 262
Scattaregia, J. H., 80
Scerbo, M. W., 457
Schachter, S., 314
Schaubroeck, J., 195, 483,
    486–488
Scheier, M. F., 486
Scheiman, P., 477
Schein, V. E., 348, 422
Schellhardt, T. D., 200, 337
Schiewe, A., 447
Schippmann, J. S., 60, 123
Schmidt, F. L., 40, 78, 83, 96,
    103–104, 106–108, 111,
    120, 196
Schmidt, S. M., 304
Schmidtke, J. M., 455–457
Schmit, M. J., 61, 74, 116–117, 238
Schmitt, N. W., 52, 78, 83, 85,
    100, 115, 124, 126–127,
    186, 191
Schneer, J. A., 350
Schneider, B., 38, 216, 314, 394
Schneider, J. R., 124
Schneider, R. J., 117
Schneider, S. L., 82
Schneier, C. E., 273
Schoorman, F. D., 375, 384
Schriesheim, C. A., 279–280, 288,
    296, 299
Schriesheim, J. F., 296
Schroeder, R. G., 332
Schwab, D. P., 74, 80, 262
Schwartz, F., 354–355

Schwartz, P., 351
Schweiger, D. M., 336, 405
Schwoerer, C. E., 146, 330–331,
    467
Scifres, E. L., 104
Scott, D. R., 69, 127
Scott, K. D., 253
Scott, W. D., 1
Scott, W. E., 225
Searle, S., 353
Sechrest, L. B., 459
Segal, J. A., 125
Segal, N. L., 248–249
Sego, D. J., 135, 137, 325
Seidman, B., 364
Seltzer, J., 299
Selye, H., 482
Semple, C. A., 149
Settoon, R. P., 104, 398
Shaffer, G. S., 78
Shaffer, M. A., 250
Shalley, C. E., 224
Sharp, W., 326
Shartle, C. L., 286
Shaw, B., 464
Shaw, M. E., 323, 362
Shea, C., 285
Shea, G. P., 311, 317
Shellenbarger, S., 267
Shenshaw, Y., 360
Shepard, H. A., 316, 412
Sheppard, B. H., 431
Shepperd, J. A., 219
Sheridan, D., 144
Sheridan, J., 90, 395–396
Sherman, P. A., 474–476
Shine, L., 108–109
Shore, L. M., 123, 239
Shore, T. H., 123, 239
Shulman, H. G., 463
Silbey, V., 109
Silver, N. C., 458
Silverhart, T. A., 83
Silverman, S. B., 115
Silvers, R. C., 425
Sime, W. E., 487
Simon, H. G., 342, 379
Simon, M. C., 348

Simon, S. J., 146
Simons, T., 354
Simpson, D. D., 477
Sims, H. P., 296
Sincich, T., 239
Singer, A. D., 259
Sinha, K. K., 332
Sinks, T., 454
Skinner, B. F., 219
Slack, J. D., 493
Slaven, G., 445
Smalley, M. M., 179
Smith, Adam, 10
Smith, C. A., 239
Smith, D. B., 384
Smith, D. C., 497
Smith, D. E., 105, 118, 124, 168
Smith, E. M., 135
Smith, G. M., 90
Smith, K. G., 386
Smith, L. M., 333
Smith, M., 39, 83
Smith, M. J., 466
Smith, N. R., 209–210
Smith, P. C., 171, 177, 242, 244
Smith, R. A., 27
Smith, R, G., 115
Smith, T. J., 443
Smith-Jentsch, K. A., 157
Smither, J. W., 105, 118, 192, 197
Smither, R. D., 10, 77, 123, 209,
   224, 278, 384, 413, 422, 438
Snell, A. F., 78–79
Snow, R. E., 155
Snyder, M., 275
Snyderman, B., 207
Sommer, S. M., 31, 220
Sonnenstuhl, W. J., 496
Sorra, J. S., 137
Sosik, J. J., 461
Spector, P. E., 255, 485
Spencer, C. C., 77
Spencer, B. A., 335
Spera, S. P., 254
Sperduto, W. A., 220
Spitz, C., 147
Spreitzer, G. M., 224–225
Spring, B., 82

Springbett, B. M., 80
Sproull, L., 461
Spychalski, A. C., 124
Srinivasan, D., 221
Stahl, M. J., 210
Stalker, C. M., 388–389, 393
Stamoulis, D. T., 193
Stamps, D., 142
Stanton, J. M., 190
Starke, F. A., 434
Stathatos, P., 67
Staw, J., 32, 219, 296
Stecher, M. D., 118
Steel, R. P., 225, 251, 255, 257
Steers, R. M., 250–251
Steffy, B. D., 475, 486
Stein, J. A., 90, 480
Steiner, D. D., 105, 179, 189
Sterk-Elifson, C., 477
Stevens, C. K., 73, 137, 330, 351
Stevens, M. J., 142
Stewart, G. L., 117, 156, 317
Stewart, K., 445
Stierwalt,, S. L., 116
Stilwell, D., 301
Stoffey, R. W., 105, 118
Stogdill, R. M., 283
Stokes, G. S., 77–79
Stokes, J. P., 248
Stokols, D., 494
Stone, D. L., 480
Stone, V. K., 258
Stone-Romero, E. F., 238
Strasser, S., 261
Straus, S. G., 327
Strauss, J. P., 117, 229, 254
Strickland, W., 99
String, J., 149
Stroh, L. K., 263
Strong, E. K., 121
Stuart, P., 474, 480, 482
Sullivan, L. A., 349
Suls, J., 353
Sulsky, L. M., 187, 190, 193
Sumer, H. C., 189
Summala, H., 444
Summer, C. E., 386
Summers, T. P., 219

Suresh, S., 274
Sutton, C. D., 193, 487
Svinicki, M., 436
Swaroff, P. G., 75
Swim, J. K., 346
Switzer, F. S., 60
Syme, S. L., 484
Sytsma, M. R., 191
Syvantek, D. J., 420

Tabachnik, B. G., 27
Taber, T. D., 306
Tait, M., 237
Talaga, J. A., 362
Tane, L. D., 267
Tannenbaum, S. I., 137, 156–157
Tansey, R., 39
Tarulli, B. A., 152
Tarullo, G. M., 151
Tatsuoka, M. M., 115
Taylor, F. W., 1–2, 10, 12–13, 15,
   204, 402, 445–446
Taylor, G. S., 253
Taylor, H. C., 108–110
Taylor, L. R., 126
Taylor, M. S., 73, 218
Taylor, R., 17
Taynor, J., 190
Teachout, M. S., 153, 182, 184
Tedeschi, J. T., 280
Tellegen, A., 251
Teo, A. C., 275
Tepas, D. I., 443
Tepper, B. J., 288, 350
Terpestra, D. E., 58, 356, 427
Terris, W., 120
Tesluk, P. E., 337
Testa, M., 315
Tetrault, L. A., 288
Tetrick, L. E., 238
Tett, R. P., 114, 238
Tharenou, P., 346
Thatchenkery, T. J., 401
Thayer, J., 487–488
Thiele, G., 447
Thierry, H., 219
Thomas, D. A., 359
Thomas, J., 127

Thomas, J. B., 218
Thomas, K. M., 218
Thomas, K. W., 224, 324
Thomas, L. T., 353–354
Thomas, M. H., 458
Thomas, R. R., 343, 345
Thompson, C., 108
Thorndike, R. L., 171
Thornton, G. C., 123–124, 480–481
Thornton, W., 446
Tiegs, R. B., 192
Timbrook, C., 454
Tindale, R. S., 82
Tippins, N., 187
Tomasek, H., 335
Tomkiewicz, J., 348
Tower, S. L., 83
Townsend, A. M., 461
Townsend, B., 366
Tracey, J. B., 137
Trattner, M. H., 104
Treacy, M. E., 267
Trevor, G. O., 261
Triands, H. C., 357
Trist, E. L., 390–391
Trost, M. R., 189
Tsui, A. S., 275, 300
Tubbs, M. E., 225, 228–229
Tuckman, B. W., 316–317
Turban, D. B., 82, 102, 351
Turnage, J. J., 124
Tushman, M. L., 410, 427
Tuttle, J. M., 256
Tuzzolino, F., 210
Tversky, A., 328
Tziner, A., 80, 228

Urban, J. M., 442

Valacich, J. S., 327
Vance, R. J., 228, 337
Van Cott, H. P., 448
Vancouver, J. B., 351, 394
Vandenberg, R. J., 74, 262
Van de Ven, A. H., 372–373, 385, 415
Van de Vliert, E., 324, 455
Van Dyne, L., 324

Van Eerde, W., 219
Van Fleet, D. D., 205
Van Orden, K. F., 454
Van Ryn, M., 484
Van Scotter, J. R., 190
Van Velsor, E., 346
Van Velzen, D., 482
Van Yperen, N. W., 455
Vasilopoulous, N. L., 197
Vecchio, R. P., 215–216, 289
Vejvoda, M., 447
Velthouse, B. A., 224
Veres, J. G., 82
Veroff, J., 210
Vest, J. M., 491–492
Vest, M. J., 491–492
Villanova, P., 188, 243–244
Vinokur, A. D., 484
Viswesvaran, C., 40, 48, 120, 196
Vitkovic, L., 484
Vollrath, D. A., 331
Von Glinow, M. A., 296
Vroom, V. H., 216–217, 262, 292–295, 401

Wade, K. J., 189
Wagener, D. K., 465
Waggert, J. L., 458
Wagner, J. A., 319, 336, 357
Wagner, R. J., 151
Wahba, M. A., 210
Wakabayashi, M., 299
Waldersee, R., 415
Waldman, D. A., 185, 191, 196, 364
Wall, P., 474
Wall, T. D., 333
Wallace, M., 262
Walton, A. E., 420, 422, 427–428, 437
Walton, R., 429
Wan, C. K., 353
Wanek, J. E., 120
Wanous, J. P., 74–75, 210, 417
Warm, J. S., 456
Warner, J. L., 77
Warr, P., 152
Warrick, M. J., 448
Watanabe, A., 236–237

Waterman, R. H., 322, 393
Watson, C., 318
Watson, J., 422
Watson, J. B., 219
Watson, W. E., 326, 358
Waxman, H. S., 490
Wayne, S. J., 188, 240, 299, 301
Weaver, C. N., 362
Weaver, J. L., 442
Weber, M., 301, 375–376, 380, 401–402, 438
Webster, E. C., 80, 82, 86
Webster, J., 138, 485
Weekley, J., 190
Weekley, J. A., 128, 168
Weeks, J. L., 153
Wegmann, R. G., 395
Weingart, L. R., 229, 324
Weisner, W. H., 84
Weiss, D. J., 242, 246
Weiss, H. M., 177
Weiss, R. M., 475
Weitzel, J., 289–290
Welbourne, T. M., 262
Welsh, D. H. B., 31, 220
Werbell, J. D., 84
Werner, J. M., 146, 171, 185
West, M., 399
Westley, B., 422
Wexley, K. N., 147, 179, 188, 322
Wheeler, D. D., 326, 329
Whetzel, D. L., 83
White, J. B., 238
White, J. R., 296
White, L. A., 189, 191, 193, 274
White, M., 39
White, R. P., 346
White, W., 398
Whitman, M. E., 461
Whitmore, M. D., 124
Whitney, D. J., 78, 83
Wholey, D. R., 334
Whyte, G., 111, 328
Wiersma, M. F., 403
Wilk, S. L., 32, 65, 112
Wilkins, A. L., 394
Williams, C. R., 228, 254
Williams, J. R., 196
Williams, K., 319

Williams, K. D., 205
Williams, K. J., 75, 353–354
Williams, L. J., 238
Williams, M. L., 261
Williams, R. E., 169
Williams, S., 326, 486
Willis, C. E., 189
Willis, R. P., 159
Wing, A. L., 493
Winkleby, M., 484
Winkler, H., 90
Winn, D. W., 465
Wise, L., 258
Woehr, D. J., 189, 193
Wohlers, A. J., 194, 196
Wolf, S., 397
Wong, C. S., 204
Wong, D. T., 120
Woo, J., 489
Wood, R., 226, 290
Woodman, R. W., 193, 389, 420

Woodward, J., 385, 387–388, 393
Wormley, W. M., 191
Worrell, D. L., 361
Wotton, E., 452
Wrench, D., 350
Wright, P. M., 84, 219, 228–229
Wuebker, L., 486
Wyndham, C., 454

Xin, K. R., 275, 483

Yammarino, F. J., 196, 348
Yandrick, R., 498
Yang, H., 161
Yarborough, M. H., 489
Yates, V. L., 191
Yetton, P. W., 292–295, 326
York, K. M., 356
Young, S. M., 405
Youngblood, S. A., 75, 253, 255
Yu, J., 197

Yukl, G. A., 188, 280–281, 322

Zaccaro, S. J., 283
Zajac, D., 238–239
Zalesny, M., 189
Zaleznic, A., 273
Zander, A., 316–317
Zarkin, G. A., 474, 498
Zedeck, S., 80, 106, 179, 186, 188
Zeiss, C., 353
Zeitlin, L. R., 466
Zeitz, K., 126
Zemke, R., 116, 148
Zenke, L. L., 108
Zhou, J., 455–457
Zickar, M. J., 17, 126
Zmund, R. W., 460
Zuk, Y., 218
Zulley, J., 447
Zwany, A., 210

Subject Index

Abilities, 111
Abilities requirements approach, 71
Ability testing, 95–96, 111–114
Ability to attend, 250
Absence culture, 252
Absenteeism, 249–253, 257
Academic settings, 16–17
Academy of Management, 18
Academy of Management Journal, 18
Academy of Management Review, 18
Accidents, 444, 452, 463–467
Accommodating, 324
Achievement, need for, 209
Achievement motivation theory, 209–211
Acquired immune deficiency syndrome. *See* AIDS
Acting on other, 212
Action research, 424–426
Adarand Constructors v. Pena (1995), 63
Addictive behavior, 474–482
Adjourning stage, groups, 317
Adjustment-to-stress theory, 465
Adverse impact, 61
Affective commitment, 239–240
Affiliation, need for, 209
Affirmative action, 66–67
African Americans, 342, 344–345, 357–361, 465, 487
After-only method, 162
Age, 191–192, 361–365, 465
Age Discrimination Act (1967), 64
Ahmedabad Manufacturing Company, 15–16, 333, 380, 389, 412

AIDS (acquired immune deficiency syndrome), 490–493
Air Force, U.S., 135, 147, 184, 190, 462
Alcohol abuse, 471–472, 474–476
Alcohol Abuse and Alcoholism Prevention, Treatment, and Rehabilitation Act (1970), 472
Alcoholics Anonymous (AA), 499
Allport Ascendance-Submission Test, 95
Altered inputs/outputs, 212
Altering objects of comparison, 212
American Airlines, 498
American College Testing Program, 59
American Hotel and Motel Association, 143
American Medical Association, 490
American Psychological Association, 2, 17–18, 34
American Psychological Society, 2, 18
American Society for Training and Development, 18
Americans with Disabilities Act (1990), 64, 126, 473, 493
Analyses of covariance, 34
Analyses of variance, 34
Analysis, 413–415
Application blanks, 76–77
Applications of theories, 8–11
Applied research, 53
Applied sciences, 4
Applied settings, 9
Appraisal interviews, 181–182

Appraisals. *See* Performance appraisals
Apprenticeship, 132, 141
Aptitudes, 111
Aptitude testing, 95–96, 111–114
Armed Services Vocational Aptitude Battery, 156, 184
Army, U.S., 95, 176, 189
Arousal-alertness theory, 465–466
Asian Americans, 345, 357, 487
Assessment. *See* Testing
Assessment centers, 122–125, 197–198
Assessment of trainability, 153, 155–158
Astronauts, 447
AT&T, 93–95, 122, 284, 344
Attendance motivation, 250–251
Attraction-selection-attrition, 314, 394–395
Attributional approaches to leadership, 298, 304–307
Audiovisual methods, 143–144
Australia, 333
Automatic speech recognition systems, 457–458
Automation, 459–463
Authoritarian leadership, 278–279
Autonomous work groups, 333, 391
Availability heuristic, 68

Babcock & Wilcox, 149
Bakke v. Regents of University of California (1978), 62
BankAmerica, 344
Base rates, 46
Baseball, 186–187, 214–219
Behavior, 160, 259–260, 310–313, 474–482

Behavioral approaches to motivation, 219–223
Behaviorally anchored rating scales, 177–179
Behavioral observation scales, 179
Behavioral performance appraisal, 184–185
Behavioral standards, 169
Behavioral theories of leadership, 282, 286–291, 297
Behavior descriptions, 87–88
Behavior modeling, 145–146
Benefits, 265–268
Benevolent authoritative systems, 382–383
Benevolents, 213
Bennett Mechanical Comprehension Test, 112
Bethlehem Steel, 402, 445–446
Biases of raters, 190–194
Biodata, 77–81
Biographical inventory, 77–81
Blue-collar workers, 367–368
Boeing Corporation, 238
Bona fide occupational qualification, 76, 125
Bounded rationality, 342
Britain, 95, 390, 412, 464
British Airways, 410–411, 425
Brogden-Cronbach-Gleser model, 109
Bureaucracy, 375–376
Bureau of Labor Statistics, 463
Burnout, 482
Business leadership, 273

California Psychological Inventory, 115, 121
Campbell Soup, 498
Canada, 302
Cardiopulmonary resuscitation, 467
Cardiovascular endurance, 112
Career-and-family women, 354–355
Career-primary women, 354–355

Case studies, 48–49, 150, 161–162, 312–313
Case Western Reserve University, 58
Catalyst study, 349
Categorization, 343
Causality, 27
Cautious shifts, 327
CD-ROMs, 147–148
Center for Creative Leadership, 275
Central Intelligence Agency, 95
Central tendency errors, 188
Chain of command, 377
Change, 409
    models of, 420–428
    resistance to, 415–420
Change agents, 411
Change-based models, 414
Charisma, 301–302
Charismatic leadership, 298, 301–302, 306
Charismatic power, 280
Checklists, 176–177, 466
Chief executive officers, 366
Child care, 267–268
China, 197
Chrysler Corporation, 366, 374, 417
Citizenship behavior, organizational, 397–398
Civil Rights Act (1964), 60–61, 65, 125–126, 170, 199, 341–342, 356, 385
Civil Rights Act (1991), 61, 64–66, 106, 125–126
Civil Service, 67
Civil War, U.S., 286–287
Classical organization theory, 375–380
Climate, organizational, 398–399
Cliques, 312–313
Code of Hammurabi, 132
Coercive power, 279
Coffee breaks, 332
Cognitive ability, 111–112

Cognitive theories of leadership, 282, 291–296, 298
Collective action approach, 373
Collectivism, 357–358, 360
Collegial organizations, 416
Commitment, organizational, 7, 238–240
Comparable worth, 351–353
Comparative methods, 175–176
Compensation, 213, 261–264, 266–267, 349–353, 362–363
Compensatory models, 262
Competence, 224
CompuServe, 267
Computer-adaptive testing, 126, 147
Computer-assisted instruction, 147–148
Computerized interviews, 88
Computerized performance monitoring, 190
Computers, 459–460
Concurrent validity, 99
Conferences, 144–145
Conflict model, 429, 431
Conflict resolution, 323–324
Conformity, 321
Congress, U.S., 12, 60–61, 64–67, 118, 140, 341–342, 374
Connecticut State Teachers College, 411
Conscientiousness, 254
Consideration, 286, 302
Consortium model, 497
Construct equivalence, 102
Constructivism, 401
Construct validity, 52, 101–103
Consultative systems, 382
Content validity, 100–101, 103
Context errors, 189–190
Contingency theory, 287–288, 297, 384–393
Contingent reward, 320
Continuance commitment, 239–240

Continuous reinforcement, 222
Contractor-model, 497
Contracts, 213
Control groups, 28, 162–163
Controlled experiments, 27
Conversations for closure, 416
Conversations for performance, 416
Conversations for understanding, 416
Corning, 150
Correlation, 36
Correlational method, 36–42
Correlational studies, 36–42
Correlation coefficient, 37
Cost effectiveness, of training, 164
Cray Research, 144
Criterion, 36, 59, 171
Criterion contamination, 172–174
Criterion deficiency, 172–173
Criterion development, 171–174
Criterion-referenced standards, 169
Criterion-related validity, 98–100, 103
Criterion relevance, 172–173
Criterion usefulness, 174
Critical incidents technique, 70, 180
Cross-functional teams, 334–335
Cuba, 328
Cummins Engine, 391
Customer service, 19, 38
Cytogenetic monitoring, 125

Decision making, 325–329
Decision-making models, participative, 331–338
Decision-making theory, 292–295, 298
Decisions, group, 325–327
Decision training, 193
Defamation, 88–89
Defense Department, U.S., 335, 446
Deindividuation, 319

Dell, 267
Delphi method, 329
Demands-abilities fit, 483
Departmentalization, 377–378
Dependent variables, 28, 36
Design, system, 443, 450, 466–467
Designated groups, 315–316
Detroit Edison Company, 412
Deviance, 319–322, 419
Deviant behavior, 259–260
Diagnosis, 413–415
Dialectical theory, 415
Differential Aptitude Test, 112, 184
Differentiation, 387–388
Diffusion of responsibility, 319
Digital Equipment, 442
Discrepancy theory, 261
Discrimination, 60–68
DISC test, 429
Disparity studies, 66
Dispositional stress, 485–487
Dispute resolution, 323–324
Dissatisfaction, job, 249–260
Dissonance theory, 211–212
Distributed expertise, 325
Distributions, 34–35
Diversity programs, 343
Diversity in workplace, 341–368
Doctoral programs, 17–18
Dominance cues, 318
Downsizing, 167, 349, 361
Drug abuse, 472, 477–481
Drug testing, 89–90, 478–481
Dunkin' Donuts, 142–143
DuPont, 94, 458, 471
Dynamic criteria, 185–186

Early retirement, 362
Earnings-at-risk plans, 262
Eastman Kodak, 471
Education, 19, 251, 349–351, 493–496
Effectiveness
  group, 318, 337–338
  leadership, 273
Elite organizations, 416

E-mail, 461–462
Emergence, leadership, 273
Emotional labor, 43–44
Employee assistance programs, 470–473, 496–499
Employee Benefit Research Institute, 349
Employee involvement programs, 331–338
Employment interviews, 80–88
Employment testing. *See* Testing
Empowerment, 224–225
Enlargement, job, 264–265
Enrichment, job, 264–265
Entitleds, 213
Entrepreneurship, 210
Environmental design, 443
Environmental stress, 484–485
Equal employment opportunity, 58, 66, 87, 114, 182
Equal Employment Opportunity Commission (EEOC), 61, 66, 93, 170, 356
Equal Pay Act (1963), 67, 352
Equitable Life Assurance, 488–489
Equity sensitives, 213
Equity theory, 211–216, 247
Equivalent forms method, 97–98
Ergonomics, 442
Errors in rating, 186–190
Escalating commitment, 486
Essays, evaluation, 179–180
Ethnicity, 341–342, 356–363, 487
Evaluation essays, 179–180
Evaluations
  of change models, 427–428
  of employee assistance programs, 497–499
  of leadership, 284–286, 291, 296, 305–307
  of methods, 35–36, 40, 42, 44, 46, 53
  of motivation, 207, 210–211, 215–216, 218–219, 223, 225, 229–232

Evaluations (*Continued*)
  of organization development, 434, 436–438
  of organizational theory, 378–380, 382–384, 391–393, 399–400
  of performance appraisals, 199–201
  of training programs, 136, 159–164
Evolutionary theory, 415
Evolved contexts, 399
Exceptioning, 352
Exchanges, 211
Executive Order 11246, 66
Executives, 365–367
  alcoholic, 475–476
  leadership of, 274–275
  minorities as, 358–361
  selection of, 94
  women as, 346–349
Existence/relatedness/growth, 207
Expectancy, 217
Expectancy theory, 216–219, 247
Experience-based questions, 85
Experimental groups, 28
Experimental research, 26–36, 311–312
Experiments, 9, 26–27
  evaluation of method, 35–36
  field, 30–32, 311
  laboratory, 27–30, 311
  natural, 32–33
  statistical analysis of data, 33–35
Expert power, 280
Exploitative authoritative systems, 382–383
Ex post facto studies, 32–33
External validity, 53
Extinction, 220
Exxon Corporation, 94, 412
Face validity, 104–105
Facet approach, 241–243
Facet satisfaction theory, 247
Factor analysis, 39–41
Factor Evaluation System, 67

Factory schools, 132
Fairness in selection, 60–65
Family-responsive policies, 354
Family–work conflicts, 353–355
Fatigue, 443–444
Federal Aviation Administration, 465
Federal Express, 148
Feedback, 197–198
Fidelity, 136–137
Field experiments, 30–32, 311
Films, 143
Fire prevention, 467
First aid, 467
Fit, 84
Five-factor theory, 116
Fixed criteria, 185
Fixed interval, 222
Fixed ratio, 222
Flat organizational structures, 377–379
Flexible compensation systems, 266–267
Flextime, 265–266
Flight simulation, 149
Focus groups, 49
Followers, of organizations, 374
Force, 217
Forced-choice checklists, 176–177
Forced distribution, 175–176
Forcing, 324
Ford Motor Company, 238, 417
Ford Motor Credit Company, 238
Formal groups, 313
Forming stage, groups, 316
Four-function typology, 382–383
Frame-of-reference training, 193
F ratios, 34
Free riding, 205
Frequencies, 48
Functionalism, 376–377
Functional job analysis, 70
Functional principle, 377–378

Gamblers Anonymous, 480
Gambling, 480, 482
Games, 150

Gender, 19, 341–342, 345, 362–363
  and absenteeism, 251
  and bias, 190–191
  and compensation, 263, 349–353
  and group behavior, 318
  and leadership, 273, 278, 348
  and management, 346–349
  and military service, 448
  and retirement, 362
  and sexual harassment, 355–356
  and work–family conflicts, 353–355
General Electric, 96
General Foods, 412
General mental ability, 112, 254
General Motors, 167, 366, 417, 471–472
Generic work behavior, 71
Genetic screening, 125–126
Genetic theory, 248–249
Germany, 95
Glass ceiling, 346
Glass Ceiling Initiative, 346, 359
Global approach, 241–242
Goal attainment, 434
Goals, training, 135–136
Goal-setting theory, 225–229
Goals-freedom-alertness theory, 466
Graphic rating scales, 177
Gravitational hypothesis, 32
"Great Man" theory of leadership, 281, 306
Great Depression, 14
Griggs v. Duke Power Company (1971), 62, 64
Group behavior, 310–313
Group characteristic bias, 173–174
Group cohesion, 322–323
Group decisions, 325
Group deviants, 322
Group mind, 310
Group polarization, 327–328
Groups, 310–311

characteristics of, 316–324
cohesiveness of, 322–323
conflict resolution, 323–324
decision making in, 325–329
deindividuation in, 319
employee involvement programs, 331–338
formation of, 316–318
interpersonal skills, 329–330
leadership of, 317–318, 326
norms/deviance, 319–322
primary/secondary, 313–315
reference/designated, 315–316
tasks/processes, 318
types of, 313–316
Group status, 321
Groupthink, 328–329
Grumman Corporation, 364
Gulf War, 271–273

Halo effects, 186–188
Harassment, sexual, 355–356
Harley-Davidson, 144–145
Hawthorne effect, 13, 26, 33, 43, 151–152, 162, 337
Hawthorne studies, 13–15, 44, 204, 310, 380–381, 471
Headsets, stereo, 456–457
Health promotion programs, 493–496
Health of workers, 8, 470–471, 499
addictive behavior, 474–482
AIDS, 490–493
employee assistance programs, 472–473, 496–499
health promotion programs, 493–496
historical background, 471–472
stress, 482–489
violence in workplace, 489–490
Hewlett Packard, 147
Hierarchy of needs theory, 205–207
High performance work practices, 255–256
Hiring. See Selection of personnel
Hispanics, 342, 345, 357–361, 487

HIV-infected workers, 490–493
Hogan Personality Inventory, 115
Hogan Personnel Selection Series, 120
Honda, 403
Hopwood v. State of Texas (1996), 63
Hostile environment, and sexual harassment, 356
Hot-line model, 497
Human factors, 7, 441–445
accidents, 463–467
and automation, 459–463
fatigue, 443–444
human-machine system, 448–451
origins of, 445–448
work environment design, 450, 452–459
Human Factors, 448
Human Factors and Ergonomics Society, 18, 448
Human factors psychology, 442
Human Interaction Research Institute, 491–492
Human-machine system, 448–451
Human relations theory, 381–384
Humidity, 453
Hygiene factors, 207–208
Hypotheses, 27

IBM, 141, 167, 366, 389
Idiosyncrasy credits, 321
Illinois Fair Employment Practices Commission, 60
Illumination, 450, 452–453
Impact, 225
Imperial Food Products, 441–442
Implementation of training program, 138
In-basket activity, 123
Incentive programs, 466
Increasing chronic tardiness, 259
Independent variables, 27, 36
India, 15–16
Individual assessment, 120–121
Individual interventions, 429–430

Individualized consideration, 302
Individuals, perspective of, 4–5
Industrial democracy, 425
Industrial organizational model, 385–387
Industrial and organizational (I/O) psychologists, 16
professional life, 18
training, 17–18
work environments, 16–17
Industrial and organizational (I/O) psychology, 2–3
areas of, 5–8
characteristics of, 2, 4
and measurement, 5
research methods, 25–53
theories/applications, 8–11
and workplace of future, 18–21
Inferences, 29
Informal groups, 314
Information power, 280
Ingroups, 298–300
Initiating structures, 287
Initiative conversations, 416
Inputs, 212
Instructional materials, 136–137
Integration, 387–388
Integrity tests, 118–120
Intellectual stimulation, 303
Intention to quit, 257–258
Interest measures, 121
Intergroup development, 434
Inter-Group Relations Workshop, 411
Intermittent manufacturing, 386
Internal consistency, 97–98
Internal referencing, 164
Internal Revenue Service, 170
Internal validity, 52
International employees, 41
International Ladies Garment Workers Union, 474
International Personnel Management Association, 18
Internet, 148
Interpersonal interaction/disclosure, 429–430

Interpersonal interventions, 429, 431

Interpersonal skills groups, 329–330

Interval scales, 50

Intervenors, 421

Interventions, 409, 428–436

Intervention theory, 421–422

Interviews
appraisal, 181–182
employment, 80–88
survey, 46–47

Intimate distance, 458

Intrinsic motivation, 223–225

Inventory of Managerial Potential, 101–103

I/O psychologists. *See* Industrial and organizational psychologists

I/O psychology. *See* Industrial and organizational psychology

Iraq, 271–272

Isolates, 312–313

Japan, 299, 332, 335, 384, 401–405, 417, 485

J coefficient, 105

Job analyses, 6, 67, 69–72

Job burnout, 482

Job Characteristics Model, 265

Job Compatibility Questionnaire, 243–245

Job Components Model, 105

Job descriptions, 72

Job Descriptive Index, 242, 244

Job design, 204–205, 443

Job Diagnostic Survey, 264

Job dissatisfaction, 249–260

Job elements approach, 70

Job enlargement, 264–265

Job enrichment, 264–265

Job evaluations, 67

Job involvement, 238

Job performance. *See* Performance appraisals

Job previews, 74–76

Job rotation, 141–142

Job samples, 122–125

Job satisfaction, 7, 235–236
and dissatisfaction, 249–260
increasing, 260–268
and life satisfaction, 236–238
measurement of, 240–246
organizational commitment, 238–240
theories of, 245–249

Job scope, 483

Job specifications, 72

Job transitions, 275–276

Johari Window, 429–430

Johnson v. Transportation Agency (1987), 62

Journal of Applied Psychology, 18

Kaiser-Permanente Medical Center, 473

Kemper Insurance, 471

Kimberly-Clark, 494

Kirkland v. New York Department of Correctional Services (1974), 100–101

Kirkpatrick's criteria, 160–161

Knowledge enlargement, 265

Knowledge of predictor bias, 174

Knowledge/skills/abilities, 135

Kuder Occupational Interest Inventory, 121

Kunin faces scale, 242, 245

Laboratory experiments, 27–30, 311

Laboratory-seminar training, 433–434

Labor Department, U.S., 19, 70, 346, 349, 359, 463

Laissez-faire leadership, 279

Land's End, 142

Large batch production firms, 386–387

Leader Match Program, 288

Leader-member exchange, 297–301, 305–306

Leadership, 8, 271–273

authoritarian, 278–279

behavioral theories of, 282, 286–291

cognitive theories of, 282, 291–292

and gender, 273, 278, 348

of groups, 317–318, 326

participative, 278–279

personological theories of, 281–286

position, 273–281

and power, 279–281, 284–285

social interaction, 282, 296–307

Leadership Behavior Description Questionnaire, 287

Leadership effectiveness, 273

Leadership emergence, 273

Leadership Grid, 433–435

Leadership Institute, 144

Leadership motivation patterns, 284

Leadership Opinion questionnaire, 287

Leadership organizations, 416

Learning, 160

Least Preferred Coworker, 288

Leaving the field, 212

Lectures, 142–143

Legitimate power, 279–280

Leniency errors, 188

Letters of recommendation, 88–89

Lewin's model of change, 420–421

Lie detector tests, 118–119

Life cycle theory, 415

Life satisfaction, 236–238

Life of Virginia, 143

Lifetime employment, 402–404

Lighting, 450, 452–453

Line-staff principle, 377

Log-linear modeling, 39

Logical errors, 188–189

London House Employment Productivity Index, 120

London House Personnel Selection Inventory, 118

Machine design, 443
Mafia, 319
Mail surveys, 46–47
Maloney v. B & L Motor Freight
    (1986), 89
Management
    minorities in, 358–361
    top, 365–366
    women in, 346–349
Management consulting, 17
Management of diversity, 342–345
Management by exception, 302
Management fashion, 272
Management by objectives,
    180–181, 226–227, 261
Marquette University, 144
Marriott International, 140
Mass production firms, 386–387
Matrix management, 333–335
Matsushita Electric, 404
MBA programs, 350–351
McDonald's Corporation, 494
McDonnell-Douglas Corporation,
    497–498
Meaning, 224
Means, 48
Measurement scales, 49
Mechanistic systems, 388–389
Medical services, 473
Mental health. *See* Health of
    workers
Mentors, 278, 350
Merit pay, 262
Meritocratic organizations, 416
Meta-analyses, 40
Microsoft Corporation, 267
Midvale Steel Company, 12
Midwestern Industrial Manage-
    ment Association, 67
Military leadership, 272
Minnesota Multiphasic Personality
    Inventory, 115, 121
Minnesota Satisfaction Question-
    naire, 242–243, 246, 248
Minority workers, 19, 341–342,
    356–363, 487
Mixed-standard scales, 177–178

Modern organizations, 401–402
Modesty biases, 196–197
"Mommy track," 355
Mood, and absenteeism, 257
Motivated distortion, 116
Motivating potential score, 265
Motivation, 8, 203–204
    attendance, 250
    behavioral approach, 219–223
    definitions, 204–205
    equity theory, 211–216
    evaluations of, 230–232
    expectancy theory, 216–219
    goal-setting theory, 225–229
    intrinsic, 223–225
    need theories, 205–211
    trainee, 153, 156–157
Motivators, 207–208
Motorola, 60, 148
Movement quality, 112
Multidisciplinary approaches, 4
Multimedia training, 148–149
Multiple regression, 39
Multirater feedback, 197–198
Multivariate analyses of variance, 34
Muscular strength, 112
Myart v. Motorola (1963), 60, 62,
    101
Myers-Briggs Type Indicator, 116,
    121, 429

Narrative methods, 179–180
National Institute of Alcohol
    Abuse and Alcoholism, 472
National Institute of Occupational
    Safety and Health, 441, 484
National Research Council, 477
National Safety Council, 463
National Security Decision Direc-
    tive 84, 119
National Training Laboratories,
    411–412
Natural experiments, 32–33
Natural selection approach, 373
Navy, U.S., 446
Naylor-Shine model, 109
Need for achievement, 209

Need for affiliation, 209
Need for power, 210, 284–285
Needs, training, 134–135
Need theories, 205–211, 246
Negative affectivity, 248, 314
Negative reinforcement, 220–221
Negligent hiring, 89
Noise, 455–457
Nominal scales, 50
Nordson Corporation, 463
Normal distributions, 34–35
Normative commitment, 239
Norming stage, groups, 317
Norms, 319–322
Northwestern Mutual Life Insur-
    ance, 483
Norway, 412
Nuclear power plants, 149

Objective criteria, 185
Objective personality measures,
    115
Objectives, training, 135–136
Obligations, 214
Observational method, 43–46,
    312
Observational skill training, 193
Observational studies, 42–46
Observations, 43, 312
Obstacles, 275, 277
Occupational Outlook Quarterly,
    20
Occupational Safety and Health
    Act (1970), 468
Occupational Safety and Health
    Administration, 489
Occupations, fastest growing, 19,
    21
Office of Strategic Services, 95,
    122
*Officers for Justice v. Civil Rights
    Commission* (1992), 106
Offshore oil rigs, 444–445
Ohio Civil Rights Commission, 60
Ohio Mechanics Institute, 132
Ohio State University, 286–287,
    297

Older workers, 191–192,
    361–365
Olympic Games, 168
On-the-job training, 139–140
Open learning, 152–153
Operant conditioning, 219
Opportunistic management, 433
Opportunity bias, 173
Ordinal scales, 50
Organic systems, 388–389
Organizational analyses, 134
Organizational architecture, 413
Organizational behavior, 4–5
Organizational behavior modifica-
    tion, 219
Organizational change. *See* Change
Organizational citizenship behav-
    ior, 397–398
Organizational climate, 398–399
Organizational commitment, 7,
    238–240
Organizational culture, 393–400
Organizational goal setting, 434
Organizational leadership. *See*
    Leadership
Organizational life, stages of,
    385–386
Organizational principles, 374
Organizational psychology, 4–5,
    372
Organizational socialization,
    395–397
Organizational structures, 7,
    377–379
Organizational theory
    approaches to, 372–374
    classical, 375–380
    contingency, 384–393
    human relations, 381–384
    organizational culture, 393–400
Organizational transformation,
    425–426
Organization development,
    409–411, 438
    change models, 420–428
    diagnosis/analysis, 413–415

ethical issues, 434, 436–437
evaluation of, 434, 436–438
interventions, 428–436
methodological concerns,
    437–438
origins of, 411–413
resistance to change, 415–420
Organizations, 371–372
    classical organization theory,
        375–380
    contingency theories, 384–393
    human relations theory,
        381–384
    Japanese, 401–405
    modern, 401–402
    organizational culture perspec-
        tive, 393–400
    postmodern, 400–402
    premodern, 400, 402
    qualities of, 374–375, 377–378
    study of, 372–374
    types of, 415–416
Organizationwide interventions,
    433–436
Organizing arrangements, 414
Other, equity theory, 212
Outcomes, 169, 216–217
Outdoor experiential training,
    151–152
Outgroups, 299–300
Outputs, 212, 374
Overlearning, 159
Ownership power, 280

Paired comparisons, 175
Pairs, 312–313
Parallel forms method, 97–98
Partial reinforcement, 222
Participants, 27
Participative decision-making
    models, 331–338
Participative leadership, 278–279
Participative systems, 382–383
Paternalistic management, 433
Path–goal theory, 293, 295–296,
    298

Pay Satisfaction Questionnaire, 262
PDI Employment Inventory, 71,
    120
Pearson product moment, 39
Peer ratings, 194–197
Pepsi, 494
Perceptions, 215–216
Performance
    and fatigue, 443–444
    predictions of, 59–60, 96–107
    and ratio, 222
    team, 337–338
Performance appraisals, 7–8,
    167–168
    criterion development, 171–172
    evaluations of, 199–201
    importance of, 170–171
    measurement of, 182–187
    methods of, 174–182
    political aspects of, 200
    role of, 169–171
    social factors in, 194–195
    sources of error, 182–198
    systems for, 198–199
    uses of, 169–170
Performance Research Associates,
    38
Performing stage, groups, 317
Person, equity theory, 212
Personal aggression, 260
Personality, 114
Personality assessment, 114–118
Personality measures, 114–118
Personal power, 279
Personal space, 458
Person-environment fit, 483
Personological theories of leader-
    ship, 281–286, 297
Persons analyses, 135
Personnel Psychology, 18
Personnel Testing Council, 18
Persuasive power, 280
Physical ability, 112–114
Physical fidelity, 136–137
Physical health. *See* Health of
    workers

Physical setting factors, 414
Physiological motivations, 204
Piecework, 12, 204
Planned change, 391
Planned change model, 422–424
Polarization, group, 327–328
Political deviance, 260
Political leadership, 272–273
Politics, and performance appraisals, 200
Polygraphs, 118–119
Populations, 29
Position Analysis Questionnaire, 70–71
Position power, 279
Positive affectivity, 251–252, 314
Positive reinforcement, 220–221
Postal Service, 450–451, 489
Postmodern organizations, 400–402
Postmodernism, 400
Power, 210, 279–281, 284–285, 297
Predictive validity, 99–100
Predictor, 27, 36, 59, 174
Pregnancy Discrimination Act (1978), 64
Premodern organizations, 400, 402
Prestige power, 280
Pretest-posttest method, 161–162
Price Waterhouse v. Hopkins (1988), 63
Primary groups, 313–315
Principles, organizational, 374
Private self-consciousness, 486
Proactive personality, 117–118
Problem solving, 324
Processes, 169, 318, 432
Process production firms, 385
Production deviance, 260
Professional life, I/O psychologists, 18
Programmed instruction, 146–147
Projective personality measures, 115

Property deviance, 260
Prospect theory, 328
Protégés, 278, 350
Proximity errors, 188–189
Psychological contracts, 374–375
Psychological Corporation, 95
Psychological fidelity, 137
Psychological motivations, 204
Psychological space, 312
Psychology, 2
Psychotherapy, 473
Public Broadcasting System, 462
Public distance, 459
Punctuated equilibrium, 317, 426–427
Punishment, 220–221
Purdue Mechanical Adaptability Test, 112
Pygmalion effect, 193–194

Qualitative studies, 43
Quality circles, 335–336, 404
Quantitative studies, 43
Quasi-experiments, 31
Questar Data Systems, 38
Questions
    interview, 81, 85
    trade test, 112–113
Quid pro quo, and sexual harassment, 356

Race, 191, 341–342, 356–363, 465, 487
Random samples, 31
Ranking systems, 175
Raters, biases of, 190–195
Rating errors, 186–190
Ratings, peer, 194–197
Rating scales, 177–179
Ratio, and performance, 222
Ratio scales, 50
Reactions, 160
Readiness, trainee, 153, 155–156
Realistic job previews, 74–76
Realistic recruitment, 74
Recruitment, 72–76

Reduced effects training, 193
Reference groups, 315–316
References, 88–89
Referent power, 280
Reframing, 425
Rehabilitation Act (1973), 64, 126
Reid Report, 118
Reinforcement theory, 220–223, 289–291, 297
Reliability, 52–53, 96–98
Reliability Scale, 120
Remedial training programs, 155
Representative samples, 29
Research methods, 25–26
    case studies, 47–49
    correlational studies, 36–42
    evaluations, 53
    experimental research, 26–36
    focus groups, 49
    measurement scales, 49–50
    observational studies, 42–46
    reliability/validity in, 52–53
    selection of, 50–51
    surveys, 46–47
Reservation wage model, 262
Restrictions in range, 99
Results, 160
Reverse discrimination, 66
Reward power, 279
Risky shifts, 327
Robotics, 462–463
Role ambiguity, 483
Rorschach Inkblot Test, 121

Saab, 16, 412
Safety, 463–467, 484, 489–490
Safety committees, 467
Salary. *See* Compensation
Sales, 45
Samples, 29, 31
Satisfaction. *See* Job satisfaction
Scabs, 320
Scalar principle, 377–378
Scales, measurement, 49–50
Scholastic Aptitude Tests, 59

Scientific management, 10, 12–13

Scientific theories, 8–9

Scientist-practitioners, 9

Score banding, 106–107

Sears, Roebuck & Company, 94, 167, 374

Seat design, 450, 452

Secondary groups, 313–315

Selection of personnel, 6, 57, 443
  application blanks, 76–81
  biodata, 76–81
  drug testing, 89–90
  effective procedures, 57–58
  executives, 94
  interviews, 80–88
  job analyses, 67, 69–72
  letters of recommendation, 88–89
  predictor/criterion in, 58–68
  recruitment, 72–76
  references, 88–89
  See also Testing

Selection ratio, 61, 108

Self-actualization, 206

Self-assessments, 194–197

Self-determination, 224

Self-Directed Search, 121

Self-efficacy, 156, 218, 330

Self-management, worker, 137

Self-monitoring, 275–276

Semistructured interviews, 85–86

Sensitivity training, 144–145

Service industries, 19

Service Management Practices Inventory, 38

Seven S theory, 404–405

Severity errors, 188

Sex. *See* Gender

Sex-stereotyping of jobs, 352

Sexual harassment, 355–356

Shell Oil, 148, 391

Shiftwork, 265–266, 443–44

Shirking, 205

Similar-to-me errors, 188

Simulated speech, 457–458

Simulations, 149–150

Situational leadership, 289–290, 297

Situational questions, 85

Situational specificity, 102–104

Situations, 399

16PF, 115, 120–121

Skewed distributions, 34–35

Small batch production firms, 387

Smoking, 496

Social distance, 459

Social factors, 194–195, 414

Social influence errors, 189

Social information processing, 211, 247–248

Social interaction theories of leadership, 282, 296–307

Socialization, organizational, 395–397

Social loafing, 205, 319

Social Security, 362

Social Security Administration, 472

Social stratification, 365–368

Social support, 322–323

Society of Human Resource Management, 81

Society for Industrial and Organizational Psychology, 16–18

Sociometry, 312–313

Sociotechnical systems, 16, 389–392

Software psychology, 460

Solomon four-group design, 162–163

Soroka v. Dayton Hudson (1991), 63, 104–105

Sounds, common, 456

Southern California Edison, 464

Soviet Union, 12, 351

Space arrangements, 458–459

Space program, 447

Space Relations Test, 112

Span of control, 377, 379

Specification, 343

Speech, simulated, 457–458

Split-half reliability, 97–98

Sports, 68, 186–187, 214–219

Stabilization, 434

Stable periodic tardiness, 259

Standard deviations, 48

Standards, 169

Stanton Survey, 118

Stars, 312–313

State Department, U.S., 104

Statistical analyses of data
  correlational method, 39–41
  experiments, 33–35
  surveys, 48

Statistical inference validity, 52

Stereo headsets, 456–457

Storming stage, groups, 316–317

Strategic choice approach, 372–373

Stress, 353, 482–489

Stress interviews, 86

Stress management programs, 488–489

Strong-Campbell Interest Inventory, 121

Structure, 375

Structured interviews, 84–85

Subgroup norming, 65, 107

Subject matter experts, 325

Substance abuse, 474–481

Supervisors, 256, 262

Supplies-values fit, 483

Supreme Court, U.S., 60, 62–66, 100–101, 104–106

Survey Research Center, 412

Surveys, 46–48

Survival, by organizations, 374

Sweden, 412

Synthetic validity, 105–106

System design, 443, 450, 466–467

Systems of organizations, 382–383

System-structural approach, 372–373

Systems theory, 384–393

Taiwan, 196

Tall organizational structures, 377–379

Tardiness, 259
Task analyses, 134–135
Task cues, 318
Task enlargement, 265
Task motivation theory, 210
Task-related characteristics, 275–277
Tasks, 318, 432
Tavistock Institute of Human Relations, 15, 389, 412
Taxonomies, 20–22
Taylor-Russell model, 108–109
Taylor-Russell tables, 108, 110
Team building, 431–433
Team development, 434
Team development interventions, 431–433
Teams, 331–333, 336–338
Technology, 414
Telecommunications, 460–462
Teleconferences, 144, 461
Teleological theory, 415
Telephones, 460–461
Telephone surveys, 46–47
Temperature, 453–455
Terry v. EEOC (1996), 66
Test bias, 107
Testing, 93–94
    drug, 89–90, 478–481
    history of, 95–96
    improvement of procedures, 107–111
    of instructional materials, 137
    new approaches, 125–128
    prediction of performance from, 96–107
    types of, 111–125
Test-retest method, 96
Tests of significance, 33
Texaco, 58
T-groups, 411–412
Thematic Apperception Test, 210, 284
Theoretical sciences, 4
Theories, 8–11
Theory X, 381–382, 404, 412

Theory Y, 381–382, 404, 412
Theory Z, 404–405
Third-party interventions, 429, 431
Third-variable problem, 42
360° feedback, 197
Three Mile Island disaster, 149
Thurstone Personality Scale, 95
Time-and-motion studies, 12
Title VII, 60–61, 170, 199
Total quality management, 335–336, 434, 436
Toyota, 403
Trade tests, 112–113
Traditional interviews, 84
Trainability, assessment of, 153, 155–158
Trainers, training of, 158–159
Training, 6–7, 131–132, 443
    evaluations of, 159–164
    history of, 132–133
    of international employees, 41
    of I/O psychologists, 17–18
    methods of, 138–155
    multimedia, 148–149
    on-the-job, 139–140
    optimization of, 153, 155–159
    outdoor experiential, 151–152
    programs for, 133–138
    safety, 466
    sensitivity, 144–145
    of trainers, 158–159
    transfer of, 136–137, 149
    vestibule, 139–141
Trait-based standards, 169
Trait rating forms, 182–183
Traits, 182–184
Trait theories, 281, 283, 297
Transactional leadership, 302–303
Transfer of training, 136–137, 149
Transformational leadership, 298, 302–304, 306
t test, 33–34
Turnover, 253–258
Turnover culture, 256
Two-factor theory, 207–208

Type A behavior, 486–488
Type B behavior, 487–488
Type I errors, 33
Type II errors, 33

Ultimate criterion, 171–172
Unavoidable tardiness, 259
Unfolding model of turnover, 258
Unfreezing-moving-freezing model, 420–421
Uniform Guidelines on Employee Selection Procedures, 61
Union Carbide, 412
United Auto Workers, 238
United States Employment Service, 65
Unity of command, 377
University of Michigan, 287, 412
University of Minnesota, 144
University of Texas, 433, 436
Upward feedback, 197–198
User-friendly systems, 460, 463
Utility analysis, 108
Utility companies, 149
Utility models, 108–111

Valences, 217
Validity, 52–53, 97–106
Validity generalization, 102–104
Value discrepancy theory, 247
Values, 217
Variability, 34
Variable interval, 222
Variable ratio, 222
Variables, 27–28, 36
Vertical dyad linkage, 297–301, 304–305
Vestibule training, 139–141
Vibration, 455, 457
Video-based assessment, 126–128
Videocommunication, 461
Videotapes, 143
Vietnam Era Veterans Readjustment Assistance Act (1974), 64

Vigilance, 456–457
Violence in workplace, 489–490
Virtual reality simulations, 462
Visual display terminals, 460
Voice mail, 460–461
Volvo, 16, 391, 412
Vroom-Yetton decision-making
    model, 292–295, 298

Wages. *See* Compensation
Walt Disney World, 267
*Wards Cove Packing Company v.
    Antonio* (1987), 62–65
Watson-Glaser Critical Thinking
    Appraisal, 120–121
Weahkee v. Perry (1978), 170
Wechsler Adult Intelligence Scale
    Revised, 121

Weighted application blanks, 76
Weighted checklists, 176
Welfare Reform Act (1996), 140
Welfare-to-work programs, 140
Western Electric Company, 13,
    471
Westinghouse Corporation,
    433
Whistleblowers, 379
Women. *See* Gender
Women's Legal Defense Fund,
    351
Wonderlic Personnel Test, 112
Work
    avoidance of, 205
    psychology of, 2, 5
Work centrality, 238
Work conditions, 7

and absenteeism, 252–253
design of, 443, 450, 452–459,
    466–467
and human factors, 441–467
I/O psychologists, 16–17
Work–family conflicts,
    353–355
Workforce, projected changes in,
    19–20
Work groups. *See* Groups
Work restriction, 14
Workstation design, 459
World War I, 95, 464
World War II, 95, 122, 176, 267,
    335
World Wide Web, 148

Xerox Corporation, 238, 344